New York City

"All you've got to do is decide to go
and the hardest part is over.

So go!"

TONY WHEELER, COFOUNDER – LONELY PLANET

THIS EDITION WRITTEN AND RESEARCHED BY

Regis St Louis, Cristian Bonetto

Contents

(left) Wander through picturesque **Central Park (p230)**.

(above) Take in the view of the Empire State Building from the **Top of the Rock (p185)**.

(right) View the beautiful clock at **Grand Cental Terminal (p186)**.

Welcome to New York City

Epicenter of the arts. Dining and shopping capital. Trendsetter. New York City wears many crowns, and spreads an irresistible feast for all.

Urban Wanderers

With its compact size and streets packed with eye candy of all sorts – architectural treasures, old-world cafes, atmospheric booksellers and curiosity shops – NYC is an urban wanderer's delight. You can lose yourself in the crowds of Chinatown amid brightly painted Buddhist temples, steaming noodle shops and fragrant fishmongers, then stroll up to Nolita for enticing boutiques and coffee-tasting among the craft-minded scenesters. Every neighborhood offers a dramatically different version of New York City – from the 100-year-old Jewish delis of the Upper West Side to the cobblestone lanes of Greenwich Village. And the best way to experience this city is to walk its streets.

Nexus of the Arts

The Met, the MoMA and the Guggenheim are just the beginning of a dizzying list of art-world icons. You'll find museums devoted to everything from fin de siècle Vienna to immigrant life in the Lower East Side, and sprawling galleries filled with Japanese sculpture, postmodern American painting, Himalayan textiles and New York City lore. Delve into the cutting-edge galleries of Chelsea and the Lower East Side, with their myriad exhibition spaces, and festive opening-night parties (usually on Thursday nights).

The Night Is Young

When the sun sinks slowly beyond the Hudson and luminous skyscrapers light up the night, New York transforms into one grand stage. Well-known actors take to the legendary theaters of Broadway as world-class soloists, dancers and musicians perform at venues large and small across town. Whether high culture or low, New York embraces it all: in-your-face rock shows at Williamsburg dives, lavish opera productions at the Lincoln Center, and everything in between. This is a city of experimental theater, improv comedy, indie cinema, ballet, poetry readings, burlesque, world music, jazz and so much more.

Culinary Capital

There's never been a better time to dine in New York. The city has become a hotbed of seasonal and locally sourced cuisine, with restaurants raising vegetables on roof gardens or their own upstate farms, and sourcing meats and seafood from sustainable outfits nearby. Bars have also taken creativity to new heights, with pre-Prohibition-era cocktails, served alongside delectable small plates. Though of course, you can also hit the gourmet food-truck scene, or dine more traditionally at one of NYC's 20,000-plus sit-down restaurants.

Why I Love New York City

By Regis St Louis, Author

I've lived in NYC since 2001, and I'm excited about how green the city has become in recent years. The Brooklyn Bridge Park in my neighborhood, the High Line, the Hudson River Park, the growing number of farmers markets around town, the new Citi Bike program, Bloomberg's plant-a-million-trees campaign: New York is no longer 'the concrete jungle' of yesteryear. Culturally speaking, it's an exciting time to be in New York, with the arrival of new theaters, cultural centers and sporting arenas (Theatre for a New Audience, BRIC, Barclays Center). I also feel fortunate to be here during the Brooklyn renaissance, when there's so much creativity in the air. **For more about our authors, see p448.**

New York City's
Top 16

Food Scene (p38)

1 One of New York's greatest assets is the sheer variety of its restaurants. In a single neighborhood you'll find vintage-filled gastropubs, sushi counters, tapas bars, French bistros, barbecue joints, pizza parlours, vegan cafes and good old-fashioned delis, whipping up toasted bagels with lox and cream cheese. And that's just the beginning. There's no wrong way to eat a meal, whether that means ordering off a food truck, nibbling your way through a market or sliding into that soft leather booth for a 4am feast after a night on the town. KATZ'S DELICATESSEN, LOWER EAST SIDE (P118)

✕ *Eating*

Markets (p50)

2 New York's markets are packed with treasures. On weekends, one parking garage in Chelsea transforms into an antique-lover's paradise, with vintage clothes, Victorian housewares, mid-century furniture, and hundreds of other curios from the past. Foodies meanwhile focus on New York's sprawling food markets – like the Union Square Greenmarket or the brick-walled Chelsea Market, an ideal spot for snacking, dining and browsing gourmet grocery sellers. And for an enticing mash-up of antiques, food and artisanal goods and crafts, one market rules supreme: the vast Brooklyn Flea. UNION SQUARE GREENMARKET (P173)

🛍 *Shopping*

HUW JONES / GETTY IMAGES ©

Brooklyn Bridge
(p266)

3 Completed in 1883, this Gothic Revival masterpiece – crafted entirely from granite – has inspired poetry (Jack Kerouac's 'Brooklyn Bridge Blues'), music (Frank Sinatra's 'Brooklyn Bridge') and plenty of art (Walker Evans' photography). It is also the most scenic way to cross from Manhattan into Brooklyn. Go early in the morning (we're talking sun-up) to have the bridge largely to yourself. Come at sunset for romantic views as the amber skies form a magnificent backdrop to Lower Manhattan.

⊙ *Brooklyn*

Metropolitan Museum of Art
(p212)

4 With more than two million objects in its collections, the Met is simply dazzling. Its great works span the world, from the chiseled sculptures of ancient Greece to the evocative tribal carvings of Papua New Guinea. The Renaissance galleries are packed with old-world masters, while the relics of ancient Egypt fire the imagination – particularly the Temple of Dendur, complete with its 2000-year-old stone walls covered in hieroglyphics and carvings of papyrus seemingly growing from a pond. After you think you've seen enough, head up to the rooftop for a sweeping view over Central Park.

⊙ *Upper East Side*

Shopping *(p50)*

5 Take it from the likes of Holly Golightly and Carrie Bradshaw, New York is a beacon of the material world. Hundreds of creators – both local and international – descend upon the city with alacrity to display their wares. You'll find dozens of ways to empty your coffers, but at the end of the day shopping in New York isn't about collecting a closet full of items, it's about accessing the city's myriad subcultures through their art and artifacts. BROOKLYN WINDOW DISPLAY

🛍 *Shopping*

Central Park (p230)

6 London has Hyde Park, Paris has the Bois de Boulogne, and New York City has Central Park. One of the world's most renowned green spaces, it checks in with 843 acres of rolling meadows, boulder-studded outcrops, elm-lined walkways, manicured European-style gardens, a lake and a reservoir – not to mention an outdoor theater, a memorial to John Lennon, an idyllic waterside eatery (the Loeb Boathouse) and one very famous statue of Alice in Wonderland. The big challenge? Figuring out where to begin.

👁 *Upper West Side & Central Park*

Music & Nightlife (p42)

7 Trendy all-night lounges tucked behind the walls of a Chinese restaurant; taco shops that clandestinely host late-night tranny cabarets; stadium-size clubs that clang to the thump of DJ beats; and after-after-after-parties on the roof as the sun rises – an alternate universe lurks between the cracks of everyday life, and it welcomes savvy visitors just as much as locals in the know. If New York doesn't turn into a pumpkin come midnight, why should you?

🍷 *Drinking & Nightlife*

Empire State Building *(p179)*

8 The striking art deco skyscraper may no longer be New York's tallest building, but it remains one of its most recognizable icons. The ESB has appeared in dozens of films and still provides one of the best views in town – particularly around sunset when the twinkling lights of the city (and neighboring states) switch on. The beloved landmark hasn't stopped turning heads, especially since the addition of LED lights which create more than 16 million color possibilities. Keep your eye to the sky on big holidays, when dramatic displays light up the night sky.

◉ *Midtown*

Statue of Liberty & Ellis Island *(p62)*

9 Since its unveiling in 1886, Lady Liberty has welcomed millions of immigrants sailing into New York Harbor in the hope of a better life. It now welcomes millions of tourists, many of whom head up to her crown for one of New York City's finest skyline and water views. Close by lies Ellis Island, the American gateway for over 12 million new arrivals between 1892 and 1954. These days it's home to one of the city's most moving museums, paying tribute to these immigrants and their indelible courage.

⊙ *Lower Manhattan & the Financial District*

The High Line *(p131)*

10 A resounding triumph of urban renewal, the High Line is – without a doubt – New York's proudest testament to the continuous effort to transform the scarring vestiges of the city's industrial past into eye-pleasing spaces. Once an unsightly elevated train track that snaked between slaughterhouses and low-end domestic dwellings, the High Line is today an unfurled emerald necklace of park space that encourages calm, crowds, and has, unsurprisingly, acted as a veritable real estate magnet luring world-class architects to the neighborhood to create gorgeous iterations of residential eye candy.

⊙ *Greenwich Village, Chelsea & the Meatpacking District*

Broadway & Times Square *(p176)*

11 Sizzling lights, electrifying energy: this is the America of the world's imagination. Stretching from 40th St to 54th St, between Sixth and Eighth Aves, Broadway is NYC's dream factory – a place where romance, betrayal, murder and triumph come with dazzling costumes and stirring scores. The district's undisputed star is bright, blinding Times Square. More than the meeting point of Broadway and Seventh Ave, this is America concentrate – an intense, intoxicating rush of Hollywood billboards, shimmering cola signs, and buffed topless cowboys. Welcome to the 'crossroads of the world'.

⊙ *Midtown*

9

MoMA *(p181)*

12 Quite possibly the greatest hoarder of modern masterpieces on earth, the Museum of Modern Art (MoMA) is a cultural promised land. It's here that you'll see Van Gogh's *The Starry Night,* Cézanne's *The Bather,* Picasso's *Les Demoiselles d'Avignon,* Pollock's *One: Number 31,* and Warhol's *Campbell's Soup Cans.* Just make sure you leave time for Chagall, Dix, Rothko, de Kooning and Haring, a free film screening, a glass of vino in the Sculpture Garden, a little designer retail therapy, and a fine-dining feed at its lauded in-house restaurant, the Modern.

⊙ *Midtown*

Out on the Water *(p384)*

13 Step off the island of Manhattan onto a ferry and you'll have a new appreciation for those pedestrian-clogged streets as the city skyline rises slowly into view. Governors Island makes a fine destination, with new parkland, art exhibitions and peaceful, car-free lanes to stroll or cycle along. You can also hop across to Brooklyn aboard the East River Ferry. The dock near the Brooklyn Bridge Park makes an excellent entry point to the borough.

Lower Manhattan & the Financial District

Neighborhood Rambling *(p138)*

14 One of the best ways to see New York is to pick a neighborhood, lace on your walking shoes and spend the day exploring. Greenwich Village is a fine place to start, with picturesque cobblestone streets dotted with sunlit shops, narrow sidewalk cafes and quaint restaurants that beckon you inside. For a different take on New York, head over to the bohemian East Village, overload your senses down in Chinatown, or take in the local scene in gallery-filled Chelsea. This is a city that invites endless wandering.
GREENWICH VILLAGE (P129)

Greenwich Village, Chelsea & the Meatpacking District

National September 11 Memorial & Museum *(p66)*

15 Rising from the ashes of Ground Zero, the National September 11 Memorial and Museum is a beautiful, dignified response to the city's darkest chapter. Where the Twin Towers once soared, two reflecting pools now weep like dark, elegant waterfalls. Framing them are the names of those who lost their lives on September 11 and in the 1993 World Trade Center bombing. Deep below lies the Memorial Museum, a powerful, poignant exploration of these catastrophic events, the later of which was the deadliest attack on American soil.

⊙ *Lower Manhattan & the Financial District*

Williamsburg *(p271)*

16 Retro cocktail lounges peddling a Depression-era vibe. Artsy eateries dishing out everything from barbecue ribs to Michelin-starred gastronomy. And enough music halls and rowdy beer gardens to keep the most dedicated night owls up for weeks. Prefer the daylight hours? Williamsburg is stocked with an array of designer homeware shops, in addition to fashion outposts of all stripes, from vintage thrift emporiums to high-design boutiques. It's not for nothing that this Brooklyn neighborhood – just one subway stop from downtown Manhattan – is the city's trendiest hangout.

⊙ *Brooklyn*

What's New

Brooklyn Pride

If you haven't heard, the Brooklyn renaissance is well underway. This epicenter of creativity boasts some of the city's best locavore-focused restaurants, cocktail bars, artisanal shops and coffee roasters; it even has a buzzing new hotel scene. Brooklyn now has a pro basketball team (the Nets), a grand arena and new theaters and cultural spaces including the Theater for a New Audience, devoted to Shakespeare and classical works.

Remembering September 11

Within the memorial grounds of the World Trade Center site, the National September 11 Museum delves into the tragic events that forever changed NYC. (p66)

Leslie Lohman Museum of Gay & Lesbian Art

This SoHo gem, which gained its museum charter in 2011, is finally poised to draw in the crowds. It's the first LGBT-specific art museum in the world. (p87)

The Coffee Scene

Artisanal roasters and celebrated coffee makers have opened shop, transforming NYC's once humble java scene. Brooklyn Roasting Company (p282), Stumptown Coffee Roasters (p200), Blue Bottle Coffee (p290), Toby's Estate (p170) and Little Collins (p200) are leading the charge.

Queens is Back

After a $70-million renovation, the Queens Museum is back - bigger and better than ever. It's quickly becoming an icon of NYC's most ethnically diverse borough. (p306)

Governors Island Park

A new 30-acre park has been added to the wonderful car-free island in New York's harbor, bringing a hammock grove, ball fields, a formal garden and climbable play areas for kids. (p71)

Franklin D Roosevelt Four Freedoms Park

On Roosevelt Island, Louis Kahn's arresting memorial pays homage to one of America's greatest presidents. Striking skyline views link the memorial with the UN, one of FDR's most visible achievements. (p193)

One World Trade Center

The soaring, 104-story icon – costing some $4 billion, and eight years in the making – has at last arrived. Its observation deck is set to open in 2015. (p67)

High Line 3.0

The celebrated green space will open its final section, bringing a lush new design courtesy of Diller Scofidio + Renfro. Up next? The $15-billion commercial development of the Hudson Yards, adjoining the final section. (p131)

Greener Days in Brooklyn

The magnificent 1.3-mile-long Brooklyn Bridge Park, with its staggering views of Manhattan, has transformed a once inaccessible waterfront into a green oasis. (p265)

For more recommendations and reviews, see **lonelyplanet. com/usa/new-york-city**

Need to Know

For more information, see Survival Guide (p379)

Currency
US dollar (US$)

Language
English

Visas
The US Visa Waiver program allows nationals of 37 countries to enter the US without a visa.

Money
ATMs widely available; credit cards accepted at most hotels, stores and restaurants. Farmers markets, food trucks and some restaurants and bars are cash only.

Cell Phones
Most US cell phones, apart from the iPhone, operate on CDMA, not the European standard GSM; check compatibility with your phone service provider.

Time
Eastern Standard Time (GMT/UTC minus five hours)

Tourist Information
There are official NYC Visitor Information Centers (☎212-484-1222; www.nycgo.com; 53rd St at Seventh Ave, Midtown) throughout the city. The main office is in Midtown.

Daily Costs

Budget: less than $100
➡ Dorm bed: $40–$70
➡ Slice of pizza: around $4
➡ Food-truck taco: from $2.50
➡ Bus or subway ride: $2.50)

Midrange: $100–$300
➡ Double room in a midrange hotel: from $150
➡ Brunch for two at Cafe Mogador: $70
➡ Dinner for two at Red Farm: $130
➡ Innovative cocktail at a speakeasy-style lounge: $14-18
➡ Discount TKTS tickets to a Broadway show: $80
➡ Brooklyn Academy of Music orchestra seats: from $84

Top End: $300 plus
➡ Luxury stay at the NoMad Hotel: $325–$850
➡ Tasting menu at Le Bernadin: 155–%198
➡ A 90-minute massage in the atmospheric Great Jones Spa: $200
➡ Metropolitan Opera orchestra seats: $100–$390

Advance Planning

Two months before Book hotel reservations – prices increase the closer you get to your arrival date. Snag tickets to your favorite Broadway blockbuster.

Three weeks before If you haven't already, score a table at your top-choice restaurant.

One week before Surf the web for the latest openings. Join email news blasts as well.

Useful Websites
➡ **Lonely Planet** (www.lonelyplanet.com/usa/new-york-city) Destination information, hotel bookings, traveler forum and more.
➡ **NYC: The Official Guide** (www.nycgo.com) New York City's official tourism portal.
➡ **Visit Brooklyn** (www.visitbrooklyn.org) NYC & Co's Brooklyn-specific website.
➡ **New York Magazine** (www.nymag.com) Comprehensive, listings for bars, restaurants, entertainment and shopping.
➡ **New York Times** (www.nytimes.com) Excellent local news coverage and theater listings.
➡ **Village Voice** (www.villagevoice.com) Solid resource for the various goings-on about town.
➡ **Time Out** (www.timeout.com/newyork) The lowdown on what's happening around town.

WHEN TO GO

Summers can be scorching hot; winters cold and not without their blizzards. Spring or autumn are the best times to explore.

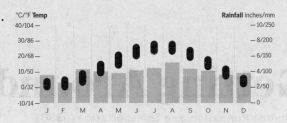

°C/°F Temp — Rainfall inches/mm

Arriving in New York

John F Kennedy International Airport (JFK) The AirTrain ($5) links to the Metropolitan Transport Authority's (MTA's) subway ($2.50), which makes the one-hour journey into Manhattan; express bus to Grand Central or Port Authority is $16; shared vans to Manhattan hotels run $20 to $25; taxis cost a flat rate of $52 excluding tolls and tip.

LaGuardia Airport (LGA) This is the closest airport to Manhattan but least accessible by public transit: take the Q70 express bus from the airport to the 74th St–Broadway subway station (7 line, or the E, F, M and R lines at the connecting Jackson Hts Roosevelt Ave station). Express bus to Midtown costs $13. Taxis range from $26 to $48 (excluding tolls and tip) depending on traffic.

Newark Liberty International Airport (EWR) Take the AirTrain to Newark Airport rail station, and board any train bound for New York's Penn Station ($12.50). Express bus to Port Authority or Grand Central costs $16. Shared shuttles to Midtown cost $20 to $26. Taxis range from $60 to $80 (excluding the unavoidable $13 toll and tip). Allow 45 minutes to one hour of travel time.

For much more on **arrival,** see p380

Tipping

Tipping is *not* optional; only withhold tips in cases of outrageously bad service.

➡ **Restaurant servers** 15%–20%, unless a gratuity is already charged on the bill (usually only for groups of five or more)

➡ **Bartenders** 10%–15% per round, minimum per drink $1 for standard drinks, and $2 per specialty cocktail

➡ **Taxi drivers** 10%–15%, rounded up to the next dollar

➡ **Airport & hotel porters** $2 per bag, minimum per cart $5

➡ **Hotel maids** $2–$4 per night, left in envelope or under the card provided

For much more on **money,** see p387

Sleeping

In general, accommodation prices in New York City do not abide by any high-season or low-season rules; wavering rates usually reflect availability. With over 54 million visitors to the city in 2013, you can expect that hotel rooms fill up quickly – especially in summer.

Useful Websites

➡ **newyorkhotels.com** (www.newyorkhotels.com) The self-proclaimed official website for hotels in NYC.

➡ **airbnb** (www.airbnb.com) Choose furnished apartment or rooms in a New Yorker's house rather than pricey hotel digs.

➡ **Jetsetter** (www.jetsetter.com) Great selection of international sales on luxury hotels; excellent NYC selection.

For much more on **sleeping,** see p325

Getting Around

For more information, see Transportation (p380)

Subway

Often the quickest way around, with color-coded lines each with express and local service. Runs 24 hours, though only local (and less frequent) services late at night.

Bus

Slow but scenic. Very useful for getting 'crosstown' (going east–west or west–east). Catch crosstown buses on 14th, 23rd, 34th, 42nd, 49th/50th, 57th, 72nd, 79th and 86th Sts.

Bicycle

Use one of Citi Bike's 330 stations for a speedy 30-minute jaunt across town.

Taxi

Everywhere, except when you need one. Wave or whistle them down. Fares: around $15 to $26 from downtown to Midtown.

Boat

The free Staten Island Ferry runs from Lower Manhattan. The more useful East River Ferry travels between Wall St/Pier 11 and E 34th St in Manhattan, stopping en route in Brooklyn (Dumbo, South Williamsburg, North Williamsburg, Greenpoint) and Queens (Long Island City).

Key Phrases

Car service You can phone a car service (often a black sedan) to pick you up. Useful on return trips to the airport or if needing outer-borough transport (where taxis are in short supply).

Citi Bike The ubiquitous blue bikes that are part of NYC's bike-sharing scheme, with hundreds of quick-hire kiosks around town.

Express train/local train Express subway trains make limited stops, skipping many stations; local trains stop at every station. To switch between the two, often you just have to cross the platform.

LIRR The Long Island Rail Road, useful for speedy transport to JFK and for beach getaways.

MetroCard The flimsy yellow-and-blue card, which you load with credit, then swipe through for every ride on the subway or bus.

Uptown/Downtown Uptown means going north (Upper East Side, Harlem, etc), downtown means going south (Soho, Lower Manhattan, etc).

Key Routes

Scenic views Take the J, M or Z line over the Williamsburg Bridge or the B, D, N or Q line over the Manhattan Bridge for great views of Manhattan. There's also the Roosevelt Island Tramway.

Uptown bound The 4, 5 or 6 lines go to the Upper East Side; for the Upper West Side take the B, C, 1, 2 or 3 trains.

Taxi Etiquette

➡ To hail one of NYC's yellow cabs, look for one with its roof light lit (if it's not lit, the cab is taken).

➡ Stand in a prominent place on the side of the road and stick out your arm.

➡ Once inside the cab, tell them your destination (it's illegal for drivers to refuse you a ride somewhere).

➡ Pay your fare at the end, either with cash or credit card (via the touch screen in back). Don't forget to tip (typically 10% to 15%).

TOP TIPS

➡ Pay attention to 'downtown' vs 'uptown' subway station entrances. Sometimes there are separate entrances (usually across the street from one another) depending on which direction the train is going.

➡ Plan your route carefully. Sometimes, walking a few blocks can get you to a faster or more direct subway line, thereby saving you time in the end.

➡ For short trips, consider hopping on a Citi Bike.

When to Travel

➡ Rush hour is never just an hour! On weekdays, from 8am to 9:30am and 4:30pm to 6:30pm, trains and buses are frustratingly packed.

➡ If it's not possible to avoid traveling at these peak times, allow extra time to get places (particularly to/from the airport).

➡ Hailing a cab can be difficult on weekdays from 4pm to 5pm when many drivers change shifts. And when it's raining, finding an available taxi can seem a monumental challenge.

Etiquette

➡ Have your MetroCard ready before you go through the gate. New Yorkers are skilled at moving through the ticket barriers without breaking stride.

➡ On subway platforms, stand to the side of the train doors and wait for passengers to exit before boarding.

➡ On escalators, stand on the right-hand side or use the left if you want to walk down/up.

➡ When walking on the sidewalk, think of yourself as a car on the street: don't stop short, pay attention to the speed limit, and pull off to the side if you need to look at a map or dig through your bag for an umbrella.

Tickets & Passes

➡ MetroCards are the swipe cards used for all of NYC's public transportation. Each ride on the subway or bus (except for express buses) deducts $2.50 from the card.

➡ Purchase a MetroCard ($1) at kiosks in subway stations, and load it with credit ($20, which will give you eight rides and change, is a good start). If you plan to ride a lot, buy a seven-day unlimited pass ($30).

➡ The subway kiosks take credit or ATM cards (larger machines also take cash). When you need to add more credit, just insert your card and follow the prompts (tip: when it asks for your ZIP, input '99999' if you're not from the USA).

➡ Transfers from subway to bus, or bus to subway, are free. Just swipe/insert your card, and no extra charge will be deducted.

CITI BIKES

To use a Citi Bike, here's how it works: purchase a 24-hour or seven-day access pass (around $11 or $28 including tax) at any Citi Bike kiosk. You will then be given a five-digit code to unlock a bike. Return the bike to any station within 30 minutes to avoid incurring extra fees. Reinsert your credit card (you won't be charged) and follow the prompts to check out a bike again. You can make an unlimited number of 30-minute check-outs during those 24 hours or seven days.

For much more on **getting around**, see p380

Top Itineraries

Day One

Upper West Side & Central Park (p228)

 Spend the morning exploring the wonders of **Central Park**, taking in the fortresslike walls of skyscrapers surrounding the green. Start at **Columbus Circle**, then head northeast, passing the **Central Park Zoo**, the **Bethesda Fountain**, the **Conservatory Water** and **Strawberry Fields** on the west side. If you have the kids in tow, check out the dinosaur skeletons at the **American Museum of Natural History** then hit up the **Loeb Boathouse** to rent rowboats for a paddle around the lake.

> ✕ **Lunch** Pick up supplies at Zabar's (p235) for a picnic in Central Park.

Midtown (p174)

 After a morning exploring the green, it's time to uncover some of the city's architectural wonders, like **Grand Central Terminal**, the **Chrysler Building**, the **New York Public Library** and **Rockefeller Center**. Round off the afternoon with a visit to the city's museum darling: **Museum of Modern Art (MoMA)**.

> ✕ **Dinner** For Broadway-goers, do an early dinner at Marseille (p200).

Midtown (p174)

 Spend the evening under the starry lights of **Broadway**, checking out a blockbuster show or something distinctly ahead of the curve at **Playwrights Horizon** or **Signature Theatre**. Soak up the Las Vegas–like atmosphere of **Times Square** from the **TKTS Booth**, swig cocktails at **Rum House**, then climb to the top of the **Empire State Building** to wish the city 'goodnight'.

Day Two

Upper East Side (p210)

 Start at the staggering **Metropolitan Museum of Art**. Wander through the Egyptian and Roman collections, take in European masters, then head up to the rooftop (in summer) for a view over Central Park. Visit the nearby **Neue Galerie** for a feast of German and Austrian art in a 1914 mansion.

> ✕ **Lunch** Lunch on Austrian specialties at elegant Cafe Sabarsky (p224).

SoHo & Chinatown (p82)

 Head down to **SoHo** for an afternoon of shopping amid crowds of tourists seeking the best brands in the world. Wander over to **Chinatown**, which feels worlds away from mainstream consumerism, but is – in reality – only a few blocks over. Stroll by the neighborhood's **Buddhist temples**, stopping for snacks like custard tarts and almond ice cream.

> ✕ **Dinner** Savor soup dumplings at Joe's Shanghai (p93), a Chinatown staple.

Upper West Side & Central Park (p228)

 If you have concert tickets, then skip dinner downtown and hit up **Barcibo Enoteca** for a preshow glass of expertly curated Italian wine. Then it's off to the **Lincoln Center** for opera at the **Metropolitan Opera House** or a symphony in **Avery Fisher Hall**. Afterwards, dine at **Burke & Wills** for modern Australian cuisine, followed by drinks upstairs at the **Manhattan Cricket Club**.

Village Vanguard (p153), Greenwich Village

Day Three

Brooklyn (p263)

 Catch the East River Ferry over to Dumbo, and admire the magnificent view of Manhattan from the lush new **Brooklyn Bridge Park**. Afterwards stroll through the cobblestone streets of Dumbo, browsing bookstores, boutiques and cafes. Don't miss the vintage **Jane's Carousel** and more great views from the Empire Fulton Ferry.

> **Lunch** Fill up on good-value lunch specials at atmospheric AlMar (p283).

Brooklyn (p263)

Travel up to the **Brooklyn Museum** for a look at fascinating works from Africa, the Americas and Ancient Egypt, plus excellent temporary shows. Afterwards take a stroll in **Prospect Park**, pausing for refreshments at the scenic new **Lakeside** complex.

> **Dinner** Partake of Brooklyn's culinary renaissance by dining at Rye (p281).

Brooklyn (p263)

 Jump in a 'Boro Taxi' up to **Williamsburg**, on the north side of the borough, for oysters and bespoke cocktails at **Maison Premiere**. Head up to rooftop bar, the **Ides** for a fabulous view over the city. End the night across the street at the **Brooklyn Bowl**, with a side of bowling and some groovy musical acts.

Day Four

Lower Manhattan & the Financial District (p60)

 Catch the **Staten Island Ferry** in the early morning and watch the sun come up over Lower Manhattan's skyscrapers. Then visit the moving **National September 11 Memorial** before honoring some of New York's greatest luminaries buried in the cemetery at **Trinity Church**.

> **Lunch** Find your way into the alley for creative cooking at Freemans (p118).

East Village & Lower East Side (p104)

Wander through the **Lower East Side**, doing a bit of window-shopping and gallery-hopping. Then visit the **Lower East Side Tenement Museum** for insight into the city's fascinating immigration history. Afterwards, walk up to the East Village for a wander along **St Mark's Place** and nearby 9th St.

> **Dinner** Dine on rich seafood plates at iconic Jeffrey's Grocery (p140).

Greenwich Village, Chelsea & the Meatpacking District (p129)

 Stroll the lovely, meandering streets of Greenwich Village. Delve into the its soul-filled roots for an evening of live jazz at **Blue Note**, **Smalls** or the **Village Vanguard**. Afterwards, slip behind the inconspicuous brown door to swig bathtub gin cocktails amid Prohibition-era-style surrounds at **Little Branch**, then head up to **Cielo** for dancing in one of the city's best little clubs.

If You Like...

Museums

Museum of Modern Art (MoMA) NYC's darling museum has brilliantly curated spaces boasting the best of the world's modern art. (p181)

Metropolitan Museum of Art The most incredible encyclopedic museum in the Americas comes stocked with its own Egyptian temple and the country's most famous canvas of George Washington. (p212)

Guggenheim Museum The exhibits can be uneven, but the architecture is the real star in this Frank Lloyd Wright–designed building. (p216)

Frick Collection A Gilded Age mansion has Vermeers, El Grecos and Goyas and a stunning courtyard fountain. (p219)

Cloisters Museum & Gardens Medieval treasures including a beguiling 16th-century tapestry that depicts a unicorn hunt. (p255)

Brooklyn Museum Ancient Egyptian treasures, a stellar collection of American painting and a cutting-edge feminist arts center. (p267)

Lower East Side Tenement Museum Fantastic insight into life as an immigrant during the 19th and early 20th centuries. (p106)

Whitney Museum of American Art Celebrated for cutting-edge contemporary and 20th-century works. See future American greats at the Whitney Biennial on even-numbered years. (p218)

BEN KLAUS / GETTY IMAGES ©

Japanese garden, Brooklyn Botanic Garden (p278)

Places of Worship

St Patrick's Cathedral
A glorious neo-Gothic masterpiece – it's the largest cathedral in America. (p190)

Trinity Church This gorgeous Anglican church was the tallest building in NYC in the mid-1800s. (p69)

Cathedral Church of St John the Divine The largest house of worship in the US was begun in 1892 – and still isn't completely finished (hence its nickname, St John the Unfinished). (p249)

Temple Emanu-el A Romanesque structure with gilded ceilings serves as one of New York's most beautiful synagogues. (p219)

Plymouth Church This Brooklyn Heights place of worship was a center of abolitionist activity in the 19th century. (p272)

Eldridge Street Synagogue Glittering after a multi-million-dollar restoration, the hallowed hall is now a museum space. (p112)

Staying Up Late

Smalls Catch 1am 'after hours' shows at this atmospheric West Village jazz spot. (p153)

Veselka The go-to place when you've just got to have pierogi (homemade dumplings) and other Ukrainian fare at 4am. (p113)

Landmark Sunshine Cinema Watch midnight screenings on weekends at this Lower East Side classic. (p125)

Chinatown A secreted scatter of late-night lounges tucked behind the unassuming facades of hole-in-the-wall chow spots. (p97)

Output Get your groove on at this late-night dance club in Williamsburg. (p294)

Der Schwarze Köelner A Fort Greene beer hall is the place for a late-night brew on weekends. (p292)

Sing Sing Karaoke Croon your heart out (till the sun comes up on weekends) at this East Village space. (p125)

Gray's Papaya You can't say you've done New York until you've eaten a recession special (two hot dogs and a papaya drink). (p237)

Skyline Views

Brooklyn Bridge Park Brooklyn's newest park has wide open views of downtown Manhattan and the Brooklyn and Manhattan Bridges. (p265)

Top of the Strand Go one better than staring at Midtown's mix of scrapers and swig a drink while you're part of the view. (p200)

The Standard Hotel Check out the downtown views from the sleek bathrooms tucked high up between the Boom Boom Room and Le Bain. (p150)

Brooklyn Heights Promenade Staggering view of Manhattan 24 hours a day. (p274)

Roosevelt Island River and skyscraper views from Louis Kahn's spectacular Franklin D Roosevelt Four Freedoms Park. (p193)

Roof Garden Café & Martini Bar From late April through October, the rooftop garden at the Metropolitan Museum of Art offers incredible views of Central Park and the Midtown skyline. (p225)

Bargemusic Classical music with views of the Brooklyn Bridge and Manhattan – just beautiful. (p295)

East River State Park Take in an inspiring sweep of Midtown from the Williamsburg waterfront. (p271)

Green Spaces

Central Park The city's most famous park has more than 800 acres of rolling meadows and boulder-topped hillocks. (p230)

Hudson River Park Manhattan's looking greener than ever thanks to new parkland running up its west side. (p136)

Brooklyn Bridge Park A brand-new park lines the waterfront along Dumbo, all the way to the foot of Atlantic Ave. (p265)

High Line A thin stripe of green with wild plants and surprising vantage points atop a former rail line. (p131)

Green-Wood Cemetery A lush oasis with great views and rambling paths that dates back to the 1830s. (p279)

Prospect Park Brooklyn's favorite outdoor space for picnics, kite-flying, running, cycling, and ambling amid beautifully landscaped scenery. (p268)

Brooklyn Botanic Gardens Three-season beauty with cherry blossoms in spring, vibrant summery blooms and red, gold and yellow blazes in autumn. (p278)

For more top New York City spots, see the following:

➡ Eating (p38)
➡ Drinking & Nightlife (p42)
➡ Gay & Lesbian (p45)
➡ Entertainment (p47)
➡ Shopping (p50)
➡ Sports & Activities (p53)

PLAN YOUR TRIP IF YOU LIKE...

Historic Sights

Ellis Island The gateway to freedom and opportunity for so many of America's immigrants. (p64)

Frick Collection A rare mansion from the Gilded Age survives to this day as a museum on the Upper East Side. (p219)

Gracie Mansion A graceful Federal-style structure now serves as the mayor's home. (p222)

Jane's Carousel A 1922 carousel in Brooklyn Bridge Park is in the National Register of Historic Places. (p265)

Morris–Jumel Mansion Museum A Georgian-Federal structure is the oldest house in Manhattan. (p255)

Historic Richmond Town A time-stuck village in Staten Island that's home to the country's oldest schoolhouse. (p72)

Venturing off the Beaten Path

Flushing Go on a foodie safari deep in the heart of Queens and browse a sprawling lesser-known Chinatown. (p308)

New York Botanical Garden A vast garden in the Bronx is home to 50 acres of forest and a Victorian-style conservatory. (p261)

Inwood Hill Park It's part of Manhattan, but it doesn't feel like it – this park remains wonderfully wild. (p255)

Queens Museum Excellent exhibits without the fanfare and crowds of some of Manhattan's other museum spaces. (p306)

Dyckman Farmhouse Museum Manhattan's last surviving Dutch farmhouse. (p255)

Gowanus An old industrial canal popular with urban decay types (and the Environmental Protection Agency). (p278)

Old School New York

Coney Island An amusement center that dates back to the early days of the 20th century; don't forget the hot dogs at Nathan's Famous. (p269)

Barney Greengrass After a century in the business, BG still serves up some of the best smoked fish in the city. (p237)

Russian & Turkish Baths Steam your stress away in this East Village classic, now over 120 years old. (p128)

Katz's Smoked meat that will please even the biggest kvetchers. (p118)

Marie's Crisis Show tunes and singing patrons at this legendary West Village gay bar. (p147)

Zabar's An emporium for all types of Upper West Side food-a-holics since the 1930s. (p235)

McSorley's Old Ale House Abraham Lincoln, Boss Tweed and Woody Guthrie are among the many who've raised a glass or two at this sawdust-on-the-floor pub. (p119)

Ultimate Indulgences

Retail therapy at Barney's The fashionista's aspirational closet comes with a hefty price tag. (p206)

Dough Head to Bed-Stuy for the best doughnuts on the planet (or find them at the Brooklyn Flea). (p284)

Pegu Club Stylish lounge, with great ambience and a welcome lack of pretension (never mind the $15 cocktails). (p97)

Brandy Library Nurse a glass of rare, amber-hued armagnac at this gentlemanly retreat. (p78)

Exhale From four-handed massage to beginner yoga classes to acupuncture, you'll find it all at this zen Upper East Side spa. (p227)

Hidden Hangouts

Beauty & Essex Hidden behind a pawnshop facade is an enchanting drinking den. (p123)

Bathtub Gin Slide behind a false wall at the back of a modest coffee shop for Prohibition-chic styling and retro cocktails. (p152)

Mulberry Project An unassuming set of stairs leads to the swank cocktail laboratory of the international owners and their coterie of server-friends. (p97)

Smith & Mills Push the unmarked door to find a kooky industrial interior (think 1900s factory) and smooth libations. (p79)

Freemans Walk down a tiny alley to find quaint cabinlike surrounds and legions of faithful brunchers. (p118)

Little Branch You'd never guess that great cocktails are crafted inside this seemingly abandoned West Village building. (p146)

Larry Lawrence Concealed drinking spot in Williamsburg with an old-time vibe. (p291)

Month By Month

TOP EVENTS
. . . .
Tribeca Film Festival,
April

**Cherry Blossom
Festival**, April or May

SummerStage, June
through August

Independence Day, July

**Village Halloween
Parade**, October

February

**The odd blizzard
and below-freezing
temperatures make
February a good time to
stay indoors nursing a
drink or a warm meal at a
cozy bar or bistro.**

✕ Winter
Restaurant Week

Celebrate dreary February
with slash-cut meal deals
at some of the city's finest eating establishments
during Winter Restaurant
Week, which actually runs
for about three weeks. Price
for a three-course lunch is
around $26 ($40 for dinner).

✿ Mercedes-Benz
Fashion Week

The infamous Bryant Park
fashion shows (www.mb-
fashionweek.com) are sadly

not open to the public. But
whether you're invited or
not, being in the city this
week – when the couture
world descends upon Man-
hattan to swoon over new
looks – could provide a
vicarious thrill, especially if
you find the after-parties.

✿ Lunar New Year

One of the biggest Lunar
(Chinese) New Year celebrations in the country, this
display of fireworks and
dancing dragons draws
mobs of thrill-seekers into
the streets of Chinatown.
The date of Chinese New
Year fluctuates from year
to year, but typically falls in
early February.

March

**After months of freezing
temperatures and
thick winter coats, the
odd warm spring day
appears and everyone
rejoices – though it's
usually followed by a
week of sub-zero drear as
winter lingers on.**

✿ St Patrick's
Day Parade

A massive audience, rowdy
and wobbly from cups
of green beer, lines Fifth

Ave on March 17 for this
popular parade of bagpipe
blowers, sparkly floats
and clusters of Irish-lovin'
politicians. The parade,
which was first held here in
1762, is the city's oldest and
largest.

April

**Spring finally appears:
optimistic alfresco joints
have a sprinkling of
streetside chairs as the
city squares overflow with
bright tulips and blossom-
covered trees.**

☆ Tribeca Film
Festival

Created in response to the
tragic events of Septem-
ber 11, Robert De Niro's
downtown film festival
(www.tribecafilm.com)
has quickly become a star
in the indie movie circuit.
You'll have to make some
tough choices: over 150
films are screened during
the 10-day fest.

May

**April showers bring May
flowers...in the form
of brilliant bursts of
blossoms adorning the
flowering trees all around**

the city. The weather is warm and mild without the unpleasant humidity of summer.

✿ Cherry Blossom Festival

Known in Japanese as Sakura Matsuri, this annual tradition, held on one weekend in late April or early May, celebrates the magnificent flowering of cherry trees in the Brooklyn Botanic Garden. It's complete with entertainment and activities (*taiko* drumming, folk dancing, origami workshops, ikebana flower displays, samurai sword showmanship), plus refreshments and awe-inspiring beauty.

✿ Fleet Week

For one week at the end of the month, Manhattan resembles a 1940s movie set as clusters of fresh-faced, uniformed sailors go 'on the town' to look for adventures (www.fleetweeknewyork. com). For nonswabby visitors, this is a chance to take free tours of ships that have arrived from various corners of the globe. See them docked off Manhattan (around Midtown) and Brooklyn (just south of Brooklyn Bridge Park's pier 6).

🚴 Five Boro Bike Tour

May is Bike Month, featuring two-wheelin' tours, parties and other events for pedal-pushing New Yorkers. TD Bank Five Boro Bike Tour (www.bikenewyork. org), the main event, sees thousands of cyclists hit the pavement for a 42-mile ride, much of it on roads closed to traffic or on waterfront paths through each of the city's five boroughs.

June

Summer's definitely here and locals crawl out of their office cubicles to relax in the city's green spaces. Parades roll down the busiest streets and portable movie screens are strung up in several parks.

✿ Puerto Rican Day Parade

The second weekend in June attracts thousands of flag-waving revelers for the annual Puerto Rican Day Parade (www.nationalpuertoricandayparade.org). Now in its fifth decade, it runs up Fifth Ave from 44th to 86th Sts.

☆ SummerStage

Central Park's SummerStage (www.summerstage. org), which runs from June through August, features an incredible lineup of music and dance throughout the summer. Django Django, Femi Kuti, Shuggie Otis and the Martha Graham Dance Company are among recent standouts. Most events are free. There's also a SummerStage Kids program just in case you've got the little ones in tow. Other parks throughout the city also host events.

✿ Gay Pride

June is Gay Pride Month, and it culminates in a major march down Fifth Ave on the last Sunday of the month. NYC Pride (www. nycpride.org) is a five-hour spectacle of dancers, drag queens, gay police officers, leathermen, lesbian soccer moms and representatives of just about every other queer scene under the rainbow.

☆ HBO Bryant Park Summer Film Festival

Beginning in June and ending in August, Bryant Park hosts Monday-night outdoor screenings of classic Hollywood films, which kick off after sundown. Arrive early (the lawn opens at 5pm; folks line up by 4pm).

✿ Mermaid Parade

Celebrating sand, sea and the beginning of summer is this wonderfully quirky afternoon parade. It's a flash of glitter and glamour, as elaborately costumed folks display their fishy finery along the Coney Island boardwalk. Held on the last Saturday of the month. It's even more fun to take part (all in costume are welcome).

July

As the city swelters, locals flee to beachside escapes on Long Island. It's a busy month for tourism, however, as holidaying North Americans and Europeans fill the city.

✿ Independence Day

America's Independence Day is celebrated on the 4th of July with dramatic fireworks and fanfare. From 2009 to 2013, the fiery show happened over the Hudson, but it may return to the East River in coming years (good news for Manhattan East Siders, Brooklynites and Queens residents).

☆ Shakespeare in the Park

The much-loved Shakespeare in the Park (www. shakespeareinthepark.org) pays tribute to the Bard, with free performances in

(Top) Mermaid Parade, Coney Island
(Bottom) Military ships on the Hudson River for Fleet Week

MICHAEL MARQUAND / GETTY IMAGES ©

DENNIS K JOHNSON / GETTY IMAGES ©

Central Park. The catch? You'll have to wait hours in line to score tickets, or win them in the online lottery. Tickets are given out at noon on show days; arrive no later than 10am for a seat.

August

Thick waves of summer heat slide between skyscrapers as everyone heads to the seashore nearby or gulps cool blasts of air-conditioning when stuck in the city. Myriad outdoor events and attractions add life to the languid urban heat.

☆ Fringe Festival

This annual mid August theater festival (www.fringenyc.org) presents two weeks of performances by companies from all over the world. It's the best way to catch the edgiest, wackiest and most creative up-and-comers around.

September

Labor Day officially marks the end of the Hampton's share-house season as the blistering heat of summer fades to more tolerable levels. As locals return to work, the cultural calendar ramps up.

☆ BAM! Next Wave Festival

Celebrated for 30 years in 2012, the Brooklyn Academy of Music's Next Wave Festival (www.bam.org), which runs through December, showcases world-class avant-garde theater, music and dance.

☆ Electric Zoo

Celebrated over Labor Day Weekend, Electric Zoo (www.madeevent.com/electriczoo) is New York's electronic music festival held in sprawling Randall's Island Park. Past headliners have included Moby, Afrojack, David Guetta, Martin Solveig and The Chemical Brothers.

October

Brilliant bursts of orange, red and gold fill the trees in Central and Prospect Parks as temperatures cool and alfresco cafes finally shutter their windows. Along with May, October is one of the most pleasant and scenic months to visit NYC.

✳ Open House New York

The country's largest architecture and design event, Open House New York (www.ohny.org) features special, architect-led tours, as well as lectures, design workshops, studio visits and site-specific performances all over the city.

☆ Comic-Con

Enthusiasts from near and far gather at this annual beacon of nerd-dom (www.newyorkcomiccon.com) to dress up as their favorite characters and cavort with like-minded anime aficionados.

✳ Animal Blessing

In honor of the Feast Day of St Francis, which falls early in the month, pet owners with their sidekicks – poodles, lizards, parrots, llamas, you name it – in tow flock to the grand Cathedral Church of St John the Divine for the annual Blessing of the Animals. It's a wild and wonderful afternoon for participants and onlookers alike.

✳ Village Halloween Parade

October 31 brings riotous fun to the city, as New Yorkers don their wildest costumes for a night of revelry. See the wildest, most outrageous displays at the Village Halloween Parade (www.halloween-nyc.com) that runs up Sixth Ave in the West Village. It's fun to watch, but even better to join in the action.

November

As the leaves tumble, light jackets are replaced by wool and down. A headliner marathon is tucked into the final days of prehibernation weather, then families gather to give thanks.

🏃 NYC Marathon

Held in the first week of November, this annual 26-mile run (www.nycmarathon.org) draws thousands of athletes from around the world, and just as many excited viewers line the streets to cheer the runners on.

✳ Macy's Thanksgiving Day Parade

Massive helium-filled balloons soar overhead, high-school marching bands rattle their snares and millions of onlookers bundle up with scarves and coats to celebrate Thanksgiving with Macy's world-famous 2.5-mile-long parade.

☆ New York Comedy Festival

Funny-makers take the city by storm during the New York Comedy Festival (www.nycomedyfestival.com) with stand-up sessions, improv nights and big-ticket shows hosted by the likes of Rosie O'Donnell and Ricky Gervais.

✳ Oh, Christmas Tree

The flick of a switch ignites the massive Christmas tree in Rockefeller Center, officially ushering in the holiday season. Bedecked with over 25,000 lights, it is NYC's unofficial Yuletide headquarters and a must-see for anyone visiting the city during December.

December

Winter's definitely here, but there's plenty of holiday cheer to warm the spirit. Fairy lights adorn most buildings, and Fifth Ave department stores (as well as Macy's) create elaborate worlds within their storefront windows.

✳ New Year's Eve

The ultimate place to ring in the New Year in the northern hemisphere, Times Square swarms with millions of gatherers who come to stand squashed together like canned sardines, swig booze, freeze in subarctic temperatures, witness the annual dropping of the ball made entirely of Waterford Crystal and chant the '10...9...8...' in perfect unison.

With Kids

New York City has loads of activities for young ones, including imaginative playgrounds and leafy parks where kids can run free, plus lots of kid-friendly museums and sights. Other highs: carousel rides, puppet shows and noshing at markets around town.

Toucan, Bronx Zoo (p261)

Top Attractions

For many kids, some of New York City's top attractions are a world of fun.

Wildlife

The city has a number of zoos. The best, by far, is the Bronx Zoo (p261), which is known for its well-designed habitats. (The Congo Gorilla Forest is a stunner.) Otherwise, if you're pressed for time, the zoos in Central Park and Prospect Park are great for short visits.

Statue of Liberty

The boat ride to **Lady Liberty** (Map p408; ☏201-604-2800, 877-523-9849; www.statue-cruises.com; adult/child $17/9; ⓢevery 30min 9am-5pm, extended summer hours) offers the opportunity to chug around New York Harbor and get to know an icon that most kids only know from textbooks.

On Top of the World

A glass-roofed elevator leads to the Top of the Rock (p189), a lookout that offers glittering views of New York.

Coney Island

Hot dogs. Ice cream. Amusement-park rides. Coney Island (p269) is just the ticket if you're in need of some low-brow entertainment.

Best Museums

The American Museum of Natural History (p236), with its dinosaurs, marine world, planetarium and IMAX films, should not be missed. Other big museums – the Metropolitan Museum of Art, the Museum of Modern Art and the Guggenheim Museum – all have kids' programs, but many smaller institutions are even more appealing for young visitors.

Toddler Time

For tots aged one to five, hit the Children's Museum of the Arts (p88) in West SoHo and the Brooklyn Children's Museum (p279) in Crown Heights. Both have story times, art classes, craft hours and painting sessions.

NOT FOR PARENTS

For an insight into New York aimed directly at kids, pick up a copy of Lonely Planet's *Not for Parents: New York*. Perfect for children aged eight and up, it opens up a world of intriguing stories and fascinating facts about New York people, places, history and culture.

Five & Over

Bigger kids can clamber on vintage subway cars at the New York Transit Museum (p274), slide down a pole at the New York City Fire Museum (p87) and impose law and order in a miniature cruiser at the New York City Police Museum (p70). Book 'em.

Best Parks & Playgrounds

Central Park

More than 800 acres of green space, a lake that can be navigated by rowboat, a carousel, a zoo and a massive statue of Alice in Wonderland. Heckscher playground, near Seventh Ave and Central Park South is the biggest and best of Central Park's (p230) 21 playgrounds.

Prospect Park

Brooklyn's hilly 585-acre Prospect Park (p268) has abundant amusement for kids, including a zoo, hands-on playthings at Lefferts Historic House and a new ice-skating rink – that becomes a water park in summer.

Brooklyn Bridge Park

Hit the fun water park in the summer on Pier 6 (bring swimsuits, all will get wet) and nosh on pizza at waterfront Fornino (p266). Further north are the grassy hills of Pier 1 and Jane's Carousel.

Hudson River Park

Coursing along Manhattan's west side, this park (p136) offers loads of kiddy excitement, including mini-golf near Moore St (Tribeca), a fun playground near West St (West Village), a carousel off W 22nd St, watery fun at W 23rd & Eleventh Ave, and a science-themed play space near W 44th St.

The High Line

NYC's celebrated elevated green space (p131) has food vendors, water features (which kids can splash through) and great views, plus warm-weather family events – story time, science and craft projects, fun with food, and more. Check the website (www.thehighline.org/public-programs/kids) for details.

Riverside Park

Riverside Park (p235) on the Upper West Side has a bicycle trail with views of the Hudson River. Take a break at the River Run Playground (at W 83rd St), with fountains for cooling off in summer.

South Street Seaport

In Lower Manhattan, the **Imagination Playground** (Map p408; www.imaginationplayground.com; South Street Seaport, East River Dr & John St; ⊙10am-6pm Mon-Fri, 9am-6:30pm Sat & Sun; 🚻; ⓢA/C, 2/3, 4/5 to Fulton St/Broadway-Nassau) features oversized foam building blocks, allowing kids to construct their own play spaces.

Kid-Friendly Theater

Tiny **Puppetworks** (Map p442; ☑718-965-3391; www.puppetworks.org; 338 Sixth Ave, cnr 4th St, Park Slope; adult/child $9/8) in Brooklyn's Park Slope has amusing weekend puppet shows throughout the year.

Markets Snacks

Markets around NYC are great snack spots, particularly Brooklyn Flea (p296), which has vendors selling everything from popsicles, doughnuts and pickles to tacos and pork sandwiches.

José de Creeft's *Alice in Wonderland*, Central Park (p230)

The Chelsea Market (p143) has many temptations; assemble a picnic then head over to the Hudson River Park for a waterside picnic.

Best Bets for a Rainy Day

Craft Hour

At the Upper East Side **Craft Studio** (Map p432; ☎212-831-6626; www.craftstudionyc.com; 1657 Third Ave btwn 92nd & 93rd Sts; ⊗10am-6pm Mon-Sat, 11am-6pm Sun; 🖼; ⓢ6 to 96th St), families can drop in to create ceramic masterpieces right on the spot. Ages three and up.

Bounce Around

Little Athletes Exploration Center (Map p422; ☎212-336-6500, ext 0; www.chelseapiers. com; Chelsea Piers, Twelfth Ave at 23rd St; single session $12; ⊗9:30am-noon & 1-5pm ; 🖼; ⓢC/E to 23rd St) at the Chelsea Piers is a colorful indoor playground that lets six-month to four-year-old kids let off some steam.

Animal World

At **Art Farm in the City** (Map p432; ☎212-410-3117; www.theartfarms.org; 419 E 91st St btwn First & York Aves; 🖼; ⓢ4/5/6 to 86th St), on the Upper East Side, there are art supplies, craft sessions and a petting zoo (with bunnies, turtles and the occasional sheep or pig). Ages six months to eight years.

Story Time

NYC's public libraries have free story hour (with separate times for babies, toddlers and preschoolers) at many branches around town. Check www.nypl.org/events/calendar for Manhattan offerings and www.bklynpubliclibrary.org (click on 'Events Calendar') for Brooklyn.

Keep It Cheap

Ferry Tale

The Staten Island Ferry (p81) is free and offers spectacular views of New York Harbor and the Statue of Liberty.

Fabled Views

For kids who dig trains, the subway can be a great adventure. You can clatter across the bridges on the J, M or Z lines (Williamsburg Bridge) or B, D, N or Q lines across the Manhattan Bridge. (For views of the Brooklyn Bridge and Lower Manhattan, take the N or Q train.) And don't miss the aerial tram to Roosevelt Island (departing near 60th St and Second Ave).

Bird Brains

In Central Park, pop into Belvedere Castle (p246) for a free children's birding kit – an excellent way to get kids interested in nature.

NEED TO KNOW

➡ **Car seats** It's legal for children under the age of seven to ride on an adult's lap in a taxi, but you can also install your own car seat.

➡ **Strollers** Strollers are not allowed on public buses unless they are folded.

➡ **Babysitting** The Baby Sitters' Guild (☎212-682-0227; www.babysittersguild.com) can arrange for childcare at your hotel.

➡ **Online resources** Time Out New York Kids (www.timeout.com/new-york-kids) has event listings as does Mommy Poppins (www.mommypoppins.com).

Like a Local

New Yorkers have developed winning strategies when it comes to nightlife, dining out and partaking of the city's staggering cultural calendar. From weekend brunches to leisurely spring days in the park, there are plenty of ways to go local – without having to pay those ridiculous rents.

Commuter, Central Park West subway station

A Little Birdie Told Me

Check out the following list of our favorite members of New York's Twitterati, who are always tweeting about the city's latest musts:

Everything NYC (@EverythingNYC) Hunting down the best things to see, do and eat in the Big Apple.

Pete Wells (@pete_wells) Restaurant critic of the *New York Times*.

New York Nightlife (@NYNightlife) Party/club scene news and updates.

Paper (@papermagazine) Art, culture and music news.

Guest of a Guest (@guestofaguest) In-the-know info on NYC parties, social and fashion scenes.

Gothamist (@gothamist) News and curiosities.

Hyperallergic (@Hyperallergic) Tweets from NYC's favorite art blogazine.

Colson Whitehead (@colsonwhitehead) Manhattan native, novelist and *New Yorker* contributor.

Paul Goldberger (@paulgoldberger) Pulitzer Prize–winning architecture critic.

Tom Colicchio (@tomcolicchio) Celebrity chef and owner of the popular Craft franchise.

Sam Sifton (@samsifton) Senior editor at the *New York Times*.

Dos & Don'ts

Hail a cab only if the roof light is on. If it's not lit, the cab is taken, so put your arm down already!

➡ You needn't obey 'walk' signs – simply cross the street when there isn't oncoming traffic.

➡ When negotiating pedestrian traffic on the sidewalk think of yourself as a vehicle – don't stop short, follow the speed of the crowd around you and pull off to the side if you need to take out your map or umbrella. Most New Yorkers are respectful of personal space, but they will bump into you – and not apologize – if you get in the way.

➡ When boarding the subway, wait until the passengers disembark, then be aggressive enough when you hop on so that the doors don't close in front of you.

➡ In New York you wait 'on line' instead of 'in line'.

➡ Oh, and it's How-sten St, not Hew-sten.

Joining In

Truth be told, watching a parade is a pretty dull affair. It's much more fun to take part. Along those lines, there are many ways you can join in the action. Don an outrageous costume for the Village Halloween Parade or the summertime Mermaid Parade in Coney Island. Sign up for an organized race in the city (New York Road Runners stages dozens of annual runs). Take a rock-climbing class at Brooklyn Boulders or the Cliffs in Queens. Polish up those old poems and take the stage at open-mike night at the Nuyorican or if there's music in you, try the open mike at Sidewalk Cafe. Whatever your passion – chess, hip-hop, drawing, architecture, beer-making – you'll find it in NYC, and be surrounded by plenty of like minds.

Seasonal Activities

Winter

There's always something to look forward to; even dreary winter brings its delights – namely, ice skating! Beginning in November or December, the city's skating rinks provide ample amusement (and a good prequel to fireside drinks in a toasty bar afterwards). Locals skip tourist-swarmed Rockefeller Center and Bryant Park and head instead to Central Park, McCarren Park or Prospect Park for skating.

Spring

In spring the city's blossoming parks are the place to be for picnics, sun-drenched strolls and lazy days lounging on the grass. Top spots for flower-gazing: the New York Botanical Garden and the Brooklyn Botanic Garden. The latter hosts a lovely Cherry Blossom Festival, much adored by Brooklynites.

Summer

The summer is the time for free open-air events: film screenings in Bryant Park, street festivals around town, and concerts in Central Park, Hudson River Park, Prospect Park and other green spaces around the city.

Fall

In fall the cultural calendar ramps up again as the city's premier performing-arts halls open their seasons (which run from September through May) and galleries kick off their new shows (Thursday nights incidentally, is when the art openings happen).

Eating & Drinking

The Culture of Brunch

Brunch in New York is deeply woven into the city's social fabric, much like teatime for British royals. It typically happens between 11am and 4pm on weekends (though some places, especially in Brooklyn, have begun serving brunch every day). The meal provides a perfect setting for friends to catch up on the week's events and weekend's shenanigans over dishes constructed of breakfast materials and an indiscriminant mix of cocktails or coffee. For our top brunch picks, see p41.

The Weekends Are for Amateurs

New Yorkers tend to avoid the big clubs, packed bars and certain neighborhoods (East Village, Lower East Side) on the weekends when you find yourself among a high proportion of less sophisticated types (some might unkindly use the word 'douchebags'). Instead, weeknights can be great for going out – with fewer crowds, fewer of the aforementioned types, and more creative folk who don't work the typical nine-to-five (actors, writers, artists). Plus, you'll be able to score happy-hour and early-in-the-week specials.

Bar Food

Many of New York's best bars blur the boundary between eating and drinking. Slide onto a barstool, pick up a menu and you'll often be faced with some surprising dining options. That could be oysters at the bar, small sharing plates (seared scallops, sliders, truffle-oil fries), cheese boards and charcuterie or anything else – roasted beet salads, gourmet sandwiches, braised artichokes, rack of lamb. When planning a meal, don't limit yourself to a sit-down restaurant, you can also eat and drink your way around a neighborhood by stopping in at gastropubs.

For Free

The Big Apple isn't the world's cheapest destination. Nevertheless, there are many ways to kick open the treasure chest without spending a dime – free concerts, theater and film screenings, pay-what-you-wish nights at legendary museums, city festivals, free ferry rides, plus loads of green space.

BARRY WINKER / GETTY IMAGES ©

Hispanic Society of America (p255), Washington Heights

Live Music, Theater & Cinema

In the summer, there are scores of free events around town. From June through August, SummerStage (p244) features over 100 free performances at 17 parks around the city, including Central Park. Prospect Park has its own venerable open-air summer concert and events series: **Celebrate Brooklyn** (bricartsmedia.org/performing-arts/celebrate-brooklyn).

Summertime also brings free film screenings and events to the water's edge in both the Hudson River Park (p136) in Manhattan and the Brooklyn Bridge Park (p265). Another great option for film lovers is the free Bryant Park (p28) film screenings on Monday nights during summer.

You'll have to be tenacious to get free tickets to Shakespeare in the Park (p28) held in Central Park in the summer. But it's well worth the effort. Top actors like Meryl Streep and Al Pacino have taken the stage in years past.

A few places offer free music throughout the year. BAMcafe (p294) in Brooklyn has free concerts (world music, R&B, jazz, rock) on select Friday and Saturday nights. In Harlem, Marjorie Eliot (p261) opens her home for free jazz jams on Sundays.

On the Water

The free Staten Island Ferry (p81) provides magical views of the Statue of Liberty, and you can enjoy it with a cold beer (available on the boat).

For a bit more adventure, take out a free kayak, available in the Hudson River Park, Brooklyn Bridge Park and in Red Hook (p299). And while it's not free, for just $4 you can sail from Lower Manhattan across to Brooklyn, Queens or up to 34th St on the East River Ferry (p384) – a great alternative to the subway. On summer weekends, you can also take a free ferry over to Governors Island (p71), a car-free oasis with priceless views.

TV Tapings

Some of America's top evening shows are taped right here in New York City. The

Late Show (www.cbs.com/shows/late_show/), the **Daily Show with Jon Stewart** (www.thedailyshow.com/tickets) and **Late Night with Jimmy Fallon** all give out free tickets to their shows. Go online to reserve seats.

Walking Tours

One of the best ways to experience the city, is to have a local show you around. The highly recommended Big Apple Greeter (p388) provides free tours by locals who love showing off their city. For DIY adventures, check out our own walking tours of the following neighborhoods:

➡ Lower Manhattan (p77)
➡ Chinatown (p86)
➡ East Village (p115)
➡ Greenwich Village (p138)
➡ Union Square (p165)
➡ Midtown (p191)
➡ Upper East Side (p223)
➡ Brooklyn Heights (p272)
➡ South Brooklyn (p276)

Free Museums & Sites
Always Free

➡ The High Line (p131)
➡ National September 11 Memorial (p66)
➡ National Museum of the American Indian (p68)
➡ Hispanic Society of America Museum & Library (p255)
➡ Museum at FIT (p193)
➡ Hamilton Grange (p254)
➡ American Folk Art Museum (p235)

Admission by Donation

➡ Metropolitan Museum of Art (p212)
➡ American Museum of Natural History (p236)
➡ Cloisters Museum & Gardens (p255)
➡ Brooklyn Museum (p267)
➡ Museum of the City of New York (p222)
➡ Nicholas Roerich Museum (p235)
➡ Brooklyn Historical Society (p274)

Free or Pay-What-You-Wish on Certain Days

➡ Museum of Modern Art (MoMA; p181) 4–8pm Friday
➡ Guggenheim (p216) 5:45–7:45pm Saturday
➡ Whitney Museum of American Art (p218) 6–9pm Friday
➡ Neue Galerie (p219) 6–8pm first Friday of month
➡ Frick Collection (p219) 11am–1pm Sunday
➡ New Museum of Contemporary Art (p107) 7–9pm Thursday
➡ New-York Historical Society (p235) 6–8pm Friday
➡ Jewish Museum (p219) 5–8pm Thursday & Saturday
➡ Rubin Museum of Art (p137) 6–10pm Friday
➡ Asia Society & Museum (p222) 6–9pm Friday
➡ Japan Society (p189) 6–9pm Friday
➡ Studio Museum in Harlem (p251) Sunday
➡ MoMA PS1 (p302) Free with your MoMA ticket

Discount Tickets & Cards

For cut-rate admission to Broadway shows visit the TKTS Booth in Times Square.

If you're planning to see a lot of sights, getting one of these discount cards will save you a wad of cash. Check the websites for more details:

Downtown Culture Pass www.downtownculturepass.org

Explorer Pass www.smartdestinations.com

New York CityPASS www.citypass.com

The New York Pass www.newyorkpass.com

NEED TO KNOW

Handy websites for tracking down free and discounted events in the city include **Club Free Time** (www.clubfreetime.com) and **Free in NYC** (www.freeinnyc.net). These have daily listings of free tours, concerts, workshops, talks, art openings, book readings and more.

Italian combo sandwich

ADAM LEE KUBAN / GETTY IMAGES ©

 **Eating**

From inspired iterations of world cuisine to quintessentially local nibbles, New York City's dining scene is infinite, all-consuming and a proud testament to the kaleidoscope of citizens that call the city home. So go ahead, take a bite out of the Big Apple – we promise you won't be sorry.

To Market, to Market

Don't let the concrete streets and buildings fool you – New York City has a thriving greens scene that comes in many shapes and sizes. At the top of your list should be the Chelsea Market (p133), which is packed with gourmet goodies of all kinds – both shops (where you can assemble picnics) and food stands (where you can eat on-site).

Many neighborhoods have their own green market. One of the biggest is the Union Square Greenmarket (p173), open four days

weekly year round. Check **Grow NYC** (www.grownyc.org/greenmarket) for a list of the other 50-plus markets around the city.

The best market for noshers (rather than cook-at-home types) is the weekend Brooklyn Flea (p296), with dozens of food vendors. In summer also check out **Smorgasburg** (www.smorgasburg.com) – the food-only component of Brooklyn Flea.

Also popular are high-end market-cum-grocers like Eataly (p172) and Dean & DeLuca (p99), where fresh produce and ready-made fare are given the five-star treatment. **Whole**

Foods is another big draw, particularly its new, ecofriendly, locavore-focused Brooklyn outpost (p285).

And, in recent market gossip, food-show host Anthony Bourdain is planning to open an international market in Lower Manhattan, which will hawk street food from around the globe.

Top Dishes of New York City

Here are a few of our favorite dishes from NYC's always changing, but ever-creative restaurant scene:

Omakase, Tanoshi (p224) The unbelievably good chef's selection of sushi changes daily at this tiny, well-worn joint in the Upper East Side.

Bong-smoked oysters, Desnuda (p290) If you like oysters, don't miss the unusual smokiness of briny oysters infused with concentrated smoke of tea leaves.

Grilled Korean BBQ shortrib tacos, Kimchi Grill (p288) Who new that Korean and Mexican would go so well together?

Chapulqueso, Casa Mezcal (p123) Adventurous palates will want to try this Oaxacan invention: fresh greens and tomato topped with melted cheese and fried grasshoppers. It goes down nicely with a smoky mezcal margarita.

Ike's Vietnamese fish sauce wings, Pok Pok (p288) Flavorfully rich and complex, these chicken wings are the most famous dish at Andy Ricker's celebrated new restaurant.

Food Trucks & Carts

Skip the bagel- and hot-dog-vending food carts. These days, there's a new mobile crew in town dishing up high-end treats and unique fusion fare. The trucks ply various routes, stopping in designated zones throughout the city – namely around Union Square, Midtown and the Financial District – so if you're looking for a particular grub wagon, it's best to follow them on Twitter. Here are a few of our favorites:

Cinnamon Snail Vegan Lunch Truck (www.twitter.com/VeganLunchTruck)

Kimchi Taco (www.twitter.com/kimchitruck)

Red Hook Lobster Pound (twitter.com/lobstertruckny)

Big Gay Ice Cream (www.twitter.com/biggayicecream)

NEED TO KNOW

Price Guide

For this guide, the following price symbols apply for a main dish, exclusive of tax and tip:

$	under $10
$$	$10–$20
$$$	more than $20

Opening Hours

Generally speaking, meal times often bleed together as New Yorkers march to the beat of their own drum: breakfast is served from 7am to noon, lunch goes from 11am to around 3pm, and dinner stretches between 5pm and 11pm. The popular Sunday brunch (often served on Saturdays too) lasts from 11am until 4pm.

Websites

→ **Yelp** (www.yelp.com) Comprehensive user-generated content.

→ **Open Table** (www.opentable.com) Click-and-book reservation service for many restaurants.

→ **Tasting Table** (www.tastingtable.com) Sign up for handy news blasts about the latest and greatest.

Tipping

New Yorkers tip between 15% and 20% of the final price of the meal. For takeaway, it's polite to drop a dollar or two in the tip jar.

Reservations

Popular restaurants abide by one of two rules: either they take reservations and you need to plan in advance (weeks or months early for the real treasures) or they only seat patrons on a first-come basis, in which case you should arrive when it opens, and eat early. Otherwise, you might be looking at a two-hour wait.

Korilla BBQ (www.twitter.com/korillabbq)

Calexico Cart (www.twitter.com/calexiconyc)

Kelvin Natural Slush (www.twitter.com/kelvinslush)

Wafels & Dinges (www.twitter.com/waffletruck)

Souvlaki GR (www.witter.com/souvlakitruck)

Eating by Neighborhood

Harlem & Upper Manhattan
Comfort cuisine meets Caribbean and Latin American (p256)

Upper West Side & Central Park
A few top eats tucked between apartment blocks (p236)

Central Park

Upper East Side
Ladies-who-lunch meet cafe culture (p222)

Midtown
Fine dining, cocktail-literate bistros and old-school delis (p197)

Queens
A multicultural borough that cures all cravings (p307)

Greenwich Village, Chelsea & the Meatpacking District
See-and-be-seen brunch spots, wine bars and New American darlings (p137)

Union Square, Flatiron District & Gramercy
Everything from after-work tapas to parkside burgers (p164)

Manhattan

East Village & Lower East Side
Unpretentious spectrum of eats, from Asia to the Middle East (p113)

SoHo & Chinatown
Bargain-basement fare beside high-end markets (p90)

Lower Manhattan & the Financial District
Celebrity-chef hot spots and a locavore market (p76)

Brooklyn
Neighborhood pizzerias, Michelin-star dining and retro–New American fare (p280)

Tours & Courses

There's no better way to engage with the city's infinite dining scene than to link up with a savvy local for a food tour or cooking class. Check out the following winners:

Institute of Culinary Education (p173) America's largest cooking school offers accessible, top-notch cooking courses, as well as foodie tours.

Urban Oyster (www.urbanoyster.com) High-quality, themed foodie tours mostly in Lower Manhattan and Brooklyn.

Scott's Pizza Tours (www.scottspizzatours.com) Offbeat and fun, Scott promises to unveil all of the secrets of the city's pizza-pie scene.

Joshua M Bernstein (www.joshuambernstein.com) Respected food blogger and journalist, his tours have a special focus on craft and home-brewed beer.

I Want More Food (www.iwantmorefood.com) Food blogger specializing in Queens food-truck crawls.

Pizza A Casa (www.pizzaacasa.com) Much-loved pie school on the Lower East Side specializing in rolling and decorating dough.

Food Reviews & Blogs

New Yorkers are famous for offering their opinion, so why not capitalize on their taste-bud experiences and click through scores of websites catering to the discerning diner. Some of our favorite blog-style rags:

Eater (http://ny.eater.com)

New York Magazine (www.nymag.com)

Serious Eats (http://newyork.seriouseats.com)

Grub Street (http://www.grubstreet.com/)

Gothamist (http://gothamist.com/food)

Immaculate Infatuation (www.immaculateinfatuation.com)

Checkmark Eats (http://chekmarkeats.com)

Lonely Planet's Top Choices

Le Bernardin (p199) Triple Michelin-star earner and New York's holy grail of fine dining.

Saxon + Parole (p92) Revamped comfort grub meets sneaky bar at this buzzing NoHo must.

RedFarm (p139) Savvy Sino-fusion dishes boast bold flavors but it doesn't take itself too seriously.

Dovetail (p239) Simplicity is key at this Upper West Side stunner – vegetarians unite on Mondays for a divine tasting menu.

Foragers City Table (p143) A triumph of farm-to-table cooking with flavorful sustainable recipes.

Best by Budget

$
Taïm (p139) Outstanding falafel sandwiches.

Le Grainne (p143) Good-value French restaurant in Chelsea.

Golden Shopping Mall (p308) All things Asian and edible in Queens.

Moustache (p137) Tiny West Village gem serving satisfying Middle Eastern dishes.

$$
Upstate (p116) A seafood feast awaits in the East Village.

Jeffrey's Grocery (p140) Much-loved West Village neighborhood spot.

Amy Ruth's Restaurant (p260) Rich soul food served with flair in Harlem.

Vinegar Hill House (p283) Inventive dishes in an off-the-beaten path location in Brooklyn.

$$$
Rouge Tomate (p197) Sustainable, healthy and delectable dishes.

Café Boulud (p225) French icon by celebrated chef Daniel Boulud.

Dutch (p93) High-end farm-to-table fare in SoHo.

Best by Cuisine

Asian
Danji (p199) Michelin-starred eatery serving exquisite Korean fare.

Ippudo NY (p114) Upscale ramen spot in the East Village.

Italian
Rosemary's (p140) A beautifully designed West Village spot with memorable cooking.

Morandi (p140) A downtown gem that invites lingering.

Vegetarian
Butcher's Daughter (p91) Inventive vegetarian menu in Nolita.

Hangawi (p197) Meat-free (and shoe-free) Korean restaurant in Koreatown.

Best Brunch

Balthazar (p93) A buzzing SoHo bistro with years of excellence.

Cookshop (p143) Great indoor-outdoor dining spot in west Chelsea.

Peaches (p284) Southern perfection in less-traveled Bed-Stuy.

Cafe Mogador (p114) An icon of the East Village brunch scene.

Café Luxembourg (p239) A picture-perfect French bistro near Lincoln Center.

Marseille (p200) The best place to brunch in Hell's Kitchen.

Best for Old-School New York City

Barney Greengrass (p237) Perfect plates of smoked salmon and sturgeon for over 100 years.

Katz's Deli (p118) Perhaps the most famous Jewish eatery in the universe.

Zabar's (p235) Store selling gourmet, kosher foods since the 1930s.

El Margon (p198) Unfussy, unchanged Cuban lunch counter in Midtown.

Sant Ambroeus (p224) Fanciful Upper East Side restaurant and cafe.

Best Bakeries

Dough (p284) Probably NYC's best doughnut.

Billy's Bakery (p143) When in Chelsea, stop here for cupcakes, pastries and more.

Make My Cake Head uptown for wondrous dessert temptations.

City Bakery (p166) Decadent hot chocolate, baked goods and full meals.

Best Upscale Market Groceries

Chelsea Market (p133) Sprawling, atmospheric space with dozens of eating temptations.

Eataly (p172) A mecca for lovers of Italian food.

Whole Foods (p285) Ecofriendly shopping in the reinvented Gowanus neighborhood.

Union Square Greenmarket (p173) Delicious veggies and bakery items.

Bartender, Brooklyn

🍷 Drinking & Nightlife

Considering that 'Manhattan' is thought to be a derivation of the Munsee word manahactanienk *(place of general inebriation), it shouldn't be surprising that New York truly lives up to its nickname: 'the city that never sleeps.' In fact, some 20 years after the city was founded, Peter Stuyvesant lashed out, stating that a quarter of New Amsterdam's buildings were taverns. Sometimes it feels like things have barely changed.*

Historic Cocktails, Crafty Beers

Here in the land where the term 'cocktail' was born, mixed drinks are still stirred with the utmost gravitas. From Jack McGarry at Dead Rabbit (p78) to Kenta Goto at Pegu Club (p97), the city's top barkeeps are virtual celebrities, their obsession with precision creating some of the world's most sophisticated libations. Often, it's a case of history in a glass: New York's obsession with rediscovered recipes and Prohibition-era style shows no signs of abaiting.

The city's craft-beer culture is equally dynamic, with an ever-expanding booty of breweries, bars and shops showcasing local artisan brews. While Brooklyn may no longer be the major beer exporter of yesteryear, hipster breweries like Brooklyn Brewery (p273) and Sixpoint have put it back on the map. Neighboring Queens has also jumped on the craft-brew bandwagon, with start-ups including SingleCut Beersmiths and Big Alice Brewery making amber waves.

The Coffee Evolution

A boom in specialty coffee roasters is transforming New York's once-dismal caffeine culture. More locals are cluing in on single-origin beans and different brewing techniques, with numerous roasters now offering cupping classes for curious drinkers. Many are transplants from A-list coffee cities, among them Portland's Stumptown (p200) and the Bay Area's Blue Bottle (p290). The Australian influence is especially notable. One of the latest is Midtown's Little Collins (p200), named in honor of a trendy Melbourne street.

Clubbing

New Yorkers are always looking for the next big thing, so the city's club scene changes faster than a New York minute. Promoters drag revelers around the city for weekly events held at all of the finest addresses, and, when there's nothing on, it's time to hit the dance-floor stalwarts.

When clubbing it never hurts to plan ahead; having your name on a guest list can relieve unnecessary frustration and disappointment. If you're an uninitiated partier, dress the part. If you're fed the 'private party' line, try to bluff – chances are high that you've been bounced. Also, don't forget a wad of cash as many nightspots (even the swankiest ones) often refuse credit cards, and in-house ATMs scam a fortune in fees.

Drinking & Nightlife by Neighborhood

➡ **Lower Manhattan & the Financial District** Office slaves loosen their ties in everything from specialist beer and brandy bars to speakeasy-style cocktail hot spots. In the warmer months, crowds pack pedestrianized Stone St. (p78)

➡ **East Village & Lower East Side** Proud home of the original-flavor dive bar, the East Village is brimming with options. In the cool 'n' edgy Lower East Side, hit Stanton and Rivington Sts. (p97)

➡ **Greenwich Village, Chelsea & the Meatpacking District** Jet setters flock to the Meatpacking District, with wine bars, backdoor lounges and gay hangouts radiating out into the West Village and Chelsea. (p119)

➡ **Union Square, Flatiron District & Gramercy** Vintage drinking dens packed with after-work ties, swinging cocktail bars jammed with slinky night owls, and a string of fun student hangouts – this NYC trio spans all tastes and budgets. (p170)

NEED TO KNOW

Websites

➡ **New York Magazine** (www.nymag.com/nightlife) Brilliantly curated nightlife options by the people who know best.

➡ **Thrillist** (www.thrillist.com) An on-the-ball round up of what's hot or coming soon on the NYC bar scene, including interviews with industry peeps.

➡ **Urbandaddy** (www.urbandaddy.com) More up-to-the-minute info and a handy 'hot right now' list.

➡ **Time Out** (www.timeout.com/newyork/clubs-nightlife) Articles, reviews and on-the-ball listings of where to drink and dance.

Business Hours

Opening times vary, though most places get rollin' around 5pm – some start as early as 8am. Most bars stay open until the legal closing time of 4am, though a few stop at 2am.

How Much

Happy-hour beers start at around $2; expect to pay about $6 for a regular draft, and from $8 for imported bottles. Glasses of wine start at around $7. Specialty cocktails run from $12 to well over $20.

Tipping

If you grab a beer at the bar, bartenders will expect at least a $1 tip *per drink;* tip $2 to $3 for fancier cocktails. Sit-down bars with waitstaff may expect more of a standard restaurant-style 15% to 20% tip, particularly if you snacked along with your boozing.

➡ **Midtown** Rooftop bars with skyline views, historic cocktail salons and time-warped dive bars: welcome to Midtown. (p200)

➡ **Harlem & Upper Manhattan** North of Central Park, the drinking scene is a burgeoning mix of speakeasy-style bars, hipster hangouts pouring craft suds, and old-school dives where the drinks are strong, cheap and swilled to soul-stirring jazz and blues. The heart of the action is Harlem. (p261)

➡ **Brooklyn** Brooklyn offers everything on the nightlife spectrum with Williamsburg as its heart. (p290)

Lonely Planet's Top Choices

Campbell Apartment (p187) Sip Kentucky Gingers in the lavish railway office of a 1920s bigwig.

Little Branch (p146) Speakeasy-chic is all the craze, but no one does it quite like this West Village hideout.

Maison Premiere (p290) Absinthe, juleps and oysters shine bright at this Big Easy tribute in Williamsburg, Brooklyn.

Bohemian Hall & Beer Garden (p310) Czech brews served with thick accents at NYC's favorite beer garden in underrated Queens.

Best Cocktails

Dead Rabbit (p78) Meticulously researched cocktails, punches and pop-inns – lightly hopped ales spiked with different flavors – in a cozy Financial District den.

Weather Up (p78) The place barkeeps go for a well-crafted drink in Tribeca.

Angel's Share (p122) Perfect mixology in an intimate East Village hideout.

Penrose (p225) Artful concoctions in a vintage Upper East Side joint.

Best Mocktails

North End Grill (p76) Vibrant juices and artisanal flavours at Danny Meyer's downtown bar and grill.

NoMad (p337) Sophisticated mocktails in a luxe, Victoriana oasis.

Flatiron Lounge (p170) Fresh, seasonal mocktails and deco design in Flatiron.

Clover Lounge (p292) Vintage-inspired classics (with or without alcohol) served with verve on Brooklyn's Smith St.

Best Wine Lists

Gramercy Tavern (p167) Extraordinary top-shelf and lower-priced surprises in a bar/fine-dining hybrid.

Barcibo Enoteca (p239) Go-to spot for wine lovers before or after a show at the nearby Lincoln Center.

Immigrant (p122) Excellent wines and service in a skinny East Village setting.

Terroir (p201) An encyclopedic wine list in Murray Hill, Midtown East.

Best for Craft Beer

Spuyten Duyvil (p292) A much-loved Williamsburg spot serving unique, high-quality crafts.

Astoria Bier & Cheese (p310) Artisan suds meet gourmet cheeses in Astoria, Queens.

Birreria (p170) Unfiltered, unpasteurized Manhattan ales on a Flatiron rooftop.

Proletariat (p119) Tiny East Village bar serving up extremely uncommon brews.

Best for Spirits

Brandy Library (p78) Blue-blooded cognacs, brandies and more for Tribeca connoisseurs.

Rum House (p201) Unique, coveted rums and a pianist to boot in Midtown.

Mayahuel (p123) A sophisticated East Village temple to mescal and tequila.

Dead Rabbit (p78) NYC's finest collection of rare Irish whiskeys in the Financial District.

Best Dive Bars

Spring Lounge (p97) Soaks, ties and cool kids unite at this veteran Nolita rebel.

Malachy's The perfect place for a 1pm pick-me-up in the Upper West Side.

Sunny's (p293) Our favorite Red Hook dive, near the Brooklyn waterfront.

Best for Date Night

Metropolitan Museum Roof Garden Café & Martini Bar (p225) Exhibition-inspired cocktails with inspiring Central Park views.

Pegu Club (p97) Made-from-scratch concoctions in a Burma-inspired SoHo hideaway.

Ten Bells (p123) Candlelit beauty with great drinks and tapas in the Lower East Side.

Best for Coffee Snobs

Stumptown Coffee Roasters (p200) Hipster baristas serving Portland's favorite joe.

Blue Bottle Coffee (p290) Specialty coffee roasted on-site in Brooklyn.

La Colombe (p97) Sucker-punch roasts for the downtown cognoscenti.

Little Collins (p200) Australia's famous cafe culture comes to Midtown East.

Best Dance Clubs

Cielo (p150) An icon of the Meatpacking District.

Le Bain (p147) Well-dressed crowds pack this club favorite near the High Line.

Output (p294) Williamsburg heats up at this huge warehouse with panoramic roof deck.

Gay & Lesbian

The future has arrived in NYC: men seek out other men using apps, drag queens are so 'out' that they're practically 'in,' bouncers thumb through guest lists on their iPads, and gay wedding bells are chiming. It may not always be perfect, but few cities make being queer so utterly fabulous.

Weekdays are the New Weekend

Here in the Big Apple, any night of the week is fair game to paint the town rouge – especially for the gay community, who attack the weekday social scene with gusto. Wednesdays and Thursdays roar with a steady stream of parties, and locals love raging on Sundays (especially in summer). While there's undoubtedly much fun to be had on Friday and Saturday nights, weekend parties tend to be more 'bridge and tunnel' – Manhattanites often use these nonwork days to catch up with friends, check out new restaurants and attend house parties.

Promoters

One of best ways to dial into the party hotline is to follow the various goings-on of your favorite promoter. Some of ours:

Josh Wood (www.joshwoodproductions.com)

Rafferty Mazur Events (www.raffertymazurevents.com)

Spank (www.spankartmag.com)

Daniel Nardicio (www.danielnardicio.com)

Erich Conrad (Twitter @ZIGZAGLeBain)

Gay & Lesbian by Neighborhood

➡ **East Village & Lower East Side** Slightly grittier, sweatier, grungier versions of the west side haunts.

➡ **Greenwich Village, Chelsea & the Meatpacking District** The original flavor of gay New York, with classic bars and clubs.

➡ **Union Square, Flatiron District & Gramercy** Hosts a spillover of gay venues from the East Village, West Village and Chelsea.

➡ **Midtown** Hell's Kitchen is the city's new gay epicenter, with an ever-expanding choice of gay and gay-friendly eateries, bars, clubs and shops.

➡ **Brooklyn** Multineighborhood borough with gays of every ilk, and diverse watering holes peppered throughout.

RESOURCES & SUPPORT

For over 30 years, the **LGBT Community Center** (☎212-620-7310; www.gaycenter.org; 208 W 13th St btwn Seventh & Greenwich Aves; suggested donation $5; 🕒9am-10pm Mon-Sat, to 9pm Sun; [S]1/2/3 to 14th St) has been the nexus of the Village's queer community. The second-largest center of its kind in the world, it plays host to over 300 groups who meet here, as well as providing a ton of regional publications about Lesbian, Gay, Bisexual and Transgender (LGBT) events and nightlife. It also offers frequent special events, from yoga classes, art exhibits and political panels to dance parties and Broadway-caliber performances.

NEED TO KNOW

Websites

There are tons of websites geared towards the goings-on of the city's gay community. Check out the following sites:

➡ **Next Magazine** (www.nextmagazine.com) Online version of the print guide to all things gay in NYC.

➡ **Get Out!** (http://getoutmag.com) Online version of a guide to all things queer in town.

➡ **Gayletter** (www.gayletter.com) E-newsletter covering queer-related culture, musings and parties.

Lonely Planet's Top Choices

NYC Pride Parade (p28) Rainbow-clad pomp and circumstance.

LGBT Community Center (p45) NYC's hub of gay life, culture and politics.

Leslie-Lohman Museum of Gay & Lesbian Art (p87) The world's first LGBT art museum.

Industry (p202) Still one of the hottest bar-clubs in town.

Best for School Nights

Therapy (p202) Late-night music and drag give school nights razzle-dazzle.

Flaming Saddles (p202) Bootscootin' barmen pouring liquor down your throat – who said weeknights were boring?

Boxers NYC (p171) From postwork to late-night, this sports bar sees dudes tackling the tighter ends on and off the field.

Best Festivals

NYC Pride (p28) A month-long celebration in June, with parties, cultural events and the famous march down Fifth Ave.

NewFest NYC's premier queer film fest in July, with a week-long program of homegrown and foreign flicks in September.

HOT! Festival A month of LGBT theater and performance art in July.

MIX New York Queer Experimental Film Festival Six days of avant-garde and political queer cinema in November.

Best for Dancing Queens

XL Nightclub (p202) A sprawling danceteria of hot, sweat-soaked muscle in where-it's-at Hell's Kitchen.

Industry (p202) As night deepens, this Hell's Kitchen hit turns from buzzing bar to thumping club.

Monster Cheeky go-go boys and cheekier drag queens keep the punters purring in the basement.

BarTini Ultra Lounge Cocktails, crowds and anthems in a white-on-white space.

Best Daytime Scene

Brunch on Ninth Avenue Pick a sidewalk table and do your bit for Neighborhood Watch, Hell's Kitchen–style.

Shopping in Chelsea Style-up at Universal Gear and other fab Chelsea boutiques.

Pier 45 (Christopher Street Pier) (p135) Butt-hugging trunks and loved-up couples make this a summertime sunbaking staple.

Fire Island Mingle with the hot and rich at this sand-dune-swept playground.

Best for Women

Ginger's Happy-hour specials, karaoke and Sunday bingo pull the girls at Brooklyn's G-Spot.

Cubbyhole A no-attitude Village veteran, with jukebox tunes and chatty regulars.

Henrietta Hudson (p150) A fun, classic dive packed with supercool rocker chicks.

Best Old-School Hangouts

Marie's Crisis (p147) One-time hooker hangout turned show-tune piano bar.

Stonewall Inn (p150) Scene of rioting drag queens during the Stonewall riots of '69.

Julius Bar The oldest gay bar in the Village.

Cock Tongue-in-cheek sleaze in a former gay/punk hangout.

Best Places to Slumber

Out NYC (p335) The world's first straight-friendly urban resort in gaycentric Hell's Kitchen.

Ink48 (p336) Skyline views and a hop away from Hell's Kitchen bars and clubs.

Standard East Village (p333) Crisp, fresh boutique chic in the funky East Village.

Chelsea Pines Inn (p332) Hollywood posters, diva-moniker rooms and a Chelsea address.

Hotel Gansevoort (p333) Jet-setter cool and a rooftop pool in the Meatpacking District.

Entertainment

Hollywood may hold court when it comes to the motion picture, but it's NYC that reigns supreme over the pantheon of other arts. Actors, musicians, dancers and artists flock to the bright lights of the Big Apple like moths to a flame. It's like the old saying goes: if you can make it here, you can make it anywhere.

Comedy

A good laugh is easy to find in the Big Apple, where comedians sharpen their stand-up and improv chops practising new material or hoping to get scouted by a producer or agent. The best spots for some chuckles are downtown, particularly around Chelsea and Greenwich Village. Several festivals, like ComicCon, draw big names throughout the year. You can also snag seats to tapings of America's popular late-night variety shows. See p206 for more details.

Dance

Dance fans are spoiled for choice in this town, which is home to both the New York City Ballet (p243) and the American Ballet Theatre (p244). Another key venue dedicated to dance is the Joyce Theater (p154), which stages acclaimed contemporary productions by dance companies from every corner of the globe. There are also modern dance companies galore, including those of masters Alvin Ailey, Paul Taylor, Merce Cunningham, Martha Graham, Bill T Jones, Mark Morris and a slew of up-and-comers, which often take to the stage downtown and at the Brooklyn Academy of Music (p295).

Note that there are two major dance seasons: first in spring from March to May, then in late fall from October to December. But rest assured that there's always someone putting on the moves.

Film, Television & Radio

Feasting on films in NYC is quite a different experience to the traditional American blockbuster-at-the-multiplex scene. Filmgoing is a serious venture here, as evidenced by the preponderance of movie houses that show indie, classic, avant-garde, foreign and otherwise nonstandard fare. Frequent film festivals, like the Tribeca Film Festival (p27), with different themes provide additional texture to the movie-going scene.

One of the least known gems for films is the Museum of Modern Art (p181), which has a rich collection of movies spanning all genres and corners of the world. The Film Society of Lincoln Center (p243) stages an incredible array of documentary and art house films. Also worth checking is the BAM Rose Cinemas (p295), which does similar fare as well as revivals.

Live Music

NYC is the country's capital of live music, and just about every taste can be catered for here. For current listings check out *New York Magazine* (www.nymag.com), the *Village Voice* (www.villagevoice.com) and *Time Out* (http://newyork.timeout.com).

Jazz You'll find big-band shindigs, jazz brunches and swank dress-up clubs on the Upper West Side and in Times Square. Harlem and the West Village are they city's veritable jazz ghettos.

Rock Big name indie rockers earned their stripes downtown, but these days that scene has largely flocked to North Brooklyn.

NEED TO KNOW

Calendar & Reviews

➜ **Playbill** (www.playbill.com) The publisher of the ubiquitous yellow-and-white programs; offers theater news, listings and a ticket-purchase system.

➜ **Talkin' Broadway** (www.talking-broadway.com) A less formal site, with dishy reviews as well as a board for posting extra tickets to buy or sell.

➜ Print publications include *Time Out, New York Magazine, New York Times* and *Village Voice.*

Websites & Tickets

To purchase tickets for shows, you can either head directly to the venue's box office, or use one of several ticket-service agencies (most of which add a surcharge) to order by phone or online.

➜ **Broadway Line** (www.livebroadway. com)

➜ **SmartTix** (www.smarttix.com)

➜ **Telecharge** (www.telecharge.com)

➜ **Theatermania** (www.theatermania. com)

➜ **Ticketmaster** (www.ticketmaster. com) An old chestnut, Ticketmaster sells tickets for every conceivable form of big-time entertainment.

➜ TKTS booths offer cut-price same-day tickets in **Midtown** and **downtown**.

Opera & Classical Music

When thinking about opera, one name rules the roost: the Metropolitan Opera (p242), which stages lavish and exceptional productions. However, many other forms live within the city limits. The laudable downtown company Amore Opera (p125) performs impressive works in the intimate 99-seat Connelly Theater. Other roving companies include **Opera on Tap** (www. operaontap.org/newyork), which stages performances not at grand theaters, but at bars around Brooklyn. Another creative Brooklyn outfit is **LoftOpera** (www.loftopera.com), which, true to name, performs condensed operas in a loft in Gowanus.

In NYC, the choices for orchestras, chamber music and opera are abundant, with the more cutting-edge options often stealing center stage. For all things traditional on a grand scale, don't miss Lincoln Center (p234), the Brooklyn Academy of Music (p295) and the famously stunning Carnegie Hall (p203).

Theater

From the legendary hit factories of Broadway to the scruffy black-box theaters that dot countless downtown blocks, NYC boasts the full gamut of theater experiences. The most celebrated scene is, of course, that of Broadway – nicknamed the Great White Way in 1902 for its bright billboard lights. There's something truly magical about sitting in one of the ornate Broadway theaters and letting the show take you to another world as the lights dim.

The term 'off Broadway' is not a geographical one – it simply refers to theaters that are smaller in size (200 to 500 seats) and usually have less of a glitzy production budget than the Broadway big hitters. 'Off off Broadway' takes place in even smaller theaters, with shows that are often inexpensively produced and experimental in nature.

Entertainment by Neighborhood

➜ **East Village & Lower East Side** Experimental performance spaces, poetry slams and stand-up comics fill basements with laughter. (p124)

➜ **Greenwich Village, Chelsea & the Meatpacking District** Unofficial headquarters of the world's jazz club scene, plus dance troupes galore in Chelsea. (p153)

➜ **Midtown** Razzle-dazzle extravaganzas, fresh American theater, world-class jazz sessions, stand-up comedy blue bloods: when the sun sinks, no neighborhood does 'classic New York' better than Midtown. (p202)

➜ **Upper West Side & Central Park** The Lincoln Center supplies an endless amount of high culture, while other venues (the Beacon Theatre and Cleopatra's Needle) provide more intimate settings for live music. (p242)

➜ **Brooklyn** There's a little bit of everything in America's fourth largest city, from the classical offerings at **BAM** (p295) and **Theater for a New Audience** (p293), to the indie rock bands in Williamsburg.

Lonely Planet's Top Choices

Book of Mormon (p203) Uproariously brilliant Broadway musical appreciated citywide for its wit, charm and pitch-perfect performances.

Kinky Boots (p203) A feel-good tale of an old English shoe factory saved by a drag queen. Great costumes.

Jazz at Lincoln Center (p202) Glittering evening views of Central Park and world-class musical acts.

Carnegie Hall (p203) Legendary concert hall, blessed with perfect acoustics; hosts everything from opera to jazz.

Brooklyn Academy of Music (p295) This hallowed theater hosts cutting-edge works, particularly during its celebrated Next Wave Festival.

Best for Laughs

Upright Citizens Brigade Theatre (p154) Hilarious comedy sketches and improv

Comedy Cellar (p154) A well-loved basement comedy joint in Greenwich Village.

Caroline's on Broadway (p205) The go-to spot for seeing famous comics perform.

Comic Strip Live (p226) Best spot for upcoming talent.

Best for Dance

Joyce Theater (p154) NYC's best venue devoted solely to dance.

New York Live Arts (p154) Experimental leanings with performances by troupes from around the globe.

New York City Center (p205) Excellent lineup of dance companies and mini-festivals.

Brooklyn Academy of Music (p295) Catch Mark Morris Dance Group and many others.

Best for Film

Angelika Film Center (p154) Foreign and indie films in an unfancy but much-loved setting.

Anthology Film Archives (p124) Screens obscure works and revivals.

BAM Rose Cinemas (p295) A good mix of first-run and foreign films in a landmark building.

Film Society of Lincoln Center (p243) Two excellent theaters at the epicenter of NYC creativity.

Best Broadway Shows

Book of Mormon (p203) Brilliantly funny, award-winning show by the creators of South Park.

Chicago (p204) One of the most scintillating shows on Broadway.

Kinky Boots (p203) Book well ahead to score seats for this over-the-top musical.

Matilda (p204) Roald Dahl's classic tale brought to the stage.

Best for Theater (Non-Broadway)

Playwrights Horizons (p204) Showcase of powerfully written plays.

Signature Theatre (p204) Stages works by some of the world's top playwrights.

Flea Theater (p79) Some of the city's best off-Broadway shows.

Theater for a New Audience (p293) Brooklyn's new theater opened to much fanfare in 2013.

Best for Jazz

Jazz at Lincoln Center (p202) Innovative fare under the guidance of jazz luminary Wynton Marsalis.

Village Vanguard (p153) Legendary West Village jazz club.

Smalls (p153) Tiny basement joint that evokes the feel of decades past.

Birdland (p205) Sleek Midtown space that hosts big-band sounds, Afro-Cuban jazz and more.

Best for Rock

Bowery Ballroom (p125) Celebrated downtown concert hall.

Music Hall of Williamsburg (p293) Indie rock galore out in Brooklyn.

Rockwood Music Hall (p125) Music all the time at this Lower East Side spot.

Bell House (p295) South Brooklyn charmer with an innovative lineup of indie and folk sounds.

Best for Classical Music & Opera

Metropolitan Opera House (p242) Enchanting setting for seeing some of the world's best opera.

Amore Opera (p125) Intimate setting for opera in a downtown location.

Brooklyn Academy of Music (p295) Innovative works by Brooklyn's renowned hit-maker.

Bargemusic (p295) String quartets on a barge parked on the East River.

Barneys shop window, Madison Ave (p206)

INGOLF POMPE / GETTY IMAGES ©

Shopping

New York City is quite simply one of the best shopping destinations on the planet. Fashion boutiques, flea markets, booksellers, record stores, antique shops, Asian emporiums and gourmet grocers selling edibles from every corner of the globe are just a few places to begin the shopping adventure. And while it's quite easy to spend a fortune, sample sales and designer outlets yield some startlingly good deals.

Boutiques & Department Stores

One of the world's fashion capitals, NYC is ever setting trends for the rest of the country to follow. For checking out the latest designs hitting the streets, it's worth browsing some of the city's best-loved boutiques around town – regardless of whether you intend to spend. A few favorites include Opening Ceremony, Issey Miyake, Marc Jacobs, Steven Alan, Rag & Bone, John Varvatos, By Robert James and Piperlime.

If time is limited, or you simply want to browse a plethora of labels in one go, then head to those heady conglomerations known worldwide as department stores. New York has a special blend of alluring draws – in particular don't miss Barneys (p206), Bergdorf Goodman (p207), Macy's (p208) and Bloomingdale's (p206).

New York City Icons

A few stores in this city have cemented their status as NYC legends. The city just wouldn't quite be the same without them. For label hunters, Century 21 (p80) is a Big Apple institution, with wares by D&G, Prada, Marc Jacobs and many others at low prices. Other Music (p101) is a long-running indie music store (CDs and some vinyl) that thrives despite the odds. Book lovers of the world unite at the Strand (p155), the city's biggest and best bookseller. Run by Hassidic Jews and employing mechanized whimsy, B&H (p208) is a mecca for digital and audio geeks. For secondhand clothing, home furnishings and books, good-hearted Housing Works (p158), with many locations around town, is a perennial favorite.

Flea Markets & Adventures

As much as New Yorkers gravitate towards all that's shiny and new, it can be infinitely fun to rifle through closets of unwanted wares and threads. The most popular flea market is the Brooklyn Flea (p296), housed in all sorts of spaces throughout the year. The East Village is the city's de facto neighborhood for secondhand stores – the uniform of the unwavering legion of hipsters.

For antiques and assorted ephemera from the past (records, artwork, books, home furnishings, toys) don't miss the sprawling Antiques Garage Flea Market (p158) held on weekends in Chelsea.

Shopping by Neighborhood

→ **Lower Manhattan & the Financial District** While not a shopping hot spot per se, Lower Manhattan serves up a trickle of gems, from vintage film posters and hard-to-find vino to hipster-chic threads and outrageous retro fabrics. (p80)

→ **SoHo & Chinatown** West Broadway is a veritable outdoor mall of encyclopedic proportions. It's like the UN of retail – if you can't find what you're looking for then it hasn't been invented yet. Try Mott St for something a bit more subdued. (p98)

→ **East Village & Lower East Side** Hipster treasure trove of vintage wares and design goods. Go wild on E 9th St, St Marks Place and Orchard St. (p126)

→ **Greenwich Village, Chelsea & the Meatpacking District** Bleecker St, running off Abingdon Sq is lined with boutiques with a handful on nearby W 4th St. Other high-end shops lurk around Washington St, Hudson St and W 14th St in the Meatpacking District. (p155)

NEED TO KNOW

Websites

→ **Racked** (www.ny.racked.com) Informative shopping blog with its finger on the pulse.

→ **New York Magazine** (www.nymag. com) Trustworthy opinions on the Big Apple's best places to swipe your plastic.

→ **Daily Candy** (www.dailycandy.com) Curated selection of the best NYC has to offer.

Ones to Follow

→ **Bill Cunningham** (www.nytimes. com/video/on-the-street) Legendary fashion photographer who captures the zeitgeist for the New York Times.

→ **Andre Leon Talley** (twitter.com/ OfficialAL) Anna Wintour's top fashion editor in the know at Vogue.

→ **Women's Wear Daily** (twitter.com/ womensweardaily) Everything that's happening in the fashion industry.

Opening Hours

In general, most business are open from 10am to around 7pm on weekdays and 11am to around 8pm Saturdays. Sundays can be variable – some stores stay closed while others keep weekday hours. Stores tend to stay open later in the neighborhoods downtown. Small boutiques often have variable hours – many open at noon.

Sales Tax

Clothing and footwear that costs less than $110 is exempt from sales tax. For everything else, you'll pay 8.875% retail sales tax on every purchase.

→ **Midtown** Epic department stores, global chains, historic music stores and the odd in-the-know treasure – window-shoppers unite! (p206)

→ **Upper East Side** The country's most expensive boutiques along Madison Ave, but plenty of price-conscious consignment shops can be scouted as well. (p226)

→ **Brooklyn** A healthy mix of independent boutiques and thrift stores. Good shopping streets include Bedford Ave and Grand Ave in Williamsburg, Smith St in Boerum Hill and Fifth Ave in Park Slope. (p295)

Lonely Planet's Top Choices

Barneys (p206) Serious fashionistas shop (or at least browse) at Barneys, well known for its spot-on collections of in-the-know labels.

Brooklyn Flea (p296) Brooklyn's collection of flea markets offers plenty of vintage furnishings, retro clothing and bric-a-brac, plus great food stalls.

ABC Carpet & Home (p172) Spread over six floors, ABC is packed with treasures large (furniture) and small (designer jewelry, global gifts).

MoMA Design & Bookstore (p207) The perfect one-stop shop for coffee-table tomes, art prints, edgy jewellery and 'Where-did-you-get-that?' homewares.

Idlewild Books (p173) An inspiring place for travelers and daydreamers with titles (both fiction and nonfiction) spanning the globe.

Chelsea Market (p133) Culinary temptation in every shape and form at this wondrous food-focused market.

Best Fashion Boutiques

Steven Alan (p80) Stylish, heritage-inspired fashion.

Marc Jacobs (p156) A downtown and uptown favorite, particularly the West Village locations.

Rag & Bone (p98) Beautifully tailored clothes for men and women.

John Varvatos (p127) Rugged but worldly wearables in a former downtown rock club.

Odin (p102) Tiny downtown men's boutique for one-of-a-kind pieces.

Best for Unique Souvenirs & Gifts

MIN New York (p99) Unique perfumes in an apothecary-like setting.

De Vera (p101) Beautiful glasswares and art objects.

Obscura Antiques (p127) A cabinet of curiosities packed with strange and eerie objects.

Amé Amé (p208) Beautifully made umbrellas and rain gear, plus candy!

Top Hat (p127) Lovely collectibles from around the globe.

Best for Women

Spiritual America (p127) A good place to begin the shopping journey in the boutique-filled Lower East Side.

Verameat (p126) Exquisite jewelry that treads between beauty and whimsy.

Beacon's Closet (p156) Valhalla for vintage lovers with multiple locations.

Best for Men

By Robert James (p128) Rugged menswear by a celebrated new local designer.

Nepenthes New York (p208) Japanese collective selling covetable, in-the-know labels.

Best Music Stores

Rough Trade (p295) Vinyl is far from dead at this sprawling new music shop/concert space in Williamsburg.

Other Music (p101) Great selection of rare grooves at this downtown icon.

A-1 Records Endless bins of records in the East Village.

Best for Reading Material

Strand Book Store (p155) Hands down, NYC's best used bookstore.

McNally Jackson (p100) Great SoHo spot for book browsing and author readings.

Housing Works Book Store Used books and a cafe in an atmospheric setting in SoHo.

Best for Children

Dinosaur Hill (p126) Fun and creative toys, books and music that will inspire young minds.

FAO Schwarz (p207) The famed toy store near Central Park.

Yoyamart (p156) Small, pretty toy and clothing store in the Meatpacking District.

Books of Wonder (p173) Great gift ideas for kids, plus in-store readings.

Best Vintage Stores

Beacon's Closet (p156) Get a new outfit without breaking the bank at this great vintage shop.

Screaming Mimi's (p102) Lots of appealing clothes from decades past.

Resurrection (p102) Mint-condition pieces from couture labels.

Tokio 7 (p126) A fun place to browse high-end labels in the East Village.

Best Homeware & Design Stores

Shinola (p80) Unusual accessories from a cutting-edge Detroit design house.

Adobe New York (p297) Home-furnishings store in Brooklyn.

Sports & Activities

Although hailing cabs in New York City can feel like a blood sport, and waiting on subway platforms in summer heat is steamier than a sauna, New Yorkers still love to stay active in their spare time. And considering how limited the green spaces are in New York, it's surprising for some visitors just how active the locals can be.

Spectator Sports

BASEBALL

New York is one of the last remaining corners of the USA where baseball reigns supreme over football and basketball. Tickets start around $15 – a great deal for seeing the home teams playing in their recently opened stadiums. The two Major League Baseball teams play 162 games during the regular season from April to October, when the playoffs begin.

New York Yankees (www.yankees.com) The Bronx Bombers are the USA's greatest dynasty, with over two dozen World Series championship titles since 1900.

New York Mets (www.mets.com) In the National League since 1962, the Mets remain New York's 'new' baseball team.

HOCKEY

The NHL (National Hockey League) has three franchises in the greater New York area; each team plays three or four games weekly during the season from September to April.

New York Rangers (www.nyrangers.com) Manhattan's favorite hockey squad.

New York Islanders (www.newyorkislanders.com) New York City hasn't given much Islander love since the unremarkable four-consecutive-year Stanley Cup streak in the '80s. Their stock is likely to rise, however, when they move to Brooklyn's Barclay Center in 2015.

New Jersey Devils (www.newjerseydevils.com) The Devils may not be New Yorkers, but they've seen more wins than their neighbors.

BASKETBALL

Two NBA (National Basketball Association) teams, the Knicks and the Nets, now play in New York City. The season lasts from October to May or June.

New York Knicks (p209) Occasional scandal aside, NYC loves its blue-and-orange basketball team.

Brooklyn Nets Formerly the New Jersey Nets, Brooklyn's new pro team (the first since the Dodgers left town) has gained a strong local following.

FOOTBALL

Football season runs from August to January or February. Most of New York tunes into its NFL (National Football League) teams – the Giants and Jets – both of whom play at the new Metlife Stadium at the Meadowlands Sports Complex in New Jersey (from Manhattan take NJ Transit via Secaucus Junction, $10.50 return). Metlife Stadium hosted the 2014 Super Bowl.

The NFL season has 16 regular-season games (held on Sunday or Monday night), then up to three play-offs before the Super Bowl.

New York Giants (www.giants.com) One of the NFL's oldest teams, with four Super Bowl victories, most recently in 2011.

New York Jets (www.newyorkjets.com) Games are always packed and new fans easily get swept away by the contagious 'J-E-T-S!' chants.

NEED TO KNOW

Websites

➡ **NYC Parks** (www.nycgovparks.org) Details on park services, including free pools and basketball courts, plus borough biking maps.

➡ **New York Road Runners Club** (www.nyrrc.org) Organizes weekend runs citywide.

➡ **MeetUp** (www.meetup.com) Sign up and get access to thousands of citywide activity groups – many dedicated to active pursuits.

➡ **Groupon** (www.groupon.com) Loads of NYC deals, including discounted yoga, pilates, kickboxing, spa treatments and more.

Buying Tickets

With so many teams and overlapping seasons, a game is rarely a day away. Some teams' hotlines or box offices sell tickets directly (available under 'tickets' on the relevant websites), but most go via **Ticketmaster** (www.ticketmaster.com). The other major buy/sell outlet is **StubHub** (☎866-788-2482; www.stubhub.com; 539 Atlantic Ave btwn 3rd & 4th Aves; 🕒10am-6pm Mon-Sat).

Outdoor Sports

RUNNING & JOGGING

Central Park's loop roads are best during traffic-free hours, though you'll be in the company of many cyclists and in-line skaters. The 1.6-mile path surrounding the Jacqueline Kennedy Onassis Reservoir (where Jackie O used to run) is for runners and walkers only; access it between 86th and 96th Sts. Running along the Hudson River is a popular path, best from about 30th St to Battery Park in Lower Manhattan. The Upper East Side has a path that runs along FDR Dr and the East River (from 63rd St to 115th St). Brooklyn's Prospect Park has plenty of paths, and 1.3-mile-long Brooklyn Bridge Park has incredible views of Manhattan (reach it via Brooklyn Bridge to up the mileage).

The **New York Road Runners Club** (Map p432; www.nyrr.org; 9 E 89th St btwn Madison & Fifth Aves; 🕒10am-8pm Mon-Fri, to 5pm Sat, to 3pm Sun; [S]4/5/6 to 86th St) organizes weekend runs citywide, including the New York City Marathon.

BICYCLING

NYC has taken enormous strides in making the city more bike friendly, adding over 250 miles of bike lanes in the last five years. That said, we recommend that the uninitiated stick to the less hectic trails in the parks and along the waterways, like Central Park, Prospect Park, the **Manhattan Waterfront Greenway** (www.nyc.gov/html/dcp/html/mwg/mwghome.shtml) and the **Brooklyn Waterfront Greenway** (www.brooklyngreenway.org).

The new Citi Bike is handy for quick jaunts, but for longer rides, you'll want a proper rental. **Bike and Roll** (www.bikenewyorkcity.com) has loads of outdoor hire spots (including at Central Park by Columbus Circle). Check out the neighborhood chapters for more bike-rental locations.

STREET SPORTS

With all that concrete around, New York has embraced a number of sports and events played directly on the streets themselves.

Those with hoop dreams will find pick-up basketball games all over the city, the most famous courts being the West 4th Street Basketball Courts (p159), known as 'the Cage.' Or try **Holcombe Rucker Park** (Map p436; www.nycgovparks.org/parks/holcomberuckerpark; W 155th St at Frederick Douglass Blvd; [S]B/D to 155th St) up in Harlem – that's where many NBA big shots cut their teeth. You'll also find pick-up games in Tompkins Square Park (p111) and Riverside Park (p235). Hudson River Park (p73) has courts at Canal St and on W11th Ave at 23rd St.

Lesser-known handball and stickball are also popular in NYC – you'll find one-wall courts in outdoor parks all over the city. For stickball, link up with the Bronx-based **Emperors Stickball League** (☎201-658-1871; www.stickball.com) to check out its Sunday games during the warmer months.

Indoor Activities

You can't do a child's pose without bumping into one of the many yoga or Pilates studios that dot the city. **Yelp** (www.yelp.com) is a great tool for selecting a spot in the neighborhood that suits your needs.

Lonely Planet's Top Choices

Central Park (p230) The city's wondrous playground has rolling hills, forested paths, open green spaces, and a beautiful lake.

New York Yankees (p53) Even if you don't follow baseball, it's well worth trekking out to the Bronx to experience the rabid fandom.

Chelsea Piers Complex (p159) Every activity imaginable – from kickboxing to ice hockey – under one gigantic roof, just a stone's throw from the High Line.

New York Spa Castle (p311) Bathing behemoth with wallet-friendly prices. Inspired by ancient Korean traditions of wellness. You'll want to stay for days.

Brooklyn Bridge Park (p265) This brand-new green space is Brooklyn's pride and joy.

Prospect Park (p268) Escape the crowds at Brooklyn's gorgeous park, with trails, hills, a canal, lake and meadows.

Best Urban Green Spaces

Governors Island (p266) Car-free island just a quick hop from Lower Manhattan or Brooklyn.

Bryant Park (p190) A small appealing oasis amid the skyscrapers of Midtown.

Madison Square Park (p164) A pretty little park between Midtown and downtown.

Flushing Meadows Corona Park (p307) Sprawling green space with relics of the 1939 World's Fair.

Inwood Hill Park (p255) Serene setting of forest and salt marsh in upper Manhattan.

Franklin D Roosevelt Four Freedoms Park (p193) Picturesque new park with great Manhattan views.

Best Places for Garden Lovers

Brooklyn Botanic Garden (p278) Japanese gardens, native flora and photogenic springtime cherry blossoms.

New York Botanical Garden (p261) Fifty acres of old growth forest up in the Bronx.

Cloisters Museum & Gardens (p255) Pretty gardens next to a Medievalesque building.

Best Indoor Activities

Cliffs (p311) Massive new climbing center in Long Island City, Queens.

Brooklyn Boulders (p299) Another great spot for rock climbers – this one's in south Brooklyn.

Jivamukti (p173) Lavish yoga center near Union Square.

Area Yoga (p299) A great choice for yoga in health-minded Cobble Hill.

24 Hour Fitness (p209) Work out at all hours (and many locations) at this full-service fitness center.

Best Out-of-the-Box Activities

Gowanus Canal canoeing (p299) Go for a canoe ride, and help clean up a polluted waterway en route.

New York Trapeze School (p159) Channel your inner circus star at this trapeze school with two locations.

Gotham Girls Roller Derby (p299) Watch a high-jinks roller derby at various NYC locations.

Best Bowling

Brooklyn Bowl (p298) A Williamsburg classic that's equal parts hipster hangout, concert space and bowling alley.

Bowlmor Lanes (p159) Going strong since 1938, this draws New York University students and young crowds.

Best Spas

New York Spa Castle (p311) An enchanting wonderland of waterfalls and steam rooms far out in Queens.

Russian & Turkish Baths (p128) An East Village icon since 1892.

Great Jones Spa (p103) Book a massage, then enjoy the steam room, hot tub and rock sauna.

Best Spectator Sports

New York Yankees (p53) One of the country's successful baseball teams.

New York Giants (p53) Football powerhouse that, despite the name, plays their home games in New Jersey.

New York Knicks (p209) See the Knicks sink a few three-pointers at Madison Square Garden.

Brooklyn Nets (p53) The hot new NBA team in town and symbol of Brooklyn's resurgence.

Brooklyn Cyclones (p299) See a minor league baseball game near Coney Island's boardwalk.

New York Mets (p311) NYC's other baseball team play their games at Citi Field in Queens.

Explore New York City

NEW YORK CITY'S TOP SIGHTS

Neighborhoods at a Glance

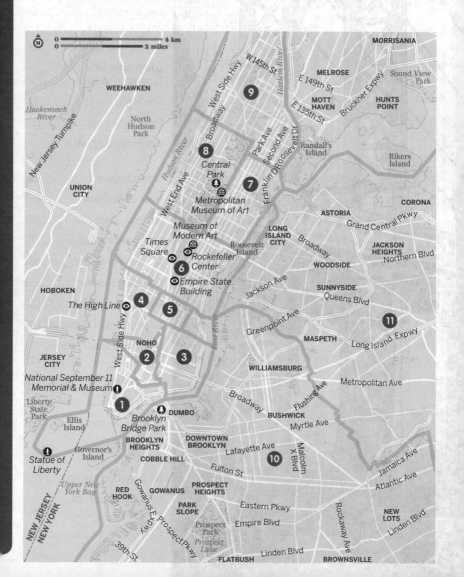

N
0 — 4 km
0 — 2 miles

MORRISANIA

WEEHAWKEN

W 145th St

MELROSE

E 149th St

Sound View Park

MOTT HAVEN

E 135th St

HUNTS POINT

Hackensack River

North Hudson Park

New Jersey Turnpike

West Side Hwy

Broadway

Hudson River

Harlem River

Park Ave

Second Ave

Franklin D Roosevelt Dr

Randall's Island

Rikers Island

9

UNION CITY

West End Ave

8

Central Park

Metropolitan Museum of Art

7

ASTORIA

Grand Central Pkwy

CORONA

Museum of Modern Art

Times Square

Rockefeller Center

Roosevelt Island

LONG ISLAND CITY

Broadway

JACKSON HEIGHTS

Northern Blvd

6

Empire State Building

WOODSIDE

HOBOKEN

The High Line

4

Jackson Ave

SUNNYSIDE

Queens Blvd

East River

5

Greenpoint Ave

11

JERSEY CITY

West Side Hwy

NOHO

2

3

MASPETH

Long Island Expwy

WILLIAMSBURG

Metropolitan Ave

National September 11 Memorial & Museum

Broadway

Flushing Ave

Liberty State Park

Ellis Island

1

DUMBO

BUSHWICK

Myrtle Ave

Metropolitan Ave

Brooklyn Bridge Park

DOWNTOWN BROOKLYN

Malcolm X Blvd

Governor's Island

BROOKLYN HEIGHTS

Lafayette Ave

10

Statue of Liberty

COBBLE HILL

Fulton St

Jamaica Ave

Atlantic Ave

Upper New York Bay

RED HOOK

GOWANUS

PROSPECT HEIGHTS

NEW LOTS

Linden Blvd

NEW JERSEY / NEW YORK

Gowanus E Prospect Pkwy

PARK SLOPE

Eastern Pkwy

Empire Blvd

Rockaway Ave

39th St

Prospect Park

Prospect Lake

Linden Blvd

FLATBUSH

BROWNSVILLE

❶ Lower Manhattan & the Financial District (p60)

Home to icons such as Wall St, the National September 11 Memorial and the Statue of Liberty, the southern end of Manhattan pulses with businesslike energy during the day before settling into quiet nights. Tribeca, however, continues to hum well after dark with its cache of restaurants and lounges.

❷ SoHo & Chinatown (p82)

Sacred temples, hawkers peddling bric-a-brac and steam-filled soup-dumpling parlors line the hurried streets of Chinatown, with SoHo, next door, providing the counterpoint with streamlined thoroughfares and storefronts representing all of the biggest-name brands in the world. Tucked somewhere in between is Little Italy (emphasis on the 'little').

❸ East Village & Lower East Side (p104)

Old meets new on every block of this downtown duo – two of the city's hottest 'hoods for nightlife and cheap eats that lure students, bankers and scruffier types alike.

❹ Greenwich Village, Chelsea & the Meatpacking District (p129)

Quaint, twisting streets and well-preserved townhouses offer endless options for intimate dining and drinking in the West Village. The Meatpacking District next door has trendy nightlife options galore; further up is Chelsea, home to hundreds of art galleries and the unofficial headquarters of NYC's gay scene.

❺ Union Square, Flatiron District & Gramercy (p160)

Though short on sights, there's lots happening on and around Union Square, which bustles with a medley of protesters, buskers and businessfolk. North of there is grassy Madison Square Park, an elegant oasis en route to Midtown. The peaceful streets around Gramercy are mostly residential with a handful of high-end eating and drinking spots.

❻ Midtown (p174)

This is the home of the NYC found on postcards: Times Square, Empire State Building, Broadway theaters, canyons of skyscrapers, and bustling crowds that rarely thin. The Museum of Modern Art (MoMA), Bryant Park, the grand shops along Fifth Ave and the gay bars of Hell's Kitchen are also here.

❼ Upper East Side (p210)

High-end boutiques line Madison Ave and sophisticated mansions run parallel along Fifth Ave, which culminates in an architectural flourish called Museum Mile – one of the most cultured strips in the city, if not the world.

❽ Upper West Side & Central Park (p228)

New York's antidote to the endless stretches of concrete, Central Park is a verdant escape from honking horns and sunless sidewalks. Lining the park with inspired residential towers, the Upper West Side is home to the Lincoln Center.

❾ Harlem & Upper Manhattan (p247)

Harlem and Hamilton Heights – a bastion of African American culture – offers good eats and jazz beats. Head up to Inwood for leafy park space, or try Morningside Heights to soak up some student life.

❿ Brooklyn (p263)

Brooklyn's sprawling checkerboard of distinct neighborhoods is over three times the size of Manhattan, not to mention more diverse and far-reaching. For skyline views and a pinch of history, try brownstone-studded Brooklyn Heights; or try Williamsburg for vintage wares and late-night bar crawls.

⓫ Queens (p300)

A patchwork of communities, Queens is trailblazer territory for return visitors and locals alike. Gorge at the ethnic delis of Astoria, ogle contemporary art in Long Island City, rip through steamed pork buns in Flushing, and ride the surf in Rockaway Beach.

NEIGHBORHOODS AT A GLANCE

Lower Manhattan & the Financial District

WALL STREET | THE FINANCIAL DISTRICT | NEW YORK HARBOR | BATTERY PARK CITY | EAST RIVER WATERFRONT | CITY HALL & CIVIC CENTER | TRIBECA

Neighborhood Top Five

1 Scaling the iconic **Statue of Liberty** (p62), peering out from her crown and seeing the world's greatest city spread out before you. Prepare to pinch yourself.

2 Reflecting on loss and hope at the **National September 11 Memorial & Museum** (p66).

3 Taking in sunset-blazing skyscrapers from the free-and-fantastic **Staten Island Ferry** (p81).

4 Conjuring up the ghosts of the past at evocative **Ellis Island** (p64).

5 Hunting down major bargains at cheap 'n' chic **Century 21** (p80).

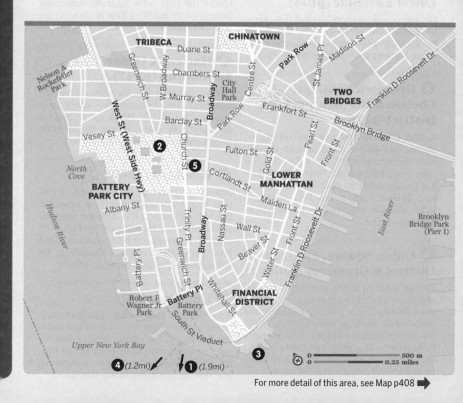

For more detail of this area, see Map p408 ➡

Explore Lower Manhattan & the Financial District

A little planning will save you a lot of time in Lower Manhattan. Book tickets online to the unmissable Ellis Island and Statue of Liberty. Alternatively, catch the first ferry and avoid weekends. You'll need a good four or five hours to explore the two sights properly, and bring a picnic lunch – the food on-site is awful. By the time this guidebook is out, you should no longer need to reserve a time slot online to visit the World Trade Center site, though it's worth double-checking online for any changes. To experience the Financial District's power-broking intensity, go during business hours, but to calmly contemplate the area's Federal homes, Greek Revival temples and early modern skyscrapers, go after hours. To avoid the hordes at shopping mecca Century 21, raid the racks by 8am on weekdays. If the weather is on your side, soak up some rays and river views on Pier 15 at South Street Seaport, or walk across the Brooklyn Bridge for jaw-dropping views of Lower Manhattan. For an evening buzz on any night, head to Tribeca's string of renowned cocktail bars and restaurants.

Local Life

→ **Coffee** Ditch the chains for in-the-know Kaffe 1668 (p78) and La Colombe (p78).

→ **Wine** Swill free vino on Sunday afternoons at Pasanella & Son (p80).

→ **Cocktails** Sip meticulously researched libations at Dead Rabbit (p78).

→ **Culture** Catch encore-provoking drama at the Flea Theater (p79).

→ **Escape** Cycle, relax and eye-up art on revamped summer oasis Governors Island.

Getting There & Away

→ **Subway** The Financial District is well serviced by subway lines, connecting the area to the rest of Manhattan, Brooklyn, Queens and the Bronx. Fulton St is the main interchange station, servicing the A/C, J/Z, 2/3 and 4/5 lines. The 1 train terminates at South Ferry, from where the Staten Island Ferry departs.

→ **Bus** From the Staten Island Ferry terminal, useful routes include the M15 (to East Village, Midtown East, Upper East Side and East Harlem) and the M20 (to Tribeca, West Village, Chelsea and Midtown West).

→ **Boat** The Staten Island Ferry terminal is at the southern end of Whitehall St. Ferries to Governors Island leave from the adjacent Battery Maritime Building. Services to Liberty and Ellis Islands depart from nearby Battery Park.

Lonely Planet's Top Tip

After cheap tickets to Broadway shows? Ditch the TKTS Booth in Times Square for the TKTS Booth at South Street Seaport. Queues usually move a little faster and you can purchase tickets for next-day matinees (something you can't do at the Times Square outlet). The TKTS Smartphone app offers real-time listings of what's on sale.

 Best Places to Eat

→ Locanda Verde (p76)
→ North End Grill (p76)
→ Les Halles (p76)

For reviews, see p76 →

 Best Places to Drink

→ Dead Rabbit (p78)
→ Weather Up (p78)
→ Brandy Library (p78)

For reviews, see p78 →

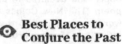 **Best Places to Conjure the Past**

→ Ellis Island (p64)
→ Historic Richmond Town (p72)
→ Fraunces Tavern Museum (p68)
→ South Street Seaport (p73)

For reviews, see p68 →

TOP SIGHT
STATUE OF LIBERTY

ANGUS OBORN / GETTY IMAGES ©

Lady Liberty has been gazing sternly across the waters to 'unenlightened Europe' since 1886. Dubbed the 'Mother of Exiles,' the statue serves as an admonishment to the rigid social structures of the Old World. 'Give me your tired, your poor, Your huddled masses yearning to breathe free, The wretched refuse of your teeming shore. Send these, the homeless, tempest-tost to me, I lift my lamp beside the golden door!' she declares in Emma Lazarus' famous 1883 poem 'The New Colossus.' Ironically, these famous words were added to the statue's base only in 1903, more than 15 years after the poet's death.

From Egypt to the Empire State

To the surprise of many, France's jumbo-sized gift to America was not originally conceived with the US in mind. Indeed, when sculptor Frédéric-Auguste Bartholdi began planning the piece, his vision was for a colossal sculpture to guard the entrance to Egypt's Suez Canal, one of France's greatest engineering achievements of the 19th century. Bartholdi's ode to Gallic ingenuity would incorporate elements of two of the Seven Wonders of the Ancient World: the Colossus of Rhodes and the lighthouse of Alexandria. Despite its appeal to human vanity, the ambitious monument failed to attract serious funding from either France or Egypt, and Bartholdi's dream seemed destined for the scrapheap. Salvation would come from Bartholdi's friend, Edouard René Lefèbvre de Laboulaye. A French jurist, writer and antislavery activist, de Laboulaye proposed a gift to America as a symbol of the triumph of Republicanism and of the democratic values that underpinned both France and the US. Seeing an opportunity too good to miss, Bartholdi quickly set to work, tweaking his vision and turning

DID YOU KNOW?

The Statue of Liberty weighs 225 tonnes and stretches 93m from ground to torch-tip.

PRACTICALITIES

- Map p408
- ☎877-523-9849
- www.nps.gov/stli
- Liberty Island
- adult/child incl Ellis Island $17/9, incl crown & Ellis Island $20/12
- 🕐9.30am-5.30pm, check website for seasonal changes
- [S]1 to South Ferry, 4/5 to Bowling Green

his Suez flop into 'Liberty Enlightening the World'; an enviable gift to commemorate America's centennial of the Declaration of Independence in 1876.

Creating the Lady

The artist spent most of 20 years turning his dream – to create the hollow monument and mount it in the New York Harbor – into reality. Along the way it was hindered by serious financial problems, but was helped in part by the fund-raising efforts of newspaper publisher Joseph Pulitzer. Lending a further hand was poet Emma Lazarus, whose ode to Lady Liberty was part of a fund-raising campaign for the statue's pedestal, designed by American architect Richard Morris Hunt. Bartholdi's work on the statue was also delayed by structural challenges – a problem resolved by the metal framework mastery of railway engineer Gustave Eiffel (yes, of the famous tower). The work of art was finally completed in France in 1884 (a bit off schedule for the centennial). It was shipped to NYC as 350 pieces packed into 214 crates, reassembled over a span of four months and placed on the US-made granite pedestal. Its spectacular October 1886 dedication included New York's first ticker-tape parade, and a flotilla of almost 300 vessels. Put under the administration of the National Park Service in 1933, the Lady's oxidized copper began to be restored in 1984, the same year the monument made it onto the UN's list of World Heritage sites.

Liberty Today

Folks who reserve their tickets in advance are able to climb the (steep) 354 steps to Lady Liberty's crown, from where the city and harbor are breathtaking. That said, crown access is extremely limited, and the only way in is to reserve your spot in advance, the further in advance you can do it, the better, as a six-month lead time is allowed. Each customer may only reserve a maximum of four crown tickets, and children must be at least 4ft tall to access the crown.

If you miss out on crown tickets, you may have better luck with tickets to the pedestal, which also offers commanding views. Like crown tickets, pedestal tickets are limited and should be reserved in advance, either online or by phone. Only crown and pedestal ticket holders have access to the Statue of Liberty museum in the pedestal.

If you don't have crown or pedestal tickets, don't fret. All ferry tickets to Liberty Island offer basic access to the grounds, including guided ranger tours or self-guided audio tours. The grounds also host a gift shop and cafeteria. (Tip: Bring your own nibbles and enjoy them by the water, the Manhattan skyline stretched out before you.)

NEED TO KNOW

Although the ferry ride from Battery Park in Lower Manhattan lasts only 15 minutes, a trip to both the Statue of Liberty and Ellis Island is an all-day affair, and only those setting out on the ferry by 1pm will be allowed to visit both sites. Security screening at the ferry terminal can take up to 90 minutes. Reservations to visit the Statue of Liberty are strongly recommended, as they give you a specific visit time and a guarantee you'll get in. Your other option is to buy a Flex Ticket (adult/child $17/9), which lets you access the grounds (excluding the crown, pedestal and museum) any time within a three-day period. The Flex Ticket is only available at the ferry ticket booth.

The book of law in her left hand is inscribed with July IV MDC-CLXXVI (4 July 1776), the date of American Independence. The rays on her crown represent the seven seas and continents; the 25 windows adorning it symbolize gemstones. At her feet, chains and a broken shackle accentuate her status as free from oppression and servitude. The torch is a 1986 replacement of the original, which is now housed at the on-site museum.

TOP SIGHT
ELLIS ISLAND

Ellis Island is America's most famous and historically important gateway – the very spot where Old World despair met New World promise. Between 1892 and 1954, over 12 million immigrants passed through this processing station, their dreams in tow. Among them were Hungarian Erik Weisz (Harry Houdini), Rodolfo Guglielmi (Rudolph Valentino) and Brit Archibald Alexander Leach (Cary Grant). An estimated 40% of Americans today have at least one ancestor who was processed here, confirming the major role this tiny harbor island has played in the making of modern America.

After a $160-million restoration, the center was reopened to the public in 1990. Now anybody who rides the ferry to the island can experience a cleaned-up, modern version of the historic new-arrival experience at the impressive Immigration Museum, the interactive exhibits of which pay homage to the hope, jubilation and sometimes bitter disappointment of the millions who came here in search of a new beginning.

DON'T MISS...

- Immigration Museum exhibits
- Main Building architecture
- American Immigrant Wall of Honor & Fort Gibson ruins

PRACTICALITIES

- Map p408
- ☎212-363-3200
- www.nps.gov/elis
- admission free, ferry incl Statue of Liberty adult/child $17/9
- 🕑9.30am-5.30pm, check website for seasonal changes
- [S]1 to South Ferry, 4/5 to Bowling Green

Immigration Museum Exhibits

The three-level Immigration Museum is a poignant tribute to the immigrant experience. To get the most out of your visit, opt for the 50-minute self-guided audio tour (free with ferry ticket, available from the museum lobby). Featuring narratives from a number of sources, including historians, architects and the immigrants themselves, the tour brings to life the museum's hefty collection of personal objects, official documents, photographs and film footage. It's an evocative experience to relive personal memories – both good and bad – in the very halls and corridors in which they occurred.

The collection itself is divided into a number of permanent and temporary exhibitions. If you're very short on time, skip the 'Journeys: The Peopling of America 1550–1890' exhibit on the 1st floor and focus on the exhibitions on the 2nd floor. It's here you'll find two of the most fascinating exhibitions. The first, 'Through America's Gate,' examines the step-by-step process faced by the newly arrived, including the chalk-marking of those suspected of illness, a wince-inducing eye examination and 29 questions in the beautiful, vaulted Registry Room. The second must-see exhibition, 'Peak Immigration Years,' explores the motives behind the immigrants' journeys and the challenges they faced once they were free to begin their new American lives. For a history of the rise, fall and resurrection of the building itself, make time for the 'Restoring a Landmark' exhibition on the 3rd floor; its tableaux of trashed desks, chairs and other abandoned possessions are strangely haunting. Best of all, the audio tour offers optional, in-depth coverage for those wanting to delve deeper into the collections and the island's history. If you don't feel like opting for the audio tour, you can always pick up one of the phones in each display area and listen to the recorded, yet affecting memories of real Ellis Island immigrants, taped in the 1980s. Another option is the free, 45-minute guided tour with a park ranger. Booked in advance, the tour is also available in American sign language.

Main Building Architecture

With their Main Building, architects Edward Lippincott Tilton and William A Boring created a suitably impressive and imposing 'prologue' to America. The designing duo won the contract after the original wooden building burnt down in 1897. Having attended the Ecole des Beaux Arts in Paris, it's not surprising that they opted for a beaux arts aesthetic for the project. The building evokes a grand train station, with majestic triple-arched entrances, decorative Flemish bond brickwork, and granite quoins (cornerstones) and belvederes. Inside, it's the 2nd-floor, 338ft-long Registry Room (also known as the Great Hall) that takes the breath away. It was under its beautiful vaulted ceiling that the newly arrived lined up to have their documents checked, and that the polygamists, paupers, criminals and anarchists were turned back. The original plaster ceiling was severely damaged by an explosion of munition barges at nearby Black Tom Wharf. It was a blessing in disguise, the rebuilt version adorned with striking, herringbone-patterned tiles by Rafael Guastavino. The Catalan-born engineer is also behind the beautiful tiled ceiling at the Grand Central Oyster Bar & Restaurant (p187) at Grand Central Terminal.

American Immigrant Wall of Honor & Fort Gibson Ruins

Accessible from the 1st-floor 'Journeys: The Peopling of America 1550-1890' exhibit is the outdoor American Immigrant Wall of Honor, inscribed with the names of over 700,000 immigrants. Believed to be the world's longest wall of names, it's a fund-raising project, allowing any American to have an immigrant relative's name recorded for the cost of a donation. Construction of the wall in the 1990s uncovered the remains of the island's original structure, Fort Gibson you can see the ruins at the southwestern corner of the memorial. Built in 1808, the fortification was part of a harbor defense system against the British that also included Castle Clinton in Battery Park and Castle Williams on Governors Island. During this time, Ellis Island measured a modest 3.3 acres of sand and slush. Between 1892 and 1934, the island expanded dramatically thanks to landfill brought in from the ballast of ships and construction of the city's subway system.

AN IRISH DEBUT

Ellis Island's very first immigrant arrival was 15-year-old Anna 'Annie' Moore. After a 12-day journey from County Cork, Ireland, on the steamship *Nevada*, the steerage passenger stepped onto the island on January 1, 1892, accompanied by her brothers Phillip and Anthony. The three siblings had headed to America to join their parents, who had migrated to New York City four years earlier. After tying the knot with German immigrant Joseph Augustus Schayer, the Irish-American gave birth to at least 11 children, only five of whom survived. Annie died on December 6, 1924 and was laid to rest at Calvary Cemetery, Queens.

At the turn of the 20th century, the since-defunct hospital on Ellis Island was one of the world's largest. Consisting of 22 buildings and dubbed the 'Hospital of all Nations,' it was America's front line in the fight against 'imported' diseases. The institution's fascinating history is vividly relayed in writer/producer Lorie Conway's documentary and accompanying book *Forgotten Ellis Island*. For more on the project, visit www.forgottenellisisland.com.

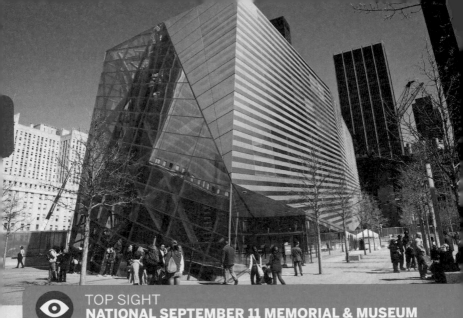

NATIONAL SEPTEMBER 11 MEMORIAL & MUSEUM

Plagued by design controversies, budget blowouts and construction delays, the core part of the World Trade Center (WTC) redevelopment – the National September 11 Museum and Memorial – is finally open to the world. Titled *Reflecting Absence,* the memorial's two massive reflecting pools are as much a symbol of hope and renewal as they are a tribute to the thousands who lost their lives to terrorism. Beside them stands the state-of-the-art Memorial Museum, a striking, solemn space documenting the events and consequences of that fateful fall day in 2001.

DON'T MISS...

➡ Reflecting Pools
➡ Memorial Museum
➡ Santiago Calatrava's oculus

PRACTICALITIES

➡ Map p408
➡ www.911memorial. org
➡ cnr Greenwich & Albany Sts
➡ admission $24
➡ Ⓢ A/C/E to Chambers St, R to Rector St, 2/3 to Park Pl

Reflecting Pools

Surrounded by a plaza planted with 400 swamp white oak trees, the September 11 Memorial's reflecting pools occupy the very footprints of the ill-fated twin towers. From their rim, a steady cascade of water pours 30ft down toward a central void. The flow of the water is richly symbolic, beginning as hundreds of smaller streams, merging into a massive torrent of collective confusion, and ending with a slow journey towardd an abyss. Bronze panels frame the pools, inscribed with the names of those who died in the terrorist attacks of September 11, 2001, and in the World Trade Center car bombing on February 26, 1993. Designed by Michael Arad and Peter Walker, the pools are both striking and deeply poignant.

Memorial Musem

The contemplative energy of the monument is further enhanced by the **National September 11 Memorial Museum** (Map p408; www.911memorial.org/museum). Standing between the reflective pools, the museum's glass entrance pavilion subtly, yet eerily, evokes a toppled tower. Inside, a gently sloping ramp leads to the museum's subterranean exhibition galleries. On the descent, visitors stand in the shadow of two 70ft-high steel tridents, originally embedded in the bedrock at the base of the North Tower. Looking like giant, rusty forks, these scorched survivors are but two of many artifacts that bear silent witness to the attacks. Among them is the so-called 'survivors staircase,' used by hundreds of workers to flee the WTC site. There's the last steel column removed from the clean-up, adorned with the messages and mementos of recovery workers, responders and loved ones of the victims. And then there's the New York City Fire Department's Engine Company 21, its burnt out cab a piercing testament to the inferno faced by those at the scene. Alongside video, images, personal effects, testimonies and real-time audio recordings, the galleries provide a dignified, reflective exploration of the day of the tragedy, the events that preceded it (including the WTC bombing of 1993), and the stories of grief, resilience and hope that followed.

One World Trade Center

Soaring skywards at the northwest corner of the WTC site is architect David M Childs' 104-floor **One World Trade Center** (Map p408; One WTC; Vesey St) – a redesign of Daniel Libeskind's original 2002 concept. Not only the loftiest building in America, this tapered giant is currently the tallest building in the western hemisphere, not to mention the fourth tallest in the world by pinnacle height. Topped by a cable-stayed antenna codesigned by sculptor Kenneth Snelson, the building's total height of 1776ft is a symbolic reference to the year of American independence. Symbolism feeds several aspects of the building: the tower's footprint is equal to those of the original towers, while the observation decks will match the heights of those in the destroyed buildings. Scheduled to open to the public in 2015, these observation decks will span floors 100 to 102, delivering unparalleled 360-degree views. Unlike the original towers, however, One WTC was built with a whole new level of safety in mind, its precautionary features including a 200ft-high blast-resistant base and 1m-thick concrete walls encasing all elevators, stairwells, and communication and safety systems. One thing that wasn't foreseen by the architects and engineers was the antenna's noisy disposition; the strong winds that race through its lattice design produce a haunting, howling sound known to keep locals up at night.

WORLD TRADE CENTER (WTC) TRANSPORTATION HUB

It was the image of a child releasing a dove that inspired Santiago Calatrava's dramatic oculus above the new WTC Transportation Hub. While budget-driven tweaks of the Spanish architect's design have led some to call it an 'immobilized stegosaurus,' there's no doubt that the soaring creation is arresting. The structure will stream natural light into the WTC's $3.74-billion (and counting) transit center, expected to serve 200,000 subway and PATH train commuters daily once completed in 2015. A whopping 2.5 times bigger than Grand Central Terminal, the project will also feature c 200,000 sq ft of retail and dining space for those who want to linger in Manhattan's latest architectural controversy.

One of the Memorial Museum's most curious (and famous) artifacts is the so-called 'Angel of 9/11,' the eerie outline of a woman's anguished face on a twisted girder believed to originate from the point where American Airlines Flight 11 slammed into the North Tower. Experts have a more prosaic explanation: natural corrosion and sheer coincidence.

◉ SIGHTS

◉ Wall Street & the Financial District

NATIONAL SEPTEMBER 11 MEMORIAL & MUSEUM   MONUMENT, MUSEUM
See p66.

FRAUNCES TAVERN MUSEUM   MUSEUM

Map p408 (www.frauncestavernmuseum.org; 54 Pearl St btwn Broad St & Coenties Slip; adult/child $7/free; ⊘noon-5pm; ⓢJ/Z to Broad St, 4/5 to Bowling Green) Combining five early-18th-century structures, this unique museum-restaurant-bar combo pays homage to the nation-shaping events of 1783, when the British relinquished control of New York at the end of the Revolutionary War, and General George Washington gave a farewell speech to the officers of the Continental Army in the 2nd-floor dining room on December 4.

The site was originally built as a tony residence for merchant Stephen Delancey's family; barkeeper Samuel Fraunces purchased it in 1762, turning it into a tavern in honor of the American victory in the Revolutionary War. After the war, when New York was the nation's first capital, the space was used by the Departments of War, Treasury and Foreign Affairs. The tavern was closed and fell into disuse in the 19th century – and soon after was damaged during several massive fires that destroyed most colonial buildings and Dutch-built structures in the area. In 1904 the Sons of the Revolution, a historical society, bought the building and returned it to an approximation of its colonial-era look – an act believed to be the first major attempt at historical preservation in the USA. Today, the museum hosts lectures, Revolutionary War paintings, occasional historical walking tours, and some surprising Washington relics, including a lock of hair and a fragment from his coffin.

NATIONAL MUSEUM OF THE AMERICAN INDIAN   MUSEUM

Map p408 (www.nmai.si.edu; 1 Bowling Green; ⊘10am-5pm Fri-Wed, to 8pm Thu; 🛜; ⓢ4/5 to Bowling Green, R to Whitehall St) FREE An affiliate of the Smithsonian Institution, this elegant museum of Native American culture is set in Cass Gilbert's spectacular 1907 Custom House, one of NYC's finest beaux arts buildings. Beyond a vast elliptical rotunda, sleek galleries play host to changing exhibitions documenting Native American art, culture, life and beliefs. The museum's permanent collection includes stunning decorative arts, textiles and ceremonial objects that document the diverse native cultures across the Americas.

It's an ironically grand space for the country's leading museum on Native American art, established by oil heir George Gustav Heye in 1916. The four giant female sculptures outside the building are the work of Daniel Chester French, who would go on to sculpt the seated Abraham Lincoln at Washington, DC's Lincoln Memorial. Representing (from left to right) Asia, North America, Europe and Africa, the figures of-

---

BLAST FROM THE PAST

If you wander past the former headquarters of JP Morgan Bank on the southeast corner of Wall and Broad Sts, take a minute to examine its limestone facade on the Wall St side. The pockmarks you see are the remnants of the so-called Morgan Bank bombing – America's deadliest terrorist attack until the Oklahoma City bombing of 1995.

The fateful day was Thursday, September 16, 1920, when at exactly 12.01pm, 500lb of lead sash weights and 100lb of dynamite exploded from a horse-drawn carriage. Thirty-eight people were killed and around 400 injured. Among the latter was John F Kennedy's father, Joseph P Kennedy.

The bomb's detonation outside America's most influential financial institution at the time led many to blame anticapitalist groups, from Italian anarchists to stock-standard Bolsheviks. Yet the crime has yet to be solved, with the decision to reopen both the bank and New York Stock Exchange the following day leading to a swift clean-up of both debris and vital clues. Almost 100 years on, the shrapnel marks remain, purposely left by banker Jack Morgan as an act of remembrance and defiance.

fer a revealing look at America's world view at the beginning of the 20th century; Asia 'bound' by its religions, America 'youthful and virile,' Europe 'wise yet decaying' and Africa 'asleep and barbaric.' The museum also hosts a range of cultural programs, including dance and music performances, readings for children, craft demonstrations, films and workshops. The museum shop is well stocked with Native American jewelry, books, CDs and crafts.

TRINITY CHURCH CHURCH

Map p408 (www.trinitywallstreet.org; Broadway at Wall St; ⌚church 7am-6pm Mon-Fri, 8am-4pm Sat, 7am-4pm Sun, churchyard 7am-4pm Mon-Fri, 8am-3pm Sat, 7am-3pm Sun; [S]R to Rector St, 2/3, 4/5 to Wall St) New York City's tallest building upon completion in 1846, Trinity Church features a 280ft-high bell tower, an arresting stained-glass window over the altar, and a small museum of historical church artifacts. Famous residents of its serene cemetery include founding father Alexander Hamilton, while its excellent music series includes Concerts at One (1pm Thursdays) and magnificent choir concerts, including an annual December rendition of Handel's *Messiah*.

The original Anglican parish church was founded by King William III in 1697 and once presided over several constituent chapels, including St Paul's Chapel at the corner of Fulton St and Broadway. Its huge landholdings in Lower Manhattan made it the country's wealthiest and most influential church throughout the 18th century. Burnt down in 1776, its second incarnation was demolished in 1839. The third and current church, designed by English architect Richard Upjohn, helped launch the picturesque neo-Gothic movement in America.

ST PAUL'S CHAPEL CHURCH

Map p408 (www.trinitywallstreet.org; Broadway at Fulton St; ⌚10am-6pm Mon-Fri, to 4pm Sat, 8am-4pm Sun; [S]A/C, J/Z, 2/3, 4/5 to Fulton St) Despite George Washington worshipping here after his inauguration in 1789, this classic revival brownstone chapel found new fame in the aftermath of September 11. With the World Trade Center destruction occurring just a block away, the mighty structure became a spiritual support and volunteer center, movingly documented in its exhibition 'Unwavering Spirit: Hope & Healing at Ground Zero.'

Through photographs, personal objects and messages of support, the exhibition honors both the victims and the volunteers who worked round the clock, serving meals, setting up beds, doling out massages and counseling rescue workers.

FEDERAL HALL MUSEUM

Map p408 (www.nps.gov/feha; 26 Wall St, entrance on Pine St; ⌚9am-5pm Mon-Fri; 📶; [S]J/Z to Broad St, 2/3, 4/5 to Wall St) [FREE] A Greek Revival masterpiece, Federal Hall houses a museum dedicated to postcolonial New York. Themes include George Washington's inauguration, Alexander Hamilton's relationship with the city, and the struggles of John Peter Zenger – jailed, tried and acquitted of libel here for exposing government corruption in his newspaper. There's also a visitor information hall which covers downtown cultural happenings.

Distinguished by a huge statue of George Washington, the building itself stands on the site of New York's original City Hall. It was here that the first US Congress convened and that Washington took the oath of office as the first US president on April 30, 1789. The museum's artifacts include the very slab of stone on which Washington stood while taking that oath. After that structure's demolition in the early 19th century, the current building rose in its place between 1834 and 1842, serving as the US Customs House until 1862.

NEW YORK STOCK EXCHANGE NOTABLE BUILDING

Map p408 (www.nyse.com; 11 Wall St; ⌚closed to the public; [S]J/Z to Broad St, 2/3, 4/5 to Wall St) Home to the world's best-known stock exchange (the NYSE), Wall St is an iconic symbol of US capitalism. About one billion shares change hands daily behind the portentous Romanesque facade, a sight no longer accessible to the public due to security concerns. Feel free to gawk outside the building, protected by barricades and the hawk-eyed New York Police Department (NYPD).

Frantic buying and selling by those familiar red-faced traders screaming 'Sell! Sell!' goes on at the **New York Mercantile Exchange** (Map p408; ☎212-299-2000; www.nymex.com; 1 North End Ave; [S]2/3 to Park Pl, E to World Trade Center), near Vesey St. This exchange deals in gold, gas and oil commodities, but no longer with tourists; like the NYSE, it's closed to visitors.

BOWLING GREEN PARK

Map p408 (cnr Broadway & State St; ☎; [S]4/5 to Bowling Green) New York's oldest – and possibly tiniest – public park is purportedly the spot where Dutch settler Peter Minuit paid Native Americans the equivalent of $24 to purchase Manhattan Island. At its northern edge stands Arturo Di Modica's 7000lb bronze *Charging Bull,* placed here permanently after it mysteriously appeared in front of the New York Stock Exchange in 1989, two years after a market crash.

The tree-fringed triangle was leased by the people of New York from the English crown beginning in 1733, for the token amount of one peppercorn each. But an angry mob, inspired by George Washington's nearby reading of the Declaration of Independence, descended upon the site in 1776 and tore down a large statue of King George III; a fountain now stands in its place.

MUSEUM OF AMERICAN FINANCE MUSEUM

Map p408 (www.moaf.org; 48 Wall St btwn Pearl & William Sts; adult/child $8/free; ⏲10am-4pm Tue-Sat; [S]2/3, 4/5 to Wall St) Money makes this museum go round, its focus on historic moments in American financial history. Permanent collections include rare historic currency (including Confederate currency used by America's southern states during the Civil War), stock and bond certificates from the Gilded Age, the oldest-known photograph of Wall St and a stock ticker from c 1875.

Once the headquarters for the Bank of New York, the building is a lavish spectacle, with 30ft ceilings, high arched windows, a majestic staircase to the mezzanine, glass chandeliers, and murals depicting historic scenes of banking and commerce.

NEW YORK CITY POLICE MUSEUM MUSEUM

Map p408 (www.nycpolicemuseum.org; 45 Wall St at William St; admission $5; ⏲10am-5pm Mon-Sat, noon-5pm Sun; 👪; [S]J/Z to Broad St; 2/3, 4/5 to Wall St) Until its Hurricane Sandy-damaged landmark location at 100 Old Slip reopens, this tribute to 'New York's Finest' will remain on Wall St. Exhibitions span both past and present aspects of city crime fighting, from the mug shots and weapons of notorious New York mobsters, to historic NYPD uniforms, to rare photographic images documenting the September 11 terrorist attacks. Check the website for updates on the museum's move back to its permanent address.

FEDERAL RESERVE BANK OF NEW YORK NOTABLE BUILDING

Map p408 (☎212-720-6130; www.newyorkfed.org; 33 Liberty St at Nassau St, entry via 44 Maiden Lane; ⏲reservation required, guided tours 11.15am, noon, 12.45pm, 1.30pm, 2.15pm & 3pm Mon-Fri, museum 10am-3pm; [S]A/C, J/Z, 2/3, 4/5 to Fulton St) [FREE] The best reason to visit the Federal Reserve Bank is the chance to (briefly) ogle at its high-security vault – more than 10,000 tons of gold reserves reside here, 80ft below ground. You'll only see a small part of that fortune, but signing on to a free tour (the only way down; book several months ahead) is worth the effort.

While you don't need to join a guided tour to browse the bank's interactive museum, which delves into the bank's history and research, you will still need to book a time online. Bring your passport or other official ID.

⊙ New York Harbor

STATUE OF LIBERTY MONUMENT

See p62.

ELLIS ISLAND LANDMARK, MUSEUM

See p64.

⊙ Battery Park City

★**MUSEUM OF JEWISH HERITAGE** MUSEUM

Map p408 (www.mjhnyc.org; 36 Battery Pl; adult/child $12/free, 4-8pm Wed free; ⏲10am-5:45pm Sun-Tue & Thu, to 8pm Wed, to 5pm Fri Apr-Sep, to 3pm Fri Oct-Mar; ☎; [S]4/5 to Bowling Green) This evocative waterfront museum explores all aspects of modern Jewish identity, with often poignant personal artifacts, photographs and documentary films. Its outdoor *Garden of Stones* – created by artist Andy Goldsworthy – in which 18 boulders form a narrow pathway for contemplating the fragility of life, is dedicated to those who lost loved ones in the Holocaust.

The building itself features a six-sided shape and three tiers to symbolize the Star of David and the six million Jews who perished in WWII. The museum also hosts films, music concerts, ongoing lecture series and special holiday performances. Frequent, free workshops for families with children are also on offer, while the on-site kosher cafe serves light food.

WORTH A DETOUR

GOVERNORS ISLAND

Off-limits to the public for 200 years, former military outpost **Governors Island** (☎212-514-8285; www.nps.gov/gois; admission free; ⏰10am-7pm Sat & Sun late May-late Sep; ferries leave from Battery Maritime Bldg, Slip 7, hourly 10am-3pm Fri & every 30min 10am-5pm Sat & Sun May-Oct, [S]4, 5 to Bowling Green, 1 to South Ferry) is now one of New York's most popular seasonal playgrounds. Each summer, free ferries make the seven-minute trip from Lower Manhattan to the 172-acre oasis. In 2014, 30 new acres of island parkland opened to the public, with features including the 6-acre, art-studded Liggett Terrace; the 10-acre Hammock Grove (complete with 50 hammocks); and the 14-acre Play Lawn, with a duo of natural turf ball fields for adult softball and Little League baseball. Things get even better in 2015, with the completion of The Hills, an ambitious quartet of artifical hills offering spectacular city and harbor views, squeal-inducing slides and site-specific art.

Art is the focus at **Figment** (www.figmentproject.org), a one-weekend-only interactive art festival in June, while inspiring views are also on tap along the Great Promenade. Running for 2.2 miles along the island's perimeter, the path takes in everything from Lower Manhattan and Brooklyn, to Staten Island and New Jersey. Those who want to hit the pedal can rent bikes from Bike and Roll for $20 per half-day.

Besides serving as a successful military fort in the Revolutionary War, the Union Army's central recruiting station during the Civil War, and the take-off point for Wilbur Wright's famous 1909 flight around the Statue of Liberty, Governors Island is where the 1988 Reagan-Gorbachev summit signaled the beginning of the end of the Cold War. You can visit the spot where that famous summit took place at the **Admiral's House**, an 1843 military residence that's part of the elegant ghost-town area of Nolan Park. Other historic spots include **Fort Jay**, fortified in 1776 for what became a failed attempt to prevent the Brits from invading Manhattan; **Colonel's Row**, a collection of lovely, 19th-century brick officers' quarters; and the creepy **Castle Williams**, a 19th-century fort that was eventually used as a military penitentiary. The best way to explore it all is with the **National Park Service** (www.nps.gov/gois/planyourvisit), the rangers of which conduct 45- to 60-minute guided tours of the historic district. See the website for specific days and times.

SKYSCRAPER MUSEUM — MUSEUM

Map p408 (www.skyscraper.org; 39 Battery Pl; admission $5; ⏰noon-6pm Wed-Sun; [S]4/5 to Bowling Green) Fans of phallic architecture will appreciate this compact, high-gloss gallery, examining skyscrapers as objects of design, engineering and urban renewal. Temporary exhibitions dominate the space, with one recent exhibition exploring New York's new generation of superslim residential towers. Permanent fixtures include information on the design and construction of the Empire State Building and World Trade Center.

The museum is also home to the cutting-edge technology known as VIVA – the Visual Index to the Virtual Archive. This visual-based interface uses a 3-D computer model of Manhattan as a clickable map, allowing users to see the city's past and present, and to explore the museum's collections through an online database (accessed via the museum's website).

CASTLE CLINTON — HISTORIC SITE

Map p408 (www.nps.gov/cacl; Battery Park; ⏰8:30am-5pm; 📶; [S]1 to South Ferry, 4/5 to Bowling Green) Built as a fort to defend the New York Harbor during the war of 1812, this national monument has played numerous roles, including opera house, entertainment complex and aquarium. It's now a visitors center, with historical displays, a ticket booth for ferries to the Statue of Liberty and Ellis Island, a gift shop, as well as a performance space for summer concerts under the stars.

The circular structure got its current moniker in 1817 to honor then mayor DeWitt Clinton. Later, and before Ellis Island opened to immigrants, Castle Garden (as it was then known) served as the major processing center for new immigrant arrivals, welcoming more than eight million people between 1855 and 1890. Rangers lead historic tours of the site daily at 10am, noon and 2pm, subject to staff availability.

STATEN ISLAND

Most visitors to Staten Island exit the ferry – which docks in downtown St George, on the northern tip of the 58-sq-mile island – then reboard right away. Indeed, if not for its namesake ferry – or Robert Redford and Jane Fonda's wild night out with Armenians in *Barefoot in the Park* – New York's 'forgotten borough' might be a complete unknown. Despite its unfashionable reputation for suburbanism and conservatism, Staten Island is not without its drawcards, and a day out here promises a surprisingly different take on NYC life.

From the ferry terminal, turn left onto Richmond Tce (which becomes Bay St) and walk 0.3 miles south to the **Staten Island Chamber of Commerce** (☑718-727-1900; www.sichamber.com; 130 Bay St; ⊙9am-5pm Mon-Fri) for tourist information. For organic coffee, books, political talks or, later on, live music, walk a further 0.2 miles south on Bay St to **Everything Goes Book Café & Neighborhood Stage** (www.etgstores.com/bookcafe; 208 Bay St; ⊙10.30am-6.30pm Tue-Thu, to 10pm Fri & Sat, noon-5pm Sun; ⊛), a Berkeley-style arts community. Close by you'll find its sibling, **Everything Goes Furniture & Gallery** (☑718-273-0568; 17 Brook St; ⊙10:30am-6:30pm Tue-Sat), which sells eclectic antiques, collectibles and art. An easy 0.3 miles northwest of the ferry terminal, the **Staten Island Museum** (☑718-727-1135; www.statenislandmuseum.org; 75 Stuyvesant Pl at Wall St; adult/child $5/free; ⊙11am-5pm Mon-Fri, 10am-5pm Sat, noon-5pm Sun) offers an eclectic collection of local history, natural science and art. By the time you read this, the museum will also run exhibitions at its new building at Snug Harbor.

Staten Island's buses – which accept the MTA MetroCard and leave from outside the ferry terminal – are your best bet for reaching the island's more distant attractions. Top of the list is **Snug Harbor Cultural Center & Botanical Garden** (☑718-448-2500; www.snug-harbor.org; 1000 Richmond Tce; galleries & gardens adult/child $8/free, gardens only $5/free, galleries only $5/free; ⊙grounds dawn-dusk daily, Chinese Scholar's Garden 10am-4pm Tue-Sun, art galleries noon-5pm Wed-Sun; ⊟S40 to Snug Harbor), a beautiful complex of themed gardens, historic buildings, art spaces and museums 2 miles west of the ferry terminal. Highlights include an ancient-style Chinese Scholar's Garden, a Tuscan Garden modeled on the Villa Gamberaia in Florence, and the Newhouse Center for Contemporary Art, which showcases changing exhibitions of modern art. From Henderson St on the southern edge of the Snug Harbor complex, the Staten Island Mall–bound S44 bus leads to **Denino's Pizzeria & Tavern** (www.deninos.com; 524 Port Richmond Ave; pizzas $11.50-20; ⊙10am-10pm Mon-Thu, to 11pm Fri-Sun; ⊟S44). The pizzas here are insanely good and revered by gastronomes across the city.

In the very center of Staten Island, **Historic Richmond Town** (☑718-351-1611; www.historicrichmondtown.org; 441 Clarke Ave; adult/child $8/5; ⊙1-5pm Wed-Sun Sep-Jun, 10am-5pm Wed-Sat, 1-5pm Sun Jul & Aug; ⊟S74 to Richmond Rd & St Patrick's Pl) consists of 27 historic buildings (some dating back to a 1690s Dutch community) standing in a 100-acre preservation project maintained by the Staten Island Historical Society. The town includes the island's former county seat. Its most famous building, the two-story, redwood Voorlezer's House, is the USA's oldest schoolhouse, dating back to c 1695. Guides lead tours (included with admission) at 2pm and 3:30pm. From the ferry, catch bus S74; journey time is 40 minutes.

Another cultural drawcard is **Alice Austen House** (☑718-816-4506; www.aliceausten.org; 2 Hylan Blvd; admission $3; ⊙11am-5pm Tue-Sun Mar-Dec; ⊟S51 to Hylan Blvd & Bay St), the harborside home of the early-20th-century photographer. The museum offers glimpses into her world, including her life on Staten Island, as well as exhibiting many of her works. It's located just north of the Verrazano-Narrows Bridge, or about a 15-minute ride south from the ferry terminal on bus S51.

IRISH HUNGER MEMORIAL MEMORIAL

Map p408 (290 Vesey St at North End Ave; admission free; [S]2/3 to Park Pl) Artist Brian Tolle's compact labyrinth of low limestone walls and patches of grass pays tribute to the Great Irish Famine and Migration (1845–52), which prompted hundreds of thousands of immigrants to leave Ireland for better opportunities in the New World. Representing abandoned cottages, stone walls and potato fields, the work was created with stones from each of Ireland's 32 counties.

HUDSON RIVER PARK PARK

Map p408 (www.hudsonriverpark.org; Manhattan's west side from Battery Park to 59th St; [S]1 to Franklin St, 1 to Canal St) Stretching from Battery Park to Hell's Kitchen, the 5-mile, 550-acre Hudson River Park runs along the lower western side of Manhattan. Diversions include a bike/run/skate path that snakes along its entire length, community gardens, playgrounds, sculpture exhibitions, and renovated piers reinvented as riverfront esplanades, miniature golf courses, alfresco summertime movie theaters and concert venues. Visit the website for a detailed map or check out p136 for more information.

East River Waterfront

SOUTH STREET SEAPORT NEIGHBORHOOD

Map p408 (www.southstreetseaport.com; [S]A/C, J/Z, 2/3, 4/5 to Fulton St) This 11-block enclave of cobbled streets, maritime warehouses and shops combines the best and worst in historic preservation. It's not on the radar for most New Yorkers, but tourists are drawn to the nautical air, the frequent street performers and the mobbed restaurants.

In late 2013 the area's historic Pier 17 was condemned to the wrecking ball, with plans for a new retail, entertainment and marina complex provoking mixed reactions from locals. The future of the pier's neighboring **New Amsterdam Market** (Map p408; www.newamsterdammarket.org; South St btwn Peck Slip & Beekman St; [S]A/C, J/Z, 1/2, 4/5 to Fulton St) – a much-loved Sunday locavore food market held outside the old Fulton Fish Market – was also up in the air, while the cash-strapped **South Street Seaport Museum** (Map p408; www.seany.org; 12 Fulton St; adult/child $5/free; [S]2/3, 4/5, A/C, J/M/Z to Fulton St) and its galleries of historic maritime artifacts remained closed indefinitely. The museum's booty extends to the iron-hulled **Pioneer** (Map p408; ☎212-742-1969; www.nywatertaxi.com; Pier 16, South Street Seaport; adult/child $45/35) at Pier 16, a 19th-century vessel that continues to offer wonderful two-hour sailing journeys through the warmer months. Happy times also await at neighboring **Pier 15** (Map p408; South St btwn Fletcher & John Sts; 🕒6am-dusk), a striking, two-level pier with swaths of soothing lawn and spectacular water views.

City Hall & Civic Center

WOOLWORTH BUILDING NOTABLE BUILDING

Map p408 (http://woolworthtours.com; 233 Broadway at Park Pl; 30/60/90min tours $15/30/45; 🕒tour times vary; [S]R to City Hall, 4/5/6 to Brooklyn Bridge-City Hall) The world's tallest building upon completion in 1913, Cass Gilbert's 57-story, 792ft-tall Woolworth Building is a neo-Gothic marvel, elegantly clad in masonry and terracotta. Surpassed in height by the Chrysler Building in 1930, its landmarked lobby is a breathtaking spectacle of dazzling, Byzantine-like mosaics. The lobby is only accessible on prebooked guided tours, which also offer insight into the building's more curious original features, among them a dedicated subway entrance and a secret swimming pool.

At its dedication, the building was described as a 'cathedral of commerce'; though meant as an insult, FW Woolworth, head of the five-and-dime chain store empire headquartered there, took the comment as a compliment and began throwing the term around himself.

AFRICAN BURIAL GROUND MEMORIAL

Map p408 (www.nps.gov/afbg; 290 Broadway btwn Duane & Elk Sts; 🕒memorial 9am-5pm daily, visitor center 10am-4pm Tue-Sat; [S]4/5 to Wall St) [FREE] In 1991, construction workers here uncovered over 400 stacked wooden caskets, just 16ft to 28ft below street level. The boxes contained the remains of enslaved Africans (nearby Trinity Church graveyard had banned the burial of Africans at the time). Today, a memorial and visitors center honors an estimated 15,000 Africans buried here during the 17th and 18th centuries.

The visitors center requires airportlike security screenings, so leave your nail files in the hotel.

1. Hudson River Park (p73)
Explore this 5-mile park along Manhattan's western side.

2. Brooklyn Bridge (p266)
Watch the sun set over Lower Manhattan from this vantage point.

3. Squirrel in Battery Park (p70)
Make your way to Castle Clinton in Battery Park, a visitors center selling tickets to the Statue of Liberty and Ellis Island.

4. One World Trade Center (p67)
Check out New York City's tallest skyscraper.

Tribeca

HARRISON STREET HOUSES — HISTORIC BUILDING

Map p408 (Harrison St; [S]1 to Franklin St) Built between 1804 and 1828, the eight townhouses on the block of Harrison St immediately west of Greenwich St constitute the largest collection of Federal architecture left in NYC. Yet only the buildings at 31 and 33 Harrison St remain where they were originally constructed. The other six once stood two blocks away, on a stretch of Washington St that no longer exists.

In the early 1970s, that site was home to the Washington Market, a wholesale fruit and vegetable shopping complex. But development of the waterfront – which resulted in the construction of the Borough of Manhattan Community College and the Soviet-style concrete apartment complex that now looms over the townhouses – meant the market had to move uptown and the historic row of houses had to be relocated.

🍴 EATING

Frenzied lunch rushes for financial types fuel two extremes in Lower Manhattan: fast-food storefronts and masculine dining rooms catering to steak-chomping bigwigs. Both genres offer plenty of satisfying experiences, whether it's faux *filet Bercy* at Les Halles or frozen custard at Shake Shack. Head north into Tribeca and the vibe is hipper and more fashion-forward, with a string of celeb-chef favorites.

SHAKE SHACK — BURGERS $

Map p408 (www.shakeshack.com; 215 Murray St btwn West St & North End Ave; burgers from $3.60; 🕐11am-11pm; [S]A/C, 1/2/3 to Chambers St) Danny Meyer's cult burger chain is fast food at its finest: cotton-soft burgers made with prime, freshly ground mince; Chicago-style hot dogs in poppy-seed potato buns; and seriously good cheesy fries. Leave room for the legendary frozen custard and drink local with a beer from Brooklyn brewery Sixpoint.

NORTH END GRILL — AMERICAN $$

Map p408 (☎646-747-1600; www.northendgrillnyc.com; 104 North End Ave at Murray St; 3-course lunch $39, dinner mains $17-34; 🕐11:30am-2pm & 5:30-10pm Mon-Thu, to 10:30pm Fri, 11am-2pm & 5:30-10:30pm Sat, 11am-2:30pm & 5:30-9pm Sun; [S]1/2/3, A/C to Chambers St, E to World Trade Center) Handsome, smart and friendly, this is celeb chef Danny Meyer's take on the American grill. Top-tier produce (including stuff from the restaurant's own rooftop garden) forms the basis for modern takes on comfort grub, happily devoured by suited money-makers and a scattering of more casual passersby.

Dishes are given a kiss of smoke, either in the charcoal-fired oven or on the smokier wood-fired grill, with standouts including clam pizza with chili flakes, whole European branzino, and the feel-good roasted chicken for two. In true Meyer style, waitstaff are hawk-eyed and charming.

LES HALLES — FRENCH $$

Map p408 (☎212-285-8585; www.leshalles.net; 15 John St btwn Broadway & Nassau St; mains $14.50-32; 🕐7am-midnight; 📶; [S]A/C, J/Z, 2/3, 4/5 to Fulton St) Vegetarians need not apply at Anthony Bourdain's serious brasserie. Among the elegant light-fixture balls, dark-wood paneling and stiff white tablecloths, you'll find a buttoned-up, meat-lovin' crowd who've come for rich and decadent favorites like *cote de boeuf* and steak au poivre.

Standards like French onion soup, *moules frites* and salade Niçoise are equally sublime, while the lists of wine, single-malt scotches and other liquors are impressive.

★LOCANDA VERDE — ITALIAN $$$

Map p408 (☎212-925-3797; www.locandaverdenyc.com; 377 Greenwich St at Moore St; lunch $19-29, dinner mains $28-34; 🕐7am-11pm Mon-Fri, 8am-11pm Sat & Sun; [S]A/C/E to Canal St, 1 to Franklin St) Step through the velvet curtains into a sassy scene of loosened Brown Brothers' shirts, black dresses, and slick bartenders behind a long, crowded bar. Part of the Greenwich Hotel (p328), this brasserie is owned by celebrity chef Andrew Carmellini, whose modern Italian grub sees pumpkin agnolotti get it on with sage and amaretti, or roasted scallops join forces with Sicilian cauliflower, pine nuts and capers.

Bookings recommended.

TINY'S & THE BAR UPSTAIRS — AMERICAN $$$

Map p408 (☎212-374-1135; 135 W Broadway btwn Duane & Thomas Sts; mains $22-36; 🕐11:30am-11pm Mon-Thu, to midnight Fri, 10:30am-midnight

Neighborhood Walk
Lower Manhattan Landmarks

START LA COLOMBE
END FEDERAL HALL
LENGTH 2.5 MILES; THREE HOURS

Intimate and sometimes confusing side streets, Gothic churches and a fine collection of early-20th-century skyscrapers: Lower Manhattan is an area steeped in history.

Start with coffee at **1 La Colombe** (p78). In the 19th century the site was a stop on the antislavery 'underground railway,' a secret network of routes and safe houses allowing African Americans to reach free states and Canada. A plaque on the Lispenard St side of the building commemorates the fact. Further west, the intersection of Varick and N Moore Sts is where you'll find **2 Hook & Ladder 8**, better known as ghost-control headquarters in '80s film *Ghostbusters*. Continue south on Varick St, turn left into Leonard St. On the southeast corner at the intersection with Church St stands the **3 Textile Building**, built in 1901. Its architect, Henry J Hardenbergh, subsequently designed Midtown's monumental Plaza Hotel. Further south on Church St, turn left into Park Pl and right into Broadway. Before you is the neo-Gothic **4 Woolworth Building** (p73), the world's tallest skyscraper upon completion in 1913. Continue south on Broadway, cross Vesey St and you'll see **5 St Paul's Chapel** (p69) on your right – it's the only pre–Revolutionary War church left intact in the city. Directly behind it lies the World Trade Center site, now home to the **6 National September 11 Memorial & Museum** (p66). The museum houses artifacts relating to the 2001 terrorist attacks, while the memorial itself features two giant reflecting pools set in the footprints of the collapsed towers. Soaring above them is the 1776ft One World Trade Center, America's tallest skyscraper. Further south on Broadway, **7 Trinity Church** (p69) was NYC's tallest building upon completion in 1846. Its cemetery is the final resting place of steamboat inventor Robert Fulton. Head east onto Wall St to the **8 New York Stock Exchange** (p69) and **9 Federal Hall** (p69). You can visit the latter, in which John Peter Zenger was acquitted of seditious libel in 1735 – the first step, historians say, in establishing a democracy committed to a free press.

Sat, 10:30am-11pm Sun; [S]A/C, 1/2/3 to Chambers St) Snug and adorable (book ahead!), Tiny's comes with a crackling fire in the back room and an intimate bar upstairs. Served on vintage porcelain, dishes are soulful, subtly retweaked delights; think *burrata* with date puree, lemon honey glaze and pistachios, or pan-seared scallops getting zesty with grapefruit and Thai chili-ginger coconut sauce.

DRINKING & NIGHTLIFE

Corporate types don't always bolt for the 'burbs when 5pm hits, many loosening their ties in the smattering of wine bars and pubs around Stone St, Wall St and South Street Seaport. Tribeca keeps its cool with artisan coffee shops and plush cocktail dens. Thankfully, the drinks here tend to be stirred with a little more precision than over on the East Side.

★DEAD RABBIT — COCKTAIL BAR

Map p408 (www.deadrabbitnyc.com; 30 Water St; 🕐11am-4am; [S]R to Whitehall St, 1 to South Ferry) Far from dead, this new kid on the cocktail block has wasted no time swagging awards, among them World's Best New Cocktail Bar, Best Cocktail Menu and International Bartender of the Year at the 2013 Tales of the Cocktail Festival.

During the day, hit the sawdust-sprinkled taproom for specialty beers, historic punches and pop-inns (lightly hopped ale spiked with different flavors). Come evening, scurry upstairs to the cozy Parlour for 72 meticulously researched cocktails.

LA COLOMBE — CAFE

Map p408 (www.lacolombe.com; 319 Church St at Lispenard St; 🕐7:30am-6:30pm Mon-Fri, 8:30am-6:30pm Sat & Sun; [S]A/C/E to Canal St) Coffee and a few baked treats is all you'll get at this roaster but, man, are they good. The espresso is dark and intense, brewed by hipster baristas and swilled by an endless stream of cool kids and clued-in Continentals. Don't leave without a bottle of 'Pure Black Coffee,' steeped in oxygen-free stainless steel wine tanks for 16 hours.

KAFFE 1668 — CAFE

Map p408 (www.kaffe1668.com; 275 Greenwich St btwn Warren & Murray Sts; 🕐6:30am-10pm Mon-Fri, 7am-9pm Sat & Sun; 📶; [S]A/C, 1/2/3 to Chambers St) A coffee-geek mecca, with espresso machine, coffee urns and dual Synessos pumping out single-origin magic. There's a large communal table speckled with suits and laptop-tapping creatives, and more seating downstairs. For a hair-raising thrill, order a triple ristretto.

WEATHER UP — COCKTAIL BAR

Map p408 (www.weatherupnyc.com; 159 Duane St btwn Hudson St & W Broadway; 🕐5pm-2am; [S]1/2/3 to Chambers St) Softly lit subway tiles, amiable barkeeps and seductive cocktails make for a bewitching trio at Weather Up. Sweet talk the staff over a Whizz Bang (scotch whiskey, dry vermouth, house-made grenadine, orange bitters and absinthe). Failing that, comfort yourself with some seriously fine snacks, including spectacular oysters slapped with gin-martini granita.

WARD III — COCKTAIL BAR

Map p408 (www.ward3tribeca.com; 111 Reade St btwn Church St & W Broadway; 🕐4pm-4am Mon-Fri, 5pm-4am Sat & Sun; [S]A/C, 1/2/3 to Chambers St) Dark and bustling, Ward III channels old-school jauntiness with its elegant libations, vintage vibe (including old Singer sewing tables behind the bar) and gentlemanly house rules (No 2: 'Don't be creepy'). Reminisce over a Moroccan martini, or line the stomach first with top-notch bar grub, available every day till close.

MACAO — COCKTAIL BAR

Map p408 (☎212-431-8750; www.macaonyc.com; 311 Church St btwn Lispenard & Walker Sts; 🕐bar 4pm-5am; [S]A/C/E to Canal St) Though we love the '40s-style 'gambling parlor' bar-restaurant, it's the downstairs 'opium den' (open Thursday to Saturday) that gets our hearts racing. A Chinese-Portuguese fusion of grub and liquor, both floors are a solid spot for late-night sipping and snacking, especially if you've got a soft spot for sizzle-on-the-tongue libations.

BRANDY LIBRARY — BAR

Map p408 (www.brandylibrary.com; 25 N Moore St at Varick St; 🕐5pm-1am Sun-Wed, 4pm-2am Thu, 4pm-4am Fri & Sat; [S]1 to Franklin St) When sipping means serious business, settle in at this uberluxe 'library', its handsome club chairs facing floor-to-ceiling, bottle-lined shelves. Go for top-shelf cognac, malt scotch or vintage brandies (prices range from $9 to $235), expertly paired with nibbles such as the house-specialty *gougères* (Gruyere-cheese puffs). Reservations are recommended.

KEG NO 229 BEER HALL

Map p408 (www.kegno229.com; 229 Front St btwn Beekman St & Peck Slip; ⏲noon-midnight Sun-Wed, to 2am Thu-Sat; [S]A/C, J/Z, 1/2, 4/5 to Fulton St) If you know that a Flying Dog Raging Bitch is a craft beer – not a nickname for your ex – this curated beer bar is for you. From Mother's Milk Stout to Abita Purple Haze, its battalion of drafts, bottles and cans are a who's who of boutique American brews. Across the street, sibling Bin No 220 is its wine-loving sibling.

SMITH & MILLS COCKTAIL BAR

Map p408 (www.smithandmills.com; 71 N Moore St btwn Hudson & Greenwich Sts; ⏲11am-2am Mon-Wed, to 3am Thu-Sat, to 1am Sun; [S]1 to Franklin St) Petite Smith & Mills ticks all the cool boxes: unmarked exterior, kooky industrial interior and expertly crafted cocktails – the 'Carriage House' is a nod to the space's previous incarnation. Space is limited so head in early if you fancy kicking back on a plush banquette. A seasonal menu spans light snacks to a particularly notable burger.

☆ ENTERTAINMENT

FLEA THEATER THEATER

Map p408 (www.theflea.org; 41 White St btwn Church St & Broadway; [S]1 to Franklin St, A/C/E, N/Q/R, J/Z, 6 to Canal St) One of NYC's top off-Broadway companies, Flea is famous for performing innovative, timely new works in its two performance spaces. Luminaries including Sigourney Weaver and John Lithgow have trodden the boards here, and the year-round program also includes music and dance performances.

TRIBECA CINEMAS CINEMA

Map p408 (www.tribecacinemas.com; 54 Varick St at Laight St; [S]A/C/E, N/Q/R, J/Z, 6 to Canal St) This is the physical home of the Tribeca Film Festival (p27), founded in 2003 by Robert De Niro and Jane Rosenthal. Throughout the year, the space hosts a range of screenings and educational panels, including festivals dedicated to themes like architecture and design. See the website for details.

LOCAL KNOWLEDGE

DOWNTOWN DRINKING

Sean Muldoon, co-owner of award winning bar Dead Rabbit gives the lowdown on downtown's best drinking holes:

Best Cocktails

My favorite bar is Mayahuel (p123) in the East Village. From the cocktails and bartenders, to the food and music, it's exactly what a tequila cocktail bar should be. It uses a lot of mezcal, a smoky, tequila-like spirit. For New York's best Negroni, reserve a spot at nearby **PDT** (Map p414; ☎212-614-0386; www.pdtnyc.com; 113 St Marks Pl btwn First Ave & Ave A; [S]L to 1st Ave).

Best Newcomers

Notable newbies include Alphabet City's **Pouring Ribbons** (Map p414; www.pouringribbons.com; 225 Avenue B, 2nd floor; ⏲6pm-2am; [S]L to 1st Ave), from the team behind the Death & Co), and the Lower East Side's **Attaboy** (Map p416; 134 Eldridge St btwn Delancy & Broome Sts; ⏲6:45pm-4am; [S]B/D to Grand St).

Old Favorites

In the West Village, Employees Only (p147) offers a different take on the speakeasy bar, with interesting art deco touches. The place was once only open to people in the hospitality industry, hence the name. While I don't necessarily love its drinks – I usually opt for a beer – the bartenders, music and vibe are brilliant.

Down in Tribeca, don't miss the decor at Macao and the effortless cool of Weather Up.

🛍 SHOPPING

While the Financial District is not a shopping destination per se, it is where you'll find the cut-price fashion mecca Century 21. Further north in Tribeca, hit the lower end of Hudson St and surrounding streets for high-end interior design, antiques and a handful of trendy boutiques.

★ **CENTURY 21**   FASHION
Map p408 (www.c21stores.com; 22 Cortlandt St btwn Church St & Broadway; ⊙7:45am-9pm Mon-Wed, to 9:30pm Thu & Fri, 10am-9pm Sat, 11am-8pm Sun; ⓢA/C, J/Z, 2/3, 4/5 to Fulton St, N/R to Cortlandt St) For penny-pinching fashionistas, this giant, cut-price department store is dangerously addictive. Raid the racks for designer duds at up to 70% off. Not everything is a knockout or a bargain, but persistence pays off. You'll also find accessories, shoes, cosmetics, homewares and toys.

PHILIP WILLIAMS POSTERS   VINTAGE
Map p408 (www.postermuseum.com; 122 Chambers St btwn Church St & W Broadway; ⊙11am-7pm Mon-Sat; ⓢA/C, 1/2/3 to Chambers St) You'll find over half a million posters in this cavernous treasure trove, from oversized French advertisements for perfume and cognac to Soviet film posters and retro-fab promos for TWA. Prices range from $15 to a few thousand bucks, and most of the stock is original. There is a second entrance at 52 Warren St.

STEVEN ALAN   FASHION
Map p408 (www.stevenalan.com; 103 Franklin St btwn Church St & W Broadway; ⊙11.30am-7pm Mon-Wed, Fri & Sat, 11.30am-8pm Thu, noon-6pm Sun; ⓢA/C/E to Canal St, 1 to Franklin St) New York designer Steven Alan mixes his hip, heritage-inspired threads for men and women with a beautiful edit of clothes from indie-chic labels like Scandinavia's Hope, Our Legacy and Won Hundred. Accessories include hard-to-find fragrances, bags, jewelry and a selection of shoes by cognoscenti brands such as Common Projects and No. 6.

SHINOLA   ACCESSORIES
Map p408 (www.shinola.com; 177 Franklin St btwn Greenwich & Hudson Sts; ⊙11am-7pm Mon-Sat, noon-6pm Sun; ⓢ1 to Franklin St) Well known for its coveted wrist watches, Detroit-based Shinola branches out with a supercool se-

lection of Made-in-USA life props. Bag anything from leather tablet and journal covers to limited-edition bicycles with customized bags, even jewelry made with metal from torn-down buildings in Detroit.

There's an in-house espresso bar, **Smile** (Map p408; ⊙7am-7pm Mon-Sat, to 6pm Sun), too.

MYSTERIOUS BOOKSHOP   BOOKS
Map p408 (www.mysteriousbookshop.com; 58 Warren St at W Broadway; ⊙11am-7pm Mon-Sat; ⓢ1/2/3, A/C to Chambers St) With more crime per square inch than any other corner of the city, this mystery-themed bookstore peddles everything from classic espionage and thrillers to contemporary Nordic crime fiction and literary criticism. You'll find both new and secondhand titles, including rare first editions, signed copies, obscure magazines, and picture books for budding sleuths.

Check the website for in-store events.

PASANELLA & SON   WINE
Map p408 (www.pasanellaandson.com; 115 South St btwn Peck Slip & Beekman St; ⊙10am-9pm Mon-Sat, noon-7pm Sun; ⓢA/C, J/Z, 2/3, 4/5 to Fulton St) Oenophiles adore this savvy wine peddler, with its 400-plus drops both inspired and affordable. The focus is on small producers, with a number of biodynamic and organic winemakers in the mix. There's an impressive choice of American whiskeys, free wine tastings of the week's new arrivals on Sundays, and themed wine and cheese tastings throughout the year.

BEST MADE COMPANY   ACCESSORIES, FASHION
Map p408 (www.bestmadeco.com; 36 White St at Church St; ⊙noon-7pm Mon-Sat, to 6pm Sun; ⓢA/C/E to Canal St, 1 to Franklin St) Give your next camping trip a Manhattan makeover at this store/design-studio hybrid. Pick up cool, handcrafted axes, rucksacks, sunglasses, even designer dartboards and first-aid kits. A small, smart edit of threads for men includes designer graphic T-shirts, sweatshirts, flannel pullovers, and rugged knitwear from Portland's Dehen Knitting Mills.

CITYSTORE   SOUVENIRS
Map p408 (www.nyc.gov/citystore; Municipal Bldg, North Plaza, 1 Centre St; ⊙10am-5pm Mon-Fri; ⓢJ/Z to Chambers St, 4/5/6 to Brooklyn Bridge-City Hall) Score all manner of New York memorabilia, including authentic taxi

medallions, manhole coasters, Brooklyn Bridge posters, NYPD baseball caps and actual streets signs ('No Parking,' 'Don't Feed the Pigeons'). There's also a great collection of city-themed books.

SPORTS & ACTIVITIES

★STATEN ISLAND FERRY FERRY

Map p408 (www.siferry.com; Whitehall Terminal at Whitehall & South Sts; 24hr; [S]1 to South Ferry) [FREE] Staten Islanders know these hulking, dirty-orange ferryboats as commuter vehicles, while Manhattanites like to think of them as their secret, romantic vessels for a spring-day escape. Yet many a tourist is clued into the charms of the Staten Island Ferry: its 5.2-mile journey between Lower Manhattan and the Staten Island neighborhood of St George is one of NYC's finest free adventures.

In service since 1905, the ferry service carries around 20 million passengers each year. Whether you choose to simply ride it to Staten Island and back in one run – enjoying cinematic views of the city skyline, the Verrazano-Narrows Bridge (which connects Staten Island to Brooklyn) and the Statue of Liberty – or stay and explore New York's least-known borough before catching a later ferry, you're guaranteed a memorable experience.

BIKE AND ROLL BICYCLE RENTAL

Map p408 (☎212-260-0400; www.bikenewyorkcity.com; State & Water Sts; rentals per day from $44, tours from $50; 8am-8pm late May-Aug, shorter hours in winter; [S]4/5 to Bowling Green, 1 to South Ferry) Located just north of the Staten Island Ferry terminal, this is one of several Bike and Roll bike rental outlets in the city. It also leads bike tours, including across the Brooklyn Bridge and along the Hudson River.

BATTERY PARK CITY PARKS CONSERVANCY COURSE, TOUR

(☎212-267-9700; www.bpcparks.org) Offers a range of free and payable activities, from drawing classes and walking tours to parent and baby yoga, storytelling sessions and volunteer gardening. Check the website for upcoming events.

SoHo & Chinatown

SOHO | NOHO | NOLITA | CHINATOWN | LITTLE ITALY

Neighborhood Top Five

1 Maxing out the credit cards on SoHo's concrete catwalks, followed by boozy lunching at New York classic **Balthazar** (p93) and cool hunting on the streets of nearby Nolita.

2 Slurping soup dumplings and haggling for designer wares of ambiguous authenticity amid the sizzling lights of **Chinatown** (p84).

3 Snooping around time-jarred **Merchant's House Museum** (p88), imagining NYC life in the wild and dusty 1800s.

4 Reimagining Little Italy's action-packed past, with prized *porchetta* (roast pork) sandwich from **Di Palo** (p96) in hand.

5 Escaping the urban frenzy for a meditative moment at the **Mahayana Buddhist Temple** (p85) – the largest in Chinatown.

For more detail of this area, see maps on p410 and p413 ➡

Explore SoHo & Chinatown

Like a colorful quilt of subneighborhoods sewn together in mismatched patches, the areas orbiting SoHo (or SOuth of HOuston) feel like a string of mini republics. Style mavens boutique-hop in booming Nolita (NOrth of LIttle ITAly), Italo Americans channel Napoli in ever-shrinking Little Italy and Chinese extended families gossip over *xiao long bao* (soup dumplings) in hyperactive Chinatown.

Lower-rise buildings inject these streets with a cozy, villagelike vibe (main drags Broadway and Canal St excepted). Celebrities, cast-iron lofts and A-list boutiques stud SoHo's cobbled side streets, while humbler 19th-century tenements and quirkier one-off boutiques flavor neighboring Nolita.

In Chinatown, an anything-goes spirit wafts up like stall smoke, with frenzied crowds and hawkers mingling and haggling under faded billboards. The best way to weave your way around here is on foot. And don't bother planning your route of attack. It's all about letting your senses guide you. Whether you're following your nose down an alleyway for freshly baked pork buns, or your ears to a prayer gong in a heady Buddhist temple, unexpected surprises are always at the ready.

Local Life

→ **Family style** Hit Chinatown's bustling dining dens (p93) with a handful of friends and eat 'family style' (order a ton of dishes and sample spoonsful of each). You'll think the waiter left a zero off the bill.

→ **Side streets** The multilaned thoroughfares of SoHo are reserved for the legions of tourists – you'll find New Yorkers scouring the one-of-a-kind boutiques on the side streets for idiosyncratic buys and slashed prices.

→ **Cultural breaks** It's not all retail therapy in SoHo. Take time to explore the area's artistic legacy at spaces like Artists Space (p88), New York Earth Room (p87) and the Leslie-Lohman Museum of Gay & Lesbian Art (p87).

Getting There & Away

→ **Subway** The subway lines dump off along various points of Canal St (J/Z, N/Q/R and 6). Once you arrive it's best to explore on foot. The neighborhood's downtown location makes it easy to access from Midtown and Brooklyn.

→ **Bus and taxi** Avoid taking cabs or buses – especially in Chinatown, as the traffic is full-on. For SoHo, have your taxi let you off along Broadway if you aren't fussed about your final destination. Don't take cabs south of Canal St if you're simply planning to wander around Chinatown.

Lonely Planet's Top Tip

Serious shopaholics should consult the city's in-the-know retail blogs before hitting SoHo and surrounds – there's always some sort of 'sample sale' or offer going on, not to mention the opening of yet another boutique stocking fresh, emerging design talent. For a list of top blogs, see p51.

SOHO & CHINATOWN

Best Places to Eat

→ Dutch (p93)

→ Saxon + Parole (p92)

→ Balthazar (p93)

→ Public (p93)

→ Joe's Shanghai (p93)

For reviews, see p90

Best Places to Drink

→ Pegu Club (p97)

→ Spring Lounge (p97)

→ Mulberry Project (p97)

→ Madam Geneva (p97)

For reviews, see p97

Best Places to Shop

→ MoMA Design Store (p100)

→ Rag & Bone (p98)

→ MIN New York (p99)

→ Piperlime (p100)

→ INA Men (p100)

For reviews, see p98 →

ANGUS OBORN / GETTY IMAGES ©

TOP SIGHT
CHINATOWN

Endless exotic moments await in New York City's most colorfully cramped community, where a walk through the neighborhood is never the same no matter how many times you pass through. Catch the whiff of fresh fish and ripe persimmons, hear the clacking of mah-jongg tiles on makeshift tables, drool over dangling duck roasts swinging in store windows, and shop for anything imaginable, from rice-paper lanterns and 'faux-lex' watches to tire irons and a pound of pressed nutmeg. America's largest congregation of Chinese immigrants is your oyster – dipped in piquant soy sauce, of course.

Canal Street

Walking down Canal St is like a game of Frogger played on the streets of Shanghai. This is Chinatown's spine, where you'll dodge oncoming human traffic as you scurry into side streets to scout treasures from the Far East. You'll pass stinky seafood stalls hawking slippery fish; mysterious herb shops peddling a witch's cauldron's worth of roots and potions; storefront bakeries with steamy windows and the tastiest 70¢ pork buns you've ever had; restaurants with whole, roasted ducks and pigs hanging by their skinny necks in the windows; produce markets piled high with fresh lychees, bok choy and Asian pears; and street vendors selling every iteration of knock-off, from Gucci sunglasses to Prada bags.

Buddhist Temples

Chinatown is home to Buddhist temples large and small, public and obscure. They are easily stumbled upon during a full-on stroll of the neighborhood, and at least two such

DON'T MISS...

- ➡ A family-style meal at a bustling, back-alley dive
- ➡ Museum of Chinese in America
- ➡ Canal St vendors and street life
- ➡ Mahayana Buddhist Temple

PRACTICALITIES

- ➡ Map p413
- ➡ www.explorechinatown.com
- ➡ south of Canal St & east of Broadway
- ➡ [S] N/Q/R, J/Z, 6 to Canal St, B/D to Grand St, F to East Broadway

temples are considered landmarks. The **Eastern States Buddhist Temple** (Map p413; 64 Mott St, btwn Bayard & Canal Sts; ⌚9am-6pm; [S]J/M/Z, 6 to Canal St) is filled with hundreds of Buddhas, while the **Mahayana Buddhist Temple** (Map p413; 133 Canal St, at Manhattan Bridge Plaza; ⌚8am-6pm; [S]B/D to Grand St, J/Z, 6 to Canal St) holds one golden, 16ft-high Buddha, sitting on a lotus and edged with offerings of fresh oranges, apples and flowers. Mahayana is the largest Buddhist temple in Chinatown, and its entrance, which overlooks the frenzied vehicle entrance to the Manhattan Bridge, is guarded by two proud and handsome golden lions for protection. Step inside and you'll find a simple interior of wooden floor and red paper lanterns, dramatically upstaged by the temple's magnificent golden Buddha, thought to be the largest in the city.

Food Glorious Food

The most rewarding experience for Chinatown neophytes is to access this wild and wonderful world through their taste buds. More than any other area of Manhattan, Chinatown's menus sport wonderfully low prices, uninflated by ambience, hype or reputation. But more than cheap eats, the neighborhood is rife with family recipes passed between generations and continents. Food displays and preparation remain unchanged and untempered by American norms; it's not unusual to walk by storefronts sporting a tangled array of lacquered animals – chickens, rabbit and duck, in particular – ready to be chopped up and served at a family banquet. Steaming street stalls clang down the sidewalk serving pork buns and other finger-friendly food. Don't forget to wander down the back alleys for a Technicolor assortment of spices and herbs to perfect your own Eastern dishes.

Museum of Chinese in America

Housed in a 12,350-sq-ft space designed by architect Maya Lin (designer of the famed Vietnam Memorial in Washington, DC), the **Museum of Chinese in America** (Map p413; ☎212-619-4785; www.mocanyc.org; 211-215 Centre St, btwn Grand & Howard Sts; adult/child $10/free, Thu free; ⌚11am-6pm Tue, Wed & Fri-Sun, to 9pm Thu; 📶; [S]N/Q/R, J/Z, 6 to Canal St) is a multifaceted space with exhibit galleries, a bookstore and a visitors lounge, which, all together, serve as a national center of information about Chinese American life. Browse through interactive multimedia exhibits, maps, timelines, photos, letters, films and artifacts. Its anchor exhibit, 'With a Single Step: Stories in the Making of America,' provides an often intimate, interactive glimpse into subjects such as immigration, politics, history and food.

HISTORY

The history of Chinese immigrants in New York City is a long and tumultuous one. The first Chinese people to arrive in America came to work under difficult conditions on the Central Pacific Railroad; others were lured to the West Coast in search of gold. When prospects dried up, many moved east to NYC to work in factory assembly lines and in the laundry houses of New Jersey.

A rising racist sentiment gave way to the Chinese Exclusion Act (1882–1943), which made naturalization an impossibility, and largely squashed the opportunity for mainland Chinese to find work in the US. When the ban was lifted, the Chinese were given a limited immigration quota that eventually expanded and grew. Today it's estimated that over 150,000 citizens fill the bursting, tenement-like structures orbiting Mott St.

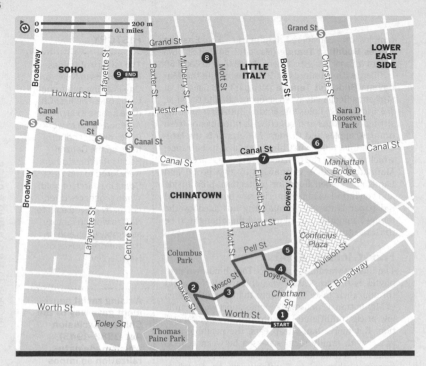

🏃 Neighborhood Walk
Chinatown

START CHATHAM SQ
END MUSEUM OF CHINESE IN AMERICA
LENGTH 0.9 MILES; 1½ HOURS

Begin exploring at **1 Chatham Square**, home to the Kim Lau Memorial Arch, erected in 1962 to honor the Chinese Americans who have fallen in battle. There's also a statue of Lin Ze Xu, a Qing-dynasty scholar whose anti-drug-trafficking stance largely led to the First Opium War in 1839.

From Chatham Sq head northwest on Worth St until you hit **2 Columbus Park**, Chinatown's unofficial living room. In the 19th century this was NYC's notorious Five Points slum, about which Charles Dickens wrote: 'Debauchery has made the very houses prematurely old.' To the east, slip into **3 Mosco St**, known in the 19th century as Bandits Roost, a menacing hangout for Irish gangs. Turn left into Mott St, right into Pell St, then right into **4 Doyers St**, a crooked lane dubbed 'Barbers Row' for its bounty of hair snippers. The lane's popular-

ity with feuding tongs (secret societies) early last century earned it the nickname Bloody Angle. American composer and lyricist Irving Berlin practiced upstairs at number 10, while at number 12 stands the neighborhood's oldest Chinese restaurant, wokking since 1920.

Turn left into Bowery and head north. At the southwest corner of Pell St and Bowery stands **5 Edward Mooney House**, NYC's oldest townhouse, built in 1785 by butcher Edward Mooney. This Georgian Federal–style veteran has housed a store, hotel, billiards parlor and Chinese social club; it's now a bank. Continue north on Bowery to Canal St, where you'll see Manhattan Bridge and, just beyond that, the **6 Mahayana Buddhist Temple**. See the massive golden Buddha inside, then dive into **7 Canal St**, Chinatown's hyperactive spine and NYC's one-time Jewish Diamond District. Make a right on Mott St for superlative steamed *bao* (buns) at **8 Golden Steamer**. Turn left into Grand St and left again at Centre St, delving into the Chinese American experience at the **9 Museum of Chinese in America**.

SIGHTS

SoHo, NoHo & Nolita

SoHo (SOuth of HOuston), NoHo (NOrth of HOuston) and Nolita (NOrth of LIttle ITAly) represent three of the coolest city neighborhoods, known for their tangled thickets of hipness in the form of boutiques, bars and eateries. This is the NYC of incognito, coffee-clutching celebrities and prized cast-iron lofts. It's also home to a string of cultural surprises. So slip on those shades, perfect that pout and get yourself a fix of downtown NYC cool.

DRAWING CENTER GALLERY

Map p410 (☎212-219-2166; www.drawingcenter.org; 35 Wooster St, btwn Grand & Broome Sts; adult/child $5/free; 🕒noon-6pm Wed & Fri-Sun, to 8pm Thu; [S]A/C/E, 1 to Canal St) America's only nonprofit institute focused solely on drawings, the Drawing Center uses work by masters as well as unknowns to juxtapose the medium's various styles. Historical exhibitions have included work by Michelangelo, James Ensor and Marcel Duchamp, while contemporary shows have showcased heavyweights like Richard Serra, Ellsworth Kelly and Richard Tuttle. As to the themes themselves, expect anything from the whimsical to the politically controversial.

Artist lectures and performance-art programs are hot tickets here – as is the Big Draw event (usually in summer), which invites folks of all ages to bring a sketchpad to any of several artist-led, hands-on happenings at locations around the city.

NEW YORK CITY FIRE MUSEUM MUSEUM

Map p410 (☎212-219-1222; www.nycfiremuseum.org; 278 Spring St, btwn Varick & Hudson Sts; adult/child $8/5; 🕒10am-5pm; 👪; [S]C/E to Spring St) In a grand old firehouse dating from 1904, this ode to firefighters includes a fantastic collection of historic equipment, from gold, horse-drawn firefighting carriages to early rescue gear like stovepipe firefighter hats. Exhibits trace the development of the NYC firefighting system, and the museum's friendly staff (and the heavy equipment) make this a great spot to bring kids.

The New York Fire Department (FDNY) lost half of its members in the collapse of the World Trade Center on September 11, 2001, and memorials and exhibits have become a permanent part of the collection. Fans can stock up on books about firefighting history and official FDNY clothing and patches in the gift shop.

NEW YORK EARTH ROOM GALLERY

Map p410 (www.earthroom.org; 141 Wooster St, btwn Prince & W Houston Sts; 🕒noon-6pm Wed-Sun, closed 3-3:30pm mid-Jun–mid-Sep; [S]N/R to Prince St) [FREE] Since 1980 the oddity of the New York Earth Room, the work of artist Walter De Maria, has been wooing the curious with something not easily found in the city: dirt (250 cu yd, or 280,000lb, of it, to be exact). Walking into the small space is a heady experience, as the scent will make you feel like you've entered a wet forest; the sight of such beautiful, pure earth in the midst of this crazy city is surprisingly moving.

A short walk away is De Maria's equally arresting **Broken Kilometer** (Map p410; 393 W Broadway, btwn Spring & Broome Sts; 🕒noon-6pm Wed-Sun, closed 3-3:30pm mid-Jun–mid-Sep; [S]N/R to Prince St), five rows of perception-toying brass rods inside a stark SoHo loft.

AMERICAN NUMISMATIC SOCIETY MUSEUM

Map p410 (☎212-234-3130; www.numismatics.org; 1 Hudson Sq, at Varick & Watts Sts; 🕒9am-5pm Mon-Fri; [S]1 to Houston St) [FREE] The holdings here of more than 800,000 coins, medals and notes are rivaled by only one similar collection in Europe. The items are from all over the map and throughout history, including Greek, Roman, East Asian, medieval and Islamic items, and the center's small special exhibitions and lectures focus on the history of currency. If you're especially interested in seeing a particular part of the collection, it's best to make an appointment ahead of time.

LESLIE-LOHMAN MUSEUM OF GAY & LESBIAN ART MUSEUM

Map p410 (☎212-431-2609; www.leslielohman.org; 26 Wooster St, btwn Grand & Canal Sts; 🕒noon-6pm Tue-Sat; [S]A/C/E to Canal St) [FREE] The world's first museum dedicated to LGBT themes stages six to eight annual exhibitions of both homegrown and international art. To date, offerings have included solo-artist retrospectives to themed shows exploring the likes of art and sex along the New York waterfront. Much of the work on display is from the museum's own collection, which consists of over 50,000 works. The space also hosts queer-centric lectures, readings, film screenings and performances; check the website for updates.

ARTISTS SPACE GALLERY

Map p410 (☎212-226-3970; www.artistsspace.org; 38 Greene St, 3rd fl, btwn Grand & Broome Sts; ⏲noon-6pm Wed-Sun; [S]A/C/E, J/Z, N/Q/R, 1, 6 to Canal St) [FREE] One of the first alternative spaces in New York, Artists Space made its debut in 1972. Its mission was to support contemporary artists working in the visual arts, from video, electronic media and performance to architecture and design. More than 40 years on, it remains a solid choice for those seeking crisp, provocative and experimental creativity.

CHILDREN'S MUSEUM OF THE ARTS MUSEUM

Map p410 (☎212-274-0986; www.cmany.org; 103 Charlton St, btwn Greenwich & Hudson Sts; admission $11, suggested donation 4-6pm Thu; ⏲noon-5pm Mon & Wed, noon-6pm Thu & Fri, 10am-5pm Sat & Sun; 👪; [S]1 to Houston St, C/E to Spring St) This small but worthy stop exhibits paintings, drawings and photographs by local school kids, with adorable exhibit titles like 'Beyond the Refrigerator Door.' For more hands-on activities, check out the museum's vast offering of public programs for kids of all ages, including guided workshops on art forms ranging from sculpture to collaborative mural painting, as well as movie nights and other special treats.

ST PATRICK'S OLD CATHEDRAL CHURCH

Map p410 (www.oldsaintpatricks.com; 263 Mulberry St, entrance on Mott St; ⏲8am-6pm; [S]N/R to Prince St) Though St Patrick's Cathedral is now famously located on Fifth Ave in Midtown, its first congregation was housed here, in this 1809–15 Gothic Revival church designed by Joseph-François Mangin. Back in its heyday, the church was the seat of religious life for the archdiocese of New York, as well as an important community center for new immigrants, mainly from Ireland.

When the church was built, the city hadn't yet spread this far north, the build-

TOP SIGHT
MERCHANT'S HOUSE MUSEUM

Bought in 1821 by merchant magnate Seabury Tredwell, this red-brick mansion remains the most authentic Federal house (of which there are about 300) in town. It's an antiquarian's dream, as much about the city's mercantile past as it is a showcase of 19th-century high-end domestic furnishings. Everything in the house is a testament to what money could buy, from the mahogany pocket doors, bronze gasoliers and marble mantelpieces, to the elegant parlor chairs, attributed to noted furniture designer Duncan Phyfe. Even the elaborate system of multilevel call bells for the servants works to this day.

Many believe that the Tredwell ancestors haunt the old mansion, making cameo appearances late in evenings and sometimes at public events. At a Valentine's Day concert a few years back several attendees witnessed the shadow of a woman walk up to the performers and take a seat in the parlor chairs – it was supposedly the ghost of Gertrude Tredwell, Seabury's youngest child and the home's last resident. Appropriately, the museum offers **ghost tours** after dark (usually in late October), as well as lectures, special events and historical walking tours of NoHo. Check the website.

DON'T MISS...

- Chairs attributed to Duncan Phyfe
- Servant call bells
- Maid's quarters
- Ghost Tours

PRACTICALITIES

- Map p410
- ☎212-777-1089
- www.merchantshouse.org
- 29 E 4th St, btwn Lafayette St & Bowery
- adult/child $10/free
- ⏲noon-5pm Thu-Mon, guided tours 2pm
- [S]6 to Bleecker St

ing's calculated isolation a welcome relief from the hostility of the New York's Protestant majority. Anti-Catholic sentiments also led to the construction of the church grounds' brick wall, an attempt to hinder stone-throwers.

The church and its beautiful graveyard feature in Martin Scorsese's celluloid classic *Mean Streets* (1973). It's a spot well known to the Italian American auteur, who grew up in nearby Elizabeth St.

Chinatown & Little Italy

Although Chinatown and Little Italy are immigrant communities with yin and yang relationships, they have several points in common: both neighborhoods make for brilliant DIY adventures. Put down the guidebook and get lost on their scented streets and sidewalks.

CHINATOWN STREET

See p84.

CANAL STREET STREET

See p84.

MUSEUM OF CHINESE IN AMERICA MUSEUM

See p85.

MAHAYANA TEMPLE TEMPLE

See p84.

MULBERRY STREET STREET

Map p413 ([S]N/Q/R, J/Z, 6 to Canal St, B/D to Grand St) Named for the mulberry farms that once stood here, Mulberry St is now better known as the meat in Little Italy's sauce. It's an animated strip, packed with smooth-talking restaurant hawkers (especially between Hester and Grand Sts), wisecracking baristas and a healthy dose of kitschy souvenirs.

Despite the neighborhood's many changes over the years, history looms large. It was inside restaurant **Da Gennaro** (Map p413; 129 Mulberry St, at Hester St), formerly Umberto's Clam House, that 'Crazy Joe' Gallo was gunned down on April 2, 1972, an unexpected birthday surprise for the Brooklyn-born mobster. One block further north stands fourth-generation **Alleva** (Map p413; 188 Grand St, at Mulberry St), one of the city's original cheese shops and famed for its mozzarella. Across the street on Grand lies another veteran, **Ferrara Cafe & Bakery** (Map p413; 195 Grand St), celebrated for its classic Italian pastries and gelati. Back on Mulberry, old-time **Mulberry Street Bar** (Map p413; ☎212-226-9345; 176½ Mulberry St, btwn Broome & Grand Sts) was a favorite haunt of the late Frank Sinatra, its own TV cameos including *Law & Order* and the *Sopranos*. Alcohol was openly traded on the corner of Mulberry and Kenmare Sts during Prohibition, leading to its nickname, the 'Curb Exchange.' That police headquarters at the time were only a block away at 240 Center St is testament to the power of good old-fashioned bribes. From this point north, the old-school delis and restaurants of Little Italy give way to the new-school boutiques, galleries and restaurants of Nolita. Take a gander at what was once the **Ravenite Social Club** (Map p410; 247 Mulberry St; [S]6 to Spring St, N/R to Prince St) to see how things have really changed around here. Now a designer shoe store, it was once a mobster hangout (originally known as the Alto Knights Social Club). Indeed, it was right here that big hitters such as Lucky Luciano and John Gotti (as well as the FBI, who kept a watchful eye from the building across the street) logged time. Only the shop's tile floor remains from the day, the shop windows once an intimidating brick wall.

COLUMBUS PARK PARK

Map p413 (Mulberry & Bayard Sts; [S]J/Z, N/Q/R, 6 to Canal St) Mah-jongg meisters, slow-motion tai chi practitioners and old aunties gossiping over homemade dumplings: it might feel like Shanghai, but this leafy oasis is core to NYC history. In the 19th century this was part of the infamous Five Points neighborhood, the city's first tenement slums and the inspiration for Martin Scorsese's *Gangs of New York*.

The 'five points' were the five streets that used to converge here; now you'll find the intersection of only Mosco, Worth and Baxter Sts. Aside from serving up an intriguing slice of multicultural life, the park's other perk these days is its public bathroom, making it the perfect place for a pit stop.

CHURCH OF THE TRANSFIGURATION CHURCH

Map p413 (☎212-962-5157; www.transfigurationnyc.org; 29 Mott St, btwn Bayard & Mosco Sts; donation welcome; 🕐2-5pm Sat; [S]J/Z, N/Q/R,

6 to Canal St) It's been serving New York's immigrant communities since 1801, and the Church of the Transfiguration doesn't stop adapting. First it was the Irish, then Italians and now Chinese. The same priest delivers sermons in Cantonese, English and sometimes even Latin. This small landmark is not far from Pell and Doyers Sts, two winding paths worth exploring.

🍴 EATING

In the land of acronyms there are only three letters you need to know: YUM. Though the area may not have a plethora of headliners like the East and West Villages just beyond, it has its fair share of worthy hot spots. You 99%ers should make a beeline for Chinatown, where heaping portions are served up for pennies.

🍴 SoHo, NoHo & Nolita

TACOMBI MEXICAN $

Map p410 (www.tacombi.com; 267 Elizabeth St, btwn E Houston & Prince Sts; tacos from $3.95; ⏲11am-late Mon-Fri, from 9am Sat & Sun; [S]B/D/F/M to Broadway-Lafayette St, 6 to Bleecker St) Festively strung lights, foldaway chairs and Mexican men flipping tacos in an old VW Kombie: if you can't make it to the Yucatan shore, here's your Plan B. Casual, convivial and ever-popular, Tacombi serves up fine, fresh tacos, including breakfast numbers like *huevos con chorizo* (eggs with chorizo). Wash down the goodness with a pitcher of sangria and start plotting that south-of-the-border getaway.

LOVELY DAY THAI $

Map p410 (www.lovelydaynyc.com; 196 Elizabeth St, btwn Spring & Prince Sts; dishes $5.50-15; ⏲11am-11pm Sun-Thu, to midnight Fri & Sat; [S]6 to Spring St, J to Bowery, N/R to Prince St) With a look best described as 'doll house meets retro diner,' supercute Lovely Day seems like an incongruous setting for cheap, scrumptious Thai-inspired grub. But life is full of surprises, and you'll find a steady stream of fans chowing down competent pad thai, spicy green curry or salty-sweet Thai *chow fun* (flat-rice noodles, Chinese broccoli and hoisin sauce).

Fusion dishes are equally moreish, from ginger fried chicken with spicy aioli to the wholewheat challah bread French toast with coconut and honey-orange graze.

RUBY'S CAFE $

Map p410 (www.rubyscafe.com; 219 Mulberry St, btwn Spring & Prince Sts; breakfast $5-12, lunch & dinner dishes $9.50-13.50; ⏲9:30am-10:30pm; [S]6 to Spring St, N/R to Prince St) Good things come in small packages, including this five-table, cash-only, Aussie-inspired cafe. All bases are covered, from 'brekkie'-friendly avo toast (mashed avocado and fresh tomato on seven-grain toast) and buttermilk pancakes, to posh panini and pastas, vibrant salads and lusty burgers named after Australian surf beaches.

Flat-white coffees, Down Under brews and a surfboard behind the door complete your antipodean experience.

ESTELA MODERN AMERICAN, MEDITERRANEAN $$

Map p410 (☎212-219-7693; www.estelanyc.com; 47 E Houston St, btwn Mulberry & Mott Sts; dishes $12-32; ⏲5:30-11pm Mon-Thu, to 11:30pm Fri & Sat, to 10:30pm Sun; [S]B/D/F/M to Broadway-Lafayette St, 6 to Bleecker St) Estela might be hopeless at hide-and-seek (its sneaky location up some nondescript stairs hardly tricks the hipster masses), but this busy, skinny wine bar kicks butt in the kitchen. Pick and graze from a competent string of sharing plates, market driven and Mediterranean inspired. Well-executed seafood and meats dominate the menu, with standouts including a phenomenal beef tartare, spiked with beef heart, pickled elderberry and fish sauce.

If they're on the menu, don't miss the salted cod and potato croquettes with *borani* (Iranian yogurt-based dip), or the addictively smooth ricotta dumplings lavished with earthy mushrooms and *pecorino sardo* (firm Italian sheep-milk cheese). Book ahead.

IL BUCO ALIMENTARI & VINERIA ITALIAN $$

Map p410 (www.ilbucovineria.com; 53 Great Jones St, btwn Bowery & Lafayette St; lunch $15-32, dinner mains $19-42; ⏲cafe 7am-late Mon-Fri, from 9am-late weekends, restaurant noon-3pm & 5:30-late Mon- Fri, 11am-3pm & 5:30pm-late weekends; 📶; [S]6 to Bleecker St, B/D/F/M to Broadway-Lafayette St) Whether it's wham-bam espresso at the front bar, a panino

TOP SIGHT LITTLE ITALY

In the last 50 years, New York's Little Italy has shrunk from a big, brash boot to an ultraslim sandal. A mid-century exodus to the suburbs of Brooklyn and beyond would see this once-strong Italian neighborhood turn into a micropastiche of its former self. Indeed, Little Italy is little more than **Mulberry St** (p89) these days, an endearingly kitsch strip of gingham tablecloths, mandolin muzak and nostalgia for the old country.

Come late September, the street turns into a raucous, 11-day block party for the **San Gennaro Festival**, a celebration honoring the patron saint of Naples. It's a loud, convivial affair, with food and carnival stalls, free entertainment, and more big hair than *Jersey Shore*.

It's also on Mulberry St that you'll find the tiny **Italian American Museum** (Map p413; www.italianamericanmuseum.org; 155 Mulberry St, at Grand St; suggested donation $5; ⏲noon-6pm Sat & Sun; [S]J/Z, N/Q/R, 6 to Canal St, B/D to Grand St) [FREE], a random mishmash of historical artifacts and documents, from Sicilian marionettes to old Italian comics starring New York's famous mafia-busting cop, Giuseppe 'Joe' Petrosino. The building was once the Banca Stabile, which helped immigrants sort their monetary needs and provided a lifeline back to the homeland.

DON'T MISS...

- Mulberry St
- San Gennaro Festival in September
- Pizza by the slice

PRACTICALITIES

- Map p413
- [S]N/Q/R, J/Z, 6 to Canal St, B/D to Grand St

to go from the deli, or long-and-lazy Italian feasting in the sunken dining room, Il Buco's trendier spin-off delivers the goods. Brickwork, hessian and giant industrial lamps set a hip-n-rustic tone, echoed in the menu's bold, nostalgic flavors.

Whet the appetite with crunchy Casareccio bread, linger over beautiful pasta dishes, and ponder the adage 'less is more' over mains such as salt-baked whole branzino (European sea bass) with thyme and charred lemons.

RUBIROSA PIZZERIA $$

Map p410 (☎212-965-0500; www.rubirosanyc.com; 235 Mulberry St, btwn Spring & Prince Sts; pizzas $16-26, mains $12-28; ⏲11:30am-late; [S]N/R to Prince St, B/D/F/M to Broadway-Lafayette St, 6 to Spring St) Rubirosa's infallible family recipe for the perfect, whisper-thin pie crust lures a steady stream of patrons from every corner of the city. Shovel slices from the bar stools or grab a table amid cozy surrounds and make room for savory appetizers and antipasti. Gluten-free diners have their own dedicated menu.

BUTCHER'S DAUGHTER VEGETARIAN $$

Map p410 (www.thebutchersdaughter.com; 19 Kenmare St, at Elizabeth St; meals $9-16; ⏲8am-3:45pm Mon, to late Tue-Sat; 📶🌿; [S]J to Bowery, 6 to Spring St) The butcher's daughter certainly has rebelled, peddling nothing but fresh herbivorous fare in her white-washed cafe. While healthy it is, boring it's not: everything from the organic muesli, to the spicy kale Caesar salad with almond Parmesan, to the dinnertime Butcher's burger (kasha portobello patty with cashew cheddar cheese) is devilishly delish.

Add a glow to your halo with a juice spritzer, or get buzzy with a craft beer or biodynamic vino. Warning: service can be painfully slow.

LA ESQUINA MEXICAN $$

Map p410 (☎646-613-6700; www.esquinanyc.com; 114 Kenmare St, at Petrosino Sq; tacos from $3.25, mains $12-32; ⏲noon-late; [S]6 to Spring St) This megapopular and quirky little spot is three places really: a stand-while-you-eat taco window (open till 2am), a casual Mexican cafe and, downstairs, a dim, slinky, cavernous brasserie requiring reservations. Standouts include chorizo tacos, rubbed pork tacos, and mango and jicama salad, among other authentic and delicious options (many of which are also available upstairs at the anyone-welcome area).

SIGGI'S
CAFE $$

Map p410 (www.siggysgoodfood.com; 292 Elizabeth St, btwn E Houston & Bleecker Sts; dishes $10-22; ⊙11am-10:30pm Mon-Sat; ⓐ; ⓢ6 to Bleecker St, B/D/F/M to Broadway-Lafayette St) Organic deliciousness awaits at this casual, art-slung cafe (bonus points for the wintertime fireplace). All bases are covered, from soups and salads to made-from-scratch burgers, vegetarian lasagna, even slow-cooked organic stews. Virtuous libations include smoothies and freshly squeezed juices, with optional health-boosting supplements. Vegan and gluten-free diners won't go hungry either.

CAFÉ GITANE
MOROCCAN, MEDITERRANEAN $$

Map p410 (ⓙ212-334-9552; www.cafegitanenyc.com; 242 Mott St, at Prince St; mains $14-16; ⊙8:30am-midnight Sun-Thu, to 12:30am Fri & Sat; ⓢN/R to Prince St, 6 to Spring St) Clear the Gauloise smoke from your eyes and blink twice if you think you're in Paris: bistroesque Gitane has that kind of louche vibe, *mon amour*. This is a classic see-and-be-seen haunt, popular with salad-picking models and the odd Hollywood regular. Join the beautiful and their minions for a fashionable nibble on the likes of blueberry and almond *friands* (small French cake), heart-of-palm salad or Moroccan couscous with organic chicken.

★ SAXON + PAROLE
MODERN AMERICAN $$$

Map p410 (ⓙ212-254-0350; www.saxonandparole.com; 316 Bowery, at Bleecker St; lunch $8-17, dinner mains $18-37; ⊙11:30am-late Fri, from 10am weekends; ⓢ6 to Bleecker St, B/D/F/M

CULTURAL TREASURES

Massimiliano Gioni – art critic, associate director of the New Museum and curator of the Venice Biennale – reveals some of his favorite cultural treasures.

Underrated Standouts
Walter De Maria's New York Earth Room (p87) is one of NYC's best-kept secrets. It's like a mysterious chapel or a vision from some prehistoric age. It's minimalism at its dirtiest and at its purest, and now that Walter De Maria has passed away, it doubles as an involuntary memorial to one of the greatest artists of our time. Close by is De Maria's Broken Kilometer (p87), the closest minimalism ever got to Gothic ecstasy. Also in SoHo is Donald Judd's recently restored **home studio** (Map p410; ⓙ212-219-2747; www.juddfoundation.org/new_york; 101 Spring St, at Mercer St; adult $25; ⊙by prebooked guided tour only at 1pm, 3pm and 5pm Tue & Thu-Sat, also 11am Sat; ⓢN/R to Prince St, 6 to Spring St). Amid masterpieces by Judd, Dan Flavin and Carl Andre, one sees how the high priest of minimalism lived, which is pretty cool... if you like sleeping on the floor, with no curtains and basking in the light of a neon tube sculpture. The Drawing Center (p87) puts on small, jewel-like exhibitions covering both historical and contemporary artists, while the Artists Space (p88) is one of NYC's most legendary not-for-profits.

Personal Favorites
At the Metropolitan Museum of Art (p212), I'm always happy to see Florine Stettheimer's wonderful paintings, while James Turrell's *Meeting* at MoMA PS1 (p302) offers a very special way to contemplate the New York sky. Chelsea is home to quite possibly NYC's most invisible artwork, Joseph Beuys' installation *7000 Oaks*, a combination of planted trees and basalt stone columns on W 22nd St (between Tenth and Eleventh Aves). Practically unnoticeable, they're also a strong reminder of how art can quietly transform a city.

New Museum: A Unique Space
The New Museum (p107) is located far from 'Museum Mile' and doesn't have a collection. Instead, it focuses on commissioning new works from artists, many of whom are emerging or have been overlooked.

to Broadway-Lafayette St) A fun, fashionable bistro-bar named in honor of two 19th-century racing horses, Saxon and Parole (pronounced 'pearl') leads the charge with competent twists on comfort surf and turf. You might tuck into tuna tartare paired with *yuzu* (citrus fruit), avocado-wasabi and root chips, or an extraordinary Long Island duck, smoked to bacon-sweet perfection.

Desserts are equally coaxing, a place where chocolate soufflé gets its groove on with jam and whiskey ice cream. Belly full, trot through the secret door and kick on at cocktail den Madam Geneva (p97).

★BALTHAZAR FRENCH $$$

Map p410 (☎212-965-1414; www.balthazarny.com; 80 Spring St, btwn Broadway & Crosby St; mains $17 45; 🕐7:30am late Mon-Fri, from 8am weekends; [S]6 to Spring St, N/R to Prince St) Still the king of bistros, bustling (OK, *loud*) Balthazar is never short of a discriminating mob. That's all thanks to three winning details: its location in SoHo's shopping-spree heartland; the uplifting Paris-meets-NYC ambience; and, of course, the stellar something-for-everyone menu.

Highlights include the outstanding raw bar, steak frites, salade Niçoise, as well as the roasted beet salad. The kitchen stays open till 1am Friday and Saturday, and weekend brunch here is a very crowded (and delicious) production. For a decadent treat to go, grab a pastry from the Balthazar bakery next door.

★DUTCH MODERN AMERICAN $$$

Map p410 (☎212-677-6200; www.thedutchnyc.com; 131 Sullivan St, btwn Prince & Houston Sts; mains $19-52; 🕐11:30am-3pm & 5:30-late Mon-Fri, from 10am-3pm weekends; [S]C/E to Spring St, N/R to Prince St, 1 to Houston St) Whether perched at the front bar or dining snugly in the back room, you can always expect smart, farm-to-table soul grub at this see-and-be-seen stalwart. Slurp on silky Maine oysters, warm up with the juicy dry-aged burger, or keep it light with the likes of pillow-soft sea scallops spiked with arbol and chile salsa. Reservations are recommended.

PUBLIC MODERN AMERICAN $$$

Map p410 (☎212-343-7011; www.public-nyc.com; 210 Elizabeth St, btwn Prince & Spring Sts; mains $21-34; 🕐6pm-late Mon-Fri, 10:30am-3:30pm & 6pm-late weekends; [S]6 to Spring St, N/R to Prince St) What was once a muffin factory is now a svelte foodie hot spot, complete with sultry bar, industrial touches and masterfully textured dishes deserving of their Michelin star. Global twists surprise and delight, whether it's kangaroo paired with coriander falafel and lemon tahini, or New Zealand venison loin matched with Cabrales-cheese dumplings.

Add sharp service and a list of beautiful wines, and you have the perfect date spot.

CHARLIE BIRD ITALIAN, MODERN AMERICAN $$$

Map p410 (www.charliebirdnyc.com; 5 King St, entrance on Sixth Ave; small plates $12-16, mains $27-39; 🕐5:30pm-late; [S]C/E to Spring St, 1 to Houston St) Tweeting away on SoHo's western fringe, loud-n-skinny Charlie Bird is winning regulars with its passion for local produce, rustic Italian know-how, and clever homespun twists. Mingle at the marble bar, or slip into a hand-sewn leather chair for artful dishes like grilled peach with prosciutto and fresh basil, or guanciale (Italian cured meat) spiked duck-egg spaghetti, the latter a subtle play on Rome's classic carbonara. The wine list is packed with pleasant surprises.

TORRISI ITALIAN SPECIALTIES ITALIAN $$$

Map p410 (☎212-965-0955; www.torrisinyc.com; 250 Mulberry St, btwn Spring & Prince Sts; degustation menu $100; 🕐6-10:30pm Mon-Sun, also noon-2pm Fri-Sun; [S]N/R to Prince St, B/D/F/M to Broadway-Lafayette St; 6 to Spring St) Italian-inspired, Michelin-starred Torrisi is a slave to perfect produce; its celebrated eight- and 10-course tasting menus changing daily to reflect the very best of the morning's offerings. This obsession with freshness and immediacy extends to the dining experience itself, with dishes often prepared, plated or explained by the chefs themselves.

🍴 Chinatown & Little Italy

JOE'S SHANGHAI CHINESE $

Map p413 (☎212-233-8888; www.joeshanghairestaurants.com; 9 Pell St, btwn Bowery & Doyers St; mains $5-26; 🕐11am-11pm; [S]N/Q/R, J/Z, 6 to Canal St, B/D to Grand St) Gather a gaggle of friends and descend upon this Flushing transplant en masse to spin the plastic lazy Susans and gobble down some of the juiciest *xiao long bao* in town. Dumplings aside, charge your chopsticks at budget-friendly thrills like spicy buffalo carp fish belly or jalapeno-sautéed pork and squid with dry bean curd. Cash only.

PAUL DE GREGORI/ GETTY IMAGES ©

1. Cannoli
Sample authentic Italian cuisine in NYC's Little Italy (p91).

2. Mahayana Buddhist Temple (p85)
See the 16ft-high Buddha statue in Chinatown's largest Buddhist temple.

3. Chinatown (p84)
Explore Chinatown's colourful streets and food stalls.

4. SoHo shopping (p98)
Keep your eye out for emerging design talent and boutique shops.

5. SoHo apartments
Wander through SoHo's cobbled streets and towering apartment blocks.

DI PALO DELI $

Map p413 (☎212-226-1033; www.dipaloselects.com; 200 Grand St, at Mott St; sandwiches from $7; ⏰9am-6:30pm Mon-Sat, to 4pm Sun; [S]B/D to Grand St, N/Q/R, J/Z, 6 to Canal St) Food bloggers revere the *porchetta* sandwich from this family-run deli; a crusty baguette stuffed with melt-in-your-mouth roast pork seasoned with garlic, fennel and herbs. Not only is it sinfully good, it's huge, so opt for just one slice of *porchetta* when asked. Normally available from 1:30pm, the prized meat sells out in 20 minutes, so get there at 1:15pm or call ahead. Not available Mondays.

PHO VIET HUONG VIETNAMESE, CHINESE $

Map p413 (☎212-233-8988; www.phoviethuong.com; 73 Mulberry St, btwn Bayard & Walker Sts; mains $5.50-17.50; ⏰11am-10:30pm; [S]N/Q/R, J/Z, 6 to Canal St) Shockingly cheap, drool-inducing Vietnamese and Chinese classics will have you coming back for seconds at this Chinatown staple. Feast on slurp-worthy bowls of *pho* (noodle soup) and dripping *bánh mì* (Vietnamese baguettes with roast pork, piles of sliced cucumber, pickled carrots, hot sauce and cilantro), all to the sound of loose change in your pocket.

BÁNH MÌ SAIGON BAKERY VIETNAMESE $

Map p413 (☎212-941-1514; www.banhmisaigonnyc.com; 198 Grand St, btwn Mulberry & Mott Sts; sandwiches $3.50-5.75; ⏰8am-6pm; [S]N/Q/R, J/Z, 6 to Canal St) This no-frills storefront doles out some of the best *bánh mì* in town – we're talking crisp, toasted baguettes generously stuffed with hot peppers, pickled carrots, daikon, cucumber, cilantro and your choice of meat. Top billing goes to the classic BBQ pork version. Lunch for under $6? Count us in!

GREAT NEW YORK NOODLE TOWN CHINESE $

Map p413 (☎212-349-0923; www.greatnynoodletown.com; 28 Bowery St, at Bayard St; dishes $3.50-16; ⏰9am-4am; [S]N/Q/R, J/Z, 6 to Canal St) This Chinatown stalwart peddles endless incarnations of the long and slippery strands, from noodle soup with roast pork or duck, beef *chow fun*, spicy Singapore *mai fun* (rice vermicelli), wide Cantonese noodles with shrimp and egg or Hong Kong–style *lo mein* (wheat flour noodles) with ginger and onions. And, trust us, what this place lacks in ambience, it makes up for in characters, especially after 2am.

GOLDEN STEAMER CHINESE $

Map p413 (143a Mott St, btwn Grand & Hester Sts; buns from 70¢; ⏰7am-7:30pm; [S]B/D to Grand St, N/Q/R, 6 to Canal St, J to Bowery) Squeeze into this hole-in-the-wall for the fluffiest, tastiest *bao* (steamed buns) in Chinatown. Made on-site by bellowing Chinese cooks, fillings include succulent roast pork, Chinese sausage, salted egg and the crowd favorite, pumpkin. For something a little sweeter, try the dreamy egg custard tart.

NICE GREEN BO CHINESE $

Map p413 (New Green Bow; ☎212-625-2359; www.nicegreenbo.com; 66 Bayard St, btwn Elizabeth & Mott Sts; mains $3.75-12.95; ⏰11am-11pm; [S]N/Q/R, J/Z, 6 to Canal St, B/D to Grand St) Not a shred of effort – not even a new sign (you'll see!) – has been made to spruce up Nice Green Bo, and that's the way we like it. It's all about the food here: gorgeous *xiao long bao* served in steaming drums, heaping portions of noodles and scrumptious scallion pancakes.

ORIGINAL CHINATOWN ICE CREAM FACTORY ICE CREAM $

Map p413 (☎212-608-4170; www.chinatownicecreamfactory.com; 65 Bayard St; scoop $4; ⏰11am-10pm; 👪; [S]N/Q/R, J/Z, 6 to Canal St) Chinatown's favorite ice-cream peddler keeps it local with flavors like green tea, ginger, durian and lychee sorbet. If you're feeling reckless, try the zen butter (creamy peanut butter ice cream laced with toasted sesame seeds). The Factory also sells ridiculously cute, trademark T-shirts with an ice cream–slurping happy dragon on them.

NYONYA MALAYSIAN $$

Map p413 (☎212-334-3669; 199 Grand St, btwn Mott & Mulberry Sts; mains $6.75-24; ⏰11am-late; [S]N/Q/R, J/Z, 6 to Canal Street, B/D to Grand St) Take your palate to steamy Melaka at this bustling, cash-only temple to Chinese-Malay Nyonya cuisine. Savor the sweet, the sour and the spicy in classics like pungent *kangkung belacan* (sautéed water spinach spiked with spicy Malaysian shrimp paste), rich beef *randang* (spicy dry curry) and refreshing *rojak* (savory fruit salad tossed in a piquant tamarind dressing).

Vegetarians should go warned: there's not much on the menu for you.

DRINKING & NIGHTLIFE

LA COLOMBE CAFE

Map p410 (www.lacolombe.com; 270 Lafayette St, btwn Prince & Jersey Sts; ⏰7:30am-6:30pm Mon-Fri, from 8:30am weekends; [S]N/R to Prince St, 6 to Spring St) Spent SoHo shoppers reboot at this pocket-sized espresso bar. The brews are strong, full-bodied and worthy of any bar in Italy (note the cool Rome wall mural). A small selection of edibles including cookies and croissants are on offer. You'll find a bigger branch in nearby **NoHo** (Map p410; 400 Lafayette St, at 4th St; ⏰7:30am-6:30pm Mon-Fri, 8:30am-6:30pm Sat & Sun; [S]6 to Bleecker St), with more seating but longer queues.

PEGU CLUB COCKTAIL BAR

Map p410 (www.peguclub.com; 77 W Houston St, btwn W Broadway & Wooster St; ⏰5pm-2am Sun-Wed, to 4am Thu-Sat; [S]B/D/F/M to Broadway-Lafayette St, C/E to Spring St) Elegant Pegu Club (named after a legendary gentleman's club in colonial-era Rangoon) is an obligatory stop for cocktail connoisseurs. Sink into a velvet lounge and savor seamless libations from award-winning bartender Kenta Goto – we especially love the silky-smooth Earl Grey MarTEAni (tea-infused gin, lemon juice and raw egg white).

Grazing options are suitably Asianesque, among them summer rolls and sloppy duck (braised duck with tropical fruit BBQ sauce on toasted mini-brioche buns).

SPRING LOUNGE DIVE BAR

Map p410 (www.thespringlounge.com; 48 Spring St, at Mulberry St; ⏰8am-4am Mon-Sat, noon-4am Sun; [S]6 to Spring St, N/R to Prince St) This neon red rebel has never let anything get in the way of a good time. In Prohibition days it peddled buckets of beer. In the '60s its basement was a gambling den. These days, it's best known for its kooky stuffed sharks, early-start regulars and come-one-come-all late-night revelry.

Fueling the fun are cheap drinks and free grub (hot dogs on Wednesdays from 5pm, bagels on Sundays from noon, while they last). Bottoms up, baby!

MULBERRY PROJECT COCKTAIL BAR

Map p413 (☎646-448-4536; www.mulberryproject.com; 149 Mulberry St, btwn Hester & Grand Sts; ⏰6pm-1am Sun-Thu, to 4am Fri & Sat; [S]N/Q/R, J/Z, 6 to Canal St) Lurking behind an unmarked door is this intimate, cavernous cocktail den, with its festive, 'garden-party' backyard one of the best spots to chill in the hood. Bespoke, made-to-order cocktails are the specialty, so disclose your preferences and let the barkeep do the rest. If you're peckish, choose from a competent list of bites that might include watermelon salad with goat's cheese or bacon-wrapped dates.

MADAM GENEVA COCKTAIL BAR

Map p410 (www.madamgeneva-nyc.com; 4 Bleecker St, at Bowery; ⏰6pm-2am; [S]6 to Bleecker St, B/D/F/M to Broadway-Lafayette St) Hanging lanterns, leather couches and flouncy wallpaper echo colonial Nanyang at this dark and sultry cocktail den. Gin-based cocktails dominate, meticulously crafted and suitably paired with Asian-inspired bites like duck steamed buns, prawn dumplings and chicken wings with tamarind. Next door lies hot-spot sibling restaurant Saxon + Parole (p92).

JIMMY COCKTAIL BAR

Map p410 (☎212-201-9118; www.jimmysoho.com; James Hotel, 15 Thompson St, at Grand St; ⏰5pm-1am Sun-Wed, to 2am Thu-Sat; [S]A/C/E, 1 to Canal St) Lofted atop the James Hotel in SoHo, Jimmy is a sky-high hangout with sweeping views of the city below. The summer months teem with tipsy patrons who spill out onto the open deck; in cooler weather, drinks are slung indoors from the centrally anchored bar guarded by floor-to-ceiling windows.

APOTHÉKE COCKTAIL BAR

Map p413 (☎212-406-0400; www.apothekenyc.com; 9 Doyers St; ⏰6:30pm-2am Mon-Sat, 8pm-2am Sun; [S]J to Chambers St, 4/5/6 to Brooklyn Bridge-City Hall) It takes a little effort to track down this former opium-den-turned-apothecary-bar on Doyers St. Inside, skilled barkeeps work like careful chemists, using local and organic produce from green markets or the rooftop herb garden to produce intense, flavorful 'prescriptions.' Toast to your health with the invigorating Harvest of Mexico (roasted corn, Herba Sainte, mezcal, agave, lime and habanero-infused bitters).

RANDOLPH CAFE, COCKTAIL BAR

Map p413 (www.randolphnyc.com/broome; 349 Broome St, btwn Bowery & Elizabeth St; ⏰10am-2am Mon-Wed, to 4am Thu-Sat, to midnight Sun; 📶; [S]J to Bowery) Laid-back Randolph brews coffee by day and swirls cocktails by night. Beans are sourced from top-notch roasters like Intelligentsia, while cocktails focus on the seasonal and the creative. A collection of board games seals the deal for boozy, lo-fi bonding sessions.

MILADY'S DIVE BAR

Map p410 (☎212-226-9340; 160 Prince St, at Thompson St; 🕐10:30am-4am; 📶; [S]1 to Houston St, N/R to Prince St) The last of the dive bars in SoHo, where coin-counting pensioners rub shoulders with SoHo yuppies, MiLady's rattles on with televised sports, pool games and old-school, outer-borough spirit. If you're feeling hungry, stick to the salads, chicken wings and mac 'n' cheese, best paired with a cheap, good-lovin' brewski.

SHOPPING

SoHo

Your swiping hand will get a lot of exercise in SoHo, an area bursting at its fashionable seams with stores, big and small. Hit Broadway for less-expensive chains, or the streets to the west of it for higher-end fashion, accessories and homewares. During the warmer months you'll also find street vendors hawking jewelry, art, T-shirts, hats and other crafts. Over on Lafayette, shops cater to the DJ and skate crowds with indie labels and vintage shops thrown into the mix.

If indie-chic is your thing, continue east to Nolita, home of tiny jewel-box boutiques selling unique threads, kicks and accessories at marginally lower prices than SoHo stores. Mott St is best for browsing, followed by Mulberry and Elizabeth.

RAG & BONE FASHION

Map p410 (www.rag-bone.com; 119 Mercer St, btwn Prince & Spring Sts; 🕐11am-8pm Mon-Sat, noon-7pm Sun; [S]N/R to Prince St) Downtown label Rag & Bone is a hit with many of New York's coolest, sharpest dressers, both men and women. Detail-orientated pieces range from clean-cut shirts and blazers to graphic tees, feather-light strappy dresses, leather-goods and Rag & Bone's highly prized jeans. The tailoring is generally impeccable, with higher-end suits handmade by Brooklyn master tailor Martin Greenfield.

See the website for all its city locations.

Local Life
An Artisanal Afternoon in SoHo

Shopaholics across the world drool for SoHo and its sharp, trendy whirlwind of flagship stores, coveted labels and strutting fashionistas. Look beyond the giant global brands, however, and you'll discover a whole other retail scene, one where talented artisans and independent, one-off enterprises keep things local, unique and utterly inspiring. Welcome to SoHo at its homegrown best.

1 A Shop with Single Origin

Charge up with a cup of single-origin coffee from **Café Integral** (Map p410; www.cafeintegral.com; 135 Grand St, btwn Crosby & Lafayette Sts; 🕐8am-6pm Mon-Fri, 10am-6pm Sat, noon-5pm Sun; [S]N/Q/R, J, 6 to Canal St), a teeny-tiny espresso bar inside kooky shop-cum-gallery American Two Shot. At the machine you'll probably find owner César Martin Vega, a 20-something obsessed with Nicaraguan coffee beans.

2 Perfect Jeans

3x1 (Map p410; www.3x1.us; 15 Mercer St, btwn Howard & Grand Sts; 🕐11am-7pm Mon-Sat, noon-6pm Sun; [S]N/Q/R, J, 6 to Canal St) lets you design your perfect pair of jeans. Choose buttons and hems for ready-to-wear pairs (women's from $195, men's from $285), customize fabric and detailing on existing cuts ($525 to $750) or create a pair from scratch ($1200).

3 Designer Kicks

Local craftsmanship also defines the footwear of emerging star **Alejandro Ingelmo** (Map p410; www.alejandroingelmo.com; 51 Wooster St, btwn Broome & Grand Sts; 🕐11am-7pm Mon-Fri, noon-7pm Sat & Sun; [S]1, A/C/E to Canal St), his imaginative kicks spanning sparkly basketball-style boots, to butterfly-inspired stilettos, to old-school American loafers sexed-up with a thick, downtown sole. Sneakers retail for around $600.

4 Curbside Culture

The sidewalk engraving on the northwest corner of Prince St and Broadway is the work of Japanese-born sculptor Ken

Mercer St, SoHo

Hiratsuka, who has carved almost 40 sidewalks since moving to NYC in 1982. While this engraving took five or so hours of work, its actual completion took two years (1983–84), Hiratsuka's illegal nighttime chiseling often disrupted by police.

5 A Gourmet Nibble

NYC loves its luxe grocers and **Dean & DeLuca** (Map p410; ☎212-226-6800; www.deananddeluca.com; 560 Broadway, at Prince St; ⏰7am-8pm Mon-Fri, 8am-8pm Sat & Sun; [S]N/R to Prince St, 6 to Spring St) is one of the biggest names around town. If you're feeling peckish, ready-to-eat delectables include freshly baked cheese sticks, gourmet quesadillas and sugar-dusted almond croissants.

6 Fragrance Flights

Drop into library-like apothecary **MIN New York** (Map p410; www.minnewyork.com; 117 Crosby St, btwn Jersey & Prince Sts; ⏰11am-7pm Mon-Sat, noon-6pm Sun; [S]B/D/F/M to Broadway-Lafayette St, N/R to Prince St) and request a free 'fragrance flight,' a guided exploration of the store's extraordinary collection of rare, exclusive perfumes and grooming products. Look out for homegrown fragrances like Brooklyn's MCMC and Detroit's Kerosene, as well as MIN's own coveted hair products. Prices span affordable to astronomical.

MOMA DESIGN STORE HOMEWARES, GIFTS

Map p410 (☎646-613-1367; www.momastore.org; 81 Spring St, at Crosby St; ⏰10am-8pm Mon-Sat, 11am-7pm Sun; [S]N/R to Prince St, 6 to Spring St) The Museum of Modern Art's downtown retail space carries a huge collection of sleek, smart and clever objects for the home, office and wardrobe. You'll find modernist alarm clocks, wildly shaped vases, designer kitchenware and surreal lamps, plus brainy games, hand puppets, fanciful scarves, coffee-table books and lots of other great gift ideas.

SATURDAYS FASHION, ACCESSORIES

Map p410 (www.saturdaysnyc.com; 31 Crosby St, btwn Broome & Grand Sts; ⏰8:30am-7pm Mon-Fri, 10am-7pm Sat & Sun; [S]N/Q/R, J/Z, 6 to Canal St) SoHo's version of a surf shop sees boards, wax and wetsuits paired up with designer grooming products, graphic art and surf tomes, and Saturdays' own line of high-quality, fashion-literate threads for dudes. Styled-up, grab a coffee from the in-house espresso bar, hang in the back garden and fish for some crazy, shark-dodging tales. There's a second branch in the **West Village** (Map p418; 17 Perry St; ⏰8:30am-7pm Mon-Fri, 10am-7pm Sat & Sun; [S]1/2/3 to 14th St).

ADIDAS ORIGINALS SHOES, FASHION

Map p410 (☎212-673-0398; 136 Wooster St, btwn Prince & W Houston Sts; ⏰11am-7pm Mon-Sat, noon-6pm Sun; [S]N/R to Prince St) Iconic triple-striped sneakers, many referencing Adidas' halcyon days from the '60s to the '80s, is what you get here. You can even custom-design your own. Kicks aside, pimp your look with hoodies, track wear, T-shirts and accessories including eye wear, watches and retro-funky bags. DJs occasionally work the decks.

For the big-box retail experience, head to the 29,500-sq-ft **Adidas** (Map p410; ☎212-529-0081; 610 Broadway, at Houston St; ⏰10am-10pm Mon-Sat, to 8pm Sun; [S]N/R to Prince St, B/D/F/M to Broadway-Lafayette St) sneaker emporium a few blocks back.

PIPERLIME FASHION, SHOES

Map p410 (www.piperlime.com; 121 Wooster St, btwn Prince & Spring Sts; ⏰10am-8pm Mon-Sat, 11am-7pm Sun; [S]N/R to Prince St, C/E to Spring St) Piperlime peddles cool, contemporary womenswear at midrange prices. Known for giving newer designers exposure, the store's stock is organized by categories such as 'Shortcut to Chic,' 'Girl on a Budget' and 'Guest Editor's Picks,' the latter handpicked by the likes of stylist Rachel Zoe and actor/model Jessica Alba. Oh, and did we mention the fab range of shoes?

INA MEN VINTAGE

Map p410 (www.inanyc.com; 19 Prince St, at Elizabeth St; ⏰noon-8pm Mon-Sat, to 7pm Sun; [S]6 to Spring St, N/R to Prince St) Male style-meisters love INA for preloved, luxury clothes, shoes and accessories. Edits are high quality across the board, with sought-after items including the likes of Rag & Bone jeans, Alexander McQueen wool pants, Burberry shirts and Church's brogues. Next door is the women's store. You'll find unisex branches in **NoHo** (Map p410; 15 Bleecker St) and **Chelsea** (Map p422; 207 West 18th St), as well as a women's-only store in **SoHo** (Map p410; 101 Thompson Street).

MCNALLY JACKSON BOOKS

Map p410 (☎212-274-1160; www.mcnallyjackson.com; 52 Prince St, btwn Lafayette & Mulberry Sts; ⏰10am-10pm Mon-Sat, to 9pm Sun; [S]N/R to Prince St, 6 to Spring St) Bustling, indie MJ stocks an excellent selection of magazines and books covering contemporary fiction, food writing, architecture and design, art and history. The in-store cafe is a fine spot to settle in with some reading material or to catch one of the frequent readings and book signings held here.

SCHOLASTIC BOOKS, CHILDREN

Map p410 (www.scholastic.com/sohostore; 557 Broadway, btwn Prince & Spring Sts; ⏰10am-7pm Mon-Sat, 11am-6pm Sun; [S]N/R to Prince St) Bright and sprawling, this bookstore is a wonderland for young readers (and the young at heart). Books are divided by age group, and there's a fantastic selection of fun and educational toys, including Lego and science kits. Check the store's website for free weekly events like storytime sessions, character visits and sing-alongs.

KIOSK GIFTS

Map p410 (☎212-226-8601; www.kioskkiosk.com; 2nd fl, 95 Spring St, btwn Mercer St & Broadway; ⏰noon-7pm Mon-Sat; [S]N/R to Prince St, B/D/F/M to Broadway-Lafayette St) Kiosk's owners scour the planet for the most interesting and unusual items (from books and lampshades to toothpaste), which they bring back to SoHo and proudly vend with museum-worthy acumen. Shopping adventures have brought back designer curiosities from the likes of Japan, Iceland, Sweden and Hong Kong.

JOE'S JEANS FASHION

Map p410 (☎212-925-5727; www.joesjeans.com; 77 Mercer St, btwn Spring & Broome Sts; ⏰11am-7pm Mon-Sat, noon-6pm Sun; [S]N/R to Prince St, 6 to Spring St) Sex-up your pins with a pair of jeans from this cult LA label. Options include vintage reserve denim, as well as skinny jeans designed to flatter more forms than just 'Amazonian supermodel.' Mix and match with supercomfy shirts, hoodies, sweaters and the odd to-die-for leather jacket.

JACK SPADE ACCESSORIES, FASHION

Map p410 (www.jackspade.com; 56 Greene St, btwn Broome & Spring Sts; [S]N/R to Prince St, 6 to Spring St) From suede duffles and leather totes to striking wallets and supercute hats and gloves, Jack Spade has no shortage of savvy accessories for urban gentlemen. Menswear items include rustic plaid shirts, playfully preppy sweaters and blazers, selvage denim and vintage-inspired suits.

UNIQLO FASHION

Map p410 (☎917-237-8811; www.uniqlo.com; 546 Broadway, btwn Prince & Spring Sts; ⏰10am-9pm Mon-Sat, 11am-8pm Sun; [S]N/R to Prince St, 6 to Spring St) This enormous, three-story Japanese emporium owes its popularity to good-looking, good-quality apparel at discount prices. You'll find Japanese denim, Mongolian cashmere, graphic T-shirts, svelte skirts and endless racks of colorful ready-to-wear – with most things at the sub-$100 mark.

UNITED NUDE SHOES

Map p410 (☎212-420-6000; www.unitednude.com; 25 Bond St, btwn Lafayette St & Bowery; ⏰noon-7pm Sun & Mon, 11am-7pm Tue-Thu, 11am-8pm Fri & Sat; [S]6 to Bleecker St, B/D/F/M to Broadway-Lafayette St) The flagship store is stocked with improbably beautiful, statement-making footwear – flamboyant, classical, business-smart and sporty. Whether you want strappy sandals, towering stilettos or a solid pair of wedge-heeled pumps, you'll score here. The line of men's shoes is smaller but no less eye-catching.

OTHER MUSIC MUSIC

Map p410 (☎212-477-8150; www.othermusic.com; 15 E 4th St, btwn Lafayette St & Broadway; ⏰11am-9pm Mon-Fri, noon-8pm Sat, noon-7pm Sun; [S]6 to Bleecker St) This indie-run CD store feeds its loyal fan base with a clued-in selection of, well, other types of music: offbeat lounge, psychedelic, electronica, indie rock etc, available new and used. Friendly staffers like what they do, and may be able to help translate your inner musical whims and dreams to actual CD reality. OM also stocks a small but excellent selection of new and used vinyl.

ETIQUETA NEGRA FASHION, SHOES

Map p410 (☎212-219-4015; www.etiquetanegra.us; 273 Lafayette St, at Prince St; ⏰11am-7pm Mon-Sat, from noon Sun; [S]N/R to Prince St, B/D/F/M to Broadway-Lafayette St) While we love the open-topped Bugatti race car parked near the cash register, the real reason to hit this Argentine boutique is for its timeless, well-priced threads for men. Upgrade your wardrobe with handsome wool suits, button-downs, soft polo jerseys and elegant leather boots. You'll find a smaller collection of womenswear downstairs.

ATRIUM FASHION, SHOES

Map p410 (☎212-473-3980; www.atriumnyc.com; 644 Broadway, at Bleecker St; ⏰10am-9pm Mon-Sat, 11am-8pm Sun; [S]6 to Bleecker St, B/D/F/M to Broadway-Lafayette St) Head here for interesting, unisex edits of detail-orientated designer wear – including shoes and accessories – from labels like Drome, Canada Goose and T by Alexander Wang. Especially notable is the range of high-end denim from the likes of PRPS, Adriano Goldschmied and Nicolas Andreas Taralis.

DE VERA ANTIQUES

Map p410 (☎212-625-0838; www.deveraobjects.com; 1 Crosby St, at Howard St; ⏰11am-7pm Tue-Sat; [S]N/Q/R, J/Z, 6 to Canal St) Federico de Vera travels the globe in search of rare and exquisite jewelry, carvings, lacquerware and other objets d'art for this jewel-box of a store. Illuminated glass cases display works such as 200-year-old Buddhas, Venetian glassware and gilded inlaid boxes from the Meiji period, while oil paintings and carvings along the walls complete the museum-like experience.

ODIN CLOTHING, ACCESSORIES

Map p410 (☎212-966-0026; www.odinnewyork.com; 199 Lafayette St, btwn Kenmare & Broome Sts; ⏰11am-8pm Mon-Sat, noon-7pm Sun; [S]6 to Spring St, N/R to Prince St) Named after the mighty Norse god, Odin's flagship men's boutique carries hip downtown labels like

3.1 Phillip Lim, Rag & Bone and Death to Tennis. It's also a good place to browse for up-and-coming designers. Other in-store tempters include Odin candles, fragrances and skateboards, Cutler & Gross sunglasses, and footwear from cult labels like Common Projects and Grenson.

You'll find other branches in the **East Village** (Map p414; ☎212-475-0666; www.odinnewyork.com; 328 E 11th St, East Village; ⌚noon-9pm Mon-Sat, to 7pm Sun; [S]L to First Ave, L, N/Q/R, 4/5/6 to 14th St-Union Sq) and the **West Village** (Map p418; ☎212-243-4724; 106 Greenwich Ave; ⌚noon-8pm Mon-Sat, to 7pm Sun; [S]1/2/3 to 14th St).

OPENING CEREMONY FASHION

Map p410 (☎212-219-2688; www.openingceremony.us; 35 Howard St, btwn Broadway & Lafayette St; ⌚11am-8pm Mon-Sat, noon-7pm Sun; [S]N/Q/R, J/Z, 6 to Canal St) Opening Ceremony is famed for its never-boring edit of indie labels. The place showcases a changing roster of names from across the globe, complimented by Opening Ceremony's own creations. No matter who is hanging on the racks, you can always expect show-stopping, 'where-did-you-get-that?!' threads that are street-smart, bold and refreshingly avant-garde.

SCREAMING MIMI'S VINTAGE

Map p410 (☎212-677-6464; 382 Lafayette St, btwn E 4th & Great Jones Sts; ⌚noon-8pm Mon-Sat, 1-7pm Sun; [S]6 to Bleecker St, B/D/F/M to Broadway-Lafayette St) If you dig vintage threads, you may just scream too. This funtastic shop carries an excellent selection of yesteryear pieces – organized, ingeniously, by decade, from the '50s to the '90s (ask to see the small, stashed-away collection of clothing from the '20s, '30s and '40s).

From prim, beaded wool cardigans to suede minidresses and white leather go-go boots, the stock is in great condition. A selection of accessories and jewelry completes any back-to-the-future look.

RESURRECTION VINTAGE

Map p410 (☎212-625-1374; www.resurrectionvintage.com; 217 Mott St, btwn Prince & Spring Sts; ⌚11am-7pm Mon-Sat, noon-7pm Sun; [S]6 to Spring St, N/R to Prince St) Boudoir-red Resurrection gives new life to cutting-edge designs from past decades. Striking, mint-condition pieces cover the eras of mod, glam-rock and new-wave design, and design deities like Marc Jacobs have dropped by for inspiration. Top picks include Halston dresses and Courrèges coats and jackets.

SHAKESPEARE & CO BOOKS

Map p410 (☎212-529-1330; www.shakeandco.com; 716 Broadway, at Washington Pl; ⌚10am-9pm Mon-Sat, noon-7pm Sun; [S]N/R to 8th St, 6 to Astor Pl) This popular New York bookstore is one of the city's great indie institutions, with other locations, including the **Upper East Side** (Map p432; ☎212-570-0201; www.shakeandco.com; 939 Lexington Ave, at 69th St; ⌚9am-8pm Mon-Fri, 10am-7pm Sat, 11am-6pm Sun; [S]6 to 68th St). You'll find a wide array of contemporary fiction and nonfiction, art books and tomes about NYC, not to mention a steady stream of aspiring actors and directors seeking out the perfect play script downstairs.

SCOOP FASHION

Map p410 (☎212-925-3539; www.scoopnyc.com; 473 Broadway, btwn Broome & Grand Sts; ⌚11am-8pm Mon-Sat, to 7pm Sun; [S]N/Q/R to Canal St, 6 to Spring St) Scoop up contemporary threads from the likes of Theory, Diane Von Furstenberg, Michael Kors and J Brand at this handy one-stop shop. While there's nothing particularly edgy about the selections, there's a lot on offer (over 100 designers covering both men's and women's), and you can often score good deals at season-end sales. Scoop has several stores in the city.

EVOLUTION GIFTS

Map p410 (☎212-343-1114; www.theevolutionstore.com; 120 Spring St, btwn Mercer & Greene Sts; ⌚11am-7pm; [S]N/R to Prince St, 6 to Spring St) Evolution keeps things quirky with natural-history collectibles usually seen in museum cabinets. This is the place to buy – or simply gawk at – framed beetles and butterflies, bugs frozen in amber-resin cubes, stuffed parrots, zebra hides and shark teeth, as well as stony wonders, from meteorites and fragments from Mars to 100-million-year-old fossils.

PURL SOHO HANDICRAFTS

Map p410 (www.purlsoho.com/purl; 459 Broome St, btwn Greene & Mercer Sts; ⌚noon-7pm Mon-Fri, to 6pm weekends; [S]N/R to Prince St, 6 to Spring St) The brainchild of a former *Martha Stewart Living* editor, Purl is a colorful library of fabric and yarn that feels like an in-person Etsy boutique, with inspiration for DIY crafts galore and a scatter of finished products that make unique stocking stuffers.

Chinatown

IMAGE SOURCE / GETTY IMAGES ©

🛍 Chinatown

Chinatown is a great place for wandering, particularly if you're in the market for some aromatic herbs, exotic Eastern fruits (like lychees and durians in season), fresh noodles or delicious bakery goodies. Canal St is the major thoroughfare, with lots of touristy merchandise and knock-off designer gear spilling onto the sidewalks. The backstreets are the real joy, however, with bubble-tea cafes, perfumeries, video arcades, plant shops and fishmongers all hawking their wares.

AJI ICHIBAN — FOOD

Map p413 (☎212-233-7650; 37 Mott St, btwn Bayard & Mosco Sts; ⏰10am-8pm; [S]N/Q/R, J/Z, 6 to Canal St) In Japanese, the name means 'awesome,' and it's exactly what sweet-tooths think once inside this Hong Kong candy shop. Defy your dentist with sesame-flavored marshmallows, Thai durian milk candy, preserved plums, mandarin peel, blackcurrant gummies and dried guava. Savory fans can snack Asian-style on the likes of crispy spicy cod fish, crab chips, wasabi peas and dried anchovies with peanuts.

KAM MAN — HOMEWARES

Map p413 (☎212-571-0330; 200 Canal St, btwn Mulberry & Motts Sts; ⏰9am-8:30pm; [S]N/Q/R, J/Z, 6 to Canal St) Head past hanging ducks to the basement of this classic Canal St food store for cheap Chinese and Japanese tea sets, plus kitchen products such as chopsticks, bowls, stir-frying utensils and rice cookers.

🏃 SPORTS & ACTIVITIES

GREAT JONES SPA — DAY SPA

Map p410 (☎212-505-3185; www.greatjonesspa.com; 29 Great Jones St, btwn Lafayette St & Bowery; ⏰4-10pm Mon, from 9am Tue-Sun; [S]6 to Bleecker St, B/D/F/M to Broadway-Lafayette St) Don't skimp on the services at this downtown feng shui master, complete with three-story indoor waterfall. If you spend over $100 (not hard: hour-long massages start at $140, hour-long facials start at $130), you get two-hour access in the water lounge's hot tub, rock sauna, chakra-light steam room and cold pool. Swimwear is essential.

BUNYA CITISPA — DAY SPA

Map p410 (☎212-388-1288; www.bunyacitispa.com; 474 W Broadway, btwn Prince & W Houston Sts; ⏰10am-10pm Mon-Sat, to 9pm Sun; [S]N/R to Prince St, C/E to Spring St) Ex-models and fatigued shoppers retreat to this chic, Asian-inspired spa for a little Eastern pampering. Tension-soothing solutions include reflexology, head massage with green-tea hair treatment, hot stone massage and the popular 'Oriental herbal compress' Thai massage (one hour, $120).

SCOTT'S PIZZA TOURS — TOUR

(☎212-913-9903; www.scottspizzatours.com; tours from $38) Scott, pizza nerd extraordinaire, turns pizza delivery on its head by 'delivering the people to pizza' instead. Tours take in different swaths of the city, but always with the same goal in mind: scouting out the best slices in town.

East Village & Lower East Side

EAST VILLAGE | LOWER EAST SIDE

Neighborhood Top Five

❶ Admiring the off-white webbing of the boxy facade then wandering in to appreciate mind-bending iterations of art across myriad media at the **New Museum** (p107).

❷ Witnessing the shockingly cramped conditions of early immigrants at the brilliantly curated **Lower East Side Tenement Museum** (p106).

❸ Passing knickknack shops and sake bars on **St Marks Place** (p109), then heading to the neighboring streets for a quieter round of nibbling and boutique-ing.

❹ Pub-crawling through the East Village, stopping at **Immigrant** (p122) and **McSorley's Old Ale House** (p119) along the way.

❺ Snacking on a tantalizing array of global dishes such as Ukrainian dumplings at **Veselka** (p113).

For more detail of this area, see maps on p414 and p416 ➡

Explore the East Village & Lower East Side

If you've been dreaming of those quintessential New York City moments – graffiti on crimson brick, skyscrapers rising overhead, punks and grannies walking side by side, and cute cafes with rickety tables spilling out onto the sidewalks – then the East Village is your Holy Grail. Stick to the area around Tompkins Square Park, and the lettered avenues (known as Alphabet City) to its east, for interesting little nooks in which to eat and drink – as well as a collection of great little community gardens that provide leafy respites and the occasional live performance. The streets below 14th St and east of First Ave are packed with cool boutiques and excellent snack-food spots, offering styles and flavors from around the world. It's a mixed bag, indeed, and perhaps one of the most emblematic of today's city.

Local Life

➡ **One block over** Famed St Marks Place (p109) draws swarms of people shopping and carousing – though it's a bit of a circus most days. Hop a block over in either direction for some great retail and restaurant finds with half the crowds.

➡ **Taste the rainbow** The East Village and Lower East Side are like no other place in the city when it comes to sampling the finest spread of ethnic cuisine. Many of the area's restaurants don't take reservations, so have a wander and grab an open table to eat-pray-love your way through Italy, India, Indonesia or anywhere in between.

Getting There & Away

➡ **Subway** Trains don't go far enough east to carry you to most East Village locations, but it's a quick walk (and even quicker cab or bus ride) from the 6 at Astor Pl, the F, V at Lower East Side-Second Ave or the L at First or Third Aves. The subway's F line (Lower East Side-Second Ave or Delancey St stops) will let you off in the thick of the Lower East Side.

➡ **Bus** If you're traveling from the west side, it's better to take the M14 (across 14th St) or the M21 (down Houston).

Lonely Planet's Top Tip

A lot of the restaurants in this neck of the woods don't take reservations, so stop by the restaurant of your choosing in the early afternoon (2pm should do the trick) and place your name on the roster for the evening meal – chances are high that they'll take your name and you'll get seated right away when you return for dinner later on.

 Best Places to Eat

➡ Upstate (p116)
➡ Cafe Mogador (p114)
➡ Tacos Morelos (p113)
➡ Calliope (p114)
➡ Lavagna (p114)

For reviews, see p113 ➡

 Best Places to Drink

➡ Death + Co (p122)
➡ Angel's Share (p122)
➡ Golden Cadillac (p119)
➡ Wayland (p119)
➡ Ten Bells (p123)

For reviews, see p119 ➡

 Best Places to Shop

➡ Obscura Antiques (p127)
➡ Top Hat (p127)
➡ Still House (p126)
➡ Tokio 7 (p126)
➡ John Varvatos (p127)

For reviews, see p126 ➡

EAST VILLAGE & LOWER EAST SIDE

TOP SIGHT
LOWER EAST SIDE TENEMENT MUSEUM

There's no museum in New York that humanizes the city's colorful past quite like the Lower East Side Tenement Museum, which puts the neighborhood's heartbreaking but inspiring heritage on full display in several recreations of former tenements, including the 1870s home of the German-Jewish Gumpertz family, and the dwelling of the Italian-Catholic Baldizzi family who lived through the Great Depression of 1929. Always evolving and expanding, the museum has a variety of tours and talks beyond the museum's walls – a must for anyone interested in old New York.

DON'T MISS...

➡ Themed walks around the neighborhood

➡ A peek into the 1870s and the 1930s on the Hard Times tour

➡ The free 30-minute film shown in the visitor center

➡ The outhouses (though you'll have to imagine the stench)

PRACTICALITIES

➡ Map p416

➡ ☎212-982-8420

➡ www.tenement.org

➡ 103 Orchard St, btwn Broome & Delancey Sts

➡ admission $22

➡ ⊙10am-6pm

➡ ⑤B/D to Grand St, J/M/Z to Essex St, F to Delancey St

Inside the Tenement

A wide range of tenement tours lead visitors into the building where hundreds of immigrants lived and worked over the years. Hard Times, one of the most popular tours, visits apartments from two different time periods – the 1870s and the 1930s. There you'll see the squalid conditions tenants faced – no electricity or running water and a wretched communal outhouse in the early days – and what life was like for the families who lived there. Other tours focus on Irish immigrants (and the harsh discrimination they faced), sweatshop workers and 'shop life' (with a tour through a recreated 1870s German beer hall).

Neighborhood Tours

A great way to understand the immigrant experience is on a walking tour around the neighborhood. These tours, ranging from 75 minutes to two hours, explore a variety of topics. Foods of the Lower East Side looks at the ways traditional foods have shaped American cuisine; Then & Now explores the way the neighborhood has changed over the decades; Outside the Home looks at life beyond the apartment – where immigrants stored (and lost) their life savings, the churches and synagogues so integral to community life, and the meeting halls where poorly paid workers gathered to fight for better conditions.

103 Orchard St

The visitor center at 103 Orchard St has a museum shop and a small screening room that plays an original film. Several evenings a month, the museum hosts talks here, often relating to the present immigrant experience in America. The building itself was, naturally, a tenement too – ask the staff about the interesting families of East European and Italian descent that once dwelled here, or check out www.tenement.org/103-Orchard.html for black-and-white portraits of the former residents.

Meet Victoria

Travel back to 1916 and meet Victoria Confino, a 14-year-old girl from a Greek Sephardic family. Played by a costumed interpreter, Victoria interacts with visitors answering questions about what her life was like in those days. It's especially recommended for kids, as visitors are free to handle household objects. This one-hour tour is held on weekends year-round, and daily during the summer.

LONELY PLANET IMAGES / GETTY IMAGES ©

TOP SIGHT
NEW MUSEUM

For any modern-day museum worth its salt, its structure has to be as much of a statement as the artwork inside. The New Museum avatar accomplishes just that and more with its inspired design by noted Japanese architecture firm SANAA. The Lower East Side has seen its fair share of physical changes over the last two decades as the sweeping hand of gentrification has cleaned up slummy nooks and replaced them with glittering residential blocks. The New Museum manages to punctuate the neighborhood with something unique, and its cache of artistic work will dazzle and confuse just as much as its facade.

A Museum with a Mission

The mission statement of this museum – founded in 1977 by Marcia Tucker and moved to five different locations over the years – is simple: 'New art, new ideas.' The institution has given gallery space to artists Keith Haring, Jeff Koons, Joan Jonas, Mary Kelly and Andres Serrano – all at the beginning of their careers – and continues to show contemporary heavy hitters. The city's sole museum dedicated to contemporary art has brought a steady menu of edgy works in new forms, such as seemingly random, discarded materials fused together and displayed in the middle of a vast room.

The museum also houses the Hester Street Cafe, a great spot for sampling the gourmet goodies of NYC purveyors, including baked goods by Cafe Grumpy, teas by McNulty, coffee by Intelligentsia and sandwiches by Duck's Eatery.

DON'T MISS...

- The facade from across the street
- Pay-what-you-wish Thursday evening
- Hester Street Cafe
- New Museum Store

PRACTICALITIES

- Map p416
- ☎212-219-1222
- www.newmuseum.org
- 235 Bowery, btwn Stanton & Rivington Sts
- adult/child $16/free, 7-9pm Thu pay what you wish
- 🕒11am-6pm Wed & Fri-Sun, to 9pm Thu
- [S]N/R to Prince St, F to 2nd Ave, J/Z to Bowery, 6 to Spring St

NEW MUSEUM SHOP

If you aren't so keen on the current exhibits, it's still worth stopping by the museum's store to peruse the excellent coffee table books – sometimes the take-homes include savvy collaborations with showcased artists. The shop has the same hours of operation as the museum.

DISCOUNTED ADMISSION

To save cash, stop by on Thursday evening between 7pm and 9pm, when admission is pay what you wish. Depending on the show, the crowds can be sizable. We recommend lining up by 6:45pm.

FIRST SATURDAY

On the first Saturday of the month, the New Museum hosts special events for budding artists, with hands-on crafts and activities for kids aged 4 to 15. Free museum admission is included for adults (it's always free for kids).

In Orbit

It's now been several years since the New Museum has taken hold, inspiring nearby structures to adopt similarly ethereal designs. Perhaps most interestingly the museum has become somewhat of a magnetic force keeping a clutch of small workshops and creative spaces in its orbit. For more on these other galleries of the Lower East Side, see (p112).

SANAA's Vision

While exhibits rotate through the museum, regularly changing the character of the space within, the shell – an inspired architectural gesture – remains a constant, acting as a unique structural element in the diverse cityscape, while also simultaneously fading into the background and allowing the exhibits to shine.

The building's structure is the brainchild of Japanese firm SANAA – a partnership between two great minds, Sejima Kazuyo and Nishizawa Ryue. In 2010, SANAA won the much-coveted Pritzker Prize (think the Oscars of architecture) for their contributions to the world of design. Their trademark vanishing facades are known worldwide for abiding by a strict adherence to a form-follows-function design aesthetic, sometimes taking the land plot's footprint into the overall shape of the structure. The box-atop-box scheme of the New Museum provides a striking counterpoint to the clusters of crimson brick and iron fire escapes outside, while alluding to the geometric exhibition chasms within.

GARDEL BERTRAND / GETTY IMAGES ©

TOP SIGHT
ST MARKS PLACE

One of the most magical things about New York is that every street tells a story, from the action unfurling before your eyes to the dense history hidden behind colorful facades. St Marks Place is one of the best strips of pavement in the city for storytelling, as almost every building on these hallowed blocks is rife with tales from a time when the East Village embodied a far more lawless spirit.

Technically St Marks Place is 8th St between Third Ave and Ave A; it earned its saintly moniker from the like-named church nearby on 10th St.

Astor Place

To the west of St Marks Place is **Astor Place** (Map p414; 8th St, btwn Third & Fourth Aves; [S]N/R to 8th St-NYU, 6 to Astor Pl), a crowded crisscrossing of streets anchored by a curious square sculpture that's affectionately (and appropriately) known by locals as *The Cube*. A favorite meeting spot for neighborhood dwellers, this work of art – actually named *Alamo* – weighs over 1800lb and is made entirely of Cor-Tensteel.

Originally Astor Place was the home of the Astor Opera House (now gone), which attracted the city's wealthy elite for regular performances in the mid-1800s. The square was also the site of the notorious Astor Place riots, in which the city's protesting Irish population caused such a stir about their homeland potato famine that the police fired shots into the masses, injuring hundreds and killing at least 18 people.

Today the square is largely known as the home of the *Village Voice* and the **Cooper Union** (Map p414; www.cooper.edu; 51 Astor Pl) design institute.

DON'T MISS...

- The *Physical Graffiti* buildings made famous by Led Zeppelin (No 96 and 98)
- Brunch at one of the tasty cafes
- Tompkins Square Park at the end of the street
- Sake bombs at one of the basement Japanese bars
- Shopping for knick-knacks and odd souvenirs

PRACTICALITIES

- Map p414
- St Marks Pl, Ave A to Third Ave
- [S]N/R/W to 8th St-NYU, 6 to Astor Pl

EATING ON ST MARKS

In addition to all of its quirky and historical landmarks, St Marks has some wonderful places to stop for a bite. Weekend brunches in the East Village are a great bet, as the local restaurants are typically less expensive (and less scene-y) than the hot spots in neighboring 'hoods. Try Cafe Mogador (p114) and Yaffa (p114) – both fuse American favorites with an assortment of Middle Eastern plates.

Neon sign at Trash & Vaudeville

The East Village was once the home base for emerging punk rock acts – many would frequent the clothing shops along St Marks to assemble their trademark looks. Although most joints have gone the way of the dodo in favor of more tourist-friendly wares, there are still a few spots that remain, like Trash & Vaudeville at No 4 (Map p414).

Third Ave to Ave A

Easily one of NYC's most famous streets, St Marks Place is also one of the city's smallest, occupying only three blocks between Astor Pl and Tompkins Square Park. The road, however, is jam-packed with historical tidbits that would delight any trivia buff. Number 2 St Marks Place is known as the St Mark's Ale House, but for a time it was the famous Five-Spot, where jazz fiend Thelonious Monk got his start in the 1950s. A cast of colorful characters have left their mark at 4 St Marks Place: Alexander Hamilton's son built the structure, James Fenimore Cooper lived here in the 1830s and Yoko Ono's Fluxus artists descended upon the building in the 1960s. The buildings at 96 and 98 St Marks Place are immortalized on the cover of Led Zepellin's *Physical Graffiti* album. Though it closed in the 1990s, number 122 St Marks Place was the location of a popular cafe called Sin-é, where Jeff Buckley and David Gray often performed.

Tompkins Square Park

St Marks Place terminates at a welcome clearing of green deep in the heart of the East Village, the 10.5-acre Tompkins Square Park. Tompkins Square Park hosts the annual Howl! Festival of East Village Arts, which brings Allen Ginsberg–inspired theater, music, film, dance and spoken-word events to the park and various neighborhood venues each September. The Charlie Parker Jazz Festival is also held here, bringing some of the biggest jazz names to the 'hood each August.

SIGHTS

East Village

ST MARKS PLACE STREET
See p109.

TOMPKINS SQUARE PARK PARK
Map p414 (www.nycgovparks.org; E 7th & 10th Sts, btwn Aves A & B; 🕐6am-midnight; [S]6 to Astor Pl) This 10.5-acre park honors Daniel Tompkins, who served as governor of New York from 1807 to 1817 (and as the nation's vice president after that, under James Monroe). It's like a friendly town square for locals, who gather for chess at concrete tables, picnics on the lawn on warm days and spontaneous guitar or drum jams on various grassy knolls. It's also the site of basketball courts, a fun-to-watch dog run (a fenced-in area where humans can unleash their canines), frequent summer concerts and an always-lively kids' playground.

The park, which recently underwent a facelift, wasn't always a place for such clean fun, however. In the '80s, it was a dirty, needle-strewn homeless encampment, unusable for folks wanting a place to stroll or picnic. A contentious turning point came when police razed the band shell (where the legendary and now-defunct Wigstock dragfest was founded by Lady Bunny and cohorts) and evicted more than 100 squatters living in a tent city in the park in 1988 (and again in 1991). That first eviction turned violent; the Tompkins Square Riot, as it came to be known, ushered in the first wave of yuppies in the dog run, fashionistas lolling in the grass and undercover narcotics agents trying to pass as druggie punk kids.

ST MARK'S IN THE BOWERY CHURCH
Map p414 (☎212-674-6377; www.stmarksbowery.org; 131 E 10th St, at Second Ave; 🕐10am-6pm Mon-Fri; [S]L to 3rd Ave, 6 to Astor Pl) Though it's most popular with East Village locals for its cultural offerings – such as poetry readings hosted by the Poetry Project or cutting-edge dance performances from Danspace and the Ontological Hysteric Theater – this is also a historic site. This Episcopal church stands on the site of the farm, or *bouwerij*, owned by Dutch governor Peter Stuyvesant, whose crypt lies under the grounds.

EAST RIVER PARK PARK
Map p414 (FDR Dr & E Houston St; [S]F to Delancey-Essex Sts) In addition to the great ballparks, running and biking paths, 5000-seat amphitheater for concerts and expansive patches of green, this park has cool, natural breezes and stunning views of the Williamsburg, Manhattan and Brooklyn Bridges.

Although flanked by a housing project and the clogged FDR Dr on one side and the less-than-pure East River on the other, it's a fine spot for a stroll or a morning run.

COMMUNITY GARDENS

After a stretch of arboreal abstinence in New York City, the community gardens of Alphabet City are breathtaking. A network of gardens was carved out of abandoned lots to provide low-income neighborhoods with a communal backyard. Trees and flowers were planted, sandboxes were built, found-art sculptures erected and domino games played – all within green spaces wedged between buildings or even claiming entire blocks. And while some were destroyed – in the face of much protest – to make way for the projects of greedy developers, plenty of green spots have held their ground. The gardens tend to be open to the public on most weekends; many gardeners are activists within the community and are a good source of information about local politics.

Le Petit Versailles (Map p414; www.lpvtv.blogspot.com; 346 E Houston St, at Ave C; [S]F to Delancey St, J/M/Z to Essex St) is a unique marriage of a verdant oasis and an electrifying arts organization, offering a range of quirky performances and screenings to the public. The **6th & B Garden** (Map p414; www.6bgarden.org; E 6th St & Ave B; 🕐1-6pm Sat & Sun; [S]6 to Astor Pl) is a well-organized space that hosts free music events, workshops and yoga sessions; check the website for details. Three dramatic weeping willows, an odd sight in the city, grace the twin plots of **9th St Garden and La Plaza Cultural** (Map p414; www.laplazacultural.com; E 9th St, at Ave C; 🕐noon-5pm Sat & Sun Apr-Oct). Also check out the **All People's Garden** (Map p414; E 3rd St, btwn Aves B & C) and **Brisas del Caribe** (Map p414; 237 E 3rd St).

👁 Lower East Side

LOWER EAST SIDE TENEMENT MUSEUM MUSEUM

See p106.

NEW MUSEUM MUSEUM

See p112.

MUSEUM AT ELDRIDGE STREET SYNAGOGUE MUSEUM

Map p416 (☎212-219-0302; www.eldridgestreet.org; 12 Eldridge St, btwn Canal & Division Sts; adult/child $10/6; 🕒10am-5pm Sun-Thu, to 3pm Fri; [S]F to East Broadway) This landmarked house of worship, built in 1887, was once the center of Jewish life, before falling into squalor in the 1920s. Left to rot, it's only recently been reclaimed, and now shines with original splendor. Its on-site museum gives tours every half hour, with the last one departing at 4pm.

ESSEX STREET MARKET MARKET

Map p416 (☎212-312-3603; www.essexstreetmarket.com; 120 Essex St, btwn Delancey & Rivington Sts; 🕒8am-7pm Mon-Sat; [S]F to Delancey St, J/M/Z to Essex St) Founded in 1940, this market is the local place for produce, seafood, butcher-cut meats, cheeses, Latino grocery items, and even a barber's shop. Although the interior is fairly bland, there are some excellent gourmet goodies here. Stop at Rainbo's for smoked fish and Saxelby Cheesemongers for artisanal cheese, smoked sausages and housemade pâté. Pain d'Avignon bakes fresh breads and Boubouki whips up spinach pies and baklava, while Roni-Sue's Chocolates spreads sweet temptations. You can also nosh on-site at Shopsin's General Store, Brooklyn Taco Company and Davidovich Bakery.

LOWER EAST SIDE GALLERIES

Though Chelsea may be the heavy hitter when it comes to the New York gallery scene, the Lower East Side has dozens of quality showplaces. One of the early pioneers, opened in 1975, the **Sperone Westwater** (Map p416; www.speronewestwater.com; 257 Bowery; [S]F to 2nd Ave) represents big names such as William Wegman and Richard Long, and its new home was designed by the famed Norman Foster, who's already made a splash in NYC with his Hearst Building and Avery Fisher Hall designs. Nearby the avant-garde **Salon 94** has two Lower East Side outposts: one secreted away on **Freeman Alley** (Map p416; www.salon94.com; 1 Freeman Alley off Rivington; [S]F to 2nd Ave, J/Z to Bowery) and another on **Bowery** (Map p416; www.salon94.com; 243 Bowery, cnr Stanton St; [S]F to 2nd Ave, J/Z to Bowery) near the New Museum. The latter has a 20ft LCD video wall that broadcasts video art out into the street. A few blocks north is the 4000-sq-ft **Hole** (Map p414; www.theholenyc.com; 312 Bowery at Bleecker; [S]6 to Bleecker St, B/D/F/M to Broadway-Lafayette St) – known as much for its art as it is for its rowdy openings that gather both scenesters of the downtown art circuit and well-known faces like Courtney Love and Salman Rushdie.

Broome St between Chrystie and Bowery is quickly becoming the nexus of the Lower East Side art scene, with major galleries like **White Box**, **Canada**, **Jack Hanley** and **Marlborough** right next door to one another. Another buzzing strip of galleries runs down Orchard St between Rivington and Canal Sts.

The two-story **Rox** (Map p416; www.roxnyc.com; 86 Delancey St, btwn Orchard & Ludlow Sts; [S]F to Delancey St, J/M/Z to Essex St), which opened in 2013, stages provocative shows – when it opened, it stirred a bit of controversy for displaying a large-format photograph of a nude woman in the window (part of the opening show), unavoidable for all who walked down busy Delancey St.

There are popular, contemporary galleries in the area too:

Lehmann Maupin (Map p416; www.lehmannmaupin.com; 201 Chrystie St; [S]F to Delancey-Essex Sts)

Mark Miller Gallery (Map p416; www.markmillergallery.com; 92 Orchard St, btwn Delancey & Broome Sts)

Untitled (Map p416; www.nyuntitled.com; 30 Orchard St, btwn Canal & Hester Sts)

Lesley Heller (Map p416; www.lesleyheller.com; 54 Orchard St, btwn Grand & Hester Sts)

ORCHARD STREET BARGAIN DISTRICT NEIGHBORHOOD

Map p416 (Ludlow & Essex Sts, btwn Houston & Delancey Sts; ⏱Sun-Fri; [S]F, J/M/Z to Delancey-Essex Sts) Back in the day, this large intersection was a free-for-all, as Eastern European and Jewish merchants sold anything that could command a buck from their push-carts. The 300-plus shops you see now aren't as picturesque, but it's a good place to pick up some low-priced leather jackets, shirts and pants.

KEHILA KEDOSHA JANINA SYNAGOGUE & MUSEUM RELIGIOUS, SPIRITUAL

Map p416 (☎212-431-1619; www.kkjsm.org; 280 Broome St, at Allen St; ⏱11am-4pm Sun, service 9am Sat; [S]F, J/M/Z to Delancey-Essex Sts) This small synagogue is home to an obscure branch of Judaism, the Romaniotes, whose ancestors were slaves sent to Rome by ship but rerouted to Greece by a storm. This is their only synagogue in the Western Hemisphere, and includes a small museum bearing artifacts like hand-painted birth certificates, an art gallery, a Holocaust memorial for Greek Jews and costumes from Janina, the Romaniote capital of Greece.

SARA D ROOSEVELT PARK PARK

Map p416 (Houston St, at Chrystie St; [S]F to Delancey-Essex Sts) Spiffed up in recent years, this three-block-long park is a hive of activity on weekends, with basketball courts, a small soccer pitch (with synthetic turf) and a well-loved playground (just north of Hester St). Tai chi practitioners, vegetable sellers (on the nearby cross streets) and strollers of all ages and ethnic backgrounds add to the ever-evolving scene.

🍴 EATING

Here lies the epitome of what is beautiful in New York's dining scene: mind-blowing variety – which can cover the full spectrum of continents and budgets – in just a single city block. You'll find every type of taste-bud tantalizer from Ukrainian *pierogi* (dumpling) palaces and dozens of sushi joints to pizza parlors and falafel huts. There's tons of Indian fare too, especially on the carnival-esque strip of E 6th St between First and Second Aves, otherwise known as Curry Row, where cheap, decent restaurants from the subcontinent are a dime a dozen.

🍴 East Village

ABRAÇO CAFE $

Map p414 (www.abraconyc.com; 86 E 7th St, btwn First & Second Aves; snacks $2-3; ⏱8am-4pm Tue-Sat, 9am-4pm Sun; [S]F to 2nd Ave, L to 1st Ave, 6 to Astor Pl) With hardly room to move – let alone sit – Abraço is an East Village refuge that serves up some of the city's best espressos and lattes. Sip your perfectly crafted cappuccino while inhaling a slice of delicious olive oil cake.

MINCA NOODLES $

Map p414 (☎212-505-8001; www.newyorkramen.com; 536 E 5th St, btwn Aves A & B; ramen $11-14; ⏱noon-11:30pm; [S]F to Second Ave, J/M/Z to Essex St, F to Delancey St) The epitome of an East Village hole-in-the-wall, Minca focuses all of its attention on the food: cauldron-esque bowls of steaming ramen served with a recommended side order of fried gyoza.

TACOS MORELOS MEXICAN $

Map p414 (438 E 9th St, btwn First Ave & Ave A; tacos from $2.50; ⏱noon-midnight Sun-Thu, to 2am Fri & Sat; [S]L to 1st Ave) This famed food truck put down roots in a no-frills East Village storefront in 2013, quickly becoming one of Manhattan's favorite tacos. Order it with chicken, steak, roast pork, beef tongue or vegetarian. Tip: pay the 50c extra for the homemade tortilla.

KANOYAMA SUSHI $

Map p414 (☎212-777-5266; www.kanoyama.com; 175 Second Ave, near E 11th St; rolls from $5; ⏱5.30-11pm; 🍷; [S]L to Third Ave, L, N/Q/R/W, 4/5/6 to 14th St-Union Sq) Providing no-fuss sushi with fresh daily specials in the heart of the East Village, Kanoyama is a local favorite that has so far been overlooked by the city's big-name food critics (that might explain its unpretentious air). You can order sushi à la carte or in rolls, or choose from the many tempura plates.

VESELKA UKRAINIAN $

Map p414 (☎212-228-9682; www.veselka.com; 144 Second Ave, at 9th St; mains $10-18; ⏱24hr; [S]L to 3rd Ave, 6 to Astor Pl) A bustling tribute to the area's Ukrainian past, Veselka dishes out *varenyky* (handmade dumplings) and veal goulash amid the usual suspects of greasy comfort food. The cluttered spread of tables is available to loungers and carb-loaders all night long, though it's a favorite any time of day.

YAFFA AMERICAN $

Map p414 (☎212-677-9001; www.yaffacafe.com; 97 St Marks Pl, btwn First Ave & Ave A; mains $12-18; 🕒9am-6am; [S]L to First Ave, F to Second Ave, 4/6 to Astor Pl) Fun and festive Yaffa is an explosion of wild prints and animal patterns, plastic chandeliers and colored glass doodads. The menu walks the line between American comfort food and Middle Eastern flavors, while the quiet courtyard in back makes a peaceful retreat.

RAI RAI KEN RAMEN $

Map p414 (☎212-477-7030; 214 E 10th St, btwn First & Second Aves; ramen $10-13; 🕒noon-midnight Mon-Thu, noon-2am Fri & Sat; [S]L to First Ave, 4/6 to Astor Pl) Rai Rai Ken's storefront may only be the size of its door, but it's pretty hard to miss since there's usually a small congregation of hungry locals lurking out front. Inside, low-slung wooden stools are arranged around the noodle bar, where the cooks are busily churning out piping-hot portions of tasty pork-infused broth.

ANGELICA KITCHEN VEGAN, CAFE $$

Map p414 (☎212-228-2909; www.angelicakitchen.com; 300 E 12th St, btwn First & Second Aves; mains $11-19; 🕒11:30am-10:30pm; 🖉; [S]L to 1st Ave) This enduring herbivore classic has a calming vibe – candles, tables both intimate and communal, and a mellow, longtime staff – and enough creative options to make your head spin. Some dishes get too-cute names (Goodnight Mushroom, Thai Mee Up), but all do wonders with tofu, seitan, spices and soy products, and sometimes an array of raw ingredients.

CALLIOPE FRENCH $$

Map p414 (84 E 4th St, at Second Ave; mains lunch $12-17, dinner $26-39; 🕒lunch & dinner; [S]F to 2nd Ave) This rustic-chic charmer serves French farmhouse comfort fare – though given a modern twist. The menu is small, and the dishes are surprisingly well executed: spicy mackerel with avocado and black sesame, beef tongue with pickled onions, delicate rabbit pappardelle, and a marvelously tender *tête de porc* (aka pig's head). Less adventurous eaters can opt for crispy roast chicken, Newport steak and mussels.

LAVAGNA ITALIAN $$

Map p414 (☎212-979-1005; www.lavagnanyc.com; 545 E 5th St, btwn Aves A & B; mains $15-30; 🕒6-11pm Mon-Thu, to midnight Fri-Sun; 🖉 👪; [S]F to 2nd Ave) Dark wood, flickering candles and a fiery glow from a somewhat open kitchen help make homey Lavagna a late-night hideaway for lovers. But it's laid-back enough to make it appropriate for children, at least in the early hours before the smallish space fills up. Delicious pastas, thin-crust pizzas and hearty mains, such as baby rack of lamb, are standard fare.

CAFE MOGADOR MOROCCAN, MIDDLE EASTERN $$

Map p414 (☎212-677-2226; 101 St Marks Pl; mains lunch $8-14, dinner $17-21; 🕒9am-1am Sun-Thu, to 2am Fri & Sat; [S]6 to Astor Pl) Family-run Mogador is a long-standing NYC classic, serving fluffy piles of couscous, char-grilled lamb and *merguez* sausage over basmati rice and satisfying mixed platters of hummus and baba ghanoush. The standouts, however, are the tagines – traditionally spiced, long-simmered chicken or lamb dishes served up five different ways. A garrulous young crowd packs the space, spilling out onto the small cafe tables on warm days. Brunch (served weekends 9am to 4pm) is excellent.

IPPUDO NY NOODLES $$

Map p414 (☎212-388-0088; www.ippudo.com/ny; 65 Fourth Ave, btwn 9th & 10th Sts; ramen $15-16; 🕒11am-3:30pm Mon-Sat, 5-11:30pm Mon-Thu, 5pm-12:30am Fri & Sat, 11am-10:30pm Sun; [S]N/R to 8th St-NYU, 4/5/6 to 14th St-Union Sq, 6 to Astor Pl) In New York, the good folks from Ippudo have kicked things up a notch – they've taken their mouthwatering ramen recipe (truly, it's delish) and spiced it up with sleek surrounds (hello shiny black surfaces and streamers of cherry red) and blasts of rock and roll on the speakers.

WESTVILLE EAST MODERN AMERICAN $$

Map p414 (☎212-677-2033; www.westvillenyc.com; 173 Ave A; mains $11-22; 🕒10am-11pm; [S]L to 1st Ave, 6 to Astor Pl) Market-fresh veggies and mouthwatering mains is the name of the game at Westville, and it doesn't hurt that the cottage-chic surrounds are undeniably charming.

LUZZO'S PIZZERIA $$

Map p414 (☎212-473-7447; 211-213 First Ave, btwn 12th & 13th Sts; pizzas small/medium around $19/26; 🕒noon-11pm Tue-Sun, 5-11pm Mon; [S]1st Ave) Fan-favorite Luzzo's occupies a thin sliver of real estate in the East Village, which gets stuffed to the gills each evening as discerning diners feast on thin-crust pies, kissed with ripe tomatoes and cooked in a coal-fired stove.

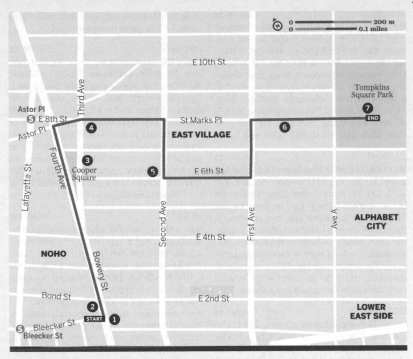

Neighborhood Walk
East Village Nostalgia

START CBGB
END TOMPKINS SQUARE PARK
LEGNTH 1.5 MILES; 1.5 HOURS

From the Bleecker St subway station, head east along the leafy like-named street for a few blocks until you reach the former **1 CBGB**, a famous music venue that opened in 1973 and launched punk rock via the Ramones. Today, it's a John Varvatos boutique selling rock-inspired leather jackets – the old walls of fading posters and wild graffiti remain untouched. The corner just north of here marks the block-long **2 Joey Ramone Place**, named after the Ramones' singer who succumbed to cancer in 2001. Head north on the Bowery to Astor Pl. Turn right and head east through the square to come to **3 Cooper Union** (p109), where in 1860 presidential hopeful Abraham Lincoln rocked a skeptical New York crowd with an arousing anti-slavery speech that ensured his candidacy. Continue east on St Marks Pl, a block full of tattoo parlors and

cheap eateries that haven't changed much at all since the 1980s. Poke your head into **4 Trash & Vaudeville**, a landmark goth-and-punk shop. Head south down Second Ave to the site of the long-defunct **5 Fillmore East**, a 2000-seat live-music venue run by promoter Bill Graham from 1968 to 1971. In the '80s the space was transformed into the Saint – the legendary, 5000-sq-ft dance club that kicked off a joyous, drug-laden, gay disco culture. Cross Second Ave at 6th St and head down the block-long strip of Indian restaurants and curry shops. At First Ave, turn left, rejoin St Marks Pl and turn right. The row of tenements is the site of Led Zeppelin's **6 Physical Graffiti album cover** (96-98 St Marks Pl), where Mick and Keith sat in 1981 in the Stones' hilarious video for 'Waiting on a Friend.' End your stroll at the infamous **7 Tompkins Square Park** (p111), where drag queens started the Wigstock summer festival at the bandshell where Jimi Hendrix played in the 1960s.

REDHEAD SOUTHERN $$

Map p414 (☎212-533-6212; www.theredheadnyc.com; 349 E 13th St, btwn First & Second Aves; mains $12-24; ⏲5:30pm-1am Mon-Sat, 5-10pm Sun; [S]L to First Ave, L to Third Ave, 6 to Astor Pl) Cozy corners of exposed brick and smiles from the staff mirror the home-style comfort food, which has a distinctly Southern bent. There are stacks of fried chicken and rounds of pucker-inducing cocktails on everyone else's table, and you should follow suit.

L'APICIO ITALIAN $$

Map p414 (13 E 1st St, btwn Bowery & Second Ave; mains $17-30; ⏲5:30-11pm daily & 11am-3pm Sat & Sun) Acclaimed chef Gabe Thompson brings contemporary Italian food to the East Village in a sleek and modern dining room that seems a touch out of place among the once solidly bohemian surrounds. Regardless, the food here is excellent, particularly the superb polenta dishes (who knew cornmeal could be so tasty) – try it with pork meatballs or braised lamb shank.

MOTORINO PIZZERIA $$

Map p414 (www.motorinopizza.com; 349 E 12th Sts, btwn First & Second Aves; pizzas $15-18; ⏲11am-midnight Sun-Thu, to 1am Fri & Sat; 🖉; [S]L to First Ave, 4/5/6 to 14th St-Union Sq) Crusts that are both chewy and pillowy at this intimate East Village restaurant.

MUD CAFE $$

Map p414 (☎212-228-9074; www.themudtruck.com; 307 E 9th St, btwn Second & First Aves; brunch $15; ⏲8am-midnight; [S]L to Third Ave, L to First Ave, 4/6 to Astor Pl) Offering trustworthy beans and a brunch that'll put some hair on the dog, this 9th St nook is a favorite among East Villagers looking for a quick caffeine fix or a friendly place to loiter with a book. Keep an eye out for the MUD trucks that roam the city streets; there's also a handy kiosk in the tiny plaza (that's been rechristened 'Mud Park') on First Ave and 1st St.

BRICK LANE CURRY HOUSE INDIAN $$

Map p414 (306 E 6th St, btwn First & Second Aves; mains $16-25; ⏲noon-11pm Sun-Thu, to 1am Fri & Sat) Modeled on the curry houses of East London, Brick Lane serves authentic tikka massala, vindaloo and tandoori that far surpasses the neighboring Indian joints lining E 6th St (though the bill certainly reflects this). Dishes are richly flavored and boast plenty of fire, if it's spiciness you seek. Skip the inconsistent lunch buffet and come for à la carte dinner instead.

UPSTATE SEAFOOD $$

Map p414 (www.upstatenyc.com; 95 First Ave, btwn 5th & 6th Sts; mains $15-30; ⏲5-11pm; [S]F to 2nd Ave) Small and often overlooked, Upstate nevertheless serves outstanding seafood dishes and craft beers. The small always-changing menu features the likes of beer-steamed mussels, seafood stew, scallops over mushroom risotto, softshell crab and wondrous oyster selections. There's no freezer – seafood comes from the market each day, so you know you'll be getting only the freshest ingredients.

HEARTH ITALIAN $$$

Map p414 (☎646-602-1300; www.restaurant-hearth.com; 403 E 12th St, at First Ave; mains $21-48; ⏲6-10pm Sun-Thu, to 11pm Fri, 11am-2pm & 6-11pm Sat, 11am-2pm Sun; [S]L to 1st Ave; L, N/Q/R, 4/5/6 to 14th St-Union Sq) A staple for finicky, deep-pocketed diners, Hearth boasts a warm, brick-walled interior. The seasonal menu includes specials such as roasted sturgeon with lentils and bacon, zucchini ravioli and rabbit pappardelle with fava beans.

PRUNE AMERICAN $$$

Map p414 (☎212-677-6221; www.prunerestaurant.com; 54 E 1st St, btwn First & Second Aves; mains brunch/dinner from $12/25; ⏲5:30-11pm daily & 10am-3:30pm Sat & Sun; [S]F/V to Lower East Side-Second Ave) Expect lines around the block on the weekend, when the hungover show up to cure their ills with Prune's brunches and excellent Bloody Marys (in 10 varieties). The small room is always busy as diners pour in for pan-roasted bass with melted leeks, seared duck breast and rich sweetbreads. Reservations available for dinner only.

🍴 Lower East Side

DIMES CAFE $

Map p416 (☎212-240-9410; 143 Division St, btwn Canal & Ludlow Sts; mains $8-12; ⏲8am-4pm Mon-Fri, from 9am Sat & Sun; 🖉) This tiny 20-seat eatery quickly garnered a local following after opening in 2013 for its friendly service and healthy, good-value dishes. A design-minded group crowds in for eggy breakfasts (served all day), bowls of açaí (that richly flavored, vitamin-rich

Amazonian berry), creative salads (with fennel, blood orange, Brussels sprouts, pumpkin seeds), roasted vegetables and pulled chicken sandwiches.

DONUT PLANT DESSERTS **$**
Map p416 (379 Grand St, at Norfolk; doughnuts $2.75; ⊙6:30am-6:30pm) Inventively flavored (eg peanut butter and jelly) doughnuts with all-natural ingredients. Another location in the Chelsea Hotel (p136) at 222 W 23rd St.

MEATBALL SHOP ITALIAN **$**
Map p416 (☑212-982-8895; www.themeatball-shop.com; 84 Stanton St, btwn Allen & Orchard Sts; mains from $10; ⊙noon-2am Sun-Thu, to 4am Fri-Sat; Ⓢ2nd Ave, F to Delancey St, J/M/Z to Essex St) Elevating the humble meatball to high art, the Meatball Shop serves up five varieties of juiciness (including a vegetable option). Order those balls on a hero, add mozzarella and spicy tomato sauce, and voilà, you have a tasty if happily downmarket meal. The Lower East Side branch

boasts a rock-and-roll vibe, with tattooed waitstaff and prominent beats. There are four other branches in NYC, including one in Williamsburg (p280).

VANESSA'S DUMPLING HOUSE CHINESE **$**
Map p416 (☑212-625-8008; 118 Eldridge St, btwn Grand & Broome Sts; dumplings $1-6; ⊙7:30am-10:30pm; ⓈB/D to Grand St, J to Bowery, F to Delancey St) Tasty dumplings – served steamed, fried or in soup – are whipped together in iron skillets at light speed and tossed into hungry mouths at unbeatable prices.

**CLINTON STREET
BAKING COMPANY** AMERICAN **$**
Map p416 (☑646-602-6263; www.clintonstreet-baking.com; 4 Clinton St, btwn Stanton & Houston Sts; mains from $9-17; ⊙8am-4pm & 6-11pm Mon-Sat, 9am-6pm Sun; ⓈJ/M/Z to Essex St, F to Delancey St, F to Second Ave) Mom-and-pop shop extraordinaire, Clinton Street Baking Company gets the blue ribbon in so many categories – best pancakes (blueberry!

EAST VILLAGE & LOWER EAST SIDE EATING

LOCAL KNOWLEDGE

TIPS FROM THE MAESTRO OF MEATBALLS

Michael Chernow – restaurateur, food writer and co-owner of the Meatball Shop – talks favorite foods and hangouts in NYC with Lonely Planet's Cristian Bonetto.

A Perfect Day in NYC

Sunday is always my favorite day in NYC. My wife and I live in Brooklyn, so we usually start with yogurt, fruit and granola at **Roebling Tea Room** (Map p438; www.roeblingtearoom.com; 143 Roebling St, Brooklyn; lunch $6-18, dinner mains $15-24; ⊙10am-11pm Sun-Thu, to 11:30pm Fri & Sat; ⓈL to Bedford Ave, G to Metropolitan Ave) before grabbing coffee to go at Toby's Estate (p291), which now also has a branch in Manhattan (p170). We then head to Brooklyn Flea for antiques, vintage clothes and some grub, before hitting the West Village for a little shopping. From here we walk down to Balthazar (p93) for more coffee and a pastry from their bakery. The benches outside Balthazar offer some of the best people-watching in the city. Dinner might be at **Tomoe** (Map p418; ☑212-777-9346; www.tomoesushi.com; 172 Thompson St, btwn Houston & Bleecker Sts; sushi rolls from $4.50, combo platters $19.95; ⊙5-11pm Mon-Sat, 1-3pm Tue-Sat, 5-10pm Sun; ⓈA/C/E to Spring St, N/R to Prince St, B/D/F, M to Broadway-Lafayette St) in Greenwich Village, which does a fantastic salmon ceviche.

Three NYC Must-Eats

In Manhattan, don't miss the burger at the Spotted Pig (p140). The meat is amazingly tender and paired with a healthy portion of Roquefort cheese. The shoestring fries with fried garlic are delicious too. In Brooklyn, pizzeria **Motorino** (Map p438; www.motorinopizza.com; 139 Broadway, at Bedford Ave, Williamsburg; pizzas $10-18; ⊙11am-midnight Sun-Thu, to 1am Fri & Sat; ⓈJ/M to Marcy Ave) gets the sauce, dough and crust just right. At my own restaurant, the meatball smash with pork meatballs, provolone cheese and spicy meat sauce is like an explosion in your mouth.

Ultimate Tip

Eat early. If you can't book a table, get to the restaurant by 6pm. Have a second meal (later that night) if you're still hungry.

swoon!), best muffins, best po'boys (southern-style sandwiches), best biscuits etc – that you're pretty much guaranteed a stellar meal no matter what time of day (or night) you stop by. Half-priced bottles of wine sweeten the deal on Monday and Tuesday, officially keeping the doors spinning every night of the week.

KUMA INN — PAN-ASIAN $$

Map p416 (212-353-8866; 113 Ludlow St, btwn Delancey & Rivington Sts; small dishes $8-14; dinner Tue-Sun; F, J/M/Z to Delancey-Essex Sts) Reservations are a must at this popular spot in a secretive 2nd-floor location (look for a small red door with 'Kuma Inn' painted on the concrete side). The Filipino-and Thai-inspired tapas runs the gamut, from vegetarian summer rolls (with jicama) to spicy drunken shrimp, and pan-roasted scallops with bacon and sake.

Bring your own beer, wine or sake (corkage fee applies).

BOIL — SEAFOOD $$

Map p416 (139 Chrystie St, btwn Delancey & Broome Sts; shrimp/crab from $12/30 per pound; 5-11pm Mon-Fri, to midnight Sat & Sun) When the waitstaff asks if you'd care for rubber gloves and a bib, you know you're in for a dining adventure. Crustaceans, of course, are the reason you're here and you'll make an ungodly mess tearing into succulent Dungeness crab, lobster, crawfish, shrimp and clams (hence the gloves). Craft beers go down nicely with the proceedings. Cash only.

'INOTECA — ITALIAN $$

Map p416 (212-614-0473; 98 Rivington St, at Ludlow St; mains $7-17; noon-1am; F/V to Lower East Side-2nd Ave) It's worth joining the crowd waiting at the cramped bar of this airy, dark-wood-paneled corner haven to choose from *tramezzini* (small sandwiches on white or whole-wheat bread), panini (pressed sandwiches) and bruschetta options, all delicious and moderately priced. The truffled egg toast, a square of bread hollowed out in its center and filled with egg, truffles and fontina cheese, is a signature favorite.

But you can't go wrong, whether you choose the beet-orange-mint salad, vegetable lasagna built with layers of eggplant rather than pasta, or a plate of garlicky mussels. There's also a list of 200 wines, 25 of them available by the glass.

HOTEL CHANTELLE — FRENCH $$

Map p416 (92 Ludlow St, btwn Broome & Delancey Sts; mains brunch $15-19, dinner $15-27; 6-11pm Mon-Fri, noon-5pm & 6-11pm Sat, noon-5pm Sun) The appeal of the Hotel Chantelle, which isn't actually a hotel, is its lovely rooftop dining area. Don't bother coming for a mediocre evening meal, or wasting time in the top-40-playing downstairs bar – instead come for the weekend brunch, when you can sip spicy Bloody Marys, nibble on fluffy servings of French toast and most importantly listen to old-timey jazz bands playing the background. For brunching alfresco, there's no better downtown spot.

KATZ'S DELICATESSEN — DELI $$

Map p416 (212-254-2246; www.katzsdelicatessen.com; 205 E Houston St, at Ludlow St; pastrami on rye $17; 8am-10:45pm Mon-Wed & Sun, to 2:45am Thu-Sat; F to 2nd Ave) Though visitors won't find many remnants of the classic, old-world-Jewish Lower East Side dining scene, there are a few stellar holdouts, among them the famous Katz's Delicatessen, where Meg Ryan faked her famous orgasm in the 1989 Hollywood flick *When Harry Met Sally,* and where, if you love classic deli grub like pastrami and salami on rye, it just might have the same effect on you.

FAT RADISH — MODERN BRITISH $$$

Map p416 (17 Orchard St, btwn Hester & Canal Sts; mains $18-28; noon-3:30pm daily, 5:30pm-midnight Mon-Sat, to 10pm Sun; F to East Broadway, B/D to Grand St) The young and fashionable pack into this dimly lit dining room with exposed white brick and industrial touches. There's a loud buzz and people checking each other out but the mains, typical of the local-seasonal-haute-pub-fare fad, are worth your attention. Start off with big briny oysters before moving on to beetroot and Swiss chard crumble or Atlantic skate with honeycrisp apples. Good vegetarian options.

FREEMANS — AMERICAN $$$

Map p416 (212-420-0012; www.freemansrestaurant.com; end of Freeman Alley; mains lunch $12-19, dinner $22-32; 11am-11:30pm Mon-Fri, from 10am Sat & Sun; F to 2nd Ave) Tucked down a back alley, the charmingly located Freemans draws a mostly hipster crowd who let their chunky jewelry clang on the wooden tables as they lean over to sip overflowing cocktails. Potted plants and taxidermic antlers lend an endearing hunting-cabin vibe – a charming escape from the bustle (when there isn't a crowd inside).

DRINKING & NIGHTLIFE

East Village

In the East Village, as a general rule, the further east you go the looser things get. Like the myriad eating options in the area, nightlife is served up across quite the gamut: you'll find dirty dive bars stuffed to the gills with NYC students, and secret swanky lounges tucked behind the Japanese restaurant right next door. Things are positively packed come the weekend.

OST CAFE CAFE

Map p414 (441 E 12th St, cnr Ave A; ⏰7:30am-10pm Mon-Fri, from 8:30am Sat & Sun; [S]L to First Ave) If you seek a charming spot to drink a frothy latte this is the place. With exposed brick walls, pressed tin ceiling, velvety armchairs and marble-topped cafe tables, Ost Cafe has class. It also has excellent coffee drinks (the kind that are topped with foam art) and wines by the glass (around $11).

WAYLAND BAR

Map p414 (700 E 9th St, cnr Ave C; ⏰5pm-4am; [S]L to 1st Ave) Whitewashed walls, weathered floorboards and salvaged lamps give this urban outpost a Mississippi flair, which goes just right with the live music on weekdays (bluegrass, jazz, folk). The drinks, though, are the real draw – in particular the 'I hear banjos,' made of apple pie moonshine, rye whiskey and applewood smoke, which tastes like a campfire (but slightly less burning). Decent drink specials and $1 oysters from 5pm to 7pm on weekdays.

PROLETARIAT BAR

Map p414 (102 St Marks Pl, btwn First Ave & Ave A; ⏰5pm-2am; [S]L to 1st Ave) The cognoscenti of NYC's beer world pack this tiny, 10-stool bar just west of Tompkins Square Park. Promising 'rare, new and unusual beers,' Proletariat delivers the goods with a changing lineup of brews you won't find elsewhere. Recent hits have included drafts from artisanal brewers like Hitachino Nest of Japan, Swiss-based BFM and Mahr's Bräu in Germany.

GOLDEN CADILLAC BAR

Map p414 (13 First Ave, cnr 1st St; ⏰5pm-2am Sun-Wed, to 4am Thu-Sat; [S]2nd Ave) This enticing new drinking spot pays homage to grittier, hard-drinking days of the 1970s, with glorious wood paneling, patterned wallpaper and groove-heavy '70s tunes (disco, funk) playing overhead – plus 1970s Playboy covers in the bathroom. The tasty, tropical-themed cocktails (around $14 a pop) go down easy – try the Mezcal Mule (mezcal, passion fruit, ginger and cucumber) – and there's vintage pub grub with a twist (steak Diane with mushroom gravy, deviled eggs with uni and caviar, veggie meatloaf and jello for dessert).

ABC BEER CO BAR

Map p414 (96 Ave C, btwn 6th & 7th Sts; ⏰noon-midnight Sun-Thu, to 2am Fri & Sat) At first glance, ABC looks like a dimly lit beer shop (indeed bottles are available for purchase), but venture deeper inside and you'll find a small indie-rock-playing gastropub in back, with a long communal table and a few plush leather sofas and chairs set against the brick walls. The generally young crowd come for craft beer (350 by the bottle and 12 constantly rotating selections on draft), plus cheese plates, smoked meats and delicious sandwiches (good value at $8 each). There's also a small patio out the back.

TERROIR WINE BAR

Map p414 (☎646-602-1300; www.wineisterroir.com; 413 E 12th St, btwn First Ave & Ave A; ⏰5pm-2am Mon-Sat, to midnight Sun; [S]L to 1st Ave, 6 to Astor Pl) Removing the pretension from the wine bar experience, Terroir spins vino by the tome-ful on smooth communal tables made from large scraps of wood. A delightful assortment of bar bites (including superlative panini) makes a strong case for teetotalers with boozy friends. There are three other locations in town, plus a seasonal outdoor spot on the High Line.

MCSORLEY'S OLD ALE HOUSE BAR

Map p414 (☎212-474-9148; 15 E 7th St, btwn Second & Third Aves; ⏰11am-1am Mon-Sat, from 1pm Sun; [S]6 to Astor Pl) Around since 1854, McSorley's feels far removed from the East Village veneer of cool: you're more likely to drink with firemen, Wall St refugees and a few tourists. It's hard to beat the cobwebs and sawdust floors and flip waiters who slap down two mugs of the house ale for every one ordered.

120

GARDEL BERTRAND / GETTY IMAGES ©

1. St Marks Place (p109)
Visit one of NYC's most famous streets, jam-packed with historical tidbits.

2. Eldridge Street Synagogue (p112)
Check out this newly restored house of worship, as well as its on-site museum.

3. Cooper Union (p109)
Marvel at the bold architecture of the Cooper Union design institute as you explore Astor Place.

4. Tompkins Square Park (p110)
Wander through this 10.5-acre park in the heart of the East Village.

DEATH + CO
LOUNGE

Map p414 (☎212-388-0882; www.deathandcompany.com; 433 E 6th St, btwn First Ave & Ave A; 🕒6pm-1am Mon-Thu & Sun, to 2am Fri & Sat; [S]F to 2nd Ave, L to 1st Ave, 6 Astor Pl) Relax amid dim lighting and thick wooden slatting and let the bartenders – with their PhDs in mixology – work their magic as they shake, rattle and roll some of the most perfectly concocted cocktails ($14 to $16) in town.

ANGEL'S SHARE
BAR

Map p414 (☎212-777-5415; 2nd fl, 8 Stuyvesant St, near Third Ave & E 9th St; 🕒5pm-midnight; [S]6 to Astor Pl) Show up early and snag a seat at this hidden gem, behind a Japanese restaurant on the same floor. It's quiet and elegant with creative cocktails, but you can't stay if you don't have a table or a seat at the bar, and they tend to go fast.

EASTERN BLOC
GAY

Map p414 (☎222-777-2555; www.easternblocnyc.com; 505 E 6th St, btwn Aves A & B; 🕒7pm-4am; [S]F to 2nd Ave) Though the theme may be 'Iron Curtain,' the drapery is most definitely velvet and taffeta at this East Village gay bar. Hang your jacket at the 'Goat Czech' and spring forth into the cramped and crowded sea of boys – some flirting with the topless barkeeps, others pretending not to stare at the retro '70s porno playing on the TVs.

TEN DEGREES BAR
WINE BAR

Map p414 (☎212-358-8600; www.10degreesbar.com; 121 St Marks Pl, btwn First Ave & Ave A; 🕒noon-4am Mon-Sun; [S]F to Second Ave, L to First Ave, L to Third Ave) This small candlelit St Marks charmer is a great spot to start out the night with leather couches, friendly bartenders and an excellent wine and cocktails list. Come from noon to 8pm for two-for-one drink specials (otherwise, it's $10 to $13-ish for cocktails), or get half-priced bottles of wine on Monday night. Go for the couches up front or grab a tiny table in the back nook.

IMMIGRANT
WINE & BEER

Map p414 (☎212-677-2545; www.theimmigrantnyc.com; 341 E 9th St, btwn First & Second Aves; 🕒5pm-1am Mon-Wed & Sun, to 2am Thu, to 3am Fri & Sat; [S]L to 1st Ave, 4/6 to Astor Pl) Wholly unpretentious, these twin boxcar-sized bars could easily become your neighborhood local if you decide to stick around town. The staff are knowledgeable and kind, mingling with faithful regulars while dishing out tangy olives and topping up glasses with imported tipplrd.

Enter the right side for the wine bar, with an excellent assortment of wines by

LOCAL KNOWLEDGE

RAIN CHECK(LIST)

Teresa Soroka, rainy day guru and owner of Amé Amé (p208), gives us her insider tips for making the most of those inevitable days of drizzle.

➡ **Circle Line** (p389) Take the Circle Line ferry around Manhattan while absorbing the changing scenery and the grand stature of New York's city skyscrapers – it's especially magical in the rain.

➡ **Lower East Side Tenement Museum** (p106) While everybody's at the Met or MoMA, check out the history of American immigrants at this wonderfully interactive museum.

➡ **Upright Citizens Brigade Theatre** (p154) There's nothing like a good laugh at one of the city's best improvisational theaters when you feel like the weather is raining on your parade.

➡ **Grand Central Station** (p186) New Yorkers hustle and bustle differently when it's raining, and you can feel it when you're at Grand Central. Don't miss the historic, celestial ceiling, and if you meet the dress code, have a chic cocktail at the Campbell Apartment.

➡ **American Museum of Natural History** (p236) No matter your age, it's hard not to let your imagination wander at the dinosaur displays at the American Museum of Natural History. Take a rainy day nap under the big blue whale.

➡ **Cloisters Museum & Gardens** (p255) A nice drizzle is the perfect background to take in the medieval architecture at the Cloisters Museum & Gardens while having a mini-escape within Manhattan. Stroll through Fort Tryon Park and then immerse yourself in the castles and arches of mystery and wonder.

the glass. The left entrance takes you into the tap room, where the focus is on unique microbrews. Both have a similar design – chandeliers, exposed brick, vintage charm.

CIENFUEGOS BAR

Map p414 (☎212-614-6818; www.cienfuegosny.com; 95 Ave A, btwn 6th & 7th Sts; ⏲6pm-2am Sun-Thu, to 3am Fri & Sat; [S]F to Second Ave, L to First Ave, 4/6 to Astor Pl) If Fidel Castro had a stretched Cadillac, its interior would look something like the inside of New York's foremost rum-punch joint. A sampler of tasty Cuban dishes makes the perfect midnight snack. If you like this place, then make a pit stop at the connected **Amor y Amargo** (Map p414; www.amoryamargo.com; 443 E 6th St, btwn Ave A & First Ave; ⏲5pm-11pm Mon-Wed & Sun, to midnight Thu, to 1am Fri-Sat; [S]F to 2nd Ave, L to 1st Ave, 4/6 to Astor Pl) – Cienfuegos' tiny bitters-centric brother.

JIMMY'S NO 43 BAR

Map p414 (☎212-982-3006; www.jimmysno43.com; 43 E 7th St, btwn Third & Second Aves; ⏲noon-2am Mon-Thu & Sun, to 4am Fri & Sat; [S]N/R to 8th St-NYU, F to Second Ave, 4/6 to Astor Pl) Barrels and stag antlers line the walls of this basement beer hall up to the ceiling as locals chug their drinks. Select from over 50 imported favorites (a dozen on draft) to go with a round of delectable locally sourced bar nibbles.

MAYAHUEL COCKTAIL BAR

Map p414 (☎212-253-5888; 304 E 6th St, at Second Ave; ⏲6pm-2am; [S]L to 3rd Ave, L to 1st Ave;,6 to Astor Pl) About as far from your typical spring break tequila bar as you can get – more like the cellar of a monastery. Devotees of the fermented agave can seriously indulge themselves experimenting with dozens of varieties (all cocktails $14); in between drinks, snack on quesadillas and tamales.

🍷 Lower East Side

The Lower East Side still clings to its status as the coolest 'hood in Manhattan. While some bars are favored by the 'bridge and tunnel' gang (not to mention tourists, ahem), the locals still adore newfound clubs that stage Manhattan's next indie-rock kings. There's something for everyone here, with booze and beer usually a lot cheaper than in most of the island's other areas – just walk up and down the tiny blocks and peek in.

TEN BELLS TAPAS BAR

Map p416 (☎212-228-4450; 247 Broome St, btwn Ludlow & Orchard Sts; ⏲5pm-2am Mon-Fri, from 3pm Sat & Sun; [S]F to Delancey St, J/M/Z to Essex St) This charmingly tucked-away tapas bar has a grotto-like design, with flickering candles, dark tin ceilings, brick walls and a U-shaped bar that's an ideal setting for conversation with a new friend. The chalkboard menu hangs on both walls and features excellent wines by the glass, which go nicely with *boquerones* (marinated anchovies), *txipirones en su tinta* (squid in ink sauce), regional cheeses and refreshing oysters (just $1.25 each before 7pm). The unsigned entrance is easy to miss. It's right next to the shop Top Hat.

STANTON SOCIAL LOUNGE

Map p416 (99 Stanton St, btwn Orchard & Ludlow Sts; ⏲5pm-1am) Skip the restaurant on the first floor, and head upstairs to the stylish lounge with a somewhat speakeasy vibe – a nondescript steel door leads into the unmarked space. Here you'll find a well-dressed downtown crowd mingling over craft cocktails ($13 each) and groovy DJs.

CASA MEZCAL BAR

Map p416 (86 Orchard St, btwn Broome & Grand Sts; ⏲noon-2am Sun-Thu, to 4am Fri & Sat) This festive three-story arts space celebrates the rich eating, drinking and musical traditions of Mexico – and Oaxaca in particular. The tall-ceilinged main room is decorated with colorful paper streamers, masks, Day-of-the-Dead skulls, and other folk art. Downstairs is Obra Negra (black sheep) featuring live concerts, DJ nights and the odd burlesque show. Upstairs is a lounge-like gallery that hosts live jazz on Wednesday nights.

BEAUTY & ESSEX BAR

Map p416 (☎212-614-0146; www.beautyandessex.com; 146 Essex St, btwn Stanton & Rivington Sts; ⏲5pm-1am; [S]F to Delancey St, J/M/Z to Essex St) This newcomer's glamour is concealed behind a tawdry pawnshop front space. Beyond lies 10,000-sq-ft of sleek lounge space, complete with leather sofas and banquettes, dramatic amber-tinged lighting and a curved staircase that leads to yet another lounge and bar area.

Ladies in need of a drink might want to bypass the bar and pay a visit to the powder room, where there's complimentary champagne (sorry, fellas).

CAKE SHOP BAR, CAFE

Map p416 (152 Ludlow St, btwn Stanton & Rivington Sts; ⌚9am-2am Sun-Thu, to 4am Fri & Sat; [S]F to Second Ave, F to Delancey St, J/M/Z to Essex St) This little cafe and bar has a downtown bohemian vibe, with a small selection of vinyl for sale up front and a few tables in back, fine for nursing an evening beer or pastry (it's not called Cake Shop for nothing) while admiring your neighbor's intriguing tattoos. There's a stage downstairs where indie bands play ($10 cover) throughout the week, but the small space can get cramped quickly.

BARRIO CHINO COCKTAIL BAR

Map p416 (☎212-228-6710; 253 Broome St, btwn Ludlow & Orchard Sts; ⌚11:30am-4:30pm & 5:30pm-1am; [S]F, J/M/Z to Delancey-Essex Sts) An eatery that spills easily into a party scene, with an airy Havana-meets-Beijing vibe and a focus on fine sipping tequilas. Or stick with fresh blood-orange or black-plum margaritas, guacamole and chicken tacos.

WELCOME TO THE JOHNSONS BAR

Map p416 (☎212-420-9911; 123 Rivington St, btwn Essex & Norfolk Sts; ⌚4:30pm-4am Mon-Fri, from 1pm Sat & Sun; [S]F, J/M/Z to Delancey-Essex Sts) Set up like a '70s game room – a bit sleazier than the one on *That '70s Show* – the Johnsons' irony still hasn't worn off for the devoted 20-something crowd. It could have something to do with the cheap beer, the pool table, the blasting garage-rock jukebox or the plastic-covered sofas.

BARRAMUNDI LOUNGE

Map p416 (☎212-529-6999; 67 Clinton St, btwn Stanton & Rivington Sts; ⌚6pm-4am; [S]F, J/M/Z to Delancey-Essex Sts) This Australian-owned arty place fills an old tenement building with convivial booths, reasonably priced drinks (including some Aussie imports) and some cool tree-trunk tables. Happy hour runs 6pm to 9pm.

☆ ENTERTAINMENT

☆ East Village

STONE LIVE MUSIC

Map p414 (www.thestonenyc.com; Ave C, at 2nd St; admission $15-25; ⌚shows 8pm & sometimes 10pm; [S]F/V to Lower East Side-Second Ave) Created by renowned downtown jazz cat John Zorn, the Stone is about the music and nothing but the music, in all its experimental and avant-garde forms. There's no bar or frills of any kind, just folding chairs on a concrete floor.

SIDEWALK CAFÉ COUNTRY, FOLK

Map p414 (☎212-473-7373; www.sidewalkmusic.net; 94 Ave A, at 6th St; [S]F/V to Lower East Side-Second Ave; 6 to Astor Pl) Anti-folk forever! Never mind the Sidewalk's burger-bar appearance outside; inside is the home of New York's 'anti-folk' scene, where the Moldy Peaches carved out their legacy before Juno got knocked up. The open-mike 'anti-hootenanny' is Monday night. Poetry slams happen most Tuesdays.

LA MAMA ETC THEATER

Map p414 (☎212-475-7710; www.lamama.org; 74A E 4th St; admission $10-20; [S]F to Second Ave) A long-standing home for onstage experimentation (the ETC stands for Experimental Theater Club), La MaMa is now a three-theater complex with a cafe, an art gallery and a separate studio building that features cutting-edge dramas, sketch comedy and readings of all kinds.

NEW YORK THEATER WORKSHOP THEATER

Map p414 (☎212-460-5475; www.nytw.org; 79 E 4th St, btwn Second & Third Aves; [S]F to 2nd Ave) Recently celebrating its 25th year, this innovative production house is a treasure to those seeking cutting-edge, contemporary plays with purpose. It was the originator of two big Broadway hits, *Rent* and *Urinetown,* and offers a constant supply of high-quality drama.

ANTHOLOGY FILM ARCHIVES CINEMA

Map p414 (☎212-505-5181; www.anthologyfilmarchives.org; 32 Second Ave, at 2nd St; [S]F to 2nd Ave) Opened in 1970, this theater is dedicated to the idea of film as an art form. It screens indie works by new filmmakers and also revives classics and obscure oldies, from Luis Buñuel to Ken Brown's psychedelia.

NUYORICAN POETS CAFÉ ARTS

Map p414 (☎212-780-9386; www.nuyorican.org; 236 E 3rd St; cover $10-20; ⌚shows 9pm or 10pm; [S] F to Lower East Side-Second Ave) Still going strong after 40-plus years, the legendary Nuyorican is home to poetry slams, hip-hop performances, plays, and film and video events. It's a piece of East Village history, but also a vibrant and still-relevant nonprofit arts organization. Buy VIP tickets online to skip the discouraging queues.

AMORE OPERA
OPERA

Map p414 (www.amoreopera.org; Connelly Theater, 220 E 4th St, btwn Aves A & B; tickets $40; SF to 2nd Ave) This company, formed by several members of the now defunct Amato Opera, presents well-known works such as *The Magic Flute*, *La Bohème*, *The Mikado* and *Hansel and Gretel*, performed at its East Village theater. The appeal? Much cheaper tickets and a more intimate setting than most opera venues.

SING SING KARAOKE
KARAOKE

Map p414 (212-387-7800; www.karaokesinging.com; 9 St Marks Pl; SN/R to 8th St-NYU, L to 3rd Ave, 6 to Astor Pl) A chuckle-worthy reference to the nearby state prison, Sing Sing is exactly as it sounds – swing by to belt your heart out.

☆ Lower East Side

SWEET
COMEDY

Map p416 (Slipper Room; 212-253-7246; www.slipperroom.com; 167 Orchard St, at Stanton St; admission $5; ⊘shows 9pm Tue; SF to 2nd Ave, F to Delancey St, J/M/Z to Essex St) There are tons of small comedy houses scattered around the city, but we're pretty sure you haven't heard of this one – a local gig hosted at the Slipper Room every Tuesday by Seth Herzog and his gang of friends (including his mother who loves to get up in front of the small crowd and discuss her weekly list of grievances).

BOWERY BALLROOM
LIVE MUSIC

Map p416 (212-533-2111; www.boweryballroom.com; 6 Delancey St, at Bowery St; J/Z to Bowery) This terrific, medium-sized venue has the perfect sound and feel for more blown-up indie-rock acts (The Shins, Stephen Malkmus, Patti Smith).

DELANCEY
LIVE MUSIC

Map p416 (212-254-9920; www.thedelancey.com; 168 Delancey St at Clinton St; SF to Delancey St, J/M/Z to Essex St) Surprisingly stylish for the Lower East Side, the Delancey hosts some popular local bands for doting indie-rock crowds. A good early-evening spot for a drink too, particularly on the palm-fringed 2nd-floor patio deck.

PIANOS
LIVE MUSIC

Map p416 (212-505-3733; www.pianosnyc.com; 158 Ludlow St, at Stanton St; cover $8-10; ⊘noon-4am; SF to 2nd Ave) Nobody's bothered to change the sign at the door, a leftover from the location's previous incarnation as a piano shop. Now it's a musical mix of genres and styles, leaning more toward pop, punk and new wave, but throwing in some hip-hop and indie for good measure. Sometimes you get a double feature – one act upstairs and another below.

SLIPPER ROOM
BURLESQUE

Map p416 (www.slipperroom.com; 212-253-7246; 167 Orchard St, entrance on Stanton St; admission $7-15; SF to 2nd Ave) Shuttered in 2010, the Slipper Room is back, and looking better than ever thanks to a major renovation. The two-story club hosts a wide range of performances, including Seth Herzog's popular variety show *Sweet* and several weekly burlesque shows, which feature a mash-up of acrobatics, sexiness, comedy and absurdity – generally well worth the admission. Tickets available online.

ROCKWOOD MUSIC HALL
LIVE MUSIC

Map p416 (212-477-4155; www.rockwoodmusichall.com; 196 Allen St, btwn Houston & Stanton Sts; SF/V to Lower East Side-Second Ave) Opened by indie rocker Ken Rockwood, this breadbox-sized concert space has three stages that see a rapid-fire flow of bands and singer/songwriters. With no cover charge, and a limit of one hour per band (die-hards can see five or more a night), what's to lose? Music kicks off at 3pm on weekends, 6pm on weeknights.

LANDMARK SUNSHINE CINEMA
CINEMA

Map p416 (212-260-7289; www.landmarktheatres.com; 143 E Houston St, btwn Forsyth & Eldridge Sts; SF/V to Lower East Side-Second Ave) A renovated Yiddish theater, the wonderful Landmark shows foreign and first-run mainstream art films on massive screens. It also has much-coveted stadium style seating, so it doesn't matter what giant sits in front of you after the lights go out.

ABRONS ARTS CENTER
THEATER, ARTS

Map p416 (212-598-0400; www.abronsartscenter.org; 466 Grand St, cnr Pitt St; ⚙; SF, J, M, Z to Delancey St-Essex St) This venerable cultural hub has three theaters, the largest being the Harry de Jur Playhouse (a national landmark), with its own lobby, fixed seats on a rise, a large, deep stage and good visibility. A mainstay of the downtown Fringe Festival, Abrons Art Center is also your best bet to catch experimental and community productions – including avant-garde jazz brought to you by the former Tonic nightclub, which was driven out of the Lower East Side by rising rents. Not afraid of difficult subjects, Abrons sponsors plays and dance and photography exhibits that don't get much play elsewhere.

SHOPPING

East Village

In the East Village – once known as the archetype of underground downtown style – you'll find urban and outsider fashion, but new local designers, sleeker shops and chain stores have also moved into the area, taking away from the neighborhood's former edginess.

VERAMEAT JEWELRY

Map p414 (☎212-388-9045; 315 E 9th St, btwn First & Second Aves; ⏰noon-8pm; [S]6 to Astor Pl) Designer Vera Balyura creates exquisite pieces with a dark sense of humor in this delightful little shop on 9th St. Tiny, artfully wrought pendants, rings, earrings and bracelets appear almost too precious, until a closer inspection reveals zombies, godzilla robots, animal heads, dinosaurs and encircling claws – bringing a whole new level of miniaturized complexity to the realm of jewelry.

DINOSAUR HILL CHILDREN

Map p414 (☎212-473-5850; www.dinosaurhill.com; 306 E 9th St; ⏰11am-7pm; [S]6 to Astor Pl) A small, old-fashioned toy store that's inspired more by imagination than Disney movies, this shop has loads of great gift ideas: Czech marionettes, shadow puppets, micro building blocks, calligraphy sets, toy pianos, art and science kits, kids' music CDs from around the globe and wooden blocks in half-a-dozen different languages, plus natural-fiber clothing for infants.

STILL HOUSE GLASSWARE

Map p414 (☎212-539-0200; 117 E 7th St; ⏰noon-8pm; [S]6 to Astor Pl) Step into this petite and peaceful boutique to browse sculptural glassware and pottery: handblown vases, geometric tabletop objects, ceramic bowls and cups and other finery for the home. You'll also find minimalistic jewelry, delicately bound notebooks and small framed artworks for the wall. In all, Still House has lots of great gift ideas, and the objects are small enough to bring home (but quite delicate, so make sure they're well wrapped).

NO RELATION VINTAGE VINTAGE CLOTHING

Map p414 (☎212-228-5201; 204 First Ave, btwn 12th & 13th Sts; ⏰noon-8pm Sun-Thu, to 9pm Fri & Sat; [S]L to First Ave) Among the many vintage shops of the East Village, No Relation is a winner for its wide-ranging collections that run the gamut from denim and leather jackets to flannels, sneakers, plaid shirts, Levi's aplenty, candy-colored T-shirts, varsity jackets, clutches and more. Sharpen your elbows: hipster crowds flock here on weekends.

TOKIO 7 CONSIGNMENT STORE

Map p414 (☎212-353-8443; www.tokio7.net; 83 E 7th St, near First Ave; ⏰noon-8pm; [S]6 to Astor Pl) This revered, hip consignment shop on a shady stretch of E 7th St, has good-condition designer labels for men and women at some fairly hefty prices. The Japanese-owned store often features lovely pieces by Issey Miyake and Yohji Yamamoto, as well as a well-curated selection of Dolce & Gabbana, Prada, Chanel and other top labels. Watch out for that giant alien thing out front (made of repurposed machine parts).

SUSTAINABLE NYC CLOTHING

Map p414 (☎212-254-5400; 139 Ave A, btwn St Marks Pl & 9th St; ⏰8am-10pm Mon-Fri, 9am-10pm Sat & Sun; [S]6 to Astor Pl) Across from Tompkins Square Park, this ecofriendly shop offers all sorts of home and office gear for living green. Organic T-shirts, wind-up radios and flashlights (no batteries required), soy and beeswax candles, recycled clocks made of vinyl records and Toms shoes are all on hand. There's a small cafe on-site.

ST MARK'S BOOKSHOP BOOKS

Map p414 (☎212-260-7853; www.stmarksbookshop.com; 31 Third Ave, btwn St Marks Pl & 9th St; ⏰10am-midnight Mon-Sat, 11am-midnight Sun; [S]6 to Astor Pl) Actually located one block away from St Marks Pl (it moved long ago), this indie bookshop specializes in political literature, poetry, new nonfiction and novels and academic journals. There's also a superior collection of magazines, both glossy and otherwise.

At press time, the bookshop was planning a move to a cheaper space a few blocks east. Check the website for the latest details.

JOHN DERIAN HOMEWARES

Map p414 (☎212-677-3917; 6 E 2nd St, btwn the Bowery & Second Ave; 🕐noon-7pm Tue-Sun; [S]F/V to Lower East Side-Second Ave) John Derian is famed for its decoupage – pieces from original botanical and animal prints stamped under glass. The result is a beautiful collection of one-of-a-kind plates, paperweights, coasters, lamps, bowls and vases.

PATRICIA FIELD FASHION

Map p414 (☎212-966-4066; 306 Bowery St, at 1st St; 🕐11am-8pm Sun-Thu, to 9pm Fri & Sat; [S]F to 2nd Ave) The fashion-forward stylist for *Sex and the City,* Patricia Field isn't afraid of flash, with feather boas, pink jackets, disco dresses, graphic and color-block T-shirts and leopard-print heels, plus colored frizzy wigs, silver spandex and some wacky gift ideas for good measure.

OBSCURA ANTIQUES ANTIQUES

Map p414 (☎212-505-9251; 207 Ave A, btwn 12th & 13th Sts; 🕐noon-8pm Mon-Sat, to 7pm Sun; [S]L to 1st Ave) This small cabinet of curiosities pleases both lovers of the macabre and inveterate antique hunters. Here you'll find taxidermic animal heads, tiny rodent skulls and skeletons, butterfly displays in glass boxes, photos of dead people, disturbing little (dental?) instruments, German landmine flags (stackable so tanks could see them), old poison bottles, glass eyes, cane-toad purses (sure to please the Aussie crowd), Zippos from Vietnam soldiers, anatomical drawings, a two-headed calf, a stuffed hyena and other items not currently available at the local department store.

KIEHL'S BEAUTY

Map p414 (☎212 677-3171; 109 Third Ave, btwn 13th & 14th Sts; 🕐10am-8pm Mon-Sat, 11am-6pm Sun; [S]L to 3rd Ave) Making and selling skincare products since it opened in NYC as an apothecary in 1851, this Kiehl's flagship store has doubled its shop size and expanded into an international chain, but its personal touch remains – as do the coveted, generous sample sizes.

JOHN VARVATOS FASHION, SHOES

Map p414 (☎212-358-0315; 315 Bowery, btwn 1st & 2nd Sts; 🕐noon-8pm Mon-Sat, to 6pm Sun; [S]F to 2nd Ave, 6 to Bleecker St) Set in the hallowed halls of former punk club CBGB, the John Varvatos Bowery store goes to great lengths to tie fashion with rock-and-roll, with records, '70s audio equipment and even electric guitars for sale alongside JV's denim, leather boots, belts and graphic tees.

🛍 Lower East Side

The downtown fashion crowd looking for that edgy, experimental or 'old-school hip-hop' look head to the shops in the Lower East Side. Sprinkled among the area's many bars and restaurants are dozens of stores selling vintage apparel, vegan shoes, old-fashioned candy, sex toys, left-wing books and more. Swing by the Essex Street Market (p112) for bagels, smoked salmon, tacos, gourmet cheeses, ice cream and other edible temptations.

TOP HAT ACCESSORIES

Map p416 (☎212-677-4240; 245 Broome St, btwn Ludlow & Orchard Sts; 🕐noon-8pm; [S]B/D to Grand St) Sporting curios from around the globe, this whimsical little shop is packed with intrigue: from vintage Italian pencils and handsomely miniaturized leather journals to beautifully carved wooden bird

UP-AND-COMING WOMEN'S CLOTHING BOUTIQUES

In NYC's ever-ephemeral shopping scene, boutiques – like style trends – come and go on a whim. The following three shops are a great starting point in seeking hot new downtown fashions:

Spiritual America (Map p416; ☎212-960-8564; www.spiritualameri.ca; 5 Rivington St, btwn the Bowery & Chrystie St; 🕐noon-8pm Mon-Fri, 11am-7pm Sat & Sun; [S]F to Lower East Side-2nd Ave)

Reformation (Map p416; ☎646-448-4925; www.thereformation.com; 156 Ludlow St, btwn Rivington & Stanton Sts; 🕐noon-8pm Mon-Sat, to 7pm Sun; [S]F to Delancey St, F to 2nd Ave, J/M/Z to Essex St)

Yumi Kim (Map p416; ☎212-420-5919; www.yumikimshop.com; 105 Stanton St, btwn Ludlow & Essex Sts; 🕐noon-7pm; [S]F to Delancey St, F to 2nd Ave, J/M/Z to Essex St)

whistles. If you're looking for an endless rain album, a toy clarinet, Japanese fabrics, a crumpled map of the night sky or geometric Spanish cups and saucers, you'll find all this and more at fanciful Top Hat.

BY ROBERT JAMES
FASHION

Map p416 (☎212-253-2121; www.byrobertjames. com; 74 Orchard St; ☺noon-8pm Mon-Sat, to 6pm Sun; ⓢF to Delancey St, J/M/Z to Essex St) Rugged, beautifully tailored menswear is the mantra of Robert James, who sources and manufactures right here in NYC (the design studio in fact is just upstairs). The racks are lined with slim-fitting denim, handsome button-downs, and classic-looking sports coats. Lola, James' black lab, sometimes roams the store. He also has a store in Williamsburg.

EDITH MACHINIST
VINTAGE

Map p416 (☎212-979-9992; 104 Rivington St, at Essex St; ☺noon-7pm Tue-Sat, to 6pm Sun; ⓢF to Delancey St, J/M/Z to Essex St) To properly strut about the Lower East Side, you've got to dress the part. Edith Machinist can help you get that rumpled but stylish look in a hurry – a bit of vintage glam via knee-high soft suede boots, 1930s silk dresses and ballet-style flats.

DRESSING ROOM
CLOTHING

Map p416 (☎212-966-7330; www.thedressing-roomnyc.com; 75a Orchard St, btwn Broome & Grand Sts; ☺1pm-midnight Tue & Wed, 1pm-2am Thu-Sat, 1:30-8pm Sun; ⓢF, J/M/Z to Delancey-Essex Sts) The Dressing Room is a creative hybrid that's equal parts indie fashion boutique and low-key drinking spot. On the 1st floor, you'll find emerging labels like Out of Print, with its catchy graphic T-shirts of vintage book covers, as well as flouncy black dresses and wildly patterned knits, while downstairs is a small selection of vintage clothes.

Adjoining the space is a casual bar – a fine spot to linger over a drink while your shopping partner browses the wares.

REED SPACE
FASHION, ACCESSORIES

Map p416 (☎212-253-0588; www.thereedspace. com; 151 Orchard St, btwn Stanton & Rivington Sts; ☺1-7pm Mon-Fri, noon-7pm Sat & Sun; ⓢF to Delancey-Essex Sts) Sneakers, accessories, youthful tees, pants and jackets for both sexes line the bright and varied shelves at Reed Space. Designer Jeff Ng has found a blueprint for the urban casual lifestyle.

MOO SHOES
SHOES

Map p416 (☎212-254-6512; www.mooshoes. com; 78 Orchard St, btwn Broome & Grand Sts; ☺11:30am-7:30pm Mon-Sat, noon-6pm Sun; ⓢF to Delancey St, J/M/Z to Essex St) This earth-and animal-friendly boutique sells surprisingly stylish microfiber (faux leather) shoes, handbags and wallets. Look for ballet flats from Love Is Mighty, rugged men's oxfords by Novacos and sleek Matt & Nat wallets.

BLUESTOCKINGS
BOOKS

Map p416 (☎212-777-6028; www.bluestockings. com; 172 Allen St, btwn Stanton & Rivington Sts; ☺11am-11pm; ⓢF/V to Lower East Side-Second Ave) This independent bookstore, which first opened with a lesbian bent, has now expanded its turf to a wide range of topics, including feminism, globalism and African American studies. It's also the site of a vegan, organic, fair-trade cafe, as well as myriad readings and speaking events.

🏃 SPORTS & ACTIVITIES

RUSSIAN & TURKISH BATHS
BATHHOUSE

Map p414 (☎212-674-9250; www.russianturkish-baths.com; 268 E 10th St, btwn First Ave & Ave A; per visit $35; ☺noon-10pm Mon-Tue & Thu-Fri, from 10am Wed, from 9am Sat, from 8am Sun; ⓢL to First Ave, 6 to Astor Pl) Since 1892, this has been the spa for anyone who wants to get naked (or stay in their swimsuit) and romp in steam baths, an ice-cold plunge pool, a sauna and on the sundeck. The baths are open to both men and women most hours (wearing shorts is required at these times), though at some times it's men or women only. Check the website for more detailed opening hours.

Greenwich Village, Chelsea & the Meatpacking District

GREENWICH VILLAGE | THE MEATPACKING DISTRICT | CHELSEA

Neighborhood Top Five

1 Packing a picnic lunch from Chelsea Market and having a uniquely pastoral moment on the thin strand of green along **The High Line** (p131) as it soars above the gridiron.

2 Checking out the city's brightest art stars at the top **Chelsea galleries** (p144).

3 Walking through **Washington Square Park** (p134), pausing under the signature arch then loitering at the fountain to cavesdrop on gossiping NYU kids.

4 Exploring fascinating exhibitions from the Himalayas and beyond at the **Rubin Museum of Art** (p137).

5 Sipping lattes alfresco on cobblestone corners and browsing the latest boutiques in the **West Village** (p146).

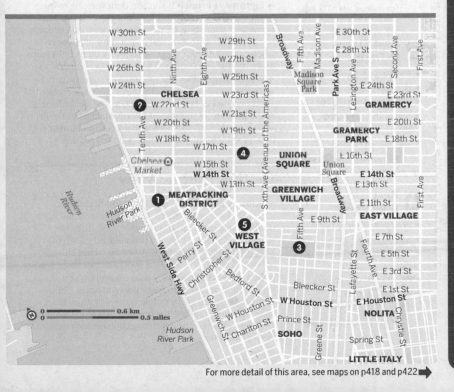

For more detail of this area, see maps on p418 and p422 ➡

Lonely Planet's Top Tip

It's perfectly acceptable to arm yourself with a map (or rely on your smartphone) to get around the West Village's charming-but-challenging side streets. Even some locals have a tricky time finding their way! Just remember that 4th St makes a diagonal turn north – breaking away from the usual east–west street grid – and you'll quickly become a Village pro.

 ### Best Places to Eat

➡ Jeffrey's Grocery (p140)
➡ Rosemary's (p140)
➡ RedFarm (p139)
➡ Chelsea Market (p143)
➡ Foragers City Table (p143)

For reviews, see p137 ➡

🍷 Best Places to Drink

➡ Bell Book & Candle (p146)
➡ Buvette (p146)
➡ Jane Ballroom (p146)
➡ Top of the Standard (p147)
➡ Marie's Crisis (p147)

For reviews, see p145 ➡

🔒 Best Bookshops

➡ Printed Matter (p158)
➡ Strand Book Store (p155)
➡ Three Lives & Company (p156)
➡ Posman Books (p158)
➡ Bonnie Slotnick Cookbooks (p156)

For reviews, see p155 ➡

Explore Greenwich Village, Chelsea & the Meatpacking District

There's a very good reason why this area is known as the Village: it actually looks like one! Quaint, quiet lanes carve their way between brown-brick townhouses offering endless strolling for locals appreciating good weather, or tourists coming to see what all the fuss is about. The Village is indeed picturesque, and the best way to uncover its treasures is to simply have a wander, and when your feet grow tired of negotiating the cobbled streets plunk yourself down at a cafe with a frothy cappuccino or a glass of wine.

Stroll through the Meatpacking District – once filled with slaughterhouses and now brimming with sleek boutiques and roaring nightclubs – to reach Chelsea just to the north. Chelsea bridges the gap between the West Village and Midtown, importing bits and bobs from both. It's the de facto neighborhood for the city's sociable gay community, and its broad avenues are lined with breezy cafes, themed bars and sweaty clubs. The neighborhood's massive gallery scene can be found in the West 20s.

Local Life

➡ **Eighth Ave brunch** If you're a dude looking to meet (or at least look at) other dudes, but the cruise-y bar scene isn't your style, then opt for the weekend brunch scene along Eighth Ave. You'll spot piles of friendly Chelsea boys drinking their hangovers off in tight jeans and even tighter T-shirts.

➡ **West Village cafes** The quizzes and surveys can't be wrong – the West Village is the most desirable residential neighborhood in Manhattan, so do as the locals do and make the most of this quaint district stacked to the brim with cute cafes. Grab a book and a latte and hunker down for a blissful afternoon of people-watching.

Getting There & Away

➡ **Subway** Sixth Ave, Seventh Ave and Eighth Ave are graced with convenient subway stations, but public transportation slims further west. Take the A/C/E or 1/2/3 lines to reach this colorful clump of neighborhoods – disembark at 14th St (along either service) if you're looking for a good place to make tracks.

➡ **Bus** Try M14 or the M8 if you're traveling across town and want to access the westernmost areas of Chelsea and the West Village by public transportation. It's a shame, however, to use the bus or a taxi to get around the West Village – the charming cobblestone streets are perfect for a stroll.

HUW JONES / GETTY IMAGES ©

TOP SIGHT
THE HIGH LINE

In the early 1900s, the western area around the Meatpacking District and Chelsea was the largest industrial section of Manhattan, and a set of elevated rail tracks were created to move freight off the cluttered streets below. As NYC evolved, the rails eventually became obsolete, and in 1999 a plan was made to convert the scarring strands of metal into a public green space. On June 9, 2009, part one of the city's most beloved urban renewal project opened with much ado, and it's been one of New York's star attractions ever since.

Industrial Past

It's hard to believe that the High Line – a shining example of brilliant urban renewal – was once a dingy rail line that anchored a rather unsavory district of thugs, trannies and slaughterhouses. The tracks that would one day become the High Line were commissioned in the 1930s when the municipal government decided to raise the street-level tracks after years of accidents that gave Tenth Ave the nickname 'Death Avenue.' The project drained over $150 million in funds (equivalent to around $2 billion by today's dime) and took roughly five years to complete. After two decades of effective use, a rise in truck transportation led to the eventual decrease in usage, and finally, in the 1980s, the rails became obsolete. Petitions were signed by local residents to remove the eyesores, but in 1999 a committee called the Friends of the High Line – founded by Joshua David and Robert Hammond – was formed to save the rusting iron and transform the tracks into a unique elevated green space.

DON'T MISS...

- The amphitheater-style viewing platforms at 17th and 26th Sts
- Spencer Finch's art installation *The River That Flows Both Ways* between 15th and 16th Sts

PRACTICALITIES

- Map p418
- ☎212 500-6035
- www.thehighline.org
- Gansevoort St
- 🕐7am-7pm
- 🚌M11 to Washington St, M11, M14 to 9th Ave, M23, M34 to 10th Ave, [S]L or A/C/E to 14th St-8th Ave, C/E to 23rd St-8th Ave

PUBLIC ART DISPLAYS

In addition to being a haven of hovering green, the High Line is also an informal art space featuring a variety of installations, both site-specific and stand-alone. For detailed information about the public art on display at the time of your visit, check out www.art.thehighline.org.

Like the smattering of ever-evolving art, the High Line also invites various gastronomic establishments from around the city to set up vending carts and stalls so that strollers can enjoy to-go items on the green. Expect a showing of the finest coffee and ice-cream establishments during the warmer months.

A Green Future

On a warm spring day in 2009, the High Line – full of blooming flowers and broad-leaved trees – opened to the public, the first of three planned phases that will one day link the Meatpacking District and Midtown. Section 1 starts at Gansevoort St and runs parallel to Tenth St up to W 20th St. Full of sitting space in various forms - from giant chaise longues to bleacher-like benching - the first part quickly became the setting for various public works and activities, many geared towards the neighborhood's growing population of families. Two years later, section 2 opened, adding another 10 blocks of green-ified tracks. The final section is slated to be completed by late 2014. Here the High Line meanders from 30th up to 34th St, going up to and around the West Side Rail Yards in a U-like fashion. As it veers west toward 12th Ave, it will go closer to the river than any of the other sections. Barring any design changes, the final stretch aims to preserve the feel of an overgrown wilderness, with the old original tracks left in place. It will also feature a dedicated children's play area – a jungle gym made up of exposed beams covered in a soft play surface.

More Than Just a Public Space

The High Line's civic influence extends far beyond being the trendsetter in the island's re-green-ification. As the West Village and Chelsea continue to embrace their new-found residential nature, the High Line is making a dedicated move towards becoming more than just a public place but an inspired meeting point for families and friends. As you walk along the High Line you'll find staffers wearing shirts with the signature double-H logo who can point you in the right direction or offer you additional information about the converted rails. There are also myriad staffers behind the scenes organizing public art exhibitions and activity sessions for family and friends. Free tours take place on Tuesday nights at 6:30pm on warmer months. Sign up near the 14th St entrance. Arrive early to get a spot. Other special tours and events explore a variety of topics: history, horticulture, design, art and food. Check the event schedule on the website for the latest details.

If you're interested in helping support the High Line through financial donations, you can become a member of the Friends of the High Line association through the website. 'Spike' level members receive a discount at stores in the area, from Diane von Furstenberg's boutique to Amy's Bread, a tasty food outlet in the Chelsea Market.

BARRY WINIKER / GETTY IMAGES ©

TOP SIGHT
CHELSEA MARKET

In a shining example of redevelopment and preservation, the Chelsea Market has taken a former factory of cookie giant Nabisco (creator of the Oreo) and turned it into an 800ft-long shopping concourse that caters to foodies. And that's only the lower part of a larger, million-sq-ft space that occupies a full city block – upstairs you'll find the current home of several TV channels, including the Food Network and NY1, the local news channel.

National Biscuit Company

Continuing the building's significance as a major landmark, the renamed Chelsea Market opened in the 1990s as a base camp for gourmet outlets and apparel boutiques.

A New Generation of Sweets

Taking the place of the old factory ovens that churned out massive numbers of biscuits are the boutique bakeries that fill the renovated hallways of this foodie haven. **Eleni's** (Map p422; ☎212-255-6804) is of special note – Eleni Gianopulos was one of the first tenants here, and her expertly designed cookies are a big hit. **Amy's Bread** (Map p422; www.amysbread.com) has fine loaves that make a brilliant tribute to the hundreds of ovens that once inhabited the buildings.

Also worth a stop is **Tuck Shop** (Map p422; www.tuckshopnyc.com), serving Aussie-style savory pies, rolls (sausage and sage, or spinach and ricotta), lamingtons and homemade sodas. Sweet-tooths will fawn over the icy outpost of **l'Arte Del Gelato** (Map p422; www.lartedelgelato.com). Gelato flavors are made fresh every day and come in over 20 varieties – it's the perfect snack to take up to the High Line. Seafood lovers will want to stroll through **Lobster Place** (Map p422; www.lobsterplace.com), with its displays of fresh fish and crustaceans. Hint: there's a sushi counter hidden inside.

DON'T MISS...

- Amy's Bread
- Lobster Place
- The High Line out back

PRACTICALITIES

- Map p422
- www.chelseamarket.com
- 75 Ninth Ave at 15th St
- 🕒7am-10pm Mon-Sat, 8am-9pm Sun
- [S]A/C/E to 14th St, L to 8th Ave

TOP SIGHT
WASHINGTON SQUARE PARK

What was once a potter's field and a square for public executions is now the unofficial town square of the Village. It plays host to lounging NYU students, fire-eating street performers, curious canines and their owners, and legions of speed-chess pros. Encased in perfectly manicured brownstones and gorgeous twists of modern architecture (all owned by NYU), Washington Square Park is one of the most striking garden spaces in the city – especially as you are welcomed by the iconic Stanford White Arch on the north side of the green.

DON'T MISS...

➡ Stanford White Arch
➡ Central fountain
➡ Greek Revival houses surrounding the park

PRACTICALITIES

➡ Map p418
➡ Fifth Ave at Washington Sq N
➡ S A/C/E, B/D/F/M to W 4th St-Washington Sq, N/R to 8th St-NYU

History

Although quite ravishing today, Washington Square Park has had a long and sordid history before finally blossoming into the paradigm of public space we now see (thanks largely to a $16 million renovation that began in 2007).

When the Dutch settled Manhattan to run the Dutch East India Company, they gave what is now the park to their freed black slaves. The land was squarely between the Dutch and Native American settlements, so, in a way, the area acted as a buffer between enemies. Though somewhat marshy, it was arable land and farming took place for around 60 years.

At the turn of the 19th century, the municipality of New York purchased the land for use as a burial ground straddling the city's limit. At first the cemetery was mainly for indigent workers, but the space quickly reached capacity during an outbreak of yellow fever. Over 20,000 bodies remain buried under the park today.

By 1830 the grounds were used for military parades, and then quickly transformed into a park for the wealthy elite who were constructing lavish townhouses along the surrounding streets.

Stanford White Arch

The iconic Stanford White Arch, colloquially known as the Washington Square Arch, dominates the park with its 72ft of beaming white Dover marble. Originally designed in wood to celebrate the centennial of George Washington's inauguration in 1889, the arch proved so popular that it was replaced with stone six years later and adorned with statues of the general in war and peace. In 1916 artist Marcel Duchamp famously climbed to the top of the arch by its internal stairway and declared the park the 'Free and Independent Republic of Washington Square.'

In Recent Years

Once it was clear that the park was here to stay, the public green became a haven for beatniks and political outcry, especially when urban planners sought to change the shape and usage of the space. Locals vehemently protested, and the square's shape has remained largely unchanged since the 1800s.

The political tradition has continued in more recent times – Barack Obama led a rally here in 2007 to drum up support for his presidential bid. Turnout was, unsurprisingly, overwhelming.

SIGHTS

Greenwich Village & the Meatpacking District

THE HIGH LINE OUTDOORS

See p131.

WASHINGTON SQUARE PARK PARK

See p134.

NEW YORK UNIVERSITY UNIVERSITY

Map p418 (NYU; ☎212-998-2222; www.nyu.edu; information center 50 W 4th St [S]A/C/E, B/D/F/M to W 4th St-Washington Sq, N/R to 8th St-NYU) In 1831 Albert Gallatin, formerly Secretary of the Treasury under President Thomas Jefferson, founded an intimate center of higher learning open to all students, regardless of race or class background. He'd scarcely recognize the place today, as it's swelled to a student population of more than 54,000, with upwards of 16,000 employees, and schools and colleges at six Manhattan locations. It just keeps growing, too – to the dismay of landmark activists and business owners, who have seen buildings rapidly bought out by the academic giant (or destroyed through careless planning, such as with the historic Provincetown Playhouse) and replaced with ugly dormitories or administrative offices. Still, some of its crevices are charming, such as the leafy courtyard at its School of Law, or impressively modern, like the Skirball Center for the Performing Arts, where top-notch dance, theater, music, spoken-word and other performers wow audiences at the 850-seat theater. NYU's academic offerings are highly regarded and wide-ranging, especially its film, theater, writing, medical and law programs. For a unique experience that will put you on the fast track to meeting locals, sign up for a weekend or one-day class – from American history to photography – offered by the School of Professional Studies and Continuing Education, and open to all.

GRACE CHURCH CHURCH

Map p418 (☎212-254-2000; www.gracechurch-nyc.org; 802 Broadway, at 10th St; ⏰10am-5pm, services daily; [S]N/R to 8th St-NYU, 6 to Astor Pl) This Gothic Revival Episcopal church, designed in 1843 by James Renwick Jr, was made of marble quarried by prisoners at 'Sing Sing,' the state penitentiary in the town of Ossining, 30 miles up the Hudson River (which, legend has it, is the origin of the expression 'being sent upriver'). After years of neglect, Grace Church is being spiffed up in a major way; now it's a National Landmark, whose elaborate carvings, towering spire and verdant, groomed yard are sure to stop you in your tracks as you make your way down this otherwise ordinary stretch of the Village. The stained-glass windows inside are stunning, and the soaring interior makes a perfect setting for the frequent organ and choir concerts. Free guided tours are offered at 1pm on Sundays.

FORBES COLLECTION MUSEUM

Map p418 (☎212-206-5548; www.forbesgalleries.com; 62 Fifth Ave, at 12th St; ⏰10am-4pm Tue-Sat; [S]L, N/Q/R, 4/5/6 to 14th St-Union Sq) [FREE] These galleries, located in the lobby of the headquarters of *Forbes* magazine, house rotating exhibits and curios from the personal collection of the late publishing magnate Malcolm Forbes. The eclectic mix of objects on display includes Fabergé eggs, toy boats, early versions of Monopoly and over 10,000 toy soldiers.

ABINGDON SQUARE SQUARE

Map p418 (Hudson St, at 12th St; [S]A/C/E to 14th St, L to Eighth Ave) This historic dot on the landscape (just a quarter acre) is a lovely little patch of green, home to grassy knolls, beds of perennial flowers and winding bluestone paths, as well as a popular Saturday greenmarket. It's a great place to enjoy a midday picnic or rest after an afternoon of wandering the winding West Village streets. After getting horizontal, look up at the southern end of the park and you'll see the *Abingdon Doughboy,* a bronze statue dedicated to servicemen from the neighborhood who gave their lives in WWI (when soldiers were commonly known as 'doughboys').

PIER 45 OUTDOORS

Map p418 (W 10th St, at Hudson River; [S]1 to Christopher St-Sheridan Sq) Still known to many as the Christopher Street Pier, this is an 850ft-long finger of concrete, spiffily renovated with a grass lawn, flower beds, a comfort station, an outdoor cafe, tented shade shelters and a stop for the New York Water Taxi as part of the Hudson River Park. And it's a magnet for downtowners of all stripes, from local families with toddlers in daylight to mobs of young gay kids who flock here at night from all over

TOP SIGHT
HUDSON RIVER PARK

The High Line may be all the rage these days, but one block away there stretches a 5-mile-long ribbon of green that has dramatically transformed the city over the past 10 years.

Covering 550 acres, and running from Battery Park at Manhattan's southern tip to 59th St in Midtown, the Hudson River Park is Manhattan's wondrous backyard. The long riverside path is a great spot for running, strolling and cycling, and the **Waterfront Bicycle Shop** (Map p418; www.bikeshopny.com; 391 West St, btwn W 10th & Christopher Sts; rentals per 1/4hr $10/20; ⏲10am-7pm) is a convenient place to rent bikes; several boathouses (p159) offer kayak hire and longer excursions for the more experienced. There's also beach volleyball, basketball courts, a skate park and tennis courts. Families with kids have loads of options, including four sparkling new playgrounds, a carousel (off W 22nd St) and mini-golf (Pier 25 off West St near N Moore St).

Those who simply need a break from the city come here to loll on the grass (those seeking something less sedate can join the sangria- and sun-loving crowds at the dockside Frying Pan (p152). And of course on the Fourth of July, there's no better place in the city to be.

DON'T MISS...

- Kayaking on the river
- Sunset strolls
- Summertime drinks at Frying Pan

PRACTICALITIES

- Map p418
- www.hudsonriverpark.org

the city (and beyond) because of the pier's long-established history as a gay cruising hangout. The spot offers sweeping views of the Hudson and cool, relieving breezes in the thick of summer.

WHITE COLUMNS GALLERY

Map p418 (☎212-924-4212; www.whitecolumns.org; 320 W 13th St, entrance on Horatio St btwn Hudson St & Eighth Ave; ⏲noon-6pm Tue-Sat; [S]A/C/E, L to Eighth Ave-14th St) [FREE] Geographically, White Columns is part of the Meatpacking District, but aesthetically speaking, it's in Chelsea. The sedate, multi-room space hosts a wide range of exhibits and installations, some of which are by fairly well-known names like Andrew Serrano, Alice Aycock, Lorna Simpson and a White Columns founder, Gordon Matta-Clark.

Chelsea

CHELSEA MARKET MARKET

See p133.

CHELSEA HOTEL HISTORIC BUILDING

Map p422 (☎212-243-3700; 222 W 23rd St, btwn Seventh & Eighth Aves; [S]1, C/E to 23rd St) It's probably not any great shakes as far as hotels go – and besides, it mainly houses long-term residents – but as a place of mythical proportions, the Chelsea Hotel is top of the line. The red-brick hotel, featuring ornate iron balconies and no fewer than seven plaques declaring its literary landmark status, has played a major role in pop-culture history.

It's where the likes of Mark Twain, Thomas Wolfe, Dylan Thomas and Arthur Miller hung out; Jack Kerouac allegedly crafted *On the Road* during one marathon session here, and it's where Arthur C Clarke wrote *2001: A Space Odyssey*. Dylan Thomas died of alcohol poisoning while staying here in 1953, and Nancy Spungen died here after being stabbed by her Sex Pistols boyfriend Sid Vicious in 1978. Among the many celebs who have logged time living at the Chelsea are Joni Mitchell, Stanley Kubrick, Dennis Hopper, Edith Piaf, Bob Dylan and Leonard Cohen, whose song 'Chelsea Hotel' recalls a romp with Janis Joplin (who spent time here, too).

Big changes are underway at the Chelsea. In 2011, the hotel was sold to a luxury developer and closed for renovations. Long-term residents, however, remained – largely because it was illegal to evict them. The property was then resold in 2013 to yet another luxury developer, and the future of the building remains uncertain.

GENERAL THEOLOGICAL SEMINARY RELIGIOUS
Map p422 (☎212-243-5150; www.gts.edu; 440 W 21st St, btwn Ninth & Tenth Aves; ⏰10am-5:30pm Mon-Fri; [S]C/E to 23rd St) [FREE] Founded in 1817, this is the oldest seminary of the Episcopal Church in America. The school, which sits in the midst of the beautiful Chelsea historic district, has been working hard lately to make sure it can preserve its best asset – the garden-like campus snuggled in the middle of its full block of buildings – even as Chelsea development sprouts up all around it.

This peaceful haven is the perfect spot for finding respite, either before or after your neighborhood gallery crawl. To visit, ring the buzzer at the garden gate, located halfway down 21st St between Ninth & Tenth Aves.

RUBIN MUSEUM OF ART MUSEUM
Map p422 (☎212-620-5000; www.rmanyc.org; 150 W 17th St, at Seventh Ave; adult/child $10/free, 6-10pm Fri free; ⏰11am-5pm Mon & Thu, to 9pm Wed, to 10pm Fri, to 6pm Sat & Sun; [S]1 to 18th St) This is the first museum in the Western world to dedicate itself to the art of the Himalayas and surrounding regions. Its impressive collections include embroidered textiles from China, metal sculptures from Tibet, Pakistani stone sculptures and intricate Bhutanese paintings, as well as ritual objects and dance masks from various Tibetan regions, spanning from the 2nd to the 19th centuries.

Rotating exhibitions have included the enlightening *Red Book of CJ Jung* and *Victorious Ones,* which comprises sculptures and paintings of Jinas, the founding teachers of Jainism. The Cafe Serai serves traditional Himalayan foods and features live music on Wednesday nights, from 5pm onwards. Later in the week, the cafe transforms into the K2 Lounge, where you can sip wine and martinis, after visiting the galleries on free Friday evenings.

ANDREA ROSEN GALLERY GALLERY
Map p422 (☎212-627-6000; www.andrearosengallery.com; 525 W 24th St; ⏰10am-6pm Tue-Sat; [S]C/E, 1 to 23rd St) Oversized installations are the norm at this spacious gallery, where curators fill every inch of space (and the annex Gallery 2 next door) in interesting ways. Rosen opened her gallery in 1990 and quickly made a name for herself. She's showcased John Currin's 'pale portraits,' Felix Gonzalez-Torres' 'Vultures' and Tetsumi Kudo's oil paintings, to name just a few of her artists.

🍴 EATING

While the West Village is known for its classy, cozy and intimate spots, the adjacent Meatpacking District's dining scene is a bit more ostentatious, complete with nightclub-like queues behind velvet ropes, bold decor and swarms of trend-obsessed patrons. Chelsea strikes a balance between the two with a brash assortment of *très* gay eateries along the uber-popular Eighth Ave (a must for see-and-be-seen brunch), and more cafes lining Ninth Ave further west. In the warmer months expect windows and doors to fling open and plenty of alfresco seating to spill out onto the streets, be they the concrete of Chelsea or the cobblestone of the Village.

🍴 Greenwich Village & the Meatpacking District

★MOUSTACHE MIDDLE EASTERN $
Map p418 (☎212-229-2220; www.moustachepitza.com; 90 Bedford Sts btwn Grove & Barrow Sts; mains $8-17; ⏰noon-midnight; [S]1 to Christopher St-Sheridan Sq) Small and delightful Moustache serves up rich, flavorful sandwiches (leg of lamb, *merguez* sausage, falafel), thin-crust pizzas, tangy salads and hearty specialties like *ouzi* (filo stuffed with chicken, rice and spices) and moussaka. The best start to a meal: a platter of hummus or baba ghanoush, served with fluffy, piping hot pitas. It's a warm, earthy space with copper-topped tables and brick walls.

OTTO ENOTECA PIZZERIA PIZZERIA, ITALIAN $
Map p418 (☎212-995-9559; www.ottopizzeria.com; 1 Fifth Ave, near 8th St; mains $9-15; ⏰lunch & dinner; [S]A/C/E, B/D/F/M to W 4th St-Washington Sq) Just north of Washington Square Park, this is a refreshingly affordable part of Mario Batali's empire, a pizza palace where thin pizzas are cooked on flat iron griddles till they crackle perfectly. They come topped with items far beyond

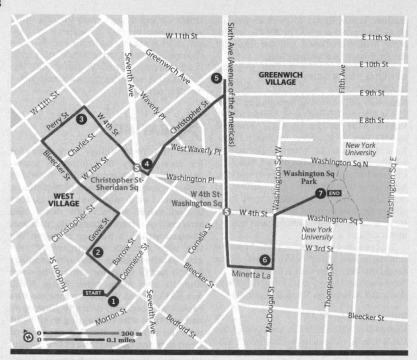

W 11th St · E 11th St · Sixth Ave (Avenue of the Americas) · Greenwich Ave · E 10th St · Seventh Ave · GREENWICH VILLAGE · Fifth Ave · E 9th St · W 11th St · Waverly Pl · Christopher St · E 8th St · Perry St · ❸ · W 4th St · Charles St · West Waverly Pl · New York University · Washington Sq N · Washington Sq E · Bleecker St · W 10th St · ❹ · Washington Pl · Washington Sq Park · Christopher St-Sheridan Sq · S · W 4th St-Washington Sq · Washington Sq W · ❼ END · WEST VILLAGE · Christopher St · Grove St · S · W 4th St · Washington Sq S · New York University · Cornelia St · W 3rd St · ❷ · Barrow St · Commerce St · Bleecker St · ❻ · Minetta La · MacDougal St · Thompson St · Hudson St · START · ❶ · Morton St · Seventh Ave · Bedford St · Bleecker St · 0 — 200 m · 0 — 0.1 miles

🏃 Neighborhood Walk
It Takes a Village...

START COMMERCE ST
END WASHINGTON SQUARE PARK
LENGTH 1 MILE; 1 HOUR

Of all the neighborhoods in New York City, Greenwich Village is the most pedestrian-friendly, with its cobbled corners that stray from the signature gridiron that unfurls across the rest of the island. Start your walkabout at the ❶ **Cherry Lane Theater** (p153). Established in 1924, the small theater is the city's longest continuously running off-Broadway establishment, and was the center of creative activity during the 1940s. Make a left on Bedford and you'll find ❷ **90 Bedford** on the right-hand side at the corner of Grove St. You might recognize the apartment block as the fictitious home of the cast of *Friends* (sadly, Central Perk was just a figment of the writers' imaginations). For another iconic TV landmark, wander up Bleecker St and make a right on Perry St, stopping at ❸ **66 Perry St**, which was used as the facade and stoop of the city's 'It Girl,' Carrie Bradshaw, in *Sex and the City*. Make a right on W 4th St until

you reach ❹ **Christopher Park**, where two white, life-sized statues of same-sex couples stand guard. On the north side of the green space is the legendary Stonewall Inn, where a clutch of fed-up drag queens rioted for their civil rights in 1969, signaling the start of what would become the gay revolution. Follow Christopher St to Sixth Ave to find the ❺ **Jefferson Market Library** straddling a triangular plot of land. The 'Ruskinian Gothic' spire was once a fire lookout tower. Today the structure houses a branch of the public library; in the 1870s it was used as a courthouse. Stroll down Sixth Ave taking in the flurry of passersby, then make a left on Minetta Lane to swing by ❻ **Cafe Wha?**, the notorious institution where many young musicians and comedians – like Bob Dylan and Richard Pryor – got their start. End your wandering further along MacDougal St in ❼ **Washington Square Park** (p134), the Village's unofficial town square, which plays host to loitering NYU students, buskers and a regular crowd of protestors chanting about various global and municipal injustices.

your standard pizza joint – fennel, goat's cheese, egg, fresh chilies, capers, the best fresh mozzarella – and sauce that has the perfect balance of smoky and sweet.

Pasta dishes (for just $11) veer toward the exotic, like penne with hazelnuts and butternut squash. And don't even think of leaving without trying the housemade gelato.

CAFE BLOSSOM VEGAN $

Map p418 (www.blossomnyc.com; 41 Carmine St, btwn Bleecker & Bedford Sts; small plates $8-16; ⏲5-10pm Mon-Fri, noon-10pm Sat, to 9pm Sun; 🌿; [S]A/C/E, B/D/F/M to W 4th St) Like the better-known Blossom in Chelsea, this romantic candlelit eatery serves first-rate organic vegan cuisine. The focus is on creative small plates meant for sharing: roasted oyster mushroom savory cakes, pizza with cashew, ricotta and smoked fennel, and agedashi crusted tofu with red Thai curry. There are also organic wines, beers and cocktails, plus luscious desserts.

TAÏM ISRAELI $

Map p418 (☎212-691-1287; www.taimfalafel.com; 222 Waverly Pl, btwn Perry & W 11th Sts; mains $6-12; ⏲11am-10pm; [S]1/2/3 to 14th St) This tiny joint whips up some of the best falafels in the city. You can order them Green (traditional style), Harissa (with Tunisian spices) or Red (with roasted peppers). Whichever you choose, you'll get them stuffed into pita bread with creamy tahini sauce and a generous dose of Israeli salad. There are also mixed platters, zesty salads and delicious smoothies (try the date, lime and banana).

THELEWALA INDIAN $

Map p418 (112 MacDougal St, btwn Bleecker & W 3rd Sts; rolls $4-6; ⏲11am-2am Sun-Thu, to 5am Fri & Sat; [S]A/C/E, B/D/F/M to W 4th St) This small, rockin' place serves up Calcutta-style street food: delicious rolls filled with the likes of minced lamb, paneer cheese, crispy okra and other ingredients. There are also *chaats* (savory snacks) and dishes like chickpea curry. Seating options – just a few stools at the counter – are limited, so get it to go, and devour your rolls (you'll want more than one) in nearby Washington Square Park.

VICTORY GARDEN ICE CREAM $

Map p418 (31 Carmine St, btwn Bleecker & Bedford Sts; ice cream $4-6; ⏲noon-11pm Mon-Sat, to 10pm Sun; [S]A/C/E, B/D/F/M to W 4th St) If you've never tried goat's milk ice cream, you're in for a treat. This small charming cafe doles out delectable soft-serve ice cream in flavors like salted caramel, chocolate made from Mexican stone-ground cocoa, and seasonal selections (watermelon, lemon poppy, roasted plum). The flavors change weekly, with four or so available each day.

SAIGON SHACK VIETNAMESE $

Map p418 (☎212-228-0588; www.saigonshacknyc.com; 114 MacDougal St, btwn Bleecker & 3rd Sts; mains $7-10; ⏲11am-11pm Sun-Thu, to 1am Fri & Sat; [S]A/B/C, B/D/F/M to W 4th St) Steaming bowls of *pho* (noodle soup), tangy *báhn mì* (baguette) sandwiches and crunchy spring rolls await at this bustling wood-lined eatery just a few strides from Washington Square Park. The prices are fair and the food arrives in a hurry. The only downside: you might have to wait for a table, as it's a popular draw for the NYU crowd.

BONSIGNOUR SANDWICHES $

Map p418 (☎212-229-9700; 35 Jane St, at Eighth Ave; mains $7-12; ⏲7:30am-10pm, to 8pm Sun; [S]L to 8th Ave, A/C/E, 1/2/3 to 14th St) Nestled on a quiet Village street, this sandwich shop offers dozens of delicious choices as well as salads, frittatas and a wonderful beef chili. Get a sandwich or a chicken curry salad to go and wander down the street to Abingdon Square for alfresco dining.

JOE'S PIZZA PIZZA $

Map p418 (☎212-366-1182; www.joespizzanyc.com; 7 Carmine St, btwn Sixth Ave & Bleecker St; slices from $3; ⏲10am-4:30am; [S]A/C/E, B/D/F/M to W 4th St; 1 to Christopher St-Sheridan Sq or Houston St) No-frills pies are served up indiscriminately to students, tourists and celebrities alike (everyone's stopped by for a bite, from Kirsten Dunst to Bill Murray).

★REDFARM FUSION $$

Map p418 (☎212-792-9700; www.redfarmnyc.com; 529 Hudson St, btwn 10th & Charles Sts; mains $19-49; ⏲5pm-11:45pm Mon-Sat, to 11pm Sun & 11am-2:30pm Sat & Sun; [S]A/C/E, B/D/F/M to W 4th St, 1 to Christopher St-Sheridan Sq) RedFarm transforms Chinese cooking into pure, delectable artistry at this small, buzzing space on Hudson St. Fresh crab and eggplant bruschetta, juicy rib steak (marinated overnight in papaya, ginger and soy) and pastrami egg rolls are among the many creative dishes that brilliantly blend East with West. Other hits include the spicy crispy beef, pan-fried lamb dumplings and the grilled jumbo shrimp red curry.

Waits can be long, so arrive early (reservations not accepted), or plan on a few cocktails at the bar on the lower level (scotch lovers: don't miss the Suntory Old-Fashioned).

★JEFFREY'S GROCERY MODERN AMERICAN $$

Map p418 (☎646-398-7630; www.jeffreysgrocery.com; 172 Waverly Pl, at Christopher St; mains $18-35; ⏰8am-11pm Sun-Wed, to 2am Thu-Sat; [S]1 to Christopher St-Sheridan Sq) A West Village classic, Jeffrey's is a lively spot that hits all the right notes. Seafood is the focus: there's an oyster bar and beautifully executed seafood selections such as razor clams with caviar and dill, whole roasted dourade with curry, and seafood platters to share. Meat dishes come in the shape of roasted chicken with Jerusalem artichoke, and a humble but juicy pastrami burger.

The scene: exposed brick, oversized windows, wood floors and a buzzing bar scene that draws more drinkers than diners as the night wears on. Brunch is fantastic.

ROSEMARY'S ITALIAN $$

Map p418 (☎212-647-1818; www.rosemarysnyc.com; 18 Greenwich Ave, at W 10th St; mains $12-26; ⏰8am-midnight; [S]1 to Christopher St-Sheridan Sq) Currently one of the West Village's hottest restaurants, Rosemary's serves high-end Italian fare that more than lives up to the hype. In a vaguely farmhouse-like setting, diners tuck into generous portions of housemade pastas, rich salads and cheese and *salumi* (cured meat) boards. Current favorites include the *acqua pazza* (seafood stew) and braised pork shoulder with roasted vegetables.

Some of the produce is grown in-house, or rather over the house, with a state-of-the art roof garden producing crisp dandelion greens, plump zucchinis and mouth-watering tomatoes. Plan for crowds (no reservations) or arrive early.

MORANDI ITALIAN $$

Map p418 (☎212-627-7575; www.morandiny.com; 211 Waverly Pl, btwn Seventh Ave & Charles St; mains $17-30; ⏰8am-midnight Mon-Fri, 10am-midnight Sat, 10am-11pm Sun; [S]1 to Christopher St-Sheridan Sq) Run by celebrated restaurateur Keith McNally, Morandi is a warmly lit space where the hubbub of garrulous diners resounds amid brick walls, wide plank floors and rustic chandeliers. Grab a seat at the copper-topped bar for wine, well-made cocktails and lighter fare (stuffed olives, antipasti, minestrone with pesto), or squeeze into a table for the full-meal experience (hand-rolled spaghetti with lemon and parmesan; meatballs with pine nuts and raisins; and grilled whole sea bream).

SPOTTED PIG PUB $$

Map p418 (☎212-620-0393; www.thespottedpig.com; 314 W 11th St, at Greenwich St; mains $16-35; ⏰11am-2am; 🍷👪; [S]A/C/E to 14th St, L to 8th Ave) This Michelin-starred gastro-pub is a favorite of Villagers, serving an upscale blend of hearty Italian and British dishes. Its two floors are bedecked with old-timey trinkets that give the whole place an air of relaxed elegance. It doesn't take reservations, so there is often a wait for a table. Lunch on weekdays is less crowded.

MINETTA TAVERN BISTRO $$

Map p418 (☎212-475-3850; www.minettatavernny.com; 113 MacDougal St; mains $19-35; ⏰5:30pm-1am Mon & Tue, 11am-3pm & 5:30pm-1am Wed-Sun; [S]A/C/E, B/D/F/M to W 4th St) Book in advance, or come early to snag a table on a weeknight, because Minetta Tavern is often packed to the rafters. The snug red-leather banquettes, dark-paneled walls with black-and-white photos, and glowing yellow bistro lamps will lure you in. The flavor-filled bistro fare – pan-seared marrow bones, roasted chicken, and mustn't-miss French dip sandwiches – will have you wishing you lived upstairs.

MALAPARTE ITALIAN $$

Map p418 (☎212-255-2122; www.malapartenyc.com; 753 Washington St, at Bethune St; mains $14-26; ⏰5:30pm-midnight Mon-Fri, from noon Sat & Sun; [S]A/C/E to 14th St, L to Eighth Ave) Tucked away on a peaceful stretch of the West Village, Malaparte is a charming neighborhood trattoria serving simple, beautifully executed Italian dishes – *garganelli* (tubular pasta) with porcini mushrooms and truffle oil, chewy crust pizzas, fennel and arugula salads, roasted cornish hen, and tiramisu (of course) for dessert. The focaccia bread basket, which arrives after you sit down, is a nice touch. Cash only.

FATTY CUE PAN-ASIAN $$

Map p418 (☎212-929-5050; www.fattycue.com; 50 Carmine St, btwn Bedford & Bleecker Sts; mains lunch $12-23, dinner $16-38; ⏰noon-11pm; [S]A/C/E to 14th St, L to Eighth Ave) On a restaurant-lined stretch of Carmine St, Fatty Cue serves up rich plates of barbecued meat with Asian accents. Stop in for brisket

LOCAL KNOWLEDGE

PARK IN THE SKY

Robert Hammond, cofounder of Friends of the High Line, talks about what, in his opinion, makes the 'park in the sky' and its surrounding neighborhood so special.

High Line Highlights

To me, the West Village is a reminder of New York's industrial past and residential future. What I love most about the High Line are its hidden moments, like at the Tenth Ave cut-out near 17th St. Most people sit on the bleachers, but if you turn the other way you can see the Statue of Liberty far away in the harbor. Architecture buffs will love looking down 18th St, and up on 30th is my favorite moment – a steel cut-out where you can see the cars underneath.

Stop-Offs

For lunch near the High Line, I recommend **Hector's Café & Diner** (Map p418; 44 Little W 12th St; mains $8-13; ⌚2am-10pm Mon-Sat). It's cheap, untouristy and not at all a see-and-be-seen spot – the cookies are great. If you're in the area, you have to visit the galleries in Chelsea – there are over 300 – and check out Printed Matter (p158), with its artist-made books. For an evening out on the town, head to the Boom Boom Room at the Top of the Standard (p147) – go early and book ahead.

Family-Friendly Activities

The High Line is also great for children with scheduled programming for kids on Saturdays and Wednesdays.

or pulled pork sandwiches at lunch, or fried chicken, dry-rub pork ribs and Isaan-spiced lamb by night. It's a stylish joint with dexterous bartenders whipping up inventive cocktails behind the bottle-lined bar.

DOMA NA ROHU CENTRAL EUROPEAN **$$**

Map p418 (☎212-929-4339; www.domanyc.com; 27½ Morton St, at 7th Ave; mains $15-21; ⌚noon-11pm Mon-Fri, 9am-midnight Sat & Sun; [S]1 to Houston St) In a charming tavern setting just off busy Seventh Ave, Doma serves up German and Czech comfort fare with a smile. Come for bratwurst, beef goulash and housemade *spaetzle* (dumplings) with seasonal vegetables, or stop in during happy hour for $3 glasses of beer and snack specials. Wednesday nights feature wild game, while *latkes* (potato pancakes) draw the weekend brunch crowd.

There's live 'gypsy jazz' on Saturday nights – or if you're around on the last Thursday of the month and feeling calorifically deprived, don't miss the pig roast, featuring abundant feasting and live music.

CAFÉ CLUNY BISTRO **$$**

Map p418 (☎212-255-6900; www.cafecluny.com; 284 W 12th St; mains lunch $14-24, dinner $18-34; ⌚8am-11:30pm Mon-Fri, 9am-11pm Sat & Sun; [S]L to 8th Ave, A/C/E, 1/2/3 to 14th St) Café Cluny brings the whimsy of Paris to the West Village, with woven bistro-style bar chairs, light wooden upholstery, and a selection of joie-de-vivre-inducing platters like *steak frîtes*, mixed green salads and roasted chicken.

ALTA TAPAS **$$**

Map p418 (☎212-505-7777; www.altarestaurant.com; 54 W 10th St, btwn Fifth & Sixth Aves; small plates $5-19; ⌚6-11pm, to midnight Fri-Sat; [S]A/C/E, B/D/F/V to W 4th St-Washington Sq) This gorgeous townhouse highlights the neighborhood's quaintness, with plenty of exposed brick, wood beams, flickering candles, massive mirrors and romantic fireplace glows. A small-plates menu of encyclopedic proportions cures indecision with the likes of succulent lamb meatballs, roasted snapper with artichoke puree, seared wild mushrooms, fried goat's cheese, and squid ink paella. The wine list is outstanding, too.

BARBUTO MODERN AMERICAN **$$**

Map p418 (☎212-924-9700; www.barbutonyc.com; 775 Washington St, btwn 12th & Jane Sts; mains $19-27; ⌚noon-11pm Mon-Wed, to midnight Thu-Sat, to 10pm Sun; [S]L to 8th Ave, A/C/E to 14th St, 1 to Christopher St-Sheridan Sq) Occupying a cavernous garage space with sweeping see-through doors that roll up and into the ceiling during the warmer months, Barbuto slaps together a delightful assortment of nouveau Italian dishes like pork loin with polenta and apple, and bruschetta smeared with duck liver, pistachio and balsamic.

EMPELLON MEXICAN $$

Map p418 (☎212-367-0999; www.empellon.com; 230 W 4th St, btwn Seventh Ave & 10th St; mains $10-24; ⏲5-11pm Mon-Wed, to midnight Thu-Sat; [S]1/2 to Christopher St-Sheridan Sq, A/C/E, B/D/F, M to W 4th St, 1/2/3 to 14th St) Chef Alex Stupak has transformed the all-important avocado into the most inventive and flavorful guacamole in town. He's also dropped the 'Tex' from Tex-Mex, creating imaginative south-of-the-corner fare that is wholly elegant and beautifully presented. The white-brick walls further accentuate the mural of luscious red petals behind the bar.

FATTY CRAB PAN-ASIAN $$

Map p418 (☎212-352-3590; www.fattycrab.com; 643 Hudson St, btwn Gansevoort & Horatio Sts; mains $16-35; ⏲noon-11pm Sun-Wed, to midnight Thu-Sat; [S]L to 8th Ave, A/C/E, 1/2/3 to 14th St) The Fatty folks have done it again with their small Malaysian-inspired joint in the thick of things on the west side. It's super hip and always teeming with locals who swing by in droves to devour fish curries and pork belly accompanied by a signature selection of cocktails.

SNACK TAVERNA GREEK $$

Map p418 (☎212-929-3499; www.snacktaverna.com; 63 Bedford St; small plates $12-14, large plates $22-28; ⏲7:30am-11pm Mon-Fri, 11am-11pm Sat, to 10pm Sun; [S]A/C/E, B/D to W 4 St, 1/2 to Christopher St-Sheridan Sq) So much more than a usual Greek restaurant, Snack Taverna eschews gyros for a seasonal selection of scrumptious small plates to accompany the flavorful selection of market mains. The regional wines are worth a miss, but the Med beers are surprisingly refreshing.

MURRAY'S CHEESE BAR CHEESE $$

Map p418 (www.murrayscheesebar.com; 246 Bleecker St; mains $12-17, cheese platters $12-16; ⏲noon-10pm Sun-Tue, to midnight Wed-Sat; [S]A/C/E, B/D/F/M to W 4th St) Lovers of fine cheeses no longer have to settle for take-out orders from Murray's famed West Village *fromagerie* (p157). Gourmet mac 'n' cheese, melted cheese sandwiches, French onion soup, and other cheese-centric dishes dominate the menu at this tile-lined eat-and-drinkery, though the cheese platters (especially the Cheesemongers Choice with five to eight cheeses, plus charcuterie items) are the things to order. There's a nicely curated wine list (from $9 a glass), and suggested wine pairings for the cheese platters.

Brunch is served on weekends (from 10am).

SUSHI NAKAZAWA SUSHI $$$

Map p418 (☎212-924-2212; www.sushinakazawa.com; 23 Commerce St, btwn Bedford St & Seventh Ave; prix-fixe $120-150; ⏲5-10pm Mon-Sat; [S]1 to Christopher St-Sheridan Sq) The price is high, but the quality is nothing short of phenomenal at this jewel-box sized sushi spot which opened to much acclaim in 2013. There are no cooked dishes and little in the way of individual choice. Instead, the meal is a 20-course fixed-price affair, with Chef Daisuke Nakazawa (who served under Jiro Ono, probably the world's finest sushi chef) serving up delectable bites of tuna belly, hay-smoked skipjack, glistening shrimp and sweet, eggy *tamago* (Japanese omelet). Match your meal with a Japanese microbrew or a flight of sake (six small glasses for around $40).

BLUE HILL AMERICAN $$$

Map p418 (☎212-539-1776; www.bluehillfarm.com; 75 Washington Pl, btwn Sixth Ave & Washington Sq W; mains $32-38; ⏲dinner; [S]A/C/E, B/D/F/M to W 4th St-Washington Sq) A place for Slow Food junkies with deep pockets, Blue Hill was an early crusader in the local-is-better movement. Gifted chef Dan Barber, who hails from a farm family in the Berkshires, Massachusetts, uses harvests from that land, as well as from farms in upstate New York, to create his widely praised fare.

Expect barely seasoned, perfectly ripe vegetables, which serve to highlight centerpieces of cod in almond broth, Berkshire pork stewed with four types of beans, and grass-fed lamb with white beans and new potatoes. The space itself, slightly below street level and housed in a landmark former speakeasy on a quaint Village block, is sophisticated and serene.

BABBO ITALIAN $$$

Map p418 (☎212-777-0303; www.babbonyc.com; 110 Waverly Pl; mains $19-34; ⏲11:30am-11:15pm, from 5pm Sun; [S]C/E, B/D/F to W 4th St, 1 to Christopher St-Sheridan Sq) Celebrity chef Mario Batali has multiple restaurants in Manhattan, but everyone has a sneaking suspicion that this two-level split townhouse is his favorite. Whether you order spicy lamb sausage with mint love letters, calf's brain *francobolli* (small, stuffed ravioli) or pig's foot *milanese,* you'll find Batali at the top of his innovative, eclectic game. Reservations are in order.

✕ Chelsea

CHELSEA MARKET   MARKET **$**
See p133.

BILLY'S BAKERY   BAKERY **$**
Map p422 (☏212-647-9956; www.billysbakery-nyc.com; 184 Ninth Ave, btwn 21st & 22nd Sts; cupcakes $3; ⏰8:30am-11pm Mon-Thu, to midnight Fri & Sat, 9am-10pm Sun; ⓢA/C/E, 1/2 to 23rd St, A/C/E to 14th St) New York's *Sex and the City*-fueled cupcake craze has come and gone, but Billy's is still cranking out its four-bite bits of heaven. Red velvet and banana cream top the recipe list, and a clutch of retro-style pastries are imagined by the I-don't-care-what-I'm-wearing hipsters in the back.

★FORAGERS
CITY TABLE   MODERN AMERICAN **$$**
Map p422 (www.foragerscitygrocer.com; 300 W 22nd St, cnr Eighth Ave; mains $22-28; ⏰6-10pm Tue-Sat, from 10:30am Sat & Sun; ✐; ⓢC/E, 1 to 23rd St) Owners of this new restaurant in Chelsea run a 28-acre farm in the Hudson Valley, from which much of their menu is sourced (and true to name, some products are indeed 'foraged'). Dishes are sustainable, locally sourced, and perhaps most importantly, delicious! A few temptations: squash soup with Jerusalem artichokes and black truffles; roasted chicken with polenta; heritage pork loin; and the season's harvest featuring toasted quinoa and a flavorful mix of vegetables. Brunch is another big draw.

Next door is the gourmet market, where you can browse many goodies, from organic produce to heavenly desserts; there's also a wine shop with reasonably priced bottles from small producers.

HEATH   SUPPER CLUB **$$**
Map p422 (☏212-564-1622; www.mckittrickhotel.com; 542 W 27th St, btwn Tenth & Eleventh Aves; mains $24-32; ⏰6pm-2am; ⓢC/E to 23rd St) In late 2013, the creators of hit interactive theater piece *Sleep No More* opened a restaurant next door to their warehouse venue. Like the fictional McKittrick Hotel in the drama, the Heath is set in another place and time (vaguely Britain, 1920s), with suspenders-wearing barkeeps, period furnishings and (fake) smoke wafting over the dining room, as a jazz band performs on stage. Actors disguised as waitstaff interact with the diners, and soon you become part of the whole theatrical experience.

The menu features heritage English recipes – spit-roasted leg of lamb, terrines, beef and ale pie, bay scallops – and is mostly unremarkable. But the evening is quite memorable, assuming you're up for a night of drama and surprises.

COOKSHOP   MODERN AMERICAN **$$**
Map p422 (☏212-924-4440; www.cookshopny.com; 156 Tenth Ave, btwn 19th & 20th Sts; mains $15-35; ⏰11:30am-4pm & 5:30-11:30pm daily, from 10:30am Sat & Sun; ⓢL to 8th Ave, A/C/E to 23rd St) A brilliant brunching pit stop before (or after) tackling the verdant High Line across the street, Cookshop is a lively place that knows its niche and does it oh so well. Excellent service, eye-opening cocktails, a perfectly baked breadbasket and a selection of inventive egg mains make this a favorite in Chelsea on a Sunday afternoon. Dinner is a sure-fire win as well. Ample outdoor seating on warm days.

LE GRAINNE   FRENCH **$$**
Map p422 (☏646-486-3000; www.legrainnecafe.com; 183 Ninth Ave, btwn 21st & 22nd Sts; mains $10-24; ⏰8am-midnight; ⓢC/E, 1 to 23rd St, A/C/E to 14th St) Tap the top of your French onion soup as you dream of that Pollyanna ingenue Amélie cracking open her crème brûlée; Le Grainne transports the senses from the busy blocks of Chelsea to the backstreets of Paris. The tin-topped eatery really excels at lunch time, when baguette sandwiches and savory crepes are scarfed down amid cramped quarters; come for dinner to breath in the wafting garlic as hearty pastas are tossed in the kitchen.

CO   PIZZERIA **$$**
Map p422 (☏212-243-1105; www.co-pane.com; 230 Ninth Ave, at 24th St; pizzas $15-20; ⏰5-11pm Mon, 11:30am-11pm Tue-Sun; ⓢC/E to 23rd St) Masterfully prepared pizza is served in trim wooden surrounds that lend a Scandinavian farmhouse vibe. Expect a faithful reproduction of the trademark Neapolitan thin-crust pies topped with an assortment of fresh-from-the-farm items like fennel and buffalo mozzarella. Salads of artichoke, beet or radicchio – as well as global wines and a sprinkling of sweets – round out the offerings.

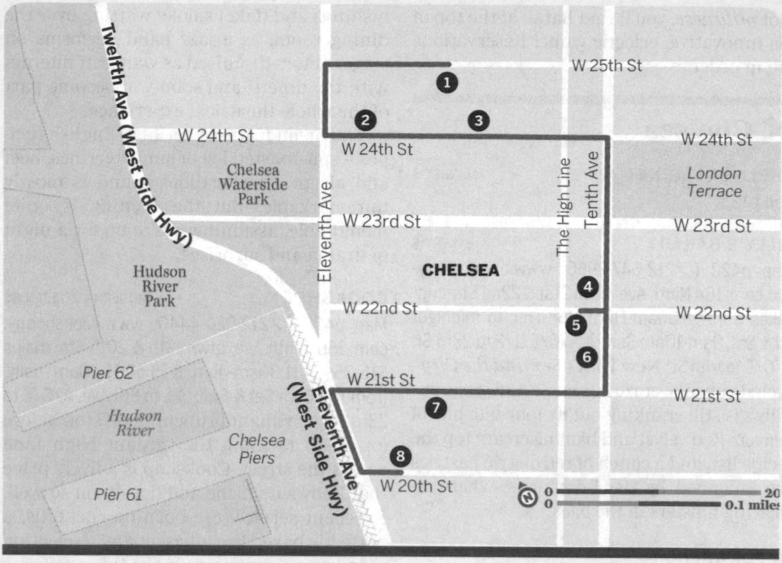

Local Life
Chelsea Galleries

Chelsea is home to the highest concentration of art galleries in the entire city. Most lie in the 20s, on the blocks between Tenth and Eleventh Aves, and openings for their new shows are typically held on Thursday evenings. Pick up Art Info's Gallery Guide (with map) available for free at most galleries, or visit www.westchelseaarts.com.

1 Pace Gallery

In a dramatically transformed garage, the **Pace Gallery** (Map p422; 534 W 25th St, btwn Tenth & Eleventh Aves; ⏰10am-6pm Tue-Sat; [S]C/E to 23rd St) has worked with some of the leading artists of recent years including Sol LeWitt, David Hockney, Chuck Close and Robert Rauschenberg. It has three locations on W 25th St, and one in Midtown.

2 Gagosian

Gagosian (Map p422; ☎212-741-1111; www.gagosian.com; 555 W 24th St; ⏰10am-6pm Tue-Sat; [S]C/E to 23rd St) offers a different vibe than most of the one-off galleries, as it's part of a constellation of showrooms that spreads well across the globe. Also check out the 21st St location, which easily rivals some of the city's museums with its large-scale installations.

3 Barbara Gladstone

The curator of the eponymous **Barbara Gladstone Gallery** (Map p422; ☎212-206-9300; www.gladstonegallery.com; 515 W 24th St, btwn Tenth & Eleventh Aves; ⏰10am-6pm Tue-Sat, closed weekends Jul & Aug; [S]C/E, 1 to 23rd St) has learned a thing or two after 30 years in the Manhattan art world. Ms Gladstone consistently puts together the most well-critiqued displays around.

4 Refuel, Spanish-Style

Wielding Spanish tapas amid closet-sized surrounds, Tía Pol (p145) is the real deal, as the hordes of swarming locals can attest.

5 Matthew Marks

Famous for exhibiting big names like Jasper Johns and Ellsworth Kelly, **Matthew Marks** (Map p422; ☎212-243-0200; www.matthew-marks.com; 522 W 22nd St; ⏰10am-6pm Tue-Sat; [S]C/E to 23rd St) is a true Chelsea pioneer. There are three other nearby locations (on 22nd and 24th Sts) besides this one.

6 Printed Matter

This tiny shop (p158) makes a fine reprieve from the big gallery experience. Inside,

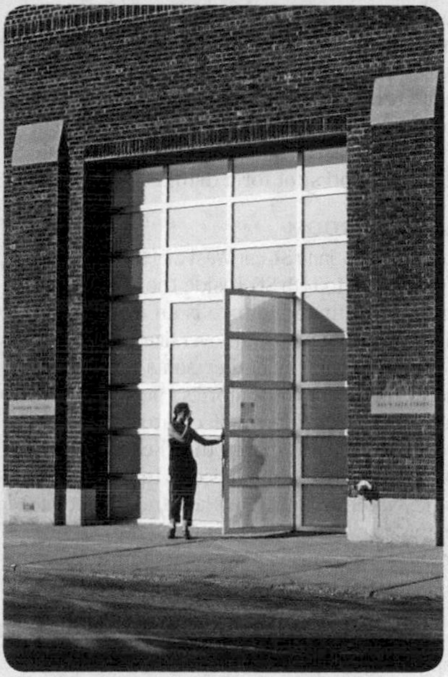

LONELY PLANET / GETTY IMAGES ©

Gagosian gallery, Chelsea

you'll find a mesmerizing selection of artists' monographs, zines and other printed curiosities.

7 Paula Cooper

An icon of the art world, **Paula** (Map p422; 534 W 21st St, btwn Tenth & Eleventh Aves; ⏱10am-6pm Tue-Sat; [S]C/E to 23rd St) was one of the first to move from SoHo to Chelsea. She continues to push boundaries and draw crowds, as she did for her 2011 exhibition *The Clock* when the gallery stayed open 24 hours a day on weekends.

8 David Zwirner

One of the major players in the art world, **David Zwirner** (Map p422; www.davidzwirner.com; 537 W 20th St, btwn Tenth & Eleventh Aves; ⏱10am-6pm Tue-Sat; [S]C/E to 23rd St) opened a five-story, LEED-certified gallery with 30,000 sq feet of exhibition space in 2013. He stages some of New York's best gallery shows. *Infinity Mirrored Room* was a major recent event which drew three-hour lines to see Yayoi Kusuma's otherworldly light installations. He also has a location at 525 W 19th St.

TÍA POL TAPAS **$$**

Map p422 (☎212-675-8805; www.tiapol.com; 205 Tenth Ave, btwn 22nd & 23rd Sts; small plates $4-16; ⏱5:30-11pm Mon, noon-11pm Tue-Sun; [S]C/E to 23rd St) Wielding Spanish tapas amid closet-sized surrounds, Tía Pol is the real deal, as the hordes of locals swarming the entrance can attest. There's a great wine list and a tantalizing array of small plates: Spanish tortillas, lemony salad topped with tuna, lima-bean-puree bruschetta and sautéed cockles with razor clams.

It's the perfect post-gallery-opening pit stop. Come on the early side to take your best stab at grabbing one of the handful of tables in the back.

BLOSSOM VEGAN **$$**

Map p422 (☎212-627-1144; www.blossomnyc.com; 187 Ninth Ave, btwn 21st & 22nd Sts; mains lunch $12-18, dinner $19-23; ⏱lunch & dinner; 🌿; [S]C/E to 23rd St) This Chelsea veg oasis – with a sinful wine and chocolate bar attached – is a peaceful, romantic dining room that offers imaginative tofu, seitan and vegetable creations, some raw, all kosher. The stellar Autumn Sweet Potato Rolls have raw strips of the orange root wrapped around tangy strips of coconut, carrots and peppers, and will leave your taste buds reeling.

Seitan scaloppini has a perfect blend of richness and a light lemony zing, while the hickory-roasted tempeh gets tempered with creamy horseradish crème fraîche. Desserts are so rich, you'll swear they're filled with butter and cream.

🍷 DRINKING & NIGHTLIFE

The key word in the West Village is 'west' – the further towards the Hudson you go, the more likely you are to sidestep the frat party scene found around the NYU campus – generally the going gets good around the crooked lanes west of Sixth Ave. Just to the north, the Meatpacking District is strictly contemporary in vibe, with sprawling, modern spaces boasting long cocktail lists, velvet-roped entrances and dins that'll rattle your brain. Chelsea is still very much the territory for gay men, but there's a handful of options for all tastes, from speakeasy-chic digs to well-worn dive bars.

🍷 Greenwich Village & the Meatpacking District

CLARKSON BAR

Map p418 (225 Varick St, at Clarkson St; ⏲11am-1:30am Mon, to 2:30am Tue-Sat, to 10pm Sun; [S]1 to Houston St) This stylish if spare newcomer has a polished wood, horseshoe-shaped bar – perfect for discreetly taking in the garrulous crowd that gathers here most nights. There's also a side room with tables set among zebra-painted columns, where folks come to dine on creative French bistro fare (deviled steak tartare, mussels with hot cherry peppers), and there's a late-night menu. The cocktails ($13 to $15) are creative and well crafted.

BELL BOOK & CANDLE BAR

Map p418 (141 W 10th St ,btwn Waverley Pl & Greenwich Ave; [S]A/B/C, B/D/F/M to W 4th St, 1 to Christopher St-Sheridan Sq) Step down into this candelit gastropub for strong, inventive libations (try the canela margarita, with cinnamon-infused tequila) and hearty pub grub. A 20-something crowd gathers around the small, packed bar (for $1 oysters and happy hour drink specials early in the night), though there's a lot more seating hidden in the back, with big booths ideal for larger groups. Many of the vegetables, incidentally, are sourced from the rooftop garden six flights up.

ARIA WINE BAR

Map p418 (☎212-242-4233; 117 Perry St, btwn Greenwich Ave & Hudson St; ⏲4pm-1am; [S]1 to Christopher St-Sheridan Sq) In the western reaches of the Village, Aria is an inviting music-filled space, with a mix of brick and tile walls and rustic wood tables. There's a good selection of wines by the glass, particularly organic labels, with prices starting around $7 a (small) glass. Recommended *cicchetti* (bite-sized plates, good for sharing) include gorgonzola-stuffed dates, crab cakes, and stewed calimari. It attracts a lively crowd most nights, and the small space can get a bit cramped.

COMMERCE BAR

Map p418 (☎212-524-2301; 50 Commerce St; ⏲5:30pm-midnight Mon-Fri, 11am-1am Sat, to 11pm Sun; [S]1 to Christopher St-Sheridan Sq) Secreted away on winding Commerce St, this art deco gem has seen many incarnations since its days as a Depression-era speakeasy. These days the buzzing space has undeniable allure with lurid Diego Rivera-style murals, a gorgeously lit interior and beautifully presented (if pricey) cuisine. We prefer coming here for a libation at the bar. With its creative cocktail menu, it's a fine neighborhood spot for a drink.

JANE BALLROOM LOUNGE

Map p418 (113 Jane St, cnr West St; [S]L to 8th Ave, A/C/E, 1/2/3 to 14th St) Inside the Jane Hotel, this high-ceilinged lounge is an explosion of wild design: beneath an oversized disco ball is a mish-mash of leather sofas and velour chairs, animal print fabrics, potted palms and various taxidermied creatures (a peacock, a ram's head over the flickering fireplace). Head up to the balcony to take in the scene, which remains low-key and loungelike during the week and morphs into a full-blown party on weekends, when revelers dance on the furniture (you've been warned).

HIGHLANDS SCOTTISH BAR

Map p418 (☎212-229-2670; 150 W 10th St; [S]1 to Christopher St-Sheridan Sq) This handsome Scottish-inspired drinkery is a fine place to while away an evening. Exposed brick, a fireplace and a mix of animal heads, pheasant wallpaper, oil paintings and Edinburgh tartans on the walls bring in more than a touch of the old country. Scottish beers and spirits, plus haggis, Scotch eggs, shepherd's pie and other traditional bites round out the menu.

LITTLE BRANCH COCKTAIL BAR

Map p418 (☎212-929-4360; 22 Seventh Ave at Leroy St; ⏲7pm-3am; [S]1 to Houston St) If it weren't for the doorman, you'd never guess that a charming drinking den lurked beyond the plain metal door positioned at this triangular intersection. When you get the go-ahead to enter, you'll find a basement bar that feels like a kickback to Prohibition times. Old-time jazz tunes waft overhead as locals clink glasses and sip inventive, artfully prepared cocktails.

BUVETTE WINE BAR

Map p418 (☎212-255-3590; www.ilovebuvette.com; 42 Grove St, btwn Bedford & Bleecker Sts; ⏲8am-2am Mon-Fri, from 10am Sat & Sun; [S]1 to Christopher St-Sheridan Sq, A/C/E, B/D/F/M to W 4th St) The rustic-chic decor here (think delicate tin tiles and a swooshing marble countertop) make it the perfect place for a glass of wine – no matter the time of day. For the full experience at this self-proclaimed *gastrotèque,* grab a seat at one of the surrounding tables, and nibble on small plates while enjoying the Old-World wines (mostly from France and Italy).

MARIE'S CRISIS BAR

Map p418 (☎212-243-9323; 59 Grove St btwn Seventh Ave & Bleecker St; ⌚4pm-4am; [S]1 to Christopher St-Sheridan Sq) Aging Broadway queens, wide-eyed out-of-town gay boys, giggly tourists and various other fans of musical theater assemble around the piano here and take turns belting out campy show tunes, often joined by the entire crowd. It's old-school fun, no matter how jaded you were when you went in.

ART BAR BAR

Map p418 (☎212-727-0244; 52 Eighth Ave, near Horatio St; ⌚4pm-4am, happy hour 4-7pm; [S]L to 8th Ave-14th St, A/C/E to 14th St) A decidedly bohemian crowd favors Art Bar, which doesn't look like much up front (booths crowded too close to the wooden bar), but has a bit more going on in the back. Grab your beer or one of the house specials (usually martinis) and head for the couches, placed under a huge *Last Supper*–esque mural featuring Jimmy Dean and Marilyn Monroe, among others. There's a roaring fire in the winter.

VIN SUR VINGT WINE BAR

Map p418 (☎212-924-4442; www.vinsur20nyc.com; 201 W 11th St, btwn Seventh Ave & Waverly Pl; ⌚5pm-2am Mon-Fri, 11am-2am Sat, to midnight Sun; [S]1/2/3 to 14th St; 1/2 to Christopher St-Sheridan Sq, L to 8th Ave) A cozy spot just off Seventh Ave's bustle, Vin Sur Vingt is a slender wine bar with a strip of bar seating and a quaint row of two-seat tables, perfect for a first date. Warning: if you come for a pre-dinner drink, you'll inevitably be charmed into staying through dinner as you munch on the excellent selection of bar bites. The reasonably priced all-French wine list keeps locals coming back for seconds.

VOL DE NUIT PUB

Map p418 (☎212-982-3388; 148 W 4th St; [S]A/C/E, B/D/F/M to W 4th St-Washington Sq) Even all the NYU students can't ruin this: a cozy Belgian beer bar, with Delirium Tremens on tap and a few dozen bottle options – like Duvel and Lindemans Framboise (raspberry beer!). You can order *moules* (mussels) and *frîtes* (fries) to share at the front patio seats, the lounge, the communal wood tables or under the dangling red lights at the bar.

TOP OF THE STANDARD LOUNGE

Map p418 (☎212-645-4646; www.standardhotels.com/high-line; 848 Washington St, btwn 13th & Little W 12th Sts; ⌚4pm-2am; [S]L to 8th Ave, 1/2/3, A/C/E to 14th St) Smooth beige surrounds, softer music and plenty of room to swig your top-shelf tipple, the Top of the Standard (also referred to as the Boom Boom Room) is strictly VIP and the favored hangout for the vogue elite (and *Vogue* elite) – expect models, their photographers and the occasional celeb sighting. Dress your best and book ahead – that's the only way to gain access if you're not a cornerstone of New York's social scene.

LE BAIN BAR, CLUB

Map p418 (☎212-645-4646; 848 Washington St, btwn 13th & Little W 12th Sts; ⌚10pm-4am Wed-Fri, 2pm-4am Sat & Sun; [S]L to 8th Ave, 1/2/3, A/C/E to 14th St) The sweeping rooftop venue at the tragically hip Standard Hotel, Le Bain sees a garish parade of party promoters who do their thang on any day of the week. Brace yourself for jaw-dropping skyline views, a heavily used fog machine steaming up the dance floor, a giant hot tub built right into the dance floor, and an ambassador from every walk of life in New York getting wasted on pricy snifters.

EMPLOYEES ONLY BAR

Map p418 (☎212-242-3021; 510 Hudson St, near Christopher St; ⌚6pm-4am; [S]1 to Christopher St-Sheridan Sq) Duck behind the neon 'Psychic' sign to find this hidden hangout. The bar gets busier as the night wears on. Bartenders are ace mixologists, fizzing up crazy, addictive libations like the Ginger Smash and the Mata Hari. Great for late-night drinking, and eating, courtesy of the on-site restaurant that serves past midnight.

KETTLE OF FISH BAR

Map p418 (☎212-414-2278; www.kettleoffishnyc.com; 59 Christopher St, near Seventh Ave; ⌚3pm-4am Mon-Fri, 2pm-4am Sat & Sun; [S]1 to Christopher St-Sheridan Sq) Step into this dimly lit spot, full of couches and plump chairs, and prepare to stay for a while because the crowd is simply beguiling. It's a dive bar, a sports bar and a gay bar in one, and everyone mixes happily. There are stacks of board games like Monopoly and checkers to while away the time, as well as a dart board. And if you get hungry, the barkeeps can offer menus from nearby restaurants that deliver here. The owner is a Packers fan, so expect raucous activity on game days.

DENNIS K JOHNSON / GETTY IMAGES ©

1. Washington Square Park (p134)
Join the buskers, students, and chess players in this striking park.

2. Rubin Museum of Art (p137)
Check out the impressive collections of art from the Himalayas and surrounding regions.

3. The Spotted Pig (p117)
Try the burger or the shoestring fries.

4. Pier 45 (p135)
Hang out on this 850ft-long pier (aka the Christopher Street Pier) and take in the views of the Hudson.

124 OLD RABBIT CLUB BAR

Map p418 (☎212-254-0575; 124 MacDougal St; ⌚6pm-4am; [S]A/C/E, B/D/F/M to W 4th St, 1 to Houston St) You'll wanna pat yourself on the back when you find this well-concealed bar (hint: look for the tiny words 'Rabbit Club Craft Beer Bar' over the door). Once you're inside the narrow, cavern-like space with its low-key vibe, grab a seat at the dimly lit bar and reward yourself with a quenching stout or one of the dozens of imported brews.

BRASS MONKEY BAR

Map p418 (☎212-675-6686; www.brassmonkeybar.com; 55 Little W 12th St, at Washington St; ⌚11am-4am; [S]A/C/E to 14th St; L to 8th Ave) While most Meatpacking District bars tend toward the chic, the Monkey is more for beer lovers than those worrying about what shoes to wear. The multifloor Monkey is at- ase and down to earth, with squeaking wood floors and a nice long list of beers and Scotch. The roof deck is fine in warm weather.

675 BAR LOUNGE

Map p418 (☎212-699-2410; www.675bar.com; 675 Hudson St, btwn 13th & 14th Sts; ⌚6pm-2am Mon-Sat; [S]L to 8th Ave, 1/2/3, A/C/E to 14th St) Tucked under Bill's Bar & Burger in the Meatpacking District is this unpretentious hangout, which feels like a cross between a '70s rec room and your uncle's library. Come for the low-priced wines and draught beers and stay for the rousing match of Mancala.

STANDARD BAR

Map p418 (☎212-645-4646, 877-550-4646; www.standardhotels.com; 848 Washington St; [S]A/C/E to 14th St, L to 8th Ave) Rising on concrete stilts over the High Line, the Standard attracts an A-list crowd, with a chichi lounge and nightclub on the upper floors – the Top of the Standard (p147) and Le Bain (p147). There's also a grill, an eating-and-drinking plaza (that becomes a skating rink in winter) and an open-air beer garden with a classic German menu and frothy drafts.

HENRIETTA HUDSON LESBIAN

Map p418 (☎212-924-3347; 438 Hudson St; [S]1 to Houston St) All sorts of cute young dykes, many from neighboring New Jersey and Long Island, storm this sleek lounge, where varying theme nights bring in spirited DJs, who stick to particular genres (hip-hop, house, rock). The owner, Brooklyn native Lisa Canistraci, is a favorite promoter in the world of lesbian nightlife, and is often on hand to mix it up with her fans.

CORNER BISTRO BAR

Map p418 (www.cornerbistrony.com; 331 W 4th St, btwn Jane & 12th Sts; ⌚noon-4am; [S]L to 8th Ave, 1/2/3, A/C/E to 14th St) An old-school dive bar with cheap beers on tap – it all sounds pretty standard until you take a mouthwatering bite out of Corner Bistro's bar burger. Nothing beats this juicy meat sandwich with a side scatter of fries.

STONEWALL INN GAY

Map p418 (53 Christopher St; [S]1 to Christopher St-Sheridan Sq) Site of the Stonewall riots in 1969, this historic bar was losing its fan base to trendier spots until new owners came along several years back, gave it a face-lift and opened it to a new and welcoming crowd. Since then, it's been pulling in varied crowds nightly for parties catering to everyone under the gay rainbow.

ONE IF BY LAND, TWO IF BY SEA BAR

Map p418 (☎212-255-8649; 17 Barrow St; ⌚dinner; [S]1 at Christopher St-Sheridan Sq; A/C/E, B/D/F/V to W 4th St-Washington Sq) Famous for its beef Wellington and graceful, aged location in Aaron Burr's old carriage house, this is quite possibly New York's favorite date restaurant. But it's even better as a quiet watering hole, perfect for those who need a break from the harried streets.

WHITE HORSE TAVERN BAR

Map p418 (☎212-243-9260; 567 Hudson St, at 11th St; [S]1 to Christopher St-Sheridan Sq) It's a bit on the tourist trail, but that doesn't dampen the century-old, pubby dark-wood, tin-ceiling atmosphere of this bar, where Dylan Thomas had his last drink (too many beers led to his 1953 death) and a tipsy Jack Kerouac got kicked out. Sit at the long oak bar inside or at sidewalk tables.

CIELO CLUB

Map p418 (☎212-645-5700; www.cieloclub.com; 18 Little W 12th St; cover charge $15-25; ⌚10:30pm-5am Mon-Sat; [S]A/C/E, L to 8th Ave-14th St) This long-running club boasts a largely attitude-free crowd and an excellent sound system. Join dance lovers on Deep Space Monday when DJ François K spins dub and underground beats. Other nights feature various DJs from Europe who mix entrancing, seductive sounds that pull everyone to their feet.

FAT CATS DIVE BAR

Map p418 (☎212-675-6056; www.fatcatmusic.org; 75 Christopher St, near Seventh Ave; cover $3; ⏲2pm-5am Mon-Fri, noon-5am Sat & Sun; [S]1 to Christopher St-Sheridan Sq, A/C/E, B/D/F/M to W 4th St) If $14 cocktails and fancy-schmancy Village boutiquery are getting you down, maybe it's time to pay a visit to this run-down little Ping-Pong hall. Fat Cats is a basement dive that draws a young, unpretentious crowd who want to hang out, shoot some pool, play a little shuffleboard, and maybe even get a Ping-Pong game going. You'll also find cheap beers, live music nightly and a no-holds-barred approach to life.

🍷 Chelsea

GALLOW GREEN BAR

Map p422 (☎212-564-1662; www.mckittrickhotel.com; 542 W 27th St, btwn Tenth & Eleventh Aves; ⏲May-Oct; [S]C/E to 23rd St, 1 to 28th St) Run by the creative team behind Sleep No More (p154), Gallow Green is a rooftop bar festooned with vines, potted plants and fairy

CAFE CULTURE

New York is no longer a second-string city when it comes to great coffee. Celebrated brewmasters, bringing technical wizardry and high-quality single-source coffee beans, have reinvented the simple cup of joe. For experiencing a mix of both classic and cutting-edge cafes, the West Village is a great place to start.

Stumptown Coffee Roasters (Greenwich Village) (Map p418; 30 W 8th St at MacDougal St; ⏲7am-8pm; [S]A/C/E, B/D/F/M to W 4th St) The renowned Portland roaster is helping to reinvent the NYC cafe scene with its exquisitely made brews. It has an elegant interior with coffered ceiling and walnut bar, though its few tables are often overtaken by the laptop-toting crowd.

Cafe Minerva (Map p418; 302 W 4th St, btwn W 12th & Bank Sts; mains $10-25; 📶) On a peaceful stretch of W 4th St, this neighborhood charmer makes a great setting for a meet-up with a friend or a fine spot to linger over a light meal (panini, mussels, salads) when you're solo. The small tables and wraparound marble-topped bar draws a cappuccino-sipping and snacking crowd by day and wine drinkers by night. The $20 bottles and $9 wines by the glass are a great deal.

Whynot Coffee & Wine (Map p418; 14 Christopher St, at Gay St; ⏲8am-midnight Mon-Thu, to 1am Fri Sat) On one of the prettiest corners in the West Village, Whynot is an airy space with soaring ceilings, a mostly vinyl soundtrack and oversized windows just right for daydreaming as the city strolls peacefully past. There's also first-rate brews from Blue Bottle Coffee and sweet temptations by Millefeuille bakery. After 5pm, wine becomes the drink of choice, though it remains very low-key even on weekends.

Joe the Art of Coffee (Map p418; ☎212-924-7400; www.joetheartofcoffee.com; 141 Waverly Pl; ⏲7am-8pm Mon-Fri, from 8am Sat & Sun; [S]A/C/E, B/D/F/M to W 4th St-Washington Sq) Superb coffee is served at this always-bustling joint sitting squarely on bucolic Waverly Pl in the heart of the Village. Some say this is the best cup of joe in town.

Third Rail (Map p418; 240 Sullivan St, btwn Bleecker & W 3rd Sts; ⏲7am-8pm Mon-Fri, from 8am Sat & Sun) Near NYU, tiny Third Rail takes its coffee seriously, using single-origin Stumptown roasts and several different espresso blends (each gets its own grinder). The cortado here is both robust and smooth – the perfect pick-me-up after a day's exploring. There's a second location in the East Village.

Grounded Organic Coffee & Tea House (Map p418; ☎212-647-0943; 28 Jane St; mains $7-9; ⏲7am-8pm; [S]A/C/E, L to 14th St) We won't blame you for flashing back to your '90s grunge look when you step into this coffeehouse, which seems as if it has been encased in amber since *Reality Bites*. In addition to brag-worthy coffee blends and loose teas, Grounded also serves up guilt-free lunches using healthy staples like quinoa.

Caffe Reggio (Map p418; ☎212-475-9557; www.caffereggio.com; 119 MacDougal St, near W 3rd St; ⏲8am-3am Mon-Thu & Sun, to 4:30am Fri & Sat; [S]A/C/E, B/D/F/M to W 4th St) This arty cafe is a visual treat of Renaissance paintings and marble-topped tables. Serving fresh pastries, panini, cakes, Italian milkshakes (try the 'delizioso') and delectable coffee since 1927, Reggio's claims to be the first American cafe to serve the cappuccino.

lights. It's a great add-on before or after experiencing the show, with waitstaff in period costume, a live band most nights and tasty rum-filled cocktails ($15).

ELECTRIC ROOM CLUB

Map p422 (355 W 16th St, btwn Eighth & Ninth Aves; ⏲10pm-4am; [S]A/C/E to 14th St) Beneath the Dream Downtown Hotel, this intimate wood-paneled lounge has a British indie-rock vibe, with couches adorned with the Union Jack, and Banksy-esque murals setting the scene. From an elevated booth, a DJ spins '60s rock, funk and Britpop to a varied crowd of models, aging rockers and artists, who fill the place around 2am. With a capacity of just 100, it's tough getting past the door. Wear your best glam-rock outfit, and arrive with a Swedish model or three.

EAGLE NYC CLUB, GAY

Map p422 (☎646-473-1866; www.eaglenyc.com; 555 W 28th St, btwn Tenth & Eleventh Aves; ⏲10pm-4am Mon-Sat; [S]C/E to 23rd St) A bi-level club full of hot men in leather, the Eagle is the choice for out-and-proud fetishists. Its two levels, plus roof deck, offer plenty of room for dancing and drinking, which are done with abandon. Thursdays are 'code' nights, meaning everyone must meet the dress code (wear leather, or nothing at all). Located in a renovated 19th-century stable, the inside joke is that 'the studs keep coming.'

BATHTUB GIN COCKTAIL BAR

Map p422 (☎646-559-1671; www.bathtubginnyc.com; 132 Ninth Ave, btwn 18th & 19th Sts; ⏲6pm-1:30am Sun-Tue, to 3:30am Wed-Sat; [S]A/C/E to 14th St, L to 8th Ave, A/C/E to 23rd St) Amid New York City's obsession with speakeasy-styled hangouts, Bathtub Gin manages to poke its head above the crowd with its super-secret front door, which doubles as a wall for an unassuming cafe. Inside, chill seating, soft background beats and kindly staff make it a great place to sling back bespoke cocktails with friends.

G LOUNGE GAY

Map p422 (☎212-929-1085; www.glounge.com; 225 W 19th St, btwn Seventh & Eighth Aves; ⏲4pm-4am; [S]1 to 18th St) Glossy and unpretentious, this gay bar is as straight-friendly as they come, and it's really all about the music. Check out the website to find out who's spinning while you're in town. For heavy drinking and dancing with no cover, you can't beat G, as locals call it – although you may have to wait in line to get in. The occasional burlesque or drag show adds to the good fun. Cash only

CHELSEA BREWING COMPANY PUB

Map p422 (☎212-336-6440; West Side Hwy, at W 18th St, Chelsea Piers, Pier 59; ⏲noon-1am; [S]C/E to 23rd St) Enjoy a quality microbrew, waterside, in the expansive outdoor area of this beer haven. It's a perfect place to re-enter the world after a day of swimming or rock climbing at the Chelsea Piers Complex (p159).

BARRACUDA GAY

Map p422 (☎212-645-8613; 275 W 22nd St, at Seventh Ave; [S]C/E to 23rd St) This longtime favorite holds its own even as newer, slicker places come and go. That's because it's got a simple, winning formula: affordable cocktails, a cozy rec-room vibe and free entertainment from some of the city's top drag queens.

PETER MCMANUS TAVERN BAR

Map p422 (☎212-929-9691; 152 Seventh Ave, at 19th St; ⏲10am-4pm Mon-Sat, noon-4pm Sun; [S]A/C/E to 14th St) Pouring drafts since the 1930s, this family-run dive is something of a museum to the world of the McManuses: photos of yesteryear, an old telephone booth and Tiffany glass. There's also greasy bar food to eat at the comfy green booths.

BAR VELOCE BAR

Map p422 (☎212-629-5300; 176 Seventh Ave, near 20th St; ⏲5pm-3am; [S]C/E to 23rd St) Sip your wine, eat a few panini, watch the well-dressed world walk by, or strike up a conversation with an interesting stranger (or two). Small and friendly Bar Veloce caters to a sophisticated crowd that likes wine and a few laughs at the end of a hard day.

FRYING PAN BAR

Map p422 (☎212-989-6363; Pier 66, at W 26th St; ⏲noon-midnight; [S]C/E to 23rd St) Salvaged from the bottom of the sea (or at least the Chesapeake Bay), the Lightship *Frying Pan* and the two-tiered dockside bar where it's parked are fine go-to spots for a sundowner. On warm days, the rustic open-air space brings in the crowds, who come to laze on deck chairs, eat burgers off the sizzling grill, drink ice-cold beers ($7 for a microbrew; $25 for a pitcher) and admire the fine views across the water to, uh, New Jersey.

ENTERTAINMENT

Greenwich Village & the Meatpacking District

LE POISSON ROUGE LIVE MUSIC

Map p418 (☎212-505-3474; www.lepoissonrouge.com; 158 Bleecker St; [S]A/C/E, B/D/F/M to W 4th St-Washington Sq) This high-concept art space (complete with dangling fish aquarium) hosts a highly eclectic lineup of live music, with the likes of Deerhunter, Marc Ribot and Cibo Matto performing in past years. There's a lot of experimentation and cross-genre pollination between classical, folk music, opera and more.

VILLAGE VANGUARD JAZZ

Map p418 (☎212-255-4037; www.villagevanguard.com; 178 Seventh Ave, at 11th St; cover $25-30, plus 1-drink minimum; [S]1/2/3 to 14th St) Possibly the city's most prestigious jazz club, the Vanguard has hosted literally every major star of the past 50 years. It started as a home to spoken-word performances and occasionally returns to its roots, but most of the time it's just big, bold jazz all night long. Mind your step on the steep stairs, and close your eyes to the signs of wear and tear – acoustically, you're in one of the greatest venues in the world.

SMALLS JAZZ

Map p418 (☎212-252-5091; www.smallsjazzclub.com; 183 W 4th St; cover 7:30pm-12:30am $20, $10 after; [S]1 to Christopher St-Sheridan Sq) This cramped but appealing basement jazz den offers a grab-bag collection of jazz acts who take the stage nightly. Cover for the evening is $20, with a come-and-go policy if you need to duck out for a slice.

BLUE NOTE JAZZ

Map p418 (☎212-475-8592; www.bluenote.net; 131 W 3rd St, btwn Sixth Ave & MacDougal St; [S]A/C/E, B/D/F/M to W 4th St-Washington Sq) This is by far the most famous (and expensive) of the city's jazz clubs. Most shows are $30 at the bar, $45 at a table, but can rise for the biggest jazz stars (there are also a few cheaper $20 shows, as well as jazz brunch on Sundays at 11:30am). Go on an off night, and be quiet – all attention is on the stage!

CORNELIA ST CAFÉ LIVE MUSIC

Map p418 (☎212-989-9319; www.corneliastreetcafe.com; 29 Cornelia St, btwn Bleecker & W 4th Sts; [S]A/C/E, B/D/F/M to W 4th St-Washington Sq) This small cafe is known for its intimate music performances with innovative jazz trios, genre-bending vocalists and other musical and visual arts combos. Cornelia St also has a literary component with monthly storytelling gatherings and open-mike poetry nights and readings.

BAR NEXT DOOR LIVE MUSIC

Map p418 (☎212-529-5945; 129 MacDougal St, btwn W 3rd & W 4th Sts; cover $12-15; ⏲6pm-2am Sun-Thu, to 3am Fri & Sat; [S]A/C/E, B/D/F/M to W 4th St) One of the loveliest hangouts in the neighborhood, the basement of this restored townhouse is all low ceilings, exposed brick and romantic lighting. You'll find mellow, live jazz nightly, as well as the tasty Italian menu of the restaurant next door, La Lanterna di Vittorio.

13TH ST REPERTORY COMPANY THEATER

Map p418 (☎212-675-6677; www.13thstreetrep.org; 50 W 13th St, btwn Fifth & Sixth Aves; [S]L to Sixth Ave; F/M, 1/2/3 to 14th St) Founded in 1972, this rep theater offers regular shows year-round, including children's theater and the New Works Reading Series on weekends. The company is also home to the longest running off-off Broadway show, *Line*.

BARROW STREET THEATER THEATER

Map p418 (☎212-243-6262; www.barrowstreettheatre.com; 27 Barrow St, btwn Seventh Ave & W 4th St, [S]1/2 to Christopher St-Sheridan Sq, A/C/E, B/D/F/M to W 4th St, 1/2 to Houston St) A fantastic off-Broadway space in the heart of the West Village showcasing a variety of local and international theater.

CHERRY LANE THEATER THEATER

Map p418 (☎212-989-2020; www.cherrylanetheater.org; 38 Commerce St; [S]1 to Christopher St-Sheridan Sq) A theater with a distinctive charm hidden in the West Village, Cherry Lane has a long and distinguished history. It was started by poet Edna St Vincent Millay and has given a voice to numerous playwrights and actors over the years. It remains true to its mission of creating 'live' theater that's accessible to the public. Readings, plays and spoken-word performances rotate frequently.

DUPLEX CABARET, KARAOKE

Map p418 (☎212-255-5438; www.theduplex.com; 61 Christopher St; cover $5-15, 2-drink minimum; ⏲4pm-4am; [S]1 to Christopher St-Sheridan

Sq) Cabaret, karaoke and campy dance moves are par for the course at the legendary Duplex. Pictures of Joan Rivers line the walls, and the performers like to mimic her sassy form of self-deprecation, while getting in a few jokes about audience members as well. It's a fun and unpretentious place, and certainly not for the bashful.

55 BAR LIVE MUSIC

Map p418 (☎212-929-9883; www.55bar.com; 55 Christopher St at Seventh Ave; cover $5-10, 2-drink minimum; ⏲1pm-4am; [S]1 to Christopher St-Sheridan Sq) Dating back to the Prohibition era, this friendly basement dive is great for low-key shows without high covers or dressing up. There are regular performances twice nightly by quality artists-in-residence, some blues bands and Miles Davis' super '80s guitarist Mike Stern.

IFC CENTER CINEMA

Map p418 (☎212-924-7771; www.ifccenter.com; 323 Sixth Ave at 3rd St; [S]A/C/E, B/D/F/M to W 4th St-Washington Sq) This arthouse cinema has a solidly curated lineup of new indies, cult classics and foreign films. Catch shorts, documentaries, '80s revivals, director-focused series, weekend classics and frequent special series, such as cult favorites *(The Shining, Taxi Driver, Aliens)* at midnight.

ANGELIKA FILM CENTER CINEMA

Map p418 (☎212-995-2570; www.angelikafilmcenter.com; 18 W Houston St, at Mercer St; tickets $10-14; 👪; [S]B/D/F/M to Broadway-Lafayette St) Angelika specializes in foreign and independent films and has some quirky charms (the rumble of the subway, long lines and occasionally bad sound). But its roomy cafe is a great place to meet and the beauty of its Stanford White–designed, beaux arts building is undeniable.

COMEDY CELLAR COMEDY

Map p418 (☎212-254-3480; www.comedycellar.com; 117 MacDougal St, btwn W 3rd & Minetta Ln; cover $12-24; ⏲shows start approx 9pm Sun-Fri, 7pm & 9:30pm Sat; [S]A/C/E, B/D/F/M to W 4th St-Washington Sq) This long-established basement club in Greenwich Village features mainstream material and a good list of regulars (Colin Quinn, *Saturday Night Live*'s Darrell Hammond, Wanda Sykes), plus an occasional high-profile drop-in like Dave Chappelle. Its success continues: Comedy Cellar now boasts another location around the corner on W 3rd St.

☆ Chelsea

★UPRIGHT CITIZENS BRIGADE THEATRE COMEDY

Map p422 (☎212-366-9176; www.ucbtheatre.com; 307 W 26th St, btwn Eighth & Ninth Aves; cover $5-10; [S]C/E to 23rd St) Pros of comedy sketches and outrageous improvisations reign at this popular 74-seat venue, which gets drop-ins from casting directors. Getting in is cheap, and so is the beer and wine. It's free Sundays after 9:30pm and Wednesdays after 11pm, when newbies take to the stage. Check the website for popular classes on sketch and improv, which spill over into an annex location on W 30th St.

SLEEP NO MORE THEATER

Map p422 (www.sleepnomorenyc.com; McKittrick Hotel, 530 W 27th St; tickets from $106; ⏲7pm-midnight Mon-Sat; [S]C/E to 23rd St) One of the most immersive theater experiences ever conceived, *Sleep No More* is a loosely based retelling of *Macbeth* set inside a series of Chelsea warehouses that have been redesigned to look like an abandoned hotel. It's a choose-your-own adventure kind of experience where audience members are free to wander the elaborate rooms (ballroom, graveyard, taxidermy shop, lunatic asylum) and interact with the actors who perform a variety of scenes that border on the bizarre to the risqué. Be prepared: you must check-in everything when you arrive (jackets, handbag, cellphone), and you will wear a mask, à la *Eyes Wide Shut*.

JOYCE THEATER DANCE

Map p422 (☎212-242-0800; www.joyce.org; 175 Eighth Ave; [S]C/E to 23rd St, A/C/E to Eighth Ave-14th St, 1 to 18th St) A favorite among dance junkies because of its excellent sight lines and offbeat offerings, this is an intimate venue, seating 472 in a renovated cinema. Its focus is on traditional modern companies such as Pilobolus, Stephen Petronio Company and Parsons Dance as well as global stars, such as DanceBrazil, Ballet Hispanico and MalPaso Dance Company.

NEW YORK LIVE ARTS DANCE

Map p422 (☎212-924-0077; www.newyorklivearts.org; 219 W 19th St, btwn Seventh & Eighth Aves; [S]1 to 18th St) You'll find a program of more than 100 experimental, contemporary performances annually at this sleek dance center, led by artistic director Carla Peterson. International troupes from Serbia, South Africa, Korea and beyond bring fresh works to the stage, with shows that will often include pre- or post-show discussions with choreographers or dancers.

IRISH REPERTORY THEATER THEATER

Map p422 (☎212-727-2737; www.irishrep.org; 132 W 22nd St, btwn Sixth & Seventh Aves; [S]1/2, F/M to 23 St, 1/2 to 18th St) This repertory troupe, with a space in a renovated Chelsea warehouse, showcases the finest contributions to the theater world from the Irish and Irish-American community.

ATLANTIC THEATER COMPANY THEATER

Map p422 (☎212-691-5919; www.atlantictheater.org; 336 W 20th St btwn Eighth & Ninth Aves; [S]C/E to 23rd St, 1 to 18th St) Founded by David Mamet and William H Macy in 1985, the Atlantic Theater is a pivotal anchor for the off-Broadway community, hosting many Tony Award and Drama Desk winners over the last 25-plus years.

KITCHEN THEATER, DANCE

Map p422 (☎212-255-5793; www.thekitchen.org; 512 W 19th St, btwn Tenth & Eleventh Aves; [S]A/C/E to 14th St, L to 8th Ave) A loft-like experimental space in west Chelsea that also produces edgy theater, readings and music performances, Kitchen is where you'll find new, progressive pieces and works-in-progress from local movers and shakers.

GOTHAM COMEDY CLUB COMEDY

Map p422 (☎212-367-9000; www.gothamcomedyclub.com; 208 W 23rd St, btwn Seventh & Eighth Aves, [S]1, C/E to 23rd St) Fancying itself as a NYC comedy hall of fame, and backing it up with regular big names and Gotham All-Stars shows, this expanded club provides space for comedians who've cut their teeth on HBO, *Letterman* and *The Tonight Show*.

CHELSEA BOW TIE CINEMA CINEMA

Map p422 (☎212-777-3456; www.bowtiecinemas.com; 260 W 23rd St, btwn Seventh & Eighth Aves; [S]C/E to 23rd St) In addition to showing first-run films, this multiscreen complex hosts weekend midnight showings of the *Rocky Horror Picture Show,* as well as a great Thursday-night series, Chelsea Classics, which has local drag star Hedda Lettuce hosting old-school camp fare from Joan Crawford, Bette Davis, Barbra Streisand and the like.

SHOPPING

Greenwich Village & the Meatpacking District

The picturesque, tranquil streets of the West Village are home to some lovely boutiques, with a few antique dealers, bookstores, record stores, and quirky gift and curio shops adding a bit of eclecticism to an otherwise fashion-focused 'hood. High-end shoppers stick to top-label stores along Bleecker St between Bank and W 10th. There's much more color along Christopher St, with its stores selling leather play gear and rainbow-colored T-shirts.

The Meatpacking District is all about that sleek, high-ceilinged industrial-chic vibe, with ultramodern designers reigning at expansive boutiques that are among the most fashionable haunts in town (some stores indeed look like sets for futuristic and beautifully stylized Kubrick films).

★STRAND BOOK STORE BOOKS

Map p418 (☎212-473-1452; www.strandbooks.com; 828 Broadway, at 12th St; ⏲9:30am-10:30pm Mon-Sat, 11am-10:30pm Sun; [S]L, N/Q/R, 4/5/6 to 14th St-Union Sq) Book fiends (or even those who have casually skimmed one or two) shouldn't miss New York's most loved and famous bookstore. In operation since 1927, the Strand sells new, used and rare titles, spreading an incredible 18 miles of books (over 2.5 million of them) among three labyrinthine floors.

Check out titles in foreign languages in the basement, browse eye-catching merchandise (smartphone covers, tote bags, paratrooper messenger bags) or sell off your own tomes before you get back on the plane, as the Strand buys or trades books at a side counter Monday through Saturday.

MONOCLE ACCESSORIES, FASHION

Map p418 (535 Hudson St, at Charles St; ⏲11am-7pm Mon-Sat, noon-6pm Sun; [S]1 to Christopher St-Sheridan Sq) Tyler Brûlé, the man behind one of the great magazines of the 21st century, founded this tiny bento-box-sized shop in 2010, and it features stylish well-made products for both the urbanite and the global traveler (leather-bound journals, elegant stationery, Japanese body soaps, passport holders, swimming trunks). If by chance you haven't heard of *Monocle* magazine, pick up a copy (or even back issues) here.

BEACON'S CLOSET
THRIFT STORE

Map p418 (10 W 13th St, btwn Fifth & Sixth Aves; ◷11am-8pm; ⓢL, N/R, 4/5/6 to Union Sq) You'll find a good selection of gently used clothing (which is of a decidedly downtown/ Brooklyn hipster aesthetic) at only slightly higher prices than Beacon's sister store in Williamsburg. Thrift shops are thin on the ground in this area, which makes Beacon's even more of a draw. Come mid-week or be prepared to brave the crowds.

PERSONNEL OF NEW YORK
FASHION, ACCESSORIES

Map p418 (9 Greenwich Ave, btwn Christopher & W 10th Sts; ◷11am-8pm Mon-Sat, noon-7pm Sun; ⓢA/C/E, B/D/F/M to W 4th St, 1 to Christopher St-Sheridan Sq) New in 2013, this small, delightful indie shop sells men's and women's designer clothing from unique labels from the East and West Coast and beyond. Look for beautifully textured wovens by Ace & Jig, rugged menswear by Hiroshi Awai, couture pieces by Rodobjer and batik shirts by All Nations. You'll also find a few housewares and crafty gifts including eye-catching Tadanori bird-shaped bottle openers.

YOYAMART
CHILDREN

Map p418 (📞212-242-5511; www.yoyamart. com; 15 Gansevoort St; ◷11am-7pm Mon-Sat, noon-6pm Sun; ⓢA/C/E to 14th St, L to Eighth Ave) Ostensibly geared toward the younger set, Yoyamart is a fun place to browse for adults – even if you're not packing a child. Sure, you'll find adorable apparel for babies and toddlers, but there are also cuddly robots, Gloomy Bear gloves, plush ninjas, build-your-own-ukulele kits, CD mixes and various anime-style amusement. For more kids' clothes and accessories, visit the nearby **Yoya** (Map p418; 📞646-336-6844; www.yoyanyc.com; 636 Hudson St; ◷11am-7pm Mon-Sat, noon-5pm Sun; ⓢA/C/E to 14th St, L to 8th Ave).

MARC BY MARC JACOBS
FASHION

Map p418 (📞212-924-0026; www.marcjacobs. com; 403-405 Bleecker St; ◷noon-8pm Mon-Sat, to 7pm Sun; ⓢA/C/E to 14th St, L to 8th Ave) With five small shops sprinkled around the West Village, Marc Jacobs has established a real presence in this well-heeled neighborhood. Large front windows allow easy peeking – assuming there's not a sale, during which you'll only see hordes of fawning shoppers.

Here's the layout: on Bleecker St, you'll find the women's line at No 403, the higher-end handbags and skincare products at No 385, and the men's collection at No 382. There's also BookMarc (for books, stationery and knickknacks) at No 400. One block over, you'll find women's accessories at 301 W 4th St, and the children's line (Little Marc) at 298 W 4th St. For men's and women's apparel from the Marc Jacobs Collection (the priciest stuff of all), head to the SoHo **Marc Jacobs** (Map p410; 📞212-343-1490; 163 Mercer St; ◷11am-7pm Mon-Sat, noon-6pm Sun; ⓢB/D/F/M to Broadway-Lafayette St, R to Prince St).

MCNULTY'S TEA & COFFEE CO, INC
FOOD & DRINK

Map p418 (📞212-242-5351; 109 Christopher St; ◷10am-9pm Mon-Sat, 1-7pm Sun; ⓢ1 to Christopher St-Sheridan Sq) Just down from a few sex shops, sweet McNulty's, with worn wooden floorboards, fragrant sacks of coffee beans and large glass jars of tea, flaunts a different era of Greenwich Village. It's been selling gourmet teas and coffees here since 1895.

BONNIE SLOTNICK COOKBOOKS
BOOKS

Map p418 (📞212-989-8962; www.bonnieslotnick-cookbooks.com; 163 W 10th St, btwn Waverly Pl & Seventh Ave; ⓢ1/2 to Christopher St-Sheridan Sq, A/C/E, B/D/F/M to W 4th St) Bonnie, the kindly owner, dotes on her customers, who are searching for the perfect cooking tome. Stocked to the ceiling with shelf after shelf of the best recipes on earth, the shop – bedecked like grandma's pantry – is bound to reveal some truly unique finds, like themed references (Jewish, gay, soup-specific etc) to antique wares.

CASTOR & POLLUX
CLOTHING

Map p418 (📞212-645-6572; www.castorandpolluxstore.com; 238 W 10th St; ◷noon-7pm Tue-Sat; ⓢ1/2 to Christopher St-Sheridan Sq or Houston St, A/C/E, B/D/F/M to W 4th St) Kerrilynn finds inspiration in the duality of the myth of Castor and Pollux to design and refine her collection of gorgeous threads. Carefully edited fashions feel wearable yet undeniably chic.

THREE LIVES & COMPANY
BOOKS

Map p418 (📞212-741-2069; www.threelives.com; 154 W 10th St, btwn Seventh Ave & Waverly Pl; ◷noon-7pm Sun-Tue, 11am-8:30pm Wed-Sat; ⓢ1/2 to Christopher St-Sheridan Sq, A/C/E, B/D/F/M to W 4th St, 1/2/3 to 14th St) Your neighborhood bookstore extraordinaire, Three Lives & Company is a wondrous spot that's tended by a coterie of exceptionally well-read individuals. A trip here is not just a pleasure, it's an adventure in the magical world of words.

BATHROOM
BEAUTY, HOMEWARES

Map p418 (☎212-929-1449; http://store.inthebathroom.com; 94 Charles St, btwn W 4th & Bleecker Sts; ⏲noon-8pm Mon-Fri, 11am-8pm Sat, noon-7pm Sun; [S]1/2 to Christopher St-Sheridan Sq, A/C/E, B/D/F/M to W 4th St) Although most New York shops tend to be kitchen obsessed, Colin Heywood's boutique pays homage to the humble bathroom. Styled like an old-school apothecary, this West Village wonder offers browsers a charming collection of handmade brands from home goods to luxury soaps.

JEFFREY NEW YORK
FASHION, ACCESSORIES

Map p418 (☎212-206-1272; www.jeffreynewyork.com; 449 W 14th St; ⏲10am-8pm Mon-Sat, 12:30-6pm Sun; [S]A/C/E to 14th St, L to Eighth Ave) One of the pioneers in the Meatpacking District's makeover, Jeffrey sells several high-end designer clothing lines – Versace, Pucci, Prada, Michael Kors and company – as well as accessories, shoes and a small selection of cosmetics. DJs spinning pop and indie add to the very hip vibe.

MURRAY'S CHEESE
FOOD & DRINK

Map p418 (☎212-243-3289; www.murrayscheese.com; 254 Bleecker St, btwn Sixth & Seventh Aves; ⏲8am-8pm Mon-Sat, 10am-7pm Sun; [S]1 to Christopher St-Sheridan Sq) Founded in 1914, this is one of New York's best cheese shops. Owner Rob Kaufelt is known for his talent of sniffing out devastatingly delicious varieties from around the world. You'll find (and be able to taste) all manner of *fromage*, be it stinky, sweet or nutty, from European nations and from small farms in Vermont and upstate New York.

There is also prosciutto and smoked meats, freshly baked breads, olives, antipasto, chocolate and all manner of goodies for a gourmet picnic – plus a counter for freshly made sandwiches and melts. Murray's also has an eat-in Cheese Bar (p142) a few doors down.

CO BIGELOW CHEMISTS
HEALTH, BEAUTY

Map p418 (☎212-473-7324; 414 Sixth Ave, btwn 8th & 9th Sts; ⏲7:30am-9pm Mon-Fri, 8:30am-7pm Sat, 8:30am-5:30pm Sun; [S]1 to Christopher St-Sheridan Sq, A/C/E, B/D/F/M to W 4th St-Washington Sq) The 'oldest apothecary in America' is now a slightly upscale fantasyland for the beauty-product obsessed (though there's still an actual pharmacy for prescriptions and standard drugstore items for sale on the premises, too). In addition to its own CO Bigelow label products, including lip balms, hand and foot salves, shaving creams and rosewater, you can browse through lotions, shampoos, cosmetics and fragrances from makers including Weleda, Yu-Be, Vichy and many more.

GREENWICH LETTERPRESS
STATIONERY

Map p418 (☎212-989-7464; www.greenwichletterpress.com; 39 Christopher St, btwn Seventh Ave & Waverly Pl; ⏲noon-6pm Sat-Mon, 11am-7pm Tue-Fri; [S]1/2 to Christopher St-Sheridan Sq, A/C/E, B/D/F/M to W 4th St, 1/2/3 to 14th St) Founded by two sisters, this cute card shop specializes in wedding announcements and other specially made letterpress endeavors, so send your loved ones a bespoke greeting card from this stalwart stationer.

EARNEST SEWN
FASHION, ACCESSORIES

Map p418 (☎212-242-3414; www.earnestsewn.com; 821 Washington St; ⏲11am-7pm Sun-Fri, 11am-8pm Sat; [S]A/C/E to 14th St, L to Eighth Ave) Earnest Sewn denim has become famous for its craftsmanship, and customers sign on to long waiting lists to order customized and tailored jeans. The atmospheric store is a fun place to browse, and you'll find an odd mix of delicate jewelry, outerwear and pocketknives among the antique (still working) machinery. You can also check out the **Lower East Side store** (Map p416; ☎212-979-5120; 90 Orchard St; ⏲noon-8pm Mon-Sat, to 7pm Sun; [S]F, J/M/Z to Essex St-Delancey St), which has a smaller selection of apparel (mostly denim).

FLIGHT 001
TRAVEL GEAR

Map p418 (☎212-989-0001; www.flight001.com; 96 Greenwich Ave; ⏲11am-8pm Mon-Sat, noon-6pm Sun; [S]A/C/E to 14th St, L to Eighth Ave) Travel is fun, sure – but getting travel gear is even more fun. Check out Flight 001's range of luggage and smaller bags by brands ranging from Bree to Rimowa, kitschy 'shemergency' kits (breath freshener, lip balm, stain remover etc), pin-up-girl flasks, brightly colored passport holders and leather luggage tags, travel guidebooks, toiletry cases and a range of mini toothpastes, eye masks, pillboxes and the like.

FORBIDDEN PLANET
COMICS

Map p418 (☎212-473-1576; 840 Broadway; ⏲9am-10pm Sun-Wed, to midnight Thu-Sat; [S]L, N/Q/R, 4/5/6 to 14th St-Union Sq) Indulge your inner sci-fi and fantasy nerd. Find heaps of comics, manga, graphic novels, posters and figurines (ranging from *Star Trek* to *Doctor Who*). Stop in, or check the website for upcoming book signings and other events.

AEDES DE VENUSTAS BEAUTY

Map p418 (☎212-206-8674; www.aedes.com; 9 Christopher St; 🕒noon-8pm Mon-Sat, 1-7pm Sun; [S]A/C/E, B/D/F/M to W 4th St; 1 to Christopher St-Sheridan Sq) Plush and inviting, Aedes de Venustas ('Temple of Beauty' in Latin) provides more than 40 brands of luxury European perfumes, including Hierbas de Ibiza, Mark Birley for Men, Costes, Odin and Shalini. It also has skincare products created by Susanne Kaufmann and Acqua di Rose, and everyone's favorite scented candles from Diptyque.

🛍 Chelsea

Better known for its dining and nightlife scenes, Chelsea has a decent selection of antiques, discount fashion, chain stores and kitsch, along with a hidden bookstore and well-edited thrift shop. The neighborhood standout is the beloved Chelsea Market (p133), a huge concourse packed with shops selling fresh baked goods, wines, veggies, imported cheeses and other temptations.

HOUSING WORKS THRIFT SHOP VINTAGE

Map p422 (☎718-838-5050; 143 W 17th St, btwn Sixth & Seventh Aves; 🕒10am-7pm Mon-Fri, to 6pm Sat, noon-5pm Sun; [S]1 to 18th St) This shop, with its swank window displays, looks more boutique than thrift, but its selections of clothes, accessories, furniture, books and records are great value. All proceeds benefit the charity serving the city's HIV-positive and AIDS homeless communities. There are 10 other branches around town.

POSMAN BOOKS BOOKS

Map p422 (☎212-627-0304; www.posmanbooks.com; 75 Ninth Ave, btwn 15th & 16th Sts; 🕒10am-9pm Mon-Fri, to 8pm Sat, to 7pm Sun; [S]A/C/E to 14th St, L to Eighth Ave, 1/2 to 18th St) Inside Chelsea Market, family-run Posman is a sleekly designed reading hub and an inviting social space that hosts talks and activities for the little ones.

PRINTED MATTER BOOKS

Map p422 (☎212-925-0325; 195 Tenth Ave, btwn 21st & 22nd Sts; 🕒11am-7pm Sat & Mon-Wed, to 8pm Thu-Fri; [S]C/E to 23rd St) Printed Matter is a wondrous two-room shop dedicated to limited-edition artist monographs and strange little zines. Here you will find nothing carried by mainstream bookstores; instead, trim little shelves hide call-to-arms manifestos, critical essays about comic books, flip books that reveal Jesus' face through barcodes and how-to guides written by prisoners.

192 BOOKS BOOKS

Map p422 (☎212-255-4022; www.192books.com; 192 Tenth Ave, btwn 21st & 22nd Sts; 🕒11am-7pm; [S]C/E to 23rd St) Located right in the gallery district is this small indie bookstore, with sections on fiction, history, travel, art and criticism. A special treat is its offerings of rotating art exhibits, during which the owners organize special displays of books that relate thematically to the featured show or artist. Weekly book readings feature acclaimed (often NY-based) authors.

UNIVERSAL GEAR FASHION

Map p422 (☎212-206-9119; www.universalgear.com; 140 Eighth Ave, btwn 16th & 17th Sts; [S]A/C/E to 14th St, L to Eighth Ave) A more accurate name might be 'Chelsea Gear,' as the place is bursting with all that's de rigueur for handsome Chelsea boys and wannabes. Here's where you'll find cute-boy staples like G-Star and Diesel denim, pouch-heightening underwear by 2(x)IST, plus button-downs by Ben Sherman, Penguin caps and swimwear, jackets, shoes and accessories.

ANTIQUES GARAGE FLEA MARKET ANTIQUES

Map p422 (112 W 25th St at Sixth Ave; 🕒9am-5pm Sat & Sun; [S]1 to 23rd St) This weekend flea market is set in a two-level parking garage, with more than 100 vendors spreading their wares. Antique lovers shouldn't miss a browse here, as you'll find clothing, shoes, records, books, globes, furniture, rugs, lamps, glassware, paintings, artwork and many other relics from the past. Weekend antique hunters should also visit the affiliated Hell's Kitchen Flea Market.

NASTY PIG CLOTHING

Map p422 (☎212-691-6067; 265 W 19th St, btwn Seventh & Eighth Aves; [S]A/C/E to 14th St, 1 to 18th St) T-shirts, socks and underwear bearing the store's namesake, along with a bit of rubber and leather fetish wear, makes this an ideal stop for Chelsea boys and their admirers.

BEHAVIOUR CLOTHING, ACCESSORIES

Map p422 (☎212-352-8380; 231 W 19th St, btwn Seventh & Eighth Aves; 🕒noon-8pm Mon-Fri, to

7pm Sat & Sun; [S]A/C/E to Eighth Ave-14th S, 1/2 to 18th St, 1/2 to 23rd St) A well-curated men's shop for the stylish dandy. From sunglasses to T-shirts, they are all excellent. Usually a dash of seersucker in the spring.

SPORTS & ACTIVITIES

CHELSEA PIERS COMPLEX — SPORTS

Map p422 (☎212-336-6666; www.chelseapiers.com; Hudson River at end of W 23rd St; [S]C/E to 23rd St) This massive waterfront sports center caters to the athlete in everyone. You can set out to hit a bucket of golf balls at the four-level driving range, ice skate on the complex' indoor rink or rent in-line skates to cruise along the new bike path on the Hudson River Park. The complex has a jazzy bowling alley, Hoop City for basketball, a sailing school for kids, batting cages, a huge gym facility with an indoor pool (day passes for nonmembers are $50), indoor rock-climbing walls – the works.

There's even waterfront dining and drinking at the Chelsea Brewing Company, which serves great pub fare and delicious home brews for you to carb-load on after your workout. Though the complex is somewhat cut off by the busy West Side Hwy (Twelfth Ave), the wide array of attractions here brings in the crowds; the M23 crosstown bus, which goes right to the main entrance, saves you the long, four-avenue trek from the subway.

WEST 4TH STREET BASKETBALL COURTS — BASKETBALL

Map p418 (Sixth Ave, btwn 3rd & 4th Sts; ⌚hours vary; [S]A/C/E, B/D/F/V to W 4th St-Washington Sq) Also known as 'the Cage,' this small basketball court that stands enclosed within chain-link fencing is home to some of the best streetball in the country. Though it's more touristy than its counterpart, Rucker Park in Harlem, that's also part of its charm, as the games held here in the center of the Village draw massive, excitable crowds, who often stand five-deep to hoot and holler for the skilled, competitive guys who play here. Prime time is summer, when the W 4th St Summer Pro-Classic League, with daily high-energy games, hits the scene. While the height of this court's popularity was back in 2001 – the year Nike capitalized on the raw energy of the place by shooting a commercial here – b'ball-lovin' throngs still storm the place on weekends.

BOWLMOR LANES — BOWLING

Map p418 (☎212-255-8188; www.bowlmor.com; 110 University Pl; bowling per person from $12, shoe rental $6; ⌚1pm-midnight Mon-Thu, noon-2am Fri & Sat, noon-midnight Sun; [S]L, N/Q/R, 4/5/6 to 14th St-Union Sq) Among retro-crazed New Yorkers, a night of bowling qualifies as quite a hoot. Open since 1938, Bowlmor has Manhattan's go-to-lanes for stars, bar mitzvah parties and beer-slugging NYU students. After 9pm Monday, it goes DJ-blasting glow-in-the-dark, with unlimited bowling for $25 including shoe rental (age 21 and up).

NEW YORK TRAPEZE SCHOOL — SPORTS

Map p418 (www.newyork.trapezeschool.com; Pier 40 at West Side Hwy; classes from $50; [S]1 to Houston St) Fulfill your circus dreams, like Carrie did on *Sex and the City,* flying trapeze to trapeze in this open-air tent by the river. It's open from May to September, on top of Pier 40. The school also has an **indoor facility** (Map p446; 53-21 Vernon Blvd, Long Island City, Queens; [S]7 to Vernon Blvd-Jackson Ave) inside the Circus Warehouse in Long Island City, Queens, open October to April. Call or check the website for daily class times. There's a one-time $22 registration fee.

DOWNTOWN BOATHOUSE — KAYAKING

Map p418 (www.downtownboathouse.org; Pier 40, near Houston St; tours free; ⌚10am-6pm Sat & Sun, 5-7pm Thu mid-May–mid-Oct; [S]1 to Houston St) New York's most active public boathouse offers free walk-up 20-minute kayaking sessions (including equipment) in a protected embayment in the Hudson River on weekends and some weekday evenings. Longer weekend three-hour trips usually go from the Midtown location at **Clinton Cove** (Map p430; Pier 96 at W 56th St; ⌚9am-6pm Sat & Sun, 5-7pm Mon-Fri mid-Jun–Aug; [S]A/C, B/D, 1 to 59th St-Columbus Circle); there's another boathouse at **Riverside Park** (Map p434; W 72nd St; ⌚10am-5pm Sun; [S]1/2/3 to 72nd St) on the Upper West Side; and a summer-only location on **Governor's Island** (⌚10:30am-4pm Sat Jun-Aug).

TONY DAPOLITO RECREATION CENTER — SWIMMING

Map p418 (☎212-242-5228; 3 Clarkson St; ⌚7am-10pm Mon-Fri, 9am-4:30pm Sat & Sun; [S]1 to Houston St) This center (formerly the Carmine) has one of Manhattan's best public pools, but it's only available to members ($75 for a six-month membership). It has an indoor and outdoor swimming pool (the latter was used for the pool scene in *Raging Bull*).

Union Square, Flatiron District & Gramercy

Neighborhood Top Five

1 Mentally configuring your fantasy loft while perusing floor after floor of wildly priced home goods at uber-gorgeous **ABC Carpet & Home** (p172).

2 Prodding fresh produce and sampling artisan treats at the **Union Square Greenmarket** (p173), which transforms into a delightful Christmas market.

3 Slurping craft brews at Eataly's secret beer garden, **Birreria** (p170), high up among the Flatiron District's clock towers.

4 Walking square around elegant **Gramercy Park**, enjoying one of the city's most intimate urban moments.

5 Snacking on coveted **Shake Shack** (p166) burgers and taking in art installations in leafy Madison Square Park.

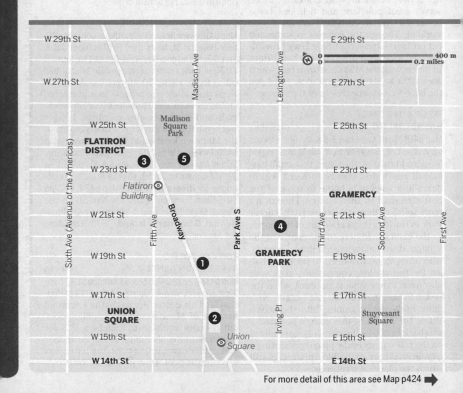

For more detail of this area see Map p424 ➡

Explore Union Square, Flatiron District & Gramercy

Union Square unifies many disparate parts of the city, acting as the veritable urban glue linking unlikely cousins. Some may criticize the area for not having a distinct personality of its own, but upon closer inspection, Union Square and the Flatiron District borrow rather cautiously and selectively from their neighbors.

There's not a lot of ground to cover, so the best plan of attack is to use the two major public spaces – Union Square and Madison Square Park – as your anchors. From Union Square you'll feel the Village vibe spilling over with the likes of quirky cafes, funky store fronts and dreadlocked buskers in the square itself. Up towards 23rd St you'll find the namesake Flatiron Building looming over the commercial quarter, replete with crowded lunch spots and after-work watering holes. East of both public spaces is Gramercy, its distinctly residential vibe tempered with buzzing restaurants.

Local Life

➡ **Mad Sq Eats** Each spring and fall, foodies flock to tiny General Worth Square – wedged between Fifth Ave and Broadway, opposite Madison Square Park – for **Mad Sq Eats** (Map p424; www.madisonsquarepark.org/tag/mad-sq-eats; General Worth Sq; [S] N/R, F/M, 6 to 23rd St), a month-long culinary pop-up market. Its 30 or so vendors include some of the city's hottest eateries, cooking up anything from proper pizza to brisket tacos using top local produce.

➡ **Gourmet groceries** Eataly (p172) had made a name for itself as the place to go for Italophile food buffs, but locals do much more of their everyday shopping at health conscious supermarket Whole Foods (p173).

Getting There & Away

➡ **Subway** A slew of subway lines converge below Union Square, shuttling passengers up Manhattan's East Side on the 4/5/6 lines, straight across to Williamsburg on the L, or up and over to Queens on the N/Q/R lines. The L also travels across to the West Side, although when there's no traffic it costs about the same to take a cab (if you're two or more people). Take the Q for an express link up to Herald Square and Times Square.

➡ **Bus** The M14 and the M23 provide cross-town service along 14th St and 23rd St respectively. Go for the bus over the subway if you're traveling between two eastern points in Manhattan – it's not worth traveling over to Union Square to walk back to First Ave.

Lonely Planet's Top Tip

Human traffic can be overwhelming in Union Square, especially along 14th St. If you're in a rush, or trying to hoof it on foot, then switch over to 13th St and you'll cover a lot more ground in much less time.

🍴 Best Places to Eat

➡ Eleven Madison Park (p167)
➡ Maialino (p167)
➡ ABC Kitchen (p170)
➡ Ess-a-Bagel (p166)

For reviews, see p164 ➡

🍷 Best Places to Drink

➡ Birreria (p170)
➡ Flatiron Lounge (p170)
➡ Raines Law Room (p171)
➡ Beauty Bar (p171)
➡ Gramercy Tavern (p167)

For reviews, see p170 ➡

👁 Best Spots to Instagram

➡ The north side of Gramercy Park, looking up Lexington Ave toward the Chrysler Building

➡ Birreria (p170), from the roof deck

➡ The south side of Madison Square Park (p164) for a full-frontal of the Flatiron Building

➡ The stone steps on the southern end of Union Square (p162), capturing the ever-changing spectacle of protestors, buskers and general eccentrics

For reviews, see p164 ➡

TOP SIGHT
UNION SQUARE

Union Square is like the Noah's Ark of New York, rescuing at least two of every kind from the curling seas of concrete. In fact, one would be hard-pressed to find a more eclectic cross-section of locals gathered in one public place. Amid the tapestry of stone steps and fenced-in foliage it's not uncommon to find denizens of every ilk: suited businessfolk gulping fresh air during their lunch breaks, dreadlocked loiterers tapping beats on their tabla, and skateboarding punks flipping tricks on the southeastern stairs.

DON'T MISS...

➜ Union Square Greenmarket

➜ Gandhi statue

➜ *Metronome* art installation

➜ Protests, sit-ins and buskers

Riches & Rags

Opened in 1831, Union Square quickly became the central gathering place for those who lived in the mansions nearby. Concert halls and artist societies further enhanced the cultured atmosphere, and high-end shopping quickly proliferated along Broadway, which was dubbed 'Ladies' Mile.'

When the Civil War broke out, the vast public space (large by New York standards, of course) was center stage for protesters of all sorts – from union workers to political activists. By the height of WWI, the area had fallen largely into disuse, allowing politically and socially driven organizations like the American Civil Liberties Union, the Communist and Socialist Parties and the Ladies' Garment Workers Union to move in.

Union Square remains a popular site for political and social protests today.

PRACTICALITIES

➜ Map p424

➜ www.union-squarenyc.org

➜ 17th St btwn Broadway & Park Ave S

➜ Ⓢ L, N/Q/R, 4/5/6 to 14th St-Union Sq

The Factory

After more than a century of the continuous push-and-pull between dapper-dom and political protest, a third – artistic, if not thoroughly hippie-ish – ingredient was tossed into the mix when Andy Warhol moved his Factory to the 6th floor of the Decker Building at 33 Union Sq West. It was here, on June 3, 1968, that disgruntled writer Valerie Solanas shot Warhol three times, seriously wounding him. The building is now a Puma sportswear store – a telling sign of the times.

Metronome

A walk around Union Square will reveal a string of whimsical, temporary sculptures. Of the permanent offerings is an imposing equestrian statue of George Washington (one of the first public pieces of art in New York City) and a statue of peacemaker Mahatma Gandhi. Trumping both on the southeast side of the square is a massive art installation that either earns confused stares or simply gets overlooked by passersby. A symbolic representation of the passage of time, *Metronome* has two parts – a digital clock with a puzzling display of numbers, and a wand-like apparatus with smoke puffing out of concentric rings. We'll let you ponder the latter while we give you the skinny on what exactly the winking orange digits denote: the 14 numbers must be split into two groups of seven – the seven from the left tell the current time (hour, minute, second, tenth-of-a-second) and the seven from the right are meant to be read in reverse order; they represent the remaining amount of time in the day.

FLATIRON BUILDING

Designed by Daniel Burnham and built in 1902, the 20-story Flatiron Building has a uniquely narrow triangular footprint that resembles the prow of a massive ship. It also features a traditional beaux arts limestone and terra-cotta facade that gets more complex and beautiful the longer you stare at it. Until 1909 it was the world's tallest building.

The Immortal Tower

Publisher Frank Munsey was one of the building's first tenants, and from his 18th-floor offices published *Munsey's Magazine,* which featured the writings of short-story writer William Sydney Porter, whose pen name was 'O Henry.' His musings (in popular stories such as 'The Gift of the Magi'), the paintings of John Sloan and the photographs of Alfred Stieglitz, best immortalized the Flatiron back in the day – along with a famous comment by actress Katherine Hepburn, who quipped that she'd like to be admired as much as the grand old building.

Today & Tomorrow

While there are plans to transform the Flatiron into a luxurious five-star hotel, progress is on hold until the final business tenants willingly vacate the premises. In the meantime, the ground floor of the building's 'prow' has been transformed into a glassed-in art space showcasing the work of guest artists. In 2013, the space featured a life-sized 3D-cutout replica of Edward Hopper's 1942 painting *Nighthawks,* its angular diner remarkably similar to the Flatiron's distinctive shape.

DON'T MISS...

➡ The view of the facade from Madison Square Park

➡ An up-close-and-personal look to appreciate the fine exterior detail

➡ Flatiron Prow Artspace

PRACTICALITIES

➡ Map p424

➡ Broadway, cnr Fifth Ave & 23rd St

➡ S N/R, F/M, 6 to 23rd St

SIGHTS

UNION SQUARE — SQUARE

See p162.

FLATIRON BUILDING — LANDMARK

See p163.

MADISON SQUARE PARK — PARK

Map p424 (www.madisonsquarepark.org; 23rd to 26th Sts, btwn Fifth & Madison Aves; ⌚6am-11pm; 📶; [S]N/R, F/M, 6 to 23rd St) This park defined the northern reaches of Manhattan until the island's population exploded after the Civil War. These days, it's a much-welcome oasis from Manhattan's relentless pace, with locals unleashing their dogs in the popular dog-run area, children squealing giddily at the impressive playground, and the hungry lining up at on-site burger joint Shake Shack (p166).

The park is the perfect spot from which to gaze up at the landmarks that surround it, including the Flatiron Building to the southwest, the art deco Metropolitan Life Insurance Tower to the southeast, and the New York Life Insurance Building, topped with a gilded spire, to the northeast.

Between 1876 and 1882 the torch-bearing arm of the Statue of Liberty was on display here, and in 1879 the first Madison Square Garden arena was constructed at Madison Ave and 26th St. In warm months, various park programs feature readings and music performances, many for kids, while eclectic sculptures are shown year-round. And, at the southeast corner of the park, you'll find one of the city's few self-cleaning, coin-operated toilets.

TIBET HOUSE — CULTURAL CENTER

Map p424 (☎212-807-0563; www.tibethouse.org; 22 W 15th St, btwn Fifth & Sixth Aves; suggested donation $5; ⌚11am-6pm Mon-Fri, to 4pm Sun; [S]F to 14th St, L to 6th Ave) With the Dalai Lama as the patron of its board, this non-profit cultural space is dedicated to presenting Tibet's ancient traditions through art exhibits, a research library and various publications. Programs on offer include educational workshops, open meditations, retreat weekends and docent-led tours to Tibet, Nepal and Bhutan.

Exhibits span a variety of subjects, from traditional Tibetan tangka painting and sculpture, to contemporary views of Tibetan Buddhist and Hindu tantric art.

THEODORE ROOSEVELT BIRTHPLACE — HISTORIC SITE

Map p424 (☎212-260-1616; www.nps.gov/thrb; 28 E 20th St, btwn Park Ave S & Broadway; adult/child $3/free; ⌚guided tours 10am, 11am, 1pm, 2pm, 3pm & 4pm Tue-Sat; [S]N/R/W, 6 to 23rd St) This National Historic Site is a bit of a cheat, since the physical house where the 26th president was actually born was demolished in his own lifetime. But this building is a worthy reconstruction by his relatives, who joined it with another family residence next door.

If you're interested in Roosevelt's extraordinary life, which has been somewhat overshadowed by the enduring legacy of his younger cousin Franklin D, visit here – especially if you don't have the time to see his spectacular summer home in Long Island's Oyster Bay. Guided tours of the property last 30 minutes.

NATIONAL ARTS CLUB — CULTURAL CENTER

Map p424 (☎212-475-3424; www.nationalartsclub.org; 15 Gramercy Park S; [S]6 to 23rd St) Founded in 1898 to promote public interest in the arts, the National Arts Club boasts a beautiful, vaulted, stained-glass ceiling above the wooden bar in its picture-lined front parlor. The building itself was designed by Calvert Vaux, one of the creators of Central Park. The club holds art exhibitions, ranging from sculpture to photography, that are open to the public from 9am to 5pm Monday to Friday (check the website for upcoming shows).

It also hosts life drawing classes on Monday evenings from 7pm to 9pm (see www.simonlevenson.com for details).

EATING

A veritable gold mine of eateries, this multinamed area stretches from E 14th St to about the mid-30s. One precious perk is the Union Square Greenmarket – a sensory delight held Monday, Wednesday, Friday and Saturday – where discerning chefs, both pro and amateur, scour the wares of upstate farmers and get inspiration for their next meals. Beyond this patch of green is a large range of offerings – both Michelin-starred fine-diners and low-key neighborhood staples. Madison Square Park is host to the popular alfresco

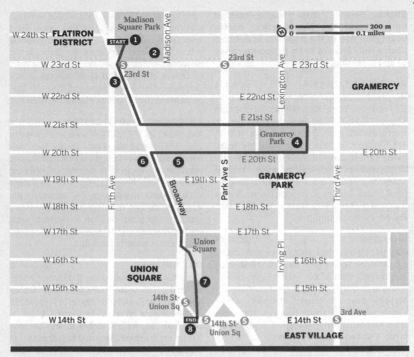

♦ Neighborhood Walk
Be There, Be Square

START MADISON SQUARE PARK
END DSW
LENGTH 2 MILES; 2 HOURS

Start off in leafy ❶ **Madison Square Park** (p164), dotted with historic statues and contemporary sculptures. If you're peckish, hit up ❷ **Shake Shack** (p166) for a gourmet burger and fries. Before exiting the park, stand at its southwest corner and take in the arresting ❸ **Flatiron Building** (p163), Chicago architect Daniel Burnham's clever response to the awkward space where Fifth Ave and Broadway meet. Its triangular, beaux arts style is mesmerizing from across the street; stand up close to admire its terra-cotta ornamentation. Follow Broadway south to 21st St and take a left. Past Park Ave S you'll find yourself alongside ❹ **Gramercy Park**, created by Samuel Ruggles in 1831 after he drained the swamp in this area and laid out streets in an English style. You can't enter the private park, but peer through the gate and imagine the likes of actor Drew Barrymore's grandfather, John Barrymore, enjoying it; the thespian

once resided at 36 Gramercy Park E. At 15 Gramercy Park S stands the National Arts Club, once home to Samuel J Tilden, governor of New York and failed presidential candidate in 1876. Head back west along 20th St and stop at the reconstructed version of ❺ **Theodore Roosevelt's Birthplace**, which offers hourly tours. On the southwest corner of Broadway and E 20th St stands the old ❻ **Lord & Taylor Building**, former home of the famous Midtown department store. A Gothic-inspired creation, it stands in an area formerly nicknamed 'Ladies' Mile' for its once-abundant emporiums. Continue south on Broadway and you'll find the northwest corner of ❼ **Union Square** (p162). Check out the produce, baked goods and flowers of the Greenmarket farmers market, seek out Gandhi near the southwest corner, or grab some food at one of the surrounding eateries for a picnic in the park. If you have any residual energy, cross Union Sq South (14th St) and dive into ❽ **DSW**, a massive warehouse dedicated to heavily discounted designer shoes and accessories.

Shake Shack, with foodie-focused burgers and the like. Further north, Lexington Ave in the high 20s is dubbed 'Curry Hill,' thanks to its preponderance of spots serving Indian fare.

DOS TOROS TAQUERIA — MEXICAN $

Map p424 (☎212-677-7300; www.dostoros.com; 137 Fourth Ave, btwn 13th & 14th Sts; burritos from $7; ⊙11:30am-10:30pm Mon, to 11pm Tue-Fri, noon-11pm Sat, noon-10:30pm Sun; ⓈL, N/Q/R, 4/5/6 to Union Sq) Skip the national Mexican-food chain in favor of this citywide favorite that promises high-quality meats tucked safely in a sea of thick guacamole and re-fried beans. Lines can be long (so you know it's good) but efficient staffers whip up your Tex-Mex treat in minutes.

SHAKE SHACK — BURGERS $

Map p424 (☎212-989-6600; www.shakeshack.com; Madison Square Park, cnr 23rd St & Madison Ave; burgers from $3.60; ⊙11am-11pm; ⓈN/R, F/M, 6 to 23rd St) The flagship of chef Danny Meyer's gourmet burger chainlet, Shake Shack whips up fresh burgers, hand-cut fries and a rotating lineup of frozen custards. Veg-heads can dip into the crisp portobello burger. Lines are long, but worth it.

ESS-A-BAGEL — DELI $

Map p424 (☎212-260-2252; www.ess-a-bagel.com; 359 First Ave, at 21st St; bagels from $1.65; ⊙6am-9pm Mon-Fri, to 5pm Sat & Sun; ⓈL, N/Q/R, 4/5/6 to Union Sq) It's simply impossible to resist the billowy tufts of sesame-scented smoke that waft out onto First Ave. Inside, crowds of lip-smacking locals yell at the bagel mongers for their classic New York snack topped with generous gobs of cream cheese. And those gaudy, jewel-dripping chandeliers jammed into the Styrofoam ceiling? You stay classy, Ess-a-Bagel.

ARTICHOKE BASILLE'S PIZZA — PIZZERIA $

Map p424 (☎212-228-2004; www.artichokepizza.com; 328 E 14th St, btwn First & Second Aves; slice from $4.50; ⊙11am-5am; ⓈL to First Ave) Run by two Italian guys from Staten Island, offering pizza that's authentic, tangy and piled high with all sorts of toppings. The signature pie is a rich, cheesy treat with artichokes and spinach; the plain Sicilian is thinner, with emphasis solely on the crisp crust and savory sauce. Lines usually form fast.

MAX BRENNER — DESSERTS $

Map p424 (Chocolate by the Bald Man; ☎646-467-8803; www.maxbrenner.com; 841 Broadway, btwn 13th & 14th Sts; desserts from $8.50; ⊙9am-midnight Mon-Thu, to 2am Fri & Sat, to 11pm Sun; ⓈL, N/Q/R, 4/5/6 to 14th St-Union Sq) Sweet-toothed Aussie Max Brenner is expanding waistlines in NYC with his cafe-cum-chocolate-bar. It's a Wonker-ful spot for a cocoa rush, whether it's from sipping a chocolate martini, gobbling down peanut butter and banana chocolate crêpes, or nibbling nicely on an artisan truffle. There is a full menu (great breakfast), but it's the chocolate that'll leave you gaga.

CURRY HILL

It's not exactly politically correct, but a small four-block section north of Union Square and Gramercy, traditionally known as Murray Hill, is sometimes also referred to as Curry Hill – a nod to the numerous Indian restaurants, shops and delis that proliferate here. Starting around E 28th St and flowing north on Lexington Ave to about E 33rd St, you'll find some of the finest Indian eateries in town – and most at bargain prices. The all-time local fave? **Curry in a Hurry** (Map p426; ☎212-683-0900; www.curryinahurrynyc.com; 119 Lexington Ave, at E 28th St; ⊙11am-10pm; Ⓢ6 to 28th St) in Midtown. It's not fancy, but even Bono of U2 fame has been spotted having a nosh here.

CITY BAKERY — BAKERY $

Map p424 (☎212-366-1414; www.thecitybakery.com; 3 W 18th St, btwn Fifth & Sixth Aves; pastries from $3, cafeteria lunch per pound $15; ⊙7:30am-7pm Mon-Fri, 8am-7pm Sat, 9am-6pm Sun; ⓈL, N/Q/R, 4/5/6 to 14th St-Union Sq) A happy marriage between gourmet mains and cafeteria service, City Bakery is best known for its scrumptious drip coffee (look how they pour the milk in first – yum!) and homemade hot chocolate. Breakfast edibles include yogurt with fresh fruit, muffins, croissants and scrambled eggs, while the Sunday brunch is particularly popular.

REPUBLIC — ASIAN $$

Map p424 (www.thinknoodles.com; 37 Union Sq W; mains $12-15; ⊙11:30am-10:30pm Sun-Wed, to 11:30pm Thu-Sat; ⓈL, N/Q/R, 4/5/6 to 14th St-Union Sq) Eat-and-go Republic feeds the masses with fresh 'n' tasty Asian staples.

Slurp away on warming broth noodles, chomp on juicy pad thai or keep it light with a green papaya and mango salad. Located right on Union Square, it's a handy spot for a cheap, uncomplicated, walk-in bite.

BOQUERIA FLATIRON TAPAS **$$**

Map p424 (☎212-255-4160; www.boquerianyc.com; 53 W 19th St, btwn Fifth & Sixth Aves; mains $5-22; ⏰noon-10:30pm Sun-Wed, to 11:30pm Thu-Sat; [S]F/M, N/R, 6 to 23rd St) A holy union between Spanish-style tapas and market-fresh fare, Boqueria woos the after-work crowd with a brilliant lineup of small plates and larger *raciones*. Lick lips and fingers over the likes of sautéed wild mushrooms with Manchego cheese and thyme, or tender baby squid seared *a la plancha* with frisée, tomato confit and crispy scallions.

A smooth selection of Spanish cheeses and wines tops it all off. *¡Buen provecho!*

★ELEVEN MADISON PARK MODERN AMERICAN **$$$**

Map p424 (☎212-889-0905; www.elevenmadisonpark.com; 11 Madison Ave, btwn 24th & 25th Sts; tasting menu $225; ⏰noon-1pm Thu-Sat, 5:30-10pm Mon-Sun; [S]N/R, F/M, 6 to 23rd St) Once overlooked in this star-studded town, this deco wonder has rocketed up the charts, coming in at number five in the 2013 San Pellegrino World's 50 Best Restaurants list. It's hardly surprising: this revamped poster child of modern, sustainable American cooking is also one of only seven NYC restaurants sporting three Michelin stars.

Behind the buzz is young-gun co-owner and chef Daniel Humm, who turns immaculate regional ingredients into indescribably pure, sublime statements. Here, a carrot is not just a carrot, it becomes a revelatory tartare, ground at the table and mixed with seasonings to create a dish that kicks the finest meat tartares off their perch. Book ahead.

★MAIALINO ITALIAN **$$$**

Map p424 (☎212 777 2410; www.maialinonyc.com; 2 Lexington Ave, at 21st St; mains lunch $19-26, dinner $28-72; ⏰breakfast, lunch & dinner; [S]6, N/R to 23rd St) Take your taste buds on a Roman holiday at this Danny Meyer must, humming away inside the forever-fashionable Gramercy Park Hotel. Created with Greenmarket produce from nearby Union Square, Maialino's iterations of rustic Italian fare are exquisite; one taste of the extraordinary *brodetto* (seafood stew), and we swear you'll agree.

Friendly staffers are solidly clued-in on the wine list, while the $35 prix fixe lunch is great value, especially if you opt for the pricier items.

GRAMERCY TAVERN AMERICAN **$$$**

Map p424 (☎212-477-0777; www.gramercytavern.com; 42 E 20th St, btwn Broadway & Park Ave S; tasting menu lunch/dinner $58/120; ⏰tavern noon-11pm Sun-Thu, to midnight Fri & Sat, dining room noon-2pm & 5:30-10pm Mon-Thu, to 11pm Fri, 5:30-11pm Sat, 5:30-10pm Sun; [S]N/R, 6 to 23rd St) 🌿 Seasonal, local ingredients drive Gramercy Tavern, a country-chic institution aglow with copper sconces, bright murals and dramatic floral arrangements. Choose from two spaces: the walk-in-only tavern and its à la carte menu, or the swankier dining room and its more ambitious prix fixe and degustation feasts.

Either way, soulful dishes like pasture-raised chicken and sausage with apples, kohlrabi and buckwheat dumplings will leave you with a postprandial glow. Desserts are suitably decadent and the wine list one of the city's best.

CASA MONO TAPAS **$$$**

Map p424 (☎212-253-2773; www.casamononyc.com; 52 Irving Pl, btwn 17th & 18th Sts; small plates $9-24; ⏰noon-midnight; [S]L, N/Q/R, 4/5/6 to Union Sq) Another success story from Mario Batali and chef Andy Nusser, Casa Mono features a great, long bar where you can sit and watch your Michelin-starred tapas getting ready, as well as tables for more discreet conversation. Either way, get set for flavor-slamming bites like cauliflower crema with raw sea urchin and Vadouvan. Around the corner lies Batali's fun, communal **Bar Jamón** (Map p424; 125 E 17th St; ⏰5pm-2am Mon-Fri, noon-2am Sat & Sun).

CRAFT AMERICAN **$$$**

Map p424 (☎212-780-0880; www.craftrestaurantsinc.com; 43 E 19th St, btwn Park Ave S & Broadway; mains $29-41, tasting menu $150; ⏰5:30-10pm Sun-Thu, to 11pm Fri & Sat; [S]L, N/Q/R, 4/5/6 to 14th St-Union Sq) When superchef Tom Colicchio opened this fine-food palace several years ago, the concept was completely new: create your own meal with à la carte items, and enjoy the feeling that not a plate on your table was cookie cutter. Copycats sprang up around town, but this spot still reigns.

168

1. Eataly (p172)
Sample gourmet produce in this 50,000-sq-ft market, or take part in a cooking class.

2. Madison Square Park (p164)
Gaze up at the park's surrounding landmarks, watch readings and music performances or view the sculptures, including *Echo*, by Jaume Plensa

3. Union Square Greenmarket (p173)
Check out the produce in the city's most famous greenmarket, which offers everything from fresh fruit and vegetables to local honey.

4. Metronome (p162)
Ponder the art installation *Metronome*, by Kristin Jones and Andrew Ginzel, a symbolic representation of the passage of time.

Menu items can be found under their appropriate subject headings – fish and shellfish, meat, pasta, salad, vegetables – and it's up to you to make the matches (or ask for some expert direction). You might wind up with a plate of roasted swordfish with sautéed Swiss chard. Or perhaps some roasted Rohan duck with roasted baby carrots will float your boat. Can't decide? Opt for the tasting menu: a seven-course feast with optional wine pairings.

ABC KITCHEN MODERN AMERICAN **$$$**

Map p424 (☎212-475-5829; www.abckitchennyc.com; 35 E 18th St, at Broadway; pizzas $15-19, dinner mains $24-34; ⏲noon-3pm & 5:30-10:30pm Mon-Wed, to 11pm Thu, to 11:30pm Fri, 11am-3:30pm & 5:30-11:30pm Sat, to 10pm Sun; ✎; [S]L, N/Q/R, 4/5/6 to Union Sq) 🍃 Looking part gallery, part rustic farmhouse, sustainable ABC Kitchen is the culinary avatar of chichi home goods department store ABC Carpet & Home. Organic gets haute in dishes like vibrant raw diver scallops with market grapes and lemon verbena, or comforting roast suckling pig with braised turnips and smoked bacon marmalade. For a more casual bite, hit the scrumptious whole-wheat pizzas.

PURE FOOD & WINE VEGETARIAN **$$$**

Map p424 (☎212-477-1010; www.oneluckyduck.com; 54 Irving Pl, btwn 17th & 18th Sts; mains $19-26; ⏲noon-4pm & 5:30-11pm; ✎; [S]L, N/Q/R, 4/5/6 to 14th St-Union Sq) 🍃 Smart and sophisticated, Pure achieves the impossible, churning out obscenely delicious creations made completely from raw organics put through blenders, dehydrators and the capable hands of its staff. The result is seductive, invigorating dishes like tomato-zucchini lasagna (sans cheese and pasta), Brazil-nut sea-vegetable croquettes, and a gorgeous lemon bar with almond coconut crust and zesty lemon custard.

There's a good-value three-course prix fixe lunch for $30, and a leafy backyard for alfresco dining among salubrious, eye-candy diners.

TRATTORIA IL MULINO ITALIAN **$$$**

Map p424 (☎212-777-8448; www.trattoriailmulino.com; 36 E 20th St, btwn Broadway & Park Ave; pasta dishes $24, mains $28-45; ⏲11:30am-11pm Sun-Thu, to 2am Fri & Sat; [S]6, N/R to 23rd St) That head chef Michele Mazza looks uncannily like Italian film star Marcello Mastroianni seems apt – his beautifully prepared dishes personify Italian dolce vita. The pasta dishes and wood-fired pizzas are particularly memorable, while cross-regional influences meet in the zingy, classic-with-a-twist limoncello tiramisu. Attentive service and a chic-yet-amiable vibe make this spot *perfetto* for a special feed.

🍷 DRINKING & NIGHTLIFE

As the Village morphs into Midtown you'll find a great diversity of drinking spots from stylish hotel lounges to fancy eatery bars and a few down-and-dirty basics thrown in for good measure. If you need a regular-guy Irish pub, look on Third Ave north of 14th St.

★BIRRERIA BEER HALL

Map p424 (www.eataly.com/birreria; 200 Fifth Ave, at 23rd St; mains $17-26; ⏲11:30am-midnight Sun-Wed, to 1am Thu-Sat; [S]N/R, F/M, 6 to 23rd St) The crown jewel of Italian food emporium Eataly (p172) is its rooftop beer garden tucked betwixt the Flatiron's corporate towers. A beer menu of encyclopedic proportions offers drinkers some of the best suds on the planet. If you're hungry, the signature pork shoulder is your frosty one's soul mate.

In case you can't find the sneaky access elevator, it's near the checkouts on the 23rd St side of the store.

★FLATIRON LOUNGE COCKTAIL BAR

Map p424 (www.flatironlounge.com; 37 W 19th St, btwn Fifth & Sixth Aves; ⏲4pm-2am Mon-Wed, to 3am Thu, to 4am Fri, 5pm-4am Sat, 5pm-2am Sun; [S]F/M, N/R, 6 to 23rd St) Until time machines hit the market, this swinging cocktail den will do just fine. Head through a dramatic archway and into a dark, deco-inspired fantasy of lipstick-red booths, racy jazz tunes and sassy grown-ups downing seasonal drinks. The Beijing Mule (Jasmine vodka, lime juice, ginger syrup and pomegranate molasses) is scrumptious, while the genial 'Flight of the Day' (a trio of mini-sized cocktails) is head-spinning enlightenment.

TOBY'S ESTATE CAFE

Map p424 (www.tobysestate.com; 160 Fifth Ave, btwn 20th & 21st Sts; ⏲7am-9pm Mon-Fri, 9am-9pm Sat, 10am-7pm Sun; [S]N/R, F/M, 6 to 23rd St) Sydney-born, Williamsburg-roasting Toby's Estate is further proof of Manhattan's evolving artisan coffee culture. Loaded with a custom-made Strada espresso machine, you'll find it tucked away in the Club Monaco store. Join coffee geeks for thick, rich brews, among them a geo-specific Flatiron Espresso Blend. Nibbles include pastries and sandwiches from local bakeries.

71 IRVING PLACE CAFE

Map p424 (Irving Farm Coffee Company; www.irvingfarm.com; 71 Irving Pl, btwn 18th & 19th Sts; ⏲7am-10pm Mon-Fri, 8am-10pm Sat & Sun; [S]4/5/6, N/Q/R to 14th St-Union Sq) Few places take coffee more seriously than Irving Farm, as you'll find out at this quaint cafe just steps away from the peaceful Gramercy Park. Hand-picked beans are lovingly roasted on a farm in the Hudson Valley (about 90 miles from NYC), and imbibers can tell – this is one of the smoothest cups of joe you'll find in Manhattan.

RAINES LAW ROOM COCKTAIL BAR

Map p424 (www.raineslawroom.com; 48 W 17th St, btwn Fifth & Sixth Aves; ⏲5pm-2am Mon-Thu, to 3am Fri & Sat, 8pm-1am Sun; [S]F/M to 14th St, L to 6th Ave, 1 to 18th St) A sea of velvet drapes and overstuffed leather lounge chairs, tin-tiled ceilings, the perfect amount of exposed brick, and expertly crafted cocktails using perfectly aged spirits – these guys are about as serious as a mortgage payment when it comes to amplified atmosphere. Walk through the unassuming entrance and let Raines Law Room transport you to a far more sumptuous era

BEAUTY BAR THEME BAR

Map p424 (☎212-539-1389; www.thebeautybar.com; 531 E 14th St, btwn Second & Third Aves; ⏲5pm-4am Mon-Fri, 2pm-4am Sat & Sun; [S]L to 3rd Ave) A kitschy favorite since the mid-'90s, this homage to old-fashioned beauty parlors pulls in a cool local crowd with its gritty soundtrack, nostalgic vibe and around-$10 manicures (with a free Blue Rinse margarita thrown in) from 6pm to 11pm weekdays and 3pm to 11pm weekends. Nightly events range from comedy to karaoke.

BOXERS NYC GAY

Map p424 (☎212-255-5082; www.boxersnyc.com; 37 W 20th St, btwn Fifth & Sixth Aves; ⏲4pm-2am Mon-Wed, to 4am Thu & Fri, 1pm-4am Sat, 1pm-2am Sun; [S]F/M, N/R, 6 to 23rd St) Dave & Busters meets David Bowie at this self-proclaimed gay sports bar in the heart of the Flatiron District. There's football on the TV, buffalo wings at the bar, and topless wait-staff keeping the pool cues polished. Monday's drag theme keeps everyone keenly aware that Boxers has a different definition of 'bromance.'

While there's now a second Boxers branch in **Hell's Kitchen** (Map p430; 742 Ninth Ave, at 50th St; ⏲4pm-2am Mon-Wed, to 4am Thu & Fri, 1pm-4am Sat, 1pm-2am Sun; [S]C/E, 1 to 50th St), locals concur that the original remains the best.

CROCODILE LOUNGE LOUNGE

Map p424 (☎212-477-7747; www.crocodileloungenyc.com; 325 E 14th St, btwn First & Second Aves; ⏲noon-4am; [S]L to 1st Ave) Hankering for Williamsburg but too lazy to cross the river? Then dive into Crocodile Lounge, outpost of Brooklyn success story Alligator Lounge. The lure of free pizza makes this hideout a big hit with East Village 20-somethings seeking a free feed. Slip on your skinny jeans and join them for on-tap microbrews, open-mike sessions and some skee-ball.

OLD TOWN BAR & RESTAURANT BAR

Map p424 (☎212-529-6732; www.oldtownbar.com; 45 E 18th St, btwn Broadway & Park Ave S; ⏲11:30am-11:30pm Mon-Fri, 10am-11:30pm Sat, 11am-11:30pm Sun; [S]L, N/Q/R, 4/5/6 to 14th St-Union Sq) It still looks like 1892 in here, with the original tile floors and tin ceilings – the Old Town is an 'old world' drinking-man's classic (and woman's: Madonna lit up at the bar here, when lighting up was still legal, in her 'Bad Girl' video). There are cocktails around, but most come for an afternoon beer and burger (from $11.50).

PETE'S TAVERN BAR

Map p424 (☎212-473-7676; www.petestavern.com; 129 E 18th St, at Irving Pl; ⏲11am-2am; [S]L, N/Q/R, 4/5/6 to 14th St-Union Sq) This dark and atmospheric watering hole has all the earmarks of a New York classic – pressed tin, carved wood and an air of literary history. You can get a respectable burger here and choose from 17 draft beers. The pub draws in everyone from post-theater couples and Irish expats to no-nonsense NYU students.

NOWHERE GAY

Map p424 (☎212-477-4744; www.nowherebarnyc.com; 322 E 14th St, btwn First & Second Aves; ⏲3pm-4am; [S]L to First Ave) Dank and rife with amiable, flannel-clad fellas,

Nowhere is everything your local gay dive bar should be (yes, there's a pool table to boot). The booze is priced for the '99%' and there's a pizza joint nearby, which keeps crowds hanging out 'til the wee hours of the morn.

ROLF'S BAR & GERMAN RESTAURANT THEME BAR

Map p424 (☎212-477-4750; www.rolfsnyc.com; 281 Third Ave, at 22nd St; ⏰noon-midnight; [S]N/R, 6 to 23rd St) During the six weeks before Christmas, Rolf's transforms itself from a standard-fare German bar into a whimsical tribute to the yuletide season that falls somewhere between Santa's workshop and an Addams Family holiday party, with bulbous ornaments and hundreds of dolls that stare at you blankly while you swig your pint.

☆ ENTERTAINMENT

PEOPLES IMPROV THEATER COMEDY

Map p424 (PIT; ☎212-563-7488; www.thepit-nyc.com; 123 E 24th St, btwn Lexington & Park Aves; 📶; [S]6, N/R, F/M to 23rd St) Aglow in red neon, this bustling comedy club serves up top-notch laughs at dirt-cheap prices (from free to a modest $20). The string of nightly acts ranges from stand-up to musical comedy, playing in either the mainstage theater or the basement lounge.

PIT also runs professional courses in everything from acting to comedy writing at its off-site location in Midtown, **Simple Studios** (Map p430; 134 W 29th St btwn Sixth & Seventh Aves; [S]1, N/R to 28th St). Courses include three-hour, drop-in improv workshops; perfect for time-pressed comics in the making. See the website for details.

🛍 SHOPPING

While this big block of neighborhoods mightn't have the retail magnetism of SoHo, Nolita or Midtown, it does claim more than a few nuggets of shoppers' gold, from independent bookstores to an artisan cheese shop. Union Square is home to the celebrated Greenmarket, which occupies the park several times a week all year round. Meanwhile, huge chain stores flank the park to the north and south, offering books, healthy groceries and discount fashion. Fourteenth St, more to the west than to the east, is a shopping adventure all of its own, with store upon store hawking discount electronics, cheap linens and a range of shoes and hit-and-miss clothing, from bargain indies to Diesel. Head up Fifth Ave for more upmarket chains, with Paul Smith, Anthropologie and Intermix among the standouts.

★EATALY FOOD & DRINK

Map p424 (www.eatalyny.com; 200 Fifth Ave, at 23rd St; ⏰8am-11pm; [S]F/M, N/R, 6 to 23rd St) A 50,000-sq-ft tribute to la dolce vita, Mario Batali's food-filled wonderland is a New York version of those dreamy Tuscan markets you find in Diane Lane films. Decked stem to the stern with gourmet edibles, Eataly is a must for a picnic lunch – though make sure to leave room for some pork shoulder at the rooftop beer garden, Birreria (p170).

Eataly also runs on-site cooking and culinary appreciation classes. See the website for details.

ABC CARPET & HOME HOMEWARES, GIFTS

Map p424 (☎212-473-3000; www.abchome.com; 888 Broadway, at 19th St; ⏰10am-7pm Mon-Wed, Fri & Sat, to 8pm Thu, noon-6pm Sun; [S]L, N/Q/R/, 4/5/6 to 14th St-Union Sq) A mecca for home designers and decorators brainstorming ideas, this beautifully curated, six-level store heaves with all sorts of furnishings, small and large. Shop for easy-to-pack knickknacks, designer jewelry and global gifts, as well as statement furniture, slinky lamps and antique carpets. Come Christmas season the shop is a joy to behold.

BEDFORD CHEESE SHOP FOOD

Map p424 (www.bedfordcheeseshop.com; 67 Irving Pl, btwn 18th & 19th Sts; ⏰8am-9pm Mon-Sat, to 8pm Sun; [S]L, N/Q/R, 4/5/6 to 14th St-Union Sq) Whether you're after local raw cow-milk cheese washed in absinthe, or garlic-infused goat-milk cheese from Australia, chances are you'll find it among the 200-strong selection at this outpost of Brooklyn's most celebrated cheese vendor. Pair the cheesy goodness with artisanal charcuterie, deli treats and ready-to-eat sandwiches ($9), as well as a proud array of Made-in-Brooklyn edibles.

The shop runs regular on-site classes, from Cheesemaking 101, to wine and olive-oil appreciation. Check the website.

UNION SQUARE GREENMARKET MARKET

Map p424 (17th St, btwn Broadway & Park Ave S; 🕐8am-6pm Mon, Wed, Fri & Sat; [S]L, N/Q/R, 4/5/6 to 14th St-Union Sq) Don't be surprised if you spot some of New York's top chefs examining the produce here: Union Square's greenmarket is arguably the city's most famous. Whet your appetite trawling the stalls, which peddle anything and everything from upstate fruit and vegetables, to artisan breads, cider, and even honey produced on NYC rooftops.

IDLEWILD BOOKS BOOKS

Map p424 (☎212-414-8888; www.idlewildbooks.com; 12 W 19th St, btwn Fifth & Sixth Aves; 🕐noon-7:30pm Mon-Thu, to 6pm Fri & Sat, to 5pm Sun; [S]L, N/Q/R, 4/5/6 to 14th St-Union Sq) Named after JFK Airport's original moniker, this indie travel bookshop gets feet seriously itchy. Books are divided by region, and cover guidebooks as well as fiction, travelogues, history, cookbooks and other stimulating fare for delving into different corners of the world. Check the website for Idlewild's lineup of readings and book-launch parties.

BOOKS OF WONDER BOOKS

Map p424 (☎212-989-3270; www.booksofwonder.com; 18 W 18th St, btwn Fifth & Sixth Aves; 🕐11am-7pm Mon-Sat, to 6pm Sun; 👪; [S]F/M, L to 6th Ave-14th St) Kid or not, expect to fall head over heels for this colorful bookstore. Devoted to children's and young-adult titles, it's a great place to take young ones on a rainy day, especially when a kids' author is giving a reading or a storyteller is on hand. The impressive range of NYC-themed picture books make for great souvenirs.

WHOLE FOODS FOOD & DRINK

Map p424 (☎212-673-5388; www.wholefoodsmarket.com; 4 Union Sq S; 🕐7.30am-11pm; 📶; [S]L, N/Q/R, 4/5/6 to 14th St-Union Sq) One of several locations of the health-food emporium that has swept the city, Whole Foods is an excellent place to fill the picnic hamper. Drool over endless rows of gorgeous produce, both organic and non-organic, plus a butcher, a bakery, ready-to-eat dishes, a health and beauty section, and aisles packed with natural packaged goods.

ABRACADABRA ACCESSORIES

Map p424 (☎212-627-5194; 19 W 21st St, btwn Fifth & Sixth Aves; 🕐11am-7pm Mon-Fri, noon-5pm Sat & Sun; [S]N/R, 4/6 to 23 St) It's not just a Steve Miller Band song, it's also an emporium of horror, costumes and magic. Those who like this sort of thing will be hard-pressed to leave without racking up some credit-card bills.

SPORTS & ACTIVITIES

INSTITUTE OF CULINARY EDUCATION COOKING COURSE

Map p424 (ICE; http://recreational.ice.edu; 50 W 23rd St, btwn Fifth & Sixth Aves; courses $30-605; [S]F/M, N/R, 6 to 23rd St) Release your inner Jean Jacques with a cooking course at the Institute of Culinary Education. The center runs the country's biggest program of cooking, baking and wine-appreciation courses, from 90-minute classes to multi-day sessions. The varied themes range from Tuscan cooking and Japanese street food, to Californian wines and coffee presentation. Restless foodies can choose from numerous culinary tours of the city.

SOUL CYCLE CYCLING

Map p424 (☎212-208-1300; www.soul-cycle.com; 12 E 18th St, btwn Fifth Ave & Broadway; classes $34; 🕐classes 6am-9:30pm; [S]L, N/Q/R, 4/5/6 to Union Sq) 'Boutique fitness' is all the buzz in NYC, and the reigning queen is Soul Cycle, whose wellness recipe (one part spinning class, one part dance party, one part therapy session) makes exercise an easy pill to swallow. There are no membership fees, so locals and tourists alike are welcome. You may even spot a celeb – Jake Gyllenhaal is known to take a class here and there.

JIVAMUKTI YOGA

Map p424 (☎212-353-0214; www.jivamuktiyoga.com; 841 Broadway, btwn 13th & 14 Sts; classes $20; 🕐classes 7am-9pm Mon-Thu, 7am-8pm Fri, 8am-8pm Sat & Sun; [S]L, N/Q/R, 4/5/6 to 14th St-Union Sq) *The* yoga spot in Manhattan, Jivamukti – in a 12,000-sq-ft locale on Union Sq – is a posh place for *vinyasa* and hatha classes (chanting alert). The center's 'open classes' are suitable for both rookies and experienced practitioners, and there's an organic, vegan cafe on-site too. Gratuitous celebrity tidbit: Uma's little bro Dechen Thurman teaches classes here.

Midtown

MIDTOWN EAST | FIFTH AVENUE | MIDTOWN WEST | TIMES SQUARE

Neighborhood Top Five

1 Playing spot the landmark at **Top of the Rock** (p189), the Rockefeller Center's jaw-dropping observation deck. Sure, the Empire State Building might be more famous, but it's from here that you'll be able to see it.

2 Hanging out with Picasso, Warhol and Rothko at the blockbuster **Museum of Modern Art** (MoMA; p181).

3 Indulging in a little **retail rampage** (p206) on and around Fifth and Madison Aves.

4 Dirty martinis, skyline views and hot evening sax at **Jazz at Lincoln Center** (p202).

5 Adding a little sparkle to life with a toe-tapping, soul-lifting **Broadway show** (p202)

For more detail of this area see maps on p426 and p430 ➡

Explore Midtown

Midtown is big, brazen and best seen on foot, so slice it up and enjoy it bit by bit. The top end of Fifth Ave (around the 50s) makes for a fabled introduction. It's here that you'll find Tiffany & Co, the Plaza Hotel, the Museum of Modern Art (MoMA), and the Rockefeller Center's Top of the Rock observation deck. A day in Midtown East could easily incorporate rare manuscripts at the Morgan Library & Museum, beaux arts architecture at Grand Central Terminal, the art deco lobby of the Chrysler Building and a tour of the United Nations. If it's a rainy day, explore the gilded New York Public Library.

In Midtown West, design and fashion buffs head to the Museum of Arts & Design and the Museum at FIT. Between the two is blinding Times Square, most spectacular at night. It's here that you'll find a TKTS Booth selling cut-price Broadway tickets. The queues are usually shortest after 5.30pm, though clever cookies buy their tickets at the less crowded South Street Seaport branch. Further west is Hell's Kitchen, famed for its restaurants and gay scene.

Local Life

→ **Dive bars** Stiff drinks, loosened ties and the whiff of nostalgia await at no-bull bars like Jimmy's Corner (p201) and Subway Inn (p201).

→ **Theater** Look beyond the glitz and kitsch of Broadway for innovative drama at Playwrights Horizons (p204).

→ **Food** Join all walks of life at time-warped Cuban diner El Margon (p198).

Getting There & Away

→ **Subway** Times Sq-42nd St, Grand Central-42nd St and 34th St-Herald Sq are Midtown's main interchange stations. A/C/E and 1/2/3 lines run north–south through Midtown West. The 4/5/6 lines run north–south through Midtown East. The central B/D/F/M lines run up Sixth Ave, while N/Q/R lines follow Broadway. The 7, E and M lines offer some crosstown service.

→ **Bus** Useful for the western and eastern extremes of Midtown. Routes include the M11 (running northbound on Tenth Ave and southbound on Ninth Ave); the M101, M102 and M103 (running northbound along Third Ave and southbound along Lexington Ave); and the M15 (running northbound on First Ave and southbound on Second Ave). Useful buses run along 34th and 42nd Sts.

→ **Train** Long-distance Amtrak and Long Island Rail Road (LIRR) trains terminate at Penn Station. Jersey's PATH trains stop at 33rd St, while Metro-North commuter trains terminate at Grand Central Terminal.

Lonely Planet's Top Tip

Savoring Midtown's A-list restaurants without mortgaging the house is possible if you go for the prix fixe lunch menu where available. Participants include Michelin starred Le Bernardin (p199) and A Voce (p200), which offer dishes featured in their evening menus. How far ahead you should book depends on the restaurant. While you can usually secure a lunch table at A Voce with a few days notice, it can sometimes be a one-month wait at Le Bernardin. Both offer online reservations.

Best Places to Eat

→ Le Bernardin (p199)
→ Danji (p199)
→ Betony (p199)
→ A Voce (p200)

For reviews, see p197 →

Best Places to Drink

→ Campbell Apartment (p187)
→ Rum House (p201)
→ Middle Branch (p201)
→ Jimmy's Corner (p201)

For reviews, see p200 →

Best Places for a Skyline View

→ Top of the Rock (p189)
→ Empire State Building (p179)
→ Top of the Strand (p200)
→ Robert (p201)

For reviews, see p189 →

TOP SIGHT
TIMES SQUARE

'I had traveled eight thousand miles around the American continent and I was back on Times Square; and right in the middle of a rush-hour, too, seeing with my innocent road-eyes the absolute madness and fantastic hoorair of New York with its millions and millions hustling forever for a buck among themselves, the mad dream...' Jack Kerouac, *On the Road*

Love it or hate it, the intersection of Broadway and Seventh Ave (better known as Times Square) is New York City's hyperactive heart. It's a restless, hypnotic torrent of glittering lights, bombastic billboards and raw urban energy. It's not hip, fashionable or in-the-know and it couldn't care less. It's too busy pumping out iconic, mass-marketed NYC, from yellow cabs and golden arches to razzle-dazzle Broadway marquees. This is the New York of collective fantasies – the place where Al Jolson 'makes it' in the 1927 film The Jazz Singer, where photojournalist Alfred Eisenstaedt famously captured a sailor and nurse lip-locked on V-J Day in 1945, and where Alicia Keys and Jay-Z waxed lyrically about this 'concrete jungle where dreams are made.'

For several decades, the dream here was a sordid, wet one. The economic crash of the early 1970s led to a mass exodus of corporations from Times Square. Billboard niches went dark, stores shut and once grand hotels were converted into SRO (single-room occupancy) dives. While the adjoining Theater District survived, its respectable playhouses shared the streets with porn cinemas and strip clubs. That all changed with tough-talking mayor Rudolph Giuliani, who, in the 1990s, boosted police numbers and lured a wave of 'respectable' retail chains, restaurants and attractions. By the new millennium, Times Square had gone from X-rated to G-rated, drawing almost 40 million visitors annually.

DON'T MISS...
➡ Taking in Times Square from the TKTS Booth steps
➡ Discount tickets to a Broadway show
➡ A drink at R Lounge, the Renaissance Hotel
➡ The Centennial Dropping Ball, Times Square Visitor Center

PRACTICALITIES
➡ Map p430
➡ www.timessquare.com
➡ Broadway at Seventh Ave
➡ S N/Q/R, S, 1/2/3, 7 to Times Sq-42nd St

For a panoramic view over the square, order a drink at the Renaissance Hotel's **R Lounge** (Map p430; www.rloungetimessquare.com; Two Times Square, 714 Seventh Ave, at 48th St; ⏰11am-midnight Sun-Thu, 11:30am-1am Fri & Sat; [S]N/Q/R to 49th St), which offers floor-to-ceiling glass windows of the neon-lit spectacle below. It might not be the best-priced sip in town, but with a view like this, who's counting?

A Subway, a Newspaper & a Very Famous Dropping Ball

At the turn of last century, Times Square was known as Longacre Square, an unremarkable intersection far from the commercial epicenter of Lower Manhattan. This would change with a deal made between subway pioneer August Belmont and *New York Times* publisher Adolph Ochs. Heading construction of the city's first subway line (from Lower Manhattan to the Upper West Side and Harlem), Belmont astutely realized that a Midtown business hub along 42nd St would maximize profit and patronage on the route. On his mission to draw business into the area, Belmont approached Ochs, who had recently turned around the fortunes of the *New York Times*. Belmont argued that moving the newspaper's operations to the intersection of Broadway and 42nd St would be a win-win for Ochs, for not only would an in-house subway station mean faster distribution of the newspaper around town, the influx of commuters to the square would also mean more sales right outside its headquarters. Belmont even convinced New York mayor George B McClellan Jr to rename the square in honor of the broadsheet. It was an irresistible offer, and in the winter of 1904–05, both subway station and the *Times'* new headquarters at One Times Square made their debut. In honor of the move, the *Times* hosted a New Year's Eve party in 1904, setting off fireworks from its skyscraper rooftop. By 1907, the square had become so built-up that fireworks were deemed a safety hazard, forcing the newspaper to come up with an alternative crowd-puller. It came in the form of a 700lb, wood-and-iron ball, lowered from the roof of One Times Square to herald the arrival of 1908.

While the *Times* may have left the building (it's now in a Renzo Piano–designed skyscraper at 620 Eighth Ave), around one million people still gather in Times Square every New Year's Eve to watch a Waterford crystal ball descend at midnight. It's a mere 90-second spectacle that is arguably one of NYC's greatest anticlimaxes. Thankfully, you don't have to endure the crowds and cold to experience this short-lived thrill: the **Times Square Museum & Visitor Center** (Map p430; ☎212-452-5283;

BRILL BUILDING

Standing at the northwest corner of Broadway and 49th St, the **Brill Building** (Map p430) is widely considered the most important generator of popular songs in the Western world. By 1962, over 160 music businesses were based here, from songwriters and managers to record companies and promoters. It was a one-stop shop for artists, who could craft a song, hire musicians, cut a demo and convince a producer without leaving the building. Among the legends who did were Carole King, Bob Dylan, Joni Mitchell and Paul Simon. One of the few surviving legacies from that gilded era is music outfitter Rudy's Music (p208) on nearby W 48th St, a street once dubbed Music Row.

Some people wish upon a star. Others scrawl their dreams on confetti and pin them to the Wishing Wall, located inside the Times Square Museum & Visitor Center. Come midnight on New Year's Eve, the mass of Technicolor hopes flutter down onto the square. Wishes can also be submitted virtually via the website.

www.timessquarenyc.org; 1560 Broadway, btwn 46th & 47th Sts, Midtown West; ⏰8am-8pm; [S]N/Q/R, S, 1/2/3, 7 to Times Sq-42nd St) offers a simulated NYE light show every 20 minutes year-round, as well as a close-up look at the Centennial Dropping Ball used in 2007 – an 11,875lb geodesic globe created using Waterford crystal and over 32,000 LEDs.

On Broadway

By the 1920s, Belmont's dream for Times Square had kicked into overdrive. Not only was it the heart of a growing commercial district, but it had overtaken Union Square as New York's theater hub. The neighborhood's first playhouse was the long-gone Empire, opened in 1893 and located on Broadway between 40th and 41st Sts. Two years later, cigar manufacturer and part-time comedy scribe Oscar Hammerstein opened the Olympia, also on Broadway, before opening the Republic – now children's theater **New Victory** (Map p430; www.newvictory.org; 209 W 42nd St, btwn Seventh & Eighth Aves, Midtown West; [S]N/Q/R, S, 1/2/3, 7 to Times Sq-42nd St, A/C/E to 42nd St-Port Authority Bus Terminal) – in 1900. This lead to a string of new venues, among them the still-beating **New Amsterdam Theatre** (Map p430; www.new-amsterdam-theatre.com; 214 W 42nd St, btwn Seventh & Eighth Aves, Midtown West; 👪; [S]N/Q/R, S, 1/2/3, 7 to Times Sq-42nd St) and **Lyceum Theatre** (Map p430; 149 W 45th St, btwn Sixth & Seventh Aves, Midtown West; [S]N/Q/R to 49th St).

The Broadway of the 1920s was well known for its lighthearted musicals, commonly fusing vaudeville and music hall traditions, and producing classic tunes like Cole Porter's *Let's Misbehave*. At the same time, Midtown's theater district was evolving as a platform for new American dramatists. One of the greatest was Eugene O'Neill. Born in Times Square at the long-gone Barrett Hotel (1500 Broadway) in 1888, the playwright debuted many of his works here, including Pulitzer Prize winners *Beyond the Horizon* and *Anna Christie*. O'Neill's success on Broadway paved the way for other American greats like Tennessee Williams, Arthur Miller and Edward Albee – a surge of serious talent that led to the establishment of the annual Tony Awards in 1947.

These days, New York's Theater District covers an area stretching roughly from 40th St to 54th St between Sixth and Eighth Aves, with dozens of Broadway and off-Broadway theaters spanning blockbuster musicals to new and classic drama. Unless there's a specific show you're after, the best – and cheapest – way to score tickets in the area is at the **TKTS Booth** (www.tdf.org), where you can line up and get same-day discounted tickets for top Broadway and off-Broadway shows. Smartphone users can download the free TKTS app, which offers rundowns of both Broadway and off-Broadway shows, as well as real-time updates of what's available on that day. Always have a back-up choice in case your first preference sells out, and never buy from scalpers on the street.

The TKTS Booth is an attraction in its own right, its illuminated roof of 27 ruby-red steps rising a panoramic 16ft 1in above the 47th St sidewalk.

RICHARD I'ANSON / GETTY IMAGES ©

TOP SIGHT
EMPIRE STATE BUILDING

The Chrysler Building may be prettier and One World Trade Center may now be taller, but the Queen Bee of the New York skyline remains the Empire State Building. It's NYC's tallest star, enjoying more than its fair share of close-ups in around 100 films, from *King Kong* to *Independence Day*. No other building screams New York quite like it, and heading up to the top is as quintessential an experience as pastrami, rye and pickles at Katz's Delicatessen.

The statistics are astounding: 10 million bricks, 60,000 tons of steel, 6400 windows and 328,000 sq ft of marble. Built on the original site of the Waldorf-Astoria, construction took a record-setting 410 days, using seven million hours of labor and costing a mere $41 million. It might sound like a lot, but it fell well below its $50 million budget (just as well given it went up during the Great Depression). Coming in at 102 stories and 1472ft from top to bottom, the limestone phallus opened for business on May 1, 1931. Generations later, Deborah Kerr's words to Cary Grant in *An Affair to Remember* still ring true: 'It's the nearest thing to heaven we have in New York.'

Observation Decks

Unless you're Ann Darrow (the unfortunate blonde caught in King Kong's grip), heading to the top of the Empire State Building should leave you beaming. There are two observation decks. The open-air 86th-floor deck offers an alfresco experience, with coin-operated telescopes for close-up glimpses of the metropolis in action. Further up, the enclosed 102nd-floor deck is New York's second-highest observation deck, trumped only by the observation deck at One World Trade Center. Needless to say, the views over the city's five boroughs (and

DON'T MISS...

- Observation decks at sunset
- Live jazz Thursday to Saturday nights

PRACTICALITIES

- Map p426
- www.esbnyc.com
- 350 Fifth Ave, at 34th St
- 86th-fl observation deck adult/child $27/21, incl 102nd-fl observation deck $44/38
- ⏰8am-2am, last elevators up 1:15am
- [S]B/D/F/M, N/Q/R to 34th St-Herald Sq

LANGUAGE OF LIGHT

Since 1976, the building's top 30 floors have been floodlit in a spectrum of colors each night, reflecting seasonal and holiday hues. Famous combos include red and pink sparkles for Valentine's Day; orange, white and green for St Patrick's Day; red and green for Christmas; and the rainbow colors for Gay Pride weekend in June. For a full rundown of the color schemes, check the website.

The Empire State Building was designed by the prolific architectural firm Shreve, Lamb and Harmon. According to legend, the skyscraper's conception began with a meeting between William Lamb and building co-financier John Jakob Raskob, during which Raskob propped up a No 2 pencil and asked, 'Bill, how high can you make it so that it won't fall down?' Shreve, Lamb and Harmon's other projects include the skyscraper at 500 Fifth Ave. To compare the soaring siblings, head to the northeast corner of Fifth Ave and 40th St.

five neighboring states, weather permitting) are quite simply exquisite. The views from both decks are especially spectacular at sunset, when the city dons its nighttime cloak in dusk's afterglow. For a little of that *Arthur's Theme* magic, head to the 86th floor between 10pm and 1am from Thursday to Saturday, when the twinkling sea of lights is accompanied by a soundtrack of live sax (yes, requests are taken). Alas, the passage to heaven will involve a trip through purgatory: the queues to the top are notorious. Getting here very early or very late will help you avoid delays – as will buying your tickets online, ahead of time, where an extra $2 convenience fee is well worth the hassle it will save you.

An Ambitious Antenna

A locked, unmarked door on the 102nd-floor observation deck leads to one of New York's most outrageous pie-in-the-sky projects to date: a narrow terrace intended to dock zeppelins. Spearheading the dream was Alfred E Smith, who went from failed presidential candidate in 1928 to head honcho of the Empire State Building project. When architect William Van Alen revealed the secret spire of his competing Chrysler Building, Smith went one better, declaring that the top of the Empire State Building would sport an even taller mooring mast for transatlantic airships. While the plan looked good on paper, there were two (major) oversights: dirigibles require anchoring at both ends (not just at the nose as planned) and passengers (traveling in the zeppelin's gondola) cannot exit the craft through the giant helium-filled balloon. Regardless, it didn't stop them from trying. In September 1931, the *New York Evening Journal* threw sanity to the wind, managing to moor a zeppelin and deliver a pile of newspapers fresh out of Lower Manhattan. Years later, an aircraft met up with the building with less success: a B-25 bomber crashed into the 79th floor on a foggy day in 1945, killing 14 people.

TOP SIGHT
MUSEUM OF MODERN ART

Superstar of the modern art scene, MoMA's booty makes many other collections look, well, endearing. You'll find more A-listers here than at an Oscars after party: Van Gogh, Matisse, Picasso, Warhol, Lichtenstein, Rothko, Pollock and Bourgeois. Since its founding in 1929, the museum has amassed over 150,000 artworks, documenting the emerging creative ideas and movements of the late 19th century through to those that dominate today. For art buffs, it's Valhalla. For the uninitiated. it's a thrilling crash course in all that is beautiful and addictive about art.

Collection Highlights

It's easy to get lost in MoMA's vast collection. To maximize your time and create a plan of attack, download the museum's free smartphone app from the website beforehand. MoMA's permanent collection spans four levels, with prints, illustrated books and the unmissable Contemporary Galleries on level two; architecture, design, drawings and photography on level three; and painting and sculpture on levels four and five. Many of the big hitters are on these last two levels, so tackle the museum from the top down before the fatigue sets in. Must-sees include Van Gogh's *Starry Night*, Cézanne's *The Bather*, Picasso's *Les Demoiselles d'Avignon* and Rousseau's *The Sleeping Gypsy*, not to mention iconic American works like Warhol's *Campbell's Soup Cans* and *Gold Marilyn Monroe*, Lichtenstein's equally poptastic *Girl With Ball*, and Hopper's haunting *House by the Railroad*.

DON'T MISS...

➡ Collection highlights
➡ Abby Aldrich Rockefeller Sculpture Garden
➡ Museum eateries
➡ Film screenings

PRACTICALITIES

➡ MoMA
➡ Map p430
➡ www.moma.org
➡ 11 W 53rd St, btwn Fifth & Sixth Aves
➡ adult/child $25/ free, 4-8pm Fri free
➡ ⊙10:30am-5:30pm Sat-Thu, to 8pm Fri; to 8pm Thu Jul-Aug
➡ 🛜
➡ S E, M to 5th Ave-53rd St

GALLERY CONVERSATIONS

To delve a little deeper into MoMA's collection, join one of the museum's lunchtime talks and readings, which sees writers, artists, curators and designers offer expert insight into specific works and exhibitions on view. The talks take place daily at 11:30am and 1:30pm. To check upcoming topics, click the 'Learn' link on the MoMA website, followed by the 'Lectures & Events' and 'Talks & Readings' links.

One of the greatest strengths of MoMA's collections is abstract expressionism, a radical movement that emerged in New York in the 1940s and boomed a decade later. Defined by its penchant for irreverent individualism and monumentally scaled works, this so-called 'New York School' helped turn the metropolis into *the* epicenter of Western contemporary art. Among the stars are Rothko's *Magenta, Black, Green on Orange*, Pollock's *One: Number 31, 1950* and de Kooning's *Painting*.

Abby Aldrich Rockefeller Sculpture Garden

With architect Yoshio Taniguchi's acclaimed reconstruction of the museum in 2004 came the restoration of the Sculpture Garden to the original, larger vision of Philip Johnson's 1953 design. Johnson described the space as a 'sort of outdoor room,' and on warm, sunny days, it's hard not to think of it as a soothing alfresco lounge. One resident that can't seem to get enough of it is Aristide Maillol's *The River*, a larger-than-life female sculpture that featured in Johnson's original garden. She's in fine company too, with fellow works from greats including Auguste Rodin, Alexander Calder and Henry Moore. Sitting sneakily above the garden's eastern end is *Water Tower*, a translucent resin installation by British artist Rachel Whiteread. The Sculpture Garden is open free of charge from 9am to 10:15am daily, except in inclement weather and during maintenance.

Artful Bites

MoMA's eateries have a stellar reputation. For communal tables and a super-casual vibe, nosh on Italian-inspired panini, pasta dishes, salads, *salumi* (cured meats) and cheeses at **Cafe 2** (Map p430; ⊙11am-5pm Sat-Mon, Wed & Thu, to 7:30pm Fri). For table service, à la carte options and Danish design, opt for **Terrace Five** (Map p430; mains $11-18; ⊙11am-5pm Sat-Mon, Wed & Thu, to 7:30pm Fri), which features an outdoor terrace overlooking the Sculpture Garden. If you're after a luxe feed, however, book a table at fine-dining **Modern** (Map p430; ☎212-333-1220; www.themodernnyc.com; 3-/4-course lunch $62/76, 4-course dinner $108; ⊙restaurant noon-2pm & 5-10:30pm Mon-Fri, 5-10:30pm Sat; bar 11:30am-10:30pm Mon-Sat, to 9:30pm Sun). Fans of *Sex and the City* will be keen to know that it was here that scribe-about-town Carrie announced her impending marriage to 'Mr Big.' (If you're on a *real* writer's wage, you can always opt for simpler, cheaper French-American grub in the adjacent Bar Room.)

Film Screenings

Not only a palace of visual art, MoMA screens an incredibly well-rounded selection of celluloid gems from its collection of over 22,000 films, including the works of the Maysles Brothers and every Pixar animation film ever produced. Expect anything from Academy Award–nominated documentary shorts and Hollywood classics to experimental works and international retrospectives. Best of all, your museum ticket will get you in for free.

TOP SIGHT
CHRYSLER BUILDING

The 77-floor Chrysler Building makes most other skyscrapers look like uptight geeks. Designed by William Van Alen in 1930, it's a dramatic fusion of art deco and Gothic aesthetics, adorned with stern steel eagles and topped by a spire that screams *Bride of Frankenstein*. The building was constructed as the headquarters for Walter P Chrysler and his automobile empire. Unable to compete on the production line with bigger rivals Ford and General Motors, Chrysler decided to trump them on the skyline. More than 80 years on, Chrysler's ambitious $15 million statement remains one of New York's most poignant symbols.

The Lobby

Although the Chrysler Building has no restaurant or observation deck, its lobby is a lavish consolation prize. Bathed in an amber glow, its Jazz Age vintage is echoed in its architecture – dark, exotic African wood and marble, contrasted against the brash, man-made steel of industrial America. The elaborately veneered elevators are especially beautiful, their Egyptian lotus motifs made of inlaid Japanese ash, Oriental walnut and Cuban plum-pudding wood. When the doors open, you almost expect Bette Davis to strut on out. Above you is painter Edward Trumbull's ceiling mural *Transport and Human Endeavor*. Purportedly the world's largest mural at 97ft by 100ft, its depiction of buildings, airplanes and industrious workers on Chrysler assembly lines shows the golden promise of industry and modernity.

The Spire

Composed of seven radiating steel arches, the Chrysler Building's 185ft spire was as much a feat of vengeance as it was of modern engineering. Secretly constructed in the stairwell,

DON'T MISS...

➡ The lobby
➡ The spire
➡ The gargoyles
➡ View from the corner of Third Ave and 44th St and the Empire State Building
➡ Chanin Building

PRACTICALITIES

➡ Map p426
➡ Lexington Ave at 42nd St, Midtown East
➡ ⏱ lobby 8am-6pm Mon-Fri
➡ Ⓢ S, 4/5/6, 7 to Grand Central-42nd St

the 200ft creation (dubbed 'the vertex') was raised through a false roof and anchored into place in an impressive 1½ hours. The novel reveal shocked and outraged architect H Craig Severance, who had hoped that his Manhattan Company skyscraper on Wall St would become the world's tallest building. The fait accompli was especially humiliating given that Severance had personally fallen out with architect William Van Alen, a former colleague. Karmic retribution may have been served with the 1931 debut of the even-taller Empire State Building, but Van Alen's crowning glory endures as a showstopping symbol of 20th-century daring.

The Gargoyles

If the spire is the building's diva, the gargoyles are its supporting cast. Pairs of gleaming steel American eagles look ready to leap from the corners of the 61st floor, giving the building a brooding, Gothic edge. Further down on the 31st floor, giant winged hubcaps echo the Chrysler radiator caps of the late 1920s. For a dramatic view of the gargoyles from street level, head to the corner of Lexington Ave and 44th St and look up.

Two Impressive Views

For a great view of the Chrysler Building, head to the corner of Third Ave and 44th St, from where you can appreciate the building's slimline profile, gargoyles and spire in one hit. If you have binoculars, bring them for a close-up view of the facade's detailing, which includes basket-weave motifs and a band of abstract automobiles. Alternatively, head to the top of the Chrysler Building's taller rival, the Empire State Building, where pay-per-view telescopes will get you up close and personal with that gleaming steel spire.

Chanin Building: A Neighboring Gem

Across the street from the Chrysler Building, on the southwest corner of Lexington Ave and 42nd St, stands another art deco gem: the **Chanin Building** (Map p426; 122 E 42nd St at Lexington Ave, Midtown East; [S]S, 4/5/6, 7 to Grand Central-42nd St). Completed in 1929, the 56-story brick and terra-cotta tower is the work of unlicensed architect Irwin S Chanin, who teamed up with the legally recognized firm Sloan & Robertson to achieve his dream. Yet, the star attractions here are the work of René Chambellan and Jacques Delamarre, creators of the exquisite bands of relief at the building's base. While birds and fish create a sense of whimsy in the lower band, the upper band of terra-cotta steals the show with its rich botanical carvings.

CLOUD CLUB

Nestled at the top of the Chrysler Building between 1930 and 1979 was the famed Cloud Club. Its regulars included tycoon John D Rockefeller, publishing magnate Condé Montrose and boxing legend Gene Tunney. The art deco-meets-hunting-lodge hangout from floors 66 to 68 featured a lounge and dining rooms (including a private room for Walter Chrysler), as well as kitchens, a barber shop and a locker room with sneak cabinets for hiding booze during Prohibition. Chrysler merrily boasted about having the highest toilet in town.

The Chrysler Building's lobby and crown feature in *Cremaster 3* (2002), an avant-garde film by award-winning visual artist and filmmaker Matthew Barney. The third installment of an epic five-part film project, it delivers a surreal take on the skyscraper's construction, fusing Irish mythology with genre elements from both zombie and gangster films. To read more about the project, check out www.cremaster.net.

TOP SIGHT
ROCKEFELLER CENTER

This 22-acre 'city within a city' debuted at the height of the Great Depression. Taking nine years to build, it was America's first multiuse retail, entertainment and office space – a modernist sprawl of 19 buildings (14 of which are the original art deco structures), outdoor plazas and big-name tenants. Developer John D Rockefeller Jr may have sweated over the cost (a mere $100 million), but it was all worth it: the center was declared a National Landmark in 1987.

DON'T MISS...

- Top of the Rock
- Public artworks
- NBC Studio Tour
- Rockefeller Plaza

PRACTICALITIES

- Map p426
- www.rockefeller-center.com
- Fifth to Sixth Aves & 48th to 51st Sts
- ⏲24hr, times vary for individual businesses
- [S]B/D/F/M to 47th-50th Sts-Rockefeller Center

Top of the Rock

There are views, and then there's *the* view from the Top of the Rock (p189). Crowning the GE Building, 70 stories above Midtown, its blockbuster vista includes one icon that you won't see from atop the Empire State Building – *the* Empire State Building. The Chrysler Building, however, is partially obscured. If possible, head up just before sunset to see the city transform from day to glittering night (if you're already in the area and the queues aren't long, purchase your tickets in advance to avoid the late-afternoon rush).

Public Artworks

Rockefeller Center features the work of 30 great artists, commissioned around the theme 'Man at the Crossroads Looks Uncertainly But Hopefully at the Future.' Paul Manship contributed *Prometheus*, overlooking the sunken plaza, and *Atlas*, in front of the International Building (630 Fifth Ave). Isamu Noguchi's *News* sits above the entrance to the Associated Press Building (50 Rockefeller Plaza), while José Maria Sert's oil *American Progress* awaits in the lobby of the GE Building. The latter work replaced Mexican artist Diego Rivera's original painting, rejected by the Rockefellers for containing 'communist imagery.'

NBC Studio Tour

TV comedy *30 Rock* gets its name from the GE Building, and the tower is the real-life home of NBC TV. Slated to reopen in late 2014, NBC Studio Tours (p209) leave from inside the NBC Experience Store, and include a sneak peak of Studio 8H, home to the legendary *Saturday Night Live* set. Tours have a strict 'no bathrooms policy ' (empty your bladder beforehand!) and advanced phone bookings are recommended. Check the website for tour recommencement updates. Across 49th St, opposite the plaza, is the glass-enclosed NBC *Today* show studio, broadcasting live from 7am to 11am daily. If you fancy some screen time, head in by 6am to be at the front of the crowd.

Rockefeller Plaza

Come the festive season, Rockefeller Plaza is where you'll find New York's most famous Christmas tree. Ceremoniously lit just after Thanksgiving, it's a tradition that dates back to the 1930s, when construction workers set up a small tree on the site. In its shadow, **Rink at Rockefeller Center** (Map p426; ☎212-332-7654; www.patinagroup.com; adult/child $27/15, skate rental $12; ⏲8:30am-midnight mid-Oct–early Apr) is the city's most famous ice-skating rink. Incomparably magical, it's also undeniably small and crowded. Opt for the first skating period (8:30am) to avoid a long wait. Come summer, the rink becomes a cafe.

FERRAN TRAITE SOLER / GETTY IMAGES ©

TOP SIGHT
GRAND CENTRAL TERMINAL

Threatened by the opening of rival Penn Station (the majestic original, that is), shipping and railroad magnate Cornelius Vanderbilt set to work on transforming his 19th-century Grand Central Depot into a 20th-century showpiece. The fruit of his envy is Grand Central Terminal, New York's most breathtaking beaux arts building. More than just a station, Grand Central is an enchanted time machine. Its swirl of chandeliers, marble and historic bars and restaurants provide a porthole into an era where train travel and romance were not mutually exclusive.

There are no teary goodbyes for people traveling across the country from here today, as Grand Central's underground electric tracks serve only commuter trains en route to northern suburbs and Connecticut. But whether you're traveling somewhere or not, Grand Central is one stop you cannot afford to miss.

42nd Street Facade

Clad in Connecticut Stony Creek granite at its base and Indiana limestone on top, Grand Central's showpiece facade is crowned by America's greatest monumental sculpture, *The Glory of Commerce*. Designed by the French sculptor Jules Félix Coutan, the piece was executed in Long Island City by local carvers Donnely and Ricci. Once completed, it was hoisted up, piece by piece, in 1914. Its protagonist is a wing-capped Mercury, the Roman god of travel and commerce. To the left is Hercules in an unusually placid stance, while looking down on the mayhem of 42nd St is Minerva, the ancient guardian of cities. The clock beneath Mercury's foot contains the largest example of Tiffany glass in the world.

DON'T MISS...

- 42nd St facade
- Main Concourse
- Whispering Gallery and the Oyster Bar & Restaurant
- Campbell Apartment
- Grand Central Market

PRACTICALITIES

- Map p426
- www.grandcentral-terminal.com
- 42nd St at Park Ave, Midtown East
- 🕒5:30am-2am
- [S]S, 4/5/6, 7 to Grand Central-42nd St

Main Concourse

Grand Central's trump card is more akin to a glorious ballroom than a thoroughfare. The marble floors are Tennessee pink, while the vintage ticket counters are Italian Bottocino marble. The vaulted ceiling is (quite literally) heavenly, its turquoise and gold-leaf mural depicting eight constellations... backwards. A mistake? Apparently not. Its French designer, painter Paul César Helleu, wished to depict the stars from God's point of view – from the out, looking in. The original, frescoed execution of Helleu's design was by New York–based artists J Monroe Hewlett and Charles Basing. Moisture damage saw it faithfully repainted (alas, not in fresco form) by Charles Gulbrandsen in 1944. By the 1990s, however, the mural was in ruins again. Enter renovation architects Beyer Blinder Belle, who restored the work, but left a tiny patch of soot (in the northwest corner) as testament to just what a fine job they did.

Whispering Gallery, Oyster Bar & Restaurant, and Campbell Apartment

The vaulted landing directly below the bridge linking the Main Concourse and Vanderbilt Hall harbors one of Grand Central's quirkier features, the so-called Whispering Gallery. If you're in company, stand facing the walls diagonally opposite each other and whisper something. If your partner proposes (it happens a lot down here), chilled champagne is just through the door at the **Grand Central Oyster Bar & Restaurant** (Map p426; www.oysterbarny.com; Grand Central Terminal, 42nd St at Park Ave; mains $14-37; ⊙11:30am-9:30pm Mon-Sat). It's hugely atmospheric (with a vaulted tiled ceiling by Catalan-born engineer Rafael Guastavino), and you're best to stick to what it does exceptionally well: oysters. An elevator beside the restaurant leads up to another historic gem: the deliciously snooty bar **Campbell Apartment** (Map p426; www.hospitalityholdings.com; Grand Central Terminal, 15 Vanderbilt Ave, at 43rd St; ⊙noon-1am Mon-Thu, to 2am Fri, 2pm-2am Sat, noon-midnight Sun).

Grand Central Market

More drooling awaits at the **Grand Central Market** (Map p426; Grand Central Terminal, Lexington Ave at 42nd St; ⊙7am-9pm Mon-Fri, 10am-7pm Sat, 11am-6pm Sun), a 240ft corridor lined with fresh produce and artisan treats. Stock up on anything from crusty bread and fruit tarts to lobsters, chicken pot pies, Spanish quince paste, fruit and vegetables, and roasted coffee beans.

GUIDED TOURS

The Municipal Art Society (p389) runs walking tours through Grand Central daily at 12:30pm. Tours start at the information booth in the Main Concourse. The Grand Central Partnership (www.grandcentralpartnership.com) leads free tours of the terminal and the surrounding neighborhood on Fridays at 12:30pm. Tours commence in the sculpture court at 120 Park Ave. Both tours run for approximately 1½ hours.

Hidden away under the Waldorf-Astoria hotel is Grand Central's little-known Platform 61. One person who did know it well was polio-afflicted president Franklin D Roosevelt. Determined to hide his affliction from public view, Roosevelt made good use of the platform's freight elevator. Upon arrival at the station, the president would be driven straight out of his train carriage, along the platform and into the elevator...his public none the wiser.

TOP SIGHT
RADIO CITY MUSIC HALL

Ladies and gentleman, boys and girls, welcome to the one and only Radio City Music Hall. A spectacular art deco diva, this 5901-seat movie palace was the brainchild of vaudeville producer Samuel Lionel 'Roxy' Rothafel. Never one for understatement, Roxy launched his venue on December 23, 1932, with an over-the-top extravaganza that included a *Symphony of the Curtains* (starring...the curtains) and the high-kick campness of precision dance troupe the Roxyettes (mercifully renamed the Rockettes).

By the 1940s, Radio City had become the greatest single attraction in New York, its red carpet well worn with a string of movie premieres. Alas, the good times didn't last, with dwindling popularity and soaring rents forcing the theater's closure in 1978. In true showbiz style, however, the venue escaped demolition with a last-minute reprieve, its interior declared a landmark worthy of a $5 million restoration.

For a real treat, join a one-hour guided tour of the sumptuous interiors, designed by Donald Deskey. But first, eye-up the building's 50th St facade, where Hildreth Meière's brass rondels represent (from left to right) dance, drama and song. Celebrated artists also lavished the interiors. Among them was Lithuanian-born William Zorach, whose nude sculpture *Spirit of the Dance* sparked enough controversy to have the work temporarily removed. Less scandalous gems include Stuart Davies' abstract wall mural *Men Without Women* in the Smoking Room, and Witold Gordon's classically inspired *History of Cosmetics* in the Women's Downstairs Lounge. The adjoining restroom (open to all) sports the world's first modern hand dryers.

While the original, wood-paneled elevators are sublime, the pièce de résistance is the main auditorium, its radiating arches evoking a setting sun. Here you'll see Radio City Music Hall's legendary pipe organ (the biggest built for a movie palace) and the landmark-listed Great Stage, famed for its still-sophisticated hydraulics. Much smaller but *très* exclusive is the VIP Roxy Suite, lavished with rich cherrywood walls, 20ft-high domed ceilings and an acoustically clever dining area.

As far as catching a show here goes, be warned: the vibe doesn't quite match the theater's splendor now that it's managed by the folks from Madison Square Garden. Latecomers are allowed, disrupting performances, and glow-in-the-dark cocktails often create an ugly sea of purple drinks that's more akin to a stadium rock concert than a sophisticated show in an elegant theater. Still, there are often some fabulous talents in the lineup, with past performers including Rufus Wainwright, Aretha Franklin and Dolly Parton. And while the word 'Rockettes' provokes eye rolling from most self-consciously cynical New Yorkers, fans of glitz and kitsch might just get a thrill from the troupe's annual Christmas Spectacular.

Tickets are available at the candy store beside the Sixth Ave entrance, though it's worth considering paying the extra $4.50 to book your ticket online given that tours can sell out quickly, particularly on rainy days.

DON'T MISS...

➜ Artworks

➜ Main auditorium

➜ Roxy Suite

➜ Vintage hand dryers

PRACTICALITIES

➜ Map p430

➜ www.radiocity.com

➜ 1260 Sixth Ave, at 51st St

➜ tours adult/child $19.95/15

➜ ⊙tours 11am-3pm

➜ Ⓢ B/D/F/M to 47th-50th Sts-Rockefeller Center

SIGHTS

Midtown East

CHRYSLER BUILDING NOTABLE BUILDING

See p183.

GRAND CENTRAL TERMINAL NOTABLE BUILDING

See p186.

MORGAN LIBRARY & MUSEUM MUSEUM

Map p426 (www.morganlibrary.org; 29 E 36th St, at Madison Ave, Midtown East; adult/child $18/12; ⏲10:30am-5pm Tue-Thu, to 9pm Fri, 10am-6pm Sat, 11am-6pm Sun; [S]6 to 33rd St) Part of the 45-room mansion once owned by steel magnate JP Morgan, this sumptuous library features a phenomenal array of manuscripts, tapestries and books (with no fewer than three Gutenberg Bibles). There's a study filled with Italian Renaissance artwork, a marble rotunda and a program of top-notch rotating exhibitions.

The program of temporary exhibitions is consistently inspiring.

UNITED NATIONS NOTABLE BUILDING

Map p426 (☎212-963-4475; http://visit.un.org; visitors' gate First Ave at 47th St, Midtown East; tours adult/child $20/11, grounds access Sat & Sun free; ⏲tours 9:15am-4:15pm Mon-Fri, visitor center also open 10am-5pm Sat & Sun; 📶; [S]S, 4/5/6, 7 to Grand Central-42nd St) Welcome to the headquarters of the UN, a worldwide organization overseeing international law, international security and human rights. While the recently spruced-up, Le Corbusier-designed Secretariat building is off-limits, one-hour guided tours do cover the Security Council Chamber, the Trusteeship Council Chamber, the Economic and Social Council (ECOSOC) Chamber, as well as exhibitions about the UN's work and artworks given by member states. Weekday tours must be booked online (at least two days ahead); children under five not admitted.

Free walk-in access to the visitor center only is permitted on weekends (enter at 43rd St). At the time of research, the iconic General Assembly – setting for the annual fall convocation of member nations – was closed for restoration and due to reopen in late 2014. To the north of the UN complex, which technically stands on international territory, is a serene park featuring Henry Moore's *Reclining Figure* as well as several other peace-themed sculptures.

JAPAN SOCIETY CULTURAL CENTER

Map p426 (www.japansociety.org; 333 E 47th St, btwn First & Second Aves, Midtown East; adult/child $12/free, 6-9pm Fri free; ⏲11am-6pm Tue-Thu, to 9pm Fri, to 5pm Sat & Sun; [S]S, 4/5/6, 7 to Grand Central-42nd St) Elegant exhibitions of Japanese art, textiles and design are the main draw at this cultural center. Its theater hosts a range of films and dance, music and theatrical performances, while those who want to dig deeper can browse through the 14,000 volumes of the research library or attend one of its myriad lectures.

Founded in 1907 by a group of NYC businesspeople with a deep admiration for Japan, this nonprofit society has played a large role in strengthening American-Japanese relations. Its expansion into a full arts and cultural center was thanks in no small part to philanthropist John D Rockefeller III, an ardent fan of the country.

MUSEUM OF SEX MUSEUM

Map p426 (www.museumofsex.com; 233 Fifth Ave, at 27th St; adult $17.50; ⏲10am-8pm Sun-Thu, to 9pm Fri & Sat; [S]N/R to 23rd St) Get the lowdown on anything from online fetishes to homosexual necrophilia in the mallard duck at this slick, smallish ode to all things hot and sweaty. The rotating program of temporary exhibitions has included explorations of cyber sex and retrospectives of controversial artists, while the permanent collection showcases the likes of erotic lithographs and awkward anti-onanism devices.

Stock up on erotic books, gifts and ergonomic sex toys in the design-savvy museum shop, or kiss a cocktail in the bar-cum-lounge.

Fifth Avenue

EMPIRE STATE BUILDING NOTABLE BUILDING, LOOKOUT

See p179.

ROCKEFELLER CENTER NOTABLE BUILDING

See p185.

TOP OF THE ROCK LOOKOUT

Map p426 (www.topoftherocknyc.com; 30 Rockefeller Plaza, at 49th St, entrance on W 50th St, btwn Fifth & Sixth Aves; adult/child $27/17, sunrise/

sunset combo $40/22; ⌚8am-midnight, last elevator at 11pm; [S]B/D/F/M to 47th-50th Sts-Rockefeller Center) This open-air observation deck at the top of Rockefeller Center first wowed New Yorkers back in 1933. Designed in homage to ocean liners popular in the day, it was an incredible place – 70 stories above Midtown – from which to view the city. But it became off-limits for almost two decades starting in 1986, when renovation of the stunning Rainbow Room restaurant five floors below cut off access to the roof. The observation deck was reopened with much fanfare in 2005, and since then it's been proving to be an even better bet than the Empire State Building: it's much less crowded and has wider observation decks that span several levels – some are indoors, some are outside with plexiglass walls, and those at the very top are completely alfresco. Though the Chrysler Building is partially obscured, you do get an excellent view of the Empire State Building, as well as Central Park's perfect patch of green. The very cool, multimedia-enhanced elevator ride to the top is an exciting bonus.

NEW YORK PUBLIC LIBRARY — CULTURAL BUILDING

Map p426 (Stephen A Schwarzman Bldg; ☎917-275-6975; www.nypl.org; Fifth Ave, at 42nd St; ⌚10am-6pm Mon & Thu-Sat, to 8pm Tue & Wed, 1-5pm Sun, guided tours 11am & 2pm Mon-Sat, 2pm Sun; 📶; [S]B/D/F/M to 42nd St-Bryant Park, 7 to 5th Ave) [FREE] Loyally guarded by 'Patience' and 'Fortitude' (the famous marble lions overlooking Fifth Ave), this beaux arts show-off is one of NYC's best free attractions. When dedicated in 1911, New York's flagship library ranked as the largest marble structure ever built in the US, and to this day, its Rose Main Reading Room will steal your breath with its lavish, coffered ceiling.

The library's Exhibition Hall contains precious manuscripts by just about every author of note in the English language, including an original copy of the Declaration of Independence and a Gutenberg Bible. The Map Division is equally astounding, with a collection that holds some 431,000 maps, 16,000 atlases and books on cartography, dating from the 16th century to the present. To properly explore this mini-universe of books, art, chandeliers and porticoes, join a free guided tour, which leaves from the information desk in Astor Hall.

BRYANT PARK — PARK

Map p426 (www.bryantpark.org; 42nd St, btwn Fifth & Sixth Aves; ⌚7am-10pm daily Apr, 7am-11pm daily May & Oct, 7am-midnight Mon-Fri, to 11pm Sat & Sun Jun-Sep, 7am-10pm Sun-Thu, to midnight Fri & Sat Nov-Feb, 7am-7pm Mar; 📶; [S]B/D/F/M to 42nd St-Bryant Park, 7 to Fifth Ave) European coffee kiosks, alfresco chess games, summer film screenings and winter ice-skating: it's hard to believe that this leafy oasis was dubbed 'Needle Park' in the '80s. Nestled behind the show-stopping New York Public Library building, it's a whimsical spot for a little time-out from the Midtown madness.

Among the park's attractions is French-inspired, Brooklyn-made **Le Carrousel** (Map p426; rides $2; ⌚11am-8pm daily Jun-Oct, 11am-9pm Sun-Thu & 11am-10pm Fri & Sat Nov & Dec, reduced hours rest of year) offering rides, as well as frequent special events. These include the Bryant Park Summer Film Festival, popular with post-work crowds lugging cheese-and-wine picnics. Come Christmastime, the place becomes a winter wonderland, with holiday gift vendors lining the park's edge and a popular ice-skating rink sprouting in its middle. Lovely **Bryant Park Grill** (Map p426; www.arkrestaurants.com; 25 W 40th St, btwn Fifth & Sixth Aves; ⌚11:30am-11pm; [S]B/D/F/M to 42nd St-Bryant Park, 7 to Fifth Ave) is the site of many a New York wedding come springtime, and when it's not closed for a private event, the patio bar is a perfect spot for a twilight cocktail. Next door you'll find its more casual alfresco sibling **Bryant Park Café** (Map p426; ⌚11am-11pm mid-Apr–mid-Nov; [S]B/D/F/M to 42nd St-Bryant Park, 7 to Fifth Ave), a much-loved spot for after-five catch-ups.

ST PATRICK'S CATHEDRAL — CHURCH

Map p426 (www.saintpatrickscathedral.org; Fifth Ave, btwn 50th & 51st Sts; ⌚6:30am-8:45pm; [S]B/D/F/M to 47th-50th Sts-Rockefeller Center) When its face-lift is complete and the scaffolding comes down in late 2015, America's largest Catholic cathedral will once more grace Fifth Ave with its neo-Gothic splendor. Built at a cost of nearly $2 million during the Civil War, the building did not originally include the two front spires; those were added in 1888. Step inside to appreciate the Louis Tiffany–designed altar and Charles Connick's stunning Rose Window, the latter gleaming above a 7000-pipe church organ.

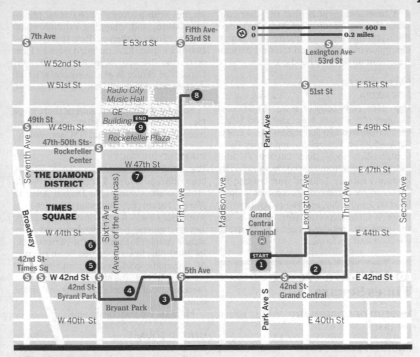

Neighborhood Walk
A Midtown Meander

START GRAND CENTRAL TERMINAL
END ROCKEFELLER CENTER
LENGTH 1.8 MILES; 3½ HOURS

Start your saunter at beaux arts marvel
1 Grand Central Terminal (p186). Star-
gaze at the Main Concourse ceiling, share
sweet nothings at the Whispering Gallery
and pick up a gourmet treat at the Grand
Central Market. Exit onto Lexington Ave and
walk one block east along 44th St to Third
Ave for a view of William Van Alen's 1930
masterpiece, the **2 Chrysler Building**
(p183). Walk down Third Ave to 42nd St,
turn right and slip into the Chrysler Building's sumptuous art deco lobby, lavished
with exotic inlaid wood and purportedly the
world's largest ceiling mural. At the corner
of 42nd St and Fifth Ave stands the stately
3 New York Public Library (p190). On
this very site, between the 1840s and 1890s,
stood the Croton Distributing Reservoir,
an aboveground, four-acre lake supplying
drinking water to the city. Step inside the
library to peek at its spectacular Rose Reading Room, then nibble on your market treat
in neighboring **4 Bryant Park** (p190).
On the northwest corner of 42nd St and
Sixth Ave soars the **5 Bank of America
Tower** (p196), NYC's third-tallest building
and one of its most ecofriendly. The next
block north along Sixth Ave is home to the
6 International Center of Photography
(p192). Take in the current exhibitions before
continuing north to 47th St. Here, between
Sixth and Fifth Aves, is the **7 Diamond
District** (p192), home to more than 2600
independent businesses selling diamonds,
gold, pearls, gemstones and watches. Walk
towards Fifth Ave, taking in its swirl of Jewish
traders. Turn left into Fifth Ave and admire
the splendor of **8 St Patrick's Cathedral**
(p190), its impressive rose window the work
of American artist Charles Connick. Your
last stop is **9 Rockefeller Center** (p185),
a magnificent complex of art deco skyscrapers and sculptures. Enter between 49th and
50th Sts to the main plaza, then head to the
70th-floor of the GE Building for an unforgettable vista at the Top of the Rock observation
deck.

A basement crypt behind the altar contains the coffins of every New York cardinal and the remains of Pierre Touissant, a champion of the poor and the first African American up for sainthood.

PALEY CENTER FOR MEDIA CULTURAL BUILDING

Map p426 (www.paleycenter.org; 25 W 52nd St, btwn Fifth & Sixth Aves; adult/child $10/5; 🕐noon-6pm Wed & Fri-Sun, to 8pm Thu; [S]E, M to 5th Ave-53rd St) Pop-culture repository Paley Center offers more than 150,000 TV and radio programs from around the world on its computer catalog. Reliving your favorite TV shows on one of the center's consoles is sheer bliss on a rainy day, and the radio-listening room is an unexpected pleasure – as are the excellent, regular screenings, festivals, speakers and performers.

Midtown West & Times Square

MUSEUM OF MODERN ART MUSEUM

See p181.

RADIO CITY MUSIC HALL NOTABLE BUILDING

See p188.

MUSEUM OF ARTS & DESIGN MUSEUM

Map p430 (MAD; www.madmuseum.org; 2 Columbus Circle, btwn Eighth Ave & Broadway; adult/child $16/free; 🕐10am-6pm Tue, Wed, Sat & Sun, to 9pm Thu & Fri; [S]A/C, B/D, 1 to 59th St-Columbus Circle) MAD offers four floors of superlative design and handicrafts, from blown glass and carved wood to elaborate metal jewelry. Its temporary exhibitions are top notch and innovative; one past show explored the art of scent. On the first Sunday of the month, professional artists lead explorations of the galleries, followed by hands-on workshops inspired by the current exhibitions. The museum gift shop sells some fantastic contemporary jewelry, while the 9th-floor restaurant-bar Robert (p201) is perfect for panoramic cocktails.

INTERNATIONAL CENTER OF PHOTOGRAPHY GALLERY

Map p430 (ICP; www.icp.org; 1133 Sixth Ave, at 43rd St; adult/child $14/free, by donation 5-8pm Fri; 🕐10am-6pm Tue-Thu, Sat & Sun, to 8pm Fri; 📶; [S]B/D/F/M to 42nd St-Bryant Park) ICP is New York's premier platform for photography, with a strong emphasis on photojournalism, and changing exhibitions on a wide range of themes. Past shows in the two-floor space have included work by Henri Cartier-Bresson, Man Ray and Robert Capa. The center is also a school, offering coursework (for credit) and a public lecture series.

Stop by the excellent gallery shop, great for instant cameras and photography tomes, cool little gifts and NYC souvenirs.

DIAMOND DISTRICT STREET

Map p430 (www.diamonddistrict.org; 47th St, btwn Fifth & Sixth Aves; [S]B/D/F/M to 47th-50th Sts-Rockefeller Center) Like Diagon Alley in *Harry Potter,* the Diamond District is a world unto itself. A frenetic whirl of Hasidic Jewish traders, pesky hawkers and love-struck couples looking for the perfect rock, its 2600-plus businesses peddle all manner of diamonds, gold, pearls, gemstones and watches. In fact, the strip handles approximately 90% of the cut diamonds sold in the country.

Marilyn, eat your heart out!

HERALD SQUARE SQUARE

Map p430 (cnr Broadway, Sixth Ave & 34th St; [S]B/D/F/M, N/Q/R to 34th St-Herald Sq) This crowded convergence of Broadway, Sixth Ave and 34th St is best known as the home of mammoth department store Macy's (p208), where you can still ride some of the original wooden elevators. As part of the city's 'traffic-free Times Square' plan, you can also (try to) relax in a lawn chair outside the store, slap-bang in the middle of Broadway.

Herald Square gets its name from a long-defunct newspaper, the *New York Herald* (1835–1924), and the small, leafy park here bustles during business hours thanks to a much-needed face-lift. Skip the indoor malls south of Macy's on Sixth Ave, packed with dull, suburban chains.

GARMENT DISTRICT NEIGHBORHOOD

Map p430 (Seventh Ave, btwn 34th St & Times Sq, Midtown West; [S]N/Q/R, S, 1/2/3 & 7 to Times Sq-42nd St) Otherwise known as the Fashion District, this thread-obsessed territory might look like an unremarkable stretch of designers' offices and wholesale and retail shops, but it's where you'll find a huge selection of fabrics, sequins, lace and, chances are, those day-glo velvet buttons you've been missing since 1986.

In the lead-up to Fashion Week (February and September), the area swarms with portfolio-clutching models on their way from one casting to the next. Whatever the time of year, look down at the sidewalk when you hit Seventh and 39th St and you'll catch the Fashion Walk of Fame, honoring the likes of Betsey Johnson, Marc Jacobs, Geoffrey Beene, Halston and other fashion visionaries. It's on the same corner as Claes Oldenburg's sculpture of the world's largest button, held upright by a 31ft-tall steel needle.

INTREPID SEA, AIR & SPACE MUSEUM MUSEUM

Map p430 (www.intrepidmuseum.org; Pier 86, Twelfth Ave at 46th St, Midtown West; adult/child Intrepid & Growler submarine $24/12, incl Space Shuttle Pavilion $31/17; ⏰10am-5pm Mon-Fri, to 6pm Sat & Sun Apr-Oct, 10am-5pm Mon-Sun Nov-Mar; 🚌M42, M50 bus westbound, [S]A/C/E to 42nd St-Port Authority Bus Terminal) The USS *Intrepid* survived both a WWII bomb and kamikaze attacks. Thankfully, this hulking aircraft carrier is now a lot less stressed, playing host to a multimillion dollar interactive military museum that tells its tale through videos, historical artifacts and frozen-in-time living quarters. The flight deck features fighter planes and military helicopters, which might inspire you to try the museum's high-tech flight simulators.

The rides include the G Force Encounter, allowing you to experience the virtual thrill of flying a supersonic jet plane, and the Transporter FX, a flight simulator promising six full minutes of 'complete sensory overload.' The museum is also home to the guided-missile submarine *Growler* (not for the claustrophobic), a decommissioned Concorde, and the former NASA space shuttle *Enterprise.*

MUSEUM AT FIT MUSEUM

Map p430 (www.fitnyc.edu/museum; 227 W 27th St, at Seventh Ave, Midtown West; ⏰noon-8pm Tue-Fri, 10am-5pm Sat; [S]1 to 28th St) [FREE] The Fashion Institute of Technology (FIT) lays claim to one of the world's richest collections of garments, textiles and accessories. At last count, there were around 50,000 items spanning the 18th century to the present day. The school's museum is the place to catch a glimpse, its innovative, rotating exhibitions showcasing both permanent collection items and on-loan curiosities.

WORTH A DETOUR

FOUR FREEDOMS PARK

Dramatic design, presidential inspiration and a refreshing perspective on the New York skyline make for an arresting trio at the **Franklin D Roosevelt Four Freedoms Park** (Map p426; www.fdrfourfreedomspark.org; ⏰9am-5pm Wed-Mon) [FREE]. Clinging to the southern tip of sinuous Roosevelt Island on the East River, this remarkable monument honors America's 32nd president and his State of the Union speech of 1941. In it, Franklin D Roosevelt addressed his desire for a world based upon four essential human freedoms: freedom of speech, freedom of worship, freedom from want and freedom from fear. Designed by renowned architect Louis Kahn in 1973, the monument would only reach completion in 2012, 38 years after Kahn's death.

The wait was worth it. Kahn's luminous granite vision is breathtakingly cinematic in its scale and effect. A sweep of grand, stark steps lead up to a sloping triangular lawn. Fringed by linden trees, the lawn gently spills down to a bronze bust of Roosevelt by American sculptor Jo Davidson. Framing the sculpture is a granite wall, hand engraved with Roosevelt's rousing speech. The wall also serves to separate the bust from 'The Room,' a contemplative granite terrace clinging to the very tip of the island. The combination of lapping waves and hovering skyline are utterly mesmerizing.

Although the F subway line will get you to Roosevelt Island, it's much more fun catching the tramway car, which glides above the East River, offering eagle-eye views of the Manhattan skyline. The monument is a 15-minute walk south of both the Roosevelt Island tramway car and subway stations. Alternatively, red island buses (25¢) make the journey from Main St, one block east of Roosevelt Island subway station or one block north of the tramway car terminal.

1. Carnegie Hall (p203)
Appreciate the accoustics of this legendary music venue at a jazz, opera or folk performance – or listen to the buskers outside.

2. Radio City Music Hall (p188)
Tour the sumptous art deco interior and the landmark listed Great Stage, designed to resemble a setting sun.

3. Times Square (p176)
See the glittering lights and bombastic billboards of this NYC icon.

4. 42nd St
Jostle with the crowds on bustling 42nd street, home to some of NYC's most famous buildings.

KOREATOWN NEIGHBORHOOD
Map p430 (31st to 36th Sts & Broadway to Fifth Ave; S B/D/F/M, N/Q/R to 34th St-Herald Sq)
For kimchi and karaoke, it's hard to beat Koreatown (Little Korea). Mainly concentrated on 32nd St, with some spillover into the surrounding streets both south and

north of this strip, it's a Seoul-ful jumble of Korean-owned restaurants, shops, salons and spas.

Authentic BBQ is available around the clock at many of the all-night spots on 32nd St, some with microphone, video screen and *Manic Monday* at the ready.

MIDTOWN SKYSCRAPERS: BEST OF THE REST

Midtown's skyline is more than just the Empire State and Chrysler Buildings, with enough modernist and postmodernist beauties to satisfy the wildest of high-rise dreams. Celebrate all things phallic with five of Midtown's finest:

Seagram Building (1956–58; 514ft)
A textbook regular, the 38-floor **Seagram Building** (Map p426; 100 E 53rd St, at Park Ave, Midtown East; S 6 to 51st St, E, M to Fifth Ave-53rd St) is one of the world's finest examples of the international style. Its lead architect, Ludwig Mies van der Rohe, was recommended for the project by Arthur Drexler, the then curator of architecture at MoMA. With its low podium, colonnade-like pillars and bronze cladding, Mies cleverly references classical Greek influences.

Lever House (1950–52; 306ft)
Upon its debut, 21-story **Lever House** (Map p426; 390 Park Ave, btwn 53rd & 54th Sts, Midtown East; S E, M to Fifth Ave-53rd St) was at the height of the cutting-edge. The UN Secretariat Building was the only other skyscraper to feature a glass skin, an innovation that would redefine urban architecture. The building's form was equally bold: two counter-posed rectangular shapes consisting of a slender tower atop a low-rise base. The open courtyard features marble benches by Japanese American sculptor Isamu Noguchi, while the lobby exhibits contemporary art commissioned for the space.

Citigroup Center (1974–77; 915ft)
With its striking triangular roof and candy-like striped facade, Hugh Stubbins' 59-story **Citigroup Center** (Map p426; 139 E 53rd St, at Lexington Ave, Midtown East; S 6 to 51st St, E, M to Lexington Ave-53rd St) signaled a shift from the flat-roof sobriety of the international style. Even more dramatic is the building's base, which is cut away at the four corners, leaving the tower to perch dramatically on a cross-shaped footing. This unusual configuration allowed for the construction of St Peter's Lutheran Church on the site's northwest corner, which replaced the original neo-Gothic church demolished during the skyscraper's construction.

Hearst Tower (2003–06; 597ft)
Foster & Partners' **Hearst Tower** (Map p430; 949 Eighth Ave, btwn 56th & 57th Ave, Midtown West; S A/C, B/D, 1 to 59th St-Columbus Circle) is hands down one of New York's most creative works of contemporary architecture. Its diagonal grid of trusses evokes a jagged glass-and-steel honeycomb, best appreciated up close and from an angle. The tower rises above the hollowed-out core of John Urban's 1928 cast-stone Hearst Magazine Building, itself originally envisioned as a skyscraper. The 46-floor structure is also one of the city's greenest creations: around 90% of its structural steel is from recycled sources. In the lobby you'll find *Riverlines*, a mural by Richard Long.

Bank of America Tower (2004–09; 1200ft)
While striking for its crystal shape and piercing, 255ft spire, the **Bank of America Tower** (Map p430; Sixth Ave, btwn 42nd & 43rd Sts; S B/D/F/M to 42nd St-Bryant Park) hit the headlines for its enviable green credentials. The stats are impressive: a clean-burning, on-site cogeneration plant providing around 65% of the tower's annual electricity requirements; CO_2-detecting air filters that channel filtered air where needed; and even destination-dispatch elevators designed to avoid empty car trips. Designed by Cook & Fox Architects, the 58-floor role model was awarded 'Best Tall Building in America' by the Council on Tall Buildings & Urban Habitat awards in 2010.

🍴 EATING

Despite the ubiquitous chains and tourist-trap deprestaurants – mostly around Times Square and the Theater District – Midtown is no culinary slouch. You'll find more than 20 Michelin-starred restaurants here, some with million-dollar skyline views. Tuck into authentic *chingudi jhola* (spicy prawn curry) in the 'Curry Hill' district (Lexington Ave around 28th St), organic Zen noodles in Koreatown, or cult-status ramen noodles on W 52nd St. Or perhaps you're more in the mood for pillow-soft cheeseburgers at a speakeasy burger joint, or Cubano sandwiches at a retro-fab diner? Then there's Ninth Ave in Hell's Kitchen, a constantly evolving see-and-be-seen, locally loved sip-and-sup strip. Ready, set, chomp!

🍴 Midtown East & Fifth Avenue

99 CENT PIZZA — PIZZERIA $

Map p426 (473 Lexington Ave, at 46th St; pizza slices $1; 🕐6am-4:30am; [S]S, 4/5/6, 7 to Grand Central-42nd St) Barebones 99 Cent Pizza does a brisk business – always a sign that you've found a good bargain. The pie ain't gourmet and doesn't claim to be, but if you're craving a decent slice to go, this is your baby.

HANGAWI — KOREAN $$

Map p426 (☎212-213-0077; www.hangawirestaurant.com; 12 E 32nd St, btwn Fifth & Madison Aves; mains lunch $10-16, dinner $16-26; 🕐noon-2:45pm & 5-10.15pm Mon-Thu, to 10:30pm Fri, 1-10:30pm Sat, 5-9:30pm Sun; 🥬; [S]B/D/F/M, N/Q/R to 34th St-Herald Sq) Flesh-free Korean is the draw at high-achieving Hangawi. Leave your shoes at the entrance and slip into a soothing, Zen-like space of meditative music, soft low seating and clean, complex dishes. Show-stoppers include the leek pancakes and a seductively smooth tofu claypot in ginger sauce.

Organic and gluten-free options add to the holistic vibe, while the $22 prix fixe lunch is good value. Book ahead for dinner.

SMITH — AMERICAN $$

Map p426 (☎212-644-2700; www.thesmithnyc.com; 956 Second Ave, at 51st St, Midtown East; mains $17-33; 🕐7:30am-midnight Mon-Wed, to 1am Thu & Fri, 10am-1am Sat, 10am-midnight Sun; 📶; [S]6 to 51st St) This cool, funky brasserie has sexed-up Midtown's far east with its industrial-chic interior, sociable bar and well-executed grub. Much of the food is made from scratch, the seasonal menus a mix of nostalgic American and Italian inspiration (we're talking hot potato chips with blue cheese fondue, chicken pot pie with cheddar chive biscuit, and handmade ravioli stuffed with goat's cheese).

Book ahead for Sunday brunch or prepare to wait.

DHABA — INDIAN $$

Map p426 (www.dhabanyc.com; 108 Lexington Ave, btwn 27th & 28th Sts, Midtown East; mains $11-23; 🕐noon-midnight Mon-Thu, to 1am Fri & Sat, to 10:30pm Sun; [S]6 to 28th St) Murray Hill (aka Curry Hill) has no shortage of subcontinental bites, but funky Dhaba packs one serious flavor punch. Mouthwatering standouts include the tangy, crunchalicious *lasoni gobi* (fried cauliflower with tomato and spices), as well as the seriously seductive *murgh bharta* (minced chicken cooked with smoked eggplant).

Concessions to the mostly Punjabi menu include a string of British curry-house classics. There's a good-value lunch buffet to boot ($10.95 Monday to Saturday, $12.95 Sunday).

EL PARADOR CAFE — MEXICAN $$

Map p426 (☎212-679-6812; www.elparadorcafe.com; 325 E 34th St, btwn First & Second Aves, Midtown East; mains $18-32; 🕐noon-midnight, closed Sun Jul & Aug; [S]6 to 33rd St) Back in the day, the far-flung location of this Mexican stalwart was much appreciated by philandering husbands. The shady regulars may have gone, but the old-school charm remains, from the beveled candleholders and dapper Latino waiters to the satisfying south-of-the-border standbys.

House classics include the *mejillones al vino* (mussels in red wine, cilantro and garlic, served with green chili corn bread), and the signature *mole poblano* (chicken stewed in a rich chili-and-chocolate-spiked sauce). End the night with a shot of the homemade pineapple tequila.

★ROUGE TOMATE — MODERN AMERICAN $$$

Map p426 (☎646-237-8977; www.rougetomatenyc.com; 10 E 60th St, btwn Fifth & Madison Aves; dinner mains $29-42; 🕐noon-3pm & 5:30-10:30pm Mon-Sat; 🥬; [S]N/Q/R to Fifth Ave-59th

St, 4/5/6 to 59th St) 🌿 Health-conscious, Michelin-starred Rouge Tomate puts the sexy in sustainable. To retain maximum nutritional value, the mostly local, seasonal ingredients are never fried or grilled. This seeming limitation is no obstacle in creating complex, sophisticated marvels like fleshy, textured eggplant tartare with garlic confit.

There's an exceptional offering of organic and biodynamic wines, swilled by a slinky, sharply dressed crowd pulled straight off the *Sex and the City* set. The three-course, $32 'Business Lunch' is good value, and it's always wise to book three or four days ahead, especially if dining Tuesday to Thursday. No booking? Head in early and try your luck at the bar.

JOHN DORY OYSTER BAR SEAFOOD **$$$**

Map p426 (www.thejohndory.com; 1196 Broadway, at 29th St; small plates $9-28; ⏲noon-midnight; [S]N/R to 28th St) Anchored to the Ace Hotel (p337) lobby, loud 'n' trendy John Dory is a fine spot to sip bubbly and slurp on plump and salty creatures of the sea. Crudo gets clever in dishes like Spanish mackerel with chili, cilantro and squid crackling, while the tapas-style 'small plates' harbor some equally creative morsels (chorizo stuffed squid with smoked tomato, anyone?).

From 5pm to 7pm and 11pm to midnight (noon to 7pm on weekends), $18 gets you six oysters or clams and a glass of sparkling vino or a pint of ale.

SPARKS STEAKHOUSE **$$$**

Map p426 (☎212-687-4855; www.sparkssteakhouse.com; 210 E 46th St, btwn Second & Third Aves, Midtown East; dinner mains $36-53; ⏲11.30am-11pm Mon-Thu, 11:30am-11:30pm Fri, 5-11:30pm Sat; 📶; [S]S, 4/5/6, 7 to Grand Central-42nd St) Get an honest-to-goodness New York steakhouse experience at this classic joint, a former mob hangout that's been around for nearly 50 years and still packs 'em in for a juicy carnivorous feed.

Rub elbows with red-meat lovers of all stripes and choose your cut: prime sirloin, filet mignon, steak *fromage* (topped with Roquefort) or medallions of beef topped with Bordelaise sauce. Thick chops of veal and lamb and various seafood options are also on tap, as are heaping portions of character thanks to the skilled waiters.

🍴 Midtown West & Times Square

★TOTTO RAMEN JAPANESE **$**

Map p430 (www.tottoramen.com; 366 W 52nd St, btwn Eighth & Ninth Aves, Midtown West; ramen from $9.75; ⏲noon-midnight Mon-Fri, noon-11pm Sat, 5-11pm Sun; [S]C/E to 50th St) Good things come to those who wait. Like tiny Totto. Write your name and number of guests on the clipboard by the door and wait for your (cash-only) ramen revelation. Skip the chicken and go for the pork, which sings in dishes like miso ramen (with fermented soybean paste, egg, scallion, bean sprouts, onion and homemade chili paste).

Behind the counter, ramen masters tackle bubbling vats of fragrant broth and char the melt-in-your-mouth pork with a blowtorch. Specials are pinned on the wall corkboards: the *ika-yaki* (skewered and torched sea urchin) is unmissable. Avoid the place on weekends as waiting times are particularly excruciating.

BURGER JOINT BURGERS **$**

Map p430 (www.burgerjointny.com; Le Parker Meridien, 119 W 56th St, btwn Sixth & Seventh Aves, Midtown West; burgers from $7.80; ⏲11am-11:30pm Sun-Thu, to midnight Fri & Sat; [S]F to 57th St) With only a small neon burger as your clue, this cash-only, speakeasy-style burger hut lurks behind the lobby curtain in the Le Parker Meridien hotel. Though it might not be as 'hip' or as 'secret' as it once was, it still delivers the same winning formula of graffiti-strewn walls, retro booths and attitude-loaded staff slapping up beef 'n' patty brilliance.

The choice is easy: hamburger or cheeseburger, cooked to your liking and pimped with your choice of garnishes. Order a side of golden fries, a pitcher of beer and scan the walls for celebrity scribbles. Head in early or late, or prepare to wait.

EL MARGON CUBAN **$**

Map p430 (136 W 46th St, btwn Sixth & Seventh Aves, Midtown West; sandwiches from $4, mains $9-15; ⏲7am-5pm; [S]B/D/F/M to 47th-50th Sts-Rockefeller Center) It's still 1973 at this ever-packed Cuban lunch counter, where orange Laminex and greasy goodness never went out of style. Go for gold with the legendary cubano sandwich (a pressed panino jammed with rich roast pork, salami, cheese, pickles, mojo and mayo). It's obscenely good.

★DANJI KOREAN $$

Map p430 (www.danjinyc.com; 346 W 52nd St, btwn Eighth & Ninth Aves, Midtown West; plates $6-20; ⏲noon-2:30pm & 5:15-10:45pm Mon-Thu, noon-2:30pm & 5:15-11:45pm Fri, 5:15-11:45pm Sat; [S]C/E to 50th St) Young-gun chef Hooni Kim makes taste buds weep with his Michelin-starred Korean 'tapas.' Served in a snug-and-slinky contemporary space, his bite-sized marvels fall into one of two categories: traditional or modern. While we hate to play favorites, we'd sell our souls for the sliders, a succulent duo of *bulgogi* beef and pork belly dressed with scallion salsa and served on butter-grilled buns. Head in early or wait.

★VICEVERSA ITALIAN $$

Map p430 (☎212-399-9291; www.viceversanyc.com; 325 W 51st St, btwn Eighth & Ninth Aves, Midtown West; pasta dishes $10-22, mains $23-30; ⏲noon-2:30pm & 5-11pm Mon-Fri, 5-11pm Sat, 11:30am-3pm & 5-10pm Sun; [S]C/E to 50th St) ViceVersa is the quintessential Italian: suave and sophisticated, affable and scrumptious. Scan the menu for refined, cross-regional dishes like arancini with black truffle and fontina cheese, or slow-roasted suckling pig with fennel pollen and grilled endives.

For a celebrated classic, order the *casoncelli alla bergamasca* (ravioli-like pasta filled with minced veal, raisins and amaretto cookies and seasoned with sage, butter, pancetta and Grana Padano), a nod to chef Stefano Terzi's Lombard heritage. The bar seating is perfect for solo diners, while the leafy courtyard is a fun spot for a see-and-be-seen Sunday brunch.

GAHM MI OAK KOREAN $$

Map p430 (43 W 32nd St, btwn Broadway & Fifth Ave; mains $10-22; ⏲24hr; [S]N/Q/R, B/D/F/M to 34th St-Herald Sq) If you're craving *yook hwe* (raw beef and Asian pear matchsticks) at 3am, this K-Town savior has you covered. The shtick here is authenticity, shining through in dishes like the house speciality *sul long tang* (a milky broth of ox bones, boiled for 12 hours and pimped with brisket and scallion), which will cure the most evil of hangovers.

★LE BERNARDIN SEAFOOD $$$

Map p430 (☎212-554-1515; www.le-bernardin.com; 155 W 51st St, btwn Sixth & Seventh Aves, Midtown West; prix fixe lunch/dinner $76/135, tasting menus $155-198; ⏲noon-2:30pm & 5:15-10:30pm Mon-Thu, noon-2:30pm & 5:15-11pm Fri, 5:15-11pm Sat; [S]1 to 50th St, B/D, E to 7th Ave) The interiors may have been subtly sexed-up for a 'younger clientele' (the stunning storm-themed triptych is by Brooklyn artist Ran Ortner), but triple Michelin-starred Le Bernardin remains a luxe, fine-dining holy grail. At the helm is celebrity chef Eric Ripert, whose deceptively simple-looking seafood often borders on the transcendental.

The menu works simply: three lunch courses for $76 or four dinner courses for $135, with ample choices per course, and two tastings menus for those with more time and money. The dishes themselves are divided into three categories (Almost Raw, Barely Touched, Lightly Cooked), and while most shine with delicious complexity, Ripert's signature tuna and foie gras creation is especially outstanding. Book at least three weeks ahead for dinner and two weeks ahead for lunch.

★BETONY MODERN AMERICAN $$$

Map p430 (☎212-465-2400; www.betony-nyc.com; 41 W 57th St, btwn Fifth & Sixth Aves; mains $27-38; ⏲5-10pm Mon-Thu, to 10:30pm Fri & Sat; [S]F to 57th St) Thrilling menus, seamless service, and a slinky downtown vibe: welcome to Midtown's latest godsend. While industrial windows, exposed brickwork and a soaring bar make Betony's front section perfect for after-five cocktails, request a table in the intimate, baroque-esque back dining room to savor chef Bryce Shuman's sophisticated albeit playful dishes.

Here, smoked pork hocks burst through seared foie gras; sauces are poured through fresh bunches of herbs; and short ribs enjoy two days in rendered dry-aged beef fat before a searing over white-hot Japanese charcoal. The result: spectacular. Book ahead.

NOMAD NEW AMERICAN $$$

Map p430 (☎347-472-5660; www.thenomadhotel.com; NoMad Hotel, 1170 Broadway, at 28th St; mains $20-37; ⏲noon-2pm & 5:30-10:30pm Mon-Thu, to 11pm Fri, 11am-2pm & 5:30-11pm Sat, 11am-3pm & 5:30-10pm Sun; [S]N/R, 6 to 28th St, F/M to 23rd St) Sharing the same name as the 'It kid' hotel it inhabits, NoMad has sealed its rep as one of Manhattan's culinary highlights. Carved up into a series of distinctly different spaces – including a see-and-be-seen Atrium, Victoriana parlor and snacks-only Library – the restaurant is the hipper, (slightly) more relaxed sibling of Michelin-starred Eleven Madison Park. The menus are eclectic, Eurocentric and – true to chef Daniel Humm's reputation – just a little playful.

While the snacks can be a bit hit-and-miss, both appetizers and mains are generally outstanding, whether it's a crispy chiffonade of snow peas paired with pancetta, pecorino and mint, or NoMad's thrilling 'chicken for two,' roasted in a wood-burning oven and served with foie-gras-rich brioche under its crackly skin. Book ahead.

A VOCE ITALIAN $$$

Map p430 (☎212-823-2523; www.avocerestaurant.com; Time Warner Center, 10 Columbus Circle, at 59th St; mains $29-45; 🕒11:30am-2:30pm & 5-10pm Mon-Thu, to 10:30pm Fri, 11am-3pm & 5-10:30pm Sat, 11am-3pm & 5-10pm Sun; [S]A/C, B/D, 1 to 59th St-Columbus Circle) Inside the salubrious Time Warner mall, Michelin-starred A Voce combines sweeping views of Central Park with high-end interpretations of Italian classics – think butternut-squash-filled ravioli with almonds, sweet gorgonzola and crispy sage. The well-versed wine list includes almost 20 drops by the glass. Book ahead.

MARSEILLE FRENCH, MEDITERRANEAN $$$

Map p430 (www.marseillenyc.com; 630 Ninth Ave, at 44th St; mains $20-29; 🕒11:30am-11pm Sun-Tue, to midnight Wed-Sat; [S]A/C/E to 42nd St-Port Authority Bus Terminal) Looking somewhere between an old cinema lobby and an art deco brasserie, this Hell's Kitchen classic is a fabulous spot to kick back with a Le Pamplemousse (Absolut Ruby Red Grapefruit vodka, Campari, elderflower and citrus) and nibble on flavor-packed French-Med fare like Provençal goat's cheese tart or Tuscan chicken with truffle jus.

DRINKING & NIGHTLIFE

The massive belly of Manhattan covers about everyone – cheesy tourist, barely legal suburbanite, martini princesses, you name it. The drinking holes east of Times Square may be a little more old-school than those to the west, but they're among the most atmospheric in town, from historic pubs to baronial hideaways. Head to Midtown West and quench your thirst anywhere from lofty cocktail bars to sleazy dive joints and even a country-and-western gay bar. Venues around Seventh Ave, Times Square and Hell's Kitchen are within easy striking distance of Broadway theaters.

Midtown East & Fifth Avenue

LITTLE COLLINS CAFE

Map p426 (www.littlecollinsnyc.com; 667 Lexington Ave, btwn 55th & 56th Sts, Midtown East; 🕒7am-6pm Mon-Fri, 9am-4pm Sat & Sun; [S]E, M to 53rd St, 4/5/6 to 59th St) Co-owned by Aussie expat Leon Unglik, Little Collins emulates the celebrated cafes of his hometown Melbourne: understatedly cool, welcoming spaces serving superlative coffee and equally tasty grub. The cafe is home to NYC's very first Modbar; high-tech, under-the-counter brewers that look like sleek chrome taps.

TOP OF THE STRAND COCKTAIL BAR

Map p426 (www.topofthestrand.com; Strand, 33 W 37th St, btwn Fifth & Sixth Aves; 🕒5pm-midnight Mon & Sun, to 1am Tue-Sat; [S]B/D/F/M to 34th St) For that 'Oh my God, I'm in New York' feeling, head to the Strand (p337) hotel's rooftop bar, order a martini (extra dirty) and drop your jaw (discreetly). Sporting slinky cabanas and a sliding glass roof, its view of the Empire State Building is unforgettable.

Expect DJ-spun tunes and a mixed crowd of post-work locals and international hotel guests.

STUMPTOWN COFFEE ROASTERS CAFE

Map p426 (www.stumptowncoffee.com; 18 W 29th St, btwn Broadway & Fifth Ave; 🕒6am-8pm Mon-Fri, 7am-8pm Sat & Sun; [S]N/R to 28th St) Hipster baristas in fedora hats brewing killer coffee? No, you're not in Williamsburg, you're at the Manhattan outpost of Portland's cult-status coffee roaster. The queue is a small price to pay for proper espresso, so count your blessings. It's standing-room only, though weary punters might find a seat in the adjacent Ace Hotel (p337) lobby.

There's a second branch in Greenwich Village (p151).

CULTURE ESPRESSO CAFE

Map p426 (www.cultureespresso.com; 72 W 38th St, at Sixth Ave; 🕒7am-7pm Mon-Fri, from 8am Sat & Sun; 📶; [S]B/D/F/M to 42nd St-Bryant Park)

Culture peddles single-origin espresso that's nutty, complex and creamy, as well as Third Wave options like Chemex and cold brew varieties (we're addicted to the Kyoto-style iced coffee). Tasty edibles include gourmet panini (with combos like prosciutto, fig jam and arugula), baked treats from local artisans, and Culture's very own super-gooey choc-chip cookies.

PJ CLARKE'S BAR

Map p426 (www.pjclarkes.com; 915 Third Ave, at 55th St, Midtown East; ⌚11:30am-4am; [S]E, M to Lexington Ave-53rd St) A bastion of old New York, this lovingly worn wooden saloon has been straddling the scene since 1884; Buddy Holly proposed to his fiancée here and Ol' Blue Eyes pretty much owned table 20. Choose a jukebox tune, order the knockout burger and settle in with a come-one-and-all crowd of collar-and-tie colleagues, college students and nostalgia-craving urbanites.

MIDDLE BRANCH COCKTAIL BAR

Map p426 (154 E 33rd St, btwn Lexington & Third Aves, Midtown East; ⌚5pm-2am; [S]6 to 33rd St) Brainchild of cocktail deity Sasha Petraske, bi-level Middle Branch injects some much-needed drinking cred in beer-and-margarita-centric Murray Hill. Eye-candy bartenders whip up some of Midtown's sharpest libations, from faithful classics to playful reinterpretations like the Enzoni (a lemon-and-grape-laced twist on the classic Negroni). Cash only.

SUBWAY INN DIVE BAR

Map p426 (143 E 60th St, btwn Lexington & Third Aves, Midtown East; ⌚11am-4am Mon-Sat, from noon Sun; [S]4/5/6 to 59th St, N/Q/R to Lexington Ave-59th St) Booze in this part of town for this cheap? Count us in. Occupying its own world across from Bloomingdale's, this old-geezer watering hole is a vintage cheap-booze spot that, despite the classic rock and worn red booths, harkens to long-past days when Marilyn Monroe would drop in.

TERROIR WINE BAR

Map p426 (439 Third Ave, btwn 30th & 31st Sts, Midtown East; ⌚5pm-1am Mon-Thu, to 2am Fri & Sat, to 11pm Sun; [S]6 to 28th St) Channeling downtown with its low-slung bulbs, brickwork and communal tables, laid-back Terroir is an oasis for oenophiles in Murray Hill. The well-versed, well-priced wine list is the size of your grandma's family photo album, with an impressive array of drops by the glass. If you're feeling peckish, graze from a string of snacks such as marinated olives, or roasted beets with orange and hazelnuts.

🍷 Midtown West & Times Square

ROBERT COCKTAIL BAR

Map p430 (www.robertnyc.com; Museum of Arts & Design, 2 Columbus Circle, btwn Eighth Ave & Broadway; ⌚11:30am-10pm Mon, 11:30am-midnight Tue-Fri, 11am-midnight Sat, 11am-10pm Sun; [S]A/C, B/D, 1 to 59th St-Columbus Circle) Perched on the 9th floor of the Museum of Arts & Design (p192), '60s-inspired Robert is technically a high-end, Modern American restaurant. While the food is satisfactory, we suggest you head in late afternoon or post-dinner, find a sofa and gaze out over Central Park with a MAD Manhattan (bourbon, blood orange vermouth and liquored cherries). Magic.

RUM HOUSE COCKTAIL BAR

Map p430 (www.edisonrumhouse.com; 228 W 47th St, btwn Broadway & Eighth Ave, Midtown West; ⌚1pm-4am; [S]N/Q/R to 49th St) Not long ago, this was Hotel Edison's crusty old piano bar. Enter the capable team from Tribeca bar Ward III, who ripped out the grubby carpet, polished up the coppertop bar and revived this slice of old New York. You'll still find a nightly pianist (Wednesday to Monday), now accompanied by well-crafted drinks and an enviable medley of whiskeys and rums.

LANTERN'S KEEP COCKTAIL BAR

Map p430 (☎212-453-4287; www.thelanternskeep.com; Iroquois Hotel, 49 W 44th St, btwn Fifth & Sixth Aves; ⌚5pm-midnight Mon-Fri, 6pm-1am Sat; [S]B/D/F/M to 42nd St-Bryant Park) Can you keep a secret? If so, cross the lobby of the Iroquois Hotel (p338) and slip into this dark, intimate cocktail salon. Its speciality is pre-Prohibition drinks, shaken and stirred by passionate, personable mixologists. If you're feeling spicy, request a Groom's Breakfast, a fiery melange of gin, hot sauce, Worcestershire sauce, muddled lime, cucumber, and salt and pepper. Reservations are recommended.

JIMMY'S CORNER DIVE BAR

Map p430 (140 W 44th St, btwn Sixth & Seventh Aves, Midtown West; ⌚11.30am-4am Mon-Sat, from 3pm Sun; [S]N/Q/R, 1/2/3, 7 to 42nd St-Times Sq, B/D/F/M to 42nd St-Bryant Park) This welcoming, completely unpretentious dive off Times Square is run by an old boxing trainer – as if you wouldn't guess by all the framed photos of boxing greats (and lesser-known fighters, too). The jukebox covers Stax to Miles Davis (plus Lionel Ritchie's most regretful moments), kept low enough for post-work gangs to chat away.

INDUSTRY GAY

Map p430 (www.industry-bar.com; 355 W 52nd St, btwn Eighth & Ninth Aves, Midtown West; 🕒4pm-4am; [S]C/E, 1 to 50th St) What was once a parking garage is now one of the hottest gay bars in Hell's Kitchen – a slick 4000-sq-ft watering hole with handsome lounge areas, a pool table and a stage for top-notch drag divas. Head in between 4pm and 9pm for the two-for-one drinks special or squeeze in later to party with the eye-candy party hordes. Cash only.

FLAMING SADDLES GAY

Map p430 (www.flamingsaddles.com; 793 Ninth Ave, btwn 52nd & 53rd Sts, Midtown West; 🕒4pm-4am Mon-Fri, noon-4am Sat & Sun; [S]C/E to 50th St) Butter my butt and call me a biscuit, a country-and-western gay bar in Midtown! *Coyote Ugly* meets *Calamity Jane* at this Hell's Kitchen hangout, complete with studly bar-dancing barmen, aspiring urban cowboys and a rough 'n' ready vibe. So slip on them Wranglers and hit the Saddle, partner. You're in for a wild and boozy ride.

XL NIGHTCLUB GAY

Map p430 (www.xlnightclub.com; 512 W 42nd St, btwn Tenth & Eleventh Aves, Midtown West; 🕒10pm-4am; [S]A/C/E to 42nd St-Port Authority Bus Terminal) Muscle boys pack this mega dance club, a hedonistic playpen featuring two dance floors, cabaret theater, lounge bar, and the prerequisite quota of go-go boys and pin-up bartenders. The venue hosts some great shows, from camp comedy to cheeky drag revues.

THERAPY GAY

Map p430 (www.therapy-nyc.com; 348 W 52nd St, btwn Eighth & Ninth Aves, Midtown West; 🕒5pm-2am Sun-Thu, to 4am Fri & Sat; [S]C/E, 1 to 50th St) Multilevel Therapy was the first gay man's lounge/club to draw throngs to Hell's Kitchen and it still pulls a crowd with its nightly shows (from music to Broadway bingo) and decent grub Sunday to Friday (chicken skewers, burger, hummus, salads). Drink monikers team with the theme: Oral Fixation and Size Queen, to name a few.

RUDY'S DIVE BAR

Map p430 (www.rudysbarnyc.com; 627 Ninth Ave, at 44th St, Midtown West; 🕒8am-4am Mon-Sat, noon-4am Sun; [S]A/C/E to 42nd St-Port Authority Bus Terminal) The big pantless pig in a red jacket out front marks Hell's Kitchen's best divey mingler, with cheap pitchers of Rudy's two beers, half-circle booths covered in red duct tape, and free hot dogs. A mix of folks come to flirt or watch muted Knicks games as classic rock plays.

☆ ENTERTAINMENT

☆ Midtown East & Fifth Avenue

NEW YORK PUBLIC LIBRARY LECTURES

Map p426 (www.nypl.org/events; 42nd St at Fifth Ave; [S]B/D/F/M to 42nd St-Bryant Park, 7 to Fifth Ave, S, 4/5/6 to 42nd St-Grand Central) Across its branches, the NYPL keeps brains lubricated with its string of lectures and public seminars, with topics ranging from contemporary art to the writings of Jane Austen. You'll find some of the best at the main branch on 42nd St. You can search all happenings at the library's website.

ST BARTHOLOMEW'S CHURCH CLASSICAL MUSIC

Map p426 (www.stbarts.org; 109 E 50th St, btwn Park & Lexington Aves, Midtown East; [S]E, M to 5th Ave-53rd St, 6 to 51st St) Several free performance series have found an extraordinary home at this landmark Anglican church, where the fine acoustics add a special touch to choir, cello, piano, violin and ensemble performances.

☆ Midtown West & Times Square

★JAZZ AT LINCOLN CENTER JAZZ

Map p430 (☎tickets to Dizzy's Club Coca-Cola 212-258-9595, tickets to Rose Theater & Allen Room 212-721-6500; www.jazzatlincolncenter.org; Time Warner Center, Broadway at 60th St; [S]A/C, B/D, 1 to 59th St-Columbus Circle) Perched high

[i] BROADWAY BARGAINS

Unless booked many months in advance, must-see Broadway musicals can be prohibitively expensive. Discount ticket agent **TKTS** (www.tdf.org) offers great deals daily, though rarely to the most in-demand shows. For these, your best bet for last-minute discounts is at the theater box office itself.

Many of the hottest shows – including *Kinky Boots*, *Book of Mormon* and *Matilda* (p204) – run ticket lotteries, entered at the theater 2½ hours before the performance. If your name is drawn, the show is yours for less than $40. The bad news: tickets are limited and in high demand.

Other shows, such as *Chicago* (p204), offer a limited number of general rush tickets, available each morning when the box office opens. Again, tickets are limited and in high demand, translating into early-morning queues and long waits.

Several shows also offer Standing Room Only (SRO) tickets, allowing patrons to stand through the performance in numbered spaces the width of a standard seat, usually at the back of the orchestra. Commonly less than $30, SRO tickets can be especially tricky to land, as they are generally only available if the show is sold out. While there's no foolproof way to predict a sold-out show in advance, shows that do often include *Book of Mormon*, *Kinky Boots* and *Matilda*. Policies can change, so always check the specific show's website before hitting the theater, toes and fingers crossed.

atop the Time Warner Center, Jazz at Lincoln Center consists of three state-of-the-art venues: the mid-sized Rose Theater; the panoramic, glass-backed Allen Room; and the intimate, atmospheric Dizzy's Club Coca-Cola. It's Dizzy's that you're likely to visit given its regular, nightly shows. The talent is often exceptional, as are the dazzling Central Park views.

★KINKY BOOTS — THEATER

Map p430 (Hirschfeld Theatre; ☎tickets 212-239-6200; www.kinkybootsthemusical.com; 302 W 45th St, btwn Eighth & Ninth Aves, Midtown West; [S]A/C/E to 42nd St-Port Authority Bus Terminal) Adapted from a 2005 British indie film, Harvey Fierstein and Cyndi Lauper's smash hit tells the story of a doomed English shoe factory unexpectantly saved by Lola, a business-savvy drag queen. Its solid characters and electrifying energy have not been lost on critics, with the musical winning six Tony Awards, including Best Musical in 2013.

Book six months ahead for standard-price tickets, or prepare to pay a premium for tickets at shorter notice. If you're feeling lucky, head to the theater 2½ hours before curtain time to enter the ticket lottery, which offers a limited number of tickets for $37.

★BOOK OF MORMON — THEATER

Map p430 (Eugene O'Neill Theatre; ☎tickets 212-239-6200; www.bookofmormonbroadway.com; 230 W 49th St, btwn Broadway & Eighth Ave, Midtown West; [S]N/Q/R to 49th St, 1 to 50th St, C/E to 50th St) Subversive, obscene and ridiculously hilarious, this cutting musical satire is the work of *South Park* creators Trey Parker and Matt Stone and *Avenue Q* composer Robert Lopez. Winner of nine Tony Awards, it tells the story of two naive Mormons on a mission to 'save' a Ugandan village.

Book half a year ahead for standard-price tickets, or pay a premium at shorter notice. Alternatively, head to the theater 2½ hours before the show to enter the lottery. Winners get in for a bargain $32. A limited number of standing-room tickets are sold an hour before the show.

★CARNEGIE HALL — LIVE MUSIC

Map p430 (☎212-247-7800; www.carnegiehall.org; W 57th St, at Seventh Ave, Midtown West; tours adult/child $15/5; ⏲tours 11:30am, 12:30pm, 2pm & 3pm Mon-Fri, 11:30am & 12:30pm Sat, 12:30pm Sun Oct-May; [S]N/Q/R to 57th St-7th Ave) This legendary music hall may not be the world's biggest, or grandest, but it's definitely one of the most acoustically blessed venues around. Opera, jazz and folk greats feature in the Isaac Stern Auditorium, with edgier jazz, pop, classical and world music in the hugely popular Zankel Hall. The intimate Weill Recital Hall hosts chamber music concerts, debut performances and panel discussions.

From October to late May, Carnegie Hall runs one-hour guided tours of the building, shedding light on the venue's storied

LOCAL KNOWLEDGE

THE NEW YORK STAGE

Jason Zinoman, theater critic for the *New York Times*, shares his tips on New York's dynamic theater scene.

Don't-Miss Musicals

The *Book of Mormon* (p203) is irreverent, obscene satire wrapped inside a truly old-fashioned Broadway musical entertainment. It's the rare show that will appeal to lovers of *South Park* and *The Music Man*. If you can't get a ticket, which is quite likely, you can't go wrong with the long-running Kander and Ebb classic *Chicago*.

For Contemporary American Theater

Playwrights Horizons, Signature Theatre and Second Stage Theatre are good places to see great new writing. But if you are in a more adventurous mood, check out PS 122 or the Brooklyn Academy of Music (p295). Troupes like the **Civilians** (www.thecivilians.org), specializing in tricky docu-dramas, and the giddy pop-culture obsessed **Vampire Cowboys** (www.vampirecowboys.com) are always worth seeing.

Talented Locals

there are far too many to mention, but Annie Baker and Young Jean Lee (YJL) are young, brilliant and prolific. Annie Baker is known for quiet, careful observed naturalism, while YJL is more experimental and provocative, playing more with form. This said, Kenneth Lonergan, Edward Albee and Tony Kushner are probably this city's greatest playwrights, with an honorable mention for Wallace Shawn.

Final Tip

Skip Broadway and see a show downtown where tickets cost barely more than a movie and popcorn, and the shows are often inspired and more accessible than you think.

history. Tour times are subject to performance and rehearsal schedules, so check the website before heading in.

SIGNATURE THEATRE THEATER

Map p430 (☎tickets 212-244-7529; www.signaturetheatre.org; 480 W 42nd St, btwn Ninth & Tenth Aves, Midtown West; [S]A/C/E to 42nd St-Port Authority Bus Terminal) Looking good in its Frank Gehry–designed home – complete with three theaters, bookshop and cafe – Signature Theatre devotes entire seasons to the body of work of its playwrights-in-residence, both past and present. To date, featured dramatists have included Tony Kushner, Edward Albee, Athol Fugard and Kenneth Lonergan. Aim to book shows one month in advance.

MATILDA THEATER

Map p430 (Shubert Theatre; ☎tickets 212-239-6200; http://us.matildathemusical.com; 225 W 44th St, btwn Seventh & Eighth Aves, Midtown West; [S]N/Q/R, S, 1/2/3, 7 to Times Sq-42nd St, A/C/E to 42nd St-Port Authority Bus Terminal) Giddily subversive, this multi-award-winning musical is an adaptation of Roald Dahl's classic children's tale. Star of the show is a precocious five-year-old who uses wit, intellect and a little telekinesis to tackle parental neglect, unjust punishment, even the Russian mafia.

The nightly ticket lottery – held at the theater 2½ hours before showtime – offers a limited number of $27 tickets. Discounted standing-room tickets are also offered at sold-out shows.

CHICAGO THEATER

Map p430 (Ambassador Theater; ☎tickets 212-239-6200; www.chicagothemusical.com; 219 W 49th St, btwn Broadway & Eighth Ave, Midtown West; [S]N/Q/R to 49th St, 1, C/E to 50th St) A little easier to score tickets to than some of the newer Broadway musicals, this beloved Bob Fosse/Kander & Ebb classic tells the story of showgirl Velma Kelly, wannabe Roxie Hart, lawyer Billy Flynn and the fabulously sordid goings-on of the Chicago underworld. Revived by director Walter Bobbie, its sassy, infectious energy more than makes up for the theater's tight-squeeze seating.

PLAYWRIGHTS HORIZONS THEATER

Map p430 (☎tickets 212-279-4200; www.playwrightshorizons.org; 416 W 42nd St, btwn Ninth & Tenth Aves, Midtown West; [S]A/C/E to 42nd St-Port Authority Bus Terminal) An excellent place to catch what could be the next big thing, this veteran 'writers' theater' is dedicated to fostering contemporary American works. Notable past productions include Bruce Norris' Tony Award–winning *Clybourne Park,* as well as *I Am My Own Wife* and *Grey Gardens,* both of which moved on to Broadway.

MAGNET THEATER
COMEDY

Map p430 (☎212-244-8824; www.magnettheater.com; 254 W 29th St, btwn Seventh & Eighth Aves, Midtown West; S1/2 to 28th St, A/C/E to 23rd St, 1/2/3 to 34th St-Penn Station) Tons of comedy in several incarnations (mostly improv) lures the crowds at this theater-cum-training ground for comics. Performances vary weekly, though regular favorites include Megawitt (featuring the theater's resident ensembles) and The Friday Night Sh*w, the latter using the audience's written rants and confessions to drive the evening's shenanigans.

BIRDLAND
JAZZ, CABARET

Map p430 (☎212-581-3080; www.birdlandjazz.com; 315 W 44th St, btwn Eighth & Ninth Aves, Midtown West; cover $20-50; ☺5pm-1am; 🚭; SA/C/E to 42nd St-Port Authority Bus Terminal) This bird's got a slick look, not to mention the legend – its name dates from bebop legend Charlie Parker (aka 'Bird'), who headlined at the previous location on 52nd St, along with Miles, Monk and just about everyone else (you can see their photos on the walls). The lineup is always stellar.

Regular highlights include David Ostwald's Louis Armstrong Eternity Band on Wednesdays and the Arturo O'Farrill Afro-Cuban Orchestra on Sundays.

CAROLINE'S ON BROADWAY
COMEDY

Map p430 (☎212-757-4100; www.carolines.com; 1626 Broadway, at 50th St; SN/Q/R to 49th St, 1 to 50th St) You may recognize this big, bright, mainstream classic from comedy specials filmed here on location. It's a top spot to catch US comedy big guns and sitcom stars.

SECOND STAGE THEATRE
THEATER

Map p430 (Tony Kiser Theatre; ☎tickets 212-246-4422; www.2st.com; 305 W 43rd St, at Eighth Ave, Midtown West; SA/C/E to 42nd St-Port Authority Bus Terminal) Second Stage is well known for debuting the work of talented emerging writers as well as that of the country's more established names. If you're after well-crafted contemporary American theater, this is a good place to find it.

DON'T TELL MAMA
CABARET

Map p430 (☎212-757-0788; www.donttellmamanyc.com; 343 W 46th St, btwn Eighth & Ninth Aves, Midtown West; ☺4pm-3am Mon-Thu, to 4am Fri-Sun; SN/Q/R, S, 1/2/3, 7 to Times Sq-42nd St) Piano bar and cabaret venue extraordinaire, Don't Tell Mama is an unpretentious little spot that's been around for more than 25 years and has the talent to prove it. Its regular roster of performers aren't big names, but true lovers of cabaret who give each show their all.

If you want your cabaret a bit more sinister and sexy, head to the **Box** (www.theboxnyc.com) on the Lower East Side. It's risqué and ribald, but its (very) late-night shows might just tickle your fancy.

NEW YORK CITY CENTER
DANCE

Map p430 (☎212-581-1212; www.nycitycenter.org; 131 W 55th St, btwn Sixth & Seventh Aves, Midtown West; SN/Q/R to 57th St-7th Ave) This Moorish, red-domed wonder almost went the way of the wrecking ball in 1943, but was saved by preservationists, only to face extinction again when its major ballet companies departed for Lincoln Center. Today, it hosts dance troupes including the Alvin Ailey American Dance Theater, theater productions, the New York Flamenco Festival in February or March, and the popular Fall for Dance Festival in September or October.

AMC EMPIRE 25
CINEMA

Map p430 (www.amctheatres.com/empire; 234 W 42nd St, at Eighth Ave, Midtown West; SN/Q/R, S, 1/2/3, 7 to 42nd St-Times Sq) It's pretty cool to gaze out over illuminated 42nd St at this massive cinema complex, and even more thrilling to settle into the stadium-style seating. While it's not the best place to catch mainstream Hollywood flicks (crowds can be massive and rowdy), it's the perfect off-the-radar spot for indies, which screen frequently to civilized numbers.

MADISON SQUARE GARDEN
STADIUM

Map p430 (www.thegarden.com; Seventh Ave, btwn 31st & 33rd Sts, Midtown West; S1/2/3 to 34th St-Penn Station) NYC's major performance venue – part of the massive complex housing Penn Station and the WaMu Theater – hosts big-arena performers, from Kanye West to Madonna. It's also a sports arena, with New York Knicks and

TV TAPINGS

Wanna be part of a live studio audience for the taping of one of your favorite shows? NYC is the place to do it. Follow the instructions below to gain access to some of TV's big-ticket tapings.

➜ **Saturday Night Live** One of the most popular NYC-based shows and known for being difficult to get into. That said, you can try your luck by getting your name into the mix in late summer, when seats are assigned by lottery. Simply send an email to snltickets@nbcuni.com in August, or line up by 7am the day of the show on the 49th St side of Rockefeller Plaza for standby lottery tickets (16 years and older only). You can choose a stand-by ticket for either the 8pm dress rehearsal or the 11:30pm live broadcast. The tickets are limited to one per person and are issued on a first-come, first-served basis. You will need to bring valid photo ID when the ticket is issued, as well as to the show later that day.

➜ **Late Show** Another late-night show that draws the crowds. You can try to request tickets for a specific date through the online request form at www.cbs.com/shows/late_show, or submit a request in person by showing up at the theater (1697 Broadway between 53rd and 54th Sts) to speak to a representative. Hours for requests are 9:30am to noon Monday to Thursday and 10am to 6pm Saturday and Sunday. Or else try for a standby ticket by calling ☎212-247-6497 at 11am on the day of the taping you would like to attend; taping begins at 5:30pm Monday to Thursday.

➜ **Daily Show with Jon Stewart** Tickets are available for specific dates through the website at thedailyshow.cc.com/tickets. Check often, as sometimes the calendar fills up and no tickets are made available. The taping occurs at 5.45pm from Monday through Thursday; ticketed guests should arrive no later than 4.30pm. The studio is on 11th Ave between 51st and 52nd Sts.

For more show ticket details, visit the websites of individual TV stations, or try www.tvtickets.com.

New York Rangers games, as well as boxing matches and events like the Annual Westminster Kennel Club Dog Show.

SHOPPING

It's here that you'll find fabled department stores like Fifth Ave's Bergdorf Goodman and Madison Ave's Barneys. Rockstars pick up pedals on W 48th St, while gem hunters scour the Diamond District on W 47th St. If you're a self-made style maven, hit the Garment District, around Seventh Ave in the 30s for massive shops peddling DIY fashion props. Down in Herald Square lies love-it-or-loathe-it Macy's, the planet's largest store.

Midtown East & Fifth Avenue

BARNEYS DEPARTMENT STORE

Map p426 (www.barneys.com; 660 Madison Ave, at 61st St, Midtown East; ⏲10am-8pm Mon-Fri, to 7pm Sat, 11am-6pm Sun; [S]N/Q/R to 5th Ave-59th St) Serious fashionistas swipe their plastic at Barneys, respected for its spot-on collections of savvy labels like Holmes & Yang, Kitsuné and Derek Lam. For (slightly) less expensive deals geared to a younger market, shop street-chic labels on the 8th floor. Recent in-store additions include a coveted basement cosmetics department and Genes, a futuristic cafe with touch-screen communal table for online shopping.

You'll find other branches in **SoHo** (Map p410; 116 Wooster St; ⏲11am-7pm Mon-Sat, noon-6pm Sun), **Upper West Side** (Map p434; 2151 Broadway; ⏲10am-8pm Mon-Fri, to 7pm Sat, 11am-7pm Sun) and **Brooklyn** (Map p440; 194 Atlantic Ave; ⏲10am-8pm Mon-Sat, 11am-7pm Sun).

BLOOMINGDALE'S DEPARTMENT STORE

Map p426 (www.bloomingdales.com; 1000 Third Ave, at E 59th St, Midtown East; ⏲10am-8:30pm Mon-Sat, 11am-7pm Sun; 📶; [S]4/5/6 to 59th St, N/Q/R to Lexington Ave-59th St) Blockbuster 'Bloomie's' is something like the Metropolitan Museum of Art (MoMA) of the shopping world: historic, sprawling, overwhelming and packed with bodies, but you'd be sorry to miss it. Raid the racks for clothes and shoes from a who's who of US and global designers, including an increasing number of 'new-blood' collections. Refuel pit stops include a branch of cupcake heaven Magnolia Bakery.

BERGDORF GOODMAN DEPARTMENT STORE

Map p426 (www.bergdorfgoodman.com; 754 Fifth Ave, btwn 57th & 58th Sts; ⏲10am-8pm Mon-Fri, to 7pm Sat, noon-6pm Sun; [S]N/Q/R to 5th Ave-59th St, F to 57th St) Not merely loved for its Christmas windows (the city's best), plush BG leads the fashion race, its fashion director Linda Fargo considered an Anna Wintour of sorts. Drawcards include exclusive collections of Tom Ford and Chanel shoes, an expanded women's shoe department, and the biggest collection of Thom Browne clothing for men and women.

The men's store is across the street.

SAKS FIFTH AVE DEPARTMENT STORE

Map p426 (www.saksfifthavenue.com; 611 Fifth Ave, at 50th St; ⏲10am-8pm Mon-Sat, 11am-7pm Sun; [S]B/D/F/M to 47th-50th Sts-Rockefeller Center, E/M to 5th Ave-53rd St) Graced with vintage elevators, Saks' 10-floor flagship store is home to the 'Shoe Salon,' NYC's biggest women's shoe department (complete with express elevator and zip code). Other fortes include the cosmetics and men's departments, the latter home to destination grooming salon John Allan's and fashion-forward labels in the 'White Room.' The store's January sale is legendary.

TIFFANY & CO JEWELRY, HOMEWARES

Map p426 (www.tiffany.com; 727 Fifth Ave, at 57th St; ⏲10am-7pm Mon-Sat, noon-6pm Sun; [S]F to 57th St, N/Q/R to 5th Ave-59th St) Ever since Audrey Hepburn gazed longingly through its windows, Tiffany & Co has won countless hearts with its glittering diamond rings, watches, silver Elsa Peretti heart necklaces, crystal vases and glassware. Swoon, drool, but whatever you do, don't harass the elevator attendants with tired 'Where's the breakfast?' jokes.

FAO SCHWARZ CHILDREN

Map p426 (www.fao.com; 767 Fifth Ave, at 58th St; ⏲10am-8pm Sun-Thu, to 9pm Fri & Sat; [S]4/5/6 to 59th St, N/Q/R to 5th Ave-59th St) The toy store giant, where Tom Hanks played footsy piano in the movie *Big,* is number one on the NYC wish list of most visiting kids. Go on, indulge them! The magical (over-the-top) wonderland, with dolls up for 'adoption,' life-size stuffed animals, gas-powered kiddie convertibles, air-hockey sets and much more, might even thrill you, too.

ARGOSY BOOKS, MAPS

Map p426 (www.argosybooks.com; 116 E 59th St, btwn Park & Lexington Aves, Midtown East; ⏲10am-6pm Mon-Fri year-round, to 5pm Sat late Sep-late May; [S]4/5/6 to 59th St, N/Q/R to Lexington Ave-59th St) Since 1925, this landmark used bookstore has stocked fine antiquarian items such as leatherbound books, old maps, art monographs and other classics picked up from high-class estate sales and closed antique shops. There's also an interesting booty of Hollywood memorabilia, from personal letters and signed books to contracts and autographed publicity stills. Prices range from costly to clearance.

UNIQLO FASHION

Map p426 (www.uniqlo.com; 666 Fifth Ave, at 53rd St; ⏲10am-9pm Mon-Sat, 11am-8pm Sun; [S]E, M to Fifth Ave-53rd St) Uniqlo is Japan's answer to H&M and this is its showstopping 89,000-sq-ft flagship megastore. Grab a mesh bag at the entrance and let the elevators woosh you up to the 3rd floor to begin your retail odyssey. The forte here is affordable, fashionable, quality basics, from tees and undergarments to Japanese denim, cashmere sweaters and super-light, high-tech parkas.

DYLAN'S CANDY BAR FOOD & DRINK

Map p426 (www.dylanscandybar.com; 1011 Third Ave, at 60th St, Midtown East; ⏲10am-9pm Mon-Thu, to 11pm Fri & Sat, 11am-9pm Sun; [S]N/Q/R to Lexington Ave-59th St) Willy Wonka has nothing on this dental nightmare of giant swirly lollipops, crunchy candy bars, glowing jars of jelly beans, softball-sized cupcakes and a luminescent staircase embedded with scrumptious, unattainable candy. Stay away on weekends to avoid being pummeled by small, sugar-crazed kids. There's a cafe on the 2nd floor.

Midtown West & Times Square

★MOMA DESIGN & BOOK STORE BOOKS, GIFTS

Map p430 (www.momastore.org; 11 W 53rd St, btwn Fifth & Sixth Aves; ⏲9:30am-6:30pm Sat-Thu, to 9pm Fri; [S]E, M to 5th Ave-53rd St) The flagship store at the Museum of Modern Art is a fab spot to souvenir shop in one fell swoop. Aside from stocking gorgeous books (from art and architecture tomes to pop culture readers and kids' picture books), you'll find art prints and posters, and one-of-a-kind knick-knacks. For furniture, lighting, homewares, jewelry, bags, and MUJI merchandise, head to the MoMA Design Store across the street.

DRAMA BOOK SHOP BOOKS

Map p430 (www.dramabookshop.com; 250 W 40th St, btwn Seventh & Eighth Aves, Midtown West; ⏲11am-7pm Mon-Wed, Fri & Sat, 11am-8pm Thu, noon-6pm Sun; [S]A/C/E to 42nd St-Port Authority Bus Terminal) Nirvana for Broadway fans, this expansive bookstore has taken its theater (both plays and musicals) seriously since 1917. Staffers are good at recommending worthy selections, which also include books on costume, stage design and other elements of performance, as well as industry journals and magazines. Check the website for regular in-store events.

RUDY'S MUSIC MUSIC

Map p430 (www.rudysmusic.com; 169 W 48th St, at Seventh Ave, Midtown West; ⏲10.30am-7pm Mon-Sat; [S]N/Q/R to 49th St) The stretch of 48th St just off Times Square was known as Music Row, and it's where rock royals like the Beatles, Jimi Hendrix and the Stones dropped in for acoustic essentials. Rudy's is one of the last vestiges of this venerable block, particularly for high-end acoustic and classical guitars.

Its newer **SoHo** (Map p410; ☎212-625-2557; 461 Broome St; [S]N/R to Prince St) store is even more impressive, with the world's best collection of D'Angelico guitars and the odd Swarovski Crystal–embedded number.

NEPENTHES NEW YORK FASHION, ACCESSORIES

Map p430 (www.nepenthesny.com; 307 W 38th St, btwn Eighth & Ninth Aves, Midtown West; ⏲noon-7pm Mon-Sat, to 5pm Sun; [S]A/C/E to 42nd St-Port Authority Bus Terminal) Occupying an old sewing shop in the Garment District, this cult Japanese collective stocks in-the-know labels like Engineered Garments and Needles, known for their quirky detailing and artisanal production value (think tweed lace-up hem pants). While there's a small edit of women's pieces, the focus is on menswear. Accessories include bags and satchels, gloves and footwear.

AMÉ AMÉ FASHION, ACCESSORIES

Map p430 (☎646-867-2342; www.amerain.com; 17 W 29th St, at Broadway; ⏲noon-7pm; [S]N/R to 28th St) Rain gear and candy? Kindly owner Teresa will explain what Amé Amé means if you're perplexed by this unusual juxtaposition. She'll also set you straight on the fallacy of buying cheap disposable umbrellas. Only well-crafted, long-lasting rain gear is sold here, in masculine styles for the gents and in beautiful shades for the ladies.

Also on hand: perfectly fitting Le Chameau boots, rugged Barbour coats, elegant stationery, stylish scarves and hats, and delectable candy from around the globe – all inspired by Teresa's own extensive travels.

MACY'S DEPARTMENT STORE

Map p430 (www.macys.com; 151 W 34th St, at Broadway; ⏲9am-9:30pm Mon-Fri, 10am-9:30pm Sat, 11am-8:30pm Sun; [S]B/D/F/M, N/Q/R to 34th St-Herald Sq) Fresh from a much-needed face-lift, the world's largest department store covers most bases, with fashion, furnishings, kitchenware, sheets, cafes, hair salons and even a branch of the Metropolitan Museum of Art gift store. It's more mid-priced than exclusive, with mainstream labels and big-name cosmetics.

HOUSING WORKS VINTAGE

Map p430 (www.housingworks.org; 730-732 Ninth Ave, btwn 49th & 50th Sts, Midtown West; ⏲11am-8pm Mon-Sat, to 6pm Sun; [S]C/E to 50th St) As one shopper put it: 'They have some fabulous shit in here.' Welcome to the Hell's Kitchen branch of this much-loved thrift store, where Burberry shirts go for $25 and Joseph suede pants are yours for $40. While it's all about luck, the daily consignments mean a sterling find is never far off. Profits go to helping homeless people living with HIV/AIDS.

B&H PHOTO VIDEO ELECTRONICS

Map p430 (www.bhphotovideo.com; 420 Ninth Ave, btwn 33rd & 34th Sts, Midtown West; ⏲9am-7pm Mon-Thu, to 1pm Fri, 10am-6pm Sun; [S]A/C/E to 34th St-Penn Station) Visiting NYC's most popular camera shop is an experience in itself – it's massive and crowded, and bustling with black-clad (and tech-savvy) Hasidic Jewish salesmen. Your chosen item is dropped into a bucket, which then moves up and across the ceiling to the purchase area (which requires a second queue).

It's all very orderly and fascinating, and the selection of cameras, camcorders, computers and other electronics is outstanding.

TIME WARNER CENTER MALL

Map p430 (www.theshopsatcolumbuscircle.com; Time Warner Center, 10 Columbus Circle; [S]A/C, B/D, 1 to 59th St-Columbus Circle) A great add-on to an adventure in Central Park, the swank Time Warner Center has a fine lineup of largely upscale vendors including Coach, Stuart Weitzman, Williams-Sonoma, True Religion, Sephora and J Crew. For delectable picnic fare, visit the enormous **Whole Foods** (www.wholefoodsmarket.com; ⏰7:30am-11pm) in the basement.

SPORTS & ACTIVITIES

NBC STUDIO TOURS GUIDED TOUR

Map p426 (☎reservations 212-664-6298; www.nbcstudiotour.com; 30 Rockefeller Plaza at 49th St; tours adult/child $24/20; [S]B/D/F/M to 47th-50th Sts-Rockefeller Center) Slated to reopen in late 2014, NBC Studio Tours take TV fans on a walking tour through parts of the NBC Studios, home to iconic TV shows *Saturday Night Live* and *The Tonight Show Starring Jimmy Fallon*. Check the NBC Studio Tour website for updates. Competition is stiff for TV show tapings. Children under six not admitted.

CENTRAL PARK BIKE TOURS BICYCLE RENTAL

Map p430 (www.centralparkbiketours.com; 203 W 58th St, at Seventh Ave, Midtown West; rentals per 2hr/day $20/40, tours adult/child from $49/40; ⏰8am-7pm Mon-Sat, to 5pm Sun Apr-Sep, 9am-5pm Mon-Sun Oct-Mar; [S]A/C, B/D, 1 to 59th St-Columbus Circle) This place rents good quality bikes and leads various tours of the city, including a two-hour tour of the park, a three-hour tour of Midtown and Downtown, as well as themed movie-location and architecture tours. Rental prices include lock and helmet. See the website for tour times.

24 HOUR FITNESS GYM

Map p426 (☎212-401-0660; www.24hourfitness.com; 153 E 53rd St, btwn Lexington & Third Aves, Midtown East; day/week pass $30/100; ⏰gym 24hr, pool 5am-11pm; 📶; [S]E, M to Lexington Ave-53rd St) Work up a sweat at this smart, well-equipped chain, which includes top-of-the-range cardio equipment, weights, classes (including BodyPump, BodyCombat and Pilates), a sauna, a steamroom and a whirlpool. This branch also has a lap pool. Check the website for information on all three Manhattan branches.

NEW YORK KNICKS BASKETBALL

Map p430 (www.nyknicks.com; Madison Sq Garden, Seventh Ave btwn 31st & 33rd Sts, Midtown West; tickets from $109; [S]A/C/E, 1/2/3 to 34th St-Penn Station) Occasional scandal aside, NYC loves its blue-and-orange basketball team. Indeed, the first song to popularize hip-hop gives it up for the beloved Knickerbockers (Sugarhill Gang sang '*I have a color TV so I can watch the Knicks play basketball*'). Yet, despite crowds consisting of Spike Lee and 18,999 others at the Garden, the Knicks haven't won a championship since 1973.

LUCKY STRIKE BOWLING

Map p430 (☎646-829-0170; www.bowlluckystrike.com; 624 W 42nd St, btwn Eleventh & Twelfth Aves, Midtown West; individual games from $10, shoe rental $6; ⏰noon-midnight Sun-Wed, to 1am Thu, to 2am Fri & Sat; 📶; [S]A/C/E to 42nd St-Port Authority Bus Terminal) One of the world's few bowling alleys with a dress code, Lucky Strike has pricey drinks, plush lounge fittings and a fashion-conscious crowd – which makes the whole experience more akin to a nightclub than a bowling alley. Book ahead.

Upper East Side

Neighborhood Top Five

1 Spending a few hours (or weeks) wandering amid the priceless treasures of the **Metropolitan Museum of Art** (p212), from mesmerizing Egyptian artifacts to Renaissance masterpieces.

2 Walking the spiral ramps of Frank Lloyd Wright's architectural masterpiece, the **Guggenheim Museum** (p216).

3 Gazing at the gilded masterpieces of Gustav Klimt at the **Neue Galerie** (p219).

4 Listening to Sunday classical music in a beaux arts mansion at **Frick Collection** (p226).

5 Sipping an early evening cocktail at the elegant, mural-lined **Bemelmans Bar** (p226).

For more detail of this area, see Map p432 ➡

Explore Upper East Side

There are infinite ways to tackle this large, well-moneyed neighborhood. Begin with a walk south down Fifth Ave, starting at about 96th St. This will take you down storied Museum Mile, which is studded with vintage mansions and prestigious museums. At 72nd St, scoot east to Madison Ave and head south, where you can then enjoy the sight of some of the country's most extravagant flagship boutiques (Vera Wang, Prada and Lanvin, to name a few). The path is strewn with old-world cafes and opulent restaurants. Welcome to the rarefied air of uptown.

Local Life

➡ **Lunch with the upper crust** The Upper East Side is all about lunch – specifically ladies who lunch, a well-coiffed breed known for dispensing air kisses while armed with designer handbags the size of steam trunks. The best places to see 'em include Sant Ambroeus (p224) and Café Boulud (p225), on weekdays.

➡ **(Window) shop 'til you drop** Skip the ritzy Madison Ave boutiques, and hit the neighborhood's high-end consignment shops. Places like Encore (p226) and Michael's (p226) offer good deals on mildly worn frocks tossed aside by New York society types.

➡ **Get jittery with it** The neighborhood seems to have the highest per capita ratio of coffee emporiums anywhere in the city. And when the locals aren't shopping or doing Pilates, they're sipping steamy skim-milk macchiatos at cafes like Via Quadronno (p222), Sant Ambroeus (p224) and Oslo Coffee Roasters (p225).

Getting There & Away

➡ **Subway** The sole subway lines here are the 4/5/6 which travel north and south on Lexington Ave. A new stretch of subway track underneath Second Ave is expected to be completed by late 2016.

➡ **Bus** The M1, M2, M3 and M4 buses all make the scenic drive down Fifth Ave beside Central Park. The M15 is handy for getting around the far east side, traveling up First Ave and down Second. Cross-town buses at 66th, 72nd, 79th, 86th and 96th Sts take you across the park and into the Upper West Side.

Lonely Planet's Top Tip

The Upper East Side is ground zero for all things luxurious, especially the area that covers the blocks from 60th to 86th Sts between Park and Fifth Aves. If you're looking for eating and drinking spots that are easier on the wallet, head east of Lexington Ave. First, Second and Third Aves are lined with less pricey neighborhood spots.

UPPER EAST SIDE

✕ Best Places to Eat

➡ Tanoshi (p224)
➡ James Wood Foundry (p224)
➡ ABV (p224)
➡ Earl's Beer & Cheese (p222)
➡ Café Boulud (p225)

For reviews, see p222

Best Places to Drink

➡ Metropolitan Museum Roof Garden Café & Martini Bar (p225)
➡ JBird (p225)
➡ Penrose (p225)
➡ Vinus and Marc (p225)

For reviews, see p225

Best Places to Shop

➡ Encore (p226)
➡ Crawford Doyle Booksellers (p227)
➡ Zitomer (p227)
➡ Housing Works Thrift Shop (p226)

For reviews, see p226

JEAN-PIERRE LESCOURRET / GETTY IMAGES ©

TOP SIGHT
METROPOLITAN MUSEUM OF ART (MET)

This sprawling encyclopedic museum, founded in 1870, houses one of the biggest art collections in the world. Its permanent collection has more than two million individual objects, from Egyptian temples to American paintings. Known colloquially as the 'Met,' the museum attracts over six million visitors a year to its 17 acres of galleries – making it the largest single-site attraction in New York City. In other words, plan on spending some time here.

Egyptian Art

The museum has an unrivaled collection of ancient Egyptian art, some of which dates back to the Paleolithic era. Located to the north of the Great Hall, the 39 Egyptian galleries open dramatically with one of the Met's prized pieces: the Mastaba Tomb of Perneb (c 2300 BC), an Old Kingdom burial chamber crafted from limestone. From here, a web of rooms is cluttered with funerary stele, carved reliefs and fragments of pyramids. (Don't miss the intriguing Models of Meketre, clay figurines meant to help in the afterlife, in Gallery 105.) These eventually lead to the Temple of Dendur (Gallery 131), a sandstone temple to the goddess Isis that resides in a sunny atrium gallery with a reflecting pool – a must-see for the first-time visitor.

European Paintings

Want Renaissance? The Met's got it. On the museum's 2nd floor, the European Paintings' galleries display a stunning collection of masterworks. This includes more than 1700 canvases from the roughly 500-year-period starting in the

DON'T MISS...

- The Temple of Dendur
- Paintings by Caravaggio, El Greco, Vermeer and other old masters.
- The Damascus Room inside the Islamic Art galleries
- Roof Garden Café & Martini Bar

PRACTICALITIES

- Map p432
- ☎212-535-7710
- www.metmuseum.org
- 1000 Fifth Ave at 82nd St
- suggested donation adult/child $25/free
- 🕒10am-5.:30pm Sun-Thu, to 9pm Fri & Sat
- [S]4/5/6 to 86th St

13th century, with works by every important painter from Duccio to Rembrandt. In fact, everything here is, literally, a masterpiece. In Gallery 621 are several Caravaggios, including the masterfully painted *The Denial of St Peter*. Gallery 611, to the west, is packed with Spanish treasures, including El Greco's famed *View of Toledo*. Continue south (to Gallery 632) to see various Vermeers, including the *Young Woman with a Water Pitcher*. Nearby (in Gallery 634) gaze at several Rembrandts, including a 1660 *Self-Portrait*. And that's just the beginning. You could spend hours exploring these many powerful works.

Art of the Arab Lands

On the 2nd floor you'll find the Islamic galleries with 15 incredible rooms showcasing the museum's extensive collection of art from the Middle East and Central and South Asia. In addition to garments, secular decorative objects and manuscripts, you'll find gilded and enameled glassware (Gallery 452) and a magnificent 14th-century *mihrab*, or prayer niche, lined with elaborately patterned polychrome tilework (Gallery 455). There is also a superb array of Ottoman textiles (Gallery 459), a medieval-style Moroccan court (Gallery 456) and an 18th-century room from Damascus (Gallery 461).

American Wing

In the northwest corner, the American galleries showcase a wide variety of decorative and fine art from throughout US history. These include everything from colonial portraiture to Hudson River School masterpieces to John Singer Sargent's unbearably sexy *Madame X* (Gallery 771) – not to mention Emanuel Leutze's massive canvas of *Washington Crossing the Delaware* (Gallery 760).

Greek & Roman Art

The 27 galleries devoted to classical antiquity are another Met doozy. From the Great Hall, a passageway takes viewers through a barrel vaulted room flanked by the chiseled torsos of Greek figures. This spills right into one of the Met's loveliest spaces: the airy Roman sculpture court (Gallery 162), full of marble carvings of gods and historical figures. The statue of a bearded Hercules from AD 68–98, with a lion's skin draped about him, is particularly awe-inspiring.

UPPER EAST SIDE METROPOLITAN MUSEUM OF ART (MET)

THE MET FOR KIDS

The most popular galleries with children are generally the Egyptian, African and Oceania galleries (great masks) and the collection of medieval arms and armor. The Met hosts plenty of kid-centric happenings (check the website) and distributes a special museum brochure and map made specifically for the tykes.

One of the best spots in the museum is the roof garden, which features rotating sculpture installations by contemporary and 20th century artists. (Jeff Koons, Andy Goldsworthy and Imran Qureshi have all shown here.) But its best feature are the views it offers of the city and Central Park. It's also home to the Roof Garden Café & Martini Bar, an ideal spot for a drink – especially at sunset. The roof garden is open from April to October.

SEEING THE MUSEUM

A desk inside the Great Hall has audio tours in several languages ($7), while docents offer guided tours of specific galleries. These are free with admission. Check the website or information desk for details. If you can't stand crowds, avoid weekends.

Metropolitan Museum of Art

PLAN OF ATTACK

Standing in the aptly named Great Hall, past the main entrance, head into the Egyptian galleries and make your way to the dramatic ❶ **Temple of Dendur**.

Stroll through the Charles Engelhard Court, a soaring sunlit atrium packed with American sculptures, and dip into the Arms and Armor galleries. See the meticulous craftsmanship of the 16th-century ❷ **Armor of Henry II of France**. The next room (Gallery 371) has four mounted fully armoured horsemen.

Head back into the American Wing and up to the second floor for a look at the ❸ **Washington Crossing the Delaware**. Also on the second floor is a jaw-dropping collection of European masters. Don't miss the Caravaggios in Gallery 621, in particular ❹ **The Denial of St Peter**.

Staying on the second floor, wind your way over to the Islamic Art galleries, where you'll find an elaborate ❺ **Mihrab**, or prayer niche; it's right next to a medieval-style Moroccan court with gurgling fountain (Gallery 456).

Nearby you'll find works by Monet, Renoir, Van Gogh and Gauguin. There are several masterpieces by Picasso, including the ❻ **Blind Man's Meal**.

Head downstairs and into Oceania exhibition halls for vivid tribal art from New Guinea and beyond. Have a look at tribal costumes such as the ❼ **Asmat Body Mask**; overhead is a ceiling lined with shields.

The Met has a trove of ancient Greek and Roman works. In the largest gallery you'll find the intricate marble sarcophagus, ❽ **Triumph of Dionysos and the Seasons**.

The Denial of Saint Peter Gallery 621
Painted in the final months of Caravaggio's short, tempestuous life, this magnificent work is a masterpiece of storytelling.

The Blind Man's Meal Gallery 830
Picasso's painting of a blind man at a table alludes to human suffering in general; the bread and wine also have undertones of Christian symbolism.

Mihrab (prayer niche) Gallery 455
One of the world's finest religious architectural decorations, this 8th-century piece from Iran was created by joining cut glazed tiles into a richly ornate mosaic.

Asmat Body Mask Gallery 354
A New Guinea costume like this was worn to represent the spirit of someone who recently died, and featured in ritual dances of the Asmat people.

Triumph of Dionysos and the Seasons Gallery 162
On this marble sarcophagus, you'll see the god Dionysos seated on a panther, joined by four figures representing (from left to right) winter, spring, summer and fall.

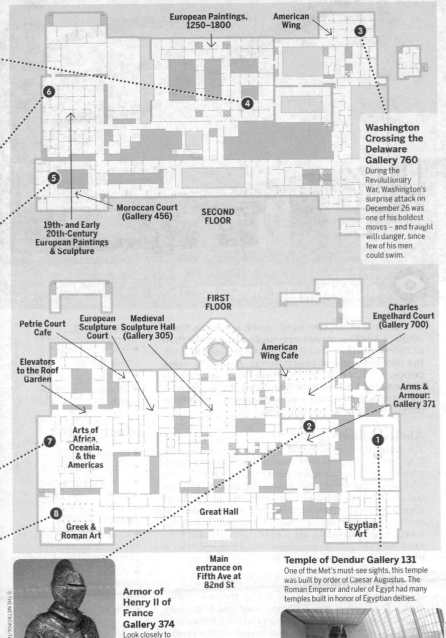

European Paintings, 1250–1800

American Wing

3

Washington Crossing the Delaware Gallery 760
During the Revolutionary War, Washington's surprise attack on December 26 was one of his boldest moves – and fraught with danger, since few of his men could swim.

6

4

5

19th- and Early 20th-Century European Paintings & Sculpture

Moroccan Court (Gallery 456)

SECOND FLOOR

FIRST FLOOR

Petrie Court Cafe

European Sculpture Court

Medieval Sculpture Hall (Gallery 305)

Charles Engelhard Court (Gallery 700)

American Wing Cafe

Elevators to the Roof Garden

Arms & Armour: Gallery 371

Arts of Africa, Oceania, & the Americas

7

2

1

8

Greek & Roman Art

Great Hall

Egyptian Art

Main entrance on Fifth Ave at 82nd St

Armor of Henry II of France Gallery 374
Look closely to see creatures, gods and warriors among the dense foliate scrolls, including Apollo chasing the nymph Daphne on the shoulders.

Temple of Dendur Gallery 131
One of the Met's must-see sights, this temple was built by order of Caesar Augustus. The Roman Emperor and ruler of Egypt had many temples built in honor of Egyptian deities.

TOP SIGHT
GUGGENHEIM MUSEUM

A sculpture in its own right, architect Frank Lloyd Wright's building almost overshadows the collection of 20th-century art that it houses. Completed in 1959, the inverted ziggurat structure was derided by some critics, but it was hailed by ofthers who welcomed it as a beloved architectural icon. Since it first opened, this unusual structure has appeared on countless postcards, TV programs and films.

Abstract Roots
The Guggenheim came out of the collection of Solomon R Guggenheim, a New York mining magnate who began acquiring abstract art in his 60s at the behest of his art adviser, an eccentric German baroness named Hilla Rebay. In 1939, with Rebay serving as director, Guggenheim opened a temporary museum on 54th St titled Museum of Non-Objective Painting. (Incredibly, it had grey velour walls, piped-in classical music and burning incense.) Four years later, the pair commissioned Wright to construct a permanent home for the collection.

Years in the Making
Like any development in New York City, the project took forever to come to fruition. Construction was delayed for almost 13 years due to budget constraints, the outbreak of WWII and outraged neighbors who weren't all that excited to see an architectural spaceship land in their midst. Construction was completed in 1959, after both Wright and Guggenheim had passed away.

DON'T MISS...
- Permanent Collection Galleries
- Cafe 3
- Exterior views of the facade

PRACTICALITIES
- Map p432
- ☎212-423-3500
- www.guggenheim.org
- 1071 Fifth Ave, at 89th St
- adult/child $22/free, by donation 5:45-7:45pm Sat
- 🕒10am-5:45pm Sun-Wed & Fri, to 7:45pm Sat
- [S]4/5/6 to 86th St

Bring on the Critics

When the Guggenheim opened its doors in October 1959, the ticket price was 50¢ and the works on view included pieces by Kandinsky, Alexander Calder and abstract expressionists Franz Kline and Willem De Kooning.

The structure was savaged by the *New York Times,* which lambasted it as 'a war between architecture and painting in which both come out badly maimed.' But others quickly celebrated it as 'the most beautiful building in America.' Whether Wright intended to or not, he had given the city one of its most recognizable landmarks.

To the Present

A renovation in the early 1990s added an eight-story tower to the east, which provided an extra 50,000 sq ft of exhibition space. These galleries show the permanent collection and other exhibits, while the ramps are occupied by rotating exhibits.

The museum's holdings include works by Kandinsky, Picasso and Jackson Pollock. Over time, other key additions have been made, including paintings by Monet, Van Gogh and Degas, photographs by Robert Mapplethorpe, and key surrealist works donated by Guggenheim's niece Peggy.

Visiting the Museum

The museum's ascending ramp is occupied by rotating exhibitions of modern and contemporary art. Though Wright intended visitors to go to the top and wind their way down, the cramped, single elevator doesn't allow for this. Exhibitions, therefore, are installed from bottom to top.

There are two good on-site food options: **Wright** (Map p432; ☎212-427-5690; www.thewrightrestaurant.com; Guggenheim Museum, 1071 Fifth Ave, at 89th St; mains $23-28; ⏰11:30am-3:30pm Fri & Sun-Wed, to 6pm Sat; [S]4/5/6 to 86th St), at ground level, a space-age eatery serving steamy risotto and classic cocktails, and **Cafe 3** (Map p432; www.guggenheim.org; Guggenheim Museum, 1071 Fifth Ave, at 89th St; sandwiches $9-10; ⏰10:30am-5pm Fri-Wed; [S]4/5/6 to 86th St), on the 3rd floor, which offers sparkling views of Central Park and excellent coffee and light snacks.

A PINK GUGGENHEIM

Wright made hundreds of sketches and pondered the use of various materials for the construction of the museum. At one point, he considered using red marble for the exterior facade – a 1945 model sketch shows a pink building – but the color scheme was rejected.

While Wright was thrilled to create a museum, the idea of working in Manhattan didn't exactly captivate him. 'I can think of several more desirable places in the world to build his great museum,' wrote the famously acerbic architect in 1949, 'but we will have to try New York.'

SAVE TIME

The line to get in to the museum can be brutal. You'll save time if you purchase tickets online in advance.

SIGHTS

METROPOLITAN MUSEUM OF ART MUSEUM
See p212.

GUGGENHEIM MUSEUM MUSEUM
See p216.

WHITNEY MUSEUM OF AMERICAN ART MUSEUM
Map p432 (☎212-570-3600; www.whitney.org; 945 Madison Ave, cnr 75th St; adult/child $20/free, by donation 6-9pm Fri; ⏰11am-6pm Wed, Thu, Sat & Sun, 1-9pm Fri; [S]6 to 77th St) The Whitney makes no secret of its mission to provoke, which starts with its imposing Brutalist building, a structure that houses works by 20th century masters Edward Hopper, Jasper Johns, Georgia O'Keeffe and Mark Rothko. In addition to rotating exhibits, there is a biennial on even years, an ambitious survey of contemporary art that rarely fails to generate controversy.

The museum was opened in 1931 by society doyenne Gertrude Vanderbilt Whitney, who was known for her lively Greenwich Village salons. During her lifetime, she collected more than 600 works of art, including canvases by painters such as Thomas Hart Benton and George Bellows. These works comprise the core of the museum's permanent collection, which is displayed on the 5th floor.

After inhabiting various locations downtown, the Whitney moved to its current Marcel Breuer–designed building in 1966. But, having outgrown these digs, it is set to move again. A new Renzo Piano–designed structure in the Meatpacking District was nearing completion as this book went to press. Located right next to the High Line (at Washington and Gansevoort Sts), the 200,000-square-foot space will open in 2015.

For food, try the museum's Danny Meyer comfort eatery in the basement, **Untitled** (Map p432; www.untitledatthewhitney.com; 945 Madison Ave, Whitney Museum of American Art; mains $13-24; ⏰11am-6pm Wed & Thu, to 9pm Fri, 10am-6pm Sat & Sun). Cedar plank salmon, gourmet burgers, smoked trout sandwiches and all-day breakfast are among the hits.

WORTH A DETOUR

ROOSEVELT: THE ISLAND OFF THE ISLAND OF MANHATTAN

Roosevelt Island, the tiny sliver of land that sits in the middle of the East River, has never had much to offer in the way of sights. For much of the 19th century, when it was known as Welfare Island, it was cluttered with hospitals, including a mental hospital and a crenelated small-pox ward. In the 1970s, a series of cookie-cutter apartment buildings were built along the island's only road. For years, the only thing Roosevelt Island really had going for it were the good views of Manhattan and the picturesque ruins of the old small-pox hospital (which is under restoration and will eventually open to the public).

But the island hit the architectural map in 2012, when a five-acre memorial (p193) to President Franklin D Roosevelt opened on the southern tip. Designed by architect Louis Kahn in the 1960s, construction of the 4½-acre park stalled in the 1970s when Kahn died and New York City almost went into bankruptcy. William vanden Heuvel, chairman of the Four Freedoms Park Conservancy and a former diplomat, kept the dream alive, and spent years raising funds and lobbying for the park's completion.

Remarkably, it was built as Kahn had originally envisioned it with only minor tweaks. A tapered lawn lined with linden trees leads down to the island's southern tip. As visitors walk toward the end of V-shaped lawn, they arrive at a small viewing platform, anchored with huge slabs of North Carolina granite. This final space perched over the river is 'the room', offering views of Manhattan through the narrow openings, with the UN building among the most prominently featured landmarks – a clear reference point between the president and one of his crowning achievements. It's a peaceful and sober monument, with many subtle hidden details.

The best way to get to Roosevelt Island is to take the picturesque four-minute aerial tram trip across the East River. Trams leave from the **Roosevelt Island Tramway Station** (☎212-832-4543; www.rioc.com/transportation.htm; 60th St, at Second Ave; one-way fare $2.25; ⏰every 15 minutes 6am-2am Sun-Thu, to 3am Fri & Sat). Otherwise, take the F train to the Roosevelt Island stop.

★FRICK COLLECTION GALLERY

Map p432 (☎212-288-0700; www.frick.org; 1 E 70th St, at Fifth Ave; admission $20, by donation 11am-1pm Sun, children under 10 not admitted; 🕐10am-6pm Tue-Sat, 11am-5pm Sun; [S]6 to 68th St-Hunter College) This spectacular art collection sits in a mansion built by prickly steel magnate Henry Clay Frick, one of the many such residences that made up Millionaires' Row. The museum has over a dozen splendid rooms that display masterpieces by Titian, Vermeer, Gilbert Stuart, El Greco and Goya.

This museum is a treat for a number of reasons. One, it resides in a lovely, rambling beaux arts structure built from 1913–14 by Carrère and Hastings. Two, it is generally not crowded (one exception being during popular shows, such as a Vermeer and Rembrandt exhibit held in 2013). And, three, it feels refreshingly intimate, with a trickling indoor courtyard fountain and gardens that can be explored on warmer days. A demure Portico Gallery, opened in 2011, displays decorative works and sculpture.

A worthwhile audio tour (available in several languages) is included in the price of admission. Classical music fans will enjoy the frequent piano and violin concerts that take place on Sundays.

NEUE GALERIE MUSEUM

Map p432 (☎212-628-6200; www.neuegalerie.org; 1048 Fifth Ave, cnr E 86th St; admission $20, free 6-8pm 1st Fri of every month, children under 12 not admitted; 🕐11am-6pm Thu-Mon; [S]4/5/6 to 86th St) This restored Carrère and Hastings mansion from 1914 is a resplendent showcase for German and Austrian art, featuring works by Paul Klee, Ernst Ludwig Kirchner and Egon Schiele. In pride of place on the 2nd floor is Gustav Klimt's golden 1907 portrait of Adele Bloch-Bauer – which was acquired for the museum by cosmetics magnate Ronald Lauder for a whopping $135 million.

This is a small but beautiful place with winding staircases and wrought-iron banisters. It also boasts the lovely, street-level eatery, Café Sabarsky (p224). Avoid weekends if you don't want to deal with gallery-clogging crowds.

JEWISH MUSEUM MUSEUM

Map p432 (☎212-423-3200; www.jewishmuseum.org; 1109 Fifth Ave, at 92nd St; adult/child $15/free, Sat free, by donation 5-8pm Thu; 🕐11am-5:45pm Fri-Tue, to 8pm Thu; 👪; [S]6 to 96th St) This New York City gem is tucked into a French-Gothic mansion from 1908, which houses 30,000 items of Judaica, as well as sculpture, painting and decorative arts. It hosts excellent temporary exhibits, featuring retrospectives on influential figures such as Art Spiegelman, as well as world-class shows on the likes of Marc Chagall, Édouard Vuillard and Man Ray among other past luminaries.

There are frequent lectures and events, as well as an array of activities and concerts for children. Every January, the museum collaborates with the Film Society of Lincoln Center to present the New York Jewish Film Festival.

NATIONAL ACADEMY MUSEUM GALLERY

Map p432 (☎212-369-4880; www.nationalacademy.org; 1083 Fifth Ave, at 89th St; adult/child $15/free; 🕐11am-6pm Wed-Sun; [S]4/5/6 to 86th St) Co-founded by painter/inventor Samuel Morse in 1825, the National Academy Museum comprises an incredible permanent collection of paintings by figures such as Wlil Barnet, Thomas Hart Benton and George Bellows. (This includes some highly compelling self-portraits.) It is housed in a beaux arts structure designed by Ogden Codman Jr and featuring a marble foyer and spiral staircase.

TEMPLE EMANU-EL SYNAGOGUE

Map p432 (☎212-744-1400; www.emanuelnyc.org; 1 E 65th St, cnr Fifth Ave; 🕐10am-4:30pm Sun-Thu; [S]6 to 68th St-Hunter College) [FREE] Founded in 1845 as the first Reform synagogue in New York, this temple, completed in 1929, is now one of the largest Jewish houses of worship in the world. An imposing Romanesque structure, it is more than 175ft long and 100ft tall, with a brilliant, hand-painted ceiling that contains details in gold.

The structure also boasts 60 stained-glass windows and a massive rose window whose dozen panels represent the 12 tribes of Israel. Other stained glass elements pay tribute to notable synagogues, including the Altneuschul in Prague (the oldest continually used Jewish house of worship in the world). The ark containing the Torah scrolls, on the eastern wall, is surrounded by a glittering glass-and-marble mosaic arch.

The temple is home to the small **Herbert & Eileen Bernard Museum of Judaica**, with more than 650 pieces that date back to the 14th century.

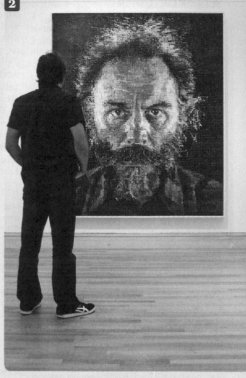

DAN HERRICK / GETTY IMAGES ©

1. Frick Collection (p219)
Browse the spectacular art collection, housed inside a beaux arts mansion.

2. Metropolitan Museum of Art (p212)
Marvel at the masterpieces inside the Met, where there are more than two million individual objects to examine. Chuck Close painting courtesy of Pace Gallery.

3. Fifth Ave (p211)
Shop in one of the many department stores or simply admire the storefront displays.

4. Madison Ave (p226)
Wander along Madison Ave and explore some of the country's most extravagant shopping boutiques.

MUSEUM OF THE CITY OF NEW YORK
MUSEUM

Map p432 (☎212-534-1672; www.mcny.org; 1220 Fifth Ave, btwn 103rd & 104th Sts; suggested admission adult/child $10/free; ⏲10am-6pm; [S]6 to 103rd St) Situated in a colonial Georgian-style mansion, this local museum focuses solely on New York City's past, present and future. Don't miss the 22-minute film *Timescapes* (on the 2nd floor), which charts NYC's growth from tiny native trading post to burgeoning metropolis.

One of the museum's star attractions is the 12-room mansion dollhouse fabricated by Carrie Stettheimer over 25 years at the turn of the 20th century – replete with tiny art works (including miniatures of pieces by Marcel Duchamp and Gaston Lachaise).

ASIA SOCIETY & MUSEUM
MUSEUM

Map p432 (☎212-288-6400; www.asiasociety.org; 725 Park Ave, at E 70th St; admission $12, 6-9pm Fri mid-Sep–Jun free; ⏲11am-6pm Tue-Sun, to 9pm Fri mid-Sep–Jun; [S]6 to 68th St-Hunter College) Founded in 1956 by John D Rockefeller (an avid collector of Asian Art), this cultural center hosts fascinating exhibits (pre-Revolutionary art of Iran, retrospectives of leading Chinese artists, block prints of Edo-era Japan), as well as Jain sculptures and Nepalese Buddhist paintings. There are tours (free with admission) at 2pm on Tuesdays year-round and at 6:30pm Fridays (excluding summer months).

The Society part of the equation brings abundant cultural fare: concerts, film screenings, lectures and culinary events (tea tastings, ramen-making demos). You'll also find great gift ideas at the small museum shop, with its silk scarves, delicate jewelry, children's stories and music from the Near and Far East. A Sunday shuttle runs from here to the Noguchi Museum in Queens.

GRACIE MANSION
HISTORIC BUILDING

Map p432 (☎tour reservations 311 or 212-639-9675; www.nyc.gov/gracie; East End Ave, at E 88th St; admission $7; ⏲tours 10am, 11am, 1pm & 2pm Wed; [S]4/5/6 to 86th St) This Federal-style home served as the country residence of merchant Archibald Gracie in 1799. Since 1942, it has been where New York's mayors have lived – with the exception of megabillionaire Mayor Michael Bloomberg, who preferred his own plush, Upper East Side digs. The house has been added to and renovated over the years. To peer inside, you'll have to call ahead to reserve a spot on one of the 45-minute house tours.

The home is bordered by the pleasant, riverside Carl Schurz Park.

COOPER-HEWITT NATIONAL DESIGN MUSEUM
MUSEUM

Map p432 (☎212-849-8400; www.cooperhewitt.org; 2 E 91st St, at Fifth Ave; [S]4/5/6 to 86th St) Part of the Smithsonian Institution in Washington, DC, this house of culture is the only museum in the country that's dedicated to both historic and contemporary design. The collection is housed in the 64-room mansion built by billionaire Andrew Carnegie in 1901. The museum closed for an extensive renovation and expansion, and is slated to reopen in 2014. Check the website for updates.

🍴 EATING

★EARL'S BEER & CHEESE
AMERICAN $

Map p432 (www.earlsny.com; 1259 Park Ave, btwn 97th & 98th Sts; grilled cheese $6-8; ⏲4pm-midnight Mon & Tue, 11am-midnight Wed-Thu & Sun, to 2am Fri & Sat Sat & Sun; [S]6 to 96th St) Chef Corey Cova's tiny comfort-food outpost channels a hipster hunting vibe, complete with a giant deer in the woods mural and a mounted buck's head. Basic grilled cheese is a paradigm shifter, served with pork belly, fried egg and kimchi. There is also mac 'n' cheese (with goat cheese and shredded chicken) and tacos (featuring braised pork shoulder and *queso fresco* - a mexican cheese). Has great craft beers too.

WILLIAM GREENBERG DESSERTS
BAKERY $

Map p432 (www.wmgreenbergdesserts.com; 1100 Madison Ave, btwn E 82nd & 83rd Sts; baked goods from $2; ⏲8am-6:30pm Mon-Fri, to 6pm Sat, 10am-4pm Sun; 👪; [S]4/5/6 to 86th St) Make a pit stop here for New York City's finest black-and-white cookies – soft vanilla discs dipped in white sugar and dark chocolate glazes. Takeout only.

VIA QUADRONNO
CAFE $

Map p432 (☎212-650-9880; www.viaquadronno.com; 25 E 73rd St, btwn Madison & Fifth Aves; sandwiches $8-15, mains $23-38; ⏲8am-11pm Mon-Fri, 9am-11pm Sat, 10am-9pm Sun; ✍; [S]6 to 77th St) A little slice of Italy that looks like it's been airlifted into New York, this cozy cafe-bistro has exquisite coffee, as well as

Neighborhood Walk
Memorable Manhattan Movie Sites

START BLOOMINGDALE'S
END METROPOLITAN MUSEUM OF ART
LENGTH 1.5 MILES; TWO HOURS

An exploration of Manhattan's most storied film sites takes you past film locations big and small.

Start outside 1 **Bloomingdale's**, where Darryl Hannah and Tom Hanks shattered televisions in *Splash* (1984) and Dustin Hoffman hailed a cab in *Tootsie* (1982). West of here, 10 E 60th St is the site of the now defunct 2 **Copacabana**, a nightclub (now a Michelin-starred restaurant) that hosted Ray Liotta and Lorraine Bracco in *Goodfellas* (1990) and a coked-up lawyer played by Sean Penn in *Carlito's Way* (1993). Continue west to 3 **Central Park** (p230), which has appeared in *The Royal Tenenbaums* (2001), *Ghostbusters* (1983), *The Muppets Take Manhattan* (1983), *Barefoot in the Park* (1967) and the cult classic *The Warriors* (1979). From here, head east to Park Ave. At 620 Park Ave at E 65th St, you'll find the building that served as 4 **John Malkovich's apartment** in Charlie Kaufman's *Being John Malkovich* (1999). And to the north at 114 E 72nd St is the 5 **high-rise** where Sylvia Miles lured Jon Voight in *Midnight Cowboy* (1969). One block to the east and south is 171 E 71st St, a townhouse featured in one of the most famous movies to star New York: this was 6 **Holly Golightly's apartment** in *Breakfast at Tiffany's* (1961). Continuing east to Third Ave, you'll find 7 **JG Melon** at the corner of E 74th St, a good spot for beer and burger – plus the site of a meeting between Dustin Hoffman and Meryl Streep in *Kramer vs. Kramer* (1979). Heading west to Madison Ave, the tony 8 **Carlyle** hotel stands at 35 E 76th St where Woody Allen and Dianne Wiest had a date from hell in *Hannah and Her Sisters* (1986). From the Carlyle, it's a short jaunt west to the 9 **Metropolitan Museum of Art** (p212) at E 82nd St and Fifth Ave, where Angie Dickinson had a fatal encounter in *Dressed to Kill* (1980) and Billy Crystal chatted up Meg Ryan in *When Harry Met Sally* (1989).

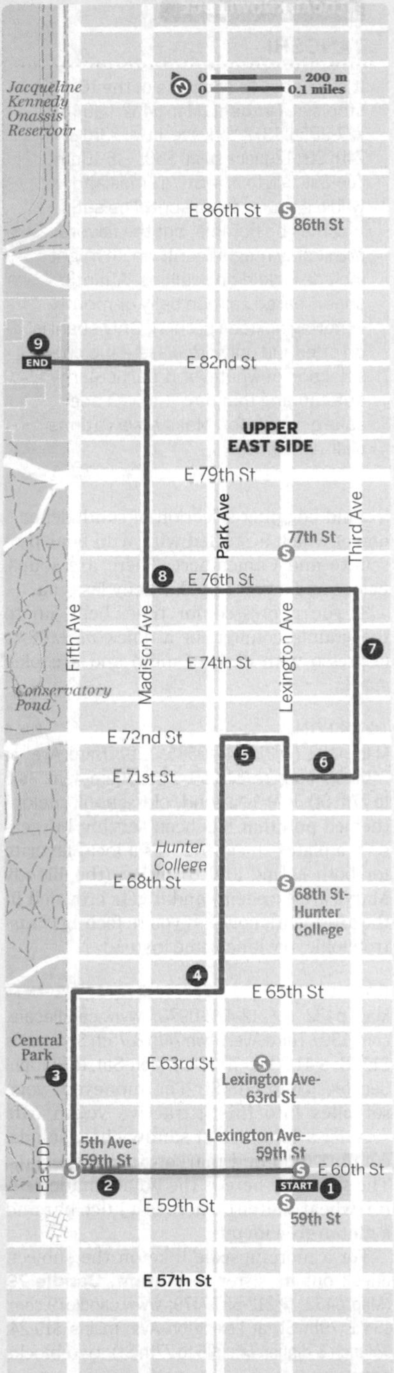

LOCAL KNOWLEDGE

TANOSHI

It's not easy to snag one of the 10 stools at **Tanoshi** (Map p432; ☎646-727-9056; 1372 York Ave, btwn 73rd & 74th Sts; 12-piece sushi $50; 🕒6-10pm Tue-Sat; [S]6 to 77th St), a small and wildly popular sushi spot. The setting may be humble, but the flavors are simply magnificent, which might include Hokkaido scallops, Atlantic shad, seared salmon belly or mouthwatering *uni* (sea urchin). Only sushi is on offer and only *omakase* – the chef's selection of whatever is particularly outstanding that day. It's BYO beer, sake or what-not. Make reservations well in advance.

a mind-boggling selection of sandwiches – one of which is stuffed with wild boar prosciutto and Camembert. There are soups, pastas and a very popular daily lasagna.

If you're pressed for time, belly up to the granite counter for a quick *macchiato* (espresso with dash of milk) and a cookie snack.

JG MELON PUB $

Map p432 (☎212-744-0585; 1291 Third Ave, at 74th St; burgers $10.50; 🕒11:30am-4am; [S]6 to 77th St) JG's is a loud, old-school, melon-themed pub that has been serving burgers on tea plates since 1972. It's a local favorite for both eating and drinking (the Bloody Marys are excellent) and it gets crowded in the after-work hours. If you're feeling claustrophobic, try lunchtime instead.

CANDLE CAFE VEGAN $$

Map p432 (☎212-472-0970; www.candlecafe.com; 1307 Third Ave, btwn 74th & 75th Sts; mains $15-21; 🕒11:30am-10:30pm Mon-Sat, to 9:30pm Sun; 🖉; [S]6 to 77th St) The moneyed, yoga set piles into this attractive vegan cafe serving a long list of sandwiches, salads, comfort food and market-driven specials. The specialty here is the house-made *seitan* (wheat/gluten). There is a juice bar and a gluten-free menu.

For a more upscale take on the subject, check out its sister restaurant, **Candle 79** (Map p432; ☎212-537-7179; www.candle79.com; 154 E 79th St, at Lexington Ave; mains $19-24; 🕒lunch & dinner; 🖉; [S]6 to 77th St), two blocks away.

SANDRO'S ITALIAN $$

Map p432 (☎212-288-7374; www.sandrosnyc.com; 306 E 81st St, near Second Ave; mains $20-40; 🕒4:30-11pm Mon-Sat, to 10pm Sun; [S]6 to 77th St) This neighborhood trattoria serves up fresh Roman dishes and homemade pastas by chef Sandro Fioriti. Specialties include crisp fried artichokes and sea urchin ravioli.

CAFÉ SABARSKY AUSTRIAN $$

Map p432 (☎212-288-0665; www.kg-ny.com/wallse; 1048 Fifth Ave, at E 86th St; mains $15-30; 🕒9am-6pm Mon & Wed, to 9pm Thu-Sun; 🖉 👪; [S]4/5/6 to 86th St) The lines get long at this popular cafe, which evokes opulent turn-of-the-century Vienna. But the well-rendered Austrian specialties make the wait worth it. Expect crepes with smoked trout, goulash soup and creamed sptäzle (dumplings). There is also a long list of specialty sweets, including a divine Sachertorte.

ABV MODERN AMERICAN $$

Map p432 (☎212-722-8959; 1504 Lexington Ave, at 97th St; 🕒5pm-midnight Mon-Thu, 4pm-1am Fri, from 11am Sat & Sun; 📶; [S]6 to 96th St.) On the borderline of East Harlem, ABV draws a young, laid-back crowd who come for eclectic sharing plates (fish tacos, foie gras mousse, scallops, veal sweetbreads), wine ($9 to $12 per glass) and craft beers. Soaring ceilings and brick walls invite lingering, and there's live music on Monday nights (from 9pm), except during football season.

JAMES WOOD FOUNDRY BRITISH $$

Map p432 (☎212-249-2700; 401 E 76th St, btwn First & York Aves; mains lunch $10-24, dinner $18-32; 🕒11am-2am; 📶; [S]6 to 77th St) Inside a narrow brick building that once housed an ironworks, the James Wood Foundry is a British-inspired gastropub serving first-rate beer-battered fish and chips, bangers and mash, lamb and rosemary pie and other temptations from the other side of the Atlantic. On warm days and nights, grab a table on the enclosed courtyard patio.

SANT AMBROEUS CAFE, ITALIAN $$$

Map p432 (☎212-570-2211; www.santambroeus.com; 1000 Madison Ave, btwn 77th & 78th St; panini $12-18, mains $23-64; 🕒7am-11pm; 🖉; [S]6 to 77th St) Behind a demure facade lies this dressy Milanese bistro and cafe that oozes old-world charm. Up front, a long granite counter dispenses rich cappuccinos, pastries and panini (grilled with the likes of parma ham and fontina), while the elegant dining room in the back dishes up northern Italian specialties such as breaded veal chop and saffron risotto. Don't bypass the famed gelato.

CAFÉ BOULUD   FRENCH $$$

Map p432 (☎212-772-2600; www.danielnyc.com/cafebouludny.html; 20 E 76th St, btwn Fifth & Madison Aves; mains $24-48; ⊗breakfast, lunch & dinner; 🖋; 🚇6 to 77th St) This Michelin-starred bistro – part of Daniel Boulud's gastronomic empire – attracts a staid crowd with its globe-trotting French cuisine. Seasonal menus include classic dishes such as coq au vin, as well as more inventive fare such as scallop *crudo* (raw) with white miso. Foodies on a budget will be interested in the three-course, $43 prix fixe lunch.

The adjacent 40-seat **Bar Pleiades** (Map p432; www.barpleiades.com; 20 E 76th St; ⊗noon-midnight) serves seasonal cocktails, along with a full bar menu (think beef sliders and grilled baby octopus).

🍷 DRINKING & NIGHTLIFE

The choices here have traditionally been extreme: luxury lounges or frat-house vomitoriums. Times are changing, however, with Brooklyn-style cocktail lounges and gastropubs opening their doors in recent years.

METROPOLITAN MUSEUM ROOF GARDEN CAFÉ & MARTINI BAR   COCKTAIL BAR

Map p432 (www.metmuseum.org; 1000 Fifth Ave, at 82nd St; ⊗10am-4:30pm Sun-Thu, to 8pm Fri & Sat, Martini Bar 5:30-8pm Fri & Sat May-Oct; 🚇4/5/6 to 86th St) The sort of setting you can't get enough of (even if you are a jaded local). Located within the Met, the roof garden's bar sits right above Central Park's tree canopy, allowing for splendid views of the park and the city skyline all around. Sunset is when you'll find fools in love – then again, it could all be those martinis.

JBIRD   BAR

Map p432 (☎212-288-8033; 339 E 75th St, btwn First & Second Aves; ⊗5:30pm-2am Mon-Thu, to 4am Fri & Sat; 🚇6 to 77th St) This rare uptown gem serves craft cocktails and seasonal pub fare in a screen-free environment that feels more downtown than

uptown. Grab a seat at the marble bar or (arrive early and) sink into a dark leather banquette. Nibble on pork sliders, grilled octopus or garlic fries, while sipping rich and complex libations made of rye whiskey, mescal, jasmine flower rum and other unusual spirits.

PENROSE   BAR

Map p432 (☎212-203-2751; 1590 Second Ave, btwn 82nd & 83rd Sts; ⊗3pm-4am Mon-Thu, noon-4am Fri, 10:30am-4am Sat & Sun; 🚇4/5/6 to 86th St) New in 2012, the Penrose brings a much-needed dose of style to the Upper East Side, with craft beers, exposed brick walls, vintage mirrors, floral wallpaper, reclaimed wood details and friendly bartenders setting the stage for fine evening outing among friends.

There's Duvel and Murphy's on draft, a decent selection of Irish whiskeys (no surprise, given the owners hail from Cork) and plenty of good pub fare: grilled portobello burger, lamb pie and fried chicken, among other bites.

OSLO COFFEE ROASTERS   CAFE

Map p432 (422 E 75th St, btwn York & First Aves; coffee from $2; ⊗7am-6pm Mon-Fri, from 8am Sat, 8am-3pm Sun; 🚇6 to 77th St) Headquartered in Williamsburg (where they do their roasting), Oslo whips up magnificent brews, espressos and lattes – all fair trade and organic, of course. Minuses: limited seating and no wi-fi.

VINUS AND MARC   LOUNGE

Map p432 (☎646-692-9015; 1825 Second Ave, btwn 95th & 94th Sts; ⊗3pm-1am Sun-Tue, to 2am Wed & Thu, to 3am Fri & Sat; 🚇6 to 96th St) Red walls, gilt-edge mirrors, vintage fixtures and a long dark-wood bar sets the stage at this inviting new lounge in Yorkville. The cocktails range from elegant inventions like the spicy Baby Vamp (tequila, mescal, strawberry and habanero bitters) to Prohibition-era classics like the Scofflaw (rye whiskey, dry vermouth and housemade grenadine). There's also good bistro fare (mussels, shrimp and grits, Angus beef tenderloin sandwich).

DRUNKEN MUNKEY   LOUNGE

Map p432 (338 E 92nd St, btwn First & Second Aves; ⊗11am-2am Mon-Thu, to 3am Fri-Sun; 🚇6 to 96th St) This playful new lounge channels colonial-era Bombay with vintage wallpaper, cricket-ball door handles and jauntily attired waitstaff. The monkey chandeliers may be pure whimsy, but the craft cocktails and tasty curries (small, meant for sharing) are serious business. Gin, not surprisingly, is the drink of choice. Try the Bramble, with Bombay gin, blackberry liqueur and fresh lemon juice and blackberries.

BEMELMANS BAR LOUNGE

Map p432 (☎212-744-1600; www.thecarlyle.com/dining/bemelmans_bar; Carlyle Hotel, 35 E 76th St, at Madison Ave; ⏰noon-2am Mon-Sat, to 12:30am Sun; [S]6 to 77th St) Sink into a chocolate leather banquette and take in the glorious 1940s elegance of this fabled bar – the sort of place where the waiters wear white jackets, a baby grand is always tinkling and the ceiling is 24-carat gold leaf. Note the charming murals by Ludwig Bemelman (famed creator of *Madeline*). Show up before 9pm if you don't want to pay a cover (per person $15 to $30).

☆ ENTERTAINMENT

CAFÉ CARLYLE JAZZ

Map p432 (www.thecarlyle.com/dining/cafe_carlyle; Carlyle Hotel, 35 E 76th St, at Madison Ave; cover $110-185; [S]6 to 77th St) This swanky spot at the Carlyle Hotel draws top-shelf talent, including Woody Allen, who plays his clarinet here with the Eddy Davis New Orleans Jazz Band on Mondays at 8:45pm (September through May). Bring bucks: the cover doesn't include food or drinks.

FRICK COLLECTION CLASSICAL MUSIC

Map p432 (www.frick.org; 1 E 70th St, at Fifth Ave; admission $35; [S]6 to 68th St-Hunter College) Once a month, this opulent mansion-museum hosts a Sunday concert that bring world-renowned performers such as cellist Yehuda Hanani and violinist Thomas Zehetmair.

92ND ST Y CULTURAL CENTER

Map p432 (www.92y.org; 1395 Lexington Ave, at 92nd St; 👪; [S]6 to 96th St) In addition to its wide spectrum of concerts, dance performances and literary readings, this nonprofit cultural center hosts an excellent lecture and conversation series. Playwright Edward Albee, cellist Yo-Yo Ma, funnyman Steve Martin and novelist Gary Shteyngart have all taken the stage.

COMIC STRIP LIVE COMEDY

Map p432 (☎212-861-9386; www.comicstriplive.com; 1568 Second Ave, btwn 81st & 82nd Sts; cover charge $15-30 plus 2-drink min; ⏰shows 8:30pm Sun-Thu, 8:30pm, 10:30pm & 12:30pm Fri, 8pm, 10:30pm & 12:30am Sat; [S]4/5/6 to 86th St) Chris Rock, Adam Sandler, Jerry Seinfeld and Eddie Murphy have all performed at this club. Not recently, but you're sure to find somebody stealing their acts here most nights. Reservations required.

🛍 SHOPPING

The Upper East Side isn't for amateurs. Madison Ave (from 60th St to 72nd St) features one of the globe's glitziest stretches of retail: the flagship boutiques of some of the world's top designers, including Gucci, Prada and Cartier. The neighborhood is also a good spot to hunt down designer deals at consignment shops.

HOUSING WORKS THRIFT SHOP VINTAGE

Map p432 (202 E 77th St, btwn Second & Third Aves; ⏰11am-7pm Mon-Fri, 10am-6pm Sat, noon-5pm Sun; [S]6 to 77th St) As at the other Housing Works around town, shopping here can be a bit hit-or-miss. On good days, you might score a designer jacket, perfectly fitting jeans or a handbag bearing a high-end label. The apparel is generally in excellent condition – if not new – and sold at decent prices. There are also books, CDs and housewares. It gets crowded on weekends.

ENCORE CLOTHING

Map p432 (www.encoreresale.com; 1132 Madison Ave, btwn 84th & 85th Sts; ⏰10:30am-6:30pm Mon-Sat, noon-6pm Sun; [S]4/5/6 to 86th St) An exclusive consignment store has been emptying out Upper East Side closets since the 1950s. (Jacqueline Kennedy Onassis used to sell her clothes here.) Expect to find a gently worn array of name brands such as Louboutin, Fendi and Dior. Prices are high but infinitely better than retail.

MICHAEL'S CLOTHING

Map p432 (www.michaelsconsignment.com; 2nd fl, 1041 Madison Ave, btwn 79th & 80th Sts; ⏰9:30am-6pm Mon-Sat, to 8pm Thu; [S]6 to 77th St) In operation since the 1950s, this is a vaunted Upper East Side resale store that is strong on high-end labels, including Chanel, Gucci and Prada. Almost everything on display is less than two years old. It's pricey, but cheaper than shopping the flagship boutiques on Madison Ave.

CRAWFORD DOYLE BOOKSELLERS BOOKS

Map p432 (1082 Madison Ave, btwn 81st & 82nd Sts; 🕐10am-6pm Mon-Sat, noon-5pm Sun; [S]6 to 77th St) This genteel Upper East Side book shop invites browsing, with stacks devoted to art, literature and the history of New York – not to mention plenty of first editions. A wonderful place to while away a chilly afternoon.

BLUE TREE FASHION, HOMEWARES

Map p432 (www.bluetreenyc.com; 1283 Madison Ave, btwn 91st & 92nd Sts; 🕐10am-6pm Mon-Fri, from 11am Sat & Sun; [S]4/5/6 to 86th St) This charming (and expensive) little boutique, owned by actress Phoebe Cates Kline (of *Fast Times at Ridgemont High*) sells a dainty array of women's clothing, cashmere scarves, Lucite objects, whimsical accessories and quirky home design.

ZITOMER BEAUTY

Map p432 (www.zitomer.com; 969 Madison Ave, btwn 75th & 76th Sts; 🕐9am-8pm Mon-Fri, to 7pm Sat, 10am-6pm Sun; [S]6 to 77th St) This multistory retro pharmacy carries a treasure trove worth of high-end, all-natural skincare products, including brands such as Kiehl's, Clarins, Kneipp, Mustela and Ahava (made from rejuvenating Dead Sea minerals). On the 3rd floor, you can browse kid's clothes and toys.

SPORTS & ACTIVITIES

ASPHALT GREEN SWIMMING

Map p432 (☎212-369-8890; www.asphaltgreen.org; 555 E 90th St, btwn York & East End Aves; gym & pool pass $35; 🕐5:30am-9:45pm Mon-Fri, 8am-7:45pm Sat & Sun; 👪; [S]4/5/6 to 86th St) Not to be confused with the 1973 Charlton Heston sci-fi film *Soylent Green,* the Asphalt Green fitness center is set in a former municipal asphalt plant. There is an excellent 50m Olympic-size pool, as well as a smaller pool for classes.

EXHALE SPA

Map p432 (☎212-561-6400; www.exhalespa.com; 980 Madison Ave, btwn 76th & 77th Sts; 1hr massage around $150; [S]6 to 77th St) This Zen-like spa offers all the standard treatments, including massages, facials and scrubs. There is also yoga, acupuncture and cupping. Prepare to emerge relaxed.

Upper West Side & Central Park

UPPER WEST SIDE | CENTRAL PARK

W 110th St (Cathedral Pkwy)
Central Park North
Harlem Meer
4
W 108th St
W 106th St (Duke Ellington Blvd)
W 104th St
Broadway
West Side Hwy
W 100th St
Central Park
Fifth Ave
W 96th St
W 94th St
W 92nd St
Riverside Park
West End Ave
Amsterdam Ave
Jacqueline Kennedy Onassis Reservoir
W 90th St
W 88th St
W 86th St
Riverside Dr
UPPER WEST SIDE
W 83rd St
1
West Dr
East Dr
5
W 81st St
W 79th St
3
W 77th St
Columbus Ave
Central Park West
Conservatory Pond
W 75th St
The Lake
Hudson River
W 72nd St
W 70th St
West Side Hwy
Broadway
W 68th St
Fifth Ave
W 66th St
Lincoln Center
W 62nd St
2
The Pond
0   500 m
0   0.25 miles
Central Park South

For more detail of this area see Map p434 ➡

Neighborhood Top Five

1 Escaping the city's urban madness with a day in **Central Park** (p230) – picnicking on Sheep's Meadow, row-boating on the lake and strolling the grand Literary Walk.

2 Going to the **Metropolitan Opera House** (p242) to wallow in the operatic trials of Rigoletto, Carmen and Figaro.

3 Walking among the world's largest dinosaurs at the **American Museum of Natural History** (p236).

4 Taking a pilgrimage to Tibet without leaving New York City at the **Nicholas Roerich Museum** (p235).

5 Stocking up on gut-filling knishes (small stuffed dough, baked or fried) and German marble cake at **Zabar's** (p235).

Explore Upper West Side & Central Park

Manhattan's midsection is a lot of ground to cover – and the best plan of attack will depend on your flavor. Traveling with tykes? Then dazzle their budding brains with a visit to the Museum of Natural History, followed by a journey through the sprawling wonderland that is Central Park. If the high arts are your pleasure, then make for Lincoln Center – where the Metropolitan Opera, the New York Philharmonic and the New York City Ballet all inject the city with vibrant doses of culture. And, if your idea of a good time is just ambling around, then take in the sights in and off Broadway in the '70s, an area cluttered with bustling shops and fine architecture.

Local Life

➡ **Go fishing** Wood-smoked lox (thinly sliced smoked salmon). Briny pickled herring. Meaty sturgeon. It doesn't get more Upper West Side than examining the seafood treats at Zabar's (p235) and Barney Greengrass (p237).

➡ **Central chill** You can pick out the tourists in Central Park (p230) because they're rushing to see sights. Make like a local by picking out a patch of green with good views and letting the world come to you.

➡ **Catch a flick** Manhattan's diehard film buffs can be found taking in quality cinema courtesy of the Film Society of Lincoln Center (p243).

➡ **Late-night munchies** Nothing is more New York than soaking up the evening's liquor damage with a midnight hot dog from Gray's Papaya (p237).

Getting There & Away

➡ **Subway** On the Upper West Side, the 1, 2 and 3 subway lines are good for destinations along Broadway and points west, while the B and C trains are best for points of interest and access to Central Park. The park can be accessed from all sides, making every subway that travels north–south through Manhattan convenient. The A, C, B, D and 1 all stop at Columbus Circle at Central Park's southwestern edge, while the N, R or Q will leave you at the southeast corner. The 2 or 3 will deposit you at the northern gate in Harlem.

➡ **Bus** The M104 bus runs north–south along Broadway, and the M10 plies the scenic ride along the western edge of the park. Crosstown buses at 66th, 72nd, 79th, 86th and 96th Sts take you through the park to the Upper East Side. Note that these pick up and drop off passengers at the edge of the park – not inside.

Lonely Planet's Top Tip

The best way to cover all 840 acres of Central Park is to rent a bicycle. Bike and Roll (p246) and the Loeb Boathouse (p245) both offer rentals. If starting at the Loeb Boathouse, pedal north along East Dr to see the Great Lawn, the reservoir, the Conservatory Garden and Harlem Meer. From the Great Hill you can coast down West Dr, past the Delacorte Theater and end up at Strawberry Fields (weather permitting).

✕ Best Places to Eat

➡ Jacob's Pickles (p237)

➡ Burke & Wills (p238)

➡ Gastronomía Culinaria (p238)

➡ Kefi (p237)

➡ Dovetail (p239)

For reviews, see p236 ➡

▤ Best Places to Drink

➡ Ding Dong Lounge (p239)

➡ Dead Poet (p239)

➡ Barcibo Enoteca (p239)

➡ Manhattan Cricket Club (p242)

➡ West 79th St Boat Basin Cafe (p236)

For reviews, see p239 ➡

☆ Best Places for Music

➡ Metropolitan Opera House (p242)

➡ SummerStage (p244)

➡ Smoke (p244)

➡ Cleopatra's Needle Club (p244)

➡ Beacon Theatre (p244)

For reviews, see p242 ➡

TOP SIGHT
CENTRAL PARK

Comprising more than 800 acres of picturesque meadows, ponds and woods, it might be tempting to think that Central Park represents Manhattan in its raw state. It does not. Designed by Frederick Law Olmsted and Calvert Vaux, the park is the result of serious engineering: thousands of workers shifted 10 million cartloads of soil to transform swamp and rocky outcroppings into the 'people's park' of today.

Birth of the Park

In the 1850s, the area was occupied by pig farms, a garbage dump, a bone-boiling operation and an African American village. It took 20,000 laborers 20 years to transform this terrain into a park. Today, Central Park has more than 24,000 trees, 136 acres of woodland, 21 playgrounds and seven bodies of water. It attracts more than 38 million visitors a year.

Strawberry Fields

This tear-shaped **garden** (Map p434; www.centralparknyc.org/visit/things-to-see/south-end/strawberry-fields.html; at 72nd St on the west side; ; S A/C, B to 72nd St) serves as a memorial to former Beatle John Lennon. The garden is composed of a grove of stately elms and a tiled mosaic that reads, simply, 'Imagine.'

Bethesda Terrace & the Mall

The arched walkways of **Bethesda Terrace** (Map p434), crowned by the magnificent Bethesda Fountain (at the level of 72nd St), have long been a gathering area for New Yorkers of all flavors. To the south is the Mall (featured in countless movies), a promenade

DON'T MISS...

➜ The Mall
➜ The Reservoir
➜ Conservatory Garden
➜ Central Park Zoo

PRACTICALITIES

➜ Map p434
➜ www.centralpark nyc.org
➜ 59th & 110th Sts, btwn Central Park West & Fifth Ave
➜ ⊘6am-1am

shrouded in mature North American elms. The southern stretch, known as **Literary Walk** (Map p434), is flanked by statues of famous authors.

Central Park Zoo

Officially known as Central Park Wildlife Center (no one calls it that), this small **zoo** (Map p434; ☎212-861-6030; www.centralparkzoo.com; 64th St, at Fifth Ave; adult/child $12/7; ⏰10am-5:30pm Apr-Nov, to 4:30pm Nov-Apr; 👪; [S]N/Q/R to 5th Ave-59th St) is home to penguins, snow leopards, dart poison frogs and red pandas. Feeding times in the sea lion and penguin tanks make for a rowdy spectacle. (Check the website for times.) The attached **Tisch Children's Zoo** (Map p434; www.centralparkzoo.com/animals-and-exhibits/exhibits/tisch-childrens-zoo.aspx; at 65th & Fifth Ave), a petting zoo, has alpacas and mini-Nubian goats and is perfect for small children.

Conservatory Water & Around

North of the zoo at the level of 74th St is Conservatory Water, where model sailboats drift lazily and kids scramble about on a toadstool-studded statue of Alice in Wonderland. There are Saturday story hours at the Hans Christian Andersen statue to the west of the water (at 11am from June to September).

Great Lawn & the Ramble

The **Great Lawn** (Map p434; btwn 79th & 86th Sts; [S]B, C to 86th St) is a massive emerald carpet at the center of the park and is surrounded by ball fields and London plane trees. (This is where Simon & Garfunkel played their famous 1981 concert.) Immediately to the southeast is **Delacorte Theater** (Map p434; enter at W 81st St), home to an annual Shakespeare in the Park festival, as well as Belvedere Castle (p246), a birdwatching lookout. Further south is the leafy **Ramble** (Map p434; mid-park from 73rd to 79th Sts), a popular birding destination (and legendary gay pick-up spot). On the southeastern end is the Loeb Boathouse (p245), home to a waterside restaurant that offers rowboat and bicycle rentals.

Jacqueline Kennedy Onassis Reservoir

The reservoir takes up almost the entire width of the park at the level of 90th St and serves as a gorgeous reflecting pool for the city skyline. It is surrounded by a 1.58-mile track that draws legions of joggers in the warmer months. Nearby, at Fifth Ave and 90th St, is a statue of New York City Marathon founder Fred Lebow, peering at his watch.

CONSERVATORY GARDEN

If you want a little peace and quiet (as in, no runners, cyclists or boom boxes), the six-acre Conservatory Garden serves as one of the park's official quiet zones. And it's beautiful, to boot: bursting with crabapple trees, meandering boxwood and, in the spring, lots of flowers. It's located at 105th St off Fifth Ave. Otherwise, you can catch maximum calm (and max bird life) in all areas of the park just after dawn.

The North Woods, on the west side between 106th and 110th Sts, is home to the park's oldest structure, the Blockhouse, a military fortification from the War of 1812.

VISITING THE PARK

Free and custom walking tours are available via the **Central Park Conservancy** (www.centralparknyc.org/walkingtours), the nonprofit organization that supports park maintenance.

Central Park

THE LUNGS OF NEW YORK

The rectangular patch of green that occupies Manhattan's heart began life in the mid-19th century as a swampy piece of land that was carefully bulldozed into the idyllic naturescape you see today. Since officially becoming Central Park, it has brought New Yorkers of all stripes together in interesting and unexpected ways. The park has served as a place for the rich to show off their fancy carriages (1860s), for the poor to enjoy free Sunday concerts (1880s) and for activists to hold be-ins against the Vietnam War (1960s).

Since then, legions of locals – not to mention travelers from all kinds of faraway places – have poured in to stroll, picnic, sunbathe, play ball and catch free concerts and performances of works by Shakespeare.

Loeb Boathouse
Perched on the shores of the Lake, the historic Loeb Boathouse is one of the city's best settings for an idyllic meal. You can also rent rowboats and bicycles and ride on a Venetian gondola.

Duke Ellington Circle

Harlem Meer

The Blockhouse

North Woods

97th St Transverse

Fifth Ave

86th St Transverse

The Great Lawn

Central Park West

Conservatory Garden
The only formal garden in Central Park is perhaps the most tranquil. On the northern end, chrysanthemums bloom in late October. To the south, the park's largest crab apple tree grows by the Burnett Fountain.

STEVEN GREAVES / GETTY IMAGES ©

Jacqueline Kennedy Onassis Reservoir
This 106-acre body of water covers roughly an eighth of the park's territory. Its original purpose was to provide clean water for the city. Now it's a good spot to catch a glimpse of waterbirds.

ANGUS OSBORN / GETTY IMAGES ©

Belvedere Castle
A so-called 'Victorian folly,' this Gothic-Romanesque castle serves no other purpose than to be a very dramatic lookout point. It was built by Central Park co-designer Calvert Vaux in 1869.

The park's varied terrain offers a wonderland of experiences. There are quiet, woodsy knolls in the north. To the south is the reservoir, crowded with joggers. There are European gardens, a zoo and various bodies of water. For maximum flamboyance, hit the Sheep Meadow on a sunny day, when all of New York shows up to lounge.

Central Park is more than just a green space. It is New York City's backyard.

FACTS & FIGURES

» **Landscape architects** Frederick Law Olmsted and Calvert Vaux

» **Year that construction began** 1858

» **Acres** 843

» **On film** Hundreds of movies have been shot on location, from Depression-era blockbusters such as *Gold Diggers* (1933) to the monster-attack flick *Cloverfield* (2008).

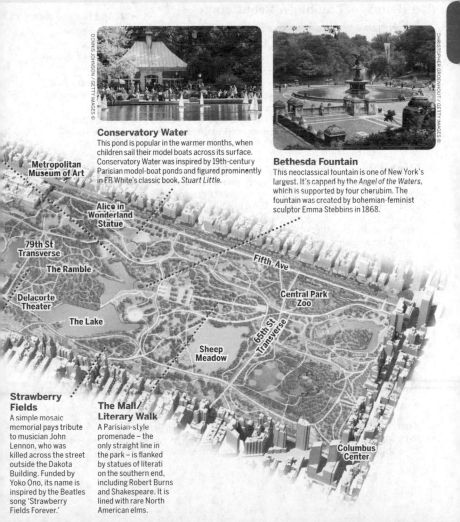

Conservatory Water
This pond is popular in the warmer months, when children sail their model boats across its surface. Conservatory Water was inspired by 19th-century Parisian model-boat ponds and figured prominently in FB White's classic book, *Stuart Little*.

Bethesda Fountain
This neoclassical fountain is one of New York's largest. It's capped by the *Angel of the Waters*, which is supported by four cherubim. The fountain was created by bohemian-feminist sculptor Emma Stebbins in 1868.

Metropolitan Museum of Art

Alice in Wonderland Statue

79th St Transverse

The Ramble

Delacorte Theater

The Lake

Fifth Ave

Central Park Zoo

65th St Transverse

Sheep Meadow

Strawberry Fields
A simple mosaic memorial pays tribute to musician John Lennon, who was killed across the street outside the Dakota Building. Funded by Yoko Ono, its name is inspired by the Beatles song 'Strawberry Fields Forever.'

The Mall / Literary Walk
A Parisian-style promenade – the only straight line in the park – is flanked by statues of literati on the southern end, including Robert Burns and Shakespeare. It is lined with rare North American elms.

Columbus Center

TOP SIGHT
LINCOLN CENTER

This stark arrangement of gleaming modernist temples contains some of Manhattan's most important performance spaces: Avery Fisher Hall (home to the New York Philharmonic), David H Koch Theater (site of the New York City ballet), and the iconic Metropolitan Opera House, whose interior walls are dressed with brightly saturated murals by painter Marc Chagall. Various other venues are tucked in and around the 16-acre campus, including a theater, two film screening centers and the renowned Juilliard School.

DON'T MISS...

- Metropolitan Opera House
- Revson Fountain at night
- Alice Tully Hall

PRACTICALITIES

- Map p434
- ☎212-875-5456
- http://lc.lincolncenter.org
- Columbus Ave btwn 62nd & 66th Sts
- public plazas free, tours adult/student $18/15
- [S]1 to 66th St-Lincoln Center

A History of Building & Rebuilding

Built in the 1960s, this imposing campus replaced a group of tenements called San Juan Hill, a predominantly African American neighborhood where the exterior shots for the movie *West Side Story* were filmed. In addition to being a controversial urban planning move, Lincoln Center wasn't exactly well received at an architectural level – it was relentlessly criticized for its conservative design, fortresslike aspect and poor acoustics. For the center's 50th anniversary (2009–10), Diller Scofidio + Renfro and other architects gave the complex a much-needed and critically acclaimed freshening up.

Highlights

A survey of the three classic buildings surrounding Revson Fountain is a must. These include the Metropolitan Opera, Avery Fisher Hall and the David H Koch Theater, the latter designed by Philip Johnson. The fountain is spectacular in the evenings when it puts on Las Vegas–like light shows. (These are all located on the main plaza at Columbus Ave, between 62nd and 65th Sts.)

Of the refurbished structures, there are a number that are worth examining, including **Alice Tully Hall** (Map p434; ☎212-875-5050; cnr 65th St & Broadway; [S]1 to 66 St-Lincoln Center), now displaying a very contemporary translucent, angled facade, and the **David Rubenstein Atrium** (Map p434; Broadway, btwn 62nd & 63rd Sts; [S]1 to 66th St-Lincoln Center), a public space offering a lounge area (free wi-fi), a cafe, an information desk and a ticket vendor plying day-of discount tickets to Lincoln Center performances. Free events are held here on Thursday evening.

Performances & Screenings

On any given night, there are at least 10 performances happening throughout Lincoln Center – including in the summer, when Lincoln Center Out of Doors (a series of dance and music concerts) and Midsummer Night Swing (ballroom dancing under the stars) lure those who love parks and culture. For details on seasons, tickets and programming – which runs the gamut from opera to dance to theater to ballet – see p243.

Tours

Daily tours of the complex explore the Metropolitan Opera House, Revson Fountain and Alice Tully Hall and are a great way to get acquainted with the complex.

SIGHTS

The stretch of Manhattan that lies to the west of Central Park was once a lively mix of African American, Latino and German Jewish immigrant communities. These days it's still holding on to its Jewish bonafides (this is where you'll find some of the best smoked fish in town), but in recent decades the neighborhood has also been a base for well-to-do artsy types, young professionals and the stroller set. While real estate developers have seen fit to carpet long stretches of Broadway with charmless chain stores, the rest of the neighborhood is an architectural bonanza, featuring residential dwellings built in beaux arts, baroque, neo-Gothic and postwar styles. You'll find some of the poshest pads lining Central Park West, among them the Dakota (on the northwest corner of 72nd St), where John Lennon once lived.

CENTRAL PARK — PARK

See p230.

LINCOLN CENTER — CULTURAL CENTER

See p234.

NICHOLAS ROERICH MUSEUM — MUSEUM

Map p434 (www.roerich.org; 319 W 107th St, btwn Riverside Dr & Broadway; suggested donation $5; ⏲noon-5pm Tue-Fri, 2-5pm Sat & Sun; [S]1 to Cathedral Pkwy) While the collection includes early modern figure paintings and religious scenes (the latter of which are quite forgettable), his mountainscapes are truly a wonder to behold: icy Tibetan peaks in shades of blue, white, green and purple, channeling a Georgia O'Keeffe/Rockwell Kent vibe. This is a curious and intriguing place. Check the calendar for periodic classical concerts – always free.

NEW-YORK HISTORICAL SOCIETY — MUSEUM

Map p434 (www.nyhistory.org; 2 W 77th St at Central Park West; adult/child $18/6, by donation 6-8pm Fri, library free; ⏲10am-6pm Tue-Thu & Sat, to 8pm Fri, 11am-5pm Sun; [S]B, C to 81st St-Museum of Natural History) As the antiquated hyphenated name implies, the Historical Society is the city's oldest museum, founded in 1804 to preserve the city's historical and cultural artifacts. Its collection of more than 60,000 objects is quirky and fascinating and includes everything from George Washington's inauguration chair to a 19th-century Tiffany ice cream dish (gilded, of course).

Other treasures include a leg brace worn by President Franklin D Roosevelt, a 19th-century mechanical bank in which a political figure slips coins into his pocket and photographer Jack Stewart's graffiti-covered door from the 1970s (featuring tags by known graffiti writers such as Tracy 168). In the lobby, be sure to look up: the ceiling mural from Keith Haring's 1986 'Pop Shop' hangs above the admissions desk.

ZABAR'S — MARKET

Map p434 (www.zabars.com; 2245 Broadway, at 80th St; ⏲8am-7:30pm Mon-Fri, to 8pm Sat, 9am-6pm Sun; [S]1 to 79th St) A bastion of gourmet Kosher foodie-ism, this sprawling local market has been a neighborhood fixture since the 1930s. And what a fixture it is: featuring a heavenly array of cheeses, meats, olives, caviar, smoked fish, pickles, dried fruits, nuts and baked goods, including pillowy fresh-out-of-the-oven knishes (Eastern European–style potato dumplings wrapped in dough). Street vendors sell knishes all over New York. Most are of the frozen-industrial variety and have all the flavor of freeze-dried hockey pucks. Zabar's is the place to try the real deal.

AMERICAN FOLK ART MUSEUM — MUSEUM

Map p434 (www.folkartmuseum.org; 2 Lincoln Sq, Columbus Ave, at 66th St; ⏲noon-7:30pm Tue-Sat, to 6pm Sun; [S]1 to 66th St-Lincoln Center) [FREE] This tiny institution contains a couple of centuries' worth of folk and outsider art treasures, including pieces by Henry Darger (known for his girl-filled battle-scapes) and Martín Ramírez (producer of hallucinatory *caballeros* – knights – on horseback). There is also an array of wood carvings, paintings, hand-tinted photographs and decorative objects. On Wednesday there are guitar concerts, and there's free music on Friday.

RIVERSIDE PARK — OUTDOORS

Map p434 (☎212-870-3070; www.riversideparknyc.org; Riverside Dr, btwn 68th & 155th Sts; ⏲6am-1am; 👪; [S]1/2/3 to any stop btwn 66th & 157th Sts) A classic beauty designed by Central Park creators Frederick Law Olmsted and Calvert Vaux, this waterside spot, running north on the Upper West Side and banked by the Hudson River from 59th to

158th Sts, is lusciously leafy. Plenty of bike paths and playgrounds make it a family favorite.

From late March through October (weather permitting), a lively waterside restaurant, the **West 79th Street Boat Basin Café** (Map p434; ☎212-496-5542; www.boatbasincafe.com; W 79th St, at Henry Hudson Parkway; mains $11-19; ⊙lunch & dinner Apr-Oct, weather permitting; ⓢ1 to 79th St) serves a light menu at the level of 79th St. Two other outdoor cafes in the riverfront in the park include the **Hudson Beach Café** (Map p434; www.hudsonbeachcafe.com; 105th St & Riverside Dr; mains around $14) and the **Pier i Café** (Map p434; ☎212-362-4450; www.piericafe.com; W 70th St & Riverside Blvd; mains $11-20; ⊙lunch & dinner; ⓘ; underground rail 1, 2, 3 to 72nd St).

CHILDREN'S MUSEUM
OF MANHATTAN
MUSEUM

Map p434 (www.cmom.org; 212 W 83rd St, btwn Amsterdam Ave & Broadway; admission $11; ⊙10am-5pm Tue-Fri & Sun, to 7pm Sat; ⓘ; ⓢB, C to 81st St-Museum of Natural History; 1 to 86th St) This small museum features interactive exhibits scaled down for the little ones. This includes toddler discovery programs

and exhibits that stimulate play, like operating a giant heart with a pedal or tumbling around a set with *Dora the Explorer* elements. It's not very exciting, but it can be a rainy-day saver if you're traveling with antsy toddlers.

 EATING

Though not known for its dining scene, this huge swath of neighborhood nonetheless manages to serve up everything from chewy bagels to fancy French cassoulets to the latest in New American cooking. It is also the best place for off-the-hook picnic fixings: head to Zabar's (p235) or Whole Foods (Map p430; Time Warner Center, 10 Columbus Circle; ⊙7:30am-11pm) in the basement of the Time Warner Center to pick up delicacies for an alfresco meal in Central Park.

LE PAIN QUOTIDIEN
SANDWICHES **$**

Map p434 (www.lepainquotidien.com; Mineral Springs Pavilion, off West Dr, Central Park; mains $10-16; ⊙7am-9pm; ✏ⓘ; underground rail B, C

⊙ TOP SIGHT
AMERICAN MUSEUM OF NATURAL HISTORY

Founded in 1869, this classic museum contains some 30 million artifacts, with its cutting-edge planetarium. From October through May, the museum is home to the Butterfly Conservatory, featuring 500-plus butterflies from around the globe. On the natural history side, the museum is perhaps best known for its Fossil Halls, containing nearly 600 specimens on view, including the skeletons of a massive mammoth and a fearsome Tyrannosaurus Rex.

There are plentiful animal exhibits, galleries devoted to gems, and an IMAX theater that plays films on natural phenomena. The Milstein Hall of Ocean Life contains dioramas devoted to ecologies, weather and conservation, as well as a beloved 94ft replica of a blue whale. At the 77th St Lobby Gallery, visitors are greeted by a 63ft canoe carved by the Haida people of British Columbia in the middle of the 19th century.

For the space set, the Rose Center For Earth & Space is the star of the show. With its mesmerizing glass box facade, home to space-show theaters and the planetarium. Every half-hour between 10:30am and 4:30pm, you can drop yourself into a cushy seat to view Dark Universe, which explores the mysteries and wonders of the cosmos.

The museum is a hit with kids and as a result it's swamped on weekends. Aim to go early on a weekday.

DON'T MISS...

➡ Tyrannosaurus Rex
➡ Milstein Hall of Ocean Life
➡ Big Bang Theater

PRACTICALITIES

➡ Map p434
➡ www.amnh.org
➡ Central Park West, at 79th St
➡ Suggested donation adult/child $22/12.50
➡ ⊙10am-5:45pm, Rose Center to 8:45pm Fri, Butterfly Conservacy Oct-May
➡ ⓢB, C to 81st St-Museum of Natural History, 1 to 79th St

to 72nd St) Fresh salads and tartines (open-faced sandwiches) are to be found inside the airy Mineral Springs Pavilion, or outside if you are lucky enough to snag a terrace seat. Other Le Pain treats include beautiful berry tarts, draft beer and big cups (bowls, really) of café au lait (plus free wi-fi). You can also hit the take-out window and have a picnic on Sheep Meadow, just a few steps away.

GRAY'S PAPAYA HOT DOGS $

Map p434 (☎212-799-0243; 2090 Broadway, at 72nd St, entrance on Amsterdam Ave; hot dog $2; ⏲24hr; [S]A/B/C, 1/2/3 to 72nd St) It doesn't get more New York than bellying up to this classic stand-up joint in the wake of a beer bender. The lights are bright, the color palette is 1970s and the hot dogs are unpretentiously good.

Granted, the papaya drink is more 'drink' than papaya, but you can't go wrong with Gray's famous (and long-running) 'Recession Special' – $4.95 for two grilled dogs and a beverage. Deal.

SHAKE SHACK BURGERS $

Map p434 (www.shakeshacknyc.com; 366 Columbus Ave, btwn 77th & 78th Sts; burgers $4-9, shakes $5-7; ⏲10:45am-11pm; 👪; [S]B, C, 1/2/3 to 72nd St) To the delight of moms, pops and kids all over the Upper West Side, organic eats guru Danny Meyer brought the Shake Shack to their 'hood. The 100% all-natural Angus beef burgers are hard to top, especially when paired with crispy curly fries and a rich, creamy milkshake – although there's also draft beer and wines by the glass or bottle. The portobello 'shroom burger is no less satisfying.

MOMOFUKU MILK BAR ASIAN $

Map p434 (www.momofuku.com; 561 Columbus Ave, btwn 87th & 88th Sts; pork buns $8; ⏲9am-11pm; [S]A/C, B to 86th St) Two words: pork buns. And not just any pork buns, but David Chang's slow-braised-pork-on-a-puffy-steamed-bun concoction, which will make you wish that pork was a major food group. There are also plenty of diabetes-inducing baked goods, including chewy-delicious cornflake-marshmallow cookies designed to rip out your fillings.

HUMMUS PLACE MIDDLE EASTERN $

Map p434 (www.hummusplace.com; 305 Amsterdam Ave, btwn 74th & 75th Sts; hummus from $8, mains $8-13; ⏲lunch & dinner; 🌿; [S]1/2/3 to 72nd St) Hummus Place is nothing special in the way of ambience – about eight tables tucked just below street level, fronting a cramped, open kitchen – but it's got amazing hummus platters. They're served warm and with various toppings, from whole chickpeas to fava-bean stew with chopped egg. You'll also find tasty salads, couscous and stuffed grape leaves. Great value.

FAIRWAY SELF-CATERING $

Map p434 (www.fairwaymarket.com/store-upper-west-side; 2127 Broadway, at 75th St; ⏲6am-1am; [S]1/2/3 to 72nd St) Like a museum of good eats, this incredible grocery spills its lovely mounds of produce into its sidewalk bins, seducing you inside with international goodies, fine cooking oils, nuts, cheeses, prepared foods and, upstairs, an organic market and cafe (look for the stairs near the check-out).

KEFI GREEK $$

Map p434 (www.kefirestaurant.com; 505 Columbus Ave, btwn 84th & 85th Sts; small sharing plates $7-10, mains $13-20; ⏲lunch & dinner daily, brunch Sat & Sun; 👪; [S]B, C to 86th St) This homey, whitewashed eatery run by chef Michael Psilakis channels a sleek taverna vibe while dispensing excellent rustic Greek dishes. Expect favorites like spicy lamb sausage, sheep-milk dumplings and grilled octopus. The platter featuring four types of spreads is delicious, as is the flat pasta with braised rabbit. The wine list features a comprehensive selection of Greek vintages (from $24 per bottle).

JACOB'S PICKLES AMERICAN $$

Map p434 (☎212-470-5566; 509 Amsterdam Ave, btwn 84th & 85th; mains $14-21; ⏲11am-2am Mon-Thu, to 4am Fri, 9am-4am Sat, to 2am Sun) Jacob's elevates the humble pickle to exalted status at this inviting and warmly lit eatery on a restaurant-lined stretch of Amsterdam Ave. Aside from briny cukes and other preserves, you'll find heaping portions of upscale comfort food, such as catfish tacos, wine-braised turkey leg dinner, and mushroom mac and cheese. The biscuits are top notch. The two dozen or so craft beers on tap showcase unique brews from New York, Maine and beyond.

BARNEY GREENGRASS DELI $$

Map p434 (www.barneygreengrass.com; 541 Amsterdam Ave, at 86th St; mains $9-20, bagel with cream cheese $5; ⏲8:30am-6pm Tue-Sun; 👪; [S]1 to 86th St) The self-proclaimed 'King of

Sturgeon' Barney Greengrass serves up the same heaping dishes of eggs and salty lox, luxuriant caviar, and melt-in-your-mouth chocolate babkas (sweet yeast cake) that first made it famous when it opened a century ago. Pop in to fuel up in the morning or for a quick lunch; there are rickety tables set amid the crowded produce aisles.

In addition to an array of Jewish delicacies (seriously, try the smoked sturgeon), you can, of course, get a perfect New York bagel. On weekends, it has fresh garlic bialys (a type of chewy, baked roll).

FIVE NAPKIN BURGER BISTRO **$$**

Map p434 (☎212-333-4488; 2315 Broadway, at 84th St; mains $14-16; ⏰11.30am-midnight; underground rail 1, 2, 3 to 86th St) This inviting spot always draws a crowd, with its juicy burgers and vaguely upmarket brasserie setting – comfy leather booths, big glass windows and outdoor seating in warm weather. The signature burger is 10 ounces of meat smothered with Gruyère, caramelized onions and aioli sauce, and served with hand-cut fries, but there are loads of other options: fish tacos, goat's cheese and beet salads, and even sushi. Good beer and wine selections.

PEACEFOOD CAFE VEGAN **$$**

Map p434 (☎212-362-2266; www.peacefood-cafe.com; 460 Amsterdam Ave, at 82nd St; paninis $12-13, mains $10-17; ⏰lunch & dinner; 🌿; [S]1 to 79th St) This bright and airy vegan haven run by Eric Yu dishes up a popular fried *seitan* (wheat gluten) panino (served on homemade focaccia and topped with cashew, arugula, tomatoes and pesto), as well as pizzas, roasted vegetable plates and an excellent quinoa salad. There are daily raw specials, organic coffees and delectable bakery selections. Healthy and good.

BURKE & WILLS MODERN AUSTRALIAN **$$**

Map p434 (☎646-823-9251; 226 W 79th St, btwn Broadway & Amsterdam Ave; mains $17-28; ⏰4pm-2am Mon-Fri, from noon Sat & Sun; [S]1 to 79th St) New in 2013, this ruggedly attractive bistro and bar brings a touch of the outback to the Upper West Side. The menu leans toward Modern Australian pub grub: juicy kangaroo burgers with triple-fried chips, grilled prawns, kale cobb salad, merguez sausage sliders, and roasted cod with cauliflower, dates and pomegranate.

Vintage framed artwork on the walls pays tribute to Oz, in particular those ill-fated European explorers (who died in the outback) for whom the restaurant is named. After the meal, head upstairs and sink into a Chesterfield while nursing a cocktail at the Manhattan Cricket Club.

SALUMERIA ROSI PARMACOTTO ITALIAN **$$**

Map p434 (☎212-877-4801; www.salumeriarosi.com; 284 Amsterdam Ave, at 73rd St; mains $12-17; ⏰11am-11pm; [S]1/2/3 to 72nd St) This is an intimate little meat-loving nook where you can dip into tasting plates that feature cheeses, salumi, slow-roasted pork loin, sausages, cured hams and every other piece of the pig you care to imagine. There are other tasty Tuscan-inspired offerings, too, including homemade lasagna, savory leek tart, escarole-anchovy salad and hand-rolled ricotta and goat's cheese gnocchi.

PJ CLARKE'S PUB **$$**

Map p434 (☎212-957-9700; www.pjclarkes.com; 44 W 63rd St, cnr Broadway; burgers $10-14, mains $18-42; ⏰11:30am-1am; [S]1 to 66th St-Lincoln Center) Right across the street from Lincoln Center, this red-checker-tablecloth spot has a buttoned down crowd, friendly bartenders and solid eats. If you're in a rush, belly up to the bar for a Black Angus burger and a Brooklyn Lager. A raw bar offers fresh Long Island Little Neck and Cherry Stone clams, as well as jumbo shrimp cocktails.

GASTRONOMÍA CULINARIA ITALIAN **$$**

Map p434 (☎212-663-1040; 53 W 106th St, btwn Columbus & Manhattan Aves; mains $14-23; ⏰11:30am-10pm Sun-Thu, to 11pm Fri & Sat; [S]B, C, 1 to 103rd St) For locals, this tongue-twister of a restaurant is more often known as 'that great Italian restaurant on 106th St'. Run by a Roman chef, GC feels like a charming old-world trattoria, its narrow brick-walled dining room the backdrop to richly prepared dishes at reasonable prices. Top selections: Tuscan kale salad with anchovies and pecorino, crispy Jewish-style artichokes, pappardelle with lamb ragu and thin-crust pizza covered in mozarella and San Daniele prosciutto. There's a small but original wine list, with equally fair prices. Overall, a great-value option.

LOEB BOATHOUSE AMERICAN **$$$**

Map p434 (☎212-517-2233; www.thecentralpark-boathouse.com; Central Park Lake, Central Park, at 74th St; mains $24-47; ⏰lunch daily & brunch

Sat & Sun year-round, dinner daily Apr-Nov; [S]A/C, B to 72nd St, 6 to 77th St) Perched on the northeastern tip of the Central Park Lake, the Loeb Boathouse, with its views of the Midtown skyline in the distance, provides one of New York's most idyllic spots for a meal. That said, what you're paying for is the setting. While the food is generally good (the crab cakes are the standout), we've often found the service to be indifferent.

If you want to experience the location without having to lay out the bucks, a better bet is to hit the adjacent Bar & Grill (plates $16), where you can still get crab cakes and excellent views.

CAFÉ LUXEMBOURG FRENCH **$$$**

Map p434 (☎212-873-7411; www.cafeluxembourg.com; 200 W 70th St, btwn Broadway & West End Ave; lunch mains $18-29, dinner mains $25-36; ⌚breakfast, lunch & dinner daily, brunch Sun; [S]1/2/3 to 72nd St) This quintessential French bistro is generally crowded with locals – and it's no mystery why: the setting is elegant, the staff friendly, and there's an outstanding menu to boot. The classics – salmon tartare, cassoulet and steak *frites* (fries) – are all deftly executed, and its proximity to Lincoln Center makes it a perfect pre-performance destination. There is a lighter lunch menu and decadent brunch offerings (try the lobster Benedict).

DOVETAIL MODERN AMERICAN **$$$**

Map p434 (☎212-362-3800; www.dovetailnyc.com; 103 W 77th St, cnr Columbus Ave; tasting menu $88, mains $36-58; ⌚5:30-10pm Mon-Sat, 11:30am-10pm Sun; 🍴; [S]A/C, B to 81st St-Museum of Natural History, 1 to 79th St) This Michelin-starred restaurant showcases its Zenlike beauty in both its decor (exposed brick, bare tables) and its delectable seasonal menus. Think: striped bass with sunchokes and burgundy truffle, and venison with bacon, golden beets and foraged greens. On Mondays, chef John Fraser has a four-course vegetarian tasting menu ($58) that is winning over carnivores with dishes like plump hen of the woods mushrooms with d'anjou pears and green peppercorns.

An encyclopedic wine list (from around $40 per bottle) features top vintages from all over the world, with charming anecdotes about some of the vineyards.

DRINKING & NIGHTLIFE

A noted family neighborhood, the Upper West Side isn't exactly the number one destination for hardcore drinkers. But it has its moments, with some good dives, pubs and wine bars.

BARCIBO ENOTECA WINE BAR

Map p434 (www.barciboenoteca.com; 2020 Broadway, cnr 69th St; ⌚4:30pm-12:30am Mon-Fri, from 3:30pm Sat & Sun; [S]1/2/3 to 72nd St) Just north of Lincoln Center, this casual chic marble-table spot is ideal for sipping, with a long list of vintages from all over Italy, including 40 different varieties sold by the glass. There is a short menu of small plates and light meals. The staff is knowledgeable; ask for recommendations.

DEAD POET BAR

Map p434 (www.thedeadpoet.com; 450 Amsterdam Ave, btwn 81st & 82nd Sts; ⌚noon-4am; [S]1 to 79th St) This skinny, mahogany-paneled pub has been a neighborhood favorite for over a decade, with a mix of locals and students nursing pints of Guinness. There are cocktails named after dead poets, including a Jack Kerouac margarita ($12) and a Pablo Neruda spiced rum sangria ($9).

DING DONG LOUNGE BAR

Map p434 (www.dingdonglounge.com; 929 Columbus Ave, btwn 105th & 106th Sts; ⌚4pm-4am; [S]B, C, 1 to 103rd St) It's hard to be too badass in the Upper West, but this former crack den turned punk bar makes a wholesome attempt by supplying graffiti-covered bathrooms to go with its exposed-brick walls. It also, interestingly, features an array of cuckoo clocks. It's popular with Columbia students and guests from nearby hostels for its can-of-beer-and-a-shot combo (only $7).

PROHIBITION BAR

Map p434 (☎212-579-3100; www.prohibition.net; 503 Columbus Ave, near W 84th St; ⌚5pm-4am; [S]B, C, 1 to 86th St) This buzzing drinking den features a live band almost every night up front, but decibel levels are low enough that your ears won't bleed. Those who want to talk can head into the back, which is band-free, and for those who prefer sports, there's a billiard table. Sexy red walls and refreshing drinks (passion fruit mojitos, agave nectar margaritas) add a little flair, and the bite-sized burgers are a perfect bar snack.

RYAN D. BUDHU / GETTY IMAGES ©

SYLVAIN SONNET / GETTY IMAGES ©

3

MEDIOIMAGES/PHOTODISC / GETTY IMAGES ©

1. Strawberry Fields (p230)

Remember former Beatle John Lennon at the tiled mosaic in this memorial garden.

2. Upper West Side

Explore streets lined with dwellings built in the beaux arts, baroque, neo-Gothic and postwar styles.

3. Belvedere Castle (p246)

Take in the views over some of Central Park's most famous landmarks, including the Turtle Pond, from Belvedere Castle.

4. American Museum of Natural History (p236)

Visit a 94ft replica of a blue whale, which is just one of the 30 million artifacts on display.

MANHATTAN CRICKET CLUB COCKTAIL BAR

Map p434 (226 W 79th St, btwn Amsterdam Ave & Broadway; 🕐7pm-2am Tue-Sat; [S]1 to 79th St) Above the Aussie bistro Burke & Wills (p238), this elegant drinking lounge is modeled on the classy Anglo-Aussie cricket clubs of the early 1900s. Sepia-toned photos of batsmen and bowlers in action adorn the gold brocaded walls, while a mahogany-lined wall of books, Chesterfield sofas and an elaborate tin ceiling all create a fine setting for quaffing well-made but pricey cocktails (at $18 each).

☆ ENTERTAINMENT

☆ Lincoln Center

This vast cultural complex is the epicenter of high art in Manhattan. In addition to the venues and companies listed below, the Vivian Beaumont Theater and the Mitzi E Newhouse Theater showcase works of drama and musical theater. Both of these have programming information listed on Lincoln Center's main website at http://lc.lincolncenter.org.

METROPOLITAN OPERA HOUSE OPERA

Map p434 (www.metopera.org; Lincoln Center, 64th St, at Columbus Ave; [S]1 to 66th St-Lincoln Center) New York's premier opera company, the Metropolitan Opera is the place to see classics such as *Carmen*, *Madame Butterfly* and *Macbeth*, not to mention Wagner's *Ring Cycle*. The Opera also hosts premieres and revivals of more contemporary works, such as Peter Sellars' *Nixon in China*, which played here in 2011. The season runs from September to April.

Ticket prices start at $30 and can get close to $500. Note that the box seats can be a bargain, but unless you're in boxes right over the stage, the views are dreadful. Seeing the stage requires sitting with your head cocked over a handrail – a literal pain in the neck.

For last-minute ticket-buyers there are other deals. You can get bargain-priced standing-room tickets ($17 to $25) starting at 10am on the day of the performance. (You won't see much, but you'll hear everything.) Two hours before shows on Monday through Thursday, 200 rush tickets are put on sale for starving artist types – just $20 for an orchestra seat (excluding galas and opening nights)! Line up early.

And don't miss the gift shop, which is chock full of operatic bric-a-brac, including Met curtain cufflinks and Rhinemaidens soap. (Seriously.)

RICHARD I'ANSON / GETTY IMAGES ©

Lincoln Center

LOCAL KNOWLEDGE

NYC'S BEST SPOTS FOR LIVE MUSIC

A jazz and pop music critic who writes for *JazzTimes* and the *New York Times*, Nate Chinen covers the music scene in New York City and beyond. (He's @natechinen on Twitter.) He gives us a list of his favorite music venues.

Village Vanguard (p153) The Vanguard is run by Lorraine Gordon, an authentic New York character with a real take-no-nonsense attitude. It's the oldest jazz club in the city, and it's sort of bare bones but the acoustics are perfect and the vibe is terrific. This is my favorite room for music in the world.

Jazz Standard (Map p426; ☎212-576-2232; www.jazzstandard.net; 116 E 27th St, btwn Lexington & Park Aves; [S]6 to 28th St) One of the city's other great jazz clubs is the Jazz Standard in Midtown. The service is impeccable. The food is great. There's no minimum and it's programmed by Seth Abramson, a guy who really knows his stuff.

Bowery Ballroom (p125) For rock and pop, this is my favorite space. The Bowery Ballroom is a room with history (it was built in the 1920s), and it has really good sound and strong bookings. This is where bigger acts will sometimes do their small shows.

Brooklyn Bowl (p293) Brooklyn Bowl is kind of a weird venue because people are also bowling, but it's where you'll find plenty of groovier gigs, including jam bands. Questlove, the drummer for The Roots, DJs every Thursday night.

Joe's Pub (Map p410; ☎212-539-8778; www.joespub.com; Public Theater, 425 Lafayette St, btwn Astor Pl & 4th St; [S]R/W to 8th St-NYU, 6 to Astor Pl) The room here feels cozy and elegant. Joe's Pub in NoHo has a high concentration of tongue-in-cheek cabaret, and the sensibility is pretty young. (It's attached to the Public Theater, located in Noho, so there's a performance aspect to it a lot of the time.)

Beacon Theatre (p244) The Beacon generally skews to classic rock. But it's a great concert hall, and the renovation was spectacular. It's like a mini–Radio City Music Hall: it doesn't swallow the artist.

FILM SOCIETY OF LINCOLN CENTER CINEMA

(☎212-875-5456; www.filmlinc.com; [S]1 to 66th St-Lincoln Center) The Film Society is one of New York's cinematic gems, providing an invaluable platform for a wide gamut of documentary, feature, independent, foreign and avant-garde art pictures. Films screen in one of two facilities at Lincoln Center: the new **Elinor Bunin Munroe Film Center** (Map p434; ☎212-875-5601, film schedule 212-875-5600; www.filmlinc.com; Lincoln Center, 144 W 65th St; [S]1 to 66 St-Lincoln Center), a more intimate, experimental venue, or the **Walter Reade Theater** (Map p434; ☎212-875-5600; www.filmlinc.com; Lincoln Center, 165 W 65th St; [S]1 to 66th St-Lincoln Center), with wonderfully wide, screening room–style seats.

Every September, both venues host the New York Film Festival, featuring plenty of New York and world premieres. In March, you'll find the New Directors/New Films series on view. For cinephiles, it's highly recommended.

NEW YORK PHILHARMONIC CLASSICAL MUSIC

Map p434 (www.nyphil.org; Avery Fisher Hall, Lincoln Center, cnr Columbus Ave & 65th St; [♿]; [S]1 to 66 St-Lincoln Center) The oldest professional orchestra in the US (dating back to 1842) holds its season every year at Avery Fisher Hall. Directed by Alan Gilbert, the son of two Philharmonic musicians, the orchestra plays a mix of classics (Tchaikovsky, Mahler, Haydn) and contemporary works, as well as concerts geared towards children.

Tickets run in the $35 to $125 range. If you're on a budget, check out its open rehearsals on Thursdays during the day (at the discretion of the conductor) for only $20. In addition, students with a valid school ID can pick up rush tickets for $13.50 up to 10 days before an event.

NEW YORK CITY BALLET DANCE

Map p434 (☎212-496-0600; www.nycballet.com; David H Koch Theater, Lincoln Center, Columbus Ave, at 62nd St; [♿]; [S]1 to 66th St-Lincoln Center) This prestigious company was first directed by renowned Russian-born choreographer George Balanchine back in the 1940s. Today, the company has 90 dancers and is the largest ballet organization in the US, performing 23 weeks a year at Lincoln Center's David H Koch Theater. During the holidays the troop is best known for its annual production of *The Nutcracker*.

Depending on the ballet, ticket prices can range from $29 to $159. Student rush tickets (valid high school or university ID required) are posted on Mondays and cost $20. Fourth-ring seats are often a deal, but the views can be lousy.

AMERICAN BALLET THEATRE DANCE

Map p434 (☎212-477-3030; www.abt.org; Lincoln Center, 64th St, at Columbus Ave; [S]1 to 66th St-Lincoln Center) This seven-decades-old traveling company presents a classic selection of ballets at the Metropolitan Opera House every spring (generally in May). Tickets are by subscription only. The Orchestra, Parterre and Grand Tier sections offer the best views. Avoid the top tier or all you'll see is the dancers' heads. Box seats towards the rear have highly obscured views.

☆ Upper West Side

Outside of Lincoln Center, there are numerous other venues in the Upper West Side that cater to the cultured set.

SUMMER HAPPENINGS IN CENTRAL PARK

During the warm months, the park is home to countless cultural events, many of which are free. The two most popular are: Shakespeare in the Park (p28), which is managed by the Public Theater, and **SummerStage** (www.summerstage.org), a series of free concerts.

Shakespeare tickets are given out at 1pm on the day of the performance, but if you want to lay your hands on a seat, line up by 8am and make sure you have something to sit on and your entire group with you. Tickets are free and one per person; no latecomers are allowed in line.

SummerStage concert venues are generally opened to the public 1½ hours prior to the start of the show. But if it's a popular act, start queuing up early or you're not getting in.

BEACON THEATRE LIVE MUSIC

Map p434 (www.beacontheatre.com; 2124 Broadway, btwn 74th & 75th Sts; [S]1/2/3 to 72nd St) This historic theater from 1929 is a perfect in-between-size venue, with 2600 seats (not a terrible one in the house) and a constant flow of popular acts, from Nick Cave to the Allman Brothers. A $15 million restoration in 2009 has left the gilded interiors – a mix of Greek, Roman, Renaissance and rococo design elements – totally sparkling.

CLEOPATRA'S NEEDLE CLUB

Map p434 (www.cleopatrasneedleny.com; 2485 Broadway, btwn 92nd & 93rd Sts; 🕐4pm-late; [S]1/2/3 to 96th St) Named after an Egyptian obelisk that resides in Central Park, this venue is small and narrow like its namesake. There's no cover, but there's a $10 minimum spend. Come early and you can enjoy happy hour (3:30pm to 6pm or 7pm), when select cocktails are half-price. But be prepared to stay late: Cleopatra's is famous for all-night jam sessions that hit their peak around 4am.

SMOKE JAZZ

Map p434 (www.smokejazz.com; 2751 Broadway, btwn 105th & 106th Sts; 🕐5:30pm-3am Mon-Fri, 11am-3am Sat & Sun; [S]1 to 103rd St) This swank but laid-back lounge – with good stage views from plush sofas – brings out old-timers and local faves, such as George Coleman and Wynton Marsalis. Most nights there's a $10 cover, plus a $20 to $30 food and drink minimum. Smoke is smoke-free but then again so is the rest of NYC. Purchase tickets online for weekend shows.

MERKIN CONCERT HALL CLASSICAL MUSIC

Map p434 (www.kaufman-center.org/mch; 129 W 67th St, btwn Amsterdam Ave & Broadway; [S]1 to 66th St-Lincoln Center) Just north of Lincoln Center, this 450-seater hall, part of the Kaufman Center, is one of the city's more intimate venues for classical music, as well as jazz, world music and pop. The hall hosts Tuesday matinees (a deal at $18) that highlight emerging classical solo artists. Every January, it is home to the New York Guitar Festival.

SYMPHONY SPACE LIVE MUSIC

Map p434 (☎212-864-5400; www.symphonyspace.org; 2537 Broadway, btwn 94th & 95th Sts; 👪; [S]1/2/3 to 96th St) Symphony Space is a multidisciplinary gem supported by the local community. It often hosts three-day series that are dedicated to one musician, and has an affinity for world music, theater, film, dance and literature (with appearances by acclaimed writers).

🛍 SHOPPING

The Upper West Side is chain store central, so local flavor can be hard to find. That said, there are some good shopping stops.

GREENFLEA MARKET

Map p434 (☎212-239-3025; www.greenfleamarkets.com; Columbus Ave, btwn 76th & 77th Sts; ⏰10am-5:30pm Sun; [S]B, C to 81st St-Museum of Natural History, 1 to 79th St) One of the oldest open-air shopping spots in the city, this friendly, well-stocked flea market is a perfect activity for a lazy Upper West Side Sunday morning. You'll find a little bit of everything here, including vintage and contemporary furnishings, antique maps, custom eyewear, hand-woven scarves, handmade jewelry and so much more. The market is also open on occasional Saturdays in warm months; call ahead to check.

WESTSIDER BOOKS BOOKS

Map p434 (www.westsiderbooks.com; 2246 Broadway, btwn 80th & 81st Sts; ⏰10am-10pm; [S]1 to 79th St) This great little shop is packed to the gills with rare and used books, including a good selection of fiction and illustrated tomes. There are first editions and there's a smattering of vintage vinyl.

WESTSIDER RECORDS MUSIC

Map p434 (☎212-874-1588; www.westsiderbooks.com/recordstore.html; 233 W 72nd St, btwn Broadway & West End Ave; ⏰11am-7pm Mon-Thu, to 9pm Fri & Sat, noon-6pm Sun; [S]1/2/3 to 72nd St) Featuring more than 30,000 LPs, this shop has got you covered when it comes to everything from funk to jazz to classical (plus spoken word, film soundtracks and other curiosities). A good place to lose all track of time.

CENTURY 21 DEPARTMENT STORE

Map p434 (www.c21stores.com; 1972 Broadway, btwn 66th & 67th Sts; ⏰10am-10pm Mon-Sat, 11am-8pm Sun; [S]1 to 66th St-Lincoln Center) Exceedingly popular with fashionable locals and foreign travelers, the Century 21 chain is a bounty of season-old brand name and designer brands sold at steeply discounted prices. Featuring everything from Missoni to Marc Jacobs, prices may sometimes seem high, but compared to retail, they're a steal.

COMPTOIR DES COTONNIERS WOMEN'S CLOTHING

Map p434 (184 Columbus Ave, btwn 68th & 69th Sts; ⏰11am-8pm Mon-Fri, from 10am Sat, noon-7pm Sun) This French chain brought a much-needed dose of style to the 'hood when it opened way back in 2010. Not unlike Parisian women, the apparel here aims for timeless, effortless style – nicely tailored cardigans, skirts, blouses and dresses that will never go out of fashion.

HARRY'S SHOES SHOES

Map p434 (www.harrys-shoes.com; 2299 Broadway, at 83rd St; ⏰10am-6:45pm Tue, Wed, Fri & Sat, to 7:45pm Mon & Thu, 11am-6pm Sun; [S]1 to 86th St) Around since the 1930s, Harry's is a classic. It's staffed by gentlemen who measure your foot in an old-school metal contraption and then wait on you patiently, making sure the shoe fits. If your feet are killing you from all the walking, you'll find lots of sturdy, comfortable brands (Merrel, Dansko, Birkenstock).

TIME FOR CHILDREN TOYS

Map p434 (☎212-580-8202; www.atimeforchildren.org; 506 Amsterdam Ave, btwn 84th & 85th Sts; ⏰10am-7pm Mon-Sat, 11am-6pm Sun; 👪; [S]1 to 86th St) This small store sells adorable clothes for babies and toddlers, colorful books and plush toys, block sets, handmade cards and other treasures for the under-6 set. Bonus: feel good about your purchase. Time donates 100% of its profits to the Children's Aid Society of New York. If you can't find what you're looking for, you'll find a bigger, and also locally owned toy shop just a few doors down at **West Side Kids** (Map p434; 498 Amsterdam Ave).

🏃 SPORTS & ACTIVITIES

LOEB BOATHOUSE KAYAKING, CYCLING

Map p434 (☎212-517-2233; www.thecentralparkboathouse.com; Central Park, btwn 74th & 75th Sts; boating per hr $12, bike rentals per hr $9-15;

🕒10am-dusk Apr-Nov; 👪; [S]B, C to 72nd St, 6 to 77th St) Central Park's boathouse has a fleet of 100 rowboats plus three kayaks available for rent from April to November. In the summer, there is also a Venetian-style gondola that seats up to six (per 30 minutes $30). Bicycles are also available from April to November. Rentals require an ID and credit card and are weather permitting. Helmets included.

BIKE AND ROLL CYCLING

Map p434 (www.bikeandroll.com/newyork; Columbus Circle, at Central Park West; from per hr/day $14/44; 🕒9am-7pm Mar-May, 8am-8pm Jun-Aug, 10am-4pm Sep-Nov; 👪; [S]A/C, B/D, 1/2 to 59th St-Columbus Circle) At the southwestern entrance to the park, a small pop-up kiosk dispenses beach cruisers and 10-speeds for rides around Central Park. It also has child seats and tandem bikes.

CHAMPION BICYCLES INC CYCLING

Map p434 (☎212-662-2690; www.championbicycles.com; 896 Amsterdam Ave, at 104th St; rentals per hr/24hr from $7/40; 🕒10am-7pm Mon-Fri, to 6pm Sat & Sun; [S]1 to 103rd St) This places stocks a variety of bikes for rent and has free copies of the helpful **NYC Cycling Map** (www.nyc.gov/bikes), which details several hundred miles of bike lanes around New York City.

TOGA BIKE SHOP CYCLING

Map p434 (www.togabikes.com; 110 West End Ave, btwn 64th & 65th Sts; rentals per 24hr $35-75; 🕒11am-7pm Mon-Fri, 10am-6pm Sat, 11am-6pm Sun; [S]1 to 66th St-Lincoln Center) This friendly and long-standing bike shop is conveniently located between Central Park and the Hudson River bike path. Rental prices include a helmet.

FIVE BOROUGH BICYCLE CLUB CYCLING

(www.5bbc.org) For a $25 annual fee, you can participate in this local club's myriad day rides as well as long-haul rides. Check the website for details of upcoming rides and meeting locations.

CHARLES A DANA DISCOVERY CENTER FISHING

Map p434 (www.centralparknyc.org; Central Park at 110th St, btwn Fifth & Lenox Aves; 🕒10am-3pm Mon-Sat, to 1pm Sun; 👪; [S]2/3 to Central Park North) Get your bass on! You can borrow a rod and bait (corn kernels) for catch-and-release fishing at the Harlem Meer from April through October. Photo ID and a fishing license are required for those over the age of 15 ($15 per day for nonresidents, www.dec.ny.gov).There are also free 'Birding for Families' tours departing from here from March to May and September to November at 10am to 11am on Sunday.

BELVEDERE CASTLE BIRDWATCHING

Map p434 (☎212-772-0210; Central Park, at 79th St; 🕒10am-3pm Tue-Sun; 👪; [S]B, C, 1/2/3 to 72nd St) [FREE] For a DIY birding expedition with kids, pick up a 'Discovery Kit' at Belvedere Castle in Central Park. It comes with binoculars, a bird book, colored pencils and paper – a perfect way to get the kids excited about birds. Picture ID required.

WEST SIDE YMCA GYM

Map p434 (☎212-912-2600; www.ymcanyc.org/west-side; 5 W 63rd St, btwn Central Park West & Columbus Ave; day pass $25; 🕒5am-10:45pm Mon-Fri, 8am-7:45pm Sat & Sun; 👪; [S]A/C, B/D 1 to 59th St-Columbus Circle) Near Central Park, the West Side Y – one of 20 YMCAs in the city – boasts two swimming pools, an indoor running track, a basketball court, six racquetball/squash courts and a big weight room. Membership is $95 monthly (with a $125 initiation fee).

WOLLMAN SKATING RINK ICE SKATING

Map p434 (☎212-439-6900; www.wollmanskatingrink.com; Central Park, btwn 62nd & 63rd Sts; adult Mon-Thu/Fri-Sun $11/18, child $6, skate rentals $8, lock rental $5, spectator fee $5; 🕒Nov-Mar; 👪; [S]F to 57 St, N/Q/R to 5th Ave-59th St) Larger than the Rockefeller Center skating rink, and allowing all-day skating, this rink is at the southeastern edge of Central Park and offers nice views. It's open mid-October through April. Cash only.

CENTRAL PARK TENNIS CENTER TENNIS

Map p434 (☎212-280-0205; www.centralparktenniscenter.com; Central Park, btwn 94th & 96th Sts, enter at 96th St & Central Park West; 🕒6:30am-dusk Apr-Oct or Nov; [S]B, C to 96th St) This daylight-hours-only facility has 26 clay courts for public use and four hard courts for lessons. You can buy single-play tickets ($15) here. You can reserve a court if you pick up a $15 permit at the **Arsenal** (Map p434; ☎212-360-8131; www.nycgovparks.org; Central Park, at 5th Ave & E 64th St; 🕒9am-4pm Mon-Fri, to noon Apr-May; [S]N/R/Q to 5th Ave-59th St) [FREE]. The least busy times are roughly noon to 4pm on weekdays.

Harlem & Upper Manhattan

MORNINGSIDE HEIGHTS | HARLEM | EAST HARLEM | HAMILTON HEIGHTS | SUGAR HILL | WASHINGTON HEIGHTS | INWOOD | WEST HARLEM

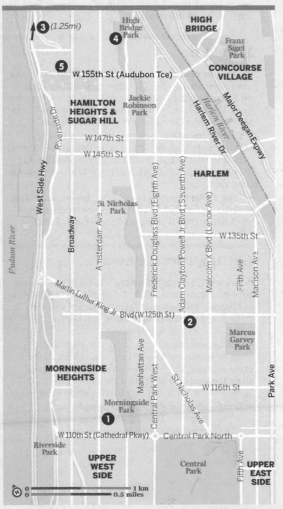

Neighborhood Top Five

1 Conceding that size *does* matter at the gloriously epic, yet still-unfinished **Cathedral Church of St John the Divine** (p249), the largest place of worship in the US.

2 Seeing the world through African American eyes at the small but savvy **Studio Museum in Harlem** (p251).

3 Escaping the rat race and modernity at the **Cloisters Museum & Gardens** (p255), an architectural mishmash of monasteries housing medieval art

4 Free Sunday jazz jams at the home of New York City's 'host with the most,' **Marjorie Eliot** (p261).

5 Quiet time with Goya, El Greco, Velázquez and friends at the underrated **Hispanic Society of America Museum & Library** (p255).

For more detail of this area, see Map p436 ➡

Lonely Planet's Top Tip

Manhattan's uptown communities tend to be locally minded, with bars, restaurants and shops catering to a neighborhood scene. These tend to be sleepiest on weekday mornings and liveliest in the evenings and on weekends.

To make the most of your visit, hit one of the museums or other historic sights in the afternoon, then stick around for dinner when these areas come to life.

✕ Best Places to Eat

➡ Charles' Pan-Fried Chicken (p260)

➡ Red Rooster (p260)

➡ Dinosaur Bar-B-Que (p256)

For reviews, see p256

🍹 Best Places to Drink

➡ Ginny's Supper Club (p261)

➡ Harlem Public (p260)

➡ Bier International (p261)

For reviews, see p261 ➡

⊙ Best Unexpected Surprises

➡ Marjorie Eliot Jazz Performance (p261)

➡ Sylvan Terrace (p256)

➡ Hispanic Society of America Museum & Library (p255)

For reviews, see p252 ➡

Explore Harlem & Upper Manhattan

The top half of Manhattan is a lot of territory to cover, with numerous points of interest a distance away from each other. So pick a neighborhood (or better yet, a couple of contiguous neighborhoods) and stick to them. If you like your cities to feel a little bit country, then start with Inwood – which has invigorating parks and an extravagant museum – and then work your way down the west side to the gargantuan Cathedral Church of St John the Divine. Prefer an urban vibe? Then it's all about Harlem and Hamilton Heights, a bastion of African American culture jammed with soul food, swinging bars and some architectural treats.

Local Life

➡ **Get your chic on** When Harlem peeps go out on the town, they usually dress to impress. For killer kicks, hit Atmos (p262) on retail-heavy 125th St. For high-end threads at preloved prices, head to in-the-know Trunk Show Designer Consignment (p262) on 113th St.

➡ **Tune in** For off-the-beaten-path musical events, nothing beats Morningside Heights. Riverside Church (p253), the Cathedral Church of St John the Divine (p249) and Columbia University (p252) all host regular concerts.

➡ **Take a hike** New Yorkers jogging, hiking and biking is what you'll find at Inwood Hill Park (p255) on any given sunny day. Tie those laces and get moving.

Getting There & Away

➡ **Subway** Harlem's main drag – 125th St – is just one subway stop from the 59th St–Columbus Circle Station in Midtown on the A and D trains. Other areas of Harlem and northern Manhattan can be reached on the A/C, B/D, 1/2/3 and 4/5/6 trains.

➡ **Bus** Dozens of buses ply the north–south route between upper and lower Manhattan along all the major avenues. The M10 bus provides a scenic trip along the west side of Central Park into Harlem. The M100 and the M101 run east to west along 125th St.

➡ **Taxi** If yellow cabs are in short supply, look for livery cabs (big town cars bearing a company name and number); negotiate a price before you get in.

STEVEN GREAVES / GETTYIMAGES ©

TOP SIGHT

CATHEDRAL CHURCH OF ST JOHN THE DIVINE

The largest place of worship in America has yet to be completed – and probably won't be any time soon. But this glorious Episcopal cathedral nonetheless commands attention with its ornate Gothic-style facade, booming vintage organ and extravagantly scaled nave – twice as wide as London's Westminster Abbey.

An Unfinished History

The first cornerstone for the cathedral was laid on St John's Day in 1892, though construction was hardly smooth. Engineers had to dig 70ft in order to find bedrock to which they could anchor the building. Architects died or were fired, and, in 1911, the initial Romanesque design was exchanged for a bigger, Gothic-inspired plan.

Depleted funds have seen construction regularly halted. The north tower remains unbuilt, and a 'temporary' domed roof, constructed out of terra-cotta tile in 1909, still shelters the crossing. A raging fire in 2001 caused significant damage, including to the north transept, which is yet to be rebuilt.

If it is ever completed, the 601ft-long cathedral will rank as the world's third-largest church, behind Rome's St Peter's Basilica and Côte d'Ivoire's Basilica of Our Lady of Peace at Yamoussoukro.

DON'T MISS...

- Portal sculptures
- Great Rose Window
- Great Organ
- Keith Haring Triptych

PRACTICALITIES

- Map p436
- ☎tours 212-932-7347
- www.stjohndivine.org
- 1047 Amsterdam Ave at W 112th St, Morningside Heights
- suggested donation $10, highlights tour $6, vertical tour $15
- ⌚7:30am-6pm
- [S]B, C, 1 to 110th St-Cathedral Pkwy

The Portal Sculptures

Framing the western entrance are two rows of sculptures carved in the 1980s and '90s by British artist Simon Verity. On the central pillar stands St John the Divine himself, author of the *Book of Revelation*. (Note the Four Horsemen of the Apocalypse under his feet.)

VISITING THE CATHEDRAL

Highlight tours are offered at 11am and 2pm Monday, 11am and 1pm Tuesday to Saturday, and at 1pm on select Sundays. Vertical tours, which take you on a steep climb to the top of the cathedral (bring your own flashlight), are at noon Wednesday and at noon and 2pm Saturday. Two services worth seeing are the Blessing of the Animals, a pilgrimage for pet owners held on the first Sunday of October, and the Blessing of the Bikes, held on a Saturday in mid- to late April, when local riders tool in on everything from sleek 10-speeds to clunky cruisers.

The cathedral was involved in civil-rights issues back in the early 1950s and has regularly worked with members of the community on issues of inequity. It is also a long-running cultural outpost, hosting holiday concerts, lectures and exhibits, and it has been the site of memorial services for many famous New Yorkers, including trumpeter Louis Armstrong and artist Keith Haring.

Interior, Cathedral Church of St John the Divine

Themes of devastation are rife, but most unnerving is the statue of Jeremiah (third on the right), which stands on a base that shows the New York City skyline – Twin Towers included – being destroyed.

The Nave

Illuminated by the **Great Rose Window** (America's largest stained-glass window), the nave is lined with two magisterial sets of 17th-century tapestries. The Barberini Tapestries depict scenes from Christ's life, while the Mortlake Tapestries, based on cartoons by Raphael, show the Acts of the Apostles.

Great Organ

One of the most powerful organs in the world, the Great Organ was originally installed in 1911, then enlarged and rebuilt in 1952. It contains 8500 pipes arranged in 141 ranks. The 2001 fire damaged the instrument, but a careful five-year restoration brought it back.

Keith Haring Triptych

Behind the choir is the white-gold and bronze triptych 'Life of Christ,' carved by '80s pop artist Keith Haring (1958–90). It's one of the last works of art he produced prior to succumbing to an AIDS-related illness aged 31.

TOP SIGHT
STUDIO MUSEUM IN HARLEM

This small, cultural treasure has been showcasing African American artists for more than four decades. Yet the museum is not just another art display center. It's an important point of connection for Harlem cultural figures of all stripes, who arrive to check out a rotating selection of exhibitions, attend film screenings or sign up for gallery talks.

From Loft to Museum

Founded in 1968, the museum originally came to life in a small loft space off 125th St that was sandwiched between a couple of garment factories and a supermarket. But it quickly became known for its thoughtful, contemporary-minded exhibits and vibrant event programming, which included concerts, poetry readings and lectures. Roughly a dozen years after its establishment, it moved to its present location, a renovated bank building that offered more room for exhibits, archives and its growing permanent collection.

Adjacent to the lobby is the museum's well-stocked **gift shop**, where you can pick everything from art tomes and exhibition catalogs to 'Black is Beautiful' T-shirts.

Collecting the Work of African American Artists

The permanent collection is small (roughly 2000 objects), but it is rich. The Studio Museum has been an important patron to African American artists and the collection features work by more than 400 of them. This includes important pieces by painter Jacob Lawrence, photographer Gordon Parks and collagist Romare Bearden – all of whom are represented in major museum collections in the US.

In addition, its photography holdings include an extensive archive of work by **James Van Der Zee** (1886–1983), an unparalleled chronicler of early-20th-century Harlem life. He shot portraits of prominent entertainers and black nationalists, and continued to take pictures well into his nineties. One well-known snap shows Jean-Michel Basquiat, the '80s graffiti artist and painter, sitting pensively with a Siamese cat on his lap.

African-American Flag

Look up on your way in. One of the museum's most iconic works hangs right outside the front door: David Hammons' 1990 piece *African-American Flag*. Replacing the red, white and blue of the stars and stripes with the red, green and black of the pan-African flag, it's a sly comment on the country's African American presence.

Artists in Residence

The museum's long-running artist-in-residence program has provided crucial support to a long list of well-known creatives, including conceptualist David Hammons, figurative painter Mickalene Thomas and portraitist Kehinde Wiley. The residents' works can often be found on display in the basement gallery or in one of the small display areas upstairs. The museum also runs regular special events, from themed discussions to music performances; check the website.

DON'T MISS...

- African American Flag
- Photography by James Van Der Zee
- The well-stocked gift shop

PRACTICALITIES

- Map p436
- ☎212-864-4500
- www.studiomuseum.org
- 144 W 125th St at Adam Clayton Powell Jr Blvd, Harlem
- suggested donation $7, Sun free
- 🕐noon-9pm Thu & Fri, 10am-6pm Sat, noon-6pm Sun
- [S]2/3 to 125th St

SIGHTS

Morningside Heights

This neighborhood (between 110th and 125th Sts on the far west side) serves as a community for Columbia University, which occupies the neighborhood's southern half.

CATHEDRAL CHURCH OF ST JOHN THE DIVINE CHURCH

See p249.

COLUMBIA UNIVERSITY UNIVERSITY

Map p436 (www.columbia.edu; Broadway at 116th St, Morningside Heights; [S]1 to 116th St-Columbia University) [FREE] Founded in 1754 as King's College downtown, the oldest university in New York is now one of the world's premiere research institutions. It moved to its current location (the site of a former asylum) in 1897, where its gated campus now channels a New England vibe and offers plenty of cultural happenings.

The principal point of interest is the main courtyard, which is surrounded by various Italian Renaissance–style structures. Here, you'll find the statue of the open-armed *Alma Mater* seated before the Low Memorial Library. On the south end of College Walk, on the corner of Amsterdam Ave, is Hamilton Hall, a key site during the infamous student uprising of 1968.

Your best bet for navigating the grounds is to download the self-guided audio tour by architectural historian Andrew Dolkart from the Columbia University website.

GENERAL ULYSSES S GRANT NATIONAL MEMORIAL MEMORIAL

Map p436 (www.nps.gov/gegr; Riverside Dr at 122nd St; 🕘9am-5pm Thu-Mon; [S]1 to 125th St) [FREE] Popularly known as Grant's Tomb ('Who's buried in Grant's Tomb?' 'Who?' 'Grant, stupid!' goes a classic joke), this landmark holds the remains of Civil War hero and 18th president Ulysses S Grant and his wife, Julia. Completed in 1897 (12 years after his death), the imposing granite structure is the largest mausoleum in America.

Seventeen Gaudí-inspired mosaic benches, designed by Chilean artist Pedro Silva in the 1970s, surround the mausoleum. It's a downright hallucinatory installation – and a good spot to contemplate the musings of the late, great comedian George Carlin, who was known to light up here back in the day.

TOP SIGHT
APOLLO THEATER

More than simply historic, Harlem's Apollo Theater is a swinging testament to Harlem's astounding musical legacy. Originally a whites-only burlesque joint, the neoclassical venue reinvented itself in 1934 with 'Jazz à la Carte.' Soon after, virtually every major black artist was crooning here, from Duke Ellington and Louis Armstrong, to Count Bassie and Billie Holiday.

The revamped Apollo also introduced the legendary 'Amateur Night,' its long-list of then-unknown competitors including Ella Fitzgerald, Gladys Night, Jimi Hendrix, the Jackson 5 and Lauryn Hill. The event still kicks on every Wednesday night, its wild and ruthless crowd as fun to watch as tomorrow's next big things. Beyond 'Amateur Night' is a thriving, year-round program of music, dance, master classes and special events, with shows spanning anything from Cuban salsa tributes to Afro-Latin jazz suites.

While guided tours of the interior are only available for groups of 20 or more with advance reservation, individuals are welcome to join group tours based on availability. Take the tour and expect to see a fragment of the 'Tree of Hope,' a long-gone elm performers would rub for good luck before taking to the stage.

DON'T MISS...

- 'Amateur Night'
- The iconic theater marquee
- Guided tours
- Tree of Hope

PRACTICALITIES

- Map p436
- ☎212-531-5300
- www.apollotheater.org
- 253 W 125th St at Frederick Douglass Blvd, Harlem
- admission varies; guided tours weekdays/weekends $16/18
- [S]A/C, B/D to 125th St

RIVERSIDE CHURCH CHURCH

Map p436 (www.theriversidechurchny.org; 490 Riverside Dr at 120th St; ⏰8am-5pm; [S]1 to 116th St) [FREE] Built by the Rockefeller family in 1930, this neo-Gothic beauty overlooks the Hudson River. The church rings its 74 carillon bells with an extraordinary 20-ton bass bell (the world's largest) at 10:30am, 12:30pm and 3pm on Sundays. Interdenominational services are held at 10:45am on Sundays, with free tours available to the public immediately after. The church also hosts high-quality events such as concerts and lectures.

Harlem

Harlem is a place that is soaked in history – and then some. And while it remains one of the country's most fabled centers of African American life, it – like everywhere else in New York – is changing. National chains now blanket 125th St, Harlem's historic main drag. Of-the-moment eateries, luxury condos and young professionals (of all creeds and races) have also moved in. But the neighborhood nonetheless retains its trademark charm, from sidewalk vendors dispensing Malcolm X T-shirts to end-of-the-world types preaching hellfire.

STUDIO MUSEUM IN HARLEM MUSEUM

See p251.

MALCOLM SHABAZZ HARLEM MARKET MARKET

Map p436 (52 W 116th St btwn Malcolm X Blvd & Fifth Ave; ⏰10am-8pm; 👪; [S]2/3 to 116th St) [FREE] This semi-enclosed market does a brisk trade in just about everything: leather goods, crafts, textiles, oils, drums, clothing, sculptures and a stupendous array of assorted African everything. It's also an excellent spot to get your hair braided. The market is run by the Malcolm Shabazz Mosque, the former pulpit of slain Muslim orator Malcolm X.

SCHOMBURG CENTER FOR RESEARCH IN BLACK CULTURE CULTURAL CENTER

Map p436 (☎212-491-2200; www.nypl.org/research/sc/sc.html; 515 Malcolm X Blvd at W 135th St; ⏰10am-6pm Mon, Fri & Sat, noon-8pm Tue-Thu; [S]2/3 to 135th St) [FREE] The nation's largest collection of documents, rare books and photographs relating to the African American experience resides at this scholarly center run by the New York Public Library. It's named after Arthur Schomburg, a black Puerto Rican activist who amassed a singular collection of manuscripts, slave narratives and other important artifacts. Regular concerts, lectures and exhibits are held on-site.

> **[i] HARLEM STREET NAMES**
>
> Many of the major avenues in the area have been renamed in honor of prominent African Americans; however, many locals still call the streets by their original names. Malcolm X Blvd is still frequently referred to as Lenox Ave.

CRACK IS WACK PLAYGROUND PARK

Map p436 (www.nycgovparks.org/parks/M208E; Harlem River Park, E 127th St & 2 Ave; ⏰dawn-dusk; [S]4/5/6 to 125th St) [FREE] This far-flung playground is named for the bright orange 'Crack is Wack' mural painted by pop graffiti artist Keith Haring on a handball court back in October 1986. It has since been restored, harkening back to a time when Haring's works covered walls all over New York.

East Harlem

The working-class district of East Harlem above 96th St and east of Fifth Ave, known colloquially as Spanish Harlem or El Barrio, has been home to one of the city's biggest Puerto Rican communities since the 1950s. Today, it remains a vibrant Latino neighborhood, infused with a mix of Puerto Rican, Dominican, Mexican and South American immigrants.

EL MUSEO DEL BARRIO MUSEUM

Map p436 (www.elmuseo.org; 1230 Fifth Ave btwn 104th & 105th Sts; suggested donation adult/child $9/free; ⏰11am-6pm Wed-Sat, to 9pm every 3rd Wed of the month; [S]6 to 103rd St) *Bienvenido* to one of New York's premiere Latino institutions, the thoughtful, rotating exhibitions of which span all media, from painting and photography to video and site-specific installations. The shows often showcase El Museo's strong permanent collection, which includes pre-Columbian artifacts, traditional folk works and a stellar array of postwar art made by a wide gamut of Latino and Latin American artists.

The museum includes pieces by well-known historical figures like Chilean surrealist Roberto Matta and established

FULL PEWS: GOSPEL CHURCH SERVICES IN HARLEM

What started as an occasional pilgrimage has turned into a tourist-industry spectacle: busloads of travelers now make their way to Harlem every Sunday to attend a gospel service. The volume of visitors is so high that some churches turn away people due to space constraints. In some cases, tourists outnumber congregants.

Naturally, this has led to friction. Many locals are upset by visitors who chat during sermons, leave in the middle of services or show up in skimpy attire. Plus, for some, there's the uncomfortable sense that African American spirituality is something to be consumed like a Broadway show. The churches, to their credit, remain welcoming spaces. But if you do decide to attend, be respectful: dress modestly (Sunday best!), do not take pictures and remain present for the duration of the service.

Sunday services generally start at 11am and can last for two or more hours. Below are just a few of the roughly five-dozen participating churches.

Abyssinian Baptist Church (Map p436; www.abyssinian.org; 132 W 138th St btwn Adam Clayton Powell Jr & Malcolm X Blvds; S2/3 to 135th St) This famed congregation, now more than a century old, is the number-one spot for foreign travelers (hence the separate tourist-seating section). It's so popular, in fact, that it offers a shorter Wednesday night service.

Canaan Baptist Church (Map p436; www.cbccnyc.org; 132 W 116th St btwn Adam Clayton Powell Jr & Malcolm X Blvds; ⏰; S2/3 to 116th St) A neighborhood church, founded in 1932.

Convent Avenue Baptist Church (Map p436; ☏212-234-6767; www.conventchurch. org; 420 W 145th St at Convent Ave; SA/C, B/D or 1 to 145th St) Traditional baptist services since the 1940s.

Greater Hood Memorial AME Zion Church (Map p436; www.greaterhood.org; 160 W 146th St btwn Adam Clayton Powell Jr & Malcolm X Blvds; ⏰; S3 to 145th) Also hosts hip-hop services on Thursdays at 6:30pm.

contemporary artists such as Félix González-Torres and Pepón Osorio. The onsite cafeteria serves pan-Latin dishes.

◉ Hamilton Heights & Sugar Hill

Basically the northwestern extension of Harlem, Hamilton Heights takes its name from the former estate of Alexander Hamilton, one of the drafters of the US Constitution.

During the Harlem Renaissance, the northern edge of the neighborhood was dubbed 'Sugar Hill' as it was here that the Harlem elite came to live the 'sweet life.' This area is also tangentially linked to hip-hop history: Sugarhill Gang (whose single 'Rapper's Delight' became the first hip-hop tune to become a mainstream hit) takes its name from here, their home turf.

HAMILTON GRANGE HISTORIC BUILDING
Map p436 (www.nps.gov/hagr; St Nicholas Park at 141st St; ⊘9am-5pm Wed-Sun, guided tours 11am, noon, 1pm, 2pm & 4pm; SA/C, B/D to 145th St) FREE This Federal-style retreat belonged to US founding father Alexander Hamilton, who owned a 32-acre country estate here

in the early 1800s. Unfortunately, Hamilton was only able to enjoy his abode for two short years, his life cut short in a fatal duel with political rival Aaron Burr. Moved from Convent Ave to its present location, the building is especially interesting to history and architecture buffs.

STRIVERS' ROW NEIGHBORHOOD
Map p436 (W 138th & W 139th Sts btwn Frederick Douglass & Adam Clayton Powell Jr Blvds; SB, C to 135th St) Also known as the St Nicholas Historic District, these streets were the darling of Harlem's elite in the 1920s. Its graceful row houses and apartments, many of which date back to the 1890s, were designed by three of the era's most celebrated architects: James Brown Lord, Bruce Price and Stanford White.

White's row of elegant Italianate creations along the north side of W 139th St are arguably the most beautiful. Keep your eyes peeled for alleyway signs advising visitors to 'walk your horses.'

HAMILTON HEIGHTS HISTORIC DISTRICT NEIGHBORHOOD
Map p436 (Convent Ave & Hamilton Tce btwn 141st & 145th Sts; SA/C, B/D to 145th St) Two parallel

streets in Hamilton Heights – Convent Ave and Hamilton Tce – contain a landmark stretch of historic limestone and brownstone townhouses from the period between 1866 and 1931. Film fans may recognize the turreted building on the southeast corner of Convent and 144th Aves from *The Royal Tenenbaums*.

⊙ Washington Heights & Inwood

Located at Manhattan's narrow, northern tip (above 155th St), Washington Heights takes its name from the first president of the US, who set up a Continental Army fort here during the Revolutionary War. For much of the 20th century, it has been a bastion of Dominican life – though it has recently seen an influx of downtown hipsters in search of affordable rent.

Inwood, at Manhattan's northern tip (from about 175th St), is a chilled-out residential zone with an almost suburban vibe.

CLOISTERS MUSEUM & GARDENS MUSEUM

(www.metmuseum.org/cloisters; Fort Tryon Park; suggested donation adult/child $25/free; ⏲10am-5:15pm Mar-Oct, to 4.45pm Nov-Feb; [S]A to 190th St) On a hilltop overlooking the Hudson River, the Cloisters is a curious architectural jigsaw, its many parts made up of various European monasteries and other historic buildings. Built in the 1930s to house the Metropolitan Museum's medieval treasures, its frescoes, tapestries and paintings are set in galleries that sit around a romantic courtyard, connected by grand archways and topped with Moorish terra-cotta roofs. Among its many rare treasures is the the beguiling 16th-century tapestry series *The Hunt of the Unicorn*.

Also worth seeking out is the arresting, well-preserved 15th-century Annunciation Triptych (Merode Altarpiece). Then there's the stunning 12th-century Saint-Guilhem Cloister and the Trie Cloister Garden, the latter adorned with plants used in medieval medicine, magic, ceremony and the arts.

HISPANIC SOCIETY OF AMERICA MUSEUM & LIBRARY MUSEUM

Map p436 (www.hispanicsociety.org; Broadway at 155th St, Washington Heights; ⏲10am-4:30pm Tue-Sat, 1-4pm Sun; [S]1 to 157th St) [FREE] Housed in the beaux arts structure where naturalist John James Audubon once lived, this treasure contains the largest collection of 19th-century Spanish art and manuscripts outside of Spain – including a substantial selection of works by El Greco, Goya and Velázquez. It's also home to a library featuring 600,000 rare books and manuscripts. Greeting visitors at the entrance is Goya's 1797 masterpiece *The Duchess of Alba*, while a majestic sculpture of *El Cid* by Anna Hyatt Huntington dominates the exterior courtyard.

DYCKMAN FARMHOUSE MUSEUM MUSEUM

(www.dyckmanfarmhouse.org; 4881 Broadway at 204th St; adult/child $1/free; ⏲11am-5pm Fri-Sun; [S]A to Inwood-207th St) Built in 1784 on a 28-acre farm, the Dyckman House is Manhattan's lone surviving Dutch farmhouse. Excavations of the property have turned up valuable clues about colonial life, and the museum includes period rooms and furniture, decorative arts, a half-acre of gardens and an exhibition on the neighborhood's history. To get here, take the subway to the Inwood–207th St station (not Dyckman St) and walk one block south.

INWOOD HILL PARK PARK

(www.nycgovparks.org/parks/inwoodhillpark; Dyckman St at the Hudson River; [S]A to Inwood-207th St) This 197-acre park contains the last natural forest and salt marsh in Manhattan. It's a cool escape in summer and a great place to explore any time, as you'll find hilly paths for hiking and mellow, grassy patches and benches for quiet contemplation. It's so bucolic, in fact, that the treetops serve as frequent nesting sites for bald eagles.

Let your sporty side rip on basketball courts, horseback-riding trails, and soccer and football fields; you can also join locals who barbecue at designated grills on summer weekends. At the time of research, the information-packed **Inwood Hill Nature Center** remained closed due to damage from Hurricane Sandy.

MORRIS-JUMEL MANSION MUSEUM HISTORIC BUILDING

Map p436 (www.morrisjumel.org; 65 Jumel Tce at 160th St, Washington Heights; adult/child $5/4, guided tours per person $6; ⏲10am-4pm Wed-Sun, other times by appointment; [S]C to 163rd St-Amsterdam Ave) Built in 1765 as a country retreat for Roger and Mary Morris, this columned mansion is the oldest house in Manhattan. It is also famous for having served as George Washington's headquarters after it was seized by the Continental Army in

1776. The mansion's rooms contain many original furnishings, including a bed that reputedly belonged to Napoleon.

Across the street, along **10-18 Jumel Terrace** (Map p436), stands a row of townhouses, designed in the 1890s by the renowned architect Henri Fouchaux. At number 16 lived prolific entertainer and civil-rights activist Paul Robeson, who subsequently moved to 555 Edgecombe Ave (p262).

Around the corner lies storybook **Sylvan Terrace** (Map p436), still graced by its original, late-19th-century gas lamps. The street's wooden houses – resplendent with their high narrow stoops, dentiled canopies and boldly paneled wooden doors – were NYC's first attempt at building affordable abodes for city workers. Equally unique are the street's cobbled stones, which, unlike those of Lower Manhattan and Brooklyn, are Belgian, not Dutch.

🍴 EATING

🍴 Morningside Heights & West Harlem

TOM'S RESTAURANT DINER $

Map p436 (www.tomsrestaurant.net; 2880 Broadway at 112th St; burgers with fries from $6.50; ⌚6am-1:30am Sun-Wed, 24hr Thu-Sat; [S]1 to 110th St) The exteriors of Tom's may look familiar if you're a fan of the TV series *Seinfeld,* but the interiors are all New York Greek diner. As in, *busy.* Reminisce about those Kramer scenes while chomping on classic burgers, gyros, or gut-warming homemade soups (the creamy broccoli is good). Breakfast is served all day. Cash only.

DINOSAUR BAR-B-QUE STEAKHOUSE $$

Map p436 (www.dinosaurbarbque.com; 700 W 125th St at Twelfth Ave; meals $6.95-26.95; ⌚11:30am-11pm Mon-Thu, to 1am Fri & Sat, noon-10pm Sun; 📶; [S]1 to 125th St) Jocks, hipsters, moms and pops: everyone dives into this honky-tonk rib bar for a rockin' feed. Get messy with dry-rubbed, slow-pit-smoked ribs, slabs of juicy steak, and succulent burgers, or watch the waist with the lightly seasoned grilled-chicken options. The very few vegetarian options include a fantastic version of Creole-spiced deviled eggs.

Local Life
Harlem Soul

Harlem. The neighborhood where Cab Calloway crooned; where Ralph Ellison penned his epic novel on truth and intolerance, *Invisible Man;* where acclaimed artist Romare Bearden pieced together his first collages. Simultaneously vibrant and effusive, brooding and melancholy, Harlem is the deepest recess of New York's soul.

1 College Campus Coffee

Rev your engine with a cuppa joe alongside Columbia University students at Community Food & Juice (p260). Across the street stands the red-neon marquee of Tom's Restaurant, famously featured in the TV comedy *Seinfeld*. The restaurant was immortalized in Suzanne Vega's iconic song *Tom's Diner*.

2 Come to Jesus

Vega's song includes the line: 'I'm listening to the bells of the cathedral.' The cathedral in question is the Cathedral Church of St John the Divine (p249), its epic scale more Old World than New. A yet-to-be-completed blend of neo-Gothic and Romanesque styles, it's the largest place of worship in the United States.

3 Rows of Cornrows

Take time to trawl the Malcolm Shabazz Harlem Market (p253), a low-key mix of African crafts and clothes, gossiping locals and dutiful men heeding the call to prayer. The market lies in the heart Little Senegal (or *Le Petit Senegal*), a strip of blocks around W 116th St packed with the colorful shops and eateries of Harlem's West African immigrants.

4 Art & Community

It might be small, but the Studio Museum in Harlem (p251) plays a vital role in the promotion and archiving of African American art. Its program of rotating exhibitions often features artists in its permanent collection, among them collagist Romare Bearden, satirical painter Robert Colescott and internationally renowned sculptor Richard Hunt.

Apollo Theater (p252)

❺ Strivers' Row

On the blocks of 138th and 139th Sts, Strivers' Row (p254) is graced with 1890s townhouses. Earning its nickname in the 1920s when aspiring African Americans first moved here, these buildings have housed some of Harlem's greatest identities, among them songwriters Eubie Blake and Noble Sissle, blues veteran WC Handy and singer/dancer Bill 'Bojangles' Robinson.

❻ Come to Jesus

Sunday gospel services at the Abyssinian Baptist Church (p254) are arguably Harlem's most famous – they even have a designated 'tourist' section. Long lines and waiting times can test the most patient of souls, so consider attending the shorter 7pm service on Wednesdays, the choir's roof-shaking voices no less enthralling.

❼ Cock-A-Doodle-Do

Taste the 'new Harlem' at Red Rooster (p260), where Ethiopian-born, Swedish-raised chef Marcus Samuelsson gives comfort food a competent, respectful makeover. The corn bread (paired with honey butter) is reason enough to roll in, while basement Ginny's Supper Club (p261) keeps the drinks and tunes flowing till the woo small hours.

❽ Cheers & Jeers

The best way to end any night in Harlem is 'where stars are born and legends are made,' the Apollo Theater (p252). Ella Fitzgerald made her singing debut here in November 1934, at one of the theater's earliest 'amateur nights.' Eighty years on, 'Amateur Night' kicks on every Wednesday, notorious crowds and all.

LOU JONES / GETTY IMAGES ©

1. Harlem
Meet the locals in one of the most fabled centers of
African American culture in the US.

2. 125th St
Explore the busy 125th St commercial district,
where you'll find the Apollo Theater and a
memorial to the late Michael Jackson.

3. Gospel services (p254)
Attend a Sunday gospel service to hear the soulful
music of the choirs.

4. Brownstones
Walk streets lined with Victorian brownstone
townhouses.

RIEGER BERTRAND / GETTY IMAGES ©

COMMUNITY FOOD & JUICE AMERICAN $$

Map p436 (www.communityrestaurant.com; 2893 Broadway btwn 112th & 113th Sts, Morningside Heights; sandwiches $11-15, dinner mains $14-29; ⏲8am-3:30pm & 5-9:30pm Mon-Thu, to 10pm Fri, 9am-3:30pm & 5-10pm Sat, 9am-3:30pm & 5-9:30pm Sun; 🥕 👪; [S]1 to 110th St) Lofty and convivial, Community is a brunch staple for frenzied families and hungover Columbia University students. Get here before 10:30am or be prepared to wait for your veggie scramble. Better yet, skip the weekend rush and bop in for a candlelit dinner. The warm lentil salad and grass-fed burger deserve an A.

🍴 Harlem

AMY RUTH'S RESTAURANT SOUTHERN $$

Map p436 (www.amyruthsharlem.com; 113 W 116th St near Malcolm X Blvd; waffles $8.95-16.95, mains $12.25-21.95; ⏲11am-11pm Mon, 8:30am-11pm Tue-Thu, 8:30am-5am Fri, 7:30am-5am Sat, 7:30am-11pm Sun; [S]B, C, 2/3 to 116th St) This perennially crowded restaurant is *the* place to go for classic soul food, serving up fried catfish, mac 'n' cheese and fluffy biscuits. But it's the waffles that are most famous – dished up 14 different ways, including with shrimp. Our favorite is the 'Rev Al Sharpton,' waffles topped with succulent fried chicken.

★**RED ROOSTER** MODERN AMERICAN $$$

Map p436 (www.redroosterharlem.com; 310 Malcolm X Blvd btwn 125th & 126th Sts; dinner mains $17-36; ⏲11:30am-10:30pm Mon-Fri, 10am-11pm Sat & Sun; [S]2/3 to 125th St) Transatlantic super-chef Marcus Samuelsson laces upscale comfort food with a world of flavors at his effortlessly cool, swinging brasserie. Here, mac 'n' cheese joins forces with lobster, dirty rice gets the aged basmati treatment, and spectacular Swedish meatballs salute Samuelsson's home country. The prix-fixe lunch is a bargain at $25, and there's a soul-lifting Sunday gospel brunch in the basement supper club, Ginny's.

🍴 East Harlem

EL AGUILA MEXICAN $

Map p436 (137 E 116th St cnr Lexington Ave; tacos $2.50, burritos $7; ⏲24hr; [S]6 to 116th St) Get messy over cheap and cheerful chicken, tongue and *bistec* (grilled steak) tacos at this no-frills, tile-clad taqueria. Tasty alternatives include tamales, tostadas, *tortas* (sandwiches) and veggie burritos, all served with a side of blaring Mexican tunes and televised Mexican soaps. If you're heading in for breakfast, dig into the *pan dulce* (a sweet Mexican bun).

🍴 Hamilton Heights

★**CHARLES' PAN-FRIED CHICKEN** SOUTHERN $

Map p436 (2839-2841 Frederick Douglass Blvd btwn 151st & 152nd Sts; fried chicken with 2 sides $12; ⏲11am-11pm Mon-Thu, to 1am Fri & Sat, to 8pm Sun; [S]B/D to 155th St) It's a hole-in-the-wall place, but the charismatic Charles Gabriel makes the best damn chicken we've ever tasted: crisp and beautifully seasoned, it's served with mountains of collard greens, mac 'n' cheese and corn bread. The setting is informal (meals are dished out in Styrofoam) and there are just four tables, but the food is wonderful and the portions are big enough for two.

HARLEM PUBLIC AMERICAN $

Map p436 (www.harlempublic.com; 3612 Broadway at 149th St; meals $8.95-13.95; ⏲3pm-2am Mon & Tue, noon-2am Wed, Thu & Sun, noon-4am Fri & Sat; 📶; [S]1, A/C, B/D to 145th St) Amicable hipsters at the bar, old-school funk on the speakers, and finger-licking pub grub: gentrification ain't *always* bad. Celebrate new beginnings with mouthwatering feel-good food, whether it's the wicked peanut butter burger (peanut butter, brown sugar bacon and New York State cheddar) or a new-school seasonal salad. Liquids focus on the local, from American craft beers and wines to small-batch New York liquors.

🍴 Inwood

NEW LEAF CAFE MODERN AMERICAN $$

(☎212-568-5323; www.newleafrestaurant.com; 1 Margaret Corbin Dr; lunch mains $12-20, dinner mains $18-30; ⏲noon-3:30pm Mon, noon-9pm Tue-Thu, noon-10pm Fri, 11am-3:30pm & 6-10pm Sat, 11am-3:30pm & 6-9pm Sun; [S]A to 190th St) Nestled into Fort Tryon Park, a short jaunt from the Cloisters Museum & Gardens (p255), this 1930s stone edifice feels like a distinguished country tavern. Settle in for seasonal produce made good in classic salads and pasta dishes, and regional seafood comforters like Maryland crab cakes. On sunny days, the outdoor patio is a perfect spot for brunch.

WORTH A DETOUR

THE BRONX

The only borough on the US mainland, the 42-sq-mile, 1.4-million-strong Bronx lies just north of Manhattan between the Hudson, Harlem and East Rivers and Long Island Sound. It was named after Scandinavian sea captain Jonas Bronck, who settled here in 1639, in an area previously inhabited by the Lenape Nation.

Known for its very expensive team, its very expensive stadium ($1.5 billion; opened in 2009), and its 27 World Series wins, **Yankee Stadium** (☎718-293-4300, tickets 212-926-5337; www.yankees.com; E 161st St at River Ave; tours $20, tickets $20-235; [S]B/D, 4 to 161st St-Yankee Stadium) channels the intimacy of the '23 original, so if you're into baseball – or *béisbol* or *beysbol* or *baseboll* – don't miss it.

For the kids, there's the **Bronx Zoo** (☎718-220-5100; www.bronxzoo.com; 2300 Southern Blvd; basic ticket adult/child $16.95/12.95, suggested donation on Wed; ⏲10am-5pm Mon-Fri, to 5:30pm Sat & Sun Apr-Oct, to 4:30pm Nov-Mar; [S]2, 5 to West Farms Sq-E Tremont Ave), while to the north is the **New York Botanical Garden** (www.nybg.org; Bronx River Pkwy & Fordham Rd; adult/child $20/8, Wed & 9-10am Sat free; ⏲10am-6pm Tue-Sun; 👪; 🚆Metro-North to Botanical Garden), opened in 1891 and featuring 50 acres of old-growth New York forest.

The **Bronx Museum** (☎718-681-6000; www.bronxmuseum.org; 1040 Grand Concourse at 165th St; ⏲11am-6pm Thu, Sat & Sun, to 8pm Fri; [S]B/D to 167th St) [FREE] hosts well-executed exhibitions of contemporary and 20th-century art, while further up the Concourse is the renovated **Edgar Allan Poe Cottage** (☎718-881-8900; www.bronxhistoricalsociety.org/poecottage; 2640 Grand Concourse at Kingsbridge Rd; adult/child $5/3; ⏲10am-4pm Sat, 1-5pm Sun; [S]B/D to Kingsbridge Rd), former abode of the brooding author (1809–49).

On the borough's northern edge, scenic **Woodlawn Cemetery** (www.thewoodlawncemetery.org; ⏲8:30am-5pm; [S]4 to Woodlawn) dates back to the Civil War (1863), its famous residents including Cuban singer Celia Cruz, jazz legends Miles Davis and Duke Ellington, and *Moby Dick* scribe Herman Melville.

For some of the best Italian food in the borough, head to Arthur Ave, the Bronx's 'Little Italy' and home to pizza-n-pasta favorite **Zero Otto Nove** (www.089bx.roberto089.com; 2357 Arthur Ave at 186th St; pizzas $8.95-15.95, mains $14.95-28.95 ; ⏲noon-2:30pm & 4:30-10pm Mon-Thu, to 11pm Fri & Sat, 1-9pm Sun; 🚆Metro-North to Fordham).

DRINKING & NIGHTLIFE

GINNY'S SUPPER CLUB COCKTAIL BAR

Map p436 (www.ginnyssupperclub.com; 310 Malcolm X Blvd btwn 125th & 126th Sts; ⏲7pm-2am Thu, 6pm-3am Fri & Sat, Sun brunch sittings 10:30am & 12:30pm, closed Sun evening; [S]2/3 to 125th St) Looking straight out of *Boardwalk Empire,* this roaring basement supper club is never short of styled-up punters, sipping cocktails, nibbling on soul and global bites (from Red Rooster's competent kitchen), and grooving to sultry jazz, blues, or fat DJ beats. Highlights include Monday night's Rakiem Walker Project (an ensemble featuring Red Rooster staffers), and Sunday's life-affirming gospel brunch.

PARIS BLUES DIVE BAR

Map p436 (2012 Adam Clayton Powell Jr Blvd cnr 121st St; ⏲noon-2am Sun-Wed, to 4am Thu-Sat; [S]A/C, B to 116th St, 2/3 to 125th St) This down-home dive is named after the 1961 Sidney Poitier and Paul Newman flick about two expats living and loving in Paris. It's a little worn in places and the booze selection is limited, but it makes up for it with buckets of charm, generous pours, and nightly jazz gigs from around 8:30pm.

BIER INTERNATIONAL BEER HALL

Map p436 (www.bierinternational.com; 2099 Frederick Douglass Blvd at 113th St; ⏲4pm-1am Mon, 4pm-2am Tue-Thu, 4pm-4am Fri, noon-4am Sat, noon-1am Sun; [S]B, C, 1 to 110th St-Cathedral Pkwy, 2/3 to 110th St-Central Park North) A fun, buzzing beer garden that peddles more than a dozen drafts and a full menu of eats to choose from. The truffle fries with Parmesan ($7) make a great accompaniment to the Bier Stiefel (beer in a boot glass; $15).

ENTERTAINMENT

MARJORIE ELIOT JAZZ

Map p436 (☎212-781-6595; Apt 3F, 555 Edgecombe Ave at 160th St, Washington Heights; [S]A/C to 163rd St-Amsterdam Ave, 1 to 157th St)

LOCAL KNOWLEDGE

555 EDGECOMBE AVENUE

If buildings could talk, **555 Edgecombe Ave** (Map p436; 555 Edgecombe Ave at 160th St, Washington Heights) would have no shortage of anecdotes. Standing high in Washington Heights, this brick-built, beaux arts giant was the neighborhood's very first luxury apartment complex. When completed in 1916, its credentials included a concierge, a separate tradesmens' entrance, and no fewer than three elevators. Initially only available to white tenants, the area's transformation from a predominantly Irish and Jewish neighborhood to an African American one saw the building become predominately black by the 1940s. Its tenants would include some of New York's most prominent African Americans, among them boxer Joe Louis and music heavyweights Lena Horne, Count Basie, Duke Ellington and Billy Strayhorn. Today, the building's cultural legacy lives on every Sunday afternoon, when veteran musician Marjorie Eliot (p261) throws open the doors of her apartment, inviting anyone and everyone into her living room for one of the city's most enchanting jazz jams.

[FREE] Each Sunday at 3:30pm, the charming Ms Eliot provides one of New York's most magical experiences: free, intimate jazz jams in her own apartment. Dedicated to her two deceased sons, the informal concerts feature a revolving lineup of talented musicians, enchanting guests from all over the globe.

MAYSLES DOCUMENTARY CENTER CINEMA
Map p436 (www.maysles.org; 343 Malcolm X Blvd btwn 127th & 128th Sts, Harlem; suggested donation $10; [S]2/3 to 125th St) This small not-for-profit cinema founded by director Albert Maysles (of *Grey Gardens* fame) shows documentary and other independent films. Check the website for details of upcoming screenings and events, which also include live performances, lectures and presentations.

SHOPPING

JUMEL TERRACE BOOKS BOOKS
Map p436 (☎212-928-9525; www.jumelterracebooks.com; 426 W 160th St, Washington Heights; 🕒by appointment; [S]C to 163rd St-Amsterdam Ave) Housed in a brownstone from 1891, this shop specializes in tomes on Africana, Harlem history and African American literature. You have to call ahead, but if you're fascinated by rare books – and a rare opportunity to shop at a beautiful home – it's worth it.

TRUNK SHOW DESIGNER CONSIGNMENT VINTAGE
Map p436 (☎212-662-0009; www.trunkshowconsignment.com; 275-277 W 113th St at Eighth Ave; 🕒1-8:30pm Tue-Fri, to 7:30pm Sat, to 6:30pm Sun; [S]B, C to 110th St-Cathedral Parkway, 2/3 to 110th St-Central Park North) Step into this hot little consignment store for a unisex edit of fabulous preloved finds, from Christian Louboutin stilettos and Louis Vuitton bags to Gucci polo shirts and Balmain denim. Opening times can vary, so consider calling ahead.

ATMOS SHOES
Map p436 (www.atmosnyc.com; 203 W 125th St at Adam Clayton Powell Jr Blvd, Harlem; 🕒11am-8pm Mon-Sat, noon-7pm Sun; [S]A/C, B/D, 2/3 to 125th St) Sneaker fetishists both high and low head here to pimp their feet (Method Man from the Wu-Tang Clan has been spotted here). A perfect place for high-end kicks, as well as limited-edition releases and rereleases.

SPORTS & ACTIVITIES

TREAD BICYCLE RENTAL
(www.treadbikeshop.com; 250 Dyckman St, Inwood; per hour $8, per day $30; 🕒10am-7pm Mon-Sat, to 6pm Sun; [S]A to Dyckman St) Located in Inwood Hill Park, right off the New York Greenway Bike Trail, is this family-friendly rentals shop – perfect for navigating the long and winding paths of upper Manhattan.

RIVERBANK STATE PARK SPORTS
Map p436 (www.nysparks.com/parks/93; 679 Riverside Dr at 145th St, Hamilton Heights; pool adult/child $2/1, fitness room $10, roller/ice skating $1.50/5, skate rental $6; 🕒park 6am-11pm; [S]1 to 145th St) This 28-acre, five-building facility, perched atop a waste refinery (not as crazy as it sounds), has an indoor Olympic-size pool, an outdoor lap pool, a fitness room, basketball and tennis courts, a running track around a soccer field, a kids' area and a roller-skating rink (with ice skating from November to March, weather permitting).

Brooklyn

WILLIAMSBURG | GREENPOINT | BUSHWICK | BROOKLYN HEIGHTS | DUMBO | DOWNTOWN BROOKLYN | FORT GREENE | CLINTON HILL | BOERUM HILL | COBBLE HILL | CARROLL GARDENS | RED HOOK | GOWANUS | PARK SLOPE | PROSPECT HEIGHTS | BEDFORD-STUYVESANT | CROWN HEIGHTS | CONEY ISLAND | BRIGHTON BEACH |

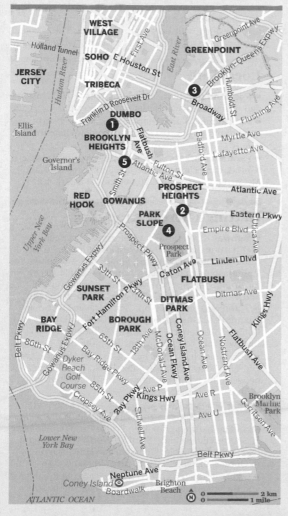

Neighborhood Top Five

1 Taking in the incredible views of Lower Manhattan from the new **Brooklyn Bridge Park** (p265) on the waterfront.

2 Catching the latest critically acclaimed art exhibitions at the **Brooklyn Museum** (p267), followed by a meal at Saul.

3 Drinking and dining your way through the creative gastropubs and cocktail joints of **Williamsburg** (p290).

4 Strolling past meadows, lakefront, scenic bridges and forest-covered hillocks at **Prospect Park** (p268).

5 Browsing the boutiques and antique shops on **Atlantic Ave**, followed by eating and drinking on **Smith St**.

For more detail, see maps on p438, p440, p442, p444 and p445 ➡

Lonely Planet's Top Tip

If you want to get a sense of what old New York was like, be sure to wander around Brighton Beach. Under the elevated tracks on Brighton Beach Ave, the bustling Russian district known as 'Little Odessa' is packed with greengrocers and emporiums dispensing smoked fish and pierogis. On the street, you'll find a cross section of humanity – from grandmas to sulky teens – chattering in dozens of different languages as the trains rumble overhead. It's unmistakably New York.

Best Places to Eat

➡ Battersby (p288)
➡ Frankies Spuntino (p288)
➡ Pok Pok (p288)
➡ Water Table (p282)
➡ Roberta's (p282)

For reviews, see p280 ➡

🍷 Best Places to Drink

➡ Maison Premiere (p290)
➡ OTB (p291)
➡ Hotel Delmano (p291)
➡ 61 Local (p293)
➡ Sunny's (p293)

For reviews, see p290 ➡

☆ Best Places for Live Music

➡ Bell House (p295)
➡ Brooklyn Bowl (p293)
➡ Cubana Social (p282)
➡ Jalopy (p295)
➡ Barbes (p294)

For reviews, see p293 ➡

BROOKLYN

Explore Brooklyn

If Brooklyn were its own city, it'd be the fourth largest in the US – bigger than Houston, Philadelphia and Phoenix. It is home to more than 2.5 million people and is a rambling 71 sq miles (easily three times larger than Manhattan). It is split in two, with one set of subway lines servicing the north end of the borough, and another set traveling to points south. So if you think you can see it all in a day, as old-school Brooklyners might say: 'Fuhgeddaboudit!'

For day-trip purposes, it is best to pick a neighborhood and stick to it. South Brooklyn, especially brownstone-studded Brooklyn Heights, offers lots of history and great Manhattan views. Fans of vintage amusement parks should head to Coney Island. For the night owls, Williamsburg lies just a single subway stop from Manhattan and is loaded with bars and restaurants. The borough may be all the rage, but it's not without its sketchy parts.

Local Life

➡ **Rock and roll** Hit the hot music spots in Williamsburg and Bushwick to hear the latest indie sounds.

➡ **Park sloping** Join the stroller brigade for a lap or two around Prospect Park. Or go window-shopping and cafe-hopping on Fifth Ave.

➡ **Farmers markets** Shop at Saturday produce markets (Grand Army Plaza, Fort Greene Park, Borough Hall, McCarren Park), followed by a picnic at a park nearby.

Getting There & Around

➡ **Subway** Sixteen subway lines travel between Manhattan and Brooklyn, with an additional line (the G) connecting the Park Slope area of Brooklyn to Williamsburg and Queens. Handy lines include A/C for Brooklyn Heights, downtown and Dumbo; 2/3 and 4/5 for Brooklyn Heights and Prospect Heights; D/F and N/Q for Park Slope, Fort Greene and Coney Island; F for Dumbo, downtown, Carroll Gardens and Cobble Hill. In north Brooklyn, Williamsburg and Bushwick are reached primarily on the L.

➡ **Bus** Handy bus routes include the B61 (Atlantic Ave) and B57 (Court St) to reach Red Hook. The B62 runs between Brooklyn's downtown (Smith & Fulton) and Williamsburg (Driggs St).

➡ **Boat** The East River Ferry (p384) runs both north and south. Heading north, boats zip from Wall St (Pier 11) in Manhattan to Brooklyn Bridge Park/Dumbo (Pier 1), South Williamsburg (S 8th St), North Williamsburg (N 6th St), Greenpoint (India St) and Long Island City in Queens, then across to E34th St in Manhattan.

➡**Taxi** New green Boro Taxis operate around Brooklyn and the other outer boroughs. Hail them on the street.

MAREMAGNUM / GETTY IMAGES ©

TOP SIGHT
BROOKLYN BRIDGE PARK

This 85-acre park is one of Brooklyn's most talked-about new sights. Wrapping around a bend on the East River, it runs for 1.3 miles from Jay St in Dumbo to the west end of Atlantic Ave in Cobble Hill. It has revitalized a once-barren stretch of shoreline, turning a series of abandoned piers into public parkland. Nearing completion, it will be the biggest new park in Brooklyn since Calvert Vaux and Frederick Olmsted designed the 585-acre Prospect Park in the 19th century.

Empire Fulton Ferry

Just east of the Brooklyn Bridge, in the northern section of Dumbo, you'll find a state park with a grassy lawn that faces the East River. Near the water is **Jane's Carousel** (Map p444; www.janescarousel.com; tickets $2; ⌚11am-7pm Wed-Mon, to 6pm Nov-Apr), a lovingly restored 1922 carousel set inside a glass pavilion designed by Pritzker Prize–winning architect Jean Nouvel. The park is bordered on one side by the **Empire Stores & Tobacco Warehouse** (Map p444), a series of Civil War–era structures that will eventually house restaurants, shops and a theater.

Pier 1

A 9-acre pier just south of the Empire Fulton Ferry is home to a stretch of park featuring a playground, walkways and the Harbor and Bridge View lawns, both of which overlook the river. On the Bridge View Lawn, you'll find artist Mark di Suvero's 30ft kinetic sculpture *Yoga* (1991). From July through August, free outdoor films are screened on the Harbor View Lawn against a stunning backdrop of Manhattan. Other free open-air events (outdoor dance parties, group

DON'T MISS...

- Views of downtown Manhattan from Pier 1
- Empire Fulton Ferry at sunset
- Refreshments at Fornino or Brooklyn Bridge Wine Bar
- A stroll across Brooklyn Bridge

PRACTICALITIES

- Map p444
- ☎718-222-9939
- www.brooklynbridgeparknyc.org
- East River Waterfront, btwn Atlantic Ave & Adams St
- ⌚6am-1am
- [S]A/C to High St, 2/3 to Clark St, F to York St

WALKING THE BROOKLYN BRIDGE

To reach the bridge on foot, take the stairs at the northeastern end of Cadman Plaza (on bicycle, enter at Tillary and Adams Sts). If you're coming from Dumbo, take Washington St straight uphill.

It's about a mile across the bridge (a 20- to 40-minute stroll depending on how often you stop to admire the view). Once on the Manhattan side, you'll arrive in City Hall Park, a 10-minute walk from Tribeca (west), Chinatown (north) or Wall Street (south).

The pedestrian walkway affords a wonderful view of lower Manhattan; observation points under the support towers offer brass 'panorama' histories of the waterfront. Take care to stay on the side of the walkway marked for pedestrians – one half is designated for cyclists, who use it en masse for both commuting and pleasure rides, and frustrated pedalers have been known to get nasty with oblivious tourists who wander, camera pressed to an eye, into the bike lane. To beat the crowds come early in the morning, when you'll have those views largely to yourself.

yoga classes, history tours) happen throughout the summer. The seasonal **Brooklyn Bridge Wine Bar** (Map p444; Pier 1; ☺May-Oct) can be found on the pier's north end. At the north end of the pier, you can catch the East River Ferry (p384).

Piers 5 & 6

At the southern end of the park, off Atlantic Ave, Pier 6 has a fantastic playground and a small water play area for tots (if you're bringing kids, pack swimsuits, towels). Neighboring Pier 5, just north, has walkways, sand volleyball courts, soccer fields and barbecue grills. There are also a few seasonal concessions (May to October), including wood-fired pizza, beer and Italian treats at **Fornino** (Map p444; www.fornino.com), which has a rooftop deck. A free seasonal ferry runs on weekends from Pier 6 to **Governors Island** (www.govisland.com; ☺10am-7pm Sat & Sun May 25-Sep 29).

Future of the Park

Work continues here. A bouncy pedestrian bridge linking Brooklyn Heights with the park opened in 2013 and there are plans to transform the west end of Pier 6 with meadows, trees and a triangular platform with unrivaled views of Lower Manhattan.

Brooklyn Bridge

The real star of the park is, of course, the architectural masterpiece linking New York's best-loved boroughs. The Brooklyn Bridge was the world's first steel suspension bridge. When it opened in 1883, the 1596ft span between its two support towers was the longest in history. Although its construction was fraught with disaster, the bridge became a magnificent example of urban design, inspiring poets, writers and painters. Today, the Brooklyn Bridge continues to dazzle.

The Prussian-born engineer John Roebling, who was knocked off a pier in Fulton Landing in June 1869, designed the bridge, which spans the East River from Manhattan to Brooklyn; he died of tetanus poisoning before construction of the bridge even began. His son, Washington Roebling, supervised construction of the bridge, which lasted 14 years and managed to survive budget overruns and the deaths of 20 workers. The younger Roebling himself suffered from the bends while helping to excavate the riverbed for the bridge's western tower, and remained bedridden for much of the project; his wife Emily oversaw construction in his stead. There was one final tragedy to come in June 1883, when the bridge opened to pedestrian traffic. Someone in the crowd shouted, perhaps as a joke, that the bridge was collapsing into the river, setting off a mad rush in which 12 people were trampled to death.

TOP SIGHT
BROOKLYN MUSEUM OF ART

This encyclopedic museum is housed in a five-story, 560,000-sq-ft beaux arts building designed by McKim, Mead & White. Construction on the building began in the early 1890s (when Brooklyn was still independent), with the intention of making it the largest single-site museum in the world. But the plan lost steam in 1898, when Brooklyn was incorporated into New York. Today, the building houses more than 1.5 million objects, including ancient artifacts, 19th-century period rooms, and sculptures and paintings from across several centuries.

DON'T MISS...

- Egyptian Collection
- Elizabeth Sackler Center for Feminist Art
- Visible Storage
- American Collection

PRACTICALITIES

- Map p442
- ☎718-638-5000
- www.brooklynmuseum.org
- 200 Eastern Pkwy
- suggested admission $12
- ⏰11am-6pm Wed & Fri-Sun, to 10pm Thu
- [S]2/3 to Eastern Pkwy-Brooklyn Museum

Egyptian Art

One of the highlights here is the excellent collection of Egyptian art, which spans a period of 5000 years. Housed in the 3rd-floor galleries, it includes bas-reliefs and Roman-era portraits, some of which are drawn from the museum's ongoing excavations in Egypt. A mummy chamber holds sarcophagi and ritual objects. But the most incredible piece is the so-called 'Bird Lady,' a delicate terracotta figurine with an abstracted face and clawlike hands, dating back to 3650–3300 BC. Look for her in a standalone vitrine.

American Collection

The Brooklyn is in possession of one of the great collections of American art. Do not miss a trip to the 5th floor to see it. Highlights include an iconic portrait of George Washington by Gilbert Stuart. Childe Hassam's celebrated urban landscape, *Late Afternoon, New York, Winter*, from 1900, and dozens of paintings by late-19th-century portraitist John Singer Sargent.

A Room of their Own

This is the rare mainstream arts institution that devotes permanent space to showcasing women. The 8300-sq-ft **Elizabeth Sackler Center for Feminist Art** on the 4th floor exhibits an engaging mix of one-person and historical shows that examine topics like women in video or pop art. At the gallery's core, you'll find Judy Chicago's seminal 1979 installation, *The Dinner Party*.

What to Know

There are other worthwhile galleries devoted to African sculpture, Latin American textiles and contemporary art. If you want a peek behind the scenes, head to the Visible Storage and Study Center on the 5th floor to see glass cases stuffed with everything from vintage bicycles to a bulbous Gaston Lachaise sculpture.

For dining, there's a casual snack counter, as well as gourmet fare in elegant **Saul** (Map p442; ☎718-935-9842; www.saulrestaurant.com; Brooklyn Museum; mains $25-32; ⏰noon-3pm Wed-Sun plus 5:30-9pm Wed & Sun, 5.30-10pm Thu, 5.30-11pm Fri & Sat; [S]F to Bergen St), which opened in late 2013.

On the first Saturday of every month (from 5pm to 11pm) the museum hosts a free evening of art, performances and live music (sometimes there's even a dance floor set up). It's a big draw with families.

TOP SIGHT
PROSPECT PARK

The creators of the 585-acre Prospect Park, Calvert Vaux and Frederick Olmsted, considered this an improvement over their other New York project, Central Park. Created in 1866, Prospect Park has many of the same features: a gorgeous meadow, a scenic lake, forested pathways and rambling hills that are straddled with leafy walkways. It receives roughly 10 million visitors a year.

Grand Army Plaza

A large, landscaped traffic circle with a massive ceremonial arch sits at the intersection of Flatbush Ave and Prospect Park West. This marks the beginning of Eastern Pkwy and the entrance to Prospect Park. The arch, which was built in the 1890s, is a memorial to Union soldiers who fought in the Civil War.

A greenmarket is held here from 8am to 4pm on Saturdays year-round. On the first and third Sundays of warmer months (May through September), the plaza also sees a circle of food trucks dispensing gourmet goodies.

Long Meadow

The 90-acre Long Meadow lies to the south of the park's formal entrance at Grand Army Plaza. It's a super strolling and lounging spot, filled with pick-up ball games and families flying kites. On the south end is the Picnic House, with a snack stand and public bathrooms.

Children's Corner

Near Flatbush Ave, the Children's Corner contains a terrific 1912 carousel, originally from Coney Island, and the **Prospect Park Zoo** (Map p442; ☎718-399-7339; www.prospectparkzoo.com; adult/child $8/5; 🕒10am-5:30pm Apr-Oct, to 4:30pm Nov-Mar), featuring sea lions, baboons, wallabies and a small petting zoo. To the northeast of the carousel is the 18th-century **Lefferts Historic House** (Map p442; ☎718-789-2822; www.prospectpark.org; 🕒noon-5pm Thu-Sun Apr-Nov, noon-4pm Sat & Sun Dec-Mar; [S]B, Q to Prospect Park) [FREE], which has plenty of old-fashioned toys to goof around with.

Audobon Center Boathouse

Sitting on a northern finger of Prospect Park Lake, the boathouse offers electric boat rides and paddle boats for rent during the summer. From here, there is a trailhead for 2.5 miles of woodsy nature trails (the route which takes you along **Lullwater Creek** is particularly scenic). Check the website for downloadable maps or ask at the boathouse for details.

Prospect Park Bandshell

To the southwest of the park's Long Meadow, this band shell hosts free outdoor concerts during the summers. Performance calendars can be found online or at the Audubon Center Boathouse.

The Lakeside Complex

After several years of construction (and a $74-million investment), Prospect Park's newest attraction opened in late 2013. The 26-acre Lakeside Complex features a pair of rinks, one for ice-skating in the winter, the other for inline skating on warmer days, as well as a cafe, new walking trails and a small concert space.

DON'T MISS

- The peaceful view from the Boathouse
- Stroll along Lullwater Creek
- Picnic and kite-flying on Long Meadow

PRACTICALITIES

- Map p442
- ☎718-965-8951
- www.prospectpark.org
- Grand Army Plaza
- 🕒5am-1am
- [S]2/3 to Grand Army Plaza, F to 15th St-Prospect Park

TOP SIGHT
CONEY ISLAND

Coney Island achieved worldwide fame as a working-class resort area at the turn of the 20th century. Though it is no longer the booming, peninsula-wide attraction it was then, it draws crowds who come for low-brow amusement – roller coaster rides, followed by hot dogs and beer on the boardwalk.

Historic Rides

Luna Park (Map p445; www.lunaparknyc.com; Surf Ave, at 10th St; ⊙late Mar-Oct; ⓘ; ⓢD/F, N/Q to Coney Island-Stillwell Ave) is one of Coney Island's most popular amusement parks and contains one of its most legendary rides: the **Cyclone** ($9), a wood roller coaster that reaches speeds of 60mph and makes near-vertical drops. The pink-and-mint-green **Deno's Wonder Wheel** (Map p445; ☎718-372-2592; www.wonderwheel.com; W 12th St, btwn Surf Ave & the Boardwalk; ride $6; ⊙mid-Mar–Oct; ⓘ; ⓢD/F, N/Q to Coney Island-Stillwell Ave) dates all the way back to 1920. It is the best place to survey Coney Island from up high.

Hot Dogs & Beer

The hot dog was invented in Coney Island in 1867, and there's no better place to eat one than **Nathan's Famous** (Map p445; 1310 Surf Ave, cnr Stillwell Ave; hot dogs from $4; ⊙breakfast, lunch & dinner till late; ⓢD/F to Coney Island-Stillwell Ave), established 1916. When thirst strikes, head to **Ruby's** (Map p445; www.rubysbar.com; 1213 Boardwalk, btwn Stillwell Ave & 12th St; ⊙11am-10pm Mon-Thu & Sun, to 1am Fri & Sat, April-Oct; ⓢD, N/Q to Coney Island-Stillwell Ave), a legendary dive bar on the boardwalk.

DON'T MISS...

➡ Cyclone roller coaster

➡ Cold beer at Ruby's

➡ Nathan's Famous hot dogs

PRACTICALITIES

➡ Map p445

➡ www.concyisland.com

➡ Surf Ave & Boardwalk, btwn W 15th & W 8th Sts

➡ ⓢD/F, N/Q to Coney Island-Stillwell Ave

Local Life
What's Going on in Williamsburg

Williamsburg is essentially a college town without a college – it's New York's of-the-moment Bohemian magnet, drawing slouchy, baby-faced artists, musicians, writers and graphic designers. Once a bastion of Latino working-class life, it's become a prominent dining and nightlife center.

❶ Seeing Green
Offering fabulous Manhattan views, the East River State Park (p271) is an open green space that becomes a major draw in the summertime – particularly during the Brooklyn Flea.

❷ Homegrown Hops
Hearkening back to a time when the area was NYC's beer-brewing center, the Brooklyn Brewery (p273) not only brews and serves tasty local suds, it also offers tours.

❸ Hipster Threads
If you want to dress the part, stop into Buffalo Exchange (p296), a much-loved vintage shop, where you'll find eye-catching fashions for men and women.

❹ Bodega Ephemera
For a glimpse for curious old objects from the days of yore, visit City Reliquary (p273), which is packed with NYC relics, including exhibits on the 1939 World's Fair.

❺ Latin American Detour
A fun little shop for browsing, Fuego 718 (p297) transports you south of the border with Day of the Dead boxes, colorful frames and mirrors, and kitsch and crafts from Mexico, Peru and beyond.

❻ Cocktails & Oysters
Crank that time machine back one more notch at Maison Premiere (p290), which features bespoke cocktails, oysters and other treats.

7 Brooklyn Art Library

Sign up for a free library card so you can browse the myriad sketchbooks from artists around the world at this space (p273). Or buy a blank book and add your work to the collection. A few doors down is the workshop/store of decadent Mast Brothers Chocolate.

8 Brooklyn Oenology Winery Tasting Room

Don't let the pretentious name deter you, with friendly **Brooklyn Oenology** (Map p438; 209 Wythe Ave, btwn 3rd & 4th Sts; ⏰4-10pm Mon, 2-10pm Tue-Fri, noon-10pm Sat & Sun) offering sample wines, whiskeys, beers, ciders and other treats, all made in New York.

9 Rough Trade

Williamsburg's massive new record shop (p295) is a dream for vinyl collectors. There are also frequent in-store concerts – many free.

SIGHTS

Williamsburg

Williamsburg is one of Brooklyn's hottest neighborhoods when it comes to eating, drinking and shopping. The neighborhood can seem a bit monochromatic after a while – you'll note plenty of hipsters with beards and high-ankled skinny jeans – but there's much creativity brimming beneath the surface. Traditional sights, however, are few, and it's best visited as an afternoon wander into evening – storefront strolling, followed by dining, drinking and catching live music. (Come earlier on weekends for markets and brunch.)

Most of the neighborhood is located along the East River waterfront, to the north of the Williamsburg Bridge. Bedford Ave serves as the main drag, with clusters of side-by-side cafes, boutiques and restaurants tucked into the area between N 10th St and Metropolitan Ave.

WILLIAMSBURG BRIDGE BRIDGE

Map p438 (www.nyc.gov/html/dot/html/bridges/willb.shtml; bike access at S 5th St & S 5th Pl; pedestrian access at Bedford Ave, btwn S 5th & S 6th Sts; [S]J/M/Z to Marcy Ave) Built in 1903 to link Williamsburg and the Lower East Side, this steel-frame suspension bridge helped transform the area into a teeming industrial center. Its foot- and bike-paths offer excellent views of Manhattan and the East River. Bonus: unlike the more attractive Brooklyn Bridge, which is capped by less-than-interesting civic center zones, the Williamsburg connects two neighborhoods with plenty of bars and restaurants, offering the possibility of refreshments on both ends.

EAST RIVER STATE PARK PARK

Map p438 (www.nysparks.com/parks/155; Kent Ave, btwn 8th & 9th Sts; ⏰9am-dusk; 👪; [S]L to Bedford Ave) The 7-acre waterfront East River State Park is Williamsburg's latest hot spot for outdoor parties and free summer concerts. Its grassy lawn is also home to a vast assortment of other events and activities. During the summer, the **Brooklyn Flea** (p296) can be found here, and there is ferry service to Manhattan and Governors Island. No pets allowed.

Neighborhood Walk
Brownstones & Bridges

START ST GEORGE HOTEL
END JANE'S CAROUSEL
LENGTH 2 MILES; TWO HOURS

Studded with historic structures, the area around Brooklyn Heights also has sublime views of Manhattan.

Start at the corner of Clark and Henry Sts, at the base of the 30-story **1 St George Hotel**. Built between 1885 and 1930, it was once the city's largest hotel with 2632 rooms. Two blocks to the north, at Orange and Hicks Sts, is **2 Plymouth Church**. In the mid-19th century, Henry Ward Beecher led abolitionist sermons here, as well as 'mock auctions' to buy a slave's freedom. Continue west on Orange and then south on Willow St. At 70 Willow, the yellow, 11-bedroom mansion served as **3 Truman Capote's house** while he was writing *Breakfast at Tiffany's*. Continue south, turning right on Pierrepont St, and follow as it bends to the left. The street turns into **4 Montague Tce**, a one-block lane lined with old brownstones. Thomas Wolfe penned *Of Time and the River* at No 5. From here, Remsen St travels west to reach the **5 Brooklyn Heights Promenade**. This scenic park, with its staggering city views, was built by planner Robert Moses in 1942, as a way of placating locals irritated by the construction of the roaring expressway below. Head north along the promenade, then north along Columbia Heights, and take the bouncy, pedestrian-only **6 Squib Park Bridge** (which opened in 2013) down into Brooklyn Bridge Park. At the bottom, admire the view from the grassy Pier 1, part of **7 Brooklyn Bridge Park**. Nearby is **8 Fulton Ferry Landing**. George Washington made an important hasty retreat here during the Battle of Long Island in 1776. From here, follow Water St under the **9 Brooklyn Bridge** (completed 1883), and past the **10 Empire Stores & Tobacco Warehouse**, two Civil War–era brick structures. The walk ends at Empire Fulton Ferry, part of Brooklyn Bridge Park and home to the gleaming **11 Jane's Carousel**.

MCCARREN PARK PARK

Map p438 (www.mccarrenpark.com; 776 Lorimer St; pool admission free, skating adult/child $8/4, skate rental $5; [S]G to Nassau) The grassy 35-acre McCarren Park makes a good picnic spot on warm days, while on sweltering days, you might want to head to the massive and historic pool that reopened in 2012 after being closed for almost three decades. Go early to avoid the worst of the crowds (and the occasional brawl that erupts from time to time). From mid-November through January, there's also an ice rink.

CITY RELIQUARY MUSEUM

Map p438 (☎718-782-4842; www.cityreliquary.org; 370 Metropolitan Ave, near Havemeyer St; admission by donation; 🕒noon-6pm Thu-Sun; [S]L to Lorimer Ave) A tiny community museum housed in a former bodega, the curiously fascinating City Reliquary is filled with New York–related ephemera. Cases and shelves are stuffed full of old shop signs, Statue of Liberty postcards, vintage pencil sharpeners, subway tokens, seltzer bottles and paint chips off the L train.

BROOKLYN BREWERY BREWERY, PUB

Map p438 (☎718-486-7422; www.brooklynbrewery.com; 79 N 11th St, btwn Berry St & Wythe Ave; tour Sat & Sun free, Mon-Thu $10; 🕒tours 5pm Mon-Thu, 1-5pm Sat, 1-4pm Sun; tasting room 6-11pm Fri, noon-8pm Sat, noon-6pm Sun; [S]L to Bedford Ave) Harkening back to a time when this area of New York was a beer-brewing center, the Brooklyn Brewery not only brews and serves tasty local suds, but offers tours of the facilities.

Tours Monday to Thursday include tastings of four beers, plus history and insight into the brewery; reserve a spot online. On weekends, tours are free (just show up) but don't include tastings. Instead, you can buy beer tokens ($5 each or four for $20) to sample the refreshing brews. Or you can skip the tour altogether and just while away a weekend afternoon in the bare-bones tasting room.

Interesting fact: the brewery's cursive logo was designed by none other than Milton Glazer, of 'I Heart New York' fame, who did the job in exchange for a share of the profits and free beer for life.

BROOKLYN ART LIBRARY GALLERY, LIBRARY

Map p438 (☎718-388-7941; www.sketchbookproject.com; 103 N 3rd St, btwn Berry St & Wythe Ave; 🕒noon-8pm) [FREE] Lining the walls of this intriguing space are over 30,000 sketchbooks, which contain a wild mix of graphic design, collage, fine art, poetry, irreverent comics and personal essays. To browse the collection, sign up for a free library card, then do a search by subject matter, theme, artist name or country. In fact, contributors from over 100 countries have added their sketchbooks to the library. Ask the friendly head librarian Chris Hueberger for his personal favorites.

If you feel inspired after paging through a few books, join in the fun. You can buy a sketch book ($25 for the basic 32-page book), which once received will be added to the collection. There are no parameters, and you can always mail it in, if you can't bring it in person.

⊙ Bushwick

A couple of subway stops to the east of Williamsburg on the L train, the ramshackle blocks of Bushwick begin to appear. Now home to a mixed community of African Americans, as well as Mexican, Ecuadorean, Puerto Rican and Dominican immigrants, it was an important beer-brewing center in the late 19th and early 20th centuries. The stately homes of beer barons still line Bushwick Ave, some in decrepit condition.

In recent years artists and musicians in search of cheap rents have begun to materialize in the area. As a result, the neighborhood's western fringes are already filling up with bars and industrial-chic restaurants. This area remains an industrial zone during the day but perks up on Friday and Saturday evenings when local bars and performance spaces come to life.

⊙ Brooklyn Heights

New York's first suburb is also its first designated historic district, with 19th-century brownstones (some of which date back to the 1820s) in the panoply of architectural styles: Victorian Gothic, Romanesque, neo-Greco, Italianate and Federal, to name but a few. This is a district of narrow streets and towering London plane trees – an ideal place to walk.

BROOKLYN HEIGHTS PROMENADE
LOOKOUT

Map p444 (btwn Orange & Remsen Sts; ⊙24hr; ⚿; S2/3 to Clark St) All of the neighborhood's east–west lanes (such as Clark and Pineapple Sts) lead to the neighborhood's number-one attraction: a narrow park with breathtaking views of Lower Manhattan and New York Harbor. Though it hangs over the busy Brooklyn–Queens Expressway (BQE), this little slice of urban perfection is a great spot for a sunset walk.

BROOKLYN HISTORICAL SOCIETY
MUSEUM

Map p444 (☎718-222-4111; www.brooklynhistory. org; 128 Pierrepont St, near Clinton St; suggested admission $10; ⊙noon-5pm Wed-Sun; SA/C, F to Jay St, M, R to Court St, 2/3, 4/5 to Borough Hall) Housed in an 1881 Queen Anne–style landmark building (a gem in itself, with striking terra-cotta details on the facade), this library and museum is devoted to all things Brooklyn. Its priceless collection contains a rare 1770 map of New York City and a signed copy of the Emancipation Proclamation.

Be sure to check out the vintage library, with its original black ash balcony from the 19th century. The society organizes regular exhibitions and neighborhood walks. Check the website for details.

◉ Dumbo

Dumbo – short for Down Under the Manhattan Bridge Overpass – is a cobblestone district lined with old 19th-century warehouses (now luxury condos) that offers incredible views of Manhattan from its waterfront areas. It's not the easiest neighborhood to navigate, so be prepared to do some walking around.

Visitors from Manhattan often combine Dumbo with a visit to Brooklyn Heights.

BROOKLYN BRIDGE PARK
PARK

See p265.

◉ Downtown Brooklyn

Jammed into the area between Cadman Plaza West and Flatbush Ave, the modern downtown consists of the borough's civic-center buildings (the courts and such), as well as functional office buildings. Here, the Fulton St Mall, a pedestrian strip, is chock-full of discount clothing and sneaker shops.

NEW YORK TRANSIT MUSEUM
MUSEUM

Map p444 (☎718-694-1600; www.mta.info/mta/ museum; Schermerhorn St, at Boerum Pl; adult/ child $7/5; ⊙10am-4pm Tue-Fri, 11am-5pm Sat & Sun; ⚿; S2/3, 4/5 to Borough Hall, R to Court St) Occupying an old subway station built in 1936 (and out of service since 1946), this kid-friendly museum takes on 100-plus years of getting around town. The best part is the downstairs area, on the platform, where you can climb aboard 13 original subway and elevated train cars dating to 1904. The museum's gift shop sells popular subway-map gifts.

◉ Fort Greene & Clinton Hill

These appealing residential districts spread east and south from the Brooklyn side of the Manhattan Bridge (along the eastern side of Flatbush Ave). The neighborhoods are marked on the southwestern end by the **Williamsburgh Savings Bank Tower** (Map p440; 1 Hanson Pl, at Ashland Pl; S2/3, 4/5 to Atlantic Ave, D, N/R to Atlantic Ave-Pacific St) FREE, which was built in 1927 and for decades was the tallest building in Brooklyn. If you're lost, looking for the tower is a good way to regain your sense of direction.

If you're on the hunt for gorgeous 19th-century architecture, Washington and Clinton Aves in Clinton Hill are home to some beautiful clusters of post–Civil War row houses.

BROOKLYN ACADEMY OF MUSIC
CULTURAL CENTRE

Map p440 (BAM; ☎718-636-4100; www.bam. org; 30 Lafayette Ave, at Ashland Pl, Fort Greene; S2/3, 4/5, B, Q to Atlantic Ave) Founded in 1861, BAM is the country's oldest performing-arts center and supplies NYC with its edgier works of modern dance, music and theater. The complex contains a 2109-seat opera house, an 874-seat theater, the four-screen Rose Cinemas and a 250-seat theater around the corner. Its stage has showcased Mercer Cunningham retrospectives, contemporary African dance and avant-garde interpretations of Shakespeare.

From September through December, BAM hosts the **Next Wave Festival**, which presents an array of avant-garde works and artists talks. The on-site bar and restaurant, BAMcafé (p294), stages free jazz, R&B and pop performances on weekends.

WORTH A DETOUR

HARBOR DEFENSE MUSEUM

Beneath the breathtaking Verrazano-Narrows Bridge and located inside Fort Hamilton, military buffs will discover a small treasure trove of artifacts at the **Harbor Defense Museum** (www.harbordefensemuseum.com; 101st St & Fort Hamilton Pkwy; ⏲10am-4pm Mon-Fri; 👪; [S]R to Bay Ridge-95 St) [FREE], the only army museum in New York City.

Built between 1825 and 1831, this arched, brick fort is still an active army base (bring photo ID to get in). The historic caponier, a freestanding bastion, houses the museum. The diverse collection includes helmets, weapons and uniforms from the Revolutionary War to WWII. There is also an array of vintage artillery.

A few blocks west, you'll find the harbor-hugging, 2.5-mile-long Shore Pkwy promenade. It's an ideal spot for a walk. North of Fort Hamilton is the old Italian district of Bay Ridge, where there are eateries and pubs along Third Ave, from 76th to 95th Sts.

To get here, take the R train to Bay Ridge–95 St and then walk half a dozen blocks to the southwest along Fourth Ave. The museum is located in a small park adjacent to the Verrazano-Narrows Bridge.

FORT GREENE PARK PARK

Map p440 (btwn Myrtle & DeKalb Aves & Washington Park & Edward's St, Fort Greene; ⏲6am-1am; 👪; [S]B, Q/R to DeKalb Ave) This 30-acre park sits on land that housed military forts during the Revolutionary War. In 1847 the area was designated Brooklyn's first park (a measure supported by newspaper editor Walt Whitman), and by 1867 Calvert Vaux and Frederick Olmsted were redesigning the place into the attractive hilltop landscape it is today. There are walkways, ball fields and a playground.

At the center of the park stands the Prison Ship Martyrs' Monument, supposedly the world's largest Doric column (it's 149ft high). Designed by Stanford White, it was built in 1905 to memorialize the 11,500 American prisoners of war who died in British prison ships during the Revolution.

BRIC HOUSE CULTURAL CENTER

Map p440 (www.bricartsmedia.org; 647 Fulton St, cnr Rockwell Pl; ⏲gallery 10am-8pm Tue-Sun; 📶) This long-running Brooklyn arts organization (responsible for free summer concerts in Prospect Park among other things) finally moved into a permanent space in 2013 – and at 40,000 sq ft, it's quite impressive. The multidisciplinary arts complex stages art exhibitions, media events, and a wide range of cultural fare – plays, concerts, dance performances – inside its 400-seat theater. There's also a branch of the Hungry Ghost cafe, and a glassworking facility (which also has exhibitions) next door.

👁 Boerum Hill, Cobble Hill & Carroll Gardens

Just south of Brooklyn Heights and Downtown Brooklyn, this cluster of tree-lined brownstone neighborhoods – Boerum Hill (east of Court St), Cobble Hill (west of Court St) and Carroll Gardens (south of Degraw St) – is short on attractions but full of great places to stroll, eat and shop.

In Boerum Hill, Smith St is a particularly enticing option. The roughly 13-block stretch south of Atlantic Ave is filled with restaurants, bookshops, bars and neat boutiques – a more chilled-out alternative to the consumer craziness of Manhattan. Atlantic Ave is broader and busier, with bars, restaurants, Middle Eastern groceries, clothing boutiques and antique shops, all concentrated into the blocks between Boerum Pl and Third Ave.

To the south of Cobble Hill is Carroll Gardens, a long-time Italian neighborhood, which continues down to the Gowanus Expwy.

INVISIBLE DOG GALLERY

Map p440 (www.theinvisibledog.org; 51 Bergen St; [S]F, G to Bergen St) In a converted factory off Smith St, the Invisible Dog is an interdisciplinary arts center that embodies the spirit of Brooklyn's creativity. Frequent exhibitions are held on the ground floor, while artists studios upstairs sometimes throw open their doors for group shows. Plays, film screenings, music

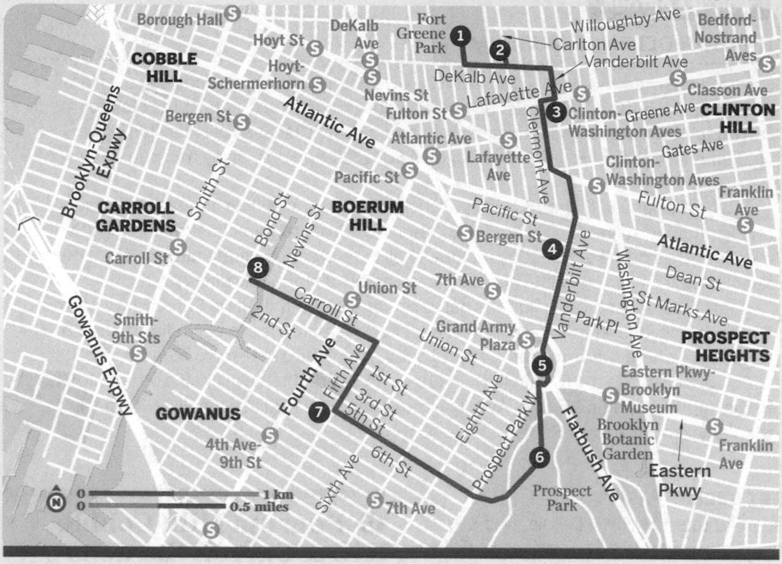

Local Life
South Brooklyn

This four-mile walk takes in some of Brooklyn's most fascinating neighborhoods, where new restaurants, shops, bars and cafes are rapidly changing the urban landscape. Along the way, you'll stroll through leafy neighborhoods, past brownstone-lined streets and across two pretty parks. To hit the flea markets and greenmarkets mentioned here, do this walk on a Saturday.

1 A Day at the Park

A stroll across pleasant 30-acre Fort Greene Park is a leisurely way to kick off the day. Climb the hill to the Prison Ship Martyr's Monument for views of Manhattan. On Saturday, there's a greenmarket just off the park on Cumberland St (we're fond of the apple cider doughnuts).

2 A Walk in Fort Greene

The leafy neighborhood surrounding the park is also called Fort Greene. Take a stroll along restaurant-lined DeKalb Ave, Fort Greene's main thoroughfare. Stop for coffee at **Smooch** (Map p440; 264 Carlton Ave, btwn DeKalb & Willoughby; [S]C to Lafayette Ave, G to Fulton St). Peak down the side streets for a glimpse of some of Brooklyn's loveliest streets.

3 Browsing New York's Best Market

Situated on the grounds of a school, the Brooklyn Flea (p296) hosts over 200 vendors who congregate to sell their wares, ranging from antiques and vintage clothes to enticing to-go snacks.

4 Wandering in Prospect Heights

Crossing Atlantic Ave you arrive in Prospect Heights, another charming Brooklyn hood. Vanderbilt Ave is the main drag, with shops, restaurants and cafes aplenty. Stop at the **Vanderbilt** (Map p442; 570 Vanderbilt Ave, cnr Bergen St; brunch mains $10-15; ⏰5-11pm daily & 11am-3pm Sat & Sun) for seasonal Modern American cooking.

5 Grand Army Plaza

Continue down to **Grand Army Plaza** (Map p442; Prospect Park, Prospect Park West & Flatbush Ave; ⏰6am-midnight; 🐾; [S]2/3 to Grand Army Plaza, B, Q to 7th Ave), a giant traffic circle crowned by a massive arch. Just south, at the Prospect Park entrance, is a popular Saturday greenmarket.

6 Brooklyn's Verdant Oasis

Prospect Park (p268), Brooklyn's version of Central Park, features many of the same

Prison Ship Martyrs' Monument, Fort Greene Park (p275)

landscape features but with far fewer crowds. A grassy meadow (perfect for picnics and kite-flying), forested trails and a scenic lake are the big draws.

7 Window-Shopping on Fifth Ave

Strolling west out of the park, you enter Park Slope, with tree-lined streets and historic brownstones in every direction. Fifth Ave is one of the commercial drags (as is Seventh Ave). Visit the curious **Brooklyn Superhero Supply Co** (Map p442; www. superherosupplies.com; 372 Fifth Ave, btwn 5th & 6th Sts; S R to 9th St, F, G to 4th Ave) for capes, disguises and particle guns.

8 Dipping into Gowanus

Just west of Park Slope is Gowanus, a once-industrial neighborhood on the make. It's named after the polluted canal that (sort of) flows there. Take the picturesque wood-plank bridge on Carroll St and have a waterside look before stopping at **Lavender Lake** (Map p440; www.lavenderlake.com; 383 Carroll St, btwn Nevins & Bond Sts; ⊙5pm-2am Mon-Fri, from 2pm Sat & Sun; S F, G to Carroll St, R to Union St), an enticing bar with a relaxing backyard open in the summer.

performances and the odd market all add to the cultural appeal of this community-focused arts center.

⊙ Red Hook

For more than a century the Statue of Liberty has fixated on this gritty neighborhood of harbor warehouses and cracked brick streets. The neighborhood is really two in one. There is 'the Back,' the popular waterfront area, which channels a rakish, 1940s kind of vibe. (It inspired the 1954 Marlon Brando drama *On the Waterfront*.) And there's the district to the south, home to the Red Hook Houses, an austere series of public housing projects that date back to the 1930s.

The area around the Back has gentrified in recent years, and a shiny Ikea housewares store sits on the waterfront, as does a gourmet-foods-stuffed Fairway supermarket. Even better is the growing array of cafes, restaurants and drinking spots that have opened their doors (Van Brunt St is good for browsing). But Red Hook's remoteness – the closest subway stop is at least a dozen blocks away – has kept development at bay.

The area around the waterfront is a good spot for a chilled-out walk in nice weather. It is best at the end of the day, when the sun starts to slip behind the Statue of Liberty; follow this with drinks or dinner at one of Red Hook's atmospheric restaurants.

To get here, climb aboard the B61 bus (which runs west on Atlantic Ave) or the B57 (southbound down Court St). You can also take the **water taxi** (Map p440; www. nywatertaxi.com/tours/ikea; one way Mon-Fri $5, Sat & Sun free; ⊙2-7.40pm Mon-Fri, 11:20am-9pm Sat & Sun) from Pier 11 in Lower Manhattan to Ikea. It's a long walk through a desolate industrial area from the Smith–9th Sts station of the F and G trains – not advisable at night.

WATERFRONT MUSEUM MUSEUM
Map p440 (☎718-624-4719; www.waterfrontmuseum.org; 290 Conover St, at Pier 44; ⊙1-5pm Sat year-round, 4-8pm Thu May-Sep; ⑪; ☐B61 Bus to Coffey St, S F train to Smith St) FREE The former Lehigh Valley Railroad Barge #79 (built 1914) was purchased for a dollar by its current owner, a juggler, who rescued it from its partially submerged state under the George Washington Bridge. Now it serves as a floating museum with exhibits

and events. The museum is free, but if you leave a donation you get a temporary tattoo. It's not a huge attraction, but sufficiently odd to be interesting.

⊙ Gowanus

To the east of the elevated subway station at Smith–9th Sts, in an area surrounded by decrepit, industrial blocks, is the Gowanus Canal. A former creek named after Gouwane, a Canarsie Native American chief, it was here that ships to New York Harbor came to unload their goods. It was also where local industrial operations unloaded all kinds of untreated waste. Today, it has been declared a clean-up site by the Environmental Protection Agency. Despite its toxic status, the area is home to a number of artists studios and frequently attracts intrepid urban explorers in search of moody waterfront pictures. With the opening of new restaurants and gourmet grocer Whole Foods, the area is Brooklyn's 'next big thing.'

⊙ Park Slope

This is New York's most earnest baby-making center, a leafy neighborhood that draws professionals in search of 19th-century brownstones and family-friendly everything.

Most businesses are located along Seventh Ave, while more youthful bars, restaurants and shops stretch along Fifth Ave. The more ornate homes – in beaux arts, Romanesque Revival and neo-Gothic styles – can be found on Prospect Park West and Eighth Ave between Union and Ninth Sts.

OLD STONE HOUSE CULTURAL BUILDING

Map p442 (☎718-768-3195; www.theoldstonehouse.org; Washington Park/JJ Byrne Playground, 3rd St, off Fifth Ave; suggested donation $3; 🕒11am-4pm Sat & Sun; 👪; [S]F, R to 4th Ave) This stone house is a replica of a 1699 Dutch farmhouse that was reconstructed by Robert Moses. There's a permanent exhibit devoted to the Battle of Long Island (what Brooklyn was known as c 1776) that includes period clothes and weapons. There's also a great playground for kids here.

MONTGOMERY PLACE NEIGHBORHOOD

Map p442 (btwn Prospect Park West & Eighth Ave; [S]2/3, 4 to Grand Army Plaza) This shady, one-block street contains a coveted series of beaux arts row houses, most of which were built by Paris-educated Charles Pierrepont Henry Gilbert in the 1880s.

⊙ Prospect Heights

Just across Flatbush Ave from Park Slope is the easygoing Prospect Heights. Once a home to Italian, Jewish and Irish residents, it began to attract African Americans and West Indians in the middle of the 20th century. Today, it draws a mix of young families and professionals who appreciate the proximity to Prospect Park. Most businesses are clustered along Vanderbilt and Washington Aves.

BROOKLYN MUSEUM MUSEUM

See p267.

BROOKLYN BOTANIC GARDEN GARDENS

Map p442 (www.bbg.org; 1000 Washington Ave, at Crown St; adult/child $10/free, Tue & 10am-noon free, Sat; 🕒8am-6pm Tue-Fri, 10am-6pm Sat & Sun; 👪; [S]2/3 to Eastern Pkwy-Brooklyn Museum) One of Brooklyn's most picturesque attractions, this 52-acre garden is home to thousands of plants and trees, as well as a Japanese garden where river turtles swim alongside a Shinto shrine. The best time to visit is late April or early May, when the blooming cherry trees (a gift from Japan) are celebrated in Sakura Matsuri, the **Cherry Blossom Festival**.

A network of trails connect the Japanese garden to other popular sections devoted to native flora, bonsai trees, a wood covered in bluebells and a rose garden.

There are multiple entrances. The best one is at Washington Ave, south of the Brooklyn Museum, which leads to a stunning new visitors center that opened in 2012. The structure, designed by Weiss/Manfredi, features a 'living' roof covered in 40,000 plants.

BROOKLYN PUBLIC LIBRARY LIBRARY

Map p442 (☎718-230-2100; www.brooklynpubliclibrary.org; 10 Grand Army Plaza, btwn Flatbush & Eastern Pkwy; 🕒9am-9pm Mon-Thu, 10am-6pm Fri & Sat, 1-5pm Sun; 👪; [S]B, Q to 7th Ave, 2/3 to Eastern Pkwy-Brooklyn Museum) [FREE] Brooklyn's Central Library is an art deco masterpiece from 1941 that contains over one million books, magazines and multimedia items. The limestone-covered building is shaped like an open book and there are 15 bronze panels above its 50ft-high entrance featuring literary characters like Tom Sawyer and Moby Dick. Free events happen throughout the year, including film screenings, classical concerts and weekly story time for babies, toddlers and preschoolers.

⊙ Bedford-Stuyvesant & Crown Heights

Bedford-Stuyvesant is NYC's largest African American district – it's where Notorious B.I.G grew up and film director Spike Lee shot *Do the Right Thing*. The neighborhood takes up a sprawling swathe of central Brooklyn between Flushing and Atlantic Aves and incorporates everything from spruced-up historic districts to sleepy streets of ramshackle row houses to bleak public housing projects. The Stuyvesant Heights Historic District (corner Lewis Ave and Decatur St; subway A/C to Utica Ave), located near Bed-Stuy's southern limits, vies with Brooklyn Heights and Park Slope for most gorgeous late-19th-century brownstones.

South of Atlantic Ave, you'll find Crown Heights, a neighborhood of African Caribbean and African American residents, who throw a resplendent West Indian Day parade (held every year on Labor Day.)

Parts of these neighborhoods bordering Bushwick and East New York can get sketchy. If you're keen on adventuring, ask around before setting out.

BROOKLYN CHILDREN'S MUSEUM MUSEUM
(www.brooklynkids.org; 145 Brooklyn Ave, at St Marks Ave, Crown Heights; admission $9, 3-5pm Thu free; ⏲10am-5pm Tue-Sun; 👪; [S]C to Kingston-Throop Aves; 3 to Kingston Ave) A bright-yellow, L-shaped structure houses this hands-on kid favorite, which was founded in 1899. The collection contains almost 30,000 cultural objects (musical instruments, masks and dolls) and natural-history specimens (rocks, minerals and a complete Asian elephant skeleton). The museum is located next to Brower Park and is about a mile from the Grand Army Plaza.

WEEKSVILLE HERITAGE CENTER HISTORIC SITE
(☎718-765-5250; www.weeksvillesociety.org; 1698 Bergen St, btwn Rochester & Buffalo Aves, Crown Heights; admission $5; ⏲tours 3pm Tue-Fri; [S]A/C to Utica Ave) In 1838 a free African American by the name of James Weeks purchased a tract of land on the fringes of Brooklyn's settled areas to build a free African American community of entrepreneurs,

GREEN-WOOD CEMETERY

If you really want to enjoy a slice of scenic Brooklyn in total peace and quiet, make for **Green-Wood Cemetery** (Map p442; www.green-wood.com; 500 25th St, at Fifth Ave; ⏲7:45am-5pm; [S]R to 25th St) [FREE]. A historic burial ground set on the borough's highest point, it covers almost 500 hilly acres. Its myriad tombs, mausoleums and patches of forest are connected by a looping network of roads and trails, making this a perfect spot for some aimless rambling.

Founded in 1838, the cemetery is the final resting place of all kinds of notable personalities. In fact, some 600,000 people are buried here – that's at least 530 miles' worth, if you laid them head-to-toe. This includes inventor Samuel Morse, mobster Joey Gallo, abolitionist Henry Ward Beecher, and '80s graffitist and Brooklyn son Jean-Michel Basquiat.

The best spot in the cemetery is **Battle Hill**, the highest point, where the Continental Army fought off British troops during the 1776 Battle of Long Island. The event is commemorated by the 7ft statue of Minerva, the Roman goddess of wisdom, who waves to the Statue of Liberty in the distance. The hill is located in the northeast sector of the cemetery, off Battle Ave. Maestro Leonard Bernstein and Brooklyn Dodgers owner Charles Ebbets are both buried in the vicinity.

You can pick up a free map at the entrance. On Wednesdays at 1pm, there is a two-hour trolley tour (per person $15). Note the squawking green parakeets nesting atop the Gothic entryway – these guys apparently broke out of an airport crate in 1980 and have lived here ever since.

Tip: pack mosquito repellent in the summer.

doctors, laborers and craftsmen. Over time, the village was absorbed into Brooklyn, but three of the historic wooden houses (aka the Hunterfly Road Houses) can be visited.

The center continues to evolve: a 19,000-sq-ft gold-certified Leadership in Energy and Environmental Design (LEED) building should have opened by the time you read this, with oral media lab, resource center, gallery space and performance hall; there will also be a new micro farm and botanic collection. It's a trek to get here, but worth it for history buffs. Call ahead to reserve a spot on the guided tour.

WYCKOFF HOUSE HISTORIC BUILDING
(☑718-629-5400; www.wyckoffassociation.org; 5816 Clarendon Rd, btwn 59th St & Ralph Ave, East Flatbush; adult/child $5/free; ⏰guided tours 1pm & 3pm Tue-Fri, 11am, 1pm & 3pm Sat & Sun Apr-Oct, closed Sun Nov-Apr; 🚌B8 to Beverley Rd/Ralph Ave, 🚊B, Q to Newkirk Plaza) Built in 1652, the Pieter Claesen Wyckoff House is NYC's oldest structure. A working farm until 1901, this Dutch Colonial H-frame house has shingled walls and split Dutch doors. It's located in the East Flatbush section of Brooklyn. Reservations required. Call or check the websites for directions out here.

◉ Coney Island & Brighton Beach

Located about an hour by subway from Lower Manhattan, these two beachside neighborhoods sit side by side, facing the Atlantic Ocean. Brighton Beach, to the east, is quieter, with coffee shops and grocery stands that display signs in Cyrillic and cater to the largely Ukrainian and Russian population. Coney Island, a mile to the west, is brassier with carnival rides, boardwalk bars and a surreal parade of humanity.

The two communities are connected by a boardwalk that runs along the beach, the best see-and-be-seen spot in Brooklyn during the steamy summer months.

CONEY ISLAND NEIGHBORHOOD
See p269.

NEW YORK AQUARIUM AQUARIUM
Map p445 (www.nyaquarium.com; Surf Ave & W 8th St; admission $10; ⏰10am-6pm Jun-Aug, to 4:30pm Sep-May; 🚼; 🚊F, Q to W 8th St-NY Aquarium) This fun, kid-friendly aquarium offers an opportunity to peek at an ocean's worth of creatures. The sea lion show is the big draw, which takes place in an outdoor Aquatheater with stadium seating. Admission on Fridays from 3pm to closing (from 4pm in the summer) is by donation.

Sadly, the New York Aquarium was badly damaged during Hurricane Sandy, and at the time of writing, some of the exhibits were closed and about half the animals had been relocated elsewhere (hence the reduced admission prices; prior to Sandy ticket prices were $15). Rebuilding and recovery aside, more changes are on the way, as the aquarium will go through a $150-million expansion, adding an ambitious exhibition entitled 'Ocean's Wonders: Sharks!' slated for completion in 2016.

EATING

A haven of all things high-end comfort, retro-vintage and bespoke, as well as plenty of ethnic joints that offer simple, unpretentious eats, Brooklyn is a place to bring your appetite. Not to mention your wallet.

✗ Williamsburg, Greenpoint & Bushwick

PETER PAN BAKERY BAKERY $
Map p438 (727 Manhattan Ave, Brooklyn; ⏰9am-7pm; 🚊G to Nassau Ave) On the main drag in Greenpoint, Peter Pan Bakery is a much-loved classic for its unfussy, well-made baked goods and excellent breakfast sandwiches on housebaked rolls or bagels (try the bacon-egg-and-cheese on a toasted poppy seed roll), all at rock-bottom prices. Take a seat at its wraparound counter only, or take it away and munch in McCarren park.

MEATBALL SHOP ITALIAN $
Map p438 (☑718-551-0520; www.themeatball-shop.com; 170 Bedford Ave, btwn 7th & 8th Sts, Williamsburg; meatballs $10-11; ⏰noon-2am Sun-Thu, to 4am Fri & Sat; 🚊L to Bedford Ave) Hot and tasty balls keep a steady stream of eaters coming back to this Williamsburg favorite, featuring vintage meat grinders on the dining-room wall. Also in the Lower East Side (p117) and West Village.

THE BEST OF BROOKLYN PIZZA

New York is known for a lot of things: screeching subways, towering skyscrapers, bright lights. It is also known for its pizza, which comes in a variety of gooey, chewy, sauce-soaked varieties. Following is a list of some of the top places in the city to grab a pie or a slice:

DiFara Pizza (www.difara.com; 1424 Ave J, cnr E 15th St; ⏲noon-4pm & 7-9pm; 👪; [S]B/Q to Avenue J) In operation since 1964 in the Midwood section of Brooklyn, this old-school slice joint is still lovingly tended to by proprietor Dom DeMarco, who makes the pies himself. Expect lines.

Totonno's (p290) The classic Coney Island pizzeria makes pies till the dough runs out.

Grimaldi's (Map p444; ☎718-858-4300; www.grimaldisbrooklyn.com; 1 Front St, cnr of Old Fulton St, Brooklyn Heights; pizzas $12-16; ⏲lunch & dinner; [S]A, C to High St) Legendary lines and legendary pizza in Dumbo.

Juliana's (p283) Celebrated return of pizza legend Patsy Grimaldi to Brooklyn in 2013.

Lucali (p284) Neapolitan-style pies started as a hobby for this noted Carroll Gardens *pizzaiolo* (pizza maker).

Franny's (p289) A contemporary eatery with an organic vibe serves simple pies in Park Slope.

Roberta's (p282) Divine pies with cheeky names like 'Gorgon Ramsay' in Bushwick's artsy district.

If you want to try several pizzas in one go, sign up for an outing with Scott's Pizza Tours (p103), which will take you to the most vaunted brick ovens around the city by foot or by bus.

CHAMPS VEGETARIAN $

Map p438 (www.champsbakery.com; 176 Ainsle St, at Leonard St; sandwiches & salads $9-12; ⏲9am-11pm; 📶✍; [S]L to Lorimer, G to Metropolitan) This airy little vegan/vegetarian spot sells baked goods (including highly popular croissants), as well as an array of sandwiches and salads. The reasonable prices and all-day breakfasts keep things busy.

PIES-N-THIGHS AMERICAN $

Map p438 (www.piesnthighs.com; 166 S 4th St, at Driggs Ave; mains $8-15; ⏲breakfast, lunch & dinner, brunch on Sun; [S]J/M/Z to Marcy Ave, L to Bedford Ave) The menu here seems designed to soak up booze: fried chicken and a mean mac 'n' cheese, plus plenty of sweet things. The most popular items are the fried chicken box (three pieces with one side) and the chicken biscuit, a puffy, fresh-baked biscuit stuffed with a fried breast and topped with hot sauce and honey. Save room for bourbon pecan pie.

MARLOW & SONS MODERN AMERICAN $$

Map p438 (☎718-384-1441; www.marlowandsons.com; 81 Broadway, btwn Berry St & Wythe Ave; mains lunch $13-16, dinner $17-27; ⏲8am-midnight; [S]J/M/Z to Marcy Ave, L to Bedford Ave) The dimly lit, wood-lined space feels like an old farmhouse cafe, which hosts a buzzing nighttime scene as diners and drinkers crowd in for oysters, tip-top cocktails and a changing menu of locavore specialties (smoked pork loin, crunchy crust pizzas, caramelized turnips, fluffy Spanish-style tortillas). Brunch is also a big draw, though prepare for lines.

RYE MODERN AMERICAN $$

Map p438 (☎718-218-8047; 247 S 1st St, btwn Roebling & Havemeyer Sts; mains $16-28; ⏲6-11pm Mon-Fri, from noon Sat & Sun; [S]L to Lorimer St, J/M to Marcy Ave) Yet another Williamsburg throwback, this inviting eat-and-drink spot with a long mahogany bar channels an early-1900s vibe. The menu is small but well executed with choices like Long Island duck breast, braised short ribs and pan-roasted skate, plus classics like mac 'n' cheese, pork belly sandwiches and raw-bar selections (oysters, shrimp cocktail). Great cocktails.

Stop in at happy hour (5:30pm to 7pm weeknights) for $5 old-fashioneds and $5 burgers.

MISS FAVELA BRAZILIAN **$$**
Map p438 (📞718-230-4040; www.missfavela.
com; 57 S 5th St, cnr Wythe St; mains $16-30;
⏰noon-midnight; 🚇J/M to Marcy Ave, L to Bed-
ford Ave) This ramsackle little spot near the
Williamsburg Bridge serves hearty plates of
Brazilian cooking like *moqueca* (a coconut-
milk-flavored fish stew) and *picanha* (a
juicy cut of prime steak), best preceded by
bolinhos de bacalhau (codfish balls) and ac-
companied by a caipirinha or three. Come
on Saturdays for live samba and *feijoada*
(black beans and pork stew) and on Sun-
days for live *forró* (music of northeastern
Brazil). Sidewalk seating on warm days.

CUBANA SOCIAL CUBAN **$$**
Map p438 (📞718-782-3334; 70 N 6th St, btwn
Kent & Wythe; mains $12-21; ⏰noon-midnight
Mon-Thu, to 4am Fri, 10am-4am Sat, 10am-
midnight Sun; 🚇L to Bedford Ave) True to
name, Cubana Social boasts an old-school
(c 1950s) Havana vibe. In an open room
fronted by a small stage, waitstaff bearing plates of slow-roasted pork, *ropa vieja*
(a kind of beef stew) and empanadas glide
among the small candelit tables. There's
live music (jazz, Afro-Cuban, Latin) Thursday to Saturday nights.

ROBERTA'S PIZZERIA **$$**
Map p438 (www.robertaspizza.com; 261 Moore St,
near Bogart St, Bushwick; individual pizzas $9-17,
mains $13-28; ⏰11am-midnight; 🅿; 🚇L to Morgan
Ave) This hipster-saturated warehouse res-
taurant in Bushwick consistently produces
some of the best pizza in New York. Serv-
ice can be lackadaisical and the waits long
(lunch is best), but the brick-oven pies are
the right combination of chewy and fresh.
The classic margherita is sublimely simple,
though more adventurous palates can opt
for the Darkwing (mozzarella, cured duck,
brussels sprouts).

There is a garden bar where you can en-
joy beer, wine or cocktails while you wait
for your name to come up. On weekends, its
brunch draws equally large crowds.

MOMO SUSHI SHACK JAPANESE **$$**
Map p438 (www.momosushishack.com; 43 Bogart
St, btwn Moore & Seigel Sts, Bushwick; sushi rolls
$5-12; ⏰noon-3:30pm daily & 6-10:30pm Mon-
Thu, to midnight Fri & Sat; 🅿; 🚇L to Morgan Ave)
Three shared tables occupy this industrial-
chic spot, where inventive Japanese tapas
all come with instructions on how to eat

them. Foodie preciousness aside, Momo's
is staggeringly good, offering superfresh
classics and flamboyant contemporary
creations, including rice croquettes with
squash, sage, walnut and mozzarella. There
are veggie options and a good list of sakes.
Cash only.

FETTE SAU BARBECUE **$$**
Map p438 (📞718-963-3404; www.fettesaubbq.
com; 354 Metropolitan Ave, btwn Havenmeyer &
Roebling Sts, Williamsburg; pork ribs or brisket per
pound $22; ⏰5-11pm Mon-Fri, from noon Sat &
Sun; 🚇L to Bedford Ave) Brooklynites craving
dry-rubbed BBQ descend en masse to the
'Fat Pig,' a cement-floored, wood-beamed
space (formerly an auto body repair shop)
that dishes up ribs, brisket and pastrami.
Everything is smoked in-house and there is
a range of accompaniments, but don't miss
the burnt-end baked beans, which are pep-
pery, not too sweet and chock-full of meaty
bits. There's a good choice of bourbon, whis-
key and beer.

WATER TABLE MODERN AMERICAN **$$$**
(www.thewatertablenyc.com; India St pier, Green-
point; prix fixe $75; ⏰7:30-10pm Fri & Sat; 🚇G to
Greenpoint Ave) Scoring high on novelty, the
Water Table is set inside a rustically converted WWII Navy patrol boat. The three-
course dinner (kale salad, clam chowder,
bouillabaisse and ricotta meatballs were
recent selections) would seem overpriced if
not for the memorable experience of sailing
past soaring skyscrapers and the Statue of
Liberty by night. Reserve a spot online.

PETER LUGER STEAKHOUSE STEAKHOUSE **$$$**
Map p438 (📞718-387-7400; www.peterluger.
com; 178 Broadway, near Driggs Ave, Wil-
liamsburg; porterhouse for 2 $100; ⏰lunch & din-
ner; 🚇J/M/Z to Marcy Ave) New York's most
storied steakhouse (in operation since
1887) serves up an amazingly tender por-
terhouse cut. Reservations essential; cash
or debit card only.

🍴 Brooklyn Heights, Downtown Brooklyn & Dumbo

BROOKLYN ROASTING COMPANY CAFE **$**
Map p444 (25 Jay St, cnr John St; coffees $1.50-
4; ⏰7am-7pm; 📶; 🚇F to York St, A/C to High
St) This sprawling coffee house is also the

headquarters of one of Brooklyn's most celebrated roasters. BRC takes its beans very seriously (all beans are fair trade and organic), and after sampling the goods (and perhaps a doughnut by Dough), you may be tempted to buy a few different roasts to take home.

BROOKLYN ICE CREAM FACTORY ICE CREAM $

Map p444 (www.brooklynicecreamfactory.com; Fulton Landing, Water & Old Fulton Sts, Brooklyn Heights; scoops/shakes $4/7; ⏲noon-10pm; 👪; [S]A/C to High St) You can grab a cone or a milkshake within view of the Manhattan and Brooklyn Bridges at this shop located inside an old fireboat house.

★VINEGAR HILL HOUSE AMERICAN $$

Map p444 (www.vinegarhillhouse.com; 72 Hudson Ave, btwn Water & Front Sts, Vinegar Hill; brunch $12-14, mains dinner $25-30; ⏲6-11pm Mon-Thu, to 11:30pm Fri & Sat, from 11am Sun; 🍸; [S]F to York St) Tucked into out-of-way Vinegar Hill, this homey spot is decked out in a charming array of thrift store bric-a-brac. But don't let the low-key decor fool you: chef Brian Leth cooks up an evolving menu that is bracingly fresh and unfussy, like veal short rib with chanterelles, carrots and cabbage or artic char with beets, yogurt, poppy seed and granola.

There is a wine list stocked with French vintages (from $38 per bottle), as well as retro cocktails. This place is popular, especially in summer when the back patio is open. Show up near opening time if you don't want to wait.

GANSO JAPANESE $$

Map p444 (25 Bond St, btwn Fulton & Livingston Sts; ramen $13-15; ⏲noon-10pm; [S]2/3 to Hoyt St; A/C, G to Hoyt-Schermerhorn) Tucked away in an unlikely corner of Brooklyn (just off the Fulton St mall) Ganso is a cozy, wood-lined spot that serves up some of the best ramen in Brooklyn. Spicy miso with pork belly is a winner (there's also a vegetaran option), and the appetizers are delicious: crispy pork *gyoza* (dumpling), *hijiki* (brown sea vegetable) salad, and plump buns stuffed with short-rib meat or pork belly.

ALMAR ITALIAN $$

Map p444 (☎718-855-5288; 111 Front St, btwn Adams & Washington Sts, Dumbo; mains $14-26; ⏲8am-10:30pm Mon-Thu, to 11pm Fri, 9am-11pm Sat, 10am-5pm Sun; 👪; [S]F to York St, A/C/E to High St) This welcoming Italian eatery serves breakfast, lunch and dinner in a homey, wood-lined space in Dumbo. Alfredo's meatballs are top-notch, as is the rich and meaty lasagna Bolognese. But if you're into seafood, don't miss the simple and delicious *cavatelli* (small pasta shells) with mussels, clams, shrimp and cherry tomatoes – it doesn't skimp on the shellfish. The small, inviting bar is an ideal spot to sip wine and nibble on olives.

JULIANA'S PIZZERIA $$

Map p444 (19 Old Fulton St, btwn Water & Front Sts; pizza $16-30; ⏲11:30am-11pm; [S]A/C to High St) The legendary 80-something pizza maestro Patsy Grimaldi makes a triumphant return to Brooklyn, with Juliana's (named after his late mother), which opened in 2012.

Patsy and his wife Carol were the original owners of Grimaldi's (they sold the business to Frank Ciolli, who now runs the still-famous Grimaldi's a few doors down). Now that there are two great pizza joints next to each other, the lines have thinned a bit, though it's still best to arrive early if you don't want a long wait. Who serves the better pie? Our money's on Juliana's, which serves up delicious thin-crust perfection, in both classic and creative combos (like the No 5, with smoked salmon, goat cheese and capers).

SUPERFINE MODERN AMERICAN $$

Map p444 (☎718-243-9005; 126 Front St, cnr Pearl Pl, Dumbo; mains $15-30; ⏲lunch & dinner Tue-Sun; [S]F to York St) This casual hangout is known for its Sunday brunches where Dumbonians sip Bloody Marys while DJs spin lazy tunes. Windows line two sides, and the rumble of the subway on the Manhattan Bridge overhead puts a bumpy thrill into the meal. The menu covers Mediterranean, Mexican and American dishes.

RIVER CAFÉ AMERICAN $$$

Map p444 (☎718-522-5200; www.rivercafe.com; 1 Water St, Brooklyn Heights; brunch $55, lunch mains $23-30, fixed price dinner 3-/6 course $100/135; ⏲lunch & dinner daily, brunch Sat & Sun; 🍸; [S]A, C to High St) Situated at the foot of the Brooklyn Bridge, this floating wonder offers beautiful views of downtown Manhattan – not to mention solidly rendered Modern American cooking. It took a beating during Hurricane Sandy and finally reopened in early 2014. Specialties include Wagyu steak tartare, Hudson Valley foie gras, crispy lavender-glazed duck breast and poached Nova Scotia lobster. The atmosphere is sedate (jackets are required after 5pm) but incurably romantic.

🍴 Fort Greene, Clinton Hill & Bedford-Stuyvesant

★DOUGH BAKERY $

(305 Franklin Ave, cnr Lafayette Ave, Clinton Hill; doughnuts around $3; ⏲7am-5pm; 📶; [S]G to Classon Ave) Situated on the border of Clinton Hill and Bed-Stuy, this small, out-of-the-way spot is a bit of a trek, but worth it if you're a pastry fan. Puffy raised doughnuts are dipped in a changing array of glazes, including pistachio, blood orange and hibiscus. Doughnut divinity for the tongue.

PEACHES SOUTHERN $$

(www.peachesbrooklyn.com; 393 Lewis Ave, Bedford-Stuyvesant; mains $14-21; ⏲lunch & dinner; [S]A/C to Utica) The homey atmosphere and tasty Southern food make Peaches a Bed-Stuy favorite. The stone-ground grits with blackened catfish is popular at all hours, while the French toast is in demand at brunch. The three-sides platter is a good veggie option; among other choices, you can put together a plate of sweet-corn succotash, sautéed spinach and gooey mac 'n' cheese.

NO 7 FUSION $$

Map p440 (☎718-522-6370; www.no7restaurant.co; 7 Greene Ave, Fort Greene; mains $18-25; ⏲5:30-11pm Tue-Sat, 4-9pm Sun, noon-3pm Sat & Sun; 🥕👪; [S]C to Lafayette Ave) This intimate Fort Greene stalwart showcases the talents of chef Tyler Kord, with imaginative dishes like ginger-chicken tortilla casserole, and fish tacos with watermelon rind, *yuzu* (Asian citrus fruit) mayo and cheddar. There's a saucy list of cocktails to choose from too.

WALTER'S MODERN AMERICAN $$

Map p440 (166 Dekalb Ave, cnr Cumberland St; mains $16-34; ⏲11am-midnight Mon-Fri, from 9am Sat & Sun; [S]B, Q/R to Dekalb Ave) On an idyllic corner just off Fort Greene Park, quaint old-timey Walter's serves up rich Southern and bistro fare with a few flourishes. Favorites: blackened catfish with red-cabbage coleslaw, spicy fisherman's stew and a reliably good burger (add bacon for a touch of decadence).

Don't neglect the raw bar (oysters, lobster, littleneck clams), the craft cocktails or brunch (fried chicken and waffles is a hit).

ROMAN'S ITALIAN $$

Map p440 (243 Dekalb Ave, btwn Clermont & Vanderbilt; mains $16-28; ⏲5-11pm daily & noon-4:30pm Sat & Sun; [S]G to Clinton-Washington Aves) In a small buzzing space on restaurant-dotted Dekalb Ave, Roman's is a celebration of seasonal locavorism, with a small menu that changes nightly. Dishes feature imaginative combinations (sourced from small, sustainable farms) and are beautifully executed: beets with oranges and anchovies, *maccheroni* (macaroni-like pasta) with pork sausage and ricotta, and striped bass fillet with green olives. Adroitly made cocktails and an esoteric wine list seal the deal.

🍴 Boerum Hill, Carroll Gardens, Gowanus & Red Hook

LUCALI PIZZERIA $

Map p440 (☎718-858-4086; 575 Henry St, at Carroll St, Carroll Gardens; pizzas $24, small calzones $10, toppings $3; ⏲6-10pm Wed-Mon; 👪; [S]F, G to Carroll St) One of New York's tastiest pizzas comes from this unlikely spot (it looks like a living room) run by Mark Iacono. Pizzas are all one size, with chewy crusts, fresh tomato sauce and superfresh mozzarella. Toppings are limited, but the Brooklyn accent is for real. Cash only; BYO beer or wine.

Plan ahead at this enormously popular spot: arrive at 6pm, give staff your cell number, and plan on dining a few hours later.

GOVINDA'S INDIAN, VEGAN $

Map p440 (305 Schermerhorn, btwn Nevins & Bond Sts; lunch $7-8; ⏲noon-3pm Mon-Fri; 🥕; [S]2/3, 4/5 to Nevins St; A/C, G to Schermerhorn St) On the bottom floor of a Hare Krishna temple, Govinda's prepares five or six different vegan options each day (eggplant Parmesan, vegetable curry, lentil soup, samosas and the like), plus rich desserts, all served cafeteria-style. There's not much ambience, but if you're vegan, you'll find this place a godsend (sorry).

BROOKLYN COOKBOOKS

Locally sourced products, sustainability and no small dose of creativity are all hallmarks of Brooklyn's celebrated new dining scene. To learn more about the magic behind the cuisine – and more importantly how to make those dishes at home – check out these titles:

- *The New Brooklyn Cookbook* (2010) Recipes, stories and culinary insight from 31 of Brooklyn's top restaurants.
- *Pok Pok* (2013) Andy Ricker delves deeply into northern Thai cooking, with precise instructions on creating those complex and heady dishes.
- *Roberta's Cookbook* (2013) Diver scallops in plum juice, orecchiette with oxtail ragu and glorious pizza perfection.
- *Four and Twenty Blackbirds Pie Book* (2013) Take your pastry skills up a notch with these tantalizing recipes by the Elsen sisters.
- *Franny's: Simple, Seasonal, Italian* (2013) An essential reference for making memorable pizzas, pastas and gelato at home.
- *The Frankies Spuntino Kitchen Companion & Cooking Manual* (2010) Beautifully designed cookbook packed with recipes of reimagined Italian-American comfort fare.
- *One Girl Cookie* (2012) Moist, tender whoopie pies and other sweet indulgences.
- *The Mile End Cookbook* (2012) Reinventing Jewish comfort food.
- *Brooklyn Brew Shop's Beer Making Book* (2011) Easy-to-follow guide for making refreshing brews at home.
- *Mast Brothers Chocolate* (2013) Compelling story of two brothers' beans-to-bars business; recipes, though, have mixed success.

For the latest on the borough's dining scene, seek out *Edible Brooklyn* magazine (www.ediblebrooklyn.com).

MILE END — DELI $

Map p440 (www.mileendbrooklyn.com; 97a Hoyt St, Boerum Hill; sandwiches $9-14; ⏲11am-4pm & 5-10pm Tue-Sun; [S]A/C/G to Hoyt Schermerhorn Sts) You can almost taste the smoked meats as you enter this small Boerum Hill eatery, which has exposed-brick walls and a couple of communal tables. Try a smoked beef brisket on rye with mustard ($14) – the bread is sticky soft and the meat will melt in your mouth. There's also classic Montreal-style bagels and that delightful Quebecois mess, *poutine* (french fries topped with gravy and cheese).

SAHADI'S — SELF-CATERING $

Map p440 (www.sahadis.com; 187 Atlantic Ave, btwn Court & Clinton Sts, Boerum Hill; ⏲9am-7pm Mon-Sat; ✎; [S]2/3, 4/5 to Borough Hall) The smell of fresh roasted coffee and spices greets you as you enter this beloved Middle Eastern delicacies shop. The olive bar boasts two-dozen options and there are also enough breads, cheeses, nuts and hummus to fulfill the self-catering needs of a whole battalion.

FAIRWAY — MARKET $

Map p440 (☎718-254-0923; 480-500 Van Brunt St, Red Hook; ⏲8am-10pm; ✎; 🚌B61 to cnr Coffey & Van Brunt Sts, [S]F, G to Carroll St) This sprawling supermarket offers an array of breads, cheeses, olives and smoked meats, as well as delicious pre-prepared foods. An on-site cafe (8am to 8pm) serves simple breakfasts and lunch, and offers excellent views of the Red Hook waterfront.

WHOLE FOODS — MARKET $

Map p440 (214 3rd St, btwn Third Ave & Bond St; ⏲8am-11pm; 📶; [S]R to Union) 🍃 Brooklyn's first Whole Foods is pretty impressive, with all the gourmet goodies you'd expect to find, plus a few surprises – including a 20,000-sq-ft greenhouse (where some of the produce is grown), an in-house coffee roaster and a sprawling prepared-foods counter (there are also records for sale). After browsing the staggering selection, head upstairs to the small bar and food counter.

You can order burgers, truffle-oil-flavored fries, mac 'n' cheese, kale salad and over a dozen unique microbrews on tap. There's outdoor seating with fine views over, uh, NYC's most polluted waterway.

MICHAEL MARQUAND / GETTY IMAGES ©

1. Prospect Heights (p278)
Check out this charming Brooklyn neighborhood, with shops, restaurants and cafes aplenty.

2. Williamsburg (p271)
Mingle with local hipsters at one of area's trendy bars or pubs.

3. Doughnuts
Indulge in tasty treats and baked goods at a Williamsburg bakery.

4. Prospect Park (p268)
Enjoy the beautiful features of this 585-acre park, which include waterfalls, forested pathways and rambling hills.

JOSEFINE STENUDD / GETTY IMAGES ©

★POK POK THAI $$

Map p440 (117 Columbia St, cnr Kane St; sharing plates $10-18; ⏲5:30-10:30pm; [S]F to Bergen St) Andy Ricker's much anticipated NYC debut has turned out to be a smashing success, with the rich and complex flavors inspired by northern Thailand street food wowing diners who make the long journey out. Fiery fish-sauce-slathered chicken wings, spicy green-papaya salad with salted black crab, smoky grilled-eggplant salad and sweet pork belly with ginger, turmeric and tamarind are among the many unique dishes.

The setting is fun and ramshackle, with a small backyard festooned with fairy lights. Waits can be long; thankfully there's a great little bar (Whiskey Soda Lounge) across the street, which serves imaginative concoctions (tamarind whiskey sours, Vietnamese coffee spiked with brandy) as well as bar nibbles from Pok Pok's menu.

FRANKIES SPUNTINO ITALIAN $$

Map p440 (www.frankiesspuntino.com; 457 Court St, btwn 4th Pl & Luquer St, Caroll Gardens; mains $16-22; ⏲11am-11pm; [S]F, G to Carroll St) Frankies is a neighborhood magnet, attracting local couples, families and plenty of Manhattanites with hearty pasta dishes like *cavatelli* with hot sausage and pappardelle with braised lamb. But as a *spuntino* (snack joint), this place is more about the small plates, with a seasonal menu that boasts excellent fresh salads, cheeses, cured meats and heavenly crostinis.

BROOKLYN CRAB SEAFOOD $$

Map p440 (24 Reed St, btwn Conover & Van Brunt Sts; mains $16-30; ⏲11:30am-10pm Wed-Sun; 🚌B61 to Van Brunt & Coffey Sts, [S]F, G to Carroll St) Across from Fairway, Brooklyn Crab is a casual three-story eatery, where diners hunker over picnic tables to feast on steamed crabs, oysters, fried cod, peel-and-eat shrimp and other delights from the sea. With waterfront views, tender crustaceans and refreshing pints of Allagash White, it's a great spot on a sunny day.

BATTERSBY MODERN AMERICAN $$

Map p440 (☎718-852-8321; 255 Smith St, btwn Douglass & Degraw Sts; mains $16-34, tasting menu $75-95; ⏲5:30-11pm; [S]F, G to Bergen St) One of Brooklyn's top new restaurants, Battersby serves magnificent seasonal dishes. The small menu changes regularly, but be on the lookout for veal sweetbreads, pappardelle with duck *ragu*, chatham cod with braised fennel and delightfully tender lamb. The space is Brooklyn-style quaint (plank floors, brick walls, tin ceiling), but tiny and cramped.

To get in without a long wait, plan ahead: arrive at opening time or make a reservation – accepted only for folks partaking of the tasting menu.

DOVER MODERN AMERICAN $$$

Map p440 (☎347-987-3545; www.doverbrooklyn.com; 412 Court St, btwn 1st & 2nd Pl; mains $28-40; ⏲5:30-10:30pm; [S]F, G to Carroll St) From the Battersby folks, Dover arrived in late 2013, offering more space, an outdoor patio and equally impressive roast meats, pastas and seafood dishes (though the prices are high). Foodies may swoon over the seven-course tasting menu ($95). Make reservations online.

🍴 Park Slope & Prospect Heights

SOUTHSIDE COFFEE CAFE $

Map p442 (☎347-599-0887; 652 Sixth Ave, btwn 19th & 20th Sts, Park Slope; 📶; [S]F to 7th Ave, R to Prospect Ave) This little spot on the southern edges of Park Slope has gained a tweaky, die-hard following for its tasty pastries, excellent coffee and friendly baristas. The cappuccinos are of the artful sort, featuring designs in the foam, and there are fresh-baked cinnamon rolls on Sundays.

BIERKRAFT SANDWICHES, BEER $

Map p442 (191 Fifth Ave, btwn Berkeley Pl & Union St; sandwiches $11; ⏲noon-11pm; 📶; [S]R to Union St) With hundreds of different beers for sale and regular tastings (currently 7pm Tuesdays), Bierkraft ranks high among Brooklyn's brew lovers. But it also prepares excellent baguette sandwiches, featuring house-roasted meats, prosciutto di Parma, cave-aged Gruyère and the like. For dessert, don't miss the impressive ice-cream-sandwiches. There's a backyard for warm days, or get it to go and head uphill to Prospect Park.

KIMCHI GRILL FUSION $

Map p442 (www.kimchitacotruck.com; 766 Washington Ave, btwn Sterling & Park Pl; mains $8-10; ⏲noon-10pm; [S]2/3 to Eastern Pkwy-Brooklyn Museum) What started as a food truck (the famous Kimchi Taco truck) is now a small, rock-and-roll eatery, with painted brick walls and just a few tables (or get it to go and eat in Prospect Park). The intriguing Korean-Mex combo features excellent BBQ beef short-rib tacos topped with kimchi, and first-rate kimchi *arancini* (rice balls); there are also vegan and gluten-free options.

TOM'S RESTAURANT DINER $

Map p442 (☎718-636-9738; 782 Washington Ave, at Sterling Pl, Prospect Heights; ⏰6am-4pm; [S]2/3 to Eastern Pkwy-Brooklyn Museum) Open since 1936, this diner looks like grandma's cluttered living room and delivers good, greasy-spoon cooking just three blocks from the Brooklyn Museum. Breakfast is served all day and it's a deal: two eggs, toast and coffee with home fries or grits comes to $4. Copious wall signs advertise specials – the blueberry-ricotta pancakes with lemon zest are unrivaled.

If you want to go old school, order an egg cream (milk, soda with chocolate syrup). Lines are loooong for weekend brunch.

CHUKO JAPANESE $

Map p442 (www.barchuko.com; 552 Vanderbilt Ave, cnr Dean St, Prospect Heights; ramen $13; ⏰5:30pm-midnight Tue-Sun; 🌿; [S]B/Q to 7th Ave, 2/3 to Bergen St) This cozy wood-lined ramen shop brings a top-notch noodle game to Prospect Heights. Steaming bowls of al dente ramen are paired with one of several spectacularly silky broths, including an excellent roasted pork and a full-bodied vegetarian. The appetizers are *very* worthwhile, particularly the fragrant salt-and-pepper chicken wings.

LOT 2 MODERN AMERICAN $$

Map p442 (☎718-499-5623; www.lot2restaurant.com; 687 Sixth Ave, btwn 19th & 20th Sts, Park Slope; mains $15-27, prix-fixe Sun supper adult/child $30/12; ⏰6-10pm; [S]F to 7th Ave, R to Prospect Ave) This intimate rustic spot serves locally sourced, high-end comfort food at the southern end of Park Slope. The menu is small but big on flavors. Try the grilled-cheese sandwich with parsnip soup, pan-seared fluke with arborio rice or a juicy grass fed burger with thick-cut, duck-fat fries.

FRANNY'S PIZZERIA $$

Map p442 (www.frannysbrooklyn.com; 348 Flatbush Ave, btwn Sterling & St Johns Pl, Park Slope; pizzas from $16; ⏰5:30-11pm Mon-Fri, noon-11pm Sat & Sun; 🌿; [S]B, Q to 7th Ave) This Park Slope icon serves bubbling thin-crust pizza baked in a brick oven, all decorated with a simple lineup of choice organic toppings such as buffalo mozzarella and oregano. There is an array of appetizers (such as chicken liver *arancini*, and wood-roasted turnips), as well as some well-rendered pastas.

CHERYL'S GLOBAL SOUL CAFE $$

Map p442 (www.cherylsglobalsoul.com; 236 Underhill Ave, btwn Eastern Pkwy & St Johns Pl, Prospect Heights; sandwiches $8-14, mains $15-25; ⏰8am-4pm Mon, to 10pm Tue-Sun; 🌿👪; [S]2/3 to Eastern Pkwy-Brooklyn Museum) Around the corner from the Brooklyn Museum and the Brooklyn Botanic Garden, this homey brick-and-wood favorite serves up fresh, unpretentious cooking that draws on a world of influences. Expect everything from sake-glazed salmon with jasmine rice to exceptional homemade quiche to a long list of tasty sandwiches. There are veggie options, as well as kid-friendly mac 'n' cheese or fish and chips.

MARCO'S ITALIAN $$

Map p442 (295 Flatbush Ave, btwn St Marks & Prospect Pl; mains $18-32; ⏰5:30-11pm daily & noon-2:30pm Sat & Sun; [S]B, Q to 7th Ave, 2/3 to Bergen St) Owned by the same folks that run Franny's, Marco's is a wee-little Italian trattoria that opened to much praise in 2013. There's no pizza and nary a red-sauce dish in sight, just imaginative rustic

LOCAL KNOWLEDGE

FOUR AND TWENTY BLACKBIRDS

At **Four and Twenty Blackbirds** (Map p440; 439 Third Ave, cnr 8th St; pie slices $5; ⏰8am-7pm Mon-Fri, from 9am Sat, 10am-6pm Sun; 📶; [S]R to 9th St), sister owners Emily and Melissa Elsen create flaky, buttery crusts and often use seasonal, regionally sourced fruits to create NYC's best pies, hands down. At this warm, old-fashioned spot, any time is just right to drop in for a slice and a steaming cup of Iriving Farm coffee. You can also come for quiches, savory galettes, sandwiches and other light bites.

Italian dishes like wood-grilled lamb chops, Ligurian fish stew and *bigoli* (long thick-tubed pasta) with cauliflower and anchovies. It's always packed, so arrive early.

🍴 Coney Island & Brighton Beach

Go Slavic on Brighton Beach Ave or hit Coney Island if you want that state-fair feel. For additional options at Coney Island, see Coney Island (p269).

VARENICHNAYA RUSSIAN $

Map p445 (☎718-332-9797; 3086 Brighton 2nd St, Brighton Beach; mains around $10; 🕓lunch & dinner; [S]B, Q to Brighton Beach) This small, family-run hideaway serves up consistently fresh dumplings from a variety of former Soviet Bloc countries. There are *pelmeni* (Siberian meat dumplings), *vareniki* (Ukrainian ravioli) and *mantis* (Uzbek lamb dumplings). The borscht is divine, as are the sturgeon and lamb kebabs. On weekends, plan on waiting for a table.

TOTONNO'S PIZZERIA $$

Map p445 (☎718-372-8606; 1524 Neptune Ave, cnr 16th St, Coney Island; pizzas $17-20; 🕓noon-8pm Wed-Sun; 🖉; [S]D/F, N/Q to Coney Island-Stillwell Ave) This old-school pizza parlor is open daily – as long as there's fresh dough. The toppings menu is slim (check the board above the open kitchen), but this is the kind of pie that doesn't need lots of overwrought decoration: coal-fired dough is topped with mozzarella first, followed by tomato sauce, so your crust never gets soggy. A place of pilgrimage, complete with real-deal New York attitude.

🍷 DRINKING & NIGHTLIFE

Dives. Cocktail lounges. And unassuming neighborhood joints. Brooklyn has got a bit of everything – including oodles of retro everything. (It's like everyone and their mother thought it'd be a good idea to resuscitate the 1920s.) Of the bunch, Williamsburg has the most hopping night scene.

🍷 Williamsburg & Bushwick

Visit the Free Williamsburg (www.freewilliamsburg.com) and Wagmag (www.wagmag.org) websites to keep tabs on the latest music gigs, art openings and more.

★MAISON PREMIERE COCKTAIL BAR

Map p438 (www.maisonpremiere.com; 298 Bedford Ave, btwn 1st & Grand Sts, Williamsburg; 🕓4pm-2am Sun-Wed, to 4am Thu-Sat; [S]L to Bedford Ave) We kept expecting to see Dorothy Parker stagger into this old-timey place, which features an elegant bar full of syrups and essences, suspendered bartenders and a jazzy soundtrack to further channel the French Quarter New Orleans vibe. The cocktails are serious business: the epic list includes more than a dozen absinthe drinks, various juleps, and an array of specialty cocktails.

A raw bar doles out delicious oysters, while there's more serious dining (and an outdoor patio) behind the bar.

DESNUDA BAR

Map p438 (221 S 1st St, btwn Roebling St & Driggs Ave; 🕓6-11pm Sun & Mon, to midnight Tue-Thu, to 2am Fri & Sat; [S]J/M to Marcy Ave, L to Lorimer St, G to Metropolitan Ave) A great way to start the night is by feasting on delectable oysters, tangy ceviches and complex libations at this charming eat-and-drinkery which arrived in Williamsburg in 2013. (There's also a Desnuda in the East Village). Come on Sunday or Monday for $1 oysters all night, served with delectable chutneys and spicy dipping sauces, or early (5pm to 8pm) the rest of the week for the same deal.

Adventurous diners: don't miss the 'bong-smoked' oysters, where fresh oysters take on just a note of smokiness (as in Lapsang tea leaves, not marijuana, lest you were wondering). Dine at the raw bar in front, or the more discreet cocktail bar in back, amid vintage map wallpaper and vaguely colonial-era decor.

BLUE BOTTLE COFFEE CAFE

Map p438 (www.bluebottlecoffee.net; 160 Berry St, btwn 4th & 5th Sts, Williamsburg; coffee from $4; 🕓7am-7pm Mon-Fri, from 8am Sat & Sun; [S]L to Bedford Ave) For the coffee connoisseurs, this top-of-the-line Williamsburg outpost (located in a former rope shop) uses a vintage Probat roaster on its beans. All drinks are brewed to order, so be prepared to wait a spell for your Kyoto iced. A small selection of baked goods includes coffee cake made with a chocolate stout from Brooklyn Brewery. Talk about locally sourced.

HOTEL DELMANO COCKTAIL BAR

Map p438 (82 Berry St, at N 9th St; ⏰5pm-late Mon-Fri, from 2pm Sat & Sun; [S]L to Bedford Ave) This low-lit cocktail bar aims for the speakeasy vibe, with old mirrors, unpolished floorboards and vintage chandeliers. Secret yourself at one of the nooks in back or have a seat at the curving marble-topped bar and watch barkeeps whip up a changing array of inventive cocktails (rye, gin and mescal are favored spirits).

There's also charcuterie, cheese boards and a raw bar (oysters, littleneck clams, shrimp cocktail). Enter on N 9th St.

TOBY'S ESTATE CAFE

Map p438 (125 N 6th St, btwn Bedford & Berry; coffee from $4; ⏰7am-7pm Mon-Thu, from 8am Sat & Sun; 📶; [S]L to Bedford Ave) This small-batch roaster brings serious flavor to the streets of Billyburg with bold aromatic pour-overs, creamy flat whites and smooth *cortados* (espresso with a dash of milk). There are a few couches and several communal tables often crowded with MacBook users.

KINFOLK STUDIOS LOUNGE

Map p438 (www.kinfolklife.com; 90 Wythe Ave, btwn 11th & 10th Sts; ⏰8:30am-late Mon-Fri, from 10am Sat & Sun) Kinfolk is a great little space for socializing, though sometimes it feels a little too cool for school. High-ceilinged cafe and art space by day morphs into high-style drinking den by night, with DJs spinning rare beats while hipsters crowd around drinking Japanese beers.

OTB BAR

Map p438 (141 Broadway, btwn Bedford & Driggs Aves; ⏰5pm-2am Sun-Thu, to 4am Fri & Sat; [S]J/M to Marcy Ave) OTB, which stands for 'off-track betting,' pays homage to those gamble-worthy thoroughbreds with horsey-themed decor (betting-form menus, black-and-white photos of shapely ponies and horse wallpaper in the bathrooms) though low-lit chandeliers, flickering candles and dark-wood furniture somehow creates a classy rather than kitschy vibe. You'll also find friendly waitstaff, a fun-time crowd, great beer selections, bespoke cocktails and oysters ($1 after 11pm or midnight).

Also has lots of other nibbles (frog legs, escargot, seared scallops, wings).

LARRY LAWRENCE BAR

Map p438 (www.larrylawrencebar.com; 295 Grand St, btwn Roebling & Havemeyer Sts; ⏰6pm-4am; [S] L to Lorimer St) This speakeasy-style bar makes a great detour while exploring Williamsburg by night. Once you find the place, you're in: no door Gestapo here; just a spacious, low-lit drinking den, with a welcoming vibe, an easygoing crowd and no overly obtrusive music. The entrance is hard to find: look for the tiny word 'bar' over a nondescript door, then head down the long concrete hallway.

There's an outdoor balcony for smokers.

CLEM'S PUB

Map p438 (☎718-387-9617; 264 Grand St, at Roebling St, Williamsburg; ⏰2pm-4am, from noon Sat & Sun; [S]L to Bedford Ave, J/M/Z to Marcy Ave) This tidy Williamsburg pub keeps things chill. There's a long bar, friendly bartenders and a few outdoor tables that are perfect for summer people-watching. It also sells beer and a shot for only $5.

IDES BAR

Map p438 (www.wythehotel.com/the-ides/; 80 Wythe Ave; ⏰5pm-2am Mon-Fri, from 2pm Sat & Sun) The rooftop bar of the Wythe Hotel offers magnificent views of Manhattan; come early to beat the crowds.

BERRY PARK BAR

Map p438 (www.berryparkbk.com; 4 Berry St, cnr 14th St; ⏰2pm-late Mon-Fri, from 11am Sat & Sun; [S]G to Nassau Ave) This sports loving bar is the go-to spot during soccer premier league matches as well as NFL games, with several huge screens for watching the action unfold. Fourteen beers on tap, and plenty of bar snacks (plus brunch till 4pm daily) keep folks from going hungry. The best part, though, is the huge rooftop deck with fabulous views of the city.

On summer days, there's no better drinking spot in the 'Burg.

PINE BOX ROCK SHOP BAR

Map p438 (www.pineboxrockshop.com; 12 Grattan St, btwn Morgan Ave & Bogart St, Bushwick; ⏰4pm-2am Mon-Fri, 2pm-4am Sat, noon-2am Sun; [S]L to Morgan Ave) The cavernous Pine Box is a former Bushwick casket factory that has 16 drafts to choose from, as well as spicy, pint-sized Bloody Marys. Run by a friendly musician couple, the walls are filled with local artwork and a performance space in the back hosts regular gigs. Tasty bar snacks consist of hearty vegan empanadas.

RADEGAST HALL & BIERGARTEN BEER HALL
Map p438 (www.radegasthall.com; 113 N 3rd St, at Berry St, Williamsburg; ⏲noon-late; [S]L to Bedford Ave) An Austro-Hungarian beer hall in Williamsburg offers up a huge selection of Bavarian brews as well as a kitchen full of munchable meats. You can hover in the dark, woody bar area, or sit in the adjacent hall, which has a retractable roof and communal tables to feast at – perfect for pretzels, sausages and burgers.

METROPOLITAN GAY & LESBIAN
Map p438 (559 Lorimer St, at Metropolitan Ave, Williamsburg; ⏲3pm-4am; [S]L to Lorimer St, G to Metropolitan Ave) This low-key Williamsburg hangout draws a good blend of arty gays and lesbians with its cool staff, cheap drinks, outdoor patio and groovy DJs. During the summer, it's known for its Sunday backyard barbecues, and on Wednesday nights, it's all about the girls.

SPUYTEN DUYVIL BAR
Map p438 (www.spuytenduyvilnyc.com; 359 Metropolitan Ave, btwn Havemayer & Roebling, Williamsburg; ⏲from 5pm Mon-Fri, from noon Sat & Sun; [S]L to Lorimer St, G to Metropolitan Ave) This low-key Williamsburg bar looks like it was pieced together from a rummage sale. The ceilings are painted red, there are vintage maps on the walls and the furniture consists of tattered armchairs. But the beer selection is staggering, the locals from various eras are chatty and there's a decent-sized patio with leafy trees that is open in good weather.

HAREFIELD ROAD PUB
Map p438 (769 Metropolitan Ave, btwn Graham Ave & Humboldt St, Williamsburg; ⏲noon-4am Mon-Fri, 11am-4am Sat & Sun; [S]L to Graham Ave) A serene crowd can be found inside this East Williamsburg bar that sports a minimalist, medieval tavern kind of look. Other than a few wines served by the glass, its focus is beer, with over a dozen brews on tap. There is also a long list of single-malt scotches, and it serves paninis.

There's a small brick courtyard in back, and a very popular weekend brunch, served from 11am to 4pm.

SPRITZENHAUS BEER HALL
Map p438 (33 Nassau Ave; ⏲4pm-4am Mon-Wed, noon-4am Thu-Sun; [S]G to Nassau Ave) Beer lovers shouldn't miss this place. On the edge of McCarren Park, this open, somewhat industrial 6000-sq-ft beer hall has 20 or so beers on tap, and dozens of other choices by the bottle. German, Belgian and North American microbrews dominate, and there's lots of meaty pub grub (sausages mostly, but the Belgian fries with truffle oil are also a hit).

Seating is at the long serpentine bar or on rustic picnic tables, though in winter you may want to linger by the fire.

🍷 Fort Greene

DER SCHWARZE KÖELNER PUB
Map p440 (www.derschwarzekoelner.com; 710 Fulton St, cnr Hanson Pl; ⏲5pm-1am Mon-Thu, to 4am Fri, 2pm-4am Sat, 2pm-1am Sun; [S]C to Lafayette Ave) This casual beer garden with checkered floors, lots of windows and a lively, mixed crowd is located just a few blocks away from the Brooklyn Academy of Music. There are 18 beers on tap, all of which go swimmingly with a hot *brezel* (soft German pretzel). A variety of other snacks are served all night.

🍷 Brooklyn Heights

FLOYD BAR
Map p444 (131 Atlantic Ave, btwn Henry & Clinton Sts; ⏲5pm-4am Mon-Thu, 4pm-4am Fri, 11am-4am Sat & Sun; [S]2/3, 4/5 to Borough Hall) This glass-front bar is home to young flirters who cuddle on tattered antique sofas while beer-swillers congregate around an indoor bocie court. A good local hang.

🍷 Cobble Hill, Carroll Gardens & Red Hook

CLOVER LOUNGE BAR
Map p440 (☎718-855-7939; 210 Smith St, btwn Baltic & Butler Sts; ⏲4pm-2am Mon-Thu, noon-4am Fri, 10:30am-4am Sat, 10:30am-1am Sun; [S]F, G to Bergen) This delightful cocktail parlor channels 19th-century elegance with a rich mahogany bar, vintage fixtures and vest-wearing barkeeps. Beautifully prepared cocktails draw in a mostly local crowd, who come for lively conversation fueled by re-

fined recipes such as the improved whiskey cocktail (rye whiskey, maraschino, absinthe and bitters). Clover also serves big weekend brunches (matched by excellent Bloody Marys and other libations).

61 LOCAL BAR

Map p440 (www.61local.com; 61 Bergen St, btwn Smith St & Boerum Pl, Cobble Hill; snacks $2-5, sandwiches $5-10; ⏲7am-late Mon-Fri, from 9am Sat & Sun; 📶; [S]F, G to Bergen) A roomy brick-and-wood hall in Cobble Hill manages to be both chic and warm, with large communal tables, a mellow vibe and a good selection of craft beers (including KelSo, Ommegang and Allagash). There's a simple menu of charcuterie, cheese boards and other snacks, including smoky ham and cheese sandwiches, quinoa salads and mezze platters (hummus, baba ghanoush, olives).

SUNNY'S BAR

Map p440 (☎718-625-8211; 253 Conover St, btwn Beard & Reed Sts, Red Hook; ⏲8pm-4am Wed-Fri, 4pm-4am Sat, to 11pm Sun; 🚌B61 to Coffey & Conover Sts, [S]F, G to Carroll St) Way out in Red Hook, this superinviting longshoreman bar – the sign says 'bar' – is straight out of *On the Waterfront*. Every Saturday at 10pm it hosts a foot-stomping bluegrass jam.

🍷 Park Slope

FREDDY'S BAR

Map p442 (www.freddysbar.com; 627 Fifth Ave, btwn 17th & 18th Sts; ⏲noon-4am; [S]R to Prospect Ave) In this old-time bar in the South Slope, you can tip one back at the vintage mahogany bar while admiring the crazy videos made by Donald, the co-owner. Check out the one behind the bar of a cat drinking. There's also live music (uke jams, honky tonk), comedy nights and the odd film screening.

DER KOMMISSAR BAR

Map p442 (www.derkommissar.net; 559 Fifth Ave & 15th St; ⏲3pm-late Mon-Wed, from noon Thu-Sun; [S]F, G, R to 4th Ave, R to Prospect Ave) This long, narrow Park Slope bar has good tunes (the Beatles, not Falco), vintage films like *Dr Strangelove*, eight beers on tap, an extensive selection of schnapps, plus no-joke Austrian sausages. Order a tasty Viennese with cheese ($6) to go with your Gösser (Austrian lager).

GREENWOOD PARK BEER HALL

Map p442 (www.greenwoodparkbk.com; 555 Seventh Ave, btwn 19th & 20th Sts; ⏲4pm-2am Mon-Fri, from noon Sat & Sun; 📶; [S]F, G to Prospect Park) Around the corner from the leafy Greenwood cemetery, this roomy beer hall is a clever reconfiguration of a former gas station and mechanic's shop. In an open, industrial setting, you'll find over two dozen beers on draft, plus panini, burgers, salads and other pub fare.

The outdoor space, with its three bocce courts and weekend barbecues, draws laid-back crowds in the summer. It's a family-friendly space in the daytime, but strictly 21-and-up after about 7pm.

☆ ENTERTAINMENT

BROOKLYN BOWL LIVE MUSIC

Map p438 (☎718-963-3369; www.brooklynbowl.com; 61 Wythe Ave, btwn 11th & 12th Sts; lane rental per hour $40-50, shoe rental $5; ⏲6pm-2am Mon-Thu, to 4am Fri, noon-4am Sat, noon-2am Sun; [S]L to Bedford Ave, G to Nassau Ave) This 23,000-sq-ft venue inside the former Hecla Iron Works Company combines bowling (p298), microbrews, food and groovy live music. In addition to the live bands that regularly tear up the stage, there are NFL game days, karaoke and DJ nights. Aside from weekends (noon to six pm), it's age 21 and up.

MUSIC HALL OF WILLIAMSBURG LIVE MUSIC

Map p438 (www.musichallofwilliamsburg.com; 66 N 6th St, btwn Wythe & Kent Aves, Williamsburg; show $15-35; [S]L to Bedford Ave) This popular Williamsburg music venue is *the* place to see indie bands in Brooklyn. (For many groups traveling through New York, this is their one and only spot.) It is intimate and the programming is solid. Recent sold-out shows include Brooklyn-based the Hold Steady and Aussie roots rockers the John Butler Trio.

THEATER FOR A NEW AUDIENCE PERFORMING ARTS

Map p440 (☎866-811-4111; www.tfana.org; 262 Ashland Pl, cnr Fulton St) Part of the emerging cultural district surrounding BAM, the Theatre for a New Audience opened in late 2013, in a grand new building modeled inspired by London's Cottesloe Theatre. It stages Shakespearean and classical

READING BROOKLYN

Brooklyn's literary roots run deep. The former Borough President Marty Markowitz described Brooklyn as 'New York's left bank,' and given the range of local talents that have shaped American literature – not to mention the countless authors living here today – he may not be far off the mark.

Here are a few quintessential Brooklyn reads from celebrated Brooklynites present and past:

➡ *Leaves of Grass* (1855) Walt Whitman's poetic celebration of life. Particularly poignant: 'Crossing Brooklyn Ferry.'

➡ *A Tree Grows in Brooklyn* (1943) Betty Smith's poignant coming-of-age story set in the squalid tenements of Williamsburg.

➡ *Sophie's Choice* (1979) William Styron's blockbuster set in a boarding house in postwar Flatbush.

➡ *Motherless Brooklyn* (1999) Jonathan Lethem's brilliant and darkly comic tale of small-time hoods set in Carroll Gardens and other parts of Brooklyn.

➡ *Literary Brooklyn* (2011) Evan Hughes provides an overview of great Brooklyn writers and their neighborhoods over the years, from Henry Miller's Williamsburg to Truman Capote's Brooklyn Heights.

dramas. Julie Taymor's wildly reconfigured *A Midsummer Night's Dream* opened the theater's first season to much acclaim.

KNITTING FACTORY LIVE MUSIC

Map p438 (☎347-529-6696; www.knittingfactory.com; 361 Metropolitan Ave, at Havemayer St, Williamsburg; shows $5-20; [S]G, L to Lorimer St) A long-time outpost for folk, indie and experimental music in New York, Williamsburg's Knitting Factory is where you go to see everything from cosmic space jazz to rock. The stage is small and intimate. A separate barroom has a soundproof window with stage views.

WARSAW LIVE MUSIC

Map p438 (www.warsawconcerts.com; Polish National Home, 261 Driggs Ave, at Eckford St, Greenpoint; [S]L to Bedford Ave, G to Nassau Ave) A burgeoning New York classic, this stage is in the Polish National Home, with good views in the old ballroom, for bands ranging from indie darlings the Dead Milkmen to legends George Clinton. Polish ladies serve pierogis and beers under the disco balls.

OUTPUT NIGHTCLUB

Map p438 (74 Wythe Ave, btwn N 12th & 11th Sts; cover $20-30; [S]L to Bedford, G to Nassau) Output boasts a great (Function-One) sound system and draws a laid-back but dance-loving crowd. The drinks are pricey but the views from the rooftop are stunning. When big-name DJs spin, arrive early to beat the long lines – and buy tickets in advance to save cash. Go online for the latest.

BAMCAFÉ LIVE MUSIC

Map p440 (☎718-636-4100; www.bam.org; 30 Lafayette Ave, at Ashland Pl, Fort Greene; [S]D, N/R to Pacific St, B, Q, 2/3, 4/5 to Atlantic Ave) This high-ceilinged restaurant and lounge in the upstairs part of the Brooklyn Academy of Music is the spot to hit for free Friday and Saturday evening shows. The room is beautiful and the lineup is generally mellow, covering jazz, R & B, world music and experimental rock.

BAMcafé also hosts 'Eat Drink & Be Literary,' a weekly Thursday reading and dinner (per person including dinner $55). Past speakers have included novelists Salman Rushdie, Jeffrey Eugenides and Jonathan Franzen.

BARBES LIVE MUSIC

Map p442 (☎347-422-0248; www.barbesbrooklyn.com; 376 9th St, at Sixth Ave; suggested donation for live music $10; ⏲5pm-2am Mon-Thu, 2pm-4am Fri & Sat, to 2am Sun; [S]F to 7th Ave) This bar and performance space, owned by two French musicians and longtime Brooklyn residents, has a world-music vibe, offering eclectic music, ranging from Lebanese diva Asmahan to traditional Mexican *bandas,* Venezuelan *joropos* and Romanian brass bands. There are readings and film screenings too.

BELL HOUSE   LIVE MUSIC

Map p440 (www.thebellhouseny.com; 149 7th St, Gowanus; ⊘5pm-4am; 🚻; §F, G, R to 4th Ave-9th St) A big, old venue in the mostly barren neighborhood of Gowanus, the Bell House features live performances, indie rockers, DJ nights, comedy shows and burlesque parties. The handsomely converted warehouse has a spacious concert area, plus a friendly little bar in the front room with flickering candles, leather armchairs and 10 or so beers on tap.

JALOPY   LIVE MUSIC

Map p440 (www.jalopy.biz; 315 Columbia St, at Woodhull St, Red Hook; §F, G to Carroll St) This fringe Carroll Gardens/Red Hook banjo shop has a fun DIY space with cold beer for its bluegrass, country and ukulele shows, including a feel-good Roots 'n' Ruckus show on Wednesday nights.

BARGEMUSIC   CLASSICAL MUSIC

Map p444 (www.bargemusic.org; Fulton Ferry Landing, Brooklyn Heights; tickets $35-45; 🚻; §A/C to High St) The chamber-music concerts held on this 125-seat converted coffee barge (built c 1899) are a unique, intimate affair. For nearly 40 years, it has been a beloved venue, with beautiful views of the East River and Manhattan. There are free children's concerts on some Saturdays.

★**BROOKLYN**
ACADEMY OF MUSIC   PERFORMING ARTS

Map p440 (BAM; www.bam.org; 30 Lafayette Ave, at Ashland Pl, Fort Greene; 🚻; §D, N/R to Pacific St, B, Q, 2/3, 4/5 to Atlantic Ave) At this performing-arts complex, the Howard Gilman Opera House and Harvey Lichtenstein Theater host their share of ballet, modern and world-dance performances. Among other groups, they've presented the Alvin Ailey American Dance Theater, the Mark Morris Dance Group and the Pina Bausch Dance Theater.

Buy tickets early for the **Next Wave Festival** (September to December), featuring cutting-edge theater and dance from around the globe. Also on-site: the elegant **BAM Howard Gilman Opera House** (Map p440) and the **BAM Rose Cinemas** (Map p440), which screen first-run, indie and foreign films. Around the corner is the **BAM Fisher Building** (Map p440; http://www.bam.org/fisher; 321 Ashland Pl) with its more intimate 250-seat theater.

ST ANN'S WAREHOUSE   THEATER

Map p444 (📞718-254-8779; www.stannswarehouse.org; 29 Jay St, Dumbo; §A/C to High St) This avant-garde performance company hosts innovative theater and dance happenings that attract the Brooklyn literati. The calendar has featured rock opera, genre-defying music by new composers, and strange and wondrous puppet theater. In the near future St Ann's will move to a new location in the historic Tobacco Warehouse facing Brooklyn Bridge Park. Check the website for updates.

BROOKLYN PUBLIC
LIBRARY   PERFORMING ARTS

Map p442 (www.brooklynpubliclibrary.org; 10 Grand Army Plaza, btwn Flatbush Ave & Eastern Pkwy, Prospect Heights; 🚻🚻; §2/3 to Grand Army Plaza) Located on the northeast edge of Brooklyn's Park Slope neighborhood, this grand library hosts a regular series of readings, including special events geared at the tots. Check their website for a schedule.

🛍 SHOPPING

Want it? Well, Brooklyn's got it. Williamsburg is chock-full of home-design shops, thrift stores, and hipster bookstores and boutiques. In South Brooklyn, you'll find some satisfying browsing (and good consignment) in the vicinity of Boerum and Cobble Hills. Atlantic Ave, running east to west near Brooklyn Heights, is sprinkled with antique stores. And Park Slope features a good selection of laid-back clothing shops.

🛍 Williamsburg & Around

ROUGH TRADE   MUSIC

Map p438 (📞718-388-4111; www.roughtradenyc.com; 64 N 9th St, btwn Kent & Wythe; ⊘9am-11pm Mon-Sat, 10am-9pm Sun; §L to Bedford Ave) This sprawling, 10,000-sq-ft record store – a London import – opened in late 2013 to much acclaim. In addition to stocking thousands of titles on vinyl and CD, it has in-store DJs, listening stations, art exhibitions, and coffee and tea from Greenpoint purveyor Five Leaves. A small concert hall on-site hosts live bands throughout the week (admission varies).

MAST BROTHERS FOOD
Map p438 (111 N 3rd St, btwn Berry St & Wythe Ave; ⏲noon-7pm; [S]L to Bedford Ave) Heavenly scents fill the air at this artisanal chocolate-maker that creates complex and flavorful perfection in beautifully wrapped chocolate bars. Prices aren't cheap ($8 or so for a 2.5-oz chocolate bar), but the Mast Brothers go to great lengths in sourcing high-quality cacao beans from small farms in Belize, Madagascar, Papua New Guinea and beyond.

You can watch the chocolate-makers in action, nibble free samples or purchase other goodies (brownies, truffles, cookies).

SPOONBILL & SUGARTOWN BOOKS
Map p438 (www.spoonbillbooks.com; 218 Bedford Ave, at 5th St, Williamsburg; ⏲10am-10pm; [S]L to Bedford Ave) Williamsburg's favorite bookstore has an intriguing selection of art and coffee-table books, cultural journals, used and rare titles, and locally made works not found elsewhere.

BUFFALO EXCHANGE CLOTHING
Map p438 (504 Driggs Ave, at 9th St, Williamsburg; ⏲11am-8pm Mon-Sat, noon-7pm Sun; [S]L to Bedford Ave) This large new and used clothing shop is a go-to spot for Brooklynites on a budget – featuring clothes (designer and not), shoes, jewelry and accessories. It takes time to find the best pieces, so plan on spending some quality time here.

BROOKLYN INDUSTRIES CLOTHING
Map p438 (www.brooklynindustries.com; 162 Bedford Ave, at 8th St, Williamsburg; ⏲10:30am-9pm;

BROOKLYN MARKETS

When the weekend arrives, Brooklynites are out and about, strolling the stoop sales and hitting the markets. Here are a few good places to unearth something unusual (and enjoy a good bite while you're at it):

Brooklyn Flea, Fort Greene (Map p440; www.brooklynflea.com; 176 Lafayette Ave, btwn Clermont & Vanderbilt Aves, Fort Greene; ⏲10am-5pm Sat Apr-Nov; 👪; [S]G to Clinton-Washington Aves) On Saturdays from April to November, some 200 vendors sell their wares on the grounds of a school in Fort Greene. You'll find antiques, records, vintage clothes, craft items and enticing food stalls stuffed with a smorgasbord of tasty treats. In winter the market moves indoors, either in Williamsburg or Fort Greene (check website for details).

Brooklyn Flea, Williamsburg (Map p438; www.brooklynflea.com; East River Waterfront, btwn 6th & 7th Sts, Williamsburg; ⏲10am-5pm Sun, Apr-Dec; [S]L to Bedford Ave) On Sundays in the summer and fall, you can get more market action at this large outdoor space at the East River Waterfront in Williamsburg. You'll also find plenty of vintage furnishings, retro clothing and bric-a-bric, not to mention an array of lobster rolls, *pupusas* (corn tortillas filled with cheese, beans, meat or vegetables), tamales and chocolate. This area is also home to the popular Smorgasburg market on Saturdays in the summer, when food vendors from all over New York City descend on the area with tasty victuals.

Artists & Fleas (Map p438; www.artistsandfleas.com; 70 N 7th Ave, btwn Berry St & Wythe Ave, Williamsburg; ⏲10am-7pm Sat & Sun; [S]L to Bedford Ave) In operation since 2003, this is a popular artists, designers and vintage market in Williamsburg, where you can find an excellent selection of crafty goodness.

Grand Army Plaza Greenmarket (Map p442; Grand Army Plaza, Prospect Park West & Flatbush Ave; ⏲8am-4pm Sat; [S]2/3 to Grand Army Plaza) Open on Saturdays year-round, this greenmarket is a good spot to put together an impromptu picnic before heading into Prospect Park.

Neighborhood Greenmarkets You'll find other year-round greenmarkets at **Brooklyn Borough Hall** (downtown Brooklyn; [S] 2/3, 4/5 to Borough Hall) on Tuesday, Thursday and Saturday; **Carroll Park** (Carroll Gardens; [S] F, G to Carroll St) on Sunday; and **Fort Greene Park** (Fort Greene; [S] B, Q/R to DeKalb Ave) on Saturday. Check www.grownyc.org for other NYC greenmarkets.

SL to Bedford Ave) This is where the cool kids shop for hooded sweatshirts, silk-screen T-shirts and slinky knit dresses. It may be a chain but this Brooklyn Industries has the cachet of actually being in Brooklyn.

DESERT ISLAND COMICS
BOOKS

Map p438 (www.desertislandbrooklyn.com; 540 Metropolitan Ave, btwn Union Ave & Lorimer St, Williamsburg; noon-9pm Mon-Sat, to 7pm Sun; SL to Lorimer St, G to Metropolitan Ave) Desert Island is an indie comic-book shop located inside a former bakery in Williamsburg. Inside, you'll find hundreds of comics, graphic novels, local zines, prints and cards. It also sells original prints and lithographs by artists like Adrian Tomine and Peter Bagge. Good tunes are provided by the turntable in back.

ACADEMY ANNEX
MUSIC

(718-218-8200; 85 Oak St, at Franklin St; noon-8pm; SG to Greenpoint) Serious vinyl vultures head to this Greenpoint mecca (formerly in Williamsburg) to browse bins stuffed full of rock, hip-hop, jazz, blues, electronica and world music.

BEACON'S CLOSET (GREENPOINT)
THRIFT STORE

Map p438 (www.beaconscloset.com; 74 Guernsey St, btwn Nassau & Norman Aves, Greenpoint; 11am-9pm Mon-Fri, to 8pm Sat & Sun; SL to Bedford Ave) Twenty-something groovers find this warehouse of vintage clothing part gold mine, part grit. Lots of coats, polyester tops and '90s-era tees are handily displayed by color, but the sheer mass can take time to conquer. Previously in Wiliamsburg, Beacon's moved to a 7500-sq-ft space in Greenpoint in early 2014.

FUEGO 718
HANDICRAFTS

Map p438 (249 Grand St, btwn Roebling St & Driggs Ave, Williamsburg; noon-8pm; SL to Bedford Ave) A kaleidoscope of kitsch and crafts, Fuego 718 packs a riotous display of Day of the Dead boxes and figurines, Haitian metal art made from recycled products, Italian *milagros* (metal charms), Lotería boards (that iconic Mexican bingo) and ornate mirrors with vividly painted frames. You can also browse the small whimsical paintings by Andras Bartos (reasonably priced at $48) and other artists, plus jewelry handcrafted by both Brooklyn and international designers.

ADOBE NEW YORK
HOMEWARES

Map p438 (www.abode-newyork.com; 179 Grand St, near Bedford Ave, Williamsburg; noon-7:30pm Mon & Wed-Sat, to 6pm Sun; SL to Bedford Ave) A contemporary home-furnishings store for urban dwellers has great last-minute gifts – including lovely wood Danish-styled trays, delicate carafes and stemware, artful vases and teacups, and creative gifts for kids like color-in placemats.

🏠 Park Slope

BEACON'S CLOSET (PARK SLOPE)
THRIFT STORE

Map p442 (718-230-1630; 92 Fifth Ave, cnr Warren St; noon-9pm Mon Fri, 11am 8pm Sat & Sun; S2/3 to Bergen St) An excellent thrift shop stocked full of shoes, jewelry and bright vintage finds. It is the sister store of the bigger Beacon's Closet in Greenpoint.

FLIRT
CLOTHING

Map p442 (www.flirt-brooklyn.com; 93 Fifth Ave, btwn Park Pl & Prospect Pl; 11:30am-7:30pm; SB/D, N/Q/R, 2/3, 4/5 to Atlantic Ave/Pacific St, G to Bergen St) The name says it all at this girlishly sexy Park Slope boutique, where a trio of stylish owners come up with funky yet feminine creations such as custommade skirts (pick your cut and fabric) and tiny tops in soft knits.

🏠 Cobble Hill, Carroll Gardens & Gowanus

NO RELATION VINTAGE
THRIFT STORE

Map p440 (654 Sackett St, btwn Third & Fourth Aves; SR to Union St) This gigantic vintage shop opened in the Gowanus area in late 2013 and has a truly staggering inventory (you'll need to spend some time here), with great deals for bargain hunters.

DRY GOODS
ACCESSORIES

Map p440 (362 Atlantic Ave, btwn Hoyt & Bond Sts; noon-7pm Tue-Sun; SA/C, G to Hoyt-Schermerhorn Sts) Strolling into this delightful little store, run by a mother-and-daughter team, is like stepping back in time. The old wooden shelves and cabinetry are packed with curiosities.

Vintage stationery and pencils, finely crafted Kent hairbrushes, papermaking kits for kids, egg-white soap from Belgium,

18th-century mouthwash (a reputed favorite of Louis XV), Saint James meridian shirts (as worn by Bardot and James Dean) and Legacy swing dresses are just a few items you'll find here. The emphasis is on heritage brands – denoting well-made products meant to last.

SMITH + BUTLER CLOTHING

Map p440 (www.smithbutler.com; 225 Smith St, cnr Butler St, Caroll Gardens; 🕐11am-7pm Mon-Sat, noon-6pm Sun; [S]F, G to Bergen St) This fashion shop in Caroll Gardens sells durable clothing that channels a nomadic Brooklyn biker vibe. It's a little pricey but has some really good finds for men and women (think hunting gear, gloves, wool scarves and plenty of plaids).

★BLACK GOLD MUSIC

Map p440 (www.blackgoldbrooklyn.com; 461 Court St, btwn 4th Pl & Luquer St, Carroll Gardens; 🕐7am-2pm Mon, to 8pm Tue-Fri, 10am-9pm Sat, to 7pm Sun; [S]F, G to Carroll St) 🍃 Records, coffee, antiques and taxidermy await you in this tiny addition to the ever-expanding Carroll Gardens Court St scene. Sample vintage vinyl on the turntable from John Coltrane to Ozzy Osborne and enjoy a damn-good cup of coffee, ground and brewed individually. Need a stuffed hyena from the Ozarks? Find one here.

Dumbo

POWERHOUSE BOOKS BOOKS

Map p444 (www.powerhousebooks.com; 37 Main St; 🕐10am-7pm Mon-Wed, to 8pm Thu & Fri, 11am-8pm Sat, to 7pm Sun; 📶; [S]A/C to High St, F to York St) An important part of Dumbo's cultural scene, Powerhouse Books hosts changing art exhibitions, book-launch parties and weird and creative events in its 5000-sq-ft space. You'll also find intriguing books on urban art, photography and pop culture – all imprints of their namesake publishing house.

PS BOOKSHOP BOOKS

Map p444 (www.psbnyc.com; cnr 76 Front & Washington Sts; 🕐10am-8pm; [S]A/C to High St, F to York St) This is a good used-bookstore with an excellent selection of art monographs, street books, children's books and vintage travelogues.

SPORTS & ACTIVITIES

BROOKLYN BRIDGE PARK OUTDOORS

Map p444 (East River Waterfront) A pretty, 6-acre greenway along Piers 3 and 4 of Brooklyn Bridge Park (p265) opened in 2013, making for a more scenic stroll or bike ride toward the northern end of the park. By the time you read this, Pier 2 should have courts for basketball, handball and bocce, plus an inline skating rink. There's also river access here for kayakers.

BROOKLYN BOWL BOWLING

Map p438 (www.brooklynbowl.com; 61 Wythe Ave, btwn 11th & 12th Sts, Williamsburg; lane rental per hour $40-50, shoe rental $5; 🕐6pm-2am Mon-Thu, 6pm-4am Fri, noon-4am Sat, noon-2am Sun; [S]L to Bedford, G to Nassau Ave) This incredible alley is housed in the 23,000-sq-ft former Hecla Iron Works Company, which provided ornamentation for several NYC landmarks at the turn of the 20th century. There are 16 lanes surrounded by cushy sofas and exposed-brick walls. In addition to bowling, you'll find plenty of music options as well.

ON THE MOVE CYCLING

Map p442 (☎718-768-4998; www.onthemovenyc.com; 400 Seventh Ave, btwn 12th & 13th Sts, Park Slope; bike rentals per day incl helmet $35; 🕐2-7pm Mon-Fri, noon-5pm Sat & Sun; [S]F to 7th Ave) A couple of blocks south from Brooklyn's Prospect Park, On the Move rents and sells all manner of bikes and gear. It is closed in inclement weather and cuts back hours from October to March.

BIKE AND ROLL BICYCLE RENTAL

Map p444 (www.bikenewyorkcity.com; Old Fulton St, Brooklyn Bridge Park; bike hire per hour/day $10/34; 🕐Mar-Nov; [S]A/C to High St) Hire bikes here for a spin through Brooklyn Bridge Park (perhaps heading down to Red Hook), around Dumbo or the uphill hoof to the very bicycle-crowded Brooklyn Bridge.

GOTHAM GIRLS ROLLER DERBY ROLLER DERBY

(☎888-830-2253; www.gothamgirlsrollerderby.com; advance $20, at the door $25-35; 🕐Apr-Nov; 👪) NYC's only all-female and skater-operated roller-derby league is made up of four home teams: the Bronx Gridlock, Brooklyn Bombshells, Manhattan Mayhem and Queens of Pain. It also has two traveling teams: the All-Stars and the Wall

Street Traitors. Matches are held all over the city, but naturally, we're partial to the Brooklyn Bombshells.

BROOKLYN CYCLONES BASEBALL

Map p445 (☎718-372-5596; www.brooklyncyclones.com; MCU Park, 1904 Surf Ave, at 17th St, Coney Island; tickets from $15, Wed $10; [S]D/F, N/Q to Coney Island-Stillwell Ave) The minor-league baseball team Brooklyn Cyclones, part of the New York–Penn League, plays at a beachside park a few steps from the Coney Island boardwalk.

RED HOOK BOATERS KAYAKING

Map p440 (www.redhookboaters.org; Louis Valentino Jr Pier Park, Coffey St, Red Hook; 🚌B61 to Van Dyke St, [S]F, G to Smith-9th Sts) [FREE] This boathouse, located in remote Red Hook, offers free kayaking (several times weekly from May to October) in the small embayment off Louis Valentino Jr Pier Park. Check the website before making the trip out.

BROOKLYN BOULDERS ROCK CLIMBING

Map p440 (www.brooklynboulders.com; 575 Degraw St, at Third Ave, Boerum Hill; day pass $25; 🕐8am-midnight; [S]R to Union St) It's Brooklyn's biggest indoor climbing arena for scaling aficionados and folks looking to reach new heights. Ceilings top out at 30ft inside this 18,000-sq-ft facility, and its caves, free-standing 17ft boulder and climbing walls offer numerous routes for beginners to experts. There are overhangs of 15 degrees, 30 degrees and 45 degrees. Climbing classes are available.

GOWANUS DREDGERS CANOE CLUB BOATING

Map p440 (☎718-243-0849; www.gowanuscanal.org; 2nd St, at Gowanus Canal; suggested donation $5; [S]F, G to Carroll St or Smith-9th St) This unusual club will supply you with gear (a canoe and a map) for self-guided tours of the canal and the surrounding area. Participants are asked to help remove any garbage they might see on the way. April through October only. Reserve in advance.

LAKESIDE SKATING, BOATING

Map p442 (www.lakesideprospectpark.com; Prospect Park, near Ocean & Parkside Aves; 🕐11am-6pm Mon-Thu, 9am-10pm Fri & Sat, to 8pm Sun; 👪; [S]B, Q to Prospect Park) Two brand-new rinks (one open and one covered) in Prospect Park opened in late 2013 as part of Lakeside Center, a $74-million project which reconfigured 26 acres of parkland in a beautiful, ecofriendly showcase. In the summer kids can splash about in wading pools and sprinklers; the other rink features outdoor inline skating.

In the summer, pedal boats are available for leisurely rides on the lake.

PROSPECT PARK TENNIS CENTER TENNIS

Map p442 (☎718-436-2500; www.prospectpark.org/tennis; Prospect Park, cnr Parkside & Coney Island Aves; 🕐7am-11pm; [S]F to Fort Hamilton Pkwy, Q to Parkside Ave) Open all year, this 11-court facility takes permits or sells single-use tickets on location from mid-May to mid-November. Hourly rates range from $38 to $82.

AREA YOGA CENTER YOGA

Map p440 (www.areayogabrooklyn.com; 320 Court St, 2nd fl, Cobble Hill; classes $12; 🕐classes 7am-8pm; [S]F, G to Carroll St) With a spa, a couple of shops and a yoga studio, Area conquers Brooklyn's Cobble Hill area for all things mind and body.

BARCLAYS CENTER BASKETBALL

Map p442 (www.barclayscenter.com; cnr Flatbush & Atlantic Aves, Prospect Heights; [S]B/D, N/Q/R, 2/3, 4/5 to Atlantic Ave) The Dodgers still play baseball in Los Angeles but the Brooklyn Nets in the NBA (formerly the New Jersey Nets) now hold court at this high-tech stadium that opened in 2012. Basketball aside, Barclays also stages major concerts and big shows – Vampire Weekend, Coldplay, Cirque de Soleil, Disney on Ice… Speaking of ice, hockey is on the way: the New York Islanders will begin playing their home games here in 2015.

Queens

LONG ISLAND CITY | ASTORIA | FLUSHING | CORONA | WOODSIDE

Neighborhood Top Five

1 Feeling inspired at **MoMA PS1** (p302), the Museum of Modern Art's cross-river sibling. From painting and sculpture to site-specific installations, this cultural 'It kid' serves up edgy, world-class artwork, not to mention lectures, performances and an electric summer party series.

2 Reliving your favorite film and TV moments at Astoria's contemporary ode to the small and silver screens, the **Museum of the Moving Image** (p306).

3 Getting soaked, pummeled and pampered at Queens' sprawling aquatic wonderworld, **New York Spa Castle** (p311).

4 Late-night Latino-food-truck crawling on melting-pot **Roosevelt Ave**.

5 Boisterous Asian street life and cheap Chinese feasting in hyperactive **Flushing**.

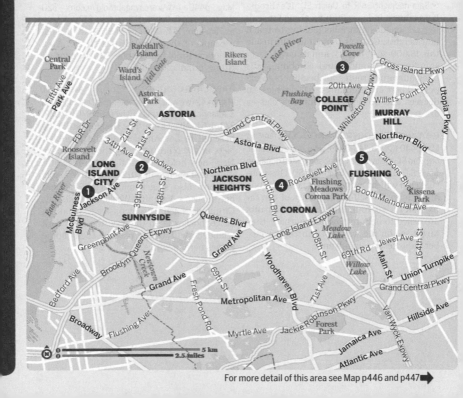

For more detail of this area see Map p446 and p447 ➡

Explore Queens

Of the city's five boroughs, Queens is top dog in size and runner-up in head count. Anywhere else, it would be a major city in its own right. So where to begin?

Assuming it's not Tuesday or Wednesday (when many galleries are closed), start with a day in Long Island City, home to contemporary-art hubs MoMA PS1, Sculpture-Center and the Fisher Landau Center for Art. Watch the sun set from Gantry Plaza State Park, and sip-and-sup on neighborly Vernon Blvd.

Spend a day or two exploring neighboring Astoria, taste-testing ethnic eateries, sipping local brews and checking out the Museum of Modern Art. If it's summer, catch an alfresco film at Socrates Sculpture Park.

With its Hong Kong jumble of street foods, Asian groceries and kitschy malls, Flushing (home to NYC's biggest Chinatown) also merits a full-day adventure. Time poor? Spend the morning on Main St and Roosevelt Ave, then hit neighboring Corona for Queens Museum or Louis Armstrong House.

If it's hot, tackle the surf at Rockaway Beach, home to NYC's best beach and fish taco.

Local Life

→ **Hangouts** Brew fans head to Astoria Bier & Cheese (p310) for local suds, while hipsters *sans* attitude down single-origin joe at Queens Kickshaw (p311).

→ **Culture** Take an aerial tour of NYC without ever leaving the ground at the better-than-ever Queens Museum (p306).

→ **Flushing** Snack on lamb dumplings in the Golden Shopping Mall (p308) basement, then ignite the palate at Hunan Kitchen of Grand Sichuan (p310) or Fu Run (p309).

Getting There & Away

→ **Subway** Twelve lines serve Queens. From Manhattan, catch the N/Q/R and M to Astoria, the 7 to Long Island City, Woodside, Corona and Flushing, and the A to Rockaway Beach. The E, J and Z lines reach Jamaica, while the G directly connects Long Island City to Brooklyn.

→ **Train** Long Island Rail Road (LIRR) has a handy connection from Manhattan's Penn Station to Flushing.

→ **Bus** Routes include the M60, which runs from La Guardia Airport to Harlem and Columbia University in Manhattan, via Astoria.

Lonely Planet's Top Tip

Don't miss the Fisher Landau Center for Art (p303) for free modern art without the crowds. Occupying an old parachute-harness factory in Long Island City, the core of its stellar collection of painting, photography, sculpture and installations spans the 1960s to today. The rotating exhibitions feature works from A-listers like Robert Rauschenberg, Cy Twombly and Jasper Johns.

QUEENS

Best Places to Eat

→ Sripraphai (p308)
→ Fu Run (p309)
→ M. Welles Dinette (p308)
→ Rockaway Taco (p306)
→ Roosevelt Ave (p309)

For reviews, see p307➡

Best Places to Chill Out

→ Rockaway Beach (p306)
→ New York Spa Castle (p311)
→ Flushing Meadows Corona Park (p307)
→ Gantry Plaza State Park (p303)

For reviews, see p303➡

Best for Culture Vultures

→ MoMA PS1 (p302)
→ Museum of the Moving Image (p306)
→ Queens Museum (p306)
→ Fisher Landau Center for Art (p303)

For reviews, see p303➡

TOP SIGHT MOMA PS1

The smaller, hipper sibling of Manhattan's Museum of Modern Art, MoMA PS1 hunts down razor-sharp art and serves it up in an ex-school locale. Forget about lily ponds in gilded frames. Here you'll be peering at videos through floorboards and debating the meaning of nonstatic structures while staring through a hole in the wall. Nothing is predictable. Best of all, admission is free with your MoMA ticket.

Roots, Radicals & PS1 Classics

PS1 first hit the scene in the 1970s. This was the age of Dia, Artists' Space and the New Museum – new-gen spaces showcasing the city's thriving experimental, multimedia art scene. In 1976, Alanna Heiss – a supporter of art in alternative spaces – took possession of an abandoned school building in Queens and invited artists like Richard Serra, James Turrell and Keith Sonnier to create site-specific works. The end result was PS1's inaugural exhibition, Rooms. Surviving remnants include Richard Artschwager's oval-shaped wall 'blimps' and Alan Saret's light-channeling *The Hole at P.S.1, Fifth Solar Chthonic Wall Temple,* on the north wing's 3rd floor. These works are part of the gallery's long-term installations, which also include Pipilotti Rist's video *Selbstlos im Lavabad* (Selfless in the Bath of Lava) – viewable through the lobby floorboards – and James Turrell's awe-inspiring *Meeting,* where the sky is the masterpiece.

Summer 'Warm Up' Parties

Head in on Saturday afternoon from July to early September and rock on at one of New York's coolest weekly music/culture events, Warm Up. It's a hit with everyone from verified hipsters to plugged-in music geeks, who spill into the MoMA PS1 courtyard to eat, drink and catch a stellar lineup of top bands, experimental music and DJs. Featured artists have included acid-house deity DJ Pierre and techno pioneer Juan Atkins. It's like one big block party, albeit with better music and art than your usual neighborhood slap-up. Linked to it is the annual Young Architects Program (YAP) competition, in which architects compete for the chance to transform the MoMA PS1 courtyard with a large-scale installation. Nabbing the prize in 2013 was Ithaca-based firm CODA; its shadow-making 'Party Wall' featured a modular skin made of ecofriendly blanks (byproducts of skateboard production).

Sunday Sessions

Another cultural treat is the Sunday Sessions, on Sunday from September to May. Spanning lectures, film screenings, music performances, even architectural projects, the lineup has included experimental comedy, postindustrial noise jams and Latin art-house dance. One week you might catch a symphony debut, the next an architectural performance from Madrid. Upcoming events are listed on the MoMA PS1 website.

DON'T MISS...

- Temporary & long-term exhibitions
- Summer 'Warm Up' parties
- Sunday Sessions

PRACTICALITIES

- Map p446
- www.momaps1.org
- 22-25 Jackson Ave, at 46th Ave, Long Island City
- adult/child $10/free, admission with MoMA ticket free, Warm Up party admission online/at venue $15/18
- ⏲noon-6pm Thu-Mon, Warm Up parties 3-9pm Sat Jul-early Sep
- [S]E, M to 23rd St-Ely Ave, G to 21st St, 7 to 45th Rd-Court House Sq

SIGHTS

The Queens Tourism Council (www.itsinqueens.com) website offers information on attractions and events, while the Queens Council on the Arts (☎347-505-3010; www.queenscouncilarts.org) promotes art in the borough. For a more personalized introduction, Hunter College urban-geography professor Jack Eichenbaum leads many unusual Walking Tours (☎718-961-8406; www.geognyc.com; tours $39) of Queens' ethnic neighborhoods, including a full-day walk/subway ride along the 7 train lines.

Long Island City

MOMA PS1 GALLERY
See p302.

★FISHER LANDAU CENTER FOR ART MUSEUM
Map p446 (www.flcart.org; 38-27 30th St; ⏲noon-5pm Thu-Mon; [S]N/Q to 39th Ave) [FREE] Surprisingly under the radar, this private art museum is a must for fans of modern and contemporary art. On any given visit you can expect to catch important works from some of the most iconic artists of the 20th and 21st centuries.

Codesigned by late British architect Max Gordon (designer of London's Saatchi Gallery), the space also hosts the Columbia University School of Visual Arts MFA Thesis Exhibition each May – a highly respected showcase for talented up-and-coming artists.

NOGUCHI MUSEUM MUSEUM
Map p446 (www.noguchi.org; 9-01 33rd Rd, at Vernon Blvd; adult/child $10/free, by donation 1st Fri of the month; ⏲10am-5pm Wed-Fri, 11am-6pm Sat & Sun; [S]N/Q to Broadway) The art and the building here are the work of eponymous Japanese American sculptor, furniture designer and landscape architect Isamu Noguchi, and both exude a Zen-like sensibility. Displayed in bare brick and concrete galleries and an outdoor rock garden, the artist's abstract stone sculptures are a meditation on the struggle between nature and the human-made world.

The building itself was once a photo-engraving plant, located across the street from Noguchi's studio. Art aside, the space also hosts a small cafe and gift shop, the latter stocking Noguchi-designed lamps and furniture, as well as a small range of other mid-20th-century design pieces. The museum is a 10-block walk from the subway stop; there's also a shuttle bus (one way/round-trip $5/10) going four times each Sunday from the northeast corner of E 70th St and Park Ave in Manhattan. See the website for times.

SCULPTURECENTER GALLERY
Map p446 (www.sculpture-center.org; 44-19 Purves St, near 43rd Ave; suggested donation $5; ⏲11am-6pm Thu-Mon; [S]7 to 45th Rd-Court House Sq, E, M to 23rd St-Ely Ave, G to Long Island City-Court Sq) In a former trolley-repair warehouse, down a dead-end street, SculptureCenter pages Berlin with its edgy art and industrial backdrop. Its dramatic exhibition spaces include a hangarlike main gallery and a cavernous underground space, providing an evocative backdrop for the gallery's rotating shows of both emerging and established artists. Expect anything from site-specific installations to video art.

SOCRATES SCULPTURE PARK ART
Map p446 (www.socratessculpturepark.org; Broadway, at Vernon Blvd; ⏲10am-dusk; [S]N/Q to Broadway) [FREE] Whimsical sculptures dot this 4.5-acre open-air space, right on the East River and close to Noguchi Museum. Try to time a visit around free events: yoga and tai chi on weekends from mid May to late September and movie screenings on Wednesday from early July to late August (prescreening performances start at 7pm, films begin at sunset – and there's food available).

GANTRY PLAZA STATE PARK PARK
Map p446 (www.nysparks.com/parks/149; 4-09 47th Rd; [S]7 to Vernon Blvd-Jackson Ave) This design-savvy, 12-acre riverside park has amazing, uninterrupted views of the Manhattan skyline (as seen in the 2005 film *The Interpreter,* with Sean Penn and Nicole Kidman), complete with four piers and public sunlounges for panoramic chilling. The restored, archlike gantries – in service until 1967 – are testament to the area's past as a loading dock for rail-car floats and barges.

Dating back to 1936, the giant Pepsi-Cola sign at the park's northern end once topped a nearby Pepsi bottling plant, which has been since demolished.

304

GAVIN HELLIER / GETTY IMAGES ©

JAMIE GRILL / GETTY IMAGES ©

BARRY WINIKER / GETTY IMAGES ©

1. Queens
Be entertained by street musicians in Queens.

2. Gantry Plaza State Park (p303)
Recline on public sunlounges and look over Long Island City's East River waterfront.

3. Flushing Meadows Corona Park (p307)
Visit Queens' most famous landmark and the world's largest globe, the *Unisphere*, by Gilmore David Clarke.

4. Rockaway Beach (p306)
Surf at NYC's best urban beach, famed for its natural scenery.

👁 Astoria

★MUSEUM OF THE MOVING IMAGE MUSEUM

Map p446 (www.movingimage.us; 36-01 35th Ave, at 37th St; adult/child $12/6, admission free 4-8pm Fri; ⏱10:30am-5pm Wed & Thu, to 8pm Fri, 11:30am-7pm Sat & Sun; 📶; [S]M/R to Steinway St) Fresh from a $65-million upgrade, this supercool complex is now one of the world's top film, television and video museums. State-of-the-art galleries show off the museum's collection of 130,000-plus TV and movie artifacts, including Elizabeth Taylor's wig from *Cleopatra,* Robin Williams' space suit from *Mork & Mindy* and the creepy stunt doll used in *The Exorcist.*

Try your hand at film editing (including redubbing the 'We're not in Kansas anymore' scene from *The Wizard of Oz*), and get nostalgic over an impressive booty of vintage TVs, cameras and retro arcade games. The museum's temporary exhibitions are usually fantastic, as are the regular film screenings; check the website for details.

👁 Flushing & Corona

QUEENS MUSEUM MUSEUM

Map p447 (QMA; www.queensmuseum.org; Flushing Meadows Corona Park; adult/child $8/free;

WORTH A DETOUR

ROCKAWAY BEACH

Immortalized by the Ramones' 1977 song 'Rockaway Beach,' America's largest urban beach – and New York's best – is just a $2.50 trip on subway line A. Come summer weekends, it's also a fun 90-minute **ferry ride** (Map p408; www.newyorkbeachferry.com; Pier 11; return adult/child $30/15; ⏱Sat, Sun & public holidays summer) from Lower Manhattan, with two Rockaway stops: Riis Landing and Beach 108th St.

Less crowded than Coney Island and famed for its surprisingly natural scenery and surf spots, Rockaway Beach is also home to a burgeoning summertime scene of hipsters, artists and locavore food options. At the heart of the revolution is the banging taco shack **Rockaway Taco** (www.rockawaytaco.com; 95-19 Rockaway Beach Blvd; tacos from $3.50; ⏱11am-8pm Mon-Wed, 9am-8pm Thu-Sun May-Sep; [S]A, S to Beach 98th St); its guacamole-topped fish tacos alone are worth the trip out here. Close by on the boardwalk, concrete concession booths peddle treats from hipster staples like Brooklyn pizza hot spot Roberta's (p282).

Beyond the May-to-September scene of oiled bodies, surfboards and cruiser bikes is a natural wonderland that feels worlds away from New York's urban chaos. Much of the area is part of the 26,000-acre **Gateway National Recreation Area**, which encompasses several parks. One of these, toward the southern tip of the Rockaways, is **Jacob Riis Park**, named for an advocate and photographer of immigrants in the late 19th century; it's also home to Fort Tilden, a decommissioned coastal artillery installation from WWI.

Extending from near JFK international airport, the salty, marshy **Jamaica Bay Wildlife Refuge** is one of the most important migratory bird and wetland habitats along the eastern seaboard. In spring and fall more than 325 bird species stop in to rest and snack, snapping up all sorts of briny sea creatures like clams, turtles, shrimp and oysters. Each season brings different visitors: spring features warblers and songbirds, and American woodcocks in late March. In mid-August shorebirds start to move south, landing here from Canada and fueling up for the trip to Mexico. Fall is when migrating hawks and raptors get mobile, along with ducks, geese, monarch butterflies and thousands and thousands of dragonflies. Birders and naturalists get the most action around the east and west ponds. Although the west pond was breached during Hurricane Sandy, it is still possible to walk the roughly 1.5-mile perimeter of the east pond. Just make sure to wear mud-resistant shoes, insect repellent and sunscreen, carry some water and watch out for poison ivy.

To get to the **visitor center** (Jamaica Bay Wildlife Refuge; ⏱8.30am-5pm), exit at Broad Channel station, walk west along Noel Rd to Cross Bay Blvd, turn right (north) and walk for 0.7 miles, and the center will be visible on the left side of the road.

⏲noon-6pm Wed-Sun; 📶; [S]7 to 111th St) The recently expanded Queens Museum is one of the city's most unexpected pleasures. Its most famous drawcard is the Panorama of New York City, a gob-smacking 9335-sq-ft miniature New York City, with all buildings accounted for and a 15-minute dusk-to-dawn light simulation of a New York day. The museum also hosts top-notch exhibitions of modern art, from contemporary photography to site-specific installations.

The QMA is housed in a historic building made for the 1939 World's Fair (and once home to the UN), and you'll find a retro-fabulous collection of memorabilia from both the '39 and '64 fairs on display (with reproductions in the gift shop).

LOUIS ARMSTRONG HOUSE CULTURAL BUILDING

Map p447 (www.louisarmstronghouse.org; 34-56 107th St, Corona Heights; admission $10; ⏲10am-5pm Tue-Fri, noon-5pm Sat & Sun; [S]7 to 103rd St-Corona Plaza) At the peak of his career and with worldwide fame at hand, Armstrong chose Queens. Armstrong spent his last 28 years in this quiet Corona Heights home, now a museum and national treasure; he died here in 1971. Guides offer free 40-minute tours of his former abode, leaving on the hour (the last starts at 4pm).

Satchmo shared the house with his fourth wife, Lucille Wilson, a dancer at the Cotton Club. The tour offers an intimate glimpse into what was a happy life together, with entertaining anecdotes and a handful of home audio recordings. Armstrong's den, of which he was most proud, features a portrait of the great painted by none other than Benedetto (aka Tony Bennett).

FLUSHING MEADOWS CORONA PARK PARK

Map p447 (www.nycgovparks.org/parks/fmcp; Grand Central Pkwy; [S]7 to Mets-Willets Point) The area's biggest attraction is this 1225-acre park, built for the 1939 World's Fair and dominated by Queens' most famous landmark, Gilmore David Clarke's stainless-steel **Unisphere** (Map p447) – it's the world's biggest globe, at 120ft high and weighing 380 tons. Facing it is the former New York City Building, now home to the surprisingly fantastic Queens Museum.

Just south are three weather-worn, Cold War–era New York State Pavilion Towers, part of the New York State Pavilion for the 1964 World's Fair. If entering the park from the subway walkway, look for the 1964 World's Fair mosaics by Salvador Dalí and Andy Warhol (just down from the pedestrian bridge from the subway). Also nearby is **Citi Field** (Map p447), and the rest of the USTA Billie Jean King National Tennis Center (p311). Head west on the pedestrian bridge over the Grand Central Pkwy to find a few more attractions, including the **New York Hall of Science** (Map p447; ☎718-699-0005; www.nysci.org; 47-01 111th St; adult/child $11/8, admission free 2-5pm Fri, 10-11am Sun Sep-Jun, daily late Aug-early Sep; ⏲9:30am-5pm Mon-Fri, 10am-6pm Sat & Sun Apr-Aug, closed Mon Sep-Mar; [S]7 to 111th St). The park has grounds too, on its eastern and southern edges. The top-notch Astroturf soccer fields are popular for organized and pick-up soccer, and there's a pitch-and-putt golf course that's lit up for drunken golfers at night.

🍴 EATING

Spanakopita? *Gai kua? Sopa de mariscos?* If it exists, you can devour it in Queens. Head to Long Island City for locavore eateries, and to Astoria for anything from Greek to bagels; hot spots here include 30th Ave, Broadway (between 31st and 35th Sts) and 31st Ave. Steinway Ave between Astoria Blvd and 30th Ave is Astoria's 'Little Cairo.' Further east, Roosevelt Ave is perfect for a Latin-food-truck crawl, while at the end of the 7 subway line lies Flushing, New York's 'Chinatown without the tourists.' For a clued-in exploration of the borough, join a World's Fare Tours (www.worldsfaretours.com; tours from $75) adventure, run by food writer Joe DiStefano – celebrity chefs Eric Ripert and Anthony Bourdain have both sought his wisdom.

🍴 Long Island City & Astoria

BROOKLYN BAGEL & COFFEE COMPANY BAKERY $

Map p446 (www.brooklynbagelandcoffeecompany.com; 35-05 Broadway, Astoria; bagels $1.20; ⏲6am-4.30pm; [S]N/Q to Broadway, M, R to Steinway St) It may be in Queens, not Brooklyn, but there's little confusion about the caliber of bagels here. Soft, dense and chewy, they come in a number of drool-inducing variations, including sesame, onion, garlic, and wholewheat with oats and raisins. The cream cheeses are to die for, their changing repertoire of flavors including wasabi lox and baked apple.

★M. WELLES DINETTE — CANADIAN $$

(www.magasinwells.com; MoMA PS1, 22-25 Jackson Ave, Long Island City; mains $9-29; 🕒noon-6pm Thu-Mon; [S]E, M to 23rd St-Ely Ave, G to 21st St, 7 to 45th Rd-Court House Sq) Just like being back at school (but with better grub), this cultish nosh spot sits inside school-turned-art gallery MoMA PS1. Desklike tables face the open kitchen, where Quebecois head chef Hugue Dufour gives regional ingredients a gutsy French-Canadian makeover. It's a predominately nose-to-tail affair, its seasonal dishes gleefully rich, comforting and confident.

Feast on the likes of frisée salad with duck hearts, smoked egg and fried bread, cleverly paired with a small, interesting selection of wines by the glass.

VESTA TRATTORIA & WINE BAR — ITALIAN $$

Map p446 (www.vestavino.com; 21-02 30th Ave, Astoria; pizzas $13-16, dinner mains $11-26; 🕒5-10pm Mon-Thu, to 11pm Fri, 11am-3pm & 4-11pm Sat, 11am-3pm & 4-10pm Sun; [S]N/Q to 30th Ave) Vesta is one of those homely neighborhood secrets, with chatty regulars at the bar, local art on the walls and organic produce from a Brooklyn rooftop farm. The menu is simple and seasonal, with nourishing *zuppe* (soups), bubbling thin-crust pizzas and tasty mains of mostly pasta and risotto dishes.

Star of the popular weekend brunch is the Warm Bankie, a hangover-friendly meal of fried eggs with creamy polenta, asparagus, wild mushrooms and truffle oil.

TAVERNA KYCLADES — GREEK $$

Map p446 (☎718-545-8666; www.tavernakyclades.com; 33-07 Ditmars Blvd, at 33rd St, Astoria; mains $11.50-35; 🕒noon-11pm Mon-Sat, to 10pm Sun; [S]N/Q to Astoria-Ditmars Blvd) Hands down our favorite spot for a decent Hellenic feed. Fresh seafood is its forte, shining through in simple classics like succulent grilled octopus and fried calamari. The grilled-fish dishes are testament to the adage that 'less is more,' while the *saganaki* (pan-fried cheese) is sinfully good. One dish not worth the price is the Kyclades Special.

LIC MARKET — CAFE $$

Map p446 (☎718-361-0013; www.licmarket.com; 21-52 44th Dr, Long Island City; lunch $8-12, dinner mains $15-24; 🕒7am-3:30pm Mon, to 10pm Tue-Sat, 10am-3:30pm Sun; 📶; [S]E, M to 23rd St-Ely Ave, 7 to 45th Rd-Court House Sq) 🍃 Everyone from local creatives to corporate high-flyers flocks to this cool little cafe, pimped with local artwork and cooking pots. Breakfast winners include the 'sausage and onions' (fried eggs, breakfast sausage, cheddar and caramelized onion on a brioche bun), while seasonal lunch and dinner options span anything from Nantucket scallops to soulful risottos and game.

EL AY SI — AMERICAN $$

Map p446 (www.elaysi.com; btwn 47th Rd & 48th Ave, Long Island City; mains $10-21; 🕒5-10pm Wed & Thu, to midnight Fri, 11am-midnight Sat, 11am-10pm Sun; [S]7 to Vernon Blvd-Jackson Ave) Good-lovin' comfort grub, camaraderie and Gen-X anthems lurk behind the velvet drapes at this feel-good, bar-style nosh spot. Squeeze in at the bar or score yourself a booth for lip-licking numbers like jalapeño sweet-corn fritters or tender, slow-cooked pork belly with caramelized apples. Get in early or prepare to wait.

🍴 Woodside

SRIPRAPHAI — THAI $$

Map p446 (www.sripraphairestaurant.com; 64-13 39th Ave; mains $9-23; 🕒11.30am-9.30pm Thu-Tue; [S]7 to 69th St) If you think NYC is a dud at Southeast Asian food, prepare to eat your words (and everything in sight) at this packed, cheap, obscenely delicious Thai legend. Musts include the crispy ground catfish topped with green mango salad and cashews, as well as the heavenly fried soft-shell crab. Go early to avoid a long wait. Cash only.

🍴 Flushing & Corona

GOLDEN SHOPPING MALL — CHINESE $

Map p447 (41-28 Main St, Flushing; meals from $3; [S]7 to Flushing-Main St) A chaotic jumble of hung ducks, airborne noodles and greasy Laminex tables, Golden Mall's basement food court dishes up fantastic hawker-style grub. Don't be intimidated by the lack of English menus. Most stalls have at least one English speaker, and the constant flow of regulars are usually happy to point out their personal favorites, whether it's Lanzhou hand-pulled noodles or spicy pig ears.

Two must-tries are the lamb dumplings from Xie Family Dishes (stall 38) – best dipped in a little black vinegar, soy sauce and chili oil – and the spicy cumin lamb burger at Xi'an Famous Foods next door.

TORTILLERIA NIXTAMAL MEXICAN $

Map p447 (www.tortillerianixtamal.com; 104-5 47th Ave, Corona; dishes $2.50-13; ⏲11am-7pm Mon-Wed, to 9pm Thu & Sun, to 11pm Fri & Sat; [S]7 to 103rd St-Corona Plaza) The red-and-yellow picnic benches at this lo-fi gem are never short of a roaming gastronome, here for super-authentic Mexican *cocina* (cuisine). The secret weapon is the Rube Goldbergian machine, which transforms additive-free masa into super-tasty tacos and tamales.

The guys here are purists, their tacos adorned with a simple garnish of cilantro, onion and lime. Other must-tries include the pork-broth posole soup, spiked with chopped onion, radish, oregano and crushed red peppers. Cool down with a *horchata fresca* (a spiced rice and almond milk drink) while cheering on El Tricolor.

FU RUN CHINESE $$

Map p447 (www.furunflushing.com; 40-09 Prince St, Flushing; mains $8.95-28.95;

ROOSEVELT AVENUE FOOD-TRUCK CRAWL

When it comes to sidewalk grazing, it's hard to beat Roosevelt Ave and its army of late-night Latino food trucks, carts and stalls. Just one stroll from 90th St to 103rd St will have you sipping on *champurrados* (a warm, thick corn-based chocolate drink), nibbling on a *cemita* (Mexican sandwich) and making a little more room for some Ecuadorian fish stew. It's cheap, authentic and quintessentially Queens. Hungry? Then set off on a taste-testing mission of Roosevelt Ave's best.

Maravillas Restaurant (37-64 90th St, at Roosevelt Ave; ⏲10am-3am; [S]7 to 90th St-Elmhurst Ave) is a hit with karaoke-singing Mexican cowboys. Ditch the indoor section for the sidewalk counter. The menu is in Spanish but ask for an El Pastor ($2.50) and an Arabes ($3.50), both types of taco topped with succulent shaved pork marinated in *chili costeño* (type of hot chili), tomato, fresh oregano, pineapple and *achiote* (annatto). Wash it all down with a *champurrado*.

From Maravillas, head back to Roosevelt Ave, cross onto the avenue's south side, and head one block east to the intersection of Benham St. Here you'll find the legendary food truck **Tia Julia** (Benham St, at Roosevelt Ave; ⏲10am-5am; [S]7 to 90th St-Elmhurst Ave), justifiably famous for its *cemitas* ($8).

A few steps further east along Roosevelt Ave lies food stall **El Coyote Dormilon** (Roosevelt Ave, btwn Benham & Aske Sts; ⏲1-11pm Mon & Tue, to 4am Wed-Sun; [S]7 to 90th St-Elmhurst Ave). The coyote might be snoozing, but the vendor is up and at it, busily turning masa from her bucket into warm, super-fresh tortillas. (Note: fresh masa and a tortilla press are a good sign at any stall.) Quesadillas ($3) are the specialty here – try the distinctive *cuitlacoche* (fungus) and *quesillo* (stringy, cow's milk cheese) combo. It's seriously fine.

Keep rolling along Roosevelt Ave to Warren St. Parked along the street is a line of mega food trucks, including the brilliant **Hornado Ecuatoriano** (Warren St, at Roosevelt Ave; ⏲6am-midnight Sun-Thu, to 4am Fri & Sat; [S]7 to Junction Blvd). If you dare, try the *guatita* (a steamy Ecuadorian dish of tender tripe cooked in a mild, curry-style peanut sauce; $9). The food on Warren St is more expensive but also more substantial.

Another Warren St star is **El Guayaquileño** (Warren St, btwn Roosevelt Ave & 40th Rd; ⏲8am-10.30pm Sun-Thu, to around 4am Fri & Sat; [S]7 to Junction Blvd), famous for its Ecuadorian fish stew made of yuca, tuna, cilantro, onion, lemon, cumin and toasted corn kernels. It's flavorsome, wonderfully textured and a meal in itself. That said, leave room for the *bollos de pescado* (mashed green plantain with tuna, steamed in a banana leaf and served with tomato and chopped onion; $10).

If you're a Latino food-truck virgin, or simply enjoy food-hunting with other curious food lovers, consider doing the **Queens Midnight Street Crawl** (www.jeffreytastes.com; tours $59), a casual, late-night tour of the area's street-food gems led by Queens food buff and blogger Jeff Orlick. Either way, *¡buen provecho!*

⌚11:30am-midnight; [S]7 to Flushing-Main St) Fu Run has a cult following for very good reason: its northeast Chinese cooking is extraordinary. Reconfigure your understanding of the country's flavors over sour cabbage-laced pork dumplings, jelly-fish flowers with shallots, or the unforgettable Muslim lamb chop (deep-fried ribs dressed in dried chilies, and cumin and sesame seeds).

HUNAN KITCHEN OF GRAND SICHUAN CHINESE $$

Map p447 (www.thegrandsichuan.com; 42-47 Main St, Flushing; mains $9.50-23; ⌚11am-12.30am; [S]7 to Flushing-Main St) Work up a sweat at this respectable Flushing restaurant, best known for its fiery specialties from Hunan, a province in south-central China. Standout dishes include a deliciously salty white pepper smoked beef, tender chicken with hot red pepper, and an incredibly flavorsome lamb with cumin. If you're in a large group order the house specialty: BBQ duck, Hunan style.

DRINKING & NIGHTLIFE

★BOHEMIAN HALL & BEER GARDEN BEER HALL

Map p446 (www.bohemianhall.com; 29-19 24th Ave, btwn 29th & 31st Sts, Astoria; ⌚5pm-1am Mon-Thu, to 3am Fri, noon-3am Sat, noon-1am Sun; [S]N/Q to Astoria Blvd) Easily one of NYC's great happy drinking grounds, this outdoor beer garden is especially brilliant when the weather is warm. The mouthwatering list of cold Czech imports on draft are served with Czech accents, as are the schnitzels, goulash and dumplings. Some warm nights, folk bands set up (with occasional cover charge of $5 or so); arrive early to ensure a spot.

ASTORIA BIER & CHEESE BEER HALL

Map p446 (www.astoriabierandcheese.com; 3414 Broadway, btwn 34th & 35th Sts, Astoria; ⌚noon-11pm Mon-Thu, to midnight Fri & Sat, to 10pm Sun; [S]N/Q to Broadway) It's a case of curds-and-brew at this funky bar-shop hybrid in As-

LOCAL KNOWLEDGE

QUEENS: THE NEW BROOKLYN

Artist Julian Lesser gives the lowdown on his favorite New York borough (and why it should be your favorite too).

The Best Thing About Queens

The cultural diversity. In Astoria alone you've got the original Greek population, plus everyone from Columbians and Brazilians to Egyptians. There's even a 'Little Egypt' on Steinway Ave, between Astoria Blvd and 30th Ave, with great kebab shops and strong coffee. Much of Queens is pretty mixed these days, but Flushing is incredibly Asian. The result is a really authentic shopping experience, with massive Asian grocery stores selling exotic-looking fruits and every conceivable type of still-wriggling seafood. Planes fly low over Flushing so it's also cool if you're a plane-spotter.

Don't-Miss Eats

I love Brooklyn Bagel & Coffee Company (p307). It has amazing, huge bagels and a wide variety of cream cheeses. Staff create a new flavor every week for their customers to try. Queens Kickshaw is also great, the team sourcing a lot of their ingredients locally. In Long Island City, I love LIC Market (p308). It's like an intimate cafe but it does full service, and puts a lot of love into the food. It's also handy if you're visiting MoMA PS1. A good dinner spot is El Ay Si (p308) – its tater tots (deep-fried potato balls) are superaddictive. It's also great for a lively evening drink.

Cultural Picks

For cutting-edge contemporary art, spend an afternoon at MoMA PS1 (p302) and the nearby SculptureCenter (p303) in Long Island City. You could easily spend a few happy hours at the impressive Museum of the Moving Image (p306) in Astoria – it's a cool place to see props from classic films and TV shows. For a lesser-known treat, join one of the fascinating walking tours run by the **Greater Astoria Historical Society** (www.astorialic.org).

toria. Foam that upper lip with 10 seasonal, mostly local drafts, or get indecisive over hundreds of canned and bottled options, yours to take home or swill on-site. Fromage fiend Mike Fisher (ex–Bedford Cheese Shop) keeps the cheese selection inspired and surprising, with pairing plates available for a refreshing twist on cheese and vino sessions.

QUEENS KICKSHAW CAFE, BAR

Map p446 (www.thequeenskickshaw.com; 40-17 Broadway, Astoria; ⏰7.30am-1am Mon-Fri, 9am-1am Sat & Sun; 📶; [S]M/R to Steinway St) If Queens is the 'new Brooklyn,' this Astoria hangout is the giveaway: think recycled bar, indie folk tunes, and communal tables lined with wi-fi-ing Macheads. Brainstorm over a single origin brew, or loosen up with a craft ale or vino. Gut liners include fantastic grilled sandwiches (try the Gouda, with black-bean hummus, guava jam and pickled jalapeños). Cash only.

SPORTS & ACTIVITIES

NEW YORK SPA CASTLE DAY SPA

(www.nyspacastle.com; 131-10 11th Ave, College Point; admission weekday/weekend $35/$45; ⏰6am-midnight; 📶; [S]7 to Flushing-Main St) Based on a Korean bathhouse, this 100,000-sq-ft spa complex is a bubbling dream of mineral and massage pools, 'healing' saunas, steam rooms and waterfalls. There's a food court, massage treatments (from $40) and a gym ($5), as well as a free shuttle-bus service to/from the corner of 39th & Union St, one block east of the Flushing–Main St subway station. Shuttle buses depart every 10 and 40 minutes past the hour.

Avoid the place on weekends as it gets packed.

CLIFFS INDOOR CLIMBING

Map p446 (☎718-729-7625; www.thecliffsclimbing.com; 1-11 44th Dr, at 23rd St, Long Island City; admission $25, shoes/harness rental $6/5; ⏰10am-11pm Mon-Fri, 9am-11pm Sat, 9am-8pm Sun; [S]E, M to 23rd St-Ely Ave, 7 to 45th Rd-Court House Sq) New York's newest and largest indoor climbing facility serves up over 30,000 sq ft of climbing surface, with more than 125 top rope stations, 16ft top-out bouldering and a rappel tower. If that's not enough thigh-blasting for you, there's also a gym with cardiovascular machines and exercise equipment.

USTA BILLIE JEAN KING NATIONAL TENNIS CENTER TENNIS

Map p447 (☎718-760-6200; www.usta.com; Flushing Meadows Corona Park; [S]7 to Mets-Willets Pt) The US Open takes place in late August; tickets usually go on sale at Ticketmaster in April or May, but are hard to get for marquee games. General admission to early rounds is easier, for about $80 (top bleachers on Court 7 can take in five matches at once). Scan the USTA website in January/February for updates.

The USTA has 12 indoor DecoTurf courts, 19 field courts, four climate-controlled clay bubbled courts, and three stadium courts that can be hired (per hour outdoor court $22 to $32, indoor court $24 to $66). Reservations can be made up to two days in advance. Hourly lessons are $90 to $120.

NEW YORK METS BASEBALL

Map p447 (☎718-507-8499; www.mets.com; Citi Field, 123-01 Roosevelt Ave, Flushing; tickets $19-130; [S]7 to Mets-Willets Pt) In the National League since 1962, the Mets remain New York's 'new' baseball team. Fans still hold onto the magic of '86, when the Mets last won the World Series in a miraculous comeback. So flip on your cap, grab an ale and cheer the boys to victory at Citi Field stadium, a 35-minute subway trip from Midtown.

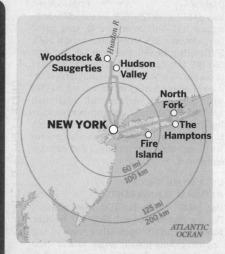

Day Trips from New York City

The Hamptons p313
New York's version of Malibu is a star-studded coastline with opulent mansions and see-and-be-seen parties, but with plenty of surprises – including Native American sites, charming village main streets and windswept state parks.

Fire Island p317
A favored gay getaway roars with dancing drag queens and a carefree summer club scene. Escape the mayhem by long walks on the seemingly endless beach.

North Fork p318
Wine tasting at Long Island's vineyards is a fun day's ramble, capped by main-street strolling and alfresco dining at waterside Greenport.

Hudson Valley p320
You could spend weeks exploring this region, with great hiking, mind-blowing art installations, charming towns and historic homes of American greats (Irving, Roosevelt and Vanderbilt included).

Woodstock & Saugerties p323
Supplement your pilgrimage to hippiedom with a round of antiquing and quiet walks in protected parks.

The Hamptons

Explore

For most of the summer this little jut of land becomes a frenetic scene mobbed with jetsetters, celebrities and throngs of curious wannabes. Luckily there's still plenty of opportunity for outdoor activity, from kayaking to mountain biking – and yes, even a few untrammeled beaches. There's no shortage of boutique shops, trendy eateries and celeb-heavy clubs in summer, and absolutely everything costs a pretty penny out here, with most inns charging well over $300 a night. Summer is high season; prices do drop a wee bit and traffic jams disappear about a month after Labor Day. This lessening of crowds, combined with the balmy weather of the fall harvest season, makes autumn an appealing time to visit.

The Best...
➡ **Sight** Southampton Historical Museum (p314)
➡ **Place to Eat** Lobster Roll (p315)
➡ **Place to Drink** Sloppy Tuna (p316)

Top Tip
Those in search of summer solitude should plan a visit on a weekday, as the weekends are stuffed to the gills with big-city refugees seeking to escape the stifling heat of the urban jungle.

Getting There & Away
➡ **Car** Take the Midtown Tunnel out of Manhattan onto I-495/Long Island Expwy. Follow this for about 1½ hours to exit 70 to Sunrise Hwy East/Rte 24. After about 10 miles merge onto Montauk Hwy/Rte 27, which goes directly to Southampton.

Continue along Rte 27 to get to all towns east of there.
➡ **Bus** The Hampton Jitney (☎212-362-8400; www.hamptonjitney.com; one way $30) is a 'luxury' express bus. Its Montauk line departs from Manhattan's East Side: 86th St between Lexington and Third Aves (in front of Victoria's Secret), then 69th St, 59th St and 40th St. It makes stops at villages along Rte 27 in the Hamptons.
➡ **Train** The Long Island Rail Road (LIRR; ☎718-217-5477; www.mta.info/lirr; one-way off-peak/peak $20/27) leaves from Penn Station in Manhattan, and Hunterspoint Ave Station and Jamaica Station in Queens, making stops in West Hampton, Southampton, Bridgehampton, East Hampton and Montauk. You can buy tickets in advance online and reserve round-trip trips in summer (a boon on Sunday night).

Need to Know
➡ **Area Code** ☎631
➡ **Location** 100 miles east (East Hampton) of Manhattan; 2½-hour drive
➡ **Tourist Office** (☎631-283-0402; www.southamptonchamber.com; 76 Main St, Southampton; ⊙10am-4pm Mon-Fri, to 2pm Sat)

⊙ SIGHTS

The Hamptons is actually a series of villages, most with 'Hampton' in the name. Those at the western end – or 'west of the canal,' as locals call the spots that are on the other side of the Shinnecock Canal – include Hampton Bays, Quogue and Westhampton. They are less frenzied than those to the east, which start with the village of Southampton.

DETOUR: LONG BEACH
Beautiful Long Beach, 30 miles from New York City (and much closer than either Jones Beach or Fire Island), is one of the best stretches of sand you can find. It's easily accessible by train and has clean beaches, a hoppin' main strip with shops and eateries within walking distance of the ocean, a thriving surfing scene and many city hipsters. The downside: the city charges $12 per person for out-of-towners. The **Long Island Rail Road** (LIRR; ☎718-217-5477; www.mta.info/lirr; 1-way fare to Long Beach $9-12.50, 'summer beach getaway' incl round-trip fare and beach admission $23) runs 'beach getaways,' which include discounted admission and round-trip train fare during the summer, with departures from both Penn Station and Atlantic Terminal in Brooklyn.

⊙ Southampton

Southampton is an old-moneyed and rather conservative spot compared to some of its neighbors. It's home to sprawling old mansions, a main street with no 'beachwear' allowed and some lovely beaches. Pick up maps and brochures about the town at the Southampton Chamber of Commerce, which is squeezed among a group of high-priced artsy-crafty shops and decent restaurants.

SOUTHAMPTON HISTORICAL MUSEUM
MUSEUM

(☑631-283-2494; www.southamptonhistorical-museum.org; 17 Meeting House Lane; adult/child $4/free; ⊙11am-4pm Wed-Sun) Don't miss the Historical Museum, which encompasses several different attractions: Rogers Mansion, built for a local whaling captain; the Pelletreau Store, where a former jeweler made his gold and silver goods; Whaley House, the residence of one of the first Southampton settlers; and Conscience Point, the point of embarkation for pilgrims coming from Lynn, Massachusetts, in search of wider religious freedom. These attractions are spread out around Southampton, but information about each can be found at the museum (which maintains the sites).

SHINNECOCK NATION CULTURAL CENTER AND MUSEUM
MUSEUM

(☑631-287-4923; www.shinnecockmuseum.com; Montauk Hwy; admission museum/village $8/10, combo ticket $15; ⊙11am-5pm Fri-Sun) Within the town of Southampton, just past Stony-brook College, is a small Native American reservation, home to the Shinnecocks, who run the tiny Shinnecock Museum, dedicated to preserving local Native art. Next to the museum is the new Wikun Village, a recreated 18th-century Native American village set in a two-acre forest. Check the website for crafts fairs, dance programs, children's activities and more.

PARRISH ART MUSEUM
MUSEUM

(☑631-283-2118; www.parrishart.org; 279 Montauk Hwy, Water Mill; adult/child $10/free, free Wed; ⊙10am-5pm Wed-Mon, to 8pm Fri) The Parrish Art Museum has quality exhibitions featuring great local artists and a cute gift shop stacked with glossy posters of famous Long Island landscapes.

⊙ Bridgehampton & Sag Harbor

To the east of Southampton, Bridgehampton has the shortest of all the main drags, but it's packed with trendy boutiques and restaurants. Seven miles north of Bridgehampton on Peconic Bay is the old whaling town of Sag Harbor. There are bunches of historic homes and points of interest here and you can pick up a historic walking-tour map at the Sag Harbor Chamber of Commerce on Long Wharf at the end of Main St.

The **Sag Harbor Whaling Museum** (☑631-725-0770; www.sagharborwhalingmuseum.org; 200 Main St, at Garden St; adult/child $6/2; ⊙10am-5pm Sat & Sun Apr-Sep) is fascinating, and the village's tiny Cape Cod–style streets are a joy to stroll; there are many excellent restaurants to discover. **Sag Harbor Cycle** (☑631-725-1110; www.saghar-

---

SLEEPING IN THE HAMPTONS

High season in the Hamptons is late May to mid-September.

Easterner Motel (☑631-283-9292; www.theeasternermotel.com; 639 East Montauk Hwy; d from $170; ✷🛜🌊) Located 5 miles from Southampton, the Easterner has comfortable if somewhat dated rooms in an old-fashioned property along the highway. Overall, good value for the area.

1708 House (☑631-287-1708; www.1708house.com; 126 Main St, Southampton; r/cottage from $200/300; ✷🛜) History buffs might gravitate toward this local standout. It's in central Southampton and prides itself on its turn-of-the-century charm.

American Hotel (☑631-725-3535; www.theamericanhotel.com; Main St, Sag Harbor; r low season $250-350, high season $350-450) An old-world hotel (but still excellent and modern), it has a popular downstairs restaurant and bar that continues to be a center of the social scene all these years later. An ideal choice for any lover of European elegance and efficiency, it has fine accommodations all set in a superb location.

borcycle.com; 34 Bay St) rents bicycles ($45 to $70 per day) and sells maps of cycling trails.

A quick ferry ride on the South Ferry (p319) from the edge of North Haven, which borders Sag Harbor, will take you to sleepy Shelter Island, nearly a third of which is dedicated to the **Mashomack Nature Preserve** (☑631-749-1001; www.nature.org; Rte 114; ☺9am-5pm Mar-Sep, to 4pm Oct-Feb), dotted with hiking trails. Take precautions while hiking – ticks are an ever-present problem. Outside the Mashomack Preserve, Shelter Island abounds in historic B&Bs and romantic restaurants, making it easy to spend a few days here soaking up the nature and history. Check out www.shelter-island.org, a listings website run by the nonprofit Shelter Island Club, for the latest information on what's available.

◉ East Hampton

This is Long Island's trendiest town.

EAST HAMPTON HISTORICAL SOCIETY　　　　　　　　　MUSEUM
(☑631 324 6850; www.easthamptonhistory.org; 101 Main St; adult/child $4/2; ☺hours vary) Check out East Hampton's colonial past with a visit to the East Hampton Historical Society. The Society tends to five historical attractions around East Hampton, including several old colonial farms, mansions and a marine museum.

POLLOCK-KRASNER HOUSE　　　　MUSEUM
(☑631-324-4929; http://sb.cc.stonybrook.edu/pkhouse/; 830 Springs-Fireplace Rd; admission $5; ☺1-5pm Thu-Sat Jun-Aug, by appt May, Sep & Oct) If you're around Thursday through Saturday, it's worth planning a visit to the Pollock-Krasner House, where Jackson Pollock lived and worked.

GUILD HALL　　　　　　CULTURAL CENTRE
(☑631-324-0806; www.guildhall.org; 158 Main St) You can catch readings and art exhibitions at Guild Hall.

◉ Montauk

Once a sleepy and humble stepsister to the Hamptons, these days Montauk, at the far eastern end of Long Island, draws a fashionable, younger crowd and even a hipster subset to its beautiful beaches. Longtime

residents, fishers and territorial surfers round out a motley mix that makes the dining and bar scene more democratic compared to other Hamptons villages.

MONTAUK POINT STATE PARK　　PARK
(☑631-668-3781; admission per vehicle $8) Covering the eastern tip of the South Fork is Montauk Point State Park, with its impressive Montauk lighthouse. You can camp in the sand nearby at windswept **Hither Hills State Park** (☑631-668-2554; www.nysparks.com; 164 Old Montauk Hwy; entrance fee per vehicle $10), a fantastic nature spot that offers a bit of everything: year-round fishing for anglers and special permits to fish at night; beach camping; the unique 'walking dunes' in Napeague Harbor (at the east end of the park); and lots of open woodlands to tramp though.

✖ EATING

ROUND SWAMP FARM　　　　　MARKET $
(☑631-324-4438; 184 Three Mile Rd, East Hampton; ☺8am-6pm Thu-Sat, to 2pm Sun) This delightful gourmet market is a great spot to assemble a picnic before hitting the beach. Abundant temptations include prepared foods (sea scallops, homemade pastas, gourmet salads, roasted meats), plus delicious pies and baked goods.

SCOOP DU JOUR　　　　ICE CREAM $
(☑631-329-4883; 35 Newton Lane, East Hampton; ice creams $4-9) This popular ice-cream parlor serves decadent selections such as pistachio and cake batter, as well as famous Dreesen's doughnuts (which have been cooking up doughy perfection since the 1950s).

★LOBSTER ROLL　　　　　SEAFOOD $$
(☑631-267-3740; 1980 Montauk Hwy; mains $14-28; ☺11:30am-10pm summer) On Rte 27, between the towns of Amagansett and Montauk, a few roadside fish shacks like this institution pop up. With its distinctive 'Lunch' sign, the Lobster Roll serves the namesake sandwich as well as fresh steamers and fried clams.

LT BURGER　　　　　AMERICAN $$
(☑631-899-4646; 62 Main St, Sag Harbor; mains $11-15; ☺8am-9pm Wed-Mon, to 11pm Fri & Sat; ♿) On restaurant-lined Main St in Sag

DETOUR: JONES BEACH

The offerings of **Jones Beach State Park** (☏516-785-1600; www.nysparks.com/parks/10/; 1 Ocean Pkwy) are simple: 6.5 miles of clean sand covered with beachgoers. The character of the beach differs depending on which 'field' you choose – for example, 2 is for the surfers and 6 is for families, and there's a gay beach followed by a nude beach way east – but it's a definite scene no matter where you choose to spread your blanket. The ocean gets quite warm by midsummer (up to about 70°F) and there are plenty of lifeguards. In between sunning and riding waves you might also hop into one of the two massive on-site pools for a swim; play shuffleboard or basketball on beachside courts; stroll the 2-mile boardwalk; or visit the still waters of the bay beach.

Biking and running are allowed along a 4-mile path that stretches through the park, and there are places to rent bikes along the beach. When the sun goes down, you can grill at one of the many barbecues in the sand, grab burgers at the few local restaurants near the beach, or head to the **Jones Beach Theater** (☏516-221-1000; www.jonesbeach.com), where alfresco concerts under the stars feature nostalgic names from the past: Steve Miller Band, Phish, Jimmy Buffett, Depeche Mode and the like.

Jones Beach is about 33 miles east of NYC, and it takes roughly 45 minutes to arrive using public transportation. The **Long Island Rail Road** (LIRR; ☏718-217-5477; www.mta.nyc.ny.us/lirr; round-trip $18.75) offers round-trips from Manhattan's Penn Station and Brooklyn's Flatbush Ave Station (transfer required at Jamaica) to Freeport Station on Long Island; a free shuttle bus runs from the station to the beach between Memorial Day Weekend and Labor Day.

If you have your own vehicle, take the Midtown Tunnel from Manhattan onto I-495/Long Island Expwy (LIE); turn off exit 38 to the eastbound Northern State Pkwy, then look for exit 33 for the Wantagh Pkwy. That goes straight to Jones Beach State Park. (You can also take the LIE to exit 31S for the Cross-Island Pkwy and then exit 25A onto the Southern State Pkwy to get to the Wantagh Pkwy.)

Harbor, this kid-friendly charmer serves up great burgers, plus excellent breakfasts and weekend brunches.

NICK & TONI'S　　　　　　　　ITALIAN $$$
(☏631-324-3550; 136 N Main St, East Hampton; mains $23-39) Flawless Italian restaurant styled to look like an old Tuscan farmhouse.

🍸 DRINKING & NIGHTLIFE

Nightlife is a seasonal (June to August) and somewhat transient affair in the Hamptons. Montauk has a buzzing nightlife scene, while in Bridgehampton new nightclubs blow in and bow out every season.

SLOPPY TUNA　　　　　　　　　BAR
(☏631-647-8000; www.thesloppytuna.com; 148 Emerson Ave, Montauk) Check out the Sloppy Tuna for beachside drinks and a rowdy dance floor.

MEMORY MOTEL　　　　　　　　BAR
(☏631-668-2702; 692 Montauk Hwy, Montauk) For a scruffy bit of fun, have a drink at the bar of the Memory Motel. This is where Mick Jagger often stayed in the 1970s and was even inspired to write the Rolling Stones song of the same name.

STEPHEN TALKHOUSE　　　　　BAR
(☏631-267-3117; www.stephentalkhouse.com; 161 Main St, Amagansett; cover $10-20) In Amagansett (4 miles west of East Hampton), this bar is a local mainstay for live rock music.

MURF'S BACKSTREET TAVERN　BAR
(☏631-725-8355; www.murfstavern.com; 64 Division St, Sag Harbor) In Sag Harbor, Murf's is a laid-back pub with a decent beer selection and a welcome lack of pretension

SURF LODGE　　　　　　　　　BAR
(☏631-483-5037; www.thesurflodge.com; 183 Edgemere St, Montauk) The place for waterside sundowners and concerts.

Fire Island

Explore

Fire Island is a skinny barrier island of sand that runs parallel to Long Island. Although several communities are famed getaways for the gay community, there's something for everyone here, including families, couples and single travelers – gay and straight alike. Along its scant 50 miles, you'll find tiny towns, wild dunes, pine forests, hiking trails and plenty of postcard-worthy beach moments atop squeaky white sands. The island is federally protected as the **Fire Island National Seashore** (☎631-687-4750; www.nps.gov/fiis) and much of the land strip is a no-go zone for cars, which fosters a serene environment while adding to the area's rugged charm. In summer, expect hamlets jam-packed with roaring nightclubs next to neighboring stretches of sand where you'll find nothing but pitched tents and deer – quite the odd juxtaposition. And don't forget bug repellent: the mosquitoes are both fierce and abundant on Fire Island.

The Best...

→ **Sight** Sunken Forest (p318)
→ **Place to Eat** Sand Castle (p318)
→ **Place to Drink** Surf's Out (p318)

Top Tip

If you're visiting during a summer weekend, make sure to skip out early on Sunday (before 3pm) or spend the night and leave Monday – the line for the ferry on Sunday evenings is impossible.

Getting There & Away

→ **Car** Take the Midtown Tunnel out of Manhattan onto I-495/Long Island Expwy. For Sayville ferries (to The Pines, Cherry Grove and Sunken Forest), get off at exit 57 on to the Vets Memorial Hwy. Make a right on Lakeland Ave and take it to the end, following signs for the ferry. For Davis Park Ferry from Patchogue (to Watch Hill), take the Long Island Expwy to exit 63 southbound (North Ocean Ave). For Bay Shore ferries (all other Fire Island destinations), take the Long Island Expwy to exit 30E, then get onto the Sagtikos Pkwy to exit 42 south, to Fifth Ave terminal in Bay Shore. To get to Robert Moses State Park by car, take exit 53 off the Long Island Expwy and travel south across the Moses Causeway.

→ **Train** The Long Island Rail Road (p313) makes stops in Bay Shore, Sayville and Patchogue, where you can catch a summer-only shuttle service (or walk or taxi) to the ferry terminal.

→ **Ferry** Fire Island Ferry Service (☎631-665-3600; www.fireislandferries.com; Bay Shore) runs to Kismet, Ocean Beach and other western communities. Sayville Ferry Service (☎631-589-0810; www.sayvilleferry.com) goes to Cherry Grove and Fire Island Pines. Davis Park Ferry (☎631-475-1665; www.davisparkferry.com) goes to Davis Park and Watch Hill, the easternmost ferry-access point of the island. Fire Island Water Taxi (☎631-665-8885; www.fireislandwatertaxi.com) also provides lateral, town-to-town service on the island.

SLEEPING ON FIRE ISLAND

Watch Hill Campground (☎631-567-6664; www.watchhillfi.com; Watch Hill; tent sites $25; ☒) Reservations are a must, as sites can fill up months in advance. There's a camp store for basics (ice, charcoal, snacks) and a good, somewhat high-end restaurant. Sites are sandy and lack shade. Take the Davis Park Ferry.

Grove Hotel (☎631-597-6600; www.grovehotel.com; Cherry Grove; r from $120; ✳☒) With beachy, basic rooms, the Grove Hotel offers the main source of entertainment at its nightclub.

Madison Fire Island (☎631-597-6061; www.themadisonfi.com; 22 Atlantic Walk, The Pines; r $200-500; ✳☞☒) Fire Island's first 'boutique' hotel, which rivals anything Manhattan has to offer in terms of amenities, but also has magnificent views from a rooftop deck and a gorgeous pool.

Need to Know

➜ **Area Code** ☑631

➜ **Location** 60 miles east of Manhattan; two hours (including ferry ride)

➜ **Tourist Office** (www.fireisland.com)

◉ SIGHTS

The gemlike parts of Fire Island are found further east of Robert Moses State Park, in the tranquil, car-free villages. Davis Park, Fair Harbor, Kismet, Ocean Bay Park and Ocean Beach combine small summer homes with tiny towns that have grocery stores, bars, nightclubs and restaurants – just keep in mind that almost everything in every town shuts down a couple of weeks after Labor Day. You can rely on the **South Bay Water Taxi** (☑631-665-8885; www.fireislandwatertaxi.com; 133 Ocean Ave; fares $10-20) service to shuttle you between villages.

Perhaps the most infamous villages are those that have evolved into gay destinations: **Cherry Grove** (www.cherrygrove.com) and the **Pines** (www.thepinesfireisland.com). While day trips are easy to Fire Island, staying for a night or two on this car-free oasis, where boardwalks serve as pathways between the dunes and homes, is wonderful.

ROBERT MOSES STATE PARK   OUTDOORS
(☑631-669-0449; www.nysparks.state.ny.us) The only part of the island that's accessible by car, Robert Moses State Park lies at the westernmost end and features wide, soft-sand beaches with mellower crowds than those at Jones Beach. It's also home to the Fire Island Lighthouse, which houses a history museum.

SUNKEN FOREST   PARK
(☑631-597-6183) If you want to skip the scene altogether and just get back to nature, enjoy a hike through the Sunken Forest, a 300-year-old forest, with its own ferry stop (called Sailor's Haven). Off-season (after the ferry shuts down), it's about a 1.5-mile walk east from Ocean Bay Park.

OTIS PIKE FIRE ISLAND WILDERNESS   OUTDOORS
At the eastern end of the island, the 1300-acre preserve of Otis Pike Fire Island Wilderness includes a beach campground and a pleasant marina restaurant at Watch Hill.

If camping or hiking, just beware of the fierce mosquitoes and ticks.

EATING & DRINKING

Expect higher prices and lower quality out on Fire Island.

SAND CASTLE   SEAFOOD $$
(http://firelslandsandcastle.com; 106 Lewis Walk, Cherry Grove; mains $15-30) One of Fire Island's only oceanfront (rather than bayfront) options, Sand Castle serves up satisfying appetizers (fried calamari, portobello fries) and lots of seafood temptations (mussels, crabcakes, seared sea scallops). Nice cocktails and people-watching.

SURF'S OUT   AMERICAN $$
(☑631-583-7400; www.surfsout.com; 1 Bay Walk; mains $18-30) Near the ferry dock in Kismet, this easygoing waterfront spot serves decent seafood and Italian fare, with occasional live music. It's a good lunchtime destination after visiting the Fire Island Lighthouse nearby – or come at sunset for oysters and white wine.

CASTAWAY   AMERICAN $$
(☑631-583-0330; 310 Bay Walk, Ocean Beach; mains $12-24) In the classic rock-loving town of Ocean Beach, the publike Castaway serves burgers, seafood platters and other unfussy fare at relatively reasonable prices (come at happy hour for clam specials). You can also belly up to the bar and order a pint of Montauk, Driftwood ale or other NY brews on tap. There are lots of other eating and drinking options nearby.

North Fork

Explore

Once synonymous with beachy hideaways, Long Island is now famous for its great grapes. Over the past three decades what was one lone winery has become a thriving industry that takes up more than 3000 acres of land. Most vineyards are at the East End's North Fork, where you can follow the green 'wine trail' signs along Rte 25 once you pass Riverhead. South Fork has

Duck Walk Vineyards (☑631-726-7555; www.
duckwalk.com; Southampton, South Fork) and
Wölffer Estate Vineyards (☑631-537-5106;
www.wolffer.com; Sagaponack, South Fork), and
you can explore them if you choose before
continuing on to the North Fork via Shelter
Island and two ferries.

The most charming town in the area is
Greenport, which has a picturesque waterfront, where kids flock to a century-old carousel. Peaceful, pedestrian-friendly streets
nearby are dotted with shops, cafes and
eateries.

The Best...
→ **Sight** Greenport
→ **Place to Eat** First and South (p320)
→ **Place to Drink** At the wineries (take
your pick!)

Top Tip
The North Folk Wineries are an easy DIY
adventure. Consider taking the train out to
Long Island and renting a car there (Riverhead is a good place to look) – prices are
cheaper than in Manhattan and you'll save
time, gas and frustration.

Getting There & Away
→ **Bus** The Hampton Jitney ☑212-362-
8400; www.hamptonjitney.com) picks
up passengers at 86th St in Manhattan
between Lexington and Third Aves, and
also 69th, 59th and 44th Sts. It makes
stops in 10 North Fork villages.

→ **Car** Take the Midtown Tunnel out of
Manhattan, which will take you onto I-495/
Long Island Expwy. Take this until it ends,
at Riverhead, and follow signs onto Rte 25.
Stay on Rte 25 for all points east.

→ **Train** The Long Island Rail Road (LIRR;
☑718-217-5477; www.mta.nyc.ny.us/lirr;

one-way fare to Greenport from $20)
has a North Fork line, usually called the
Ronkonkoma Branch, with trips leaving
from Penn Station and Brooklyn. Make
sure the stop at the end of your line is
Greenport.

→ **Ferry** To get from the North Fork to the
South Fork (or vice versa), take the North
Ferry (☑631-749-0139; www.northferry.
com) and South Ferry (☑631-749-1200;
www.southferry.com; Rte 114, North
Haven; one-way passenger/vehicle $1/17)
services to and from Shelter Island.

Need to Know
→ **Area Code** ☑631
→ **Location** 100 miles east of Manhattan;
2¼ hour drive
→ **Tourist Office** (☑631-722-2220; www.
liwines.com)

⊙ SIGHTS

Harvest time is in fall, which, combined
with foliage and pumpkin-picking opportunities, makes it an ideal time to visit North
Fork (although most places remain open
year-round). If driving yourself doesn't appeal, consider a wine-tour option. **Vintage
Tours** (☑631-765-4689; www.vintagetour1.com;
tours per person incl lunch $88-100) will shep-
herd you around in a van. **North Fork Trolley Co** (☑631-369-3031; www.northforktrolley.
com; tours per person $79) has converted
trolleys for its tours, and you can even hit
the vineyards on a bike with **Long Island
Bicycle Tours** (☑631-824-3360; www.longis-
landbicycletours.com; Mattituck; tour per person
incl lunch & bike rental $160).

Wineries are generally open from 11am
to 5pm, with closing time extended by an

SLEEPING AT THE NORTH FORK WINERIES

Quintessentials B&B Spa (☑631-477-9400; www.quintessentialsinc.com; 8585 Main
Rd, East Marion; r $200-350) A Victorian place in East Marion that's outfitted with a full-
service spa, plush quarters and peaceful, flowering grounds.

Greenporter Hotel (☑631-477-0066; www.greenporterhotel.com; 326 Front St; r from
$170; ✱✿✷) No-frills, good-value hotel in a handy central Greenport location four
blocks frrom the Long Island Rail Road (LIRR).

Pridwin Beach Hotel & Cottages (☑631-749-0476; www.pridwin.com; 81 Shore Rd,
Shelter Island; r & cottages $185-355; ✱✿) Has a wide range of rooms (some with water
views) in a forested property on Shelter Island.

hour in summer, but not all have tours or tastings every day. If you want to taste the wine without the travel, head straight to the **North Fork Tasting Room** (☑631-727-9513; www.northforktastingroom.com; 3225 Sound Ave, Riverhead; bottles from $24; ☺noon-9pm Fri-Sun), located 4.5 miles northwest of Riverhead. Here you can sample a range of wines, local brews and snacks.

A drive along the back roads of the North Fork affords some beautiful, unspoiled vistas of farms and rural residential areas. If you're too bushed to make the trip out and back in one day (a doable, but tiring, prospect), you'll find plenty of classic inns where you can rest your head for the night.

Several wineries offer full-scale tours of their facilities, including **Bedell Cellars** (☑631-734-7537; www.bedellcellars.com; Main Road, Rte 25, Cutchogue; wine tasting from $15), **Pindar Vineyards** (☑631-734-6200; www.pindar.net; Peconic; wine tasting $10) and **Raphael Vineyard & Winery** (☑631-765-1100; www.raphaelwine.com; 39390 Rte 25, Peconic; tastings from $2 per glass, winery tours incl tasting of 6 wines from $25).

 **EATING & DRINKING**

LOVE LANE KITCHEN
MODERN AMERICAN $$
(www.lovelanekitchen.com; 240 Love Lane, Matituck; mains lunch $12-15, dinner $24-30; ☺8am-9:30pm Fri-Mon, 7am-4pm Tue-Thu) In Matituck, Love Lane Kitchen serves delicious breakfasts, gourmet sandwiches and changing dinner specials.

LUNCH TRUCK
AMERICAN $$
(www.nofoti.com; 57225 Main Rd, Southold; mains $10-17; ☺11:30am-3:30pm Thu-Sun) Located in Southold, the Lunch Truck serves lobster rolls, fish tacos and juicy burgers from the parking lot of the high-end North Fork Table & Inn.

CLAUDIO'S CLAM BAR
SEAFOOD $$
(www.claudios.com; 111 Main St, Greenport; mains $15; ☺11:30am-9pm, closed Wed) For drinks and unfussy seafood (fried clams and the like) on the waterfront, don't miss Claudio's Clam Bar

FIRST AND SOUTH
MODERN AMERICAN $$$
(☑631-333-2200; www.firstandsouth.com; 100 S St, Greenport; mains around $30; ☺11am-4pm Sat-Mon & 5-10pm Thu-Sat, to 9pm Sun & Mon)

Greenport has a handful of notable restaurants well worth seeking out. First and South is a great example, serving delectable fare, much of which is locally sourced.

GREENPORT HARBOR BREWING CO
MICROBREWERY
(www.harborbrewing.com; 234 Carpenter St, Greenport) Serves refreshing microbrews.

Hudson Valley

Explore
Winding roads along the Hudson River take you by picturesque farms, Victorian cottages, apple orchards and old-money mansions built by New York's elite. Painters of the Hudson River School romanticized these landscapes – you can see their work at art museums in the area as well as in NYC. Autumn is a particularly beautiful time for a trip up this way. The east side of the river feels more populated – less so the further north you go – while the west side has a rural feel, with hills leading into the Catskills mountain region.

The Best...
➤ **Sights** Dia Beacon and Storm King Art Center (p322)

➤ **Place to Eat** Blue Hill at Stone Barns (p323)

➤ **Place to Drink** Hop (p323)

Top Tip
Foodies should gravitate towards Hudson or Rhinebeck, which have some of the best restaurants in the area.

Getting There & Away
➤ **Car** From Manhattan, take the Henry Hudson Pkwy across the George Washington Bridge (I-95) to Palisades Pkwy. Head for the New York State Thruway to Rte 9W or Rte 9, the principal scenic river routes. You can also take the Taconic State Pkwy north from Ossining, a pretty road in autumn.

➤ **Bus** Short Line Buses (☑212-736-4700; www.shortlinebus.com) runs regular trips to Rhinebeck ($51).

⇒ Train The commuter train line Metro-North (☎212-532-4900, 800-638-7646; http://mta.info; one way to Tarrytown/Cold Spring/Beacon/Poughkeepsie from $9.75/13.25/15.25/17) makes several stops on the Lower and Middle Hudson Valleys (take the Hudson Line).

Need to Know

⇒ Area Code ☎845
⇒ Location 95 miles north (Hyde Park) of Manhattan; 1¾-hour drive
⇒ Tourist Office Dutchess County Tourism (☎800-445-3131; www.dutchessny.gov; 3 Neptune Rd), Hudson Valley Network (www.hvnet.com) and Hudson Valley Tourism (☎800-232-4782; www.hudsonvalley.org)

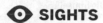

SIGHTS

Several magnificent homes and gardens can be found near Tarrytown and Sleepy Hollow, on the east side of the Hudson. Further north, the town of Cold Spring is probably the best one-stop destination if arriving by train. Within walking distance of the terminal, you'll find pretty riverfront, and a Main St lined with antique shops and restaurants.

The largest town on the Hudson's east bank, Poughkeepsie (puh-kip-see) is famous for Vassar, a private liberal-arts college that admitted only women until 1969. Further north is Rhinebeck, with a charming main street, farms and wineries. Continuing along 9G N you reach Hudson – a beautiful town with a hip, gay-friendly community of artists, writers and performers who fled the city. Warren St, the main roadway through town, is lined with antiques shops, high-end furniture stores, galleries and cafes.

KYKUIT HISTORIC BUILDING
(☎914-631-9491; Pocantico Hills, Tarrytown; adult/child/senior $22/18/20; ⊙tours 9:45am, 1:45pm & 3pm) One of the properties of the Rockefeller family, with an impressive array of Asian and European artwork, and immaculately kept gardens with breathtaking views.

LYNDHURST CASTLE CASTLE
(☎914-631-4481; www.lyndhurst.org; Rte 9, Tarrytown; castle/grounds $12/6; ⊙grounds open daily dusk-dawn) The former summer home of railroad tycoon Jay Gould is an impressive 19th-century Gothic Revival mansion set on a 67-acre estate.

SUNNYSIDE HISTORIC BUILDING
(☎914-591-8763, Mon-Fri 914-631-8200; 89 W Sunnyside Lane, Sleepy Hollow; adult/child/senior $12/6/10; ⊙10am-5pm Wed-Mon Apr-Oct, to 4pm Nov-Dec) Overlooking the Hudson River, Sunnyside was where author Washington Irving lived and wrote. Knowledgeable tour guides, dressed in period costume, provide insight into the great storyteller and life in the mid 1800s.

HUDSON HIGHLANDS STATE PARK PARK
(www.nysparks.com) There are miles of trails in the Hudson Highlands State Park just

SLEEPING ON THE HUDSON

Cheap motel chains in Poughkeepsie are clustered along Rte 9, south of the Mid-Hudson Bridge.

Bear Mountain Inn (☎845-786-2731; www.visitbearmountain.com; 55 Hessian Dr, Highland Falls; r $100-220; ☜) Amid beautiful scenery inside the state park, this extensive mountain resort is a 1915 classic, with a wood-and-stone facade and sweeping views. The vast property includes a spa, several restaurants, comfortable hotel-style rooms as well as more rustic stone cottages. Hiking trails right outside your doorstep.

Beekman Arms (☎845-876-7077; www.beekmandelamaterinn.com; 6387 Mill St, Rhinebeck; r from $175) Dating from 1766, this is America's oldest continuously operating inn. It has cozy rooms (with low ceilings) and atmospheric common areas, well located in the center of Rhinebeck.

Storm King Lodge (☎845-534-9421; www.stormkinglodge.com; 100 Pleasant Hill Rd, Mountainville; r $170-250; ☒) The charming Storm King Lodge is a stately structure from the 1800s that's filled to the brim with tasteful furnishings like cozy quilts, deep leather parlor chairs, fresh flowers and thick slats of shiny wood running across the creaky floors. It's 1.5 miles southwest of Storm King Art Center.

north of Cold Spring. Hiking trails up into the forested ridges overlooking the Hudson, begin about a half-mile from the train station (from Main St, turn left on Fair St, continue onto Rte 9D and look for the Bull Hill parking lot/trailhead on your right).

DIA BEACON GALLERY
(Beacon; ☏845-440-0100; www.diaart.org; adult $10; ⊙11am-6pm Thu-Mon mid-Apr–mid-Oct, 11am-4pm Fri-Mon mid-Oct–mid-Apr) North of Cold Spring is the town of Beacon, home to the renowned Dia Beacon, an outpost of NYC's Dia Center for the Arts. The Dia Beacon is in a former factory and is filled with huge Richard Serra ironwork pieces, as well as ever-changing installations.

The once-scruffy town of Beacon itself is undergoing a renaissance with the arrival of new eating and drinking spots, and boutique lodging options.

HARRIMAN STATE PARK OUTDOORS
(☏845-786-5003; http://nysparks.state.ny.us/parks) On the west side of the Hudson, Harriman State Park spans 72 sq miles and is a great hiking spot. Adjacent **Bear Mountain State Park** (☏845-786-2701; http://nysparks.state.ny.us/parks; ⊙8am-dusk) offers great views from its 1305ft peak. The Manhattan skyline looms beyond the river and surrounding greenery.

STORM KING ART CENTER GALLERY
(☏845-534-3115; www.stormking.org; Old Pleasant Hill Rd; adult/child $12/8; ⊙Apr-Nov) Further north from Harriman State Park, the outstanding Storm King Art Center in Mountainville is a giant open-air museum on 500 acres. Small creeks, lakes, meadows and hills form the backdrop to more than 100 massive installations by Alexander Calder, Mark di Suvero, Andy Goldsworthy, Isamu Noguchi and other major sculptors of the past and present.

WALKWAY OVER THE HUDSON PARK
(www.walkway.org; ⊙7am-sunset) Worth a stroll for its breathtaking views is the new Walkway Over the Hudson; formerly the Highland-Poughkeepsie railroad bridge and since 2009 the world's longest pedestrian bridge (at 1.3 miles)

FRANKLIN D ROOSEVELT HOME HISTORIC BUILDING
(☏845-229-5320; www.nps.gov/hofr; 4097 Albany Post Rd, Hyde Park; adult/child $18/free;

⊙9am-5pm) Sprawling modern Hyde Park isn't a very charming town, though it does have several historic sites. The beautifully preserved Franklin D Roosevelt Home provides a fascinating glimpse into the life of one of America's greatest presidents. He was born here (in 1882), lived here during his early years and even brought his wife to live here after they were married.

Visits are by one-hour guided tour only (call ahead to reserve a spot); admission also gives access to the library and museum. It's free to tour the grounds.

VAL-KILL HISTORIC BUILDING
(☏845-229-9422; www.nps.gov/elro; 54 ValKill Park Rd, Hyde Park; adult/child $10/free; ⊙9am-5pm daily May-Oct, Thu-Mon Nov-Apr) Two miles east of the Franklin D Roosevelt Home (off Rte 9G), is Eleanor Roosevelt's cottage Val-Kill – her retreat from Hyde Park, her mother-in-law and FDR himself.

VANDERBILT MANSION HISTORIC BUILDING
(☏877-444-6777; www.nps.gov/vama; 119 Vanderbilt Park Rd, Hyde Park; adult/child $10/free; ⊙9am-5pm daily Apr-Dec, Fri-Tue Jan-Mar) The Vanderbilt Mansion, a national historic site 2 miles north of the Franklin D Roosevelt Home on Rte 9, is a spectacle of lavish beaux arts and eclectic architecture.

OLANA HISTORIC BUILDING
(☏518-828-0135; www.olana.org; Rte 9G, Hudson; tours adult/child $12/free, grounds per vehicle $5; ⊙grounds 8am-sunset daily, tours 10am-5pm Tue-Sun) About 22 miles north of Rhinebeck is Olana, the wild Moorish-style home of Frederic Church, one of the primary artists of the Hudson River School of Painting. On a house tour you can appreciate the totality of Church's aesthetic vision, as well as view paintings from his own collection.

 **EATING**

HUDSON HIL'S CAFE & MARKET AMERICAN $
(www.hudsonhils.com; 129 Main St, Cold Spring; mains $9-14; ⊙8am-4pm Wed-Mon) Fill up at this great little cafe before (or after) hiking the challenging Breakneck Ridge Trail. Come for pancakes, breakfast burritos and eggs Benedict in the morning; or farm-fresh burgers, salmon BLTs and roast vegetable wraps for lunch.

HOP
MODERN AMERICAN $$

(www.thehopbeacon.com; 458 Main St, Beacon; sharing plates $8-15; ⊙noon-9pm Mon, Wed & Thu, to 11pm Fri & Sat, to 8pm Sun) In the town of Beacon, the Hop draws beer lovers with its extensive menu of microbrews. House-made sausages, artisanal cheeses, panini and salads go nicely with the craft beers.

MARKET STREET
MODERN AMERICAN $$

(☑845-876-7200; www.marketstrhinebeck.com; 19 W Market St, Rhinebeck; mains brunch $10-13, dinner $18-33; ⊙5-10pm Mon-Thu, from 11:30am Fri-Sun) A standout among Rhinebeck's excellent dining scene, the elegantly designed Market Street serves an excellent farm-to-table menu, including Hudson Valley slow-roasted duck leg or homemade pumpkin ravioli, plus wood-fired-oven pizzas. Good brunches.

★BLUE HILL AT STONE BARNS
MODERN AMERICAN $$$

(☑914-366-9600; www.bluehillfarm.com; 630 Bedford Rd, Pocantico Hills; 8-course prix fixe $148; ⊙5-10pm Wed-Sat, 1-10pm Sun) The elegant country restaurant Blue Hill at Stone Barns is a pillar of the farm-to-table movement and a locavore's dream. Even if you can't get a reservation at the restaurant (hint: plan weeks in advance), it's a fun day's outing strolling around the working **farm** (☑914-366 6200; www.stonebarnscenter.org; 630 Bedford Rd, Pocantico Hills; admission per vehicle $5; ⊙10am-5pm Wed-Sun), particularly if you have kids in tow.

CULINARY INSTITUTE OF AMERICA
INTERNATIONAL $$$

(☑845-471-6608; www.ciarestaurants.com; Hyde Park; ⊙most restaurants 11:30am-1pm & 6-8pm Mon-Sat) Trains future chefs and can satisfy anyone's gastronomic cravings. The large campus contains separate restaurants for French, Italian and Modern American cuisine.

Woodstock & Saugerties

Explore

In the southern Catskills, the town of Woodstock symbolizes the tumultuous 1960s, when young people questioned authority, experimented with freedom and redefined popular culture. Today it's a combination of quaint and hip – an artists' colony full of young urbanites. The Woodstock Guild is a good source for finding out the latest goings-on in the arts and culture scene, such as the annual Woodstock Film Festival in October, which attracts film fans from all over.

Saugerties, which sees far fewer tourists, has a quaint main street and picturesque lighthouse.

The Best...

→ **Sight** Overlook Mountain (p324)
→ **Place to Eat** Miss Lucy's Kitchen (p324)
→ **Place to Sleep** Saugerties Lighthouse

Top Tip

Bring an empty bag – you never know what you'll unearth in the many antique shops and markets (plus weekend yard sales!) found in the area.

Getting There & Away

→ **Car** Take the New York State Thruway (via the Henry Hudson Hwy north from Manhattan) or I-87 to Rte 375 for Woodstock, Rte 32 for Saugerties or Rte 28 for other points.
→ **Bus** Frequent buses to Saugerties and Woodstock are operated by Adirondack Pine Hill Trailways (☑800-858-8555; www.trailwaysny.com; round-trip from $58).

SLEEPING IN WOODSTOCK & SAUGERTIES

Village Green (☑845-679-0313; www.villagegreenbb.com; 12 Tinker St; r incl breakfast $135-165; ▣☎) You can't be any more central than this three-story Victorian, a few steps from Woodstock's main square and bus stop.

Saugerties Lighthouse (☑845-247-0656; www.saugertieslighthouse.com; d $230) This picturesque 1869 landmark is a unique and rather romantic B&B with just two guestrooms. Book well in advance.

Need to Know

➜ **Area Code** ☑845

➜ **Location** 110 miles north (Saugerties) of Manhattan

➜ **Tourist Office** (☎845-679-2079; www.woodstockguild.org; 34 Tinker St, Woodstock; ☺9am-5pm Mon-Fri)

◉ SIGHTS

Woodstock is most famous for the 1969 music festival of the same name. There's just one problem – it didn't happen here. The concert was in Bethel, a small town about 40 miles southeast. But no matter; Woodstock has embraced its hippie ethos tightly, as you'll see from the offbeat and quirky Tinker St shops and organic eateries, all decorated in vibrant hues. In summer the locals assemble at the town square (which is, of course, a peace sign) for a drum circle from 4pm to 6pm on Sundays. Just a few miles northeast you'll find Saugerties, with its own attractive downtown area and a smaller offering of galleries, cafes and eateries. A highlight is walking the half-mile trail from town out to the Saugerties Lighthouse (p323).

OPUS 40   ART

(☎845-246-3400; www.opus40.org; 50 Fite Rd; adult/child $10/3; ☺11am-5:30pm Thu-Sun May-Sep) In between the two upstate towns of Woodstock and Saugerties lies a hidden art installation that takes a bit of work to find, but is well worth the effort. *Opus 40* is the sculpture put together by artist Harvey Fite, who transformed an old slate quarry in the 1930s into an outdoor art installation.

BETHEL WOODS CENTER
FOR THE ARTS   ART

(☎866-781-2922; www.bethelwoodscenter.org; 200 Hurd Rd, Bethel) Bethel, which was all but forgotten after its cataclysmic three-day concert in 1969 is now home to the fantastic Bethel Woods Center for the Arts. The center, which hosts frequent outdoor concerts in summer, also has the **Museum at Bethel Woods** (☎866-781-2922; www.bethelwoodscenter.org; 200 Hurd Rd, Bethel; adult/child $15/6; ☺10am-7pm daily May-Sep, 10am-5pm Thu-Sun Oct-Apr), dedicated to the hippie movement and the 1960s. Woodstock's rabble-rousing spirit lives on in the museum's evocative pictures and multimedia exhibits.

CATSKILL FOREST PRESERVE   PARK

(www.dec.ny.gov/lands/5265.html) Fantastic hiking can be found in the Catskill Forest Preserve, a huge swath of land that contains the vital watershed feeding NYC's ravenous thirst, and hundreds of miles of trails.

One of the most accessible parts of the park near Woodstock is **Overlook Mountain**. Reach it by taking Rock City Rd (next to the village green), which turns into Meads Mountain Rd. The trailhead parking lot is up about 2 miles. The 4.8-mile trail takes in great views, plus the ruins of a 1920s lodge, and a metal firetower, which you can climb if you're not scared of heights.

WINDHAM MOUNTAIN   OUTDOORS

(☎518-734-4300; www.skiwindham.com) For winter skiing head north along Rtes 23 and 23A to Windham Mountain, a family-friendly resort with year-round activities (golf, spa treatments and mountain-biking).

TOWN TINKER TUBE
RENTAL   ADVENTURE SPORTS

(☎845-688-5553; www.towntinker.com; 10 Bridge St; tubes per day $15; ⛟) For a lazy outdoor day, head to Phoenicia to go innertubing down the Esopus Creek, which flows near Rte 28. Town Tinker will provide life jackets, tubes and transport back to your car.

✖ EATING

MISS LUCY'S KITCHEN   MODERN AMERICAN $$

(☎845-246-9240; www.misslucyskitchen.com; 90 Partition St, Saugerties; mains lunch $11-12, dinner $21-26; ☺lunch & dinner Wed-Sun) Old aprons, books and other homey flourishes give Miss Lucy's a country-kitchen cheerfulness that doesn't detract from the satisfying seasonal fare. Challah French toast, venison salami sandwiches and crispy braised pork belly are recent hits.

GARDEN CAFE ON THE GREEN   VEGAN $$

(☎845-679-3600; www.woodstockgardencafe.com; 6 Old Forge Rd, Woodstock; mains $10-16; ☺9am-9pm Sat-Mon, from 11:30am Wed-Fri) 🍃 On the town square, this place serves good ecofriendly food (black-bean and sweet-potato burgers, tofu scrambles, creative salads), plus regional beers and organic wines. Dine alfresco in the shaded garden.

Sleeping

Like the student with their hand up at the front of the class, NYC just seems to know how to do everything well, and its lodging scene is no exception. Brilliant minds have descended upon the 'city that never sleeps' to create some of the most inventive and memorable spaces for those who might just want to grab a bit of shut-eye during their stay.

Booking Accommodations

In New York City, the average room rate is well over $300. But don't let that scare you, there are great deals to be had – almost all of which can be found through savvy online snooping.

To get the best deals launch a two-pronged approach: if you don't have your heart set on a particular property, then check out discount juggernauts like **Booking** (www.booking. com), **Expedia** (www.expedia.com), **Orbitz** (www. orbitz.com) and **Priceline** (www.priceline.com). For those who do know where they'd like to stay – it might sound simple – but it's best to start at your desired hotel's website. These days it's not uncommon to find deals and package rates directly on the site of your accommodations of choice.

Also worth checking out are the slew of members-only websites, like **Jetsetter** (www. jetsetter.com) that offer discounted rates and 'flash sales' (limited-time only sales akin to Groupon) for their devotees. If you arrive in the city and are suddenly without accommodations, try the **Hotel Tonight** (www.hotel tonight.com) app – great deals but only for booking after noon or even later on the night you want to check in.

Room Rates

New York City doesn't have a 'high season' in the common way that beach destinations do. Sure, there are busier times of the year when it comes to tourist traffic, but at over 54 million visitor per annum, the Big Apple never needs to worry when it comes to filling up beds. As such, room rates fluctuate based on availability; in fact, most hotels have a booking algorithm in place that spits out a price quote relative to the number of rooms already booked on the same night, so the busier the evening the higher the price goes.

If you're looking to find the best room rates, then flexibility is key – weekdays are often cheaper, and you'll generally find that accommodations in winter months have smaller price tags. If you are visiting over a weekend, try for a business hotel in the Financial District, which tends to empty out when the working week ends.

Beyond Hotels & Hostels

We can all thank little Plaza-dweller Eloise for conjuring up fanciful dreams of hanging one's hat in a luxury New York City hotel room, but these days, finding a place to sleep in the city that never does is hardly restricted to the traditional spectrum of lodging.

Websites such as **Airbnb** (www.airbnb. com) are providing a truly unique – and not to mention economical – alternative to the wallet-busting glitz and glam. Selling 'unique spaces' to tourists looking for their home away from home, such sites offer locals the opportunity to rent out their apartments while they're out of town, or lease a space (be it a bedroom or pull-out couch) in their home. Airbnb is an undeniable hit in NYC, where space comes at a premium and obscenely high real estate prices act as quite the incentive for locals to supplement their housing income.

NEED TO KNOW

Prices

Prices in the guide represent the standard range in rates at each establishment regardless of the time of year. Breakfast is not included in the price of the room unless specified in the review.

$	less than $150
$$	$150 to $350
$$$	more than $350

Reservations

Reservations are essential – walk-ins are practically impossible and rack rates are almost always unfavorable relative to online deals. Reserve your room as early as possible and make sure you understand your hotel's cancellation policy. Expect check-in to always be in the middle of the afternoon and check-out times to be in the late morning.

Websites

➜ **Lonely Planet** (hotels .lonelyplanet.com) Accommodations reviews and online booking service.

➜ **Playbill** (www.play bill.com) Members get select rates on a variety of Manhattan hotels.

➜ **Kayak** (www.kayak. com) Simple all-purpose search engine.

Tipping

Always tip the maid – leave $3 to $5 per night in an obvious location with a note. Porters should receive a dollar or two, and service staff bringing items to your room should be tipped accordingly as well.

Lonely Planet's Top Choices

Ace Hotel (p337) A hipster funhouse for all wallet sizes comes with too-cool-for-school DJs spinning beats in the lobby next to hand-crafted coffee.

Jade Hotel (p333) In the West Village, this 2013 newcomer revives art deco flourishes, and upper floors have great views.

Wythe Hotel (p344) Boutique style has arrived in Brooklyn, with industrial chic rooms, a roof terrace and great Williamsburg location.

Gramercy Park Hotel (p334) This grande dame with gorgeous bars and a guest-only rooftop terrace offers keys to the coveted park below.

Andaz Fifth Avenue (p336) A boutique homage to NYC jetsetterdom that is impossibly chic yet wonderfully unpretentious.

Hôtel Americano (p332) This designer's dream is the boutique sleep of the future, stocked in an international assortment of upscale treats.

Best by Budget

$
Harlem Flophouse (p341)
Pod Hotel (p334)
East Village Bed & Coffee (p330)
3B (p342)
Jane Hotel (p331)

$$
Cosmopolitan Hotel (p328)
King & Grove (p343)
Inn on 23rd St (p332)
Nu Hotel (p343)
Bubba & Bean Lodges (p340)
Yotel (p334)
Gild Hall Wall Street (p328)

$$$
Bowery Hotel (p331)
Greenwich Hotel (p328)
Standard (p333)
Chatwal New York (p338)
Pierre (p338)

Best for Views

Standard (p333)
Aloft New York Brooklyn (p342)
Langham Place (p337)
Z Hotel (p344)

Best for Families

Hotel Beacon (p341)
70 Park (p339)
Hotel Gansevoort (p333)
Belvedere Hotel (p336)
Bubba & Bean Lodges (p340)
Nu Hotel (p343)

Best Boutique Digs

Library Hotel (p337)
King & Grove (p343)
NoMad Hotel (p337)
Bowery Hotel (p331)

Best for Honeymooners

Crosby Street Hotel (p329)
1871 House (p340)
Plaza (p338)

Best for Jetsetters

Standard (p333)
Dream Downtown (p333)
Wythe Hotel (p344)
Hotel Gansevoort (p333)

Where to Stay

Neighborhood	For	Against
Financial District & Lower Manhattan	Convenient to Tribeca's night scene and ferries. Cheap weekend rates at business hotels.	The area can feel impersonal, corporate and even a bit desolate after business hours.
SoHo & Chinatown	Shop to your heart's content right on your doorstep.	Crowds (mostly tourists) swarm the commercial streets of SoHo almost any time of day.
East Village & Lower East Side	Funky and fun, the area feels the most quintessentially 'New York' to visitors and Manhattanites alike.	Not tons to choose from when it comes to hotel sleeps.
Greenwich Village, Chelsea & the Meatpacking District	Brilliantly close-to-everything feel in a thriving, picturesque part of town that almost has a European feel.	Prices soar for traditional hotels, but remain reasonable for B&Bs. Rooms can sometimes be on the small side, even for NYC.
Union Square, Flatiron District & Gramercy	Convenient subway access to anywhere in the city. You're also steps away from the Village and Midtown in either direction.	Prices are high and there's not much in the way of neighborhood flavor.
Midtown	In the heart of the postcard's version of NYC: skyscrapers, museums, shopping and Broadway shows.	One of the most expensive areas in the city – expect small rooms. Midtown can often feel touristy and impersonal.
Upper East Side	You're a stone's throw from top-notch museums and the rolling hills of Central Park.	Options are scarce and wallet-busting prices are not uncommon; you're not particularly central.
Upper West Side & Central Park	Convenient access to Central Park and the Museum of Natural History.	Tends to swing a bit too far in the familial direction if you're looking for a livelier scene.
Harlem & Upper Manhattan	Your dollar stretches a lot further up here and there's some great eating.	You'll be commuting down to the action
Brooklyn	Better prices; great for exploring some of NYC's most creative neighborhoods.	It can be a long commute to Midtown Manhattan and points north.
Queens	Much cheaper than Manhattan. Digs in Long Island City are only a subway stop from Midtown.	Prevailing industrial setting makes the area far less charming than Manhattan and Brooklyn.

SLEEPING

🛏 Financial District & Lower Manhattan

It used to be all business all the time in the financial district around Wall Street, but these days you'll find condos, hotels, restaurants, bars and even a few nightclubs in the cozy enclave at the southern tip of Manhattan. On weekdays it fills with workers, and in summer it's particularly lively as crowds en route to the Statue of Liberty and Battery Park wander the crooked lanes dating from the days of New Amsterdam. Nearby Tribeca's a hot spot for hip hotel eateries inside the likes of forever-cool Greenwich Hotel and Smyth Tribeca.

CLUB QUARTERS WORLD TRADE CENTER
HOTEL $$

Map p408 (📞212-577-1133; www.clubquarters. com; 140 Washington St, at Albany St; r from $147; ✳🅰; 🅂 R to Cortland St, A/C, 2/3, 4/5 to Fulton St.) Right opposite the World Trade Center site, the 252-room Club Quarters keeps things affordable with clean, modern, cookie-cutter rooms at reasonable prices. Perks include free wi-fi, filtered water and coffee, complimentary use of computer work stations and printers, on-site fitness room and laundry facilities. Ten subway lines are within walking distance.

COSMOPOLITAN HOTEL
HOTEL $$

Map p408 (📞212-566-1900; www.cosmohotel. com; 95 W Broadway, at Chambers St; d from $249; ✳🅰; 🅂 1/2/3 to Chambers St) Cosmo is a hero if you'd rather save your bills for the area's chic eateries and boutiques. The 129-room hotel isn't much to brag about – clean, carpeted rooms with private bathrooms, a double bed or two, and IKEA-knock-off furnishings. But it's clean and comfortable, with major subway lines at your feet, plus all of Tribeca, Chinatown and Lower Manhattan a walk away.

GILD HALL WALL STREET
BOUTIQUE HOTEL $$

Map p408 (📞212-232-7700; www.wallstreetdis-trict.com; 15 Gold St; r from $266; ✳🅰; 🅂 2/3 to Fulton St) Boutique and brilliant, Gild Hall's entryway leads to a bi-level library and wine bar that exudes hunting lodge chic. Rooms fuse Euro elegance and American comfort, with high tin ceilings, glass-walled balconies, Sferra linens, and mini-bars stocked with Dean & DeLuca treats. Hermès designed the leather headboards on the king-size beds, which work perfectly in their warmly hued, minimalist surroundings.

Rates can drop significantly on weekends.

WALL STREET INN
LUXURY HOTEL $$

Map p408 (📞212-747-1500; www.thewallstreet inn.com; 9 S William St; r from $208; ✳🅰; 🅂 2/3 to Wall St) The sedate stone exterior of this inn belies its warm, Colonial-style interior. Beds are big and plush, and rooms have glossy wood furnishings and long drapes. The bathrooms are full of nice touches, like Jacuzzis in the deluxe rooms and tubs in the others. Wi-fi and breakfast are complimentary.

The building is a piece of history, too – the 'LB' tile in the entry dates from the previous tenants, the Lehman Brothers banking company.

★ GREENWICH HOTEL
BOUTIQUE HOTEL $$$

Map p408 (📞212-941-8900; www.greenwich-hotelny.com; 377 Greenwich St, btwn N Moore & Franklin Sts; r from $635; ✳🅰🈳; 🅂 1 to Franklin St, A/C/E to Canal St) From the plush drawing room (complete with crackling fire), to the lantern-lit pool inside a reconstructed Japanese farmhouse, nothing about Robert De Niro's Greenwich Hotel is generic. Each of the 88 individually designed rooms feature floor-to-ceiling French doors opening to the flower-filled courtyard; dark, aged wood across the floors; and opulently tiled Carrara marble or Moroccan tiled bathrooms. Wi-fi is complimentary.

ANDAZ WALL ST
HOTEL $$$

Map p408 (📞212-590-1234; http://andaz.hyatt. com; 75 Wall St, at Water St; r from $305; ✳🅰; 🅂 2/3 to Wall St) The new favorite of hipper downtown business types, the 253-room Andaz take sleek and handsome, and gives it a relaxed, new-school vibe. Guests are checked-in on iPads, and treated to complimentary wi-fi, local calls and minibar soda and snacks. Rooms are spacious, contemporary and elegantly restrained, with 7ft-high windows, oak floors, Zenlike soak tubs, and sublimely comfortable beds.

Sip on well-crafted cocktails at Bar Seven Five, nosh at farm-to-table restaurant Wall & Water, then work it all off at the 24-hour fitness center. Check online for deals, which can see rates dip below $230 in quieter periods.

SMYTH TRIBECA BOUTIQUE HOTEL **$$$**

Map p408 (☎212-587-7000; www.thompsonhotels.com; 85 W Broadway, btwn Warren & Chambers Sts; r from $299; ❄📶; [S]A/C, 1/2/3 to Chambers St) Another Thompson boutique hotel, with the same combo of luxury and laid-back hipness that you'll find at sister locations Gild Hall, 6 Columbus, 60 Thompson, and Thompson LES. Sexy Chesterfields and tartan rugs define the lobby, while the sound-proofed rooms are a soothing combo of charcoal carpets, walnut paneling, white Sferra linen and red Saarinen Womb chairs for a splash of color.

Extra in-house perks include a buzzing French bistro, two bars and a fitness center. Wi-fi is a cheeky $15 per 24 hours.

🛏 SoHo & Chinatown

Visitors swoon over the fashion-conscious streets of Soho, and hoteliers have taken note. There are a lot of fab accommodations options to choose from along these celeb-studded lanes, but they come at quite a cost. Is it worth it? Totally. You'll have some of the world's best shopping, drinking and dining at your doorstep, and you're a short subway hop or taxi ride from some of Manhattan's other great neighborhoods. Slightly cheaper digs await those that don't mind being a couple of avenues over in the borderlands of some of the area's other districts such as Nolita and Chinatown.

BEST WESTERN BOWERY HANBEE HOTEL HOTEL **$$**

Map p413 (☎212-925-1177; www.bw-boweryhanbeehotel.com; 231 Grand St, at Bowery; r from $165; ❄📶; [S]B/D to Grand St, J to Bowery) Clean, comfortable, simple rooms is what you get at this reliable chain hotel. While the place lacks any real character or charm, it's one of the few midrange options in this part of town, slap bang in Chinatown and within walking distance of uber-hip SoHo, Nolita and the Lower East Side. There's an on-site gym and breakfast is included in the price.

SOLITA SOHO HOTEL **$$**

Map p410 (☎212-925-3600; www.solitasohohotel.com; 159 Grand St, at Lafayette St; r from $289; ❄📶; [S]N/Q/R, J/Z, 6 to Canal St) Solita is great for anyone wanting to soak up the flavor of Chinatown and Little Italy. Part of the Ascend chain, the Solita's got no surprises: a clean, functional lobby accessed through a glass-topped portico on the street, and smallish, slightly octagonal rooms with wide beds and private baths that were undergoing renovation during our last visit.

Check the website for last-minute deals, which can see rooms go for as low as $151.

LAFAYETTE HOUSE BOUTIQUE HOTEL **$$**

Map p410 (☎212-505-8100; www.lafayettenyc.com; 38 E 4th St, btwn Fourth Ave & Lafayette St; ste $250-500; [S]B/D/F/V to Broadway-Lafayette St, 6 to Bleecker St) A former townhouse that's been turned into homey, spacious suites (each with a working fireplace), Lafayette House feels very Victorian. Suites have big beds, a desk, thick drapes and old-fashioned armoires. Bathrooms are large, with claw-footed tubs, and some rooms have mini kitchenettes.

Light sleepers should ask for rooms away from the street.

CROSBY STREET HOTEL BOUTIQUE HOTEL **$$$**

Map p410 (☎212-226-6400; www.firmdalehotels.com; 79 Crosby St, btwn Spring & Prince Sts; r from $686; ❄📶; [S]6 to Spring St, N/R to Prince St) Step into Crosby Street for afternoon tea and you'll never want to leave. It's not just the scones and clotted cream that will grab you, but the fun and upbeat lobby, chi-chi bar and one-of-a-kind rooms. While some of the latter are starkly black and white, and others as pretty and floral as an English garden, all are plush, playful and adorned with heavenly amenities by London perfumer Miller Harris.

NOLITAN HOTEL BOUTIQUE HOTEL **$$$**

Map p410 (☎212-925-2555; www.nolitanhotel.com; 30 Kenmare St, btwn Elizabeth & Mott Sts; r from $358; ❄📶🐾; [S]J/Z to Bowery, 6 to Spring St, B/D to Grand St) Set behind a memorable facade of floating postive-negative Tetris bricks, the Nolitan is a great find situated between two of the most popular New York neighborhoods: SoHo and the Village. Tuck into a good book in the inviting lobby lounge, or head upstairs to your stylish pad – a scene that looks straight out of a CB2 catalog.

Wi-fi is complimentary and online room rates can slide to below $300, so always keep an eye out.

TRUMP SOHO NEW YORK LUXURY HOTEL **$$$**

Map p410 (☎212-842-5500; www.trumphotelcollection.com/soho; 246 Spring St, btwn Ave of the Americas & Varick St; r from $425; ❄📶🏊; [S]A/C/E to Spring St, 1 to Houston St) Classic

American luxury comes in the form of carefully appointed rooms with oversized beds, super-plush rugs and spacious bathrooms sporting the latest in futuristic fixtures. While we don't like the $14.95 charge for wi-fi, we do love the seasonal pool, highly acclaimed spa and handful of high-end nosh spots.

JAMES NEW YORK BOUTIQUE HOTEL **$$$**
Map p410 (☎212-465-2000; www.jameshotels.com/new-york; 27 Grand St, btwn Ave of the Americas & Thompson St; r from $325; ❄📶🏊; [S]A/C/E, 1 to Canal St) The James plays with a variety of architectural elements in each of the hotel's different spaces, and somehow they all work beautifully. The public areas – especially the designated lobbies – blend abundant natural light with playful touches (we love the computer-key mural). Rooms are a handsome blend of chocolate-hued furniture and reclaimed timber floors, with a motorized screen separating each from its copper-hued bathroom.

Added sex appeal is provided by the heated rooftop pool, complete with slinky bar for see-and-be-seen cocktails.

MONDRIAN SOHO BOUTIQUE HOTEL **$$$**
Map p410 (☎212-389-1000; www.mondriansoho.com; 9 Crosby St, btwn Howard & Grand Sts; r from $380; ❄📶🐾; [S]N/Q/R, J/Z, 6 to Canal St) Mondrian playfulness underscores more than 250 rooms at the beautiful downtown property, where fairy-tale color schemes meet unusual *objets d'art*. Creamy whites and dreamy blues reign on the upper levels, making guests feel like they're gazing out at Manhattan from a cloud. The garden-inspired restaurant serves fine Italian flavors under a maelstrom of chandeliers, while winter rates can drop below $300.

MERCER BOUTIQUE HOTEL **$$$**
Map p410 (☎212-966-6060; www.mercerhotel.com; 147 Mercer St, at Prince St; r $495-695; ❄📶; [S]N/R to Prince St) Right in the heart of SoHo's brick lanes, the grand Mercer is where stars sleep. Above the leisurely lobby full of fat, plush sofas, the 75 rooms offer a slice of chic loft life in a century-old warehouse. Flat-screen TVs, dark-wood floors and white-marble, mosaic-tile bathrooms (some with soaking tubs under a skylight) add a modern touch to rooms that sport the building's industrial roots – with giant oval windows, steel pillars and exposed-brick walls.

60 THOMPSON BOUTIQUE HOTEL **$$$**
Map p410 (☎212-431-0400; www.60thompson.com; 60 Thompson St, btwn Broome & Spring Sts; r $300-700; ❄📶; [S]A/C/E, 1 to Canal St) The sexy 100-room 60 Thompson is a place to be seen, either in the futurist Thai restaurant Kittichai, or swirling cocktails on the guests-only rooftop bar A60. Rooms are small but comfy: beds have goose-down duvets and leather headboards, and you can watch DVDs on the flat-screen TVs from a wing-backed seat or plush sofa.

If the price is within reach, the extra-luxurious suites provide a lot more space and comfort. Wi-fi is free in public areas and $15 in guest rooms.

🛏 East Village & Lower East Side

Statement-making structures have been cropping up in these once grittier neighborhoods, giving the area a fun, world-in-one feel that still remains distinctly New York in style. Visitors seeking that true city feel will be perfectly happy taking up residence along these low-numbered streets, especially if you've got the dime for a room at the Bowery or Cooper Square hotels. Stay west if subway convenience is a primary concern – underground transport thins as you head east, especially beyond First Ave.

EAST VILLAGE BED & COFFEE B&B **$**
Map p414 (☎917-816-0071; www.bedandcoffee.com; 110 Ave C, btwn 7th & 8th Sts; s/d with shared bath from $130/140; ❄📶; [S]F/V to Lower East Side-Second Ave) Owner Anne has turned her family home into a quirky, arty, offbeat B&B with colorful, themed private rooms (one shared bathroom per floor) and great amenities, like free bikes, free wi-fi, and insider tips on the best the East Village has to offer. Anne's dogs roam the first two floors, but the upper ones are pet free. Each floor has shared common and kitchen space, and guests get keys so they can come and go (no curfew). Book early as it fills fast.

EAST VILLAGE B&B B&B **$**
Map p414 (☎212-260-1865; evbandb@juno.com; Apt 5-6, 244 E 7th St btwn Aves C & D; r $150-175; [S]F/V to Lower East Side-Second Ave) A popular oasis for Sapphic couples who want peace and quiet in the midst of the noisy East Village scene. Its three rooms (two black-and-white and one red) are way stylish –

bold linens, modern art, gorgeous wooden floors – and the shared living-room space is filled with light, beautiful paintings from around the globe, exposed brickwork and a big-screen TV. Two-night minimum stay.

BLUE MOON HOTEL BOUTIQUE HOTEL $$

Map p416 (☎212-533-9080; www.bluemoon-nyc.com; 100 Orchard St , btwn Broome & Delancey Sts; r incl breakfast from $210; ❄📶; [S]F to Delancey St, J/M to Essex St) You'd never guess that this welcoming brick guesthouse – full of festive yellows, blues and greens – was once a foul tenement back in the day (the day being 1879). With touches including original wood shutters and wrought-iron bed frames, Blue Moon's clean, spare rooms are vintage-inspired and comfortable, with big beds, great views from large windows and elegant marble baths.

HOTEL ON RIVINGTON BOUTIQUE HOTEL $$

Map p416 (☎212-475-2600; www.hotelonrivington.com; 107 Rivington St , btwn Essex & Ludlow Sts; r from $311; 📶; [S]F to Delancey St, J/M/Z to Essex St, F to Second Ave) This 20-floor slumber number looks like a shimmering new-Shanghai building towering over 19th-century tenements. The 'unique' rooms have enviable views over the East River and downtown's sprawl, along with hanging flat-screen TVs. The standard rooms have one glass wall with a view (instead of three) and are a tighter squeeze.

BOWERY HOTEL BOUTIQUE HOTEL $$$

Map p414 (☎212-505-9100; www.thebowery hotel.com; 335 Bowery, btwn 2nd & 3rd Sts; r from $395; ❄@📶; [S]F/V to Lower East Side-Second Ave, 6 to Bleecker St) Pick up your old-fashioned room key with its red tassel in the dark, hushed lobby – filled with antique velvet chairs and faded Persian rugs – then follow the mosaic floors to your room. There you can dock your iPod, use the wi-fi, check out the 42in plasma, watch some DVDs, or raid your bathroom goodies (courtesy of CO Bigelow, the Greenwich Village apothecary).

Rooms have huge factory windows with unobstructed views, simple white spreads with red piping, and elegant four-poster beds. The Bowery's zinc-topped bar, outside garden patio, and rustic Italian eatery, Gemma's, are always packed.

🛏 Greenwich Village, Chelsea & the Meatpacking District

Real estate in the desirable West Village in the Meatpacking District is the highest in the city, and this plays out in hotel tariffs as well. Staying here, however, is well worth opening your wallet a bit wider as you'll be treated to a wonderful neighborhood vibe at some of the more memorable properties in town. Just a few blocks up in Chelsea, you'll find a spike in new development with a horde of swankified properties promising cutting-edge design befitting the pages of a Scandinavian design magazine. Nights in Chelsea will ensure convenient (read: walkable) access to boutique shopping, eating and drinking downtown.

CHELSEA HOSTEL HOSTEL $

Map p422 (☎212-647-0010; www.chelseahostel.com; 251 W 20th St btwn Seventh & Eighth Aves; dm $40-70, s $70-95, d from $120; ❄@📶; [S]A/C/E, 1/2 to 23rd St, 1/2 to 18th St) Occupying some serious real estate in the desirable Chelsea neighborhood, this old bastion of backpackerdom is a good pick if location ranks at the top of your list. Walkable to the Village and Midtown, Chelsea Hostel capitalizes on its convenience with somewhat steep prices, but it's kept clean (even a tad sterile at times) and there's access to common rooms and kitchens where other budget travelers often meet and hang.

LARCHMONT HOTEL HOTEL $

Map p418 (☎212-989-9333; www.larchmonthotel.com; 27 W 11th St, btwn Fifth & Sixth Aves; s/d with shared bath & breakfast from $90/119; ❄📶; [S]4/5/6, N/Q/R to 14th St-Union Sq) Housed in a prewar building that blends in with the other fine brownstones on the block, a stay at the Larchmont is about location. The carpeted rooms are basic and in need of updating, as are the communal bathrooms, but it's still a good deal for the price.

JANE HOTEL HOTEL $

Map p418 (☎212-924-6700; www.thejanenyc.com; 113 Jane St, btwn Washington St & West Side Hwy; r with shared bath from $99; [P]❄📶; [S]L to Eighth Ave, A/C/E to 14th St, 1/2 to Christopher St-Sheridan Sq) The claustrophobic will want to avoid the Jane's tiny 50ft rooms, but if you can stomach living like a luxury sailor, check into this recently renovated gem.

The small cabin rooms have shared bathrooms; the more expensive captain's quarters come with private commodes. The gorgeous ballroom-bar looks like it belongs in a five-star hotel.

CHELSEA LODGE HOTEL **$**

Map p422 (☎212-243-4499; www.chelsealodge.com; 318 W 20th St btwn Eighth & Ninth Aves; s/d from $130/140; ❄📶; [S]A/C/E to 14th St, 1 to 18th St) Housed in a landmark brownstone in Chelsea's lovely historic district, the European-style, 22-room Chelsea Lodge is a super deal, with homey, well-kept rooms. Space is tight, so you won't get more than a bed, with a TV (with cable) plopped on an old wooden cabinet. There are showers and sinks in rooms, but toilets are down the hall. Six suite rooms have private bathrooms, and two come with private garden access.

COLONIAL HOUSE INN B&B **$$**

Map p422 (☎800-689-3779, 212-243-9669; www.colonialhouseinn.com; 318 W 22nd St, btwn Eighth & Ninth Aves; r $150-350; ❄📶; [S]C/E to 23rd St) Friendly and simple, this 20-room gay inn is tidy but a bit worn and small. Most rooms have small walk-in closets (with a small TV and refrigerator) and sinks. When the weather is nice, the rooftop deck sees some nude sunbathing. The smaller rooms have shared baths, while the deluxe suite has a private bath and private access to the back garden.

INCENTRA VILLAGE HOUSE B&B **$$**

Map p418 (☎212-206-0007; www.incentravillage.com; 32 Eighth Ave, btwn 12th & Jane Sts; s/d from $189/239; ❄📶; [S]A/C/E to 14th St, L to Eighth Ave) An easy walk to Chelsea clubs, these two red-brick, landmark townhouses were built in 1841 and later became the city's first gay inn. Today, the 11 rooms get booked way in advance by many queer travelers; call early to get in on its gorgeous Victorian parlor and antique-filled, serious-Americana rooms. The Garden Suite has access to a small garden in back and there's wi-fi access in the parlor.

CHELSEA PINES INN B&B **$$**

Map p418 (☎888-546-2700, 212-929-1023; www.chelseapinesinn.com; 317 W 14th St, btwn Eighth & Ninth Aves; r incl breakfast from $209; ❄📶; [S]A/C/E to 14th St, L to Eighth Ave) With its five walk-up floors coded to the rainbow flag, the 26-room Chelsea Pines is serious gay-and-lesbian central, but guests of all stripes are welcome. It helps to be up on your Hitchcock beauties, as vintage movie posters not only plaster the walls but rooms are named for starlets such as Kim Novak, Doris Day and Ann-Margret. There's a sink in the walk-in closet of standard rooms, with clean bathrooms down the hall.

The small lounge downstairs opens to a tiny courtyard out back.

MARITIME HOTEL BOUTIQUE HOTEL **$$**

Map p422 (☎212-242-4300; www.themaritimehotel.com; 363 W 16th St, btwn Eighth & Ninth Aves; r from $220; [S]A/C/E to 14th St, L to Eighth Ave) Originally the site of the National Maritime Union headquarters (and more recently a shelter for homeless teens), this white tower dotted with portholes has been transformed into a marine-themed luxury inn by a hip team of architects. It feels like a luxury *Love Boat* inside, as its 135 rooms, each with their own round window, are compact and teak-paneled, with gravy in the form of 20in flat-screen TVs and DVD players. The most expensive quarters feature outdoor showers, a private garden and sweeping Hudson views.

INN ON 23RD ST B&B **$$**

Map p422 (☎212-463-0330; www.innon23rd.com; 131 W 23rd St, btwn Sixth & Seventh Aves; r incl breakfast from $240; ❄📶; [S]F/V, 1 to 23rd St) Housed in a lone 19th-century, five-story townhouse on busy 23rd St, this 14-room B&B is a Chelsea gem. Bought in 1998 and extensively renovated by the Fisherman family (who wisely installed an elevator), the rooms are big and welcoming, with fanciful fabrics on big brass or poster beds and TVs held in huge armoires. There's an honor-system bar and an ol' piano for you to play boogie-woogie on in the lounge, and a 2nd-floor, all-Victorian library that doubles as a breakfast room.

HÔTEL AMERICANO HOTEL **$$**

Map p422 (☎212-216-0000; www.hotel-americano.com; 518 W 27th St, btwn Tenth & Eleventh Aves; r from $255; [S]A/C/E to 23rd St) Design geeks will go giddy when they walk into one of Hôtel Americano's perfectly polished rooms. It's like sleeping in a bento box, but the food's been replaced by a carefully curated selection of minimalist and muted furniture. Oh, and that thing hanging from the ceiling that looks like a robot's head? It's a dangly fireplace, of course. Other accoutrements await, from Turkish towels to Japanese washing cloths, and all controls are activated by your personal iPad. When you're ready to venture from your museum-esque cocoon, explore surrounding Chelsea on a guest bike.

JADE HOTEL BOUTIQUE HOTEL **$$**

Map p418 (☎212-375-1300; www.thejadenyc.com; 52 W 13th St; r from $260; ❄📶) New in 2013, this stylish 113-room boutique hotel does a good job blending into the townhouses and heritage buildings surrounding it. You enter by walking down the onyx-lit staircase to a cozy lounge/lobby with period furnishings, and the brick-walled bar with fireplace makes a great spot for an evening drink. Up above, it has small but attractively furnished rooms with art deco flourishes (textured wallpaper over the bed, rotary phones, modular bedside lamps).

Upper floors have excellent views over the low-rise village. Bath amenities come from the legendary pharmacy nearby, CO Bigelow.

HOTEL GANSEVOORT LUXURY HOTEL **$$**

Map p418 (☎212-206-6700; www.hotelgansevoort.com; 18 Ninth Ave, at 13th St; r from $285; ❄📶🏊🐾; [S]A/C/E, 1/2/3 to 14th St, L to Eighth Ave) Coated in zinc-colored panels, and booming up top where rooftop bar Plunge attracts block-long lines (and guests swim in the skinny pool overlooking the Hudson River), the 14-floor Gansevoort has been a swank swashbuckler of the Meatpacking District since it opened in 2004. Rooms are luscious and airy, with fudge-colored suede headboards, plasma-screen TVs and illuminated bathroom doors.

DREAM DOWNTOWN HOTEL **$$**

Map p422 (☎212-229-2559; www.dreamdowntown.com; 355 W 16th St, btwn Eighth & Ninth Aves; r from $295; [S]A/C/E to 14th St, L to Eighth Ave, 1/2 to 18th St) The newest link in the chain from the Dreamteam is a looming behemoth that sinks its circle-themed footprint deep in the heart of Chelsea. The metallic facade is punctuated by portholes that look like windows of Captain Nemo's would-be space vessel; a generous smattering of ellipses echo throughout, including bedroom walls and the subtle tiling of the lap pool – a refreshing oasis on unbearable summer days.

Ample public space is also a priority here, which takes the shape of several cocktail lounges and restaurants that attract weekenders in the know.

STANDARD BOUTIQUE HOTEL **$$$**

Map p418 (☎212-645-4646; www.standardhotels.com; 848 Washington St, at 13th St; r from $355; ❄📶; [S]A/C/E to 14th St, L to Eighth Ave) Hipster hotelier André Balazs has built a wide, boxy, glass tower that straddles the High Line. Every room has sweeping Meatpacking District views and fills with cascading sunlight that makes the Standard's glossy, wood-framed beds and marbled bathrooms glow in a particularly homey way. There's also a hyper-modern **Standard** (Map p414; ☎212-475-5700; www.standardhotels.com; 25 Cooper Sq btwn the Bowery & 4th St; r from $375; ❄📶; [S]N/R to 8th St-NYU; 4/6 to Bleecker St; 4/6 to Astor Pl) in the East Village.

Union Square, Flatiron District & Gramercy

Countless visitors like to slumber amid the glitzy lights of Times Square because of its convenient position to the many different hot spots around the city, but consider for a second that Union Sq and its neighbors are just as good. A quick glance at the subway map will show a handful of lines that crisscross in this busy downtown hub – you're a straight shot to Lower Manhattan and the museums on the Upper East Side, and the adorable nooks in the Village are at your doorstep. Try the area's cache of inns, boutique digs and rather romantic options that are a bit more subdued than the Vegas-esque lights of Broadway.

HOTEL 17 BUDGET HOTEL **$$**

Map p424 (☎212-475-2845; www.hotel17ny.com; 225 E 17th St, btwn Second & Third Aves; d $91-181; ❄📶; [S]N/Q/R, 4/5/6 to 14th St-Union Sq, L to Third Ave) Right off Stuyvesant Sq, this popular, eight-floor townhouse is where Woody Allen shot a frightening dead-body scene for his film *Manhattan Murder Mystery* (1993). Only four of the 120 rooms have private bathrooms (all free of dead bodies), and the rooms themselves are small and basic, with old-school chintzy furnishings and a lack of natural light.

If this place is booked, ask about its sister property in Midtown, **Hotel 31** (Map p426; ☎212-685-3060; www.hotel31.com; 120 E 31st St , btwn Lexington & Park Aves; r $105-220; ❄; [S]N/R/W, 6 to 28th St).

WYNDHAM GARDEN HOTEL **$$**

Map p424 (☎212-243-0800; www.wyndham.com; 37 W 24th St, btwn Fifth & Sixth Aves; r from $200; ❄📶; [S]F/M, N/R to 23rd St) Nearly equidistant from Chelsea and Union Square, the Wyndham's colorful checked entrance fits in with the surrounding unique neighborhoods. The whimsy disappears once you're inside – its beige walls, taupe carpet and plain work stations is just what you'd expect from a chain hotel (but one that caters to business folk). Still, it's a fantastic location, with free wi-fi and rooms as clean as a whistle.

HOTEL GIRAFFE BOUTIQUE HOTEL **$$$**

Map p424 (☎877-296-0009, 212-685-7700; www.hotelgiraffe.com; 365 Park Ave S, at 26th St; r $339-475; ❄📶; [S]N/R/W, 6 to 23rd St) Up a notch in posh from most of the boutiques this far south, the newish 12-floor Giraffe earns its stripes, or dots, with sleek rooms, a sunny rooftop area for drinks or tapas, complimentary breakfast and free wine and cheese between 5pm and 8pm. Most of the 72 rooms have small balconies and all come with flat-screen TVs and DVD players, and granite work desks.

Corner suites add a living room with pull-out sofa.

GRAMERCY PARK HOTEL BOUTIQUE HOTEL **$$$**

Map p424 (☎212-920-3300; www.gramercyparkhotel.com; 2 Lexington Ave, at 21st St; r from $349; ❄📶; [S]6 to 23rd St) Formerly a grand old dame, the Gramercy's major facelift has it looking young and sexy. Dark wood paneling and red suede rugs and chairs greet you in the lobby, while the rooms – overlooking nearby Gramercy Park – have customized oak furnishings, 400-count Italian linens, and big, feather-stuffed mattresses on sprawling beds. Colors are rich and alluring, fit for a Spanish grandee.

The largest rooms – sprawling suites with French doors dividing living and sleeping areas – start at $799. Be sure to visit the celebrity-studded Rose and Jade bars, the guest-only rooftop terrace, and Maialino (p167), the on-site rustic Italian eatery run by Danny Meyer. Wi-fi will set you back $16 per day.

W NEW YORK UNION SQUARE HOTEL **$$$**

Map p424 (☎888-627-9104, 212-253-9119; www.whotels.com; 201 Park Ave S, at 17th St; r from $312; ❄📶🐾; [S]L, N/Q/R/W, 4/5/6 to 14th St-Union Sq) The ultra-hip W demands a black wardrobe and credit card. The boldly accented standard rooms aren't big, but – set in a 1911, one-time insurance building – benefit from high ceilings, and are decked out with all the modern bells and whistles, from flatscreens, iPod docks and wi-fi, to mood lighting and headboards featuring abstract art.

The suites – wow and extreme wow – are spectacular, with huge, decadent bathtubs.

🛏 Midtown

If you want to be in the heart of the action, consider Midtown East, which encompasses the area around Grand Central Terminal and the UN. It's not as crazy and eclectic as Midtown West, but options are endless and prices and conditions range from $75 cheapies with shared toilets down the hall to thousand-dollar suites with private terraces overlooking the city's blinking lights.

Light sleepers beware – Midtown West is a 24-hours-a-day kind of place. Better bring your eyeshades. If the idea of sleeping under the neon sun of Times Square excites rather than depresses you, Midtown West is your perfect location. It's go-go-go all day and night long, thanks to the juxtaposition of Broadway and its fantastic theater with the heart of Manhattan's business district. To top it off, Hell's Kitchen's Ninth Ave has a huge range of restaurants with cuisines from all over the world.

POD 51 HOTEL **$**

Map p426 (☎866-414-4617; www.thepodhotel.com; 230 E 51st St, btwn Second & Third Aves, Midtown East; r from $89; ❄📶; [S]6 to 51st St, E/M to Lexington Ave-53rd St) A dream come true for folks who would like to live inside their iPod – or at least curl up and sleep with it – this affordable hot spot has a range of room types, most barely big enough for the bed. 'Pods' have bright bedding, tight workspaces, flat-screen TVs, iPod docking stations and 'raindrop' showerheads.

★**YOTEL** HOTEL **$$**

Map p430 (☎646-449-7700; www.yotel.com; 570 Tenth Ave, at 41st St, Midtown West; r from $149; ❄📶; [S]A/C/E to 42nd St-Port Authority Bus Terminal, 1/2/3, N/Q/R, S, 7 to Times Sq-42nd St) Part futuristic spaceport, part Austin Powers set, this uber-cool 669-room option bases its rooms on airplane classes: Premium Cabin (Economy), First Cabins (Business) and VIP Suites (First); the First Cabins include a private terrace with hot tub. Small but cleverly configured, Premium cabins include automated adjustable beds, while all cabins feature floor-to-ceiling windows with killer views, slick bathrooms and iPod connectivity.

You'll find coffee, tea, microwaves and fridges in the communal 'galleys'; DJ-spun tunes on weekends in the Club Lounge, and Latin-Asian dishes in the sumo-wrestling-ring-inspired Dojo restaurant-bar. There's also a gym and the city's largest outdoor hotel terrace, complete with a stunning skyscraper backdrop.

OUT NYC
BOUTIQUE HOTEL **$$**

Map p430 (☑212-947-2999; http://theoutnyc. com; 510 W 42nd St, btwn Tenth & Eleventh Aves, Midtown West; r from $207, q bed from $106; ❉ 🐾; S A/C/E to 42nd St-Port Authority Bus Terminal) Billing itself as the world's first 'straight-friendly resort', Out NYC is proud, fabulous and open to all. The svelte, stylish rooms circle three internal courtyards: the astro-turfed, bean-bag-studded Great Lawn; the dining-friendly Bamboo Garden; and the chic Spa Atrium, complete with hot tubs, cabanas and waterfall. The rooms themselves are chic yet simple, decked out in shades of charcoal and white, with heavenly beds and crisp, subway-tiled bathrooms.

On a budget? Opt for the eight hostel-style 'Quads', where each bed comes with a TV and privacy curtain. Resort-like features include spa treatments, restaurant, cocktail lounge and gay mega-club XL Nightclub (p202; light sleepers, beware). Check online for last-minute, cut-price deals.

NIGHT
BOUTIQUE HOTEL **$$**

Map p430 (☑212-835-9600; www.nighthotelny. com; 132 W 45th St, btwn Sixth & Seventh Aves, Midtown West; r from $180; ❉ 🐾; S B/D/F/M to 47th-50th Sts-Rockefeller Center) Dark, decadent and delicious, sleeping at Night feels like stepping into an Anne Rice novel. From the rocker-glam entrance, draped in crushed velvet, to the sleek-and-sexy black and white rooms (complete with gothic lettering on the carpets), celebrated hotelier Vikram Chatwal's stark, two-toned establishment stands out all the more in the glare of Times Square's neon. Rooms are small but comfy. Wi-fi will set you back $10 per 24 hours.

POD 39
HOTEL **$$**

Map p426 (☑212-865-5700, 855-763-5700; www. thepodhotel.com; 145 E 39th St, btwn Lexington & Third Aves, Midtown East; r from $119; ❉ 🐾; S S, 4/5/6, 7 to Grand Central-42nd St) It's a case of good things coming in very small packages at funky Pod 39. The newer sibling of budget-luxe Pod 51 (p334), its 366 rooms offer hip-n-functional design, private bathroom and city views in Pod's trademark tiny dimensions. Cranking up the Gen-Y cred is a Technicolor taqueria, eclectic lobby lounge, light-strung rooftop bar, and games room (complete with oh-so-retro table tennis).

Tweet away on the free wi-fi, or keep clean with the onsite laundry facilities.

AMERITANIA HOTEL
HOTEL **$$**

Map p430 (☑212-247-5000; www.ameritanianyc. com; 230 W 54th St, at Broadway, Midtown West; r from $195; ❉ 🐾; S B/D, E to Seventh Ave, N/Q/R to 57th St-Seventh Ave) Steps away from the Theater District, this 219-room slumber number delivers Midtown convenience at midrange prices. The look is smart and modern, with mid-century accents in the lobby (think floating disc lights and retro-esque sofas), and deco-inspired patterns, lamps and armchairs in the small yet comfy rooms. Bathrooms are smallish but stylish, and the beds nothing short of fabulous.

Light sleepers may find the street noise a little challenging.

414 HOTEL
HOTEL **$$**

Map p430 (☑212-399-0006; www.414hotel.com; 414 W 46th St, btwn Ninth & Tenth Aves, Midtown West; r $180-370; ❉ 🐾; S C/E to 50th St) Set up like a guesthouse, this affordable, friendly option offers 22 tidy rooms a couple of blocks west of Times Square. Rooms are simply yet tastefully decorated, with cable TV, free wi-fi and private bathroom; those facing the leafy inner courtyard are the quietest. The courtyard itself is the perfect spot to enjoy your complimentary breakfast in the warmer months.

HOTEL 373
HOTEL **$$**

Map p426 (☑888-382-7111, 212-213-3388; www. hotel373.com; 373 Fifth Ave, at 35th St, Midtown East; r $188-470; ❉ 🐾; S N/Q/R, B/D/F/M to 34th St-Herald Sq) The claustrophobic will not appreciate Hotel 373's cunning, multi-use furnishings and teeny tiny rooms, but those who like a great deal will understand that an affordable *and* clean, fun, fabulous hotel just steps from the Empire State Building always has a drawback somewhere. Wi-fi is free.

HOTEL METRO HOTEL **$$**

Map p426 (☎212-947-2500; www.hotelmetronyc.com; 45 W 35th St, btwn Fifth & Sixth Aves, Midtown East; r $140-495; ❄📶; [S]N/Q/R, B/D/F/M to 34th St-Herald Sq) Imbued with a faint whiff of 1930s art deco, the 181-room, 13-floor Metro offers somewhat plain but undeniably comfortable rooms, with caramel color schemes, flatscreen TVs and more thinking space than most hotels in its price range. Perks include free breakfast, a fitness center, and a rooftop bar with impressive views of the Empire State Building.

BELVEDERE HOTEL HOTEL **$$**

Map p430 (☎888-468-3558, 212-245-7000; www.belvederehotelnyc.com; 319 W 48th St, btwn Eighth & Ninth Aves, Midtown West; r $199-599; ❄📶; [S]C/E to 50th St) Open since 1928, the 345-room Belvedere's roots (and facade) are art deco originals, even if the makeover is a modern take on the era's glory. True to its vintage, it's built on a luxurious scale, its bathrooms bigger than many boutique hotel rooms. Rooms are classically decorated, with handy mini-kitchenettes to boot.

Wi-fi ($9.95) is complimentary in the pricier executive guestrooms.

ECONO LODGE BUDGET HOTEL **$$**

Map p430 (☎212-246-1991; www.econolodge.com; 302 W 47th St, at Eighth Ave, Midtown West; r from $150; ❄📶; [S]C/E to 50th St; N/R to 49th St) A budget option only steps away from the Times Square action, Econo Lodge has a small, no-frills lobby that leads to small, no-frills rooms. Some have double beds and can hold four, and others are kings, with just enough room to squeeze in an armoire and decent-sized bathroom. A modest continental breakfast is included in the price.

When the rates come down in off-season, the prices are more in line with the hotel's offerings.

IVY TERRACE B&B **$$**

Map p426 (☎516-662-6862; www.ivyterrace.com; 230 E 58th St, btwn Second & Third Aves, Midtown East; r $249-390; 📶; [S]4/5/6 to 59th St; N/Q/R to Lexington Ave-59th St) Especially popular with couples, Ivy Terrace is a seriously charming B&B. The spacious, Victorian-inspired rooms cozily combine elegant drapes, antique furniture (the Rose Room features a canopy bed), hardwood floors and kitchens with breakfast supplies. One of the suites even has a flagstone balcony. There's a three-night minimum stay (sometimes five to seven nights), and no elevator.

Its location is just east of the Midtown fray but close to Bloomingdales and the mega shopping strips of Madison and Fifth Aves.

INK48 BOUTIQUE HOTEL **$$**

Map p430 (☎212-757-0088; www.ink48.com; 653 Eleventh Ave, at 48th St, Midtown West; r from $255; ❄📶; [S]C/E to 50th St) The Kimpton hotel chain has braved Midtown's wild far west with Ink48, perched on the subway-starved edge of Manhattan. Occupying a converted printing house, the compensation is sweet: stellar skyline and Hudson River views; chic contemporary rooms; a boutique spa and restaurant; and a stunning rooftop bar. Topping it off is easy walking access to Hell's Kitchen's thriving restaurant scene.

HOTEL ELYSÉE BOUTIQUE HOTEL **$$**

Map p426 (☎212-753-1066; www.elyseehotel.com; 60 E 54th St, btwn Madison & Park Aves, Midtown East; r from $279; ❄📶; [S]E/M to Lexington Ave-53rd St; 6 to 51st St) Impeccably refined and lavished with antiques and classic detailing, this intimate hotel has been bedding the famous and fabulous since 1926. Come evening, star spot over complimentary wine and cheese in the lounge, or in the deco-glam Monkey Bar restaurant, co-owned by Vanity Fair editor Graydon Carter and featured in both *Mad Men* and *Sex and The City*.

There's no gym on-site but passes to NY Sports Club are complimentary.

★ANDAZ FIFTH AVENUE BOUTIQUE HOTEL **$$$**

Map p426 (☎212-601-1234; http://andaz.hyatt.com; 485 Fifth Ave, at 41st St, Midtown East; d from $380; ❄📶; [S]S, 4/5/6 to Grand Central-42nd St, 7 to Fifth Ave) Youthful, chic Andaz ditches stuffy reception desks for hip, mobile staff who check you in on iPads in the art-laced lobby. The hotel's 184 rooms are contemporary and sleek, with NYC-inspired details like 'Fashion District' rolling racks and subway-inspired lamps. We especially love the sexy, spacious bathrooms, complete with rain showers, black porcelain foot baths and CO Bigelow amenities.

There's a 'secret' basement bar pouring limited-edition spirits, a locavore-focused restaurant (you can watch the chefs in action at the second-floor showroom kitchen), and regular talks by guest artists and curators. In the low season, rates can dip as low as $195; check the website for special deals.

★NOMAD HOTEL BOUTIQUE HOTEL $$$

Map p430 (☎212-796-1500; www.thenomadhotel.com; 1170 Broadway, at 28th St, Midtown West; r $325-850; ❄📶; [S]N/R to 28th St) Crowned by a copper turret and featuring interiors designed by Frenchman Jacques Garcia, this beaux arts dream is one of the city's hottest addresses. Rooms channel a nostalgic NYC-meets-Paris aesthetic, in which recycled hardwood floors, leather steam trunk minibars and clawfoot tubs mix it with flatscreen TVs and high-tech LED lighting. Wi-fi is free, while in-house restaurant-bar NoMad (p199) is one of Manhattan's most coveted hangouts.

STRAND BOUTIQUE HOTEL $$$

Map p426 (☎212-448-1024; www.thestrandnyc.com; 33 W 37th St, btwn Fifth & Sixth Aves, Midtown East; r $255-630; ❄📶; [S]B/D/F/M, N/Q/R to 34th St-Herald Sq) This gleaming boutique option is a stone's throw from the Empire State Building, Bryant Park, Macy's, Grand Central and other Midtown icons. The eye-catching lobby features a two-story cascading waterfall and a tinkling piano bar, while even the standard rooms are large enough for a settee and a plush chair, giving them a suitelike feel.

Topping it all off (literally) is an all-weather rooftop bar with a view to die for.

LANGHAM PLACE LUXURY HOTEL $$$

Map p426 (☎212-695-4005; http://newyork.langhamplacehotels.com; 400 Fifth Avenue, at 36th St, Midtown East; r from $650; ❄📶; [S]N/Q/R to 34th St-Herald Sq) Rooms at the luxurious, skyscraping Langham Place are more akin to suites (the smallest is a generous 400 sq ft). Understatedly chic, all feature neutral hues, handsome wood paneling, Duxiana mattresses and Nespresso machines. The marble-floor bathrooms are equally impressive, with deep soaking tub and TV-embedded mirror. Local calls and garment pressing are complimentary, as is early check-in or late check-out.

We also love the luxe spa, good-sized gym, and live nightly jazz in the plush lounge. Super-centrally located, the 214-room hotel is also home to Michael White's Michelin-starred restaurant Ai Fiori.

LIBRARY HOTEL BOUTIQUE HOTEL $$$

Map p426 (☎877-793-7323, 212-983-4500; www.libraryhotel.com; 299 Madison Ave, at 41st St, Midtown East; r $279-799; ❄📶; [S]S, 4/5/6, 7 to Grand Central-42nd St) Each floor at this discreetly elegant hotel is dedicated to one of the 10 major categories of the Dewey Decimal System: Social Sciences, Literature, Philosophy and so on, with over 6000 volumes split up between quarters. The decor is equally bookish, with mahogany paneling, hushed reading rooms and a gentlemen's club atmosphere.

The petit rooms are cunningly designed with all the amenities of the larger suites, but they are only just big enough for one adult. There's a rooftop deck bar serving literary-inspired cocktails, as well as complimentary wine and cheese between 5pm and 8pm. Breakfast and wi-fi are also free, and room rates can drop dramatically in January.

ACE HOTEL BOUTIQUE HOTEL $$$

Map p426 (☎212-679-2222; www.acehotel.com/newyork; 20 W 29th St, btwn Broadway & Fifth Ave, Midtown East; r $199-799; ❄📶🐾; [S]N/R to 28th St) A hit with cashed-up creatives, the Ace's standard and deluxe rooms recall upscale bachelor pads – plaid bedspreads, quirky wall stencils, leather furnishings and fridges. Some even have Gibson guitars and turntables. All have free wi-fi. For cool kids with more 'cred' than 'coins,' there are 'mini' and 'bunk' rooms (with bunk beds), both of which can slip under $200 in the winter.

The Ace vibe is upbeat and fun, with two designer shops, a hipster-packed lobby serving up live bands and DJs, superlative espresso bar Stumptown Coffee Roasters (p200) and two of the area's top nosh spots – turf-centric **Breslin** (Map p426; 16 West 29th St; mains $18; ⏰7am-midnight; [S]N/R to 28th St) and surf-centric John Dory (p198).

BRYANT PARK HOTEL BOUTIQUE HOTEL $$$

Map p426 (☎212-869-0100, 877-640-9300; www.bryantparkhotel.com; 40 W 40th St, btwn Fifth & Sixth Aves, Midtown East; r $370-800; ❄📶; [S]B/D/F/M to 42nd St-Bryant Park, 7 to Fifth Ave) Looming to the south of cosmopolitan Bryant Park, this modish 130-room hotel (complete with red-leather elevator) dishes out bare-bone minimalist rooms, most with huge views and full-size soaking tubs, and all with high-tech sound system, flatscreen TV, travertine bathroom and cashmere blanket. If you can, opt up for a suite that faces the park (higher-priced ones have terraces).

Originally the American Standard Building (1934), this black-and-gold tower hotel also features a small fitness center, a sexy, vaulted underground bar, and an uber-sleek sushi restaurant with the odd celebrity diner.

PIERRE LUXURY HOTEL **$$$**

Map p426 (☎212-838-8000; www.tajhotels.com; 2 E 61st St, at Fifth Ave, Midtown East; r from $585; ❄📶; [S]N/Q/R to Fifth Ave-59th St) Opulent, historic and obscenely romantic, the Pierre is a destination in itself. The lobby looks like a Gilded Age period piece, the on-site restaurant (Sirio Ristorante) is owned by celebrated restaurateur Sirio Maccioni, and the spacious rooms (in muted tones with delicate accent colors) beckon with wide beds, sweeping views of Central Park (at the hotel's front door) and decadent, full-size bathrooms.

The Pierre's 49 suites have gracious sitting areas – some with fireplaces and antique desks for business – that are both lavish and tranquil, and the on-site spa beckons with treatments based on traditional Indian teachings, herbs and oils. Wi-fi will set you back $12.95 per day.

FOUR SEASONS LUXURY HOTEL **$$$**

Map p426 (☎212-758-5700; www.fourseasons.com/newyork; 57 E 57th St, btwn Madison & Park Aves, Midtown East; r from $800; ❄📶; [S]N/Q/R to Fifth Ave-59th St) Housed in a 52-floor tower designed by IM Pei, this five-star chain delivers seamless luxury. Even the smallest of the 368 neutrally hued rooms are generously sized, with spacious closets and 10in plasma TVs in the full-marble bathrooms. The views over Central Park from the 'Park View' rooms are practically unfair.

Then there's the impeccable service, the luxury spa and the 24-hour fitness center. On the downside, wi-fi is a cheeky $12.

CHATWAL NEW YORK LUXURY HOTEL **$$$**

Map p430 (☎212-764-6200; www.thechatwalny.com; 130 W 44th St, btwn Sixth Ave & Broadway, Midtown West; r from $540; 📶🏊; [S]N/Q/R, S, 1/2/3, 7 to Times Sq-42nd St) A restored art deco jewel in the heart of the Theater District, the Chatwal is as atmospheric as it is historic; the likes of Fred Astaire and Irving Berlin once supped, sipped and sang in its Lambs Club restaurant-bar. Vintage Broadway posters adorn the uber-luxe guestrooms, inspired by steamer cabin trunks and featuring 42-inch plasma screens and 400-thread Frette linen counts.

Additional perks include complimentary use of iPads, laptops and preprogrammed iPods, and there's a luxury spa for in-house pampering. The beaux arts building itself is the work of Stanton White, creator of the Washington Square Arch.

IROQUOIS HOTEL **$$$**

Map p430 (☎800-332-7220, 212-840-3080; www.iroquoisny.com; 49 W 44th St, btwn Fifth & Sixth Aves, Midtown West; r $289-559; 📶; [S]B/D/F/M to 42nd St-Bryant Park) Steeped in history (James Dean lived in room 803 from 1951 to 1953), this classic 114-room hotel radiates Old New York charm and an enviable location in the heart of Midtown.

It's a wonderfully atmospheric place, complete with a small oak library; intimate cocktail salon, Lantern's Keep (p201); and superb French-inspired restaurant, Triomphe (attracting a loyal pretheater crowd). Some rooms on the top three of its dozen floors face the Chrysler Building through a canyon of Midtown buildings. Softly colored, with classic wooden furniture, all rooms have goose-down pillows and small, Italian marble bathrooms. There's a small fitness center and sauna, as well as complimentary shoe shine service. Jimmy Dean must have dug that.

PLAZA LUXURY HOTEL **$$$**

Map p426 (☎888-850-0909, 212-759-3000; www.theplaza.com; 768 Fifth Ave, at Central Park South; r from $625; ❄📶; [S]N/R to Fifth Ave-59th St) The palatial Plaza looks even more incredible after its $400 million facelift. Suitably set in a landmark French Renaissance–style building, its 282 guestrooms are a suitably regal affair, with sumptuous Louis XV–style furniture and 24-carat gold-plated bathroom faucets. Among the hotel's long list of luxe drawcards is the fabled Palm Court, famed for its stained-glass ceiling and afternoon tea.

Add white-gloved butler service, a wine-therapy Caudelié Spa, luxury retail and dining options, and you too can expect to develop a royalty complex.

RITZ-CARLTON LUXURY HOTEL **$$$**

Map p430 (☎866-671-6008, 212-308-9100; www.ritzcarlton.com; 50 Central Park South btwn Sixth & Seventh Aves; r from $800; ❄📶; [S]N/Q/R to 57th St-Seventh Ave, F to 57th St) Pure, unadulterated luxury: this landmark building comes with views of Central Park so giant you almost can't see New York. All 259 rooms feature French colonial undertones, with tasseled armchairs, beautiful inlaid-tile bathrooms and loads of space for your countless Louis Vuitton cases, dahhhling. Park-view rooms come with a *Birds of New York* field guide set by a telescope.

The hotel's Auden Bistro offers modern takes on classic bistro fare, while the high-end spa will pamper, polish and preen you with La Prairie products.

LONDON NYC LUXURY HOTEL $$$
Map p430 (☎866-690-2029, 212-307-5000; www.thelondonnyc.com; 151 W 54th St, btwn Sixth & Seventh Aves, Midtown West; ste from $399; ❄📶; [S]B/D, E to Seventh Ave) This luxe hotel salutes the British capital in sophisticated ways, including a silk-stitched tapestry of Hyde Park (or is it Central Park?) in the lobby, and a restaurant by Gordon Ramsay. But the real draw is the huge, plush rooms – all called suites, and all with separate bedroom and living area. In winter, online prices start at $299.

Suites are subdued and sophisticated, with luxe touches including parquet floors, 2000-thread-count linens and spacious bathrooms with showers for two. Amenities include an equally sleek gym and wi-fi is free.

CHAMBERS BOUTIQUE HOTEL $$$
Map p426 (☎212-974-5656, 866-204-5656; www.chambershotel.com; 15 W 56th St, btwn Fifth & Sixth Aves; r from $350; ❄📶; [S]F to 57th St; N/Q/R to Fifth Ave-59th St) Chambers is chic and intimate, its mezzanine lounge pimped with anime-inspired wall art and area rugs. Its 77 rooms are simple yet elegant, with plush cushions on wood-frame beds, and concrete-floor bathrooms featuring giant showerheads. The on-site restaurant Ma Peche is helmed by culinary genius David Chang of Momofuku fame, and Fifth Ave's upmarket department stores are a bag swing away.

70 PARK HOTEL $$$
Map p426 (☎877-707-2752, 212-973-2400; www.70parkave.com; 70 Park Ave, at 38th St, Midtown East; r $266-665; ❄📶🐾; [S]S, 4/5/6, 7 to Grand Central-42nd St) Beyond the plush and cozy lobby lounge, complete with limestone fireplace, this slumber number offers 205 slinky rooms packed with state-of-the-art technology (including great sound systems); comfy plush beds featuring Frette linens; and a palate of black, white, purple and chrome. Adjoining rooms can be turned into large suites for families. Pets are welcome, and staff are friendly.

ROYALTON BOUTIQUE HOTEL $$$
Map p426 (☎800-635-9013, 212-869-4400; www.royalton.com; 44 W 44th St, btwn Fifth & Sixth Aves, Midtown East; d $300-700; ❄📶; [S]B/D/F/M to 42nd St) This modern-classic creation by Ian Schrager and Philippe Starck makes a grand introduction with its mahogany-rich, African art-laced lobby. Up the dark hallways are mid-size rooms with short, wide beds and soft, muted, pastel-hued furnishings. Some rooms have circular 'soaking tubs,' deluxe rooms feature a fireplace, and there's an iPad in every room. There's a fitness center to boot.

6 COLUMBUS BOUTIQUE HOTEL $$$
Map p430 (☎212-204-3000; www.thompsonhotels.com; 6 Columbus Circle, Midtown West; r $330-790; ❄📶; [S]A/C, B/D, 1 to 59th St-Columbus Circle) Flashback to the 1960s at this ultra-mod boutique hotel, brought to you by the owners of downtown 'It' spots Smyth Tribeca, Gild Hall, Thompson LES and 60 Thompson. Rooms are small but fun, with retro-cool detailing and high-tech hook-ups like LCD TVs and iPod docks. The uber-cool, intimate rooftop bar is outstanding for a twilight toast.

Then there's the location: steps from Central Park, next to Time Warner and backed by a major subway hub.

CASABLANCA HOTEL BOUTIQUE HOTEL $$$
Map p430 (☎888-922-7225, 212-869-1212; www.casablancahotel.com; 147 W 43rd St, btwn Sixth Ave & Broadway, Midtown West; r $279-599; ❄📶; [S]S, N/Q/R, 1/2/3, 7 to Times Sq-42nd St) Low-key, tourist-oriented and only steps away from Times Square, the popular 48-room Casablanca pages North Africa with its tiger statues, Moroccan murals, framed tapestries and a second-floor lounge named Rick's Cafe, after the movie. Rooms are small but pleasant and comfortable, with sisal-like carpets and a window-side seating area. Freebies include breakfast, internet, all-day espresso, and wine and cheese at 5pm.

🛏 Upper East Side

The Upper East Side contains some of the wealthiest zip codes in the country, so accommodations aren't cheap. But that's the price you pay for being walking distance from some of New York's grandest cultural attractions.

STAY THE NIGHT INN GUESTHOUSE $

Map p432 (☎212-722-8300; www.staythenight.com; 18 E 93rd St; r with shared bathroom $100-125, r $170-295; 📶; [S]6 to 96th St) Set in a 150-year-old brownstone half a block from Central Park, Stay the Night has comfortable, simply furnished rooms that are a good value for the Upper East Side. Some of the rooms are quite spacious, and can accommodate two couples – well-suited if traveling with a group of friends. A few things to keep in mind: there's no breakfast, and no common areas, and few dining options in the immediate vicinity of the guesthouse.

BUBBA & BEAN LODGES B&B $$

Map p432 (☎917-345-7914; www.bblodges.com; 1598 Lexington Ave, btwn 101st & 102nd Sts; r $120-250; ❄📶; [S]6 to 103rd St) Owners Jonathan and Clement have turned a charming Manhattan townhouse into an excellent home-away-from-home. The five guest rooms are simply furnished, with crisp, white walls, hardwood floors and navy linens, providing the place with a modern, youthful feel. All units are equipped with private bathrooms as well as kitchenettes with cookware.

FRANKLIN HOTEL $$

Map p432 (☎212-369-1000, 800-607-4009; www.franklinhotel.com; 164 E 87th St, btwn Lexington & Third Aves; r from $189; 📶; [S]4/5/6 to 86th St) Fronted by a classic red-and-gold awning, this long-time spot channels a 1930s feel – starting with the vintage elevator. As with many old-timey New York spots, the rooms and bathrooms are tiny. But the decor is modern, the staff congenial and the location couldn't be more ideal – walking distance from Central Park and many museums.

In addition, wine and cheese are served in the evenings. Rooms facing the back are quieter.

1871 HOUSE HISTORIC HOTEL $$

Map p432 (☎212-756-8823; www.1871house.com; 130 E 62nd St, btwn Park & Lexington Aves; r from $245; 📶; [S]N/Q/R to Lexington Ave-59th St) Named for the year it was built, this historic home now serves as a quaint five-room inn. Each unit (including two multi-room suites) is like a mini-apartment, with a kitchenette, private bath, queen beds, working fireplace and period-style furnishings. All the rooms are light-filled, with airy 12ft ceilings, while the suites, on the upper floors, can sleep up to five.

This is a great-value place for the neighborhood. But note that this is a characterful, vintage structure: there is no elevator, the floors are a bit creaky, and in winter, heat is provided by steam radiators.

🛏 Upper West Side & Central Park

INTERNATIONAL STUDENT CENTER HOSTEL $

Map p434 (☎212-787-7706; www.nystudentcenter.org; 38 W 88th St, btwn Columbus Ave & Central Park West; dm $30-40; [S]B, C to 86th St) Set in a converted brownstone just a short stroll from Central Park, ISC has simple dorm rooms and basic facilities, with a cozy, if well-worn, lounge on the ground floor. The hosts are friendly, but the rules can be annoying: you can't bring bags up to the rooms, and only guests aged 18 to 35 are accepted. Lack of wi-fi is a big minus. The location, however, is outstanding.

JAZZ ON THE PARK HOSTEL HOSTEL $

Map p434 (☎212-932-1600; www.jazzhostels.com; 36 W 106th St, btwn Central Park West & Manhattan Ave; dm $44-70, d $125-200; 📶; [S]B, C to 103rd St) This flophouse-turned-hostel right off of Central Park is generally a good bet, with clean dorms sporting four to 12 bunks in co-ed and single-sex configurations. This is a great place to meet other travelers, with free nightly activities (comedy and movie nights, pub crawls, summer barbecues). The downstairs lounge, aka 'the dungeon', has a pool table, couches and big-screen TV. There's also an area for eating, an accessible rooftop and several small terraces.

HOSTELLING INTERNATIONAL NEW YORK HOSTEL $

Map p434 (HI; ☎212-932-2300; www.hinewyork.org; 891 Amsterdam Ave, at 103rd St; dm $50, d from $240; ❄📶; [S]1 to 103rd St) This red-brick mansion from the 1880s houses HI's 672 well-scrubbed bunks. It's rather 19th-century industrial, but benefits include good public areas, a backyard (that sees barbecue action in the summer), a communal kitchen and a cafe. There are loads of activities on offer, from walking tours to club nights. There are attractive private rooms with private bathrooms, too. The hostel is alcohol-free. Wi-fi throughout the building.

HOTEL NEWTON HOTEL $$

Map p434 (☎212-678-6500; www.thehotelnewton.com; 2528 Broadway, btwn 94th & 95th Sts; d $120-350; ❄📶; [S]1/2/3 to 96th St) The nine-story Newton isn't going to win any interior design awards – hello, paisley 1980s bedspreads! – but it's clean and well managed, making it a solid budget option. The 110 guest rooms are small but tidy, and come stocked with TVs, mini-refrigerators, coffee makers and microwaves. The bathrooms are all well maintained. Larger 'suites' are roomier and feature a sitting area. Wi-fi costs extra.

HOTEL BELLECLAIRE HOTEL $$

Map p434 (☎212-362-7700; www.hotelbelleclaire.com; 250 W 77th St, at Broadway; d $150-370, ste $310-600; 📶; [S]1 to 79th St) A landmark beaux arts building designed by architect Emory Roth in 1903 houses a 230-room hotel that is good value for the location. Contemporary rooms come in a variety of sizes and configurations, with some units bigger or with better daylight than others. Some rooms face interior alleyways.

HOTEL BEACON HOTEL $$

Map p434 (☎212-787-1100, reservations 800-572-4969; www.beaconhotel.com; 2130 Broadway, btwn 74th & 75th Sts; d $230-350, ste $300-450; 📶👪; [S]1/2/3 to 72nd St) Adjacent to the Beacon Theatre (p244), this family favorite offers a winning mix of attentive service, comfortable rooms and convenient location. The Beacon has 260 units (including one and two bedroom suites) decorated in muted shades of Pottery Barn green. The units are well maintained and quite roomy – and all come with coffee makers and kitchenettes. Upper stories have views of Central Park in the distance. A good deal all round.

EMPIRE HOTEL HOTEL $$

Map p434 (☎212-265-7400; www.empirehotelnyc.com; 44 W 63rd St, at Broadway; r $243-553; ❄📶🏊; [S]1 to 66th St-Lincoln Center) This old hotel was remade a few years back, complete with canopied pool deck, sexy rooftop bar and a dimly lit lobby lounge studded with zebra-print settees. The 400-plus rooms come in various configurations, and feature brightly-hued walls with plush dark leather furnishings.

LUCERNE HOTEL $$

Map p434 (☎212-875-1000; www.thelucernehotel.com; 201 W 79th St, cnr Amsterdam Ave; d $244-450, ste $400-625; ❄📶👪; [S]B, C to 81st St) This unusual 1903 structure breaks away from beaux arts in favor of the baroque, with an ornately carved, terracotta-colored facade. Inside is a stately 200-room hotel, ideal for couples and families with children (Central Park and the American Museum of Natural History are a stone's throw away). Nine types of guest rooms evoke a contemporary Victorian look. Think: flowered bedspreads, scrolled headboards and plush pillows with fringe. Service is courteous and there is a nice French-Mediterranean restaurant on-site.

NYLO HOTEL BOUTIQUE HOTEL $$$

Map p434 (☎212-362-1100; www.nylo-nyc.com; 2178 Broadway, at 77th St; r from $300; ❄📶; [S]1 to 77th St) This modern boutique hotel has 285 casually stylish rooms with warm earth tones. Niceties include plush bedding, wood floors, elegant lighting, roomy (for New York) bathrooms, coffee makers and flat-screen TVs. 'Panoramic Deluxe' rooms have furnished private terraces and extravagant Manhattan views. The handsomely designed lounge and bar areas on the ground floor are great places to decamp after a day spent exploring. Friendly service and a great location.

🛏 Harlem & Upper Manhattan

HARLEM FLOPHOUSE GUESTHOUSE $

Map p436 (☎347-632-1960, www.harlemflophouse.com; 242 W 123rd St, btwn Adam Clayton Powell Jr & Frederick Douglass Blvds, Harlem; r with shared bath $125-150; 📶; [S]A/B/C/D, 2/3 to 124th St) This lovely four-room, 1890s townhouse conjures up the Jazz Age, with brass beds, polished wood floors and vintage radios (set to a local jazz station). It feels like a trip to the past – which means shared bathrooms, no air-con and no TVs. But for the real-deal retro ambience, it can't be beat.

The owner is a helpful source of information on the neighborhood, and his band rehearses at the property on Sunday afternoon. Friendly house cat Phoebe completes the homey, welcoming vibe.

★ALOFT HARLEM BOUTIQUE HOTEL $$

Map p436 (☎212-749-4000; www.aloftharlem.com; 2296 Frederick Douglass Blvd, btwn 123rd & 124th Sts, Harlem; d $179-400; ❄📶; [S]A/C,

B/D, 2/3 to 125th St) A trendy new hotel designed for younger travelers channels a W Hotel vibe but at a far cheaper price. The 124 guest rooms are snug (285 sq ft) but chic, with crisp white linens, fluffy comforters and brightly accented pillows. The modern bathrooms are small (no tubs), but are highly functional and feature amenities courtesy of Bliss.

A basement lounge with pool tables can get boisterous, but it'll be stumbling distance to your room. All around, it's convenient (the Apollo Theater and the bustling 125th St commercial district are nearby) and a good deal.

SUGAR HILL HARLEM B&B **$$**

Map p436 (☎212-234-5432; www.sugarhillharleminn.com; 460 W 141st St, btwn Amsterdam & Convent Aves, Sugar Hill; r $125-250; ❄📶; [S]A/C, B/D to 145th St) An airy townhouse has been restored to its turn-of-the-century splendor, with suites named after African American jazz greats. Well-appointed rooms feature antique-style furnishings but are equipped with modern touches like TVs and hair dryers. All units come with their own bathrooms (not necessarily en suite) and most have massive bay windows that admit lots of light; a couple have kitchens.

There is a nice garden, but no elevator (the building is three stories tall). A few additional guest rooms are located in a second renovated townhouse around the corner on Convent Ave.

MOUNT MORRIS HOUSE B&B GUESTHOUSE **$$**

Map p436 (☎917-478-6213; www.mountmorrishousebandb.com; 12 Mt Morris Park W, btwn 121st & 122nd Sts, Harlem; ste $125-325; ❄📶; [S]2/3 to 116th St) Occupying a stunning Gilded Age townhouse from 1888, this cozy inn boasts four extravagantly roomy mega-suites: the Sage, Jade, Terracotta and the Apartment. Each is appointed in period-style furnishings, with four-poster beds, Persian-style rugs and brocaded settees, as well as fireplaces and vintage bathtubs. Breakfast is not offered, though complimentary coffee, tea and cakes are available all day.

The property is an easy walk to 125th St and is located a stone's throw from the playgrounds at Marcus Garvey Park. Cash preferred.

102 BROWNSTONE HOTEL **$$**

Map p436 (☎212-222-1212; www.102brownstone.com; 102 W 118th St, btwn Malcolm X & Adam Clayton Powell Jr Blvds, Harlem; r $157-211; ❄📶; [S]A/C, B, 2/3 to 116th St) This intimate five-room guesthouse is a charming and convenient spot for travelers who want to explore the city but come to a little peace and quiet at the end of the day. All of the units have antique-style furnishings, private bathrooms and mini-fridges. The Zen suite – decorated in lemony tones – has a full kitchen and a Jacuzzi bath.

Brooklyn

A short train ride across the East River and you'll find bigger and (sometimes) brighter rooms – and a lot more bang for your buck.

Note: Brooklyn is more than 70 sq miles and transport within the borough can be a challenge, so pick an area (north or south) that offers the best proximity to the sights you want to see.

South Brooklyn

Awash in B&Bs and sleek spots, South Brooklyn covers downtown, Brooklyn Heights, Cobble Hill, Carroll Gardens, Park Slope and beyond.

3B B&B **$**

Map p444 (☎347-762-2632; www.3bbrooklyn.com; 136 Lawrence St; dm/r incl breakfast from $60/150; ❄📶; [S]A/C/F/N/R to Jay St-Metro Tech) 🍃 The 3rd floor unit of this downtown Brooklyn brownstone has been turned into a bright and contemporary four-room B&B. It has high ceilings, wood floors and comfy furnishings. On the downside: all rooms share bathroom facilities (one full bath and one half bath), and street noise may be a problem for light sleepers.

It's in a central downtown Brooklyn location, within easy walking distance of Ft Greene, Carroll Gardens or Brooklyn Heights. Hosts are friendly and eco-minded, with 100% of electricity supplied by wind energy. Good breakfasts.

ALOFT NEW YORK BROOKLYN BOUTIQUE HOTEL **$$**

Map p444 (☎718-256-3833; www.aloftnewyorkbrooklyn.com; 216 Duffield St, btwn Willoughby & Fulton Sts; d $135-$320; ❄📶🏊; [S]2 to Hoyt St) A cheery, modern boutique-y spot in downtown, Aloft is walking distance from the sights in Cobble Hill and Carroll Gardens.

Its 176 rooms are simple and cozy, with 9ft ceilings, minimalist furnishings, bright pillows and plenty of wood trim. Bath amenities are by Bliss. But the best feature is the dizzying rooftop lounge that is open til 3am on weekends.

HOTEL LE BLEU HOTEL $$

Map p440 (☎718-625-1500; www.hotellebleu.com; 370 Fourth Ave, Park Slope; d incl breakfast $140-380; [P] ❄ 📶) Situated on a charmless, industrial road on the edge of Park Slope, this hotel nonetheless manages to pull off 48 attractive units in a sleek palette of brown, white and blue. (It's not 'Le Bleu' for nothing.) Rooms are chock full of amenities, including bathrobes and coffeemakers, and the rate includes a light breakfast. During off-peak periods, the low prices make this a deal.

BPM HOTEL $$

(☎718-305-4182; www.hotelbpmbrooklyn.com; 139 E 33rd St, btwn 4th Ave & Gowanus Expy; d $150-210; ❄ 📶) Hip-hop lovers might want to check out a stay at sleek BPM (short for 'beats per minute'), which opened in 2012 in Sunset Park. Its 76 rooms are tiny (and have thin walls!) but well-appointed with 37in smart TVs, iPad-connectable mini stereos and high-end mattresses. Deep grooves, selected by owner DJ Bijal, play in heavy rotation in the lobby and lounge.

BLUE PORCH B&B $$

(☎718-434-0557; www.blueporchnyc.com; 15 DeKoven Court, at Foster Ave & Rugby Rd, Ditmas Park; r $175; 📶; [S]B/Q to Newkirk Ave) A lovely 1904 Victorian with two bright, airy guest rooms is located in the sleepy district of Ditmas Park (south of Prospect Park). The bathrooms are beautifully kept, the rooms have polished wood floors and the continental breakfasts are generous. It's a good deal if you don't mind the 40-minute trip into Manhattan. A two-night minimum is required.

NU HOTEL HOTEL $$

Map p444 (☎718-852-8585; www.nuhotelbrooklyn.com; 85 Smith St, d incl breakfast $175-400; ❄ @ 📶; [S]F, G to Bergen St) The 93 rooms in this downtown Brooklyn hotel are of the stripped-down variety, featuring lots of crisp whiteness (sheets, walls, duvets). Furnishings are made from recycled teak and the floors are cork. For something more daring, book a Nu Perspectives room, adorned with colorful murals by Brooklyn artists.

There is a small lounge and bikes are available. Ask for a room away from busy Atlantic Ave if you are a light sleeper.

🛏 North Brooklyn

This area includes the hipster enclaves of Williamsburg and Bushwick, as well as the residential district of Bedford-Stuyvesant.

★NEW YORK LOFT HOSTEL HOSTEL $

Map p438 (☎718-366-1351; www.nylofthostel.com; 249 Varet St, btwn Bogart & White Sts, Bushwick; dm $60-75; ❄ @ 📶; [S]L to Morgan Ave) This renovated 1913 warehouse building in Bushwick is a good choice for urban pioneers. It has spacious, brick-lined dorms, with two or three beds in each. Amenities include a communal kitchen, a large patio area with picnic tables and a small terrace with hot tub. With loads of activities on offer – outdoor barbecues, film screenings, bar crawls – this is a great place to meet other travelers.

It's not the prettiest part of Brooklyn, but there are plenty of good restaurants and bars nearby. A good place to get your hipster on.

HOTEL LE JOLIE BOUTIQUE HOTEL $$

Map p438 (☎718-625-2100; www.hotellejolie.com; 235 Meeker Ave, btwn Union Ave & Lorimer St, Williamsburg; d $150-400; ❄ 📶; [S]L to Bedford Ave) An unremarkable 54-room hotel sits alongside the Brooklyn Queens Expressway (leading some locals to call it 'Le Hotel BQE'), but it's comfortable and reasonable. Rooms are sleek, with beds sporting monolithic *2001: A Space Odyssey*–like headboards. There are iPod docks and flat-screen TVs. But the real deal here is the proximity to Bedford Ave.

Rooms on the upper stories with Manhattan views are best.

KING & GROVE BOUTIQUE HOTEL $$

Map p438 (☎718-218-7500; www.kingandgrove.com; 160 N 12th St, btwn Bedford Ave & Berry St, Williamsburg; d $175-360; ❄ 📶 🏊; [S]L to Bedford, G to Nassau) This hipster hotel on the fringes of Williamsburg is insufferably chic, with minimalist rooms with bamboo flooring and marble-filled bathrooms. Pricier rooms have balconies and rain showers. The large saltwater pool is surrounded by design-conscious loungers, while the upper-level bar and lounge with retractable rooftop offers jaw-dropping views of Manhattan.

There's also a superb restaurant (**The Elm** (theelmnyc.com), ranked one of the best new eateries of 2013), headed by Michelin-starred chef Paul Liebrandt, and free bicycles for guests.

AKWAABA MANSION INN
B&B $$

(☏866-466-3855, 718-455-5958; www.akwaaba.com; 347 MacDonough St, btwn Lewis & Stuyvesant Aves, Bedford-Stuyvesant; r $195; ✳ ☎; ⓢ A/C to Utica Ave) Sitting on a tree-lined block of tidy, century-old townhouses in Bedford-Stuyvesant, this graceful B&B is tucked into a sprawling mansion built by a local beer baron back in 1860. Period design flourishes include brass beds, marble fireplaces, the original parquet floors and a screened-in wraparound porch – the perfect spot to settle in with a good book.

African textiles and vintage photos add a personal touch. It has four roomy suites, each with private bathroom, while a couple of the units have Jacuzzi tubs for two.

WYTHE HOTEL
BOUTIQUE HOTEL $$

Map p438 (☏718-460-8000; wythehotel.com; 80 Wythe Ave, at N 11th St, Williamsburg; r $205-600; ✳ ☎) Set in a converted 1901 factory, the red-brick Wythe Hotel brought a serious dash of style to Williamsburg when it opened in 2013. The industrial-chic rooms have beds made from reclaimed lumber, custom-made wallpaper (from Brooklyn's own Flavor Paper), exposed brick, polished concrete floors and original 13ft timber ceilings.

On the ground floor, Reynard dishes up brasserie classics in a lovely setting of tile floors, brick walls, soaring wood ceilings and vintage fixtures. The top-floor Ides Bar is a great spot for sunset cocktails, craft brews and memorable skyline views of Manhattan.

🛏 Queens

This sprawling borough still lags behind Manhattan and Brooklyn in terms of boutique and B&B charmers, but it offers some killer views of Manhattan, easy access to Midtown, not to mention chain hotels offering some great deals.

COUNTRY INN & SUITES
HOTEL $

Map p446 (☏800-596-2375, 718-729-0111; www.countryinns.com; 40-34 Crescent St, btwn 40th & 41st Aves, Long Island City; r $90-205; ✳ ☎; ⓢ F to 21st St, N/Q to 39th Ave) An easy schlep to Manhattan and extra-large rooms –

some with kitchens and living room areas – keeps this chain hotel full year-round. Prices drop below $100 in off months, and even in peak season are still a bargain for NYC. And while it won't rate high for flair (think cookie-cutter furnishings), it's clean, has good beds, and breakfast is included.

Z HOTEL
BOUTIQUE HOTEL $$

Map p446 (☏877-256-5556, 212-319-7000; www.zhotelny.com; 11-01 43rd Ave, at 11th St, Long Island City; r $180-375; ✳ ☎; ⓢ F to 21st-Queensbridge; E, M to 23rd St-Ely Ave) Its location might scream 'industrial wasteland,' but every room at this design-savvy newbie delivers jaw-dropping views of Manhattan. The 100 rooms themselves are impressive, decked out in dark, contemporary shades, and NYC-themed stencil and designer fixtures. More astounding views (and a pizza oven) await at the rooftop bar, while the downstairs restaurant-bar is a salt-of-the-earth combo of American comfort food and Sunday football games.

Freebies include wi-fi, local and international calls, and bike rental. Rumor has it that online rates occasionally drop as low as $99 per night.

RAVEL
BOUTIQUE HOTEL $$

Map p446 (☏718-289-6101; www.ravelhotel.com; 8-08 Queens Plaza South, at Vernon Blvd, Long Island City; r from $181; ⓟ ✳ ☎; ⓢ F to 21st St-Queensbridge) The industrial location may feel a little desolate, but this Long Island City option is two short subway stops from Midtown. Rooms may not be as boutique-luxe as the hotel claims, but all are smart and contemporary, with vibrant accents, plush bedding and bathrooms featuring rainforest showers (the super-spacious superior rooms have soaking tubs). The sleek rooftop restaurant-bar offers breathtaking Manhattan views.

MARCO LAGUARDIA
HOTEL & SUITES
BUSINESS HOTEL $$

Map p447 (☏718-445-3300; www.marcolaguardiahotel.com; 137-07 Northern Blvd, at Farrington St, Flushing; r $150-199; ✳ ☎; ⓢ 7 to Flushing-Main St) For travelers whose main focus is Queens - be it the Mets at Citi Field, tennis at Flushing Meadows or taste-testing the borough's ethnic eateries – this is a convenient and welcoming choice. Located near LaGuardia Airport (free shuttle service) and JFK, it's a 30-minute ride into Manhattan on the 7 line. Rooms are designed with business travelers in mind.

Understand New York City

New York City Today

Not even Hurricane Sandy's vicious slap can stop America's biggest, boldest metropolis. The city of endless reinvention is captivating the world with its next round of showstoppers, from a national museum dedicated to 9/11, to a transport center more than twice the size of Grand Central Terminal. On the streets, bike sharing is all the rage, while at City Hall, the winds of change are blowing with a brand new Democrat mayor.

Best on Film

Annie Hall (1977) Oscar-winning romantic comedy by the king of New York neuroses, Woody Allen.
Manhattan (1979) Allen's at it again with tales of twisted love.
Taxi Driver (1976) Scorsese's tale of a troubled taxi driver and Vietnam vet.
West Side Story (1961) A modern-day *Romeo and Juliet* set on the gang-ridden streets of New York.
Requiem for a Dream (2000) An unusual tale of a Brooklyn junkie and his doting Jewish mother.

Best in Print

The Amazing Adventures of Kavalier & Clay (Michael Chabon; 2000) Beloved Pulitzer-winning novel that touches upon Brooklyn, escapism and the nuclear family.
A Tree Grows in Brooklyn (Betty Smith; 1943) An Irish American family living in the Williamsburg tenements at the beginning of the 20th century.
Down These Mean Streets (Piri Thomas; 1967) Memoirs of tough times growing up in Spanish Harlem.
Invisible Man (Ralph Ellison; 1952) Explores the situation of African Americans in the early 20th century.
The Age of Innocence (Edith Wharton; 1920) Tales and trials of NYC's social elite in the late 1800s.

After the Storm

She may have given it her best shot, but superstorm Hurricane Sandy failed to defeat NYC. Since raging through the city in October 2012, more than $1 billion worth of response and recovery work has commenced or been completed. In June 2013, then-mayor Michael Bloomberg launched a long-term plan to safeguard and strengthen the city's 520 miles of coastline, with the addition of new levees, flood walls, surge barriers and sand dunes. In another program launched by New York Governor Andrew Cuomo, Staten Island's marshy Oakwood Beach area was set to return to nature, with homeowners to be paid the pre-Sandy market value of their homes. In an effort to safeguard the city from future major blackouts, utility companies are upgrading their own systems, from Con Edison's installation of 'smart switches' to isolate damaged equipment, to Verizon's switch from copper lines to water-proof fibre optics. Full recovery is a slow and steady process. As of late 2013, work was still being carried out on damaged parts of the city, among them Battery Park, Ellis Island and South Street Seaport. What is certain, though, is that NYC is back, stronger and smarter than ever before.

WTC: From Zero to Hero

After more than a decade of sputters, spats and ballooning costs, the mammoth World Trade Center redevelopment is finally sprinting towards the finish line. While 2006 saw the completion of the 52-story 7 World Trade Center tower, September 2011 witnessed the opening of the National September 11 Memorial, its two giant reflecting pools attracting more than 10 million visitors in the two years since its debut. October 2013 debuted the 72-story, Fumihiko Maki–designed 4 World Trade Center skyscraper. The National September 11 Memorial Museum is finally open to the public, thanks in part to a $15 million push from Michael Bloomberg. Also scheduled for completion in 2014 is the 104-story One World Trade Center, the Western Hemisphere's tallest skyscraper. The tower will offer visitors the city's most enviable vantage point when its observation decks debut in 2015. In the same year, architect Santiago Calatrava's ambitious rail-and-retail complex – the WTC Transportation Hub – will also open at the site. Ground Zero is reborn.

New Mayor in Town

NYC swung to the left with the election of Mayor Bill de Blasio in November 2013, the city's first Democrat mayor since 1989. The 52 year old is also NYC's first white mayor with an African American spouse. It was a fact not lost on de Blasio in his election campaign TV commercials, which showcased his interracial family to a city in which blacks, Hispanics and Asians have outnumbered whites since the 1980s. His campaign also tapped into growing concerns about education, housing affordability and growing economic inequality, promising, among other things, to bump up taxes to fund universal pre-school and to reform then-mayor Michael Bloomberg's controversial 'stop and frisk' policy. The policy, which allows police officers to randomly stop, question and search pedestrians, had been deemed racially biased by several of its critics. It was a campaign that served de Blasio well on election day, the self-proclaimed progressive beating Republican candidate Joseph J Lhota by a breathtaking 49-point margin.

Peddle Power

New York's aim for a cleaner, greener future took another step forward in May 2013 with the launch of Citi Bike; its hugely popular bike-sharing program. By the end of the year, 4 million trips covering 8 million miles had been made, with over 80,000 people forking out the $95 for an annual membership. Yet not everyone is peddling smiles. Many residents resent the addition of Citi Bike kiosks on their streets, calling them eyesores. In fact, almost 45% of the original kiosk locations across the city were altered to appease disapproving locals. Despite these protestations, there is no stopping America's largest bike-sharing scheme. In late 2013, plans were announced for an extra 4000 bikes across the city, boosting the total fleet to 10,000. No doubt NYC's bar-hopping punters (some of the bikes' most regular users) will be toasting to that.

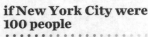
if New York City were 100 people

34 would be Caucasian
28 would be Hispanic/Latino
23 would be African American
13 would be Asian
2 would be other

housing
(% of population)

67.5 Renters
0.05 Homeless (documented)
32 Homeowners

population per sq mile
MANHATTAN   NEW YORK CITY

≈ 5,000 people

History

This is the tale of a city that never sleeps, of a kingdom where tycoons and world leaders converge, of a place that's seen the highest highs and the most devastating lows. Yet through it all, it continues to reach for the sky (both figuratively and literally). And to think it all started with $24 and a pile of beads...

NYC's Top Historical Sights

....

Ellis Island (New York Harbor)

....

Frick Collection (Upper East Side)

....

Gracie Mansion (Upper East Side)

....

Jane's Carousel (Brooklyn)

....

Historic Richmond Town (Staten Island)

Living off the Land

Long before the days of European conquest, the swath that would eventually become NYC belonged to Native Americans known as the Lenape – 'original people' – who resided in a series of seasonal campsites. They lived up and down the eastern seaboard, along the signature shoreline, and on hills and in valleys sculpted by glaciers after the Ice Age left New York with glacial debris now called Hamilton Heights and Bay Ridge. Glaciers scoured off soft rock, leaving behind Manhattan's stark rock foundations of gneiss and schist. Around 11,000 years before the first Europeans sailed through the Narrows, the Lenape people foraged, hunted and fished the regional bounty here. Spear points, arrowheads, bone heaps and shell mounds testify to their presence. Some of their pathways still lie beneath streets such as Broadway. In the Lenape language of Munsee, the term Manhattan may have translated as 'hilly island.' Others trace the meaning to a more colorful phrase: 'place of general inebriation.'

1524: A Rude Awakening

The Lenape people lived undisturbed until explorers muscled in, firstly by way of the French vessel *La Dauphine,* piloted by Florentine explorer Giovanni da Verrazano. He explored the Upper Bay in 1524, deemed it a 'very beautiful lake,' and, while anchored at Staten Island, attempted to kidnap some of the Native Americans he encountered. This began several decades of European explorers raiding Lenape villages, and cultivated the Lenape's deep mistrust of outsiders. By the time the Dutch West India Company employee Henry Hudson arrived

TIMELINE	c AD 1500	1625–26	1646
	About 15,000 Native Americans live in 80 sites around the island. The groups include the feuding Iroquois and Algonquins.	As the population of New Amsterdam reaches 200, the Dutch West India Company imports slaves from Africa to New Amsterdam to work in the fur trade and construction.	The Dutch found the village of Breuckelen on the East River shore of Long Island, naming it after Breukelen in the Netherlands; it will remain an independent city until 1898.

in 1609, encounters with Native Americans were often dichotomized into two crude stories that alternated between 'delightful primitives' and 'brutal savages.'

Buying Manhattan

The Dutch West India Company sent 110 settlers to begin a trading post here in 1624. They settled in Lower Manhattan and called their colony New Amsterdam, touching off bloody battles with the unshakable Lenape. It all came to a head in 1626, when the colony's first governor, Peter Minuit, became the city's first – but certainly not the last – unscrupulous real estate agent, by purchasing Manhattan's 14,000 acres from the Lenape for 60 guilders ($24) and some glass beads.

Peg Leg, Iron Fist

After the island's purchase, the colony quickly fell into disrepair under the governance of Willem Kieft. Then Peter Stuyvesant stepped in and busily set about fixing the demoralized settlement, making peace with the Lenape, establishing markets and a night watch, repairing the fort, digging a canal (under the current Canal St) and authorizing a municipal wharf. His vision of an orderly and prosperous trading port was partially derived from his previous experience as governor of Curaçao – and the burgeoning sugar economy in the Caribbean helped to inspire an investment in slave trading that soon boosted New Amsterdam's slave workforce to 20% of the population. After long service, some were partially freed and given 'Negroe Lots' near today's Greenwich Village, the Lower East Side and City Hall. The Dutch West India Company encouraged the fruitful connection to plantation economies on the islands, and issued advertisements and offered privileges to attract merchants to the growing port. Although these 'liberties' did not at first extend to the Jews who fled the Spanish Inquisition, the Dutch West India Company turned Stuyvesant's intolerance around. By the 1650s, warehouses, workshops and gabled houses were spreading back from the dense establishments at the river's edge on Pearl St.

By 1664, the English showed up in battleships, ready for a fight. Stuyvesant was tired, though, and avoided bloodshed by surrendering without a shot. King Charles II promptly renamed the colony after his brother the Duke of York. New York became a prosperous British port and its population rose to 11,000 by the mid-1700s. The honeymoon, however, was short lived as New York grew in prominence as the change point in the exchange of slaves and good between worlds.

NYC Names & Their Dutch Origins

Gramercy: Kromme Zee ('crooked lake')

Coney Island: Konijneneiland ('rabbits island')

Yonkers: jonker ('squire')

Bowery: bouwerij (old-fashioned word for 'farm')

Bronx: named for Jonas Bronck

1754	1784	1776	1789
The first institution of higher learning, King's College, is founded by royal charter from George II. After the American Revolution, it's reborn as Columbia University.	Alexander Hamilton founds the Bank of New York, with holdings of $500,000. Almost a decade later, it will become the first corporate stock to be traded on the NYSE.	American colonies sign the Declaration of Independence on July 4. Figures who helped create this document include John Hancock, Samuel Adams and Benjamin Franklin.	Following a seven-day procession from his home in Mount Vernon, George Washington is inaugurated at Federal Hall as the country's first president.

Tax & Press

Evidence of the rising tension could be found in the colonial press, as John Peter Zenger's *New York Weekly Journal* flayed the king and royal governor so regularly that the authorities tried to convict Zenger for seditious libel. He was acquitted, though, and that was the beginning of what we know today as 'freedom of the press.'

Meanwhile, some 2000 New Yorkers continued to resist their involuntary servitude. At the same time trade with the Caribbean accelerated and wharves lined the East River to accommodate the bulging merchant ships. By the 18th century, the economy was so robust the locals were improvising ways to avoid sharing the wealth with London. Smuggling to dodge various port taxes was commonplace, and the jagged coastline, full of coves and inlets, hid illegal activity well. And so New York was a hotbed of hotheads and tax dodgers, and provided the stage for the fatal confrontation with King George III.

Revolution & War

Patriots clashed in public spaces with Tories, who were loyal to the king, while Lieutenant Colonel Alexander Hamilton, an intellectual, became a fierce anti-British organizer. Citizens fled the scene, sensing the oncoming war, and revolutionary battle began in August of 1776, when General George Washington's army lost about a quarter of its men in just a couple of days. He retreated, and fire encompassed much of the colony. But soon the British left and Washington's army reclaimed their city. After a series of celebrations, banquets and fireworks at Bowling Green, General Washington bade farewell to his officers at what is now the Fraunces Tavern Museum and retired as commander-in-chief.

However, in 1789, to his surprise, the retired general found himself addressing crowds at Federal Hall, gathered to witness his presidential inauguration. Alexander Hamilton, meanwhile, began rebuilding New York and became Washington's secretary of the treasury, working to establish the New York Stock Exchange. But people distrusted a capitol located adjacent to the financial power of Wall St merchants, and New Yorkers lost the seat of the presidency to Philadelphia shortly thereafter.

New York City was the first capital of the United States – George Washington took his first presidential oath at Federal Hall in 1789.

Population Bust, Infrastructure Boom

There were plenty of setbacks during the 19th century: the bloody Draft Riots of 1863, massive cholera epidemics, rising tensions among 'old' and new immigrants, and the serious poverty and crime of Five Points, the city's first slum, located where Chinatown now lies. Eventually, though, the city was prosperous and found resources to build

1791	1795	1811	1825
Bill of Rights adopted as constitutional amendments articulating citizen's rights, including free speech, assembly, religion and the press; and the right to bear arms.	Just two years after turning away refugees from a yellow fever epidemic in Philadelphia, New York finds itself in the midst of its own outbreak, which kills nearly 750 people.	Manhattan's grid plan is developed by Mayor DeWitt Clinton, which leads to reshaping the city by leveling hills, filling in swamps and laying out plans for future streets.	The Erie Canal, considered one of the greatest engineering feats of the era, is ceremoniously completed, greatly influencing trade and commerce in New York.

mighty public works. A great aqueduct system brought Croton Water to city dwellers, relieving thirst and stamping out the cholera that was sweeping the town. Irish immigrants helped dig a 363-mile 'ditch' – the Erie Canal – linking the Hudson River with Lake Erie. The canal's chief backer, Mayor DeWitt Clinton, celebrated the waterway by ceremonially pouring a barrel of Erie water into the sea. Clinton was also the mastermind behind the modern-day grid system of Manhattan's street layout – a plan created by his commission to organize the city in the face of an oncoming population explosion.

And there was yet another grand project afoot – one to boost the health of the people crammed into tiny tenement apartments – in the form of an 843-acre public park. Begun in 1855 in an area so far uptown that some immigrants kept pigs, sheep and goats there, Central Park was both a vision of green reform and a boon to real-estate speculation.

Another vision was realized by German-born engineer John Roebling, who sought a solution to a series of winter freezes that had shut down the ferry system connecting downtown Manhattan to Brooklyn, then an independent city. He designed a soaring symphony of spun wire and Gothic arches to span the East River, and his Brooklyn Bridge accelerated the fusion of the neighboring cities.

Brooklyn Bridge opened with suitable fanfare on May 24, 1883. After New York Mayor Franklin Edison and Brooklyn Mayor Seth Low led President Chester Arthur and Governor Grover Cleveland across the structure, more than 150,000 members of the public followed suit, each paying a penny for the honor.

19th-Century Corruption & Immigration

Out of such growth and new prosperity came the infamous William 'Boss' Tweed – a powerful and charming politician who had served in the US House of Representatives and had become the leader of the political organization Tammany Hall, which basically looked out for the wealthy. He soon took charge of the city treasury and spent years embezzling funds – perhaps up to $200 million – which put the city in debt and contributed to citizens' growing poverty. His crimes were highlighted by Thomas Nast's biting caricatures in the 1870s, and Boss was eventually caught and thrown in jail, where he died.

By the turn of the 20th century, elevated trains carried one million people a day in and out of the city. Rapid transit opened up areas of the Bronx and Upper Manhattan, spurring mini building booms in areas near the lines. At this point, the city was simply overflowing with the masses of immigrants arriving from southern Italy and Eastern Europe, who had boosted the metropolis to around three million. The journey from immigrant landing stations at Castle Garden and Ellis Island led straight to the Lower East Side. There, streets reflected these myriad origins with shop signs in Yiddish, Italian, German and Chinese.

1853	1863	1870	1882
The State Legislature authorizes the allotment of public lands, which removes 17,000 potential building sites from the real-estate market for what will later become Central Park.	The Civil War Draft Riots erupt in New York, lasting for three days and ending only when President Lincoln dispatches combat troops from the Federal Army to restore order.	After four years of lobbying for a national institution of art by a civic group led by lawyer John Jay, New York City's Metropolitan Museum of Art is founded.	Thomas Edison switches on the city's first electric lights at the JP Morgan bank at 23 Wall St. On the same November day, electricity is delivered to 85 Manhattan addresses.

Class Lessons

All sorts of folks were living in squalor by the late 19th century, when the immigration processing center at Ellis Island opened, welcoming one million newcomers in just its first year. They crammed into packed tenements, shivered in soup lines and shoveled snow for nickels. Children collected rags and bottles, boys hawked newspapers, and girls sold flowers to contribute to family income. Family budgets were so meager that it was common to pawn the sheets to raise food money before a payday.

Meanwhile, newly wealthy folks – boosted by an economy jump-started by financier JP Morgan, who bailed out sinking railroads and led to the city to become the headquarters of Standard Oil and US Steel – began to build increasingly splendid mansions on Fifth Ave. Modeled on European chateaux, palaces such as the Vanderbilt home, on the corner of 52nd St and Fifth Ave, reached for new summits of opulence. Tapestries adorned marble halls, mirrored ballrooms reflected bejeweled revelers and liveried footmen guided grand ladies from their gilded carriages in a society where Astors, Fricks and Carnegies ruled. Reporter and photographer Jacob Riis illuminated the widening gap between the classes by writing about it in the *New York Tribune* and in his now-classic 1890 book, *How the Other Half Lives,* eventually forcing the city to pass much-needed housing reforms.

New York City has around 660 miles of subway tracks used for passenger services. Counting railyards and other non-passenger-service tracks, the figure exceeds 840 miles.

1898: Boroughs Join Manhattan

After years of governmental chaos caused by the 40 independent municipalities around the New York area, a solution came in 1898: the ratifying of the Charter of New York, which joined the five boroughs of Brooklyn, Staten Island, Queens, the Bronx and Manhattan into the largest city in America. The move brought even more development, this time in the form of skyscrapers that made good use of the steel industry and spawned many building contests to see who could reach higher into the sky. New York was home to nearly 70 skyscrapers by 1902.

Factory Tragedy, Women's Rights

Wretched factory conditions – low pay, long hours, abusive employers – in the early 20th century were illuminated with a tragic event in 1911. The infamous Triangle Shirtwaist Company fire saw rapidly spreading flames catch onto the factory's piles of fabrics, killing 146 of 500 women workers who were trapped behind locked doors. The event led to sweeping labor reforms after 20,000 female garment workers marched to City Hall. At the same time, suffragists held street-corner rallies to obtain

1883	1886	1904	1913
The Brooklyn Bridge, which was built at a cost of $15.5 million (and 27 lives) opens; 150,000 people walk across its span at the inaugural celebration.	The Statue of Liberty's pedestal is completed, allowing the large lady to be presented to New York at a dedication ceremony that takes place before thousands of citizens.	Luna Park in Coney Island opens, followed by Dreamland amusement park. Meanwhile, the IRT subway carries 150,000 passengers on its very first day of operation.	Though not yet complete, Grand Central Terminal opens for business on 2 February. Over 150,000 people visit the new station on its opening day.

the vote for women. Nurse and midwife Margaret Sanger opened the first birth-control clinic in Brooklyn, where 'purity police' promptly arrested her. After her release from jail in 1921 she formed the American Birth Control League (now Planned Parenthood), which provided services for young women and researched methods of safe birth control.

The Jazz Age

All this sassiness paved the way for what came to be known as the Jazz Age, when Prohibition outlawed the sale of alcohol, encouraging bootlegging and speakeasies. as well as organized crime. Congenial mayor James Walker was elected in 1925, Babe Ruth reigned at Yankee Stadium and the Great Migration from the South led to the Harlem Renaissance, when the neighborhood became the center of African American culture and society. It produced poetry, music, painting and an innovative attitude that continues to influence and inspire. Harlem's daring nightlife in the 1920s and '30s attracted the flappers and gin-soaked revelers who marked the complete failure of Prohibition, and gave a foretaste of the liberated nightlife that New Yorkers still enjoy today.

Hard Times

The fun times were not to last. The stock market crashed in 1929, beginning the Great Depression of the 1930s, which the city dealt with through a combination of grit, endurance, rent parties, militancy and a slew of public-works projects. The once-grand Central Park blossomed with shacks, derisively called Hoovervilles, after the president who refused to help the needy. But Mayor Fiorello LaGuardia found a friend in President Franklin Roosevelt, and worked his Washington connections to great effect to bring relief money – and subsequent prosperity – home.

WWII brought troops galore to the city, ready to party down to their last dollar in Times Square, before being shipped off to Europe. Converted to war industries, the local factories hummed, staffed by women and African American workers who had rarely before had access to good, unionized jobs. The explosion of wartime activity led to a huge housing crunch, which brought New York its much-imitated and tenant-protecting Rent Control Law.

There were few evident controls on business, as Midtown bulked up with skyscrapers after the war. The financial center marched north, while banker David Rockefeller and his brother, Governor Nelson Rockefeller, dreamed up the Twin Towers to revitalize downtown.

NYC's Tallest Building

Woolworth Building (1913–1930)

Chrysler Building (1930–31)

Empire State Building (1931–1972 & 2001–2012)

World Trade Center (1972–2001)

One World Trade Center (2012-present)

HISTORY THE JAZZ AGE

1919	**1931**	**1939**	**1941**
The Yankees acquire slugger Babe Ruth from Boston, leading to their first championship. The Red Sox's 85-year-long losing streak is finally reversed in 2004.	The Empire State Building (1454ft tall) supersedes the Chrysler Building as the world's tallest skyscraper; the World Trade Center's north tower steals the crown in 1970.	The World's Fair opens in Queens. With the future as its theme, the exposition invites visitors to take a look at 'the world of tomorrow.'	Duke Ellington's band leader Billy Strayhorn, inspired by the subway line that leads to Harlem, composes 'Take the A Train,' which becomes the band's signature song.

Enter Robert Moses

Working with LaGuardia to usher the city into the modern age was Robert Moses, an urban planner who would influence the physical shape of the city more than anyone else in the 20th century – either wonderfully or tragically, depending on whom you ask. He was the mastermind behind the Triborough Bridge (now the Robert F Kennedy Bridge), Jones Beach State Park, the Verrazano–Narrows Bridge, the West Side Hwy and the Long Island parkway system – not to mention endless highways, tunnels and bridges, which shifted this mass-transit area into one largely dependent on the automobile. His vision was one of doing away with intimate neighborhoods of brownstones and townhouses and of creating sweeping parks and soaring towers.

The approach got preservationists fired up and their efforts to stop him from bulldozing neighborhoods led to the Landmarks Preservation Commission being formed in 1965. His years of work were documented in the 1974 Pulitzer Prize–winning book *The Power Broker,* by Robert Caro, which portrayed Moses as an antipreservationist who had callously removed huge numbers of residents from ghettos to make way for development. He responded with the following statement: 'I raise my stein to the builder who can remove ghettos without removing people as I hail the chef who can make omelets without breaking eggs.'

Beats & Gays

The '60s brought an era of legendary creativity and anti-establishment expression, with many of its creators centered right downtown in Greenwich Village. One movement was Abstract Expressionism, a large-scale outbreak of American painters – Mark Rothko, Jackson Pol-

1945	1963	1969	1976–77
The UN, headquartered on Manhattan's east side, is established after representatives of 50 countries meet in San Francisco to agree on a charter.	The original Penn Station is demolished to build Madison Square Garden; outcry leads to the foundation of the Landmarks Preservation Commission.	On June 28, eight police officers raid the gay-friendly Stonewall Inn. Patrons revolt, sparking days of rioting and the birth of the modern gay rights movement.	David Berkowitz, the 'Son of Sam' killer, says a demon in a dog told him to commit a string of murders around the city. He kills six and wounds seven others using a .44 revolver.

lock, Lee Krasner, Helen Frankenthaler and Willem de Kooning among them – who offended and intrigued with incomprehensible squiggles and blotches and exuberant energy. Then there were the writers, such as Beat poets Allen Ginsberg and Jack Kerouac and novelist/playwright Jane Bowles. They gathered in Village coffeehouses to exchange ideas and find inspiration, which were often found in the form of folk music from some burgeoning big names, such as Bob Dylan. It all created an environment that was ripe for rebellion – a task that gay revelers took on with gusto, finding their political strength and voice in fighting a police raid at the Stonewall Inn in 1969. The Stonewall Riots, as they are now known, showed the city and the world that the lesbian and gay community would not accept being treated as second-class citizens.

'Drop Dead'

By the early 1970s, deficits had created a serious fiscal crisis, demoting the elected Mayor Abraham Beame to a figurehead, and turning over the city's real financial power to Governor Carey and his appointees. President Ford's refusal to lend federal aid – summed up nicely by the *Daily News* headline 'Ford to City, Drop Dead!' – marked the nadir of relationships between the US and the city it loved to hate. As massive layoffs decimated the city's working class, untended bridges, roads and parks reeked of hard times. Even the bond raters turned their thumbs down on New York's mountain of debt.

The traumatic '70s – which reached a low point in 1977 with a city-wide blackout and the terrorizing serial killer David Berkowitz – saw rents fall, which helped to nourish an exciting alternative culture that staged performances in abandoned schools, opened galleries in unused storefronts and breathed new life into the hair-dye industry with the advent of the punk rock aesthetic. The fees from shooting the movie *Fame* at PS 122 at 9th St and First Ave, for example, helped pay for the renovation of the still-popular performance space. Ramones-loving punks turned former warehouses into pulsing meccas of nightlife, transforming the former industrial precincts of SoHo and Tribeca. Immortalized in Nan Goldin's famous photographic performance piece *The Ballad of Sexual Dependency,* this renaissance challenged gender roles and turned the East Village into America's center of tattooing and independent filmmaking.

Out of the Ashes

Meanwhile, in South Bronx, a wave of arson reduced blocks of apartment houses to cinders. Amid the smoke, an influential hip-hop culture was born, both there and in Brooklyn, fueled by the percussive rhythms

Forgotten-NY.com is Queens native Kevin Walsh's compendium of historic NYC, with not-found-elsewhere tales about everything from old subway stations to cemeteries.

1977	1980	1988	1993
Following a lightning strike at a power substation, a summer blackout leaves New Yorkers in the dark for 24 sweltering hours, which leads to rioting around the city.	Mark David Chapman kills John Lennon in front of Lennon's home at the Dakota, on Manhattan's Upper West Side.	Squatters, who had turned the East Village's Tompkins Square Park into a massive homeless encampment, riot when cops attempt to remove them from their de facto home.	On February 26, terrorists detonate a bomb below the North Tower of the World Trade Center. The explosion kills six people and injures more than one thousand.

of Puerto Rican salsa. Rock Steady Crew, led by 'Crazy Legs' Richie Colon, pioneered athletic, competitive break-dancing. Kool DJ Herc spun vinyl for break beat all-night dance parties, drawing on his Jamaican apprenticeship in appropriated rhythms. Afrika Bambaataa, another founding DJ of hip-hop, formed Zulu Nation, bringing DJs, breakdancers and graffiti writers together to end violence. Daring examples of graffiti dazzled the public with their train-long graphics, with the best-known 'masterpiece' belying the graf writers' reputation as vandals: Lee 163, with the Fab 5 crew, painted a whole car of trains with the message 'Merry Christmas, New York.' Some of these maestros of the spray can infiltrated the art world, most notably Jean-Michel Basquiat, who was once known by his tag 'Samo.' Basquiat associated with Andy Warhol and sold his works with the big boys in the go-go art world of the 1980s.

Some of the money snagged in the booming stock markets of the 1980s was spent on art, but even more was blown up the noses of young traders. While Manhattan neighborhoods struggled with the spread of crack cocaine, the city reeled from the impact of addiction, citywide crime and an AIDS epidemic that cut through communities. Mayor Edward Koch could barely keep the lid on the city as homelessness burgeoned and landlords converted cheap old single-room hotels into luxury apartments. Squatters in the East Village fought back when police tried to clear a big homeless encampment, leading to the Tompkins Square Park riots of 1988.

Dot-Com Days

A *Time* magazine cover in 1990 sported a feature story on 'New York: The Rotting Apple.' Still convalescing from the real-estate crash at the end of the 1980s, the city faced crumbling bridges and roads, jobs leaking south and Fortune 500 companies hopping the rivers to suburbia. And then the dot-com market roared in, turning geeks into millionaires and the New York Stock Exchange into a speculator's fun park. Buoyed by tax receipts from IPO (initial public offering) profits, the city launched a frenzy of building, boutiquing and partying unparalleled since the 1920s.

With pro-business, law-and-order Rudy Giuliani as mayor, the dingy and destitute were swept from Manhattan's yuppified streets to the outer boroughs, leaving room for Generation X to score digs and live the high life. Mayor Giuliani grabbed headlines with his campaign to stamp out crime, even kicking the sex shops off notoriously seedy 42nd St. The energetic mayor succeeded in making New York America's safest big city, by targeting high-crime areas, using statistics to focus po-

2001	2002	2005	2008–9
On September 11, terrorist hijackers fly two planes into the Twin Towers, destroying the World Trade Center and killing nearly 3000 people.	Gambino crime family boss John Gotti (the Dapper Don), dies of cancer in prison, while serving a sentence for murder, racketeering, tax evasion and other charges.	Following a feverish bid by the group NYC 2012, founded by local rich guy Daniel Doctoroff, the city loses its bid for the 2012 Olympics.	Barack Obama becomes the first African American president. Later, the stock market crashed due to mismanagement by major American financial institutions.

lice presence, and arresting subway fare-evaders, people committing a minor infringement of city law but who often had other charges pending. In the 1990s crime dropped as a result, powering a huge appetite for nightlife in the city that never sleeps. Restaurants boomed in the spruced-up metropolis, Fashion Week gained global fame, and *Sex and the City* beamed a vision of sophisticated singles in Manolos around the world.

The city threw off the uncertainty of the David Dinkins era, a cautious politician who was NYC's first African American mayor, and residents flaunted the new wealth. To the delight of unionized plumbers, electricians and carpenters, real-estate prices sizzled, setting off a construction spree of new high-rises, converted warehouses and rejuvenated tenements. Areas of the Lower East Side that housed artist storefront galleries in the 1970s and '80s morphed overnight into blocks of gentrified dwellings with double-door security and maintenance charges equal to normal humans' take-home pay. Still, things were faltering in New York at the dawn of the new millennium, and, when that fateful day came in 2001, it forever changed the perspective of both the city and the world.

September 11
On September 11, 2001, terrorists flew two hijacked planes into the World Trade Center's Twin Towers, turning the whole complex into dust and rubble and killing nearly 3000 people. Downtown Manhattan took months to recover from the ghastly fumes wafting from the ruins of the World Trade Center as forlorn missing-person posters grew ragged on brick walls. While the city mourned its dead and recovery crews coughed their way through the debris, it also braved constant terrorist alerts and an anthrax scare. Shock and grief drew people together, uniting the oft-fractious citizenry in a determined effort not to succumb to despair. Before the year was out, community groups were already gathering together in 'Imagine New York' workshops, to develop ideas for renewal and a memorial at the World Trade Center site.

The Noughts in New York
The 10 years after 9/11 were a period of rebuilding – both physically and emotionally. In 2002, then-mayor Michael Bloomberg began the unenviable task of picking up the pieces of a shattered city that had thrust all its support behind his predecessor, mayor Giuliani, whose popularity rose in the wake of September 11. Bloomberg found his critics during his four-year campaign to build a huge sports arena atop the West Side Hwy in an effort to bring the Jets back from Jersey and to score the

The 9/11 terrorist attacks caused an estimated $60 billion in damages to the WTC site, including damage to infrastructure, the subway system and surrounding buildings. It took 3.1 million hours of labor to clean up 1.8 million tons of debris, at a cost of $750 million.

2009	2010	2011	2011
On January 15, US Airways Flight 1549 ditches in the Hudson River after losing engine power. All 150 passengers and 5 crew members are successfully evacuated.	Mayor Michael Bloomberg is sworn into a third term after winning an election that he personally made possible by abolishing the local term-limits law.	On 24 June, New York becomes the sixth US state to legalize same-sex marriage. The act is signed into law by Governor Andrew Cuomo.	The second phase of the High Line opens, effectively doubling its size. A third portion will help revamp the industrial land in the West 30s.

2012 Olympic Games. To the delight of many a New Yorker, who feared traffic build-up and cost blowouts, all three proposals failed to get the go-ahead after state capital Albany refused to supply the estimated $2.2 billion required. Despite this, Bloomberg didn't take a dent in the 2005 elections, comfortably topping Bronx Democrat Fernando Ferrer.

Much to Bloomberg's pleasure, however, New York did see much renovation and reconstruction, especially after the city hit its stride with spiking tourist numbers in 2005. MoMA was completely refurbished, and by the latter part of Bloomberg's second term as mayor, the entire city seemed to be under construction, with luxury high-rise condos sprouting up in every neighborhood.

However, in 2008 the economy buckled under its own weight, in what has largely become known as the global financial crisis. The crisis paralyzed the city, as the cornerstones of the business world were forced to close shop, while anger towards the perceived recklessness of America's financial institutions saw thousands take to the Financial District's Zuccotti Park on September 17, 2011, in a stand against the nation's unfair division of personal wealth. Known as Occupy Wall Street, the protest subsequently spread to hundreds of other cities across the world.

In the same month, the 10th anniversary of the 9/11 attacks was honored with the opening of the National September 11 Memorial, which feature two giant reflecting pools built in the footprints of the collapsed Twin Towers.

Since their initial eviction from Zuccotti Park in November 2011, Occupy Wall Street protestors have carried out numerous demonstrations at NYC landmarks, including Brooklyn Bridge and Grand Central Terminal. For more information on the movement, see www.occupywallst.org.

Superstorm Sandy

New York's resilience would be tested again in 2012 by superstorm Hurricane Sandy. With a state of emergency declared on October 28, much of the city went into virtual shutdown. Low-lying areas were evacuated; bridges, tunnels and schools were closed; and train, subway and air services suspended. While a pre-storm surge on October 28 turned parts of Brooklyn and New Jersey into a New World Venice, Sandy saved her ultimate blow for the following day. Cyclonic winds and drenching rain pounded the city, causing severe flooding and property damage in all five boroughs, including to the NYC subway system, Hugh L Carey Tunnel and World Trade Center site. A major power blackout plunged much of Lower Manhattan into surreal darkness, while trading at the New York Stock Exchange was suspended for two days in its first weather-related closure since 1888. In the neighborhood of Breezy Point, Queens, a devastating storm surge hindered the efforts of firefighters confronted with a blaze that would reduce over 125 homes to ashes. The fire would go down as one of the worst in the NYC's history, while the storm itself would claim 44 lives in the city alone.

2012	2013	2014	2015
Superstorm Sandy hits NYC in October, causing major flooding and property damage, cutting power and shutting down the New York Stock Exchange for two days.	Bill de Blasio wins the NYC mayoral election, defeating opponent Joseph J Lhota and becoming the city's first Democratic mayor in almost 20 years.	The World Trade Center redevelopment nears completion with the opening of the National September 11 Memorial Museum and One World Trade Center.	Expected opening date of the observation decks at One World Trade Center. The decks match the height of those in the original Twin Towers.

The NYC Table

Unlike California, the South or even the Southwest, New York is never really referred to as having one defining cuisine. Ask for some 'New York food' and you could wind up getting anything from a hot dog to a $190 Gallic-inspired tasting menu at Le Bernardin. Cuisine in this multicultural town is global by definition and constantly evolving by its very nature. That said, it's the edibles with the longest histories that folks usually have in mind when they refer to NYC specialties. Those at the top of the list – bagels and pizza – were introduced by Eastern European Jews and Italians, because those groups were among the earliest wave of immigrants here. But it doesn't end there, with egg creams, cheesecake and hot dogs all uncontested staples.

Food Specialties

Hot Dogs

The hot dog made its way to New York via various European butchers in the 1800s. One, Charles Feltman of Germany, was apparently the first to sell them from pushcarts along the Coney Island seashore. But Nathan Handwerker, originally an employee of Feltman's, opened his own shop across the street, offering hot dogs at half the price of those at Feltman's and putting his former employer out of business. Today, the original and legendary Nathan's still stands in Coney Island, while its empire has expanded on an international scale. There is barely a New York neighborhood that does not have at least a few hot-dog vendors on its street corners, although some locals would never touch one of those 'dirty-water dogs,' preferring the new wave of chi-chi hot-dog shops that can be found all over town. Enjoy yours, wherever it's from, with 'the works': smothered with spicy brown mustard, relish, sauerkraut and onions.

There's a plethora of books about NYC's culinary history. Top reads include William Grimes' *Appetite City: A Culinary History of New York*, Arthur Schwartz's *New York City Food: An Opinionated History and More Than 100 Legendary Recipes*, and *Gastropolis: Food & New York City*, edited by Annie Hauck Lawson and Jonathan Deutsch.

Bagels

Bagels may have been invented in Europe, but they were perfected around the turn of the 19th century in NYC – and once you've had one here, you'll have a hard time enjoying one anywhere else. It's a straightforward masterpiece: a ring of plain-yeast dough that's first boiled and then baked, either left plain or topped with various finishing touches, from sesame seeds to chocolate chips. 'Bagels' made in other parts of the country are often just baked and not boiled, which makes them nothing more than a roll with a hole. And even if they do get boiled elsewhere, bagel-makers here claim that it's the New York water that adds an elusive sweetness never to be found anywhere else. Which baker creates the 'best' bagel in New York is a matter of (hotly contested) opinion, but most agree that Manhattan's Ess-a-Bagel, Brooklyn's Bagel Hole and Queens' Brooklyn Bagel & Coffee Company rank pretty high. The most traditionally New York way to order one is by asking for a 'bagel and a schmear,' which will yield you said bagel with a small but thick swipe of cream cheese. Or splurge and add some lox (thinly sliced smoked salmon) as was originally sold from pushcarts on the Lower East Side by Jewish immigrants back in the early 1900s.

CAVAN IMAGES / GETTY IMAGES ©

New York–style pizza

THE NYC TABLE FOOD SPECIALTIES

Bargain-savvy gastronomes love the biannual NYC Restaurant Week. Taking place in January to February and July to August, it sees many of the city's restaurants, including some of its very best, serve up three-course lunches for $25, or three-course dinners for $38. Check www.nycgo.com/restaurantweek for details and reservations.

Pizza

Pizza is certainly not indigenous to Gotham. But New York–style pizza is a very particular item, and the first pizzeria in America was Lombardi's in Manhattan's Little Italy, which opened in 1905.

While Chicago–style pizza is 'deep dish' and Californian tends to be light and doughy, New York prides itself on pizza with a thin crust and an even thinner layer of sauce, and triangular slices (unless they're Sicilian-style, in which case they're rectangular). Pizza made its way over to New York in the 1900s through Italian immigrants and its regional style soon developed, the thin crust allowing for faster cooking time in a city where everyone is always in a hurry.

Today there are pizza parlors about every 10 blocks, especially in Manhattan and most of Brooklyn, where you'll find standard slices for $3. The style at each place varies slightly – some places touting cracker-thin crust, others offering slightly thicker and chewier versions, and plenty of nouveau styles throwing everything from shrimp to cherries on top. The city's booming locavore movement has also made its mark, with hipster pizzerias such as Roberta's in Brooklyn peddling wood-fired pies topped with sustainable, local produce.

Egg Creams

Now don't go expecting eggs or cream in this frothy, old-school beverage – just milk, seltzer water and plenty of chocolate syrup (preferably the classic Fox's U-Bet brand, made in Brooklyn). When Louis Auster of Brooklyn, who owned soda fountains on the Lower East Side, invented the treat back in 1890, the syrup he used was indeed made with eggs and he added cream to thicken the concoction. The name stuck, even though the ingredients were modified, and soon they were a staple of every soda fountain in New York. While Mr Auster sold them for 3¢ apiece, today they'll cost you anywhere from $1.50 to $4.50, depending on where you find one – which could be from old-school institutions such as Katz's Delicatessen in the Lower East Side or Tom's Restaurant in Brooklyn.

New York–Style Cheesecake

Sure, cheesecake, in one form or another, has been baked and eaten in Europe since the 1400s. But New Yorkers, as they do with many things, have appropriated its history in the form of the New York–style cheesecake.

This version of the cheesecake was immortalized by Lindy's restaurant in Midtown, opened by Leo Lindemann in 1921, and the particular type of confection served there – made of cream cheese, heavy cream, a dash of vanilla and a cookie crust – became wildly popular in the '40s. Today,

NYC Master Chef Cookbooks

Daniel: My French Cuisine (Daniel Boulud & Sylvie Bigar)

The Babbo Cookbook (Mario Batali)

Momofuku (David Chang & Peter Meehan)

Payard Desserts (Francois Payard & Tish Boyle)

you'll find this local favorite on many dessert menus, whether you're at a Greek diner or haute cuisine hot spot. The most famous (and arguably best) cheesecake in town is that from Brooklyn stalwart Junior's.

Urban Farm to Table

Having perfected the fast, New York City is rediscovering the slow. In recent years, a growing number of city rooftops, backyards and community gardens have been transformed into urban farms, turning America's biggest concrete jungle into an unlikely food bowl. While you can expect to find anything from organic tomatoes atop Upper East Side delis to beehives on East Village tenement rooftops, the current queen of the crop is Brooklyn Grange (www.brooklyngrangefarm.com), an organic farm covering two rooftops in Long Island City and the Brooklyn Navy Yards. At 108,000 sq ft, it's purportedly the world's biggest rooftop farm, growing everything from carrots and beans to 40 varieties of tomatoes. The project is the brainchild of young farmer Ben Flanner. Obsessed with farm-to-table eating, this former E*Trade marketing manager kick-started NYC's rooftop revolution in 2009 with the opening of its first rooftop soil farm – Eagle Street Rooftop Farm – in nearby Greenpoint. Flanner's collaborators include dining hotspots like Brooklyn's Marlow & Sons, and Roberta's, where the menus proudly showcase this homegrown goodness.

Food truck fans with a smartphone can download the free Tweat.it app, which offers real-time information on food truck locations, specials and discounts. Don't have a smartphone? Get the lowdown at www.tweat.it.

Drinks Specialties

Cocktails

New York City is a master of mixed libations. After all, this is the home of Manhattans, legendary speakeasies and Cosmo-clutching columnists with a passion for fashion. Legend has it that the city's namesake drink, Manhattan – a blend of whiskey, sweet vermouth and bitters – began life on the southeast corner of 26th St and Madison Ave, at the long-gone Manhattan Club. The occasion was a party in 1874, allegedly

---

THE COFFEE LOWDOWN

Adam Craig, Founder of Specialty Coffee Shop Culture Espresso, shares his tips on the NYC coffee scene:

What are your coffee shop recommendations? In Manhattan, definitely try Ninth Street Espresso in the East Village, Third Rail in the West Village and Stumptown Coffee Roasters in Midtown. In Brooklyn, top specialty spots include my former cafe Variety in Greenpoint, Cafe Peddler in Carroll Gardens, and Williamsburg's pioneering Cafe El Beit. Williamsburg is also home to Bay Area roaster Blue Bottle Coffee. In Astoria, Queens, head to Queens Kickshaw.

What do the coffee cognoscenti drink? Most commonly, espresso-machine drinks made using single-origin coffee; coffee sourced from a specific geographic region. African-sourced coffee is a little more citrus-like, South American varieties are nuttier and more full-bodied, while Asian coffee often has 'blueberry' and 'chocolate' coming through. Non-espresso drinks include the light-bodied 'pour over,' in which coffee is extracted through a cone over two-and-a-half to three minutes, and the 'Chemex coffee,' a filtered variety whose tea-like consistency highlights the subtler nuances of the beans.

And on a hot day? Wised-up New Yorkers opt for a 'cold brew,' prepared using two different methods. The first, known as 'full immersion', is made by steeping coarsely ground coffee in water for 16 hours to create a concentrate. The concentrate is then brought back with water to create a drink that's full-bodied, chocolatey and low in acidity. The second method, called 'Kyoto cold drip,' sees coffee passed through a ceramic filter at about one drop every two seconds for 16 to 18 hours. The result, served on ice, is super concentrated and akin to drinking cognac.

thrown by Jennie Churchill (mother of British Prime Minister Winston) to celebrate Samuel J Tilden's victory in the New York gubernatorial election. One of the barmen decided to create a drink to mark the occasion, naming it in honor of the bar.

Another New York classic was born that very year – the summer-centric Tom Collins. A mix of dry gin, sugar, lemon juice and club soda, the long drink's name stems from an elaborate hoax in which hundreds of locals were informed that a certain Tom Collins had been sullying their good names. While many set out to track him down, clued-in bartenders relished the joke by making the drink and naming it for the fictitious troublemaker. When the aggrieved stormed into the bars looking for a Tom Collins, they were served the drink to cool their tempers.

These days, NYC's kicking cocktail scene is big on rediscovered recipes, historical anecdotes and vintage speakeasy style. Once obscure bartenders like Harry Johnson and Jerry Thomas are now born-again legends, their vintage concoctions revived by a new generation of braces-clad mixologists. Historic ingredients like Crème de Violette, Old Tom gin and Batavia Arrack are back in vogue. In the Financial District, cocktail bar Dead Rabbit has gone one further, reintroducing the 17th-century practice of pop inns, drinks that fuse ale, liqueurs, spices and botanicals.

Then there are the city's revered single-spirit establishments, among them tequila- and mezcal-focused Mayahuel in the East Village and the self-explanatory Rum House in Midtown. The latter is known for its stash of Black Tot – a rare, last-consignment rum produced by the Royal British Navy (and yours for $150 a pour).

City Harvest (www.cityharvest.org) is a nonprofit organization that distributes unused food to over a million struggling New Yorkers each year. A whopping 126,000lb of food is rescued daily from city restaurants, bakeries and catering companies. Individuals wanting to make a monetary donation can do so via the City Harvest website.

Borough Brews

Beer brewing was once a thriving industry in the city – by the 1870s, Brooklyn boasted a belly-swelling 48 breweries. Most of these were based in Williamsburg, Bushwick and Greenpoint, neighborhoods packed with German immigrants with extensive brewing know-how. By the eve of Prohibition in 1919, the borough was one of the country's leading beer peddlers, as famous for kids carrying growlers (beer jugs) as for its bridges. By the end of Prohibition in 1933, most breweries had shut shop. And while the industry rose from the ashes in WWII, local flavor gave in to big-gun Midwestern brands.

Fast-forward to today and Brooklyn is once more a catchword for a decent brewski as a handful of craft breweries put integrity back on tap. Head of the pack is Brooklyn Brewery, whose seasonal offerings include a Post Road Pumpkin Ale (available August to November) and a luscious Black Chocolate Stout (a take on Imperial Stout, available October to March). The brewery's top comrades-in-craft are Sixpoint Craft Ales (www.sixpoint.com) and Kelso of Brooklyn (www.kelsoofbrooklyn.com), both of which also offer year-round classics and seasonal treats.

Not to be outdone, rival borough Queens is also abuzz with a string of new artisan breweries, from beach-born Rockaway Brewing Company (www.rockawaybrewco.com) to fusion meister Beyond Kombucha (www.beyondkombucha.com), the latter known for its fermented teas and sweet 'n' sour ale Mava Roka. Leading the Queens charge, however, is SingleCut Beersmiths (www.singlecutbeer.com), whose launch in 2012 saw Queens welcome its first brewery since Prohibition. Currently the borough's biggest player, its offerings include a highly hopped Billy Half-Stack IPA and a decadent, caffeine-inflected seasonal black called John Michael Dark Lyric Lagrrr!.

For the curious and the parched, there's no shortage of drinking holes to sip some NYC suds, among them Brooklyn's Spuyten Duyvil, Queens' Astoria Bier & Cheese, and Manhattan's Keg No 229 and Harlem Public.

The first public brewery in America was established by colonial governor Peter Minuit (1580–1638) at the Market (Marckvelt) field in what is now known as the Financial District in Lower Manhattan. Minuit is credited with 'purchasing' Manhattan from the native Lenape people in May 1626.

The Arts

The spectacles of Broadway; the gleaming white-box galleries of Chelsea; joints playing jazz, music halls blaring moody indie rock and opera houses that bellow melodramatic tales. For more than a century, NYC has been America's capital of cultural production. And while gentrification has pushed many artists out to the city's fringes and beyond, New York nonetheless remains a nerve center for the visual arts, music, theater, dance and literature.

NYC: An Art Heavyweight

That New York City claims some of the world's mightiest art museums attests to its enviable artistic pedigree. From Pollock and Rothko, to Warhol and Rauschenberg, the city has nourished many of America's greatest artists and artistic movements.

On any given week, New York is home to countless art exhibits, installations and performances. Get a comprehensive listing of happenings at www.nyart beat.com.

Birth of an Arts Hub

In almost all facets of the arts, New York really got its sea legs in the early 20th century, when the city attracted and retained a critical mass of thinkers, artists, writers and poets. It was at this time that the homegrown art scene began to take shape. In 1905, photographer (and husband of Georgia O'Keeffe) Alfred Stieglitz opened 'Gallery 291,' a Fifth Ave space that provided a vital platform for American artists and helped establish photography as a credible art form.

In the 1940s, an influx of cultural figures fleeing the carnage of WWII saturated the city with fresh ideas – and New York became an important cultural hub. Peggy Guggenheim established the Art of this Century gallery on 57th St, a space that helped launch the careers of painters like Jackson Pollock, Willem De Kooning and Robert Motherwell. These Manhattan-based artists came to form the core of the Abstract Expressionist movement (also known as the New York School), creating an explosive and rugged form of painting that changed the course of modern art as we know it.

An American Avant-Garde

The Abstract Expressionists helped establish New York as a global arts center. Another generation of artists then carried the ball. In the 1950s and '60s, Robert Rauschenberg, Jasper Johns and Lee Bontecou turned paintings into off-the-wall sculptural constructions that included everything from welded steel to taxidermy goats. By the mid-1960s, pop art – a movement that utilized the imagery and production techniques of popular culture – had taken hold, with Andy Warhol at the helm.

By the '60s and '70s, when New York's economy was in the dumps and much of SoHo lay in a state of decay, the city became a hotbed of conceptual and performance art. Gordon Matta-Clark sliced up abandoned buildings with chainsaws and the artists of Fluxus staged happenings on downtown streets. Carolee Schneeman organized performances that utilized the human body. At one famous 1964 event, she had a crew of nude dancers roll around in an unappetizing mix of paint, sausages and dead fish in the theater of a Greenwich Village church.

Art Now

Today, the arts scene is mixed and wide-ranging. The major institutions – the Metropolitan Museum of Art, the Museum of Modern Art, the Whitney Museum, the Guggenheim Museum and the Brooklyn Museum – show major retrospectives covering everything from Renaissance portraiture to contemporary installation. The New Museum, on the Lower East Side, is more daring, while countless smaller institutions, such as the excellent Bronx Museum, El Museo del Barrio and the Studio Museum in Harlem, focus on narrower slices of art history.

The gallery scene is equally diffuse, with more than 800 spaces showcasing all kinds of art all over NYC. The blue chip dealers can be found clustered in Chelsea and the Upper East Side. Galleries that showcase emerging and mid-career artists dot the Lower East Side, while the most experimental happenings generally take place in the old warehouses and basements of Brooklyn neighborhood Bushwick.

Graffiti & Street Art

Contemporary graffiti as we know it was cultivated in NYC. In the 1970s, the graffiti-covered subway train became a potent symbol of the city and work by figures such as Dondi, Blade and Lady Pink became known around the world. In addition, fine artists such as Jean-Michel Basquiat, Kenny Scharf and Keith Haring began incorporating elements of graffiti into their work.

The movement received new life in the late 1990s when a new generation of artists – many with art school pedigrees – began using materials such as cut paper and sculptural elements (all illicitly). Well-known New York City artists working in this vein include John Fekner, Stephen 'Espo' Powers, Swoon and the twin-brother duo Skewville.

Less celebratory was the 2013 closure of the iconic 5Pointz; a cluster of Long Island City warehouses dripping with Technicolor graffiti. Not even a plea from legendary British artist Banksy could save the veritable gallery, condemned to demolition. These days, spray-can and stencil hotspots include the Brooklyn side of the Williamsburg Bridge and the Brooklyn neighborhood of Bushwick.

A Musical Metropolis

This is the city where jazz players like Ornette Coleman, Miles Davis and John Coltrane pushed the limits of improvisation in the '50s. It's where various Latin sounds – from cha-cha-cha to rumba to mambo – came together to form the hybrid we now call salsa, where folk singers like Bob Dylan and Joan Baez crooned protest songs in coffeehouses, and where bands like the New York Dolls and the Ramones tore up the stage in Manhattan's gritty downtown. It was the ground zero of disco. And it was the cultural crucible where hip-hop was nurtured and grew – then exploded.

The city remains a magnet for musicians to this day. The local indie rock scene is especially vibrant: groups such as the Yeah Yeah Yeahs, LCD Soundsystem and Animal Collective all emerged out of NYC. Williamsburg is at the heart of the action, packed with clubs and bars, as well as indie record labels and internet radio stations. The best venues for rock include the Music Hall of Williamsburg and the Brooklyn Bowl, as well as Manhattan's Bowery Ballroom.

Brooklyn has a hopping indie music scene, with local bands performing regularly in Williamsburg and Bushwick. To hear the latest sounds, log on to www.newtown radio.com.

All That Jazz

Jazz, too, remains a juggernaut – from the traditional to the experimental. The best bets for jazz are the Village Vanguard in the West Village and the Jazz Standard near Madison Square Park. For more highbrow programming, there's Midtown's Jazz at Lincoln Center, which is run by trumpeter Wynton Marsalis, and features a wide array of solo outings by important musicians, as well as tribute concerts to figures such as Dizzy Gillespie and Thelonious Monk.

Classical & Opera

At Lincoln Center you'll find the classics. Here, the Metropolitan Opera puts on a wide array of well-known operas, from Verdi's *Aida* to Mozart's *Don Giovanni*. It is also here that the legendary New York Philharmonic is based (the symphony that was once directed by one of the 20th century's great maestros, Leonard Bernstein). Carnegie Hall, the Merkin Concert Hall and the Frick Collection also offer wonderful – and more intimate – spaces to enjoy great classical music.

For more avant-garde fare, try the Center for Contemporary Opera and the Brooklyn Academy of Music (BAM) – the latter is now one of the city's vital opera and classical music hubs. Another excellent venue, featuring highly experimental work, is St Ann's Warehouse in Brooklyn. If you like your performance *outré*, keep an eye on their calendar.

For comprehensive coverage of the American jazz scene log on to www.jazztimes.com, which features plenty of stories about all the established and rising New York acts.

THE ARTS ON BROADWAY & BEYOND

On Broadway & Beyond

In the early 20th century, clusters of theaters settled into the area around Times Square and began producing popular plays and suggestive comedies – a movement that had its roots in early vaudeville. By the 1920s, these messy works had evolved into on-stage spectacles like *Show Boat*, an all-out Oscar Hammerstein production about the lives of performers on a Mississippi steamboat. In 1943, Broadway had its first runaway hit – *Oklahoma!* – that remained on stage for a record 2212 performances.

Today, Broadway musicals, shown in one of 40 official Broadway theaters, the lavish early 20th-century jewels that surround Times Square, are a major component of cultural life in New York. If you're on a budget, look for off-Broadway productions. These tend to be more intimate, inexpensive, and often just as good.

A NEW YORK HIP-HOP PLAYLIST

New York is the cradle of hip-hop. Rap to the following classics from the city's finest:

'Rapper's Delight,' Sugarhill Gang (1979) The single that launched the commercial birth of hip-hop, from a New York–New Jersey trio

'White Lines,' Grandmaster Flash and the Furious Five (1983) The ultimate '80s party song from the Bronx

'It's Like That,' Run DMC (1983) That's just the way it is from the legendary Queens trio

'Fat Boys,' Fat Boys (1984) Brooklyn's ultimate beat-boxers

'No Sleep 'Til Brooklyn,' Beastie Boys (1986) The NYC trio who fought for their right to party

'Ain't No Half Steppin',' Big Daddy Kane (1988) Mellifluous rhymes from a Brooklyn master

'Shoop,' Salt-n-Pepa (1994) The Queens of Rap hail from Queens, New York

'In Da Club,' 50 Cent (2003) A global party hit produced by a rapper from South Jamaica, Queens

'99 Problems,' Jay-Z (2004) This Bed-Stuy, Brooklyn, boy is now a music mogul

NYC also bursts with theatrical offerings beyond Broadway, from Shakespeare to David Mamet to rising experimental playwrights such as Young Jean Lee. In addition to Midtown staples like Playwrights Horizons and Second Stage Theatre, the Lincoln Center theaters are hubs for works by modern and contemporary playwrights.

The Public Theater, BAM, Performance Space 122 and St Ann's Warehouse all offer edgier programming. Numerous festivals, such as Fringe NYC and Performa, the performance art biennial (held in the fall in odd years), offer good opportunities to see new work.

Bust a Move: Dance & the City

For nearly 100 years, the city has been at the center of American dance. It is here that the American Ballet Theatre (ABT) – led by the fabled George Balanchine – was founded in 1949. The company promoted the idea of cultivating American talent, hiring native-born dancers and putting on works by choreographers such as Jerome Robbins, Twyla Tharp and Alvin Ailey. The company continues to perform in New York and around the world.

But NYC is perhaps best known for nurturing a generation of modern dance choreographers – figures like Martha Graham, who challenged traditional notions of dance with boxy, industrial movements on bare, almost abstract sets. The boundaries were pushed ever further by Merce Cunningham, who disassociated dance from music. Today, companies such as STREB are pushing dance to its limits.

Lincoln Center and BAM host regular performances, and up-and-coming acts feature at spaces like Chelsea's Kitchen, Joyce Theater and New York Live Arts, and Midtown's Baryshnikov Arts Center.

New York in Letters

The city that is home to the country's biggest publishing houses has also been home to some of its best-known writers. In the 19th century, Herman Melville (*Moby Dick*), Edith Wharton (*The House of Mirth*) and Walt Whitman (*Leaves of Grass*) all congregated here. But things really got cooking in the early part of the 20th century. There were the liquor-fueled literary salons of poet-communist John Reed in the 1910s, the acerbic wisecracks of the Algonquin Round Table in the 1920s and the thinly-veiled novels of Dawn Powell in the '40s, a figure whose work often critiqued New York's media establishment.

The 1950s and '60s saw the rise of writers who began to question the status quo. Poet Langston Hughes examined the condition of African Americans in Harlem and Beat poets like Allen Ginsburg rejected traditional rhyme in favor of free-flowing musings. The last few decades of the 20th century offered a wide gamut to choose from, including chronicler of the greed and coke-fueled '80s (Jay McInerney) to new voices from underrepresented corners of the city (Piri Thomas, Audre Lorde).

NYC scribes continue to cover a vast array of realities in their work – from zombies (Colson Whitehead) and postmodern narrative techniques (Jennifer Egan), to the crazy impossibility that is New York (Michael Chabon). Hint: pick up a copy of *The Amazing Adventures of Kavalier & Clay*.

The New York Public Library and BAM host widely attended lectures and readings.

For comprehensive theater listings, news and reviews (both glowing and scathing), click onto www.nytimes.com/pages/theater.

Architecture

New York's architectural history is a layer cake of ideas and styles – one that is literally written on the city's streets. Humble colonial farmhouses and graceful Federal-style buildings can be found alongside ornate beaux arts palaces from the early 20th century. There are the revivals (Greek, Gothic, Romanesque and Renaissance) and the unadorned forms of the International Style. And, in recent years, there has been the addition of the torqued forms of deconstructivist architects. For the architecture buff, it's a bonanza. Welcome to New York.

Colonial Foundations

New York's architectural roots are modest. Early Dutch colonial farmhouses were all about function: clapboard-wood homes with shingled, gambrel roofs were positioned to take advantage of daylight and retain heat in winter. A number of these have somehow survived to the present.

Above Grand Central Terminal (p186)

The most remarkable is the Pieter Claesen Wyckoff House in East Flatbush, Brooklyn. Originally built in 1652 (with additions made over the years), it is the oldest house in the entire city.

After the Dutch colony of New Netherlands became the British colony of New York in 1664, architectural styles moved to Georgian. Boxy, brick and stone structures with hipped roofs began to materialize. In the northern Manhattan district of Inwood, the Morris-Jumel Mansion from 1765 is an altered example of this: the home was built in the Georgian style by Roger Morris, then purchased by Stephen Jumel, who added a neoclassical facade in the 19th century. Another British colonial building of interest is the Fraunces Tavern, where George Washington bid an emotional farewell to the officers who had accompanied him throughout the American Revolution. Today the structure contains a museum and restaurant.

On the ceremonial end is St Paul's Chapel, south of City Hall Park. Built in the 1760s, it is the oldest surviving church in the city. Its design was inspired by the much bigger St Martin-in-the-Fields church in London.

AIA Guide to New York (5th edition) is a comprehensive guide to the most significant buildings in the city.

Architecture in the Early Republic

In the early 1800s, architecture grew lighter and more refined. The so-called Federal style employed classical touches – slim, columned entrances, triangular pediments at the roof line and rounded fanlights over doors and windows. Some of the best surviving examples are tied to municipal government. City Hall, built in 1812, owes its French form to émigré architect Joseph François Mangin and its Federal detailing to American-born John McComb Jr. The interior contains an airy rotunda and curved cantilevered stairway.

Uptown, on the Upper East Side, Gracie Mansion (1799), the official residence of New York City's mayor since 1942, offers a fine example of a Federal residence, with its broad, river-view porch and leaded glass sidelights. This stretch of riverfront was once lined with buildings of the sort – a sight that impressed Alexis de Tocqueville during his tour of the United States in the early 19th century.

Other Federal-style specimens include the James Watson House (1793), at 7 State Street right across from Battery Park, and the Merchant's House Museum (1832), in NoHo. The latter still contains its intact interiors.

Greek, Gothic & Romanesque: The Revivals

Following the publication of an important treatise on Greek architecture in the late 1700s, architects began to show a renewed interest in pure, classical forms. In the US, a big instigator of this trend was Minard Lafever, a New Jersey–born carpenter-turned-architect-turned-author-of-pattern-books. By the 1830s, becolumned Greek Revival structures were going up all over New York.

Manhattan contains a bevy of these buildings, including the gray granite St Peter's Church (1838) and the white-marble Federal Hall National Memorial (1842) – both of which are located in the Financial District. In Greenwich Village, a row of colonnaded homes built on the north side of Washington Square (Numbers 1–13) in the 1820s are fine residential interpretations of this style.

Starting in the late 1830s, the simple Georgian and Federal styles started to give way to more ornate structures that employed Gothic and Romanesque elements. This was particularly prominent in church construction. An early example was the Church of the Ascension (1841) in Greenwich Village – an imposing brownstone structure studded with

The Chrysler Building (p183)

pointed arches and a crenelated tower. The same architect – Richard Upjohn – also designed downtown Manhattan's Trinity Church (1846) in the same style.

By the 1860s, these places of worship were growing in size and scale. Among the most resplendent are St Patrick's Cathedral (1853–79), which took over an entire city block at Fifth Ave and 51st St, and the perpetually under construction Cathedral Church of St John the Divine (1911–), in Morningside Heights. Indeed, the style was so popular that one of the city's most important icons – the Brooklyn Bridge (1870–83) – was built à la Gothic Revival.

Romanesque elements (such as curved arches) can be spotted on structures all over the city. Some of the most famous include the Joseph Papp Public Theater (formerly the Astor Library) in Greenwich Village, built between 1853 and 1881, and the breathtaking Temple Emanu-El (1927–29) on Fifth Ave on the Upper East Side.

The Beauty of Beaux Arts

At the turn of the 20th century, New York entered a gilded age. Robber barons such as JP Morgan, Henry Clay Frick and John D Rockefeller – awash in steel and oil money – built themselves lavish manses. Public buildings grew ever more extravagant in scale and ornamentation. Architects, many of whom trained in France, came back with European design ideals. Gleaming white limestone began to replace all the brownstone, first stories were elevated to allow for dramatic staircase entrances, and buildings were adorned with sculptured keystones and Corinthian columns.

McKim Mead & White's Villard Houses, from 1884 (now the Palace Hotel), show the movement's early roots. Loosely based on Rome's

Esteemed New York architecture critic Ada Louise Huxtable gathers some of her most important essays in the book *On Architecture: Collected Reflections on a Century of Change.*

One World Trade Center

Palazzo della Cancelleria, they channeled the symmetry and elegance of the Italian Renaissance. Other classics include the central branch of the New York Public Library (1911) designed by Carrère and Hastings, the 1902 extension of the Metropolitan Museum of Art by Richard Morris Hunt, and Warren and Wetmore's stunning Grand Central Station (1913), which is capped by a statue of Mercury, the god of commerce.

Reaching Skyward

By the time New York settled into the 20th century, elevators and steel-frame engineering had allowed the city to grow up – literally. This period saw a building-boom of skyscrapers, starting with Cass Gilbert's neo-Gothic 57-story Woolworth Building (1913). To this day it remains one of the 50 tallest buildings in the United States.

Public Art: New York by Jean Parker Phifer, with photos by Francis Dzikowski, is an informative guide to the city's public monuments.

Others soon followed. In 1930, the Chrysler Building, the 77-story art deco masterpiece designed by William Van Alen, became the world's tallest structure. The following year, the record was broken by the Empire State Building, a clean-lined art deco monolith crafted from Indiana limestone. Its spire was meant to be used as mooring mast for dirigibles – an idea that made for good publicity, but which proved to be impractical and unfeasible.

Modernism & Beyond

During WWII, the city became the center of everything. Displaced European architects and other thinkers landed here and, when the war was over, many chose to remain in the US, creating a lively dialogue between American and European architects. This was a period when urban planner Robert Moses furiously rebuilt vast swaths of New York – to the detriment of many neighborhoods – and designers and artists became obsessed with the clean, unadorned lines of the International Style.

One of the earliest projects in this vein were the UN buildings (1947–52), the combined effort of a committee of architects, including the Swiss-born Le Corbusier, Brazil's Oscar Niemeyer and America's Wallace K Harrison. The Secretariat employed New York's first glass curtain wall – which looms over the ski-slope curve of the General Assembly. Other significant Modernist structures from this period include Gordon Bunshaft's Lever House (1950–52), a floating, glassy structure on Park Ave and 54th St, and Mies van der Rohe's austere, 38-story Seagram Building (1956–58), located just two blocks to the south.

While these designs remain elegant, the glut in glass-box architecture resulted in a million lookalike buildings. By the late 20th century, some architects began to rebel against the hard-edged nature of Modernist design. In 1984, Philip Johnson – a figure who created more than his share of glass boxes over the course of his career – produced the pink granite AT&T Building (now the Sony Building), capping its roofline with a scrolled, neo-Georgian pediment. It mightn't be universally loved, but it certainly stands out from the crowd.

Bring on the Starchitects

The types of non-rectilinear deconstructivist buildings (as in Frank Gehry's billowy museum in Bilbao) that began to appear in other parts of the world in the mid-1990s were late getting to New York. Between the tight spaces, expensive real estate and labyrinthine nature of zoning and construction, it is a wonder that anything gets built at all. A prime example of this is the World Trade Center site, where Daniel Libeskind's twisting, angular design for the One World Trade Center tower was replaced by a boxier architecture-by-committee glass obelisk. On the same site, budget blowouts led to tweaks of Santiago Calatrava's luminous design for the WTC Transportation Hub. According to critics, what should have looked like a dove in flight now resembles a winged dinosaur. Gehry did at least get to indulge his post-structuralist tendencies with New York by Gehry (2011), a rippling 76-floor apartment tower in Lower Manhattan.

Controversies aside, New York has seen the arrival of some daring recent additions, from new kid Barclays Center (2012) – a ribbony, sci-fi arena in downtown Brooklyn – to Norman Foster's trailblazing Hearst Tower (2006), a glass tower zigzagging its way out of a 1920s sandstone structure in Midtown. Between them is a string of arresting designs, including Gehry's IAC Building (2007), a billowing white-glass structure that the locals like to compare to a wedding cake, and Renzo Piano's New York Times Building (2007), a 52-story building armored in ceramic rods. Renzo is also behind the Whitney Museum's new home in the Meatpacking District; a boldly asymmetrical structure due for completion in 2015. Eight blocks to the north is Jean Nouvel's luxe condo building 100 Eleventh Ave (2009), famed for its exuberant arrangement of angled windows. Yet even Nouvel's statement is no match for the visual drama of architect Thom Mayne's 41 Cooper Square (2009) in the East Village. With folds and slashes evoking an earthquake in motion, the building serves as a perfect metaphor for a restless megalopolis, driven to constant rebuilding and reinvention.

Painting the Town Pink

New York City is out and damn proud. It was here that the Stonewall Riots took place, that the modern gay rights movement bloomed and that America's first Pride march hit the streets. Yet even before the days of 'Gay Lib,' the city had a knack for all things queer and fabulous, from Bowery sex saloons and Village Sapphic poetry to drag balls in Harlem. It hasn't always been smooth sailing, but it's always been one hell of a ride.

Before Stonewall

Subversion in the Villages

By the 1890s, New York City's rough-and-ready Lower East Side had established quite a reputation for scandalous 'resorts' – dancing halls, saloons and brothels – frequented by the city's 'inverts' and 'fairies.' From Paresis Hall at 5th St and Bowery to Slide at 157 Bleecker St, these venues offered everything from cross-dressing spectaculars and dancing to backrooms for same-sex shenanigans. For closeted middle-class men, these dens were a secret thrill – places reached undercover on trains for a fix of camaraderie, understanding and uninhibited fun. For curious middle-class straights, they were just as enticing – salacious destinations on voyeuristic 'slumming tours.'

As New York strode into the 20th century, writers and bohemians began stepping into Greenwich Village, lured by the area's cheap rents and romantically crooked streets. The unconventionality and free thinking the area became known for turned the Village into an Emerald City for gays and lesbians, a place with no shortage of bachelor pads, more tolerant attitudes and – with the arrival of Prohibition – an anything-goes speakeasy scene. A number of gay-owned businesses lined MacDougal St, among them the legendary Eve's Hangout at number 129. A tearoom run by Polish Jewish immigrant Eva Kotchever (Eve Addams), it was famous for two things: poetry readings and a sign on the door that read 'Men allowed but not welcome.' There would have been little chance of welcome drinks when police raided the place in June 1926, charging Eve with 'obscenity' for penning her Lesbian Love anthology, and deporting her back to Europe. Three years later, Eve was honored by a Greenwich Village theater group, who staged a theatrical version of her book at Play Mart, a basement performance space on Christopher St.

Divas, Drag & Harlem

While Times Square had also developed a reputation for attracting gay men – many of them working in the district's theaters, restaurants and speakeasy bars – the hottest gay scene in the 1920s was further north in Harlem. The neighborhood's flourishing music scene included numerous gay and lesbian performers, among them Gladys Bentley and Ethel Waters. Bentley – who was as famous for her tuxedos and girlfriends as she was for her singing – had moved her way up from one-off performances at cellar clubs and tenement parties to headlining a revue at the famous Ubangi Club on 133rd St, where her supporting acts included a chorus line of female impersonators.

Even more famous were Harlem's drag balls, which had become a hit with both gay and straight New Yorkers in the Roaring Twenties. The biggest of the lot was the Hamilton Lodge Ball, organized by Lodge #710 of the Grand United Order of Odd Fellows and held annually at the swank Rockland Palace on 155th St. Commonly dubbed the Faggot's Ball, it was a chance for both gay men and women to (legally) cross-dress and steal a same-sex dance, and for fashionable 'normals' to indulge in a little voyeuristic titillation. The evening's star attraction was the beauty pageant, which saw the drag-clad competitors compete for the title of 'Queen of the Ball.' Langston Hughes proclaimed it the 'spectacles of color' and the gay writer was one of many members of New York's literati to attend the ball. It was also attended by everyone from prostitutes to high-society families, including the Astors and the Vanderbilts. Even the papers covered the extravaganza, its outrageous frocks the talk of the town.

Stonewall Revolution

Alas, the relative transgression of the early 20th century was replaced with a new conservatism in the following decades, as the Great Depression, WWII and the Cold War took their toll. Conservatism was helped along by Senator Joseph 'Joe' McCarthy, who declared that homosexuals in the State Department threatened America's security and children. Tougher policing aimed to eradicate queer visibility in the public sphere, forcing the scene further underground in the 1940s and '50s. Although crackdowns on gay venues had always occurred, they became increasingly common.

Yet when on June 28, 1969, eight police officers raided the Stonewall Inn – a gay-friendly watering hole in Greenwich Village – patrons did the unthinkable: they revolted. Fed up with both the harassment and corrupt officers receiving payoffs from the bars' owners (who were mostly organized crime figures), they began bombarding the officers with coins, bottles, bricks and chants of 'gay power' and 'we shall overcome.' They were also met by a line of high-kicking drag queens and their now legendary chant, 'We are the Stonewall girls, we wear our hair in curls, we wear no underwear, we show our pubic hair, we wear our dungarees, above our nelly knees...'.

Their collective anger and solidarity was a turning point, igniting intense and passionate debate about discrimination and forming the catalyst for the modern gay rights movement, not just in New York, but across the US and in countries from the Netherlands to Australia.

LGBT HISTORY

1927

New York State amends a public-obscenity code to include a ban on the appearance or discussion of gay people onstage in reaction to the increasing visibility of gays on Broadway.

1966

On April 21, gay rights organization Mattachine Society stages a 'Sip-In' at NYC's oldest gay drinking hole, Julius Bar, challenging a ban on serving alcohol to LGBT people.

1969

Police officers raid the Stonewall Inn in Greenwich Village on June 28, sparking a riot that lasts several days and gives birth to the modern gay rights movement.

1987

ACT UP is founded to challenge the US government's slow response in dealing with AIDS. The activist group stages its first major demonstration on March 24 on Wall St.

2011

New York's Marriage Equality Act comes into effect at 12.01am on July 24. A lesbian couple from Buffalo take their vows just seconds after midnight in Niagara Falls.

2013

Homophobic hate crimes in New York City increase significantly from 2012. On May 18, a 32-year-old gay man is abused and shot dead in Greenwich Village.

In the Shadow of AIDS

LGBT activism intensified as HIV and AIDS hit world headlines in the early 1980s. Faced with ignorance, fear and the moral indignation of those who saw AIDS as a 'gay cancer,' activists such as writer Larry Kramer set about tackling what was quickly becoming an epidemic. Out of his efforts was born ACT UP (AIDS Coalition to Unleash Power) in 1987, an advocacy group set up to fight the perceived homophobia and indifference of then President Ronald Reagan, as well as to end the price gouging of AIDS drugs by pharmaceutical companies. One of its boldest protests took place on September 14, 1989, when seven ACT UP protestors chained themselves to the VIP balcony of the New York Stock Exchange, demanding pharmaceutical company Burroughs Wellcome lower the price of AIDS drug AZT from a prohibitive $10,000 per patient per annum. Within days, the price was slashed to $6400 per patient.

The epidemic itself had a significant impact on New York's artistic community. Among its most high-profile victims were artist Keith Haring, photographer Robert Mapplethorpe and fashion designer Halston. Yet out of this loss grew a tide of powerful AIDS-related plays and musicals that would not only win broad international acclaim, but would become part of America's mainstream cultural canon. Among these are Tony Kushner's political epic *Angels in America* and Jonathan Larson's rock musical *Rent*. Both works would win Tony Awards and the Pulitzer Prize.

A Chorus Line was the first musical to highlight a gay narrative. The show debuted at the Shubert Theatre in 1975, running for 15 years.

Wedding Bells, Alarm Bells

The LGBT fight for complete equality took two massive steps forward in 2011. On September 20, a federal law banning LGBT military personnel from serving openly – the so-called 'Don't Ask, Don't Tell' policy – was repealed after years of intense lobbying. Three months earlier persistence had led to an even greater victory – the right to marry. On June 15, by a margin of 80 to 63, that the New York State Assembly passed the Marriage Equality Act. On June 24, the very eve of New York City Gay Pride, it was announced that the Act would be considered as the final bill of the legislative session. Considered and amended, the bill was approved by a margin of 33 to 29 and signed into law at 11.55pm by New York Governor Andrew Cuomo.

Causing less jubilation was the significant spike in gay hate crimes in NYC in 2013. In May alone, five attacks made the headlines, ranging from verbal and physical assaults, to the fatal shooting of Mark Carson, a 32-year-old Brooklyn man. Carson and a friend had been walking along 8th St in Greenwich Village in the early hours of May 18 when they were confronted by a group of men hurling homophobic insults. Among them was 33-year-old ex-con Elliot Morales, who asked the pair 'Do you want to die right now?' before shooting Carson at point-blank range. The attack prompted a midnight vigil in Carson's memory, as well as a sobering reminder that the city had not yet won the fight for full equality.

LGBT Reads

Dancer from the Dance (Andrew Holleran)

Last Exit to Brooklyn (Hubert Selby)

Another Country (James Baldwin)

City Boy (Edmund White)

NYC on Screen

New York City has a long and storied life on screen. It was on these streets that a bumbling Woody Allen fell for Diane Keaton in Annie Hall, that Meg Ryan faked her orgasm in When Harry Met Sally, and that Sarah Jessica Parker philosophized about the finer points of dating and Jimmy Choos in Sex & the City. To fans of American film and television, traversing the city can feel like one big déjà vu of memorable scenes, characters and one-liners.

Hollywood Roots & Rivals

Believe it or not, America's film industry is an East Coast native. Fox, Universal, Metro, Selznick and Goldwyn all originated here in the early 20th century, and, long before Westerns were shot in California and Colorado, they were filmed in the (now former) wilds of New Jersey. Even after Hollywood's year-round sunshine lured the bulk of the business west by the 1920s, 'Lights, Camera, Action' remained a common call in Gotham.

The Kaufman Astoria Legacy

The heart of the local scene was Queens' still-kicking Kaufman Astoria Studios. Founded by Jesse Lasky and Adolph Zukor in 1920 as a one-stop-shop for their Famous Players–Lasky Corporation, the complex would produce a string of silent-era hits, among them *The Sheik* (1921) and *Monsieur Beaucaire* (1924), both starring Italian-born heartthrob Rudolph Valentino, and *Manhandled* (1924), starring early silver-screen diva Gloria Swanson. Renamed Paramount Pictures in 1927, the studios became known for turning Broadway stars into big-screen icons, among them the Marx Brothers, Fred Astaire and Ginger Rogers, the latter making her feature-film debut as a flapper in *Young Man of Manhattan* (1930).

Despite Paramount moving all of its feature film shoots to Hollywood in 1932, the complex – renamed Eastern Services Studio – remained the home of Paramount's newsreel division. Throughout the 1930s, it was also known for its 'shorts,' which launched the careers of homegrown talent such as George Burns, Bob Hope and Danny Kaye. After a stint making propaganda and training films for the US Army between WWII and 1970, what had become known as the US Signal Corps Photographic Center was renamed the Kaufman Astoria Studios by George S Kaufman (the real estate agent, not the playwright) in 1983. Modernized and expanded, the studio has gone on to make a string of flicks, including *All that Jazz* (1979), *Brighton Beach Memoirs* (1986), *The Stepford Wives* (2004) and *Men in Black III* (2012). It was here that the Huxtables lived out their middle-class Brooklyn lives in '80s TV sitcom *The Cosby Show,* and it's still here that small-screen favorites *Sesame Street* and *Nurse Jackie* are taped.

Beyond Astoria

But Kaufman Astoria Studios is not alone, with numerous film and TV studios across New York City. Slap bang in the historic Brooklyn Navy Yard, the recently expanded, 26-acre Steiner Studios is the largest studio

Metro Goldwyn Mayer's famous 'Leo the Lion' logo was designed by Howard Dietz. His inspiration was the mascot of New York's Columbia University, where the publicist had studied journalism. Leo's famous roar was first added to films in 1928.

The infamous subway grill scene in *The Seven Year Itch* (1955) – in which Marilyn Monroe enjoys a dress-lifting breeze – was shot at 586 Lexington Ave, outside the since-demolished Trans-Lux 52nd Street Theatre.

complex east of LA. Its film credits to date include *The Producers* (2005), *Revolutionary Road* (2008), *Sex & the City* 1 and 2 (2008, 2010), and *Mr Popper's Penguins* (2011). The studios have also been used for numerous TV shows, among them *Pan Am* and Martin Scorsese's critically acclaimed gangster drama *Boardwalk Empire*. Back in Queens you'll find the city's other big gun, Silvercup Studios. Its list of features include NYC classics like Francis Ford Coppola's *The Godfather: Part III* (1990) and Woody Allen's *Broadway Danny Rose* (1984) and *The Purple Rose of Cairo* (1985), plus TV gems like mafia drama *The Sopranos* and the equally lauded comedy *30 Rock,* the latter starring Tina Fey as a TV sketch writer and Alec Baldwin as a network executive at the Rockefeller Center.

In reality, the Rockefeller Center is home to the NBC TV network, its long-running variety show *Saturday Night Live* the real inspiration behind Fey's *30 Rock* project. Other media networks dotted across Manhattan include the Food and Oxygen Networks, both housed in the Chelsea Market, as well as Miramax and Robert De Niro's Tribeca Productions, the latter two based in the Tribeca Film Center.

Beyond the studios and headquarters are some of the top film schools – New York University's (NYU) Tisch Film School, the New York Film Academy, the School of Visual Arts, Columbia University and the New School. But you don't have to be a student to learn, with both the Museum of the Moving Image in Astoria, Queens, and the Paley Center for Media in Midtown Manhattan acting as major showcases for screenings and seminars about productions both past and present.

Lights, Landmarks, Action!

Downtown Drama to Midtown Romance

It's not surprising that NYC feels strangely familiar to many first-time visitors – the city itself has racked up more screen time than most Hollywood divas put together and many of its landmarks are as much a part of American screen culture as its red-carpet celebrities. Take the Staten Island Ferry, which takes bullied secretary Melanie Griffiths from suburbia to Wall St in *Working Girl* (1988); Battery Park, where Madonna bewitches Aidan Quinn and Rosanna Arquette in *Desperately Seeking Susan* (1985); or the New York County Courthouse, where villains get their just deserts in *Wall St* (1987) and *Goodfellas* (1989), as well as in small-screen classics such as *Cagney & Lacey, NYPD Blue* and *Law & Order*. The latter show, famous for showcasing New York and its characters, is honored with its own road – Law & Order Way – that leads to Pier 62 at Chelsea Piers.

Few landmarks can claim as much screen time as the Empire State Building, famed for its spire-clinging ape in *King Kong* (1933, 2005), as well as for the countless romantic encounters on its observation decks. One of its most famous scenes is Meg Ryan and Tom Hanks' after-hours encounter in *Sleepless in Seattle* (1993). The sequence – which uses the real lobby but a studio-replica deck – is a tribute of sorts to *An Affair to Remember* (1959), which sees Cary Grant and Deborah Kerr make a pact to meet and (hopefully) seal their love atop the skyscraper.

Sarah Jessica Parker is less lucky in *Sex and the City* (2008), when a nervous Chris Noth jilts her and her Vivienne Westwood wedding dress at the New York Public Library. Perhaps he'd seen *Ghostbusters* (1984) a few too many times, its opening scenes featuring the haunted library's iconic marble lions and Rose Main Reading Room. The library's foyer sneakily stands in for the Metropolitan Museum of Art in *The Thomas Crown Affair* (1999), in which thieving playboy Hugh Grant meets his

In 2013, 59 TV shows were being filmed in NYC, from hit series like *The Good Wife* and *Elementary*, to long-standing classics like *Late Night with Jimmy Fallon* and *Saturday Night Live*. The city's TV industry, worth around $5 billion, supports over 100,000 jobs, with over a third of professional actors in the US based here.

NYC Film Festivals

Dance on Camera (January/ February)

New York International Children's Film Festival (March)

Tribeca Film Festival (April)

Human Rights Watch International Film Festival (June)

NewFest: LGBT Film Festival (July)

New York Film Festival (September/ October)

match in sultry detective Rene Russo. It's at the fountain in adjacent Bryant Park that DIY sleuth Diane Keaton debriefs husband Woody Allen about their supposedly bloodthirsty elderly neighbor in *Manhattan Murder Mystery* (1993). True to form, Allen uses the film to showcase a slew of New York locales, among them the National Arts Club in Gramercy Park and one of his own former hangouts, Elaine's at 1703 Second Ave. It's here, at this since-closed Upper East Side restaurant, that Keaton explains her crime theory to Allen and dinner companions Alan Alda and Ron Rifkin. The restaurant was a regular in Allen's films, also appearing in *Manhattan* (1979) and *Celebrity* (1998).

Across Central Park – whose own countless scenes include Barbra Streisand and Robert Redford rowing on its lake in clutch-a-Kleenex *The Way We Were* (1973) – stands the Dakota Building (1 W 72nd St at Central Park West), used in the classic thriller *Rosemary's Baby* (1968). The Upper West Side is also home to Tom's Restaurant (Broadway at 112th St), whose facade was used regularly in *Seinfeld*. Another neighborhood star is the elegant Lincoln Center, where Natalie Portman slowly loses her mind in

NYC CELLULOID SHORTLIST

It would take volumes to cover all the films tied to Gotham, so fire up the imagination with the following celluloid hits:

Taxi Driver (Martin Scorsese, 1976) Starring Robert De Niro, Cybill Shepherd and Jodie Foster. De Niro is a mentally unstable Vietnam War vet whose violent urges are heightened by the city's tensions. It's a funny, depressing, brilliant classic that's a potent reminder of how much grittier this place used to be.

Manhattan (Woody Allen, 1979) Starring Woody Allen, Diane Keaton and Mariel Hemingway. A divorced New Yorker dating a high-school student (the baby-voiced Hemingway) falls for his best friend's mistress in what is essentially a love letter to NYC. Catch romantic views of the Queensboro Bridge and the Upper East Side.

Desperately Seeking Susan (Susan Seidelman, 1985) Starring Madonna, Rosanna Arquette and Aidan Quinn. A case of mistaken identity leads a bored New Jersey housewife on a wild adventure through Manhattan's subcultural wonderland. Relive mid-'80s East Village and long-gone nightclub Danceteria.

Summer of Sam (Spike Lee, 1999) Starring John Leguizamo, Mira Sorvino and Jennifer Esposito. Spike Lee puts NYC's summer of 1977 in historical context by weaving together the Son of Sam murders, the blackout, racial tensions and the misadventures of one disco-dancing Brooklyn couple, including scenes at CBGB and Studio 54.

Angels in America (Mike Nichols, 2003) Starring Al Pacino, Meryl Streep and Jeffrey Wright. This movie version of Tony Kushner's Broadway play recalls 1985 Manhattan: crumbling relationships, AIDS out of control and a closeted Roy Cohn – advisor to President Ronald Reagan – doing nothing about it except falling ill himself. Follow characters from Brooklyn to Lower Manhattan to Central Park.

Party Monster (Fenton Bailey, 2003) Starring Seth Green and Macauley Culkin, who plays the famed, murderous club kid Michael Alig, this is a disturbing look into the drug-fueled downtown clubbing culture of the late '80s. The former Limelight club is featured prominently.

Precious (Lee Daniels, 2009) Starring Gabourey Sidibe and based on the novel *Push* by Sapphire. This unflinching tale of an obese, illiterate teenager who is abused by her parents takes place in Harlem, offering plenty of streetscapes and New York–ghetto 'tude.

The Great Gatsby (Baz Luhrmann, 2013) Starring Leonardo DiCaprio, Carey Mulligan, Joel Edgerton and Tobey Maguire. Although much of it was shot in Australia, this high-energy adaptation of F Scott Fitzgerald's classic American novel re-imagines the glamor and grit of Prohibition-era NYC.

Tom's Restaurant (p256)

the psychological thriller *Black Swan* (2010), and where love-struck Brooklynites Cher and Nicolas Cage meet for a date in *Moonstruck* (1987). The Center sits on what had previously been a rundown district of tenements, captured in Oscar-winning gangland musical *West Side Story* (1961).

Classic Screen Locations

Central Park
Countless cameos, including in Woody Allen's Annie Hall, Manhattan *and* Hannah & Her Sisters

64 Perry St
Carrie Bradshaw's apartment exterior in Sex & the City

Katz's Delicatessen
Where Meg Ryan faux climaxes in When Harry Met Sally

Tom's Restaurant
Stand-in for Monk's Café in Seinfeld

Tiffany & Co
Where Audrey Hepburn daydreams in Breakfast at Tiffany's

Dancing in the Streets

Knives make way for leotards in the cult musical *Fame* (1980), in which New York High School of Performing Arts students do little for the city's traffic woes by dancing on Midtown's streets. The film's graphic content was too much for the city's Board of Education, who banned shooting at the real High School of Performing Arts, then located at 120 W 46th St. Consequently, filmmakers used the doorway of a disused church on the opposite side of the street for the school's entrance, and Haaren Hall (Tenth Ave and 59th St) for interior scenes.

Fame and *West Side Story* are not alone in turning Gotham into a pop-up dance floor. In *On the Town* (1949), starstruck sailors Frank Sinatra, Gene Kelly and Jules Munshin look straight off a Pride float as they skip, hop and sing their way across this 'wonderful town,' from the base of Lady Liberty to Rockefeller Plaza and the Brooklyn Bridge. Another wave of campness hits the bridge when Diana Ross and Michael Jackson cross it in *The Wiz* (1978), a bizarre take on *The Wizard of Oz*, complete with munchkins in Flushing Meadows Corona Park and an Emerald City at the base of the WTC Twin Towers. The previous year, the bridge provided a rite of passage for a bellbottomed John Travolta in *Saturday Night Fever* (1977), who leaves the comforts of his adolescent Brooklyn for the bigger, brighter mirror balls of Manhattan. Topping them all, however, is the closing scene in Terry Gilliam's *The Fisher King* (1991), which sees Grand Central Terminal's Main Concourse turned into a ballroom of waltzing commuters.

Location Tours

Movie- and TV-location guided tours such as On Location Tours (p389) are a good way to visit some of the spots where your screen favorites were shot, including *The Devil Wears Prada*, *Spider-Man*, *How I Met Your Mother* and more. Alternatively, you can do it yourself after visiting the wonderfully comprehensive On the Set of New York website (www.onthesetofnewyork.com), which offers free downloadable location maps covering much of Manhattan.

Survival Guide

Transportation

ARRIVING IN NEW YORK CITY

With its three bustling airports, two main train stations and a monolithic bus terminal, New York City rolls out the welcome mat for the more than 50 million visitors who come to take a bite out of the Big Apple each year.

Direct flights are possible from most major American and international cities. Figure six hours from Los Angeles, seven hours from London and Amsterdam, and 14 hours from Tokyo. Consider getting here by train instead of car or plane to enjoy a mix of bucolic and urban scenery en route, without unnecessary traffic hassles, security checks and excess carbon emissions.

Flights, tours and rail tickets can be booked online at lonelyplanet.com/bookings.

John F Kennedy International Airport

JFK Airport (☑718-244-4444; www.panynj.gov) is 15 miles from Midtown in southeastern Queens, has eight terminals, serves nearly 50 million passengers annually and hosts flights coming and going from all corners of the globe.

Taxi

A yellow taxi from Manhattan to the airport will use the meter; prices (often about $60) depend on traffic – it can take 45 to 60 minutes. From JFK, taxis charge a flat rate of $52 to any destination in Manhattan (not including tolls or tip); it can take 45 to 60 minutes for most destinations in Manhattan. To/from a destination in Brooklyn, the metered fare should be about $45 (Coney Island) to $65 (downtown Brooklyn). Note that the Williamsburg, Manhattan, Brooklyn and Queensboro–59th St Bridges have no toll either way, while the Queens–Midtown Tunnel and the Hugh L Carey Tunnel (aka the Brooklyn–Battery Tunnel) cost $7.50 going into Manhattan.

Vans & Car Service

Shared vans, like those offered by **Super Shuttle Manhattan** (www.supershuttle.com), cost around $20 to $25 per person, depending on the destination. If traveling to the airport from NYC, car services have set fares from $45.

Express Bus

The **NYC Airporter** (www.nycairporter.com) runs to Grand Central Station, Penn Station or the Port Authority Bus Terminal from JFK. The one-way fare is $16.

Subway

If money is tight, the subway is the cheapest, but slowest, way of reaching Manhattan.

From the airport, hop on the AirTrain ($5, payable as you exit) to Sutphin Blvd-Archer Ave (Jamaica Station) to reach the E, J or Z line (or the Long Island Rail Road). To take the A line instead, ride the AirTrain to Howard Beach station. The E train to Midtown has the fewest stops. Expect the journey to take at least 90 minutes to Midtown.

Long Island Rail Road (LIRR)

This is by far the most relaxing way to arrive in the city. From the airport, take the AirTrain ($5, as you exit) to Jamaica Station. From there, LIRR trains go frequently to Penn Station in Manhattan or to Atlantic Terminal in Brooklyn (near Fort Greene, Boerum Hill and the Barclay Center). It's about a 20-minute journey from station to station. One-way fares to either Penn Station or Atlantic Terminal cost $7.50 ($9 at peak times).

LaGuardia Airport

Used mainly for domestic flights, **LaGuardia** (LGA; ☑718-533-3400; www.panynj.gov) is smaller than JFK but only eight miles from midtown Manhattan; it sees about 26 million passengers per year.

Taxi

A taxi to/from Manhattan costs about $42 for the approximately half-hour ride.

Car Service

A car service to LaGuardia costs around $35.

Express Bus

The **NYC Airporter** (www.nycairporter.com) costs $13.

Subway/Bus

It's less convenient to get to LaGuardia by public transportation than the other airports. The best subway link is the 74 St–Broadway station (7 line, or the E, F, M and R lines at the connecting Jackson Hts Roosevelt Ave station) in Queens, where you can pick up the new Q70 Express Bus to the airport (about 10 minutes to the airport).

Newark Liberty International Airport

Don't write off New Jersey when looking for airfares to New York. About the same distance from Midtown as JFK (16 miles), **Newark** (EWR; ☏973-961-6000; www.panynj.gov) brings many New Yorkers out for flights (there's some 36 million passengers annually).

Car Service

A car service runs about $45 to $60 for the 45-minute ride from Midtown – a taxi is roughly the same. You'll have to pay a whopping $13 to get into NYC through the Lincoln (at 42nd St) and Holland

(at Canal St) Tunnels and, further north, the George Washington Bridge, though there's no charge going back through to NJ. There are a couple of cheap tolls on New Jersey highways, too, unless you ask your driver to take Hwy 1 or 9.

Subway

NJ Transit runs a rail service (with an AirTrain connection) between Newark airport (EWR) and New York's Penn Station for $12.50 each way. The trip takes 25 minutes and runs every 20 or 30 minutes from 4:20am to about 1:40am. Hold onto your ticket, which you must show upon exiting at the airport.

Express Bus

The Newark Liberty Airport Express has a bus service between the airport and Port Authority Bus Terminal, Bryant Park and Grand Central Terminal in Midtown ($16 one way). The 45-minute ride goes every 15 minutes from 6:45am to 11:15pm and every half hour from 4:45am to 6:45am and 11:15pm to 1:15am.

Port Authority Bus Terminal

For long-distance bus trips, you'll arrive and depart from the world's busiest bus station, the **Port Authority Bus Terminal** (Map p430; ☏212-564-8484; www.panynj.gov; 41st St at Eighth Ave;

Ⓢ A, C, E, N, Q, R, 1, 2, 3, & 7), which sees nearly 70 million passengers each year. Bus companies leaving from here include the following:

Greyhound (☏800-231-2222; www.greyhound.com) Connects New York with major cities across the country.

Peter Pan Trailways (☏800-343-9999; www.peterpanbus.com) Daily express service to Boston (one way $18–32), Washington, DC ($16–25) and Philadelphia ($12–16).

ShortLine Bus (☏20 1-529 3666, 800-631-8405; www.coachusa.com) Goes to northern New Jersey and upstate New York (Rhinebeck for $25.30, Woodbury Common for $21).

Penn Station

Penn Station (☏212-582-6875, 800-872-7245; W 33rd St btwn Seventh & Eighth Aves) is the departure point for all **Amtrak** (☏800-872-7245; www.amtrak.com) trains, including the Acela Express services to Princeton, NJ, and Washington, DC (note that this express service will cost twice as much as a normal fare). All fares vary, based on the day of the week and the time you want to travel. There is no baggage-storage facility at Penn Station.

TRANSPORTATION ARRIVING IN NEW YORK CITY

CLIMATE CHANGE & TRAVEL

Every form of transport that relies on carbon-based fuel generates CO_2, the main cause of human-induced climate change. Modern travel is dependent on airplanes, which might use less fuel per kilometer per person than most cars but travel much greater distances. The altitude at which aircraft emit gases (including CO_2) and particles also contributes to their climate change impact. Many websites offer 'carbon calculators' that allow people to estimate the carbon emissions generated by their journey and, for those who wish to do so, to offset the impact of the greenhouse gases emitted with contributions to portfolios of climate-friendly initiatives throughout the world. Lonely Planet offsets the carbon footprint of all staff and author travel.

CHINATOWN BUSES

Maniacally driven Chinatown buses, operating around Canal St, were once the cheapest and probably most dangerous way to travel to Boston, Philadelphia, Washington, DC, and other areas on the East Coast. After a series of deadly accidents over the past decade (including one in 2011 that killed 15 people), the Federal Motor Carrier Safety Administration clamped down on these bus lines, some of which continued to operate illegally even after their licenses were revoked; others simply changed their names and logos. In late 2013, only two operators (both with poor safety reviews) were still in service: Eastern Travel and Lucky Star. New discount bus lines, however, have applied for (and received) permits, and will undoubtedly return to the streets, but keep in mind the risks involved in traveling with one of these cut-rate operators.

Long Island Rail Road

(LIRR; ☏718-217-5477; www.mta.info/lirr; one-way fare to Long Beach $9-12.50, 'summer beach getaway' incl round-trip fare and beach admission $23) The Long Island Rail Road serves over 300,000 commuters each day, with services from Penn Station to points in Brooklyn and Queens, and on Long Island. Prices are broken down by zones. A peak-hour ride from Penn Station to Jamaica Station (en route to JFK via AirTrain) costs $9.50 if you buy it at the station (or a whopping $16 onboard!).

New Jersey Transit

(☏800-772-2287; www.njtransit.com) Also operates trains from Penn Station, with services to the suburbs and the Jersey Shore.

New Jersey PATH

(☏800-234-7284; www.panynj.gov/path) An option for getting into NJ's northern points, such as Hoboken and Newark. Trains ($2.50) run from Penn Station along the length of Sixth Ave, with stops at 33rd, 23rd, 14th, 9th and Christopher Sts, as well as at the reopened World Trade Center site.

Metro-North Railroad

(☏212-532-4900; www.mta.info/mnr) The last line departing from Grand Central Terminal, the Metro-North Railroad serves Connecticut, Westchester County and the Hudson Valley.

Bus Stations

A growing number of budget bus lines operate from locations just outside **Penn Station** (☏212-582-6875, 800-872-7245; W 33rd St btwn Seventh & Eighth Aves):

BoltBus (☏877-265-8287; www.boltbus.com) Owned by Greyhound, BoltBus is notable for its free wi-fi (which occasionally actually works). Buses travel from New York to Philadelphia, Boston, Baltimore and Washington, DC. Prices range from $10 to $27, with better deals the earlier you buy (even $1 deals sometimes!). Buses depart from W 33rd between 11th and 12th Aves. If you're heading to Philadelphia, Baltimore or DC, buses also depart downtown, from Sixth Ave between Grand and Watts Sts. Buy tickets online.

megabus (☏877-462-6342; http://us.megabus.com) Also offering free (sometimes functioning) wi-fi and similar rates, megabus travels between New York and Boston, Washington, DC and Toronto, among other destinations.

Vamoose (☏212-695-6766, 877-393-2828; www.vamoosebus.com) Buses head to Arlington, Virginia (one way $30), near Washington, DC. Buses leave from the northwest corner of Seventh Ave and W 30th St (in front of the Bagel Maven cafe).

GETTING AROUND NEW YORK CITY

Once you've arrived in NYC, getting around is fairly easy. The 660-mile subway system is cheap and (reasonably) efficient and can whisk you to nearly every corner of the city. There are also buses, ferries, trains, pedicabs and those ubiquitous yellow taxis (though don't expect to see many available when it's raining) for zipping around and out of town when the subway simply doesn't cut it.

The sidewalks of New York, however, are the real stars in the transportation scheme – this city is made for walking. Increasingly, it's also made for bicycles, with the addition of hundreds of miles of new bike lanes and greenways over the last few years.

Subway & Buses

The New York subway system, run by the **Metropolitan Transportation Authority** (MTA; ☏718-330-1234; www.mta.info), is iconic, cheap ($2.50 per ride, regardless of the distance traveled), round-the-clock and often the fastest and most reliable way to get around the city. It's also safer and (a bit) cleaner than it used to be.

It's a good idea to grab a free map from a station attendant. If you have a smartphone, download the useful NextStop app, with map, alerts of service outages and countdowns of train arrival times. When in doubt, ask someone who looks like they know what they're doing. They may not, but subway confusion (and consternation) is the great unifier in this diverse city. And if you're new to the underground, never wear headphones when you're riding, as you might miss an important announcement about track changes or skipped stops.

Metrocards for Travelers

New York's classic subway tokens now belong to the ages: today all buses and subways use the yellow-and-blue **MetroCard** (☎718-330-1234; www.mta.info/metrocard), which you can purchase or add value to at one of several easy-to-use automated machines at any station. You can use cash or an ATM or credit card. Just select 'Get new card' and follow the prompts. Tip: if you're not from the US, when the machine asks for your zip code, enter 99999.

The card itself costs $1. You then select one of two types of MetroCard. The 'pay-per-ride' is $2.50 per ride, though the MTA tacks on a 5% bonus on Metro-Cards over $5. (Buy a $20 card, and you'll receive $21 worth of credit). If you plan to use the subway quite a bit, you can also buy an 'unlimited ride' card ($30 for a seven-day pass). These cards are handy for travelers – particularly if you're jumping around town to a few different places in one day.

Note that the MetroCard also allows free transfers between buses.

Taxi

Hailing and riding in a cab are rites of passage in New York – especially when you get a driver who's a neurotic speed demon, which is often; don't forget to buckle your seatbelt. Still, most taxis in NYC are clean and, compared to those in many international cities, pretty cheap.

The **Taxi & Limousine Commission** (TLC; ☎311), the taxis' governing body,

---

SUBWAY CHEAT SHEET

A few tips for understanding the madness of the New York subway:

Numbers, Letters, Colors

Color-coded subway lines are named by a letter or number, and most carry a collection of two to four trains on their tracks.

Express & Local Lines

A common mistake is accidentally boarding an 'express train' and passing by a local stop you want. Know that each color-coded line is shared by local trains and express trains; the latter make only select stops in Manhattan (indicated by a white circle on subway maps). For example, on the red line, the 2 and 3 are express, while the slower 1 makes local stops. If you're covering a greater distance – say from the Upper West Side to Wall St – you're better off transferring to the express train (usually just across the platform from the local) to save time.

Getting in the Right Station

Some stations – such as SoHo's Spring St station on the 6 line – have separate entrances for downtown or uptown lines (read the sign carefully). If you swipe in at the wrong one – as even crusty locals do on occasion – you'll either need to ride the subway to a station where you can transfer for free, or just lose the $2.50 and re-enter the station (usually across the street). Also look for the green and red lamps above the stairs at each station entrance; green means that it's always open, while red means that particular entrance will be closed at certain hours, usually late at night.

Lost Weekend

All the rules switch on weekends, when some lines combine with others, some get suspended, some stations get passed, others get reached. Locals and tourists alike stand on platforms confused, sometimes irate. Check the www.mta.info website for weekend schedules. Sometimes posted signs aren't visible until after you reach the platform.

CITI BIKE

Hundreds of miles of designated bike lanes were added throughout the city by former Mayor Bloomberg's very pro-cycling City Hall. And, potentially even more momentous, the Bloomberg administration launched **Citi Bike** (www.citibikenyc.com; 24hr/7 days $11/27), its long awaited bikesharing program – the largest in the country – in the summer of 2013.

Hundreds of kiosks in Manhattan and parts of Brooklyn house the iconic bright blue and very sturdy bicycles, which are free for rides of 30 minutes or less, with charges kicking in thereafter. You'll find routes and bike lanes for every borough on **NYC Bike Maps** (www.nycbikemaps.com). For downloadable maps and point-to-point route generator, visit **NYC DOT** (www.nyc.gov/html/dot/html/bicyclists/bikemaps.shtml). Free bike maps are also available at most bike shops.

has set fares for rides (which can be paid with credit or debit card). It's $2.50 for the initial charge (first one-fifth of a mile), 50¢ for each additional one-fifth mile as well as per 60 seconds of being stopped in traffic, $1 peak surcharge (weekdays 4pm to 8pm), and a 50¢ night surcharge (8pm to 6am), plus a NY State surcharge of 50¢ per ride. Tips are expected to be 10% to 15%, but give less if you feel in any way mistreated; be sure to ask for a receipt and use it to note the driver's license number.

The TLC keeps a Passenger's Bill of Rights, which gives you the right to tell the driver which route you'd like to take, or ask your driver to stop smoking or turn off an annoying radio station. Also, the driver does not have the right to refuse you a ride based on where you are going. Tip: Get in first, then say where you're going.

In 2014, new rules went into affect regarding availability. If the light on the roof is lit, it's available. It's particularly difficult to score a taxi in the rain, at rush hour and around 4pm, when many drivers end their shifts.

Private car services are a common taxi alternative in the outer boroughs. Fares differ depending on the neighborhood and length of ride, and must be determined beforehand, as they have no meters. These 'black cars' are quite common in Brooklyn and Queens, however, it's illegal if a driver simply stops to offer you a ride – no matter what borough you're in. A couple of car services in Brooklyn include **Northside** (Map p438; ☎718-387-2222; 207 Bedford Ave) in Williamsburg and **Arecibo** (Map p442; ☎718-783-6465; 170 Fifth Ave at Degraw St) in Park Slope.

Boro Taxis

In 2013, light green Boro Taxis began operating in the outer boroughs and Upper Manhattan. These allow folks to hail a taxi on the street in neighborhoods where yellow taxis rarely roam. These have the same fares and features as yellow cabs, and are a good way to get around the outer boroughs (from say Astoria to Williamsburg, or Park Slope to Red Hook). Boro Taxi drivers are reluctant (but legally obligated) to take passengers into Manhattan as they aren't legally allowed to take fares going out of Manhattan south of 96th St.

Ferry

East River Ferry (www.eastriverferry.com) runs year-round commuter service connecting a variety of locations in Manhattan, Queens and Brooklyn. **New York Water Taxi** (☎212-742-1969; www.nywatertaxi.com; hop-on-hop-off service 1-day $26) has a fleet of zippy yellow boats that provide hop-on, hop-off service around Manhattan and Brooklyn.

Another bigger, brighter ferry (this one's orange) is the commuter-oriented **Staten Island Ferry** (Map p408; www.siferry.com; Whitehall Terminal at Whitehall & South Sts; 🕒24hr; [S]1 to South Ferry) [FREE], which makes constant free journeys across New York Harbor.

Train

Long Island Rail Road (LIRR; www.mta.nyc.ny.us/lirr), **New Jersey Transit** (www.njtransit.state.nj.us) and **New Jersey PATH** (☎800-234-7284; www.panynj.gov/path) all offer useful services for getting around NYC and surrounds.

Directory A–Z

Customs Regulations

US Customs allows each person over the age of 21 to bring 1L of liquor and 200 cigarettes duty free into the USA. Agricultural items including meat, fruits, vegetables, plants and soil are prohibited. US citizens are allowed to import, duty free, up to $800 worth of gifts from abroad, while non-US citizens are allowed to import $100 worth. If you're carrying more than $10,000 in US and foreign cash, traveler's checks or money orders, you need to declare the excess amount. There is no legal restriction on the amount that may be imported, but undeclared sums in excess of $10,000 will probably be subject to investigation. If you're bringing prescription drugs, make sure they're in clearly marked containers. Obviously, leave the illegal narcotics at home. For updates, check www.cbp.gov.

Electricity

The US electric current is 110V to 115V, 60Hz AC. Outlets are made for flat two-prong plugs (which often have a third, rounded prong for grounding). If your appliance is made for another electrical system (eg 220V), you'll need a step-down converter, which can be bought at hardware stores and drugstores for around $25 to $60. Most electronic devices (laptops, camera-battery chargers etc) are built for dual-voltage use, however, and will only need a plug adapter.

Embassies & Consulates

The presence of the UN in New York City means that nearly every country in the world maintains diplomatic offices in Manhattan. You can check the local *Yellow Pages* under 'consulates' for a complete listing.

Australian Consulate (☎212-351-6500; www.newyork.usa.embassy.gov.au; 34th fl, 150 E 42nd St; 🕐9am-5pm Mon-Fri; [S]4/5/6 to Grand Central-42nd St)

Brazilian Consulate (☎917-777-7777; http://novayork.itamaraty.gov.br; 225 E 41st St, btwn 2nd & 3rd Aves; 🕐10am-1pm & 2:30-4pm Mon-Fri; [S]B/D/F/V to 47th-50th Sts-Rockefeller Ctr)

Canadian Consulate (can-am.gc.ca/new-york/menu.aspx; 1251 Sixth Ave, btwn 50th & 49th Sts; 🕐9am-3pm Mon-Fri; [S]B/D/F/V to 47th-50th Sts-Rockefeller Ctr)

French Consulate (☎212-606-3600; www.consulfrancenewyork.org; 934 Fifth Ave, btwn

PRACTICALITIES

Magazines

Magazines that give a good sense of the local flavor include the following:

New York Magazine (www.nymag.com) A biweekly magazine with feature stories and great listings about anything and everything in NYC, plus an indispensable website.

New Yorker (www.newyorker.com) This highbrow weekly covers politics and culture through its famously lengthy works of reportage, and also publishes fiction and poetry.

Time Out New York (http://newyork.timeout.com) A weekly magazine, its focus is on mass coverage, plus articles and interviews on arts and entertainment.

Newspapers

There are loads of periodicals to choose from. What else would you expect from one of the media capitals of the world? Newspapers include the following:

New York Post (www.nypost.com) The *Post* is known for screaming headlines, conservative political views and its popular Page Six gossip column.

New York Times (www.nytimes.com) 'The gray lady' has become hip in recent years, adding sections on technology, arts and dining out.

Village Voice (www.villagevoice.com) Owned by national alternative-newspaper chain New Times, the legendary *Voice* has less bite but still plenty of bark.

Wall Street Journal (www.wallstreetjournal.com) This intellectual daily focuses on finance, though its new owner, media mogul Rupert Murdoch, has ratcheted up the general coverage to rival that of the *Times*.

Radio

NYC has some excellent radio options beyond commercial pop-music stations. An excellent programming guide can be found in the *New York Times* entertainment section on Sunday. Our top pick is **WNYC** (820-AM & 93.9-FM; www.wnyc.org), NYC's public radio station that is the local NPR affiliate, and offers a blend of national and local talk and interview shows, with a switch to classical music in the day on the FM station.

Smoking

Smoking is strictly forbidden in any location that's considered a public place; this includes subway stations, restaurants, bars, taxis, and parks.

74th & 75th Sts; 🕒9am-1pm Mon-Fri; [S]6 to 77th St)

German Consulate (☎212-610-9700; www.germany.info; 871 UN Plaza, 1st Ave btwn 49th & 48th Sts; 🕒9am-noon Mon-Fri; [S]4/5/6 to Grand Central-42nd St)

Indian Consulate (☎212-774-0600; www.indiacgny.org; 3 E 64th St, btwn 5th & Madison Aves; 🕒9am-5:30pm Mon-Fri; [S]6 to 68th St-Hunter College)

Japanese Consulate (☎212-371-8222; www.ny.us.emb-japan.go.jp; 299 Park Ave btwn 48th & 49th Sts; 🕒9:30am-4pm Mon-Fri; [S]6 to 51st St; E, V to Lexington Ave-53rd St)

UK Consulate (☎212-745-0200; 845 Third Ave btwn 51st & 52nd Sts; 🕒9am-4pm Mon-Fri; [S]6 to 51st St; E, V to Lexington Ave-53rd St)

Emergency

Police, Fire, Ambulance (☎911)

Poison Control (☎800-222-1222)

Internet Access

It is rare to find accommodation in New York City that does not offer wi-fi, though it isn't always free. Public parks with free wi-fi include the High Line, Bryant Park, Battery Park, Tompkins Square Park and Union Square Park. Internet kiosks can be found at the scatter of **Staples** (www.staples.com) and **FedEx Kinko** (www.fedexkinkos.com) locations around the city. Also try Apple stores (www.apple.com).

New York Public Library (☎212-930-0800; www.nypl.org/branch/local; E 42nd St, at Fifth Ave; [S]B, D, F or M to 42nd St-Bryant Park) Offers free internet access for laptop toters and half-hour internet access via public terminals at almost all of its locations around the city. Visit the website for more information.

NYC Wireless (www.nycwireless.net) A local free-wi-fi activist group that has an online map of free access points, which requires sign-in.

Other public areas with free wi-fi include the following:

Columbia University (Map p436; www.columbia.edu; Broadway at 116th St, Morningside Heights; [S]1 to 116th St-Columbia University)

South Street Seaport (Map p408; www.southstreetseaport.com; [S]A/C, J/Z, 2/3, 4/5 to Fulton St)

Legal Matters

If you're arrested, you have the right to remain silent. There is no legal reason to speak to a police officer if you don't wish to – especially since anything you say 'can and will be used against you' – but never walk away from an officer until given permission. All persons who are arrested have the legal right to make one phone call. If you don't have a lawyer or family member to help you, call your consulate. The police will give you the number upon request.

Medical Services

Before traveling, contact your health-insurance provider to find out what types of medical care it will cover outside your hometown (or home country). Overseas visitors should acquire travel insurance that covers medical situations in the US, as non-emergency care for uninsured patients can be very expensive. For non-emergency appointments at hospitals, you'll need proof of insurance or cash. Even with insurance, you'll most likely have to pay up front for non-emergency care, and then wrangle with your insurance company afterwards in order to get your money reimbursed.

Clinics

Bolte Medical Urgent Care Center (☎212-588-9314; www.boltemedical.com; 141 E 55th St at Lexington Ave; ⏲9am-8pm Mon-Fri, to 5pm Sat & Sun; [S]6 to 51st St; E, V to Lexington Ave-53rd St) This clinic offers same-day appointments for illness diagnosis.

Callen-Lorde Community Health Center (☎212-271-7200; www.callen-lorde.org; 356 W 18th St btwn Eighth & Ninth Aves; [S]A/C/E, L to 8th Ave-14th St) This medical center, dedicated to the LGBT community and people living with HIV/AIDS, serves people regardless of their ability to pay.

Duane Reade Walk-in Medical Care (www.drwalkin.com) The drugstore chain has walk in clinics at six Manhattan locations. Hospital-affiliated doctors are available to offer diagnosis and treatment.

New York County Medical Society (☎212-684-4670; www.nycms.org) Makes doctor referrals by phone, based on type of problem and language spoken.

Planned Parenthood (☎212-965-7000; www.plannedparenthood.org; 26 Bleecker St; [S]B/D/F/V to Broadway-Lafayette St; 6 to Bleecker St) Provides birth control, STD screenings and gynecological care.

Travel MD (☎212-737-1212; www.travelmd.com) Cares specifically for visitors to NYC; hotel appointments can be made.

Emergency Rooms

Emergency services can be stress-inducing and slow (unless your medical condition is absolutely dire); a visit should be avoided if other medical services can be provided to mitigate the situation.

Bellevue Hospital Center (☎212-562-5555; 462 First Ave at 27th St; [S]6 to 28th St)

Lenox Hill Hospital (☎212-434-2000; 100 E 77th St at Lexington Ave, Upper East Side; [S]6 to 103rd St)

Mount Sinai Hospital (☎212-241-6500; 1190 Fifth Ave btwn 98th & 101st St; [S]6 to 103rd St)

New York-Presbyterian Hospital (☎212-305-2500; 630 W 168th St at Ft Washington Ave; [S]A/C, 1 to 168th St)

Pharmacies

New York is bursting with 24-hour 'pharmacies,' which are handy all-purpose stores where you can buy over-the-counter medications anytime; the pharmaceutical prescription counters have more limited hours. Check websites for locations; major pharmacy chains include the following:

CVS (www.cvs.com)

Duane Reade (www.duanereade.com)

Rite Aid (www.riteaid.com)

Walgreens (www.walgreens.com)

Money

US dollars are the only accepted currency in NYC. While debit and credit cards are widely accepted, some restaurants and cafes are cash only. It's wise to have a combination of cash and cards.

ATMs

Automatic teller machines are on practically every

corner. You can either use your card at banks – usually in a 24-hour-access lobby, filled with up to a dozen monitors at major branches – or you can opt for the lone wolves, which sit in delis, restaurants, bars and grocery stores, charging fierce service fees that average $3, but can go as high as $5.

Most New York banks are linked by the New York Cash Exchange (NYCE) system, and you can use local bank cards interchangeably at ATMs – for an extra fee if you're banking outside your system.

Changing Money

Banks and moneychangers, found all over New York City (including all three major airports), will give you US currency based on the current exchange rate.

Travelex (☑212-265-6049; 1578 Broadway at 47th St; ⏰9am-7pm Mon-Sat, 9am-5pm Sun) Features currency exchange at eight locations in the city, including this Times Sq office.

Credit Cards

Major credit cards are accepted at most hotels, restaurants and shops throughout New York City. In fact, you'll find it difficult to perform certain transactions, such as purchasing tickets to performances and renting a car, without one.

Stack your deck with a Visa, MasterCard or American Express, as these are the cards of choice here. Places that accept Visa and MasterCard also accept debit cards, which deduct payments directly from your checking or savings account. Be sure to check with your bank to confirm that your debit card will be accepted in other states or countries – debit cards from large commercial banks can often be used worldwide.

If your cards are lost or stolen, contact the company

immediately. The following are toll-free numbers for the main credit-card companies:

American Express (☑800-528-4800)

Discover (☑800-347-2683)

MasterCard (☑800-622-7747)

Visa (☑800-847-2911)

Tipping

For guidance on tipping in NYC, see the Need to Know chapter, p18.

Opening Hours

Nonstandard hours are listed in specific reviews through the neighborhood chapters in the Explore section of this guide. Standard business hours are as follows:

Banks 9am-6pm Mon-Fri, some also 9am-noon Sat

Bars 5pm-4am

Businesses 9am-5pm Mon-Fri

Clubs 10pm-4am

Restaurants Breakfast is served from 6am to 11am, lunch goes from 11am to around 3pm, and dinner stretches between 5pm and 11pm. The popular weekend brunch lasts from 10am until 2pm and sometimes later.

Shops 10am to around 7pm on weekdays, 11am to around 8pm Saturdays, and Sundays can be variable – some stores stay closed while others keep weekday hours. Stores tend to stay open later in the neighborhoods downtown.

Organized Tours

There are dozens upon dozens of organized tours around the city. The following are a few favorites; consult the Explore chapters for additional recommendations.

Sidetour (www.sidetour.com; tours $50-60) Sidetour offers unique, off-the-beaten

path experiences for those who want to delve deep into NYC. The range of experiences on offer is vast: you can attend a jazz jam in a Brooklyn brownstone, take an ethnic food walk around Astoria, take a renegade art tour through the Met or the galleries of Chelsea or explore the urban art of the Lower East Side. You can also take a class: metalworking, beatboxing, photography, homebrewing, drawing, origami making and more. Check out the enormous range of offerings online.

Big Apple Greeter Program (☑212-669-8159; www.bigapplegreeter.org) For an inside take on the NYC experience, book a walking tour, in the neighborhood of your choice, led by a local volunteer who just can't wait to show off his or her city to you. You'll be matched with a guide who suits your needs, whether that means speaking Spanish or American Sign Language, or knowing just where to find the best wheelchair-accessible spots in the city. Reserve four weeks in advance.

Bike the Big Apple (☑877-865-0078; www.bikethebigapple.com; tours incl bike & helmet around $95) Biking tours let you cover more ground than walking tours – and give you a healthy dose of exercise to boot. Bike the Big Apple, recommended by NYC & Company (the official tourism authority of New York City and operators of www.nycgo.com), offers 10 set tours. Its most popular is the six-hour Ethnic Apple Tour, 15 miles of riding that covers a bit of Queens, northern Brooklyn and the Lower East Side of Manhattan. Other tours visit the Bronx' Little Italy, city parks, Brooklyn chocolate shops and several night rides.

Circle Line Boat Tours (Map p430; ☎212-563-3200; www.circleline42.com; pier 83, 42nd St at Twelfth Ave; cruises $30-40; [S]A/C/E to 42nd-Port Authority) The classic Circle Line – whose local 1970s TV-commercial song is now the stuff of kitschy nostalgia – guides you through all the big sights from the safe distance of a boat that circumnavigates the five boroughs. It's got a bar on board and has a bit of a party reputation (especially its 90-minute evening cruise); other options include a two-and-a-half-hour full-island cruise and a shorter (90-minute) 'semi-circle' journey. From May to October, it also operates 30-minute adrenaline-fueled cruises aboard the high-speed *Beast*.

Foods of New York (☎212-913-9964; www.foodsofny.com; tours $52-65) The official foodie tour of NYC & Company offers various three-hour tours that help you eat your way through gourmet shops and eateries in one of the West Village, Chelsea, Chinatown or Nolita. Prepare yourself for a moving feast of French bread, fresh Italian pasta, sushi, global cheeses, real New York pizza, local fish and freshly baked pastries.

Gray Line (☎212-397-2620; www.newyorksightseeing.com; $44-60) The most ubiquitous guided tour in the city, Gray Line is responsible for bombarding New York streets with the red double-decker buses that aren't much loved by locals. For an overview of the city, though, it's not a bad option. The company offers various routes, the best being both the popular hop-on, hop-off loops of Manhattan. Tours are available in various languages, including Spanish, French, German, Italian and Japanese.

Liberty Helicopter Tours (Map p430; ☎1-800-542-9933; www.libertyhelicopters.com; Pier 6, East River, Lower Manhattan; per person for 15 mins $150; [S]1 to South Ferry, R to Whitehall St) Enjoy a bird's-eye view of the city in a very Donald Trump sort of way as a helicopter whisks you high above the skyscrapers. Just get ready to shell out for the privilege.

Municipal Art Society (Map p426; ☎212-935-3960; www.mas.org; 111 W 57th St; tours adult/child $20/15; [S]F to 57th St) Various scheduled tours focusing on architecture and history.

New York Gallery Tours (Map p422; ☎212-946-1548; 526 W 26th St at Tenth Ave; tours $20; [S]C/E to 23rd St) You know you're supposed to check out the array of amazing modern-art galleries in Chelsea. But where to begin? This excellent guided tour – with additional gay and lesbian tours that focus on a 'queer aesthetic' – takes you to a slew of galleries and provides helpful commentary along the way.

On Location Tours (☎212-683-2027; www.screentours.com; tours around $45) Face it: you want to sit on Carrie Bradshaw's apartment stoop and visit the design studio from *Will & Grace*. This company offers various tours – covering *Gossip Girl, Sex and the City, The Sopranos,* general TV and movie locations, and movie locations in Central Park – that let you live out your entertainment-obsessed fantasies. A couple of the tours are also available in German.

Strayboots (☎877-787-2929; www.strayboots.com; tours from $12) Self-guided hybrid tours that fuse interesting urban info and a scavenger-hunt element to help New York neophytes find their way around the neighborhood of their choice. Go at your own pace as you text in your answers to central command to receive your next clue. Download the app to give it a go.

Wildman Steve Brill (☎914-835-2153; www.wildmanstevebrill.com; sliding scale up to $20) New York's best-known naturalist – betcha didn't know there were any! – has been leading folks on foraging expeditions through city parks for more than 20 years. He'll trek with you through Central Park, Prospect Park, Inwood Park and many more, teaching you to identify natural riches including sassafras, chickweed, ginkgo nuts, garlic and wild mushrooms along the way. It's wild.

Post

Visit the **US Postal Service** (www.usps.com) website for up-to-date information about postage prices and branch locations throughout the city.

Public Holidays

Following is a list of major NYC holidays and special events. These holidays may force the closure of many businesses or attract crowds, making dining and accommodations reservations difficult.

New Year's Day January 1

Martin Luther King Day Third Monday in January

Presidents' Day Third Monday in February

Easter March/April

Memorial Day Late May

Gay Pride Last Sunday in June

Independence Day July 4

Labor Day Early September

Rosh Hashanah and Yom Kippur Mid-September to mid-October

Halloween October 31

Thanksgiving Fourth Thursday in November

Christmas Day December 25
New Year's Eve December 31

Safe Travel

Crime rates in NYC are still at their lowest in years. There are a few neighborhoods where you might feel apprehensive no matter what time of night it is (they're mainly in the outer boroughs). Subway stations are generally safe, too, though again, especially in the outer boroughs, some can be dicey. There's no reason to be paranoid, but it's better to be safe than sorry, so use common sense: don't walk around alone at night in unfamiliar, sparsely populated areas, especially if you're a woman. Carry your daily walking-around money somewhere inside your clothing or in a front pocket rather than in a handbag or a back pocket, and be aware of pickpockets, particularly in mobbed areas, such as Times Square or Penn Station at rush hour.

Taxes

Restaurants and retailers never include the sales tax – 8.875% – in their prices, so beware of ordering the $4.99 lunch special when you only have $5 to your name. Several categories of so-called 'luxury items,' including rental cars and dry-cleaning, carry an additional city surcharge of 5%, so you wind up paying an extra 13.875% in total for these services. Clothing and footwear purchases under $110 are tax free; anything over that amount has a state sales tax of 4.5%. Hotel rooms in New York City are subject to a 14.75% tax, plus a flat $3.50 occupancy tax per night. Since the US has no nationwide value-added tax (VAT), there is no opportunity for foreign visitors to make 'tax-free' purchases.

Telephone

Phone numbers within the USA consist of a three-digit area code followed by a seven-digit local number. If you're calling long distance, dial 1 + the three-digit area code + the seven-digit number. To make an international call from NYC, call ⌨011+ country code + area code + number. When calling Canada, there is no need to use the ⌨011.

Area Codes in NYC

No matter where you're calling within New York City, even if it's just across the street in the same area code, you must always dial 1 + the area code first.

Manhattan ⌨212, ⌨646
Outer boroughs ⌨347, ⌨718, ⌨929
All boroughs (usually cell phones) ⌨917

Cell Phones

Most US cell phones besides the iPhone operate on CDMA, not the European standard GSM – make sure you check compatibility with your phone service provider. North Americans should have no problem, though it is best to check with your service provider about roaming charges.

If you require a cell phone, you'll find many store fronts – most run by Verizon, T-Mobile or AT&T – where you can buy a cheap phone and load it up with prepaid minutes, thus avoiding a long-term contract.

Operator Services

Local directory ⌨411
Municipal offices and information ⌨311
National directory information ⌨1-212-555-1212
Operator ⌨0
Toll-free number information ⌨800-555-1212

Time

New York City is in the Eastern Standard Time (EST) zone – five hours behind Greenwich Mean Time (London), two hours ahead of Mountain Standard Time (including Denver, Colorado) and three hours ahead of Pacific Standard Time (San Francisco and Los Angeles, California). Almost all of the USA observes daylight-saving time: clocks go forward one hour from the second Sunday in March to the first Sunday in November, when the clocks are turned back one hour. (It's easy to remember by the phrase 'spring ahead, fall back.')

Toilets

Considering the number of pedestrians, there's a noticeable lack of public restrooms around the city. You'll find spots to relieve yourself in Grand Central Terminal, Penn Station and Port Authority Bus Terminal, and in parks, including Madison Square Park, Battery Park, Tompkins Square Park, Washington Square Park and Columbus Park in Chinatown, plus several places scattered around Central Park. The good bet, though, is to pop into a Starbucks (there's one about every three blocks), a department store (Macy's, Century 21, Bloomingdale's) or a neighborhood park like Tompkins Square in the East Village or Bleecker Playground (at W 11th & Hudson) in the West Village.

Tourist Information

In this web-based world you'll find infinite online sources to get up-to-the-minute information about New York.

In person, try one of the five official bureaus (the Midtown office is the shining star) of **NYC & Company** (☎212-484-1222; www.nycgo.com):

Midtown (Map p430; ☎212-484-1222; www.nycgo.com; 810 Seventh Ave btwn 52nd & 53rd Sts; ⌚8:30am-6pm Mon-Fri, 9am-5pm Sat & Sun; [S]B/D, E to 7th Ave)

Lower Manhattan (Map p408; ☎212-484-1222; City Hall Park at Broadway; ⌚9am-6pm Mon-Fri, 10-5pm Sat & Sun; [S]R/W to to City Hall)

Chinatown (Map p413; ☎212-484-1222; cnr Canal, Walker & Baxter Sts; ⌚10am-6pm; [S]J/M/Z, N/Q/R/W, 6 to Canal St)

Macy's Herald Square (Map p430, 151 W 34th St, ⌚9am-9:30pm Mon-Fri, 10am-9:30pm Sat, 11am-8:30pm Sun)

Times Square (Map p430; ☎212-452-5283; www.timessquarenyc.org; 1560 Broadway, btwn 46th & 47th Sts, Midtown West; ⌚8am-8pm; [S]N/Q/R, S, 1/2/3, 7 to Times Sq-42nd St)

The **Brooklyn Tourism & Visitors Center** (Map p444; ☎718-802-3846; www.visitbrooklyn.org; 209 Joralemon St btwn Court St & Brooklyn Bridge Blvd; ⌚10am-6pm Mon-Fri; [S]2/3, 4/5 to Borough Hall) has all sorts of info on this much-loved borough.

Outer Borough Tourism Portals

The outer boroughs each have a special tourism website:

Bronx ilovethebronx.com

Queens itsinqueens.info

Staten Island statenislandusa.com

Neighborhood Tourism Portals

Many of the city's most popular neighborhoods have their own websites (either official or 'unofficial') dedicated to exploring the area. Some of our favorites include the following:

Lower East Side www.lowereastsideny.com

Chinatown www.explorechinatown.com

Upper East Side www.uppereast.com

Soho www.sohonyc.com

Williamsburg www.freewilliamsburg.com

For further information check out the following websites:

Lonely Planet www.lonelyplanet.com/usa/new-york-city

New York Magazine www.nymag.com

Village Voice www.villagevoice.com

Travelers with Disabilities

Federal laws guarantee that all government offices and facilities are accessible to the disabled. For information on specific places, you can contact the mayor's **Office for People with Disabilities** (☎212-639-9675; ⌚9am-5pm Mon-Fri), which will send you a free copy of its *Access New York* guide if you call and request it.

Another excellent resource is the **Society for Accessible Travel & Hospitality** (SATH; ☎212-447-7284; www.sath.org; 347 Fifth Ave at 34th St, New York, USA, Suite 605; ⌚9am-5pm; 🚌M34 to 5th Ave, M1 to 34th St, [S]6 to 33rd St,), which gives advice on how to travel with a wheelchair, kidney disease, sight impairment or deafness.

For detailed information on subway and bus wheelchair accessibility, call or visit the **Accessibility Line** (☎511; http://web.mta.info/accessibility/) for a list of subway stations with elevators or escalators. Also visit www.nycgo.com/accessibility.

Visas

Visa Waiver Program

The USA Visa Waiver Program (VWP) allows nationals from 37 countries to enter the US without a visa, provided they are carrying a machine-readable passport. For the up-to-date list of countries included in the program and current requirements, see the website of the **US Department of State** (http://travel.state.gov/visa).

Citizens of VWP countries need to register with the **US Department of Homeland Security** (http://esta.cbp.dhs.gov) three days before their visit. There is a $14 fee for registration application; when approved, the registration is valid for two years or until your passport expires, whichever comes first.

Visas Required

You must obtain a visa from a US embassy or consulate in your home country if you:

- Do not currently hold a passport from a VWP country.
- Are from a VWP country, but don't have a machine-readable passport.
- Are from a VWP country, but currently hold a passport issued between October 26, 2005, and October 25, 2006, that does not have a digital photo on the information page or an integrated chip from the data page. (After October 25, 2006, the integrated chip is required on all machine-readable passports.)
- Are planning to stay longer than 90 days.
- Are planning to work or study in the US.

Behind the Scenes

SEND US YOUR FEEDBACK

We love to hear from travelers – your comments keep us on our toes and help make our books better. Our well-traveled team reads every word on what you loved or loathed about this book. Although we cannot reply individually to your submissions, we always guarantee that your feedback goes straight to the appropriate authors, in time for the next edition. Each person who sends us information is thanked in the next edition – the most useful submissions are rewarded with a selection of digital PDF chapters.

Visit **lonelyplanet.com/contact** to submit your updates and suggestions or to ask for help. Our award-winning website also features inspirational travel stories, news and discussions.

Note: We may edit, reproduce and incorporate your comments in Lonely Planet products such as guidebooks, websites and digital products, so let us know if you don't want your comments reproduced or your name acknowledged. For a copy of our privacy policy visit lonelyplanet.com/privacy.

OUR READERS

Many thanks to the travelers who used the last edition and wrote to us with helpful hints, useful advice and interesting anecdotes: Tora Aarberg, David Behringer, Jenn Pryor, Katrin Sosnick, Michael Zohn

AUTHOR THANKS

Regis St Louis

I'm grateful to many folks – friends and strangers alike – who shared tips and insight into their favorite places in the city. Special thanks to Florence, Phoenix, Erin, Carla and Chad. Thanks also to Cristian for his excellent contributions throughout the book. As always, biggest thanks go to my wife Cassandra and our daughters Genevieve and Magdalena, who make this whole enterprise worthwhile.

Cristian Bonetto

As always, an immeasurable thank-you to generous, on-the-ball Kathy Stromsland and her wonderful family. Many thanks also to Julian Yeo, Lane Wilson, Anthony Leung, Michael Chernow, Lucinda East, Massimiliano Gioni, Gabriel Einsohn, Rick Herron, Mark Mc-Cray, Sarah Shirley, Matt Wood, Mary Ann Gardner, Lambros Hajisava, Les Hayden, Brock Waldron, Jose Francisco Chavez and

Sean Muldoon for the tips, insight and support. Last but not least, a big shout out to my talented, ever-diligent co-author Regis St Louis.

ACKNOWLEDGMENTS

New York City Subway Map (c) 2014 Metropolitan Transport Authority. Used with permission.

Illustration p232-3 by Javier Zarracina.

Cover photograph: Flatiron Building, New York City, Pietro Canali/SIME/4Corners

THIS BOOK

This 9th edition of Lonely Planet's *New York City* guidebook was researched and written by Regis St Louis and Cristian Bonetto. Cristian also worked on the previous edition with Brandon Presser and Carolina A Miranda. Regis worked on the 7th edition with Ginger Adams and Beth Greenfield. This guidebook was commissioned in Lonely Planet's Oakland office, and produced by the following:

Commissioning Editors
Jennye Garibaldi, Katie O'Connell, Emily K Wolman

Destination Editor Dora Whitaker

Product Editor Penny Cordner

Senior Cartographer Alison Lyall

Book Designer Jessica Rose

Assisting Editors Trent Holden, Kate James, Charlotte Orr, Erin Richards, Gabrielle Stefanos, Jeanette Wall

Assisting Book Designers
Lauren Egan, Virginia Moreno, Wibowo Rusli, Wendy Wright

Cover Researcher Naomi Parker

Thanks to Sasha Baskett Brendan Dempsey, Ryan Evans, Larissa Frost, James Hardy, Anna Harris, Briohny Hooper, Genesys India, Jouve India, Kate Mathews, Wayne Murphy, Catherine Naghten, Mazzy Prinsep, Alison Ridgway, Lyahna Spencer, Angela Tinson

BEHIND THE SCENES

Index

See also separate subindexes for:

⚔ EATING P398
🍷 DRINKING & NIGHTLIFE P399
☆ ENTERTAINMENT P400
🛍 SHOPPING P401
🛏 SLEEPING P402
🏃 SPORTS & ACTIVITIES P403

INDEX SPORTS & ACTIVITIES

INDEX SPORTS & ACTIVITIES

New York City Maps

Sights

- 🏖 Beach
- 🐦 Bird Sanctuary
- Buddhist
- 🏰 Castle/Palace
- ✝ Christian
- Confucian
- Hindu
- Islamic
- Jain
- ✡ Jewish
- Monument
- Museum/Gallery/Historic Building
- Ruin
- Sento Hot Baths/Onsen
- Shinto
- Sikh
- Taoist
- Winery/Vineyard
- Zoo/Wildlife Sanctuary
- Other Sight

Activities, Courses & Tours

- Bodysurfing
- Diving
- Canoeing/Kayaking
- Course/Tour
- Skiing
- Snorkeling
- Surfing
- Swimming/Pool
- Walking
- Windsurfing
- Other Activity

Sleeping

- Sleeping
- Camping

Eating

- Eating

Drinking & Nightlife

- Drinking & Nightlife
- Cafe

Entertainment

- Entertainment

Shopping

- Shopping

Information

- Bank
- Embassy/Consulate
- Hospital/Medical
- @ Internet
- Police
- Post Office
- Telephone
- Toilet
- Tourist Information
- Other Information

Geographic

- 🏖 Beach
- Hut/Shelter
- Lighthouse
- Lookout
- ▲ Mountain/Volcano
- Oasis
- Park
-)(Pass
- Picnic Area
- Waterfall

Population

- Capital (National)
- Capital (State/Province)
- City/Large Town
- Town/Village

Transport

- Airport
- DART station
- Border crossing
- Boston T station
- Bus
- Cable car/Funicular
- Cycling
- Ferry
- Metro/Muni station
- Monorail
- Parking
- Petrol station
- Subway/SkyTrain station
- Taxi
- Train station/Railway
- Tram
- Underground station
- Other Transport

Note: Not all symbols displayed above appear on the maps in this book

Routes

- Tollway
- Freeway
- Primary
- Secondary
- Tertiary
- Lane
- Unsealed road
- Road under construction
- Plaza/Mall
- Steps
-)= = Tunnel
- Pedestrian overpass
- Walking Tour
- Walking Tour detour
- Path/Walking Trail

Boundaries

- International
- State/Province
- Disputed
- Regional/Suburb
- Marine Park
- Cliff
- Wall

Hydrography

- River, Creek
- Intermittent River
- Canal
- Water
- Dry/Salt/Intermittent Lake
- Reef

Areas

- Airport/Runway
- Beach/Desert
- Cemetery (Christian)
- Cemetery (Other)
- Glacier
- Mudflat
- Park/Forest
- Sight (Building)
- Sportsground
- Swamp/Mangrove

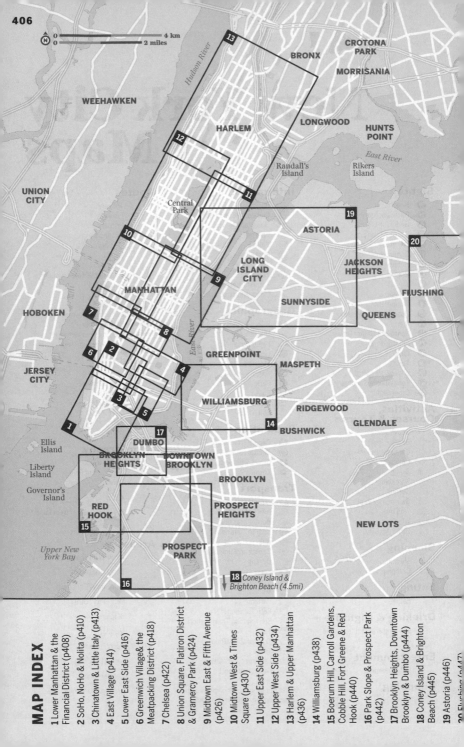

0   4 km
0   2 miles

Hudson River

WEEHAWKEN

13

BRONX

CROTONA PARK

MORRISANIA

UNION CITY

12

HARLEM

LONGWOOD

HUNTS POINT

East River

Randall's Island

Rikers Island

11

Central Park

19

ASTORIA

20

10

LONG ISLAND CITY

JACKSON HEIGHTS

FLUSHING

9

MANHATTAN

SUNNYSIDE

QUEENS

HOBOKEN

7

8

East River

GREENPOINT

MASPETH

JERSEY CITY

6

2

4

WILLIAMSBURG

RIDGEWOOD

GLENDALE

3

5

14

BUSHWICK

Ellis Island

1

17

DUMBO

Liberty Island

BROOKLYN HEIGHTS

DOWNTOWN BROOKLYN

Governor's Island

BROOKLYN

RED HOOK

15

PROSPECT HEIGHTS

NEW LOTS

Upper New York Bay

PROSPECT PARK

16

18 Coney Island & Brighton Beach (4.5mi)

LOWER MANHATTAN & THE FINANCIAL DISTRICT Map on p408

LOWER MANHATTAN & THE FINANCIAL DISTRICT

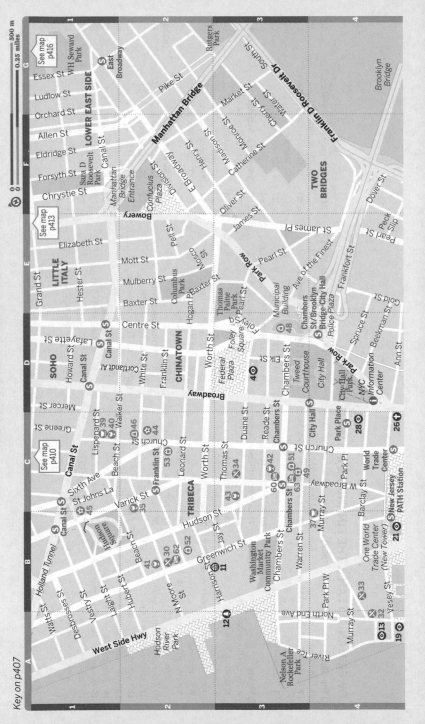

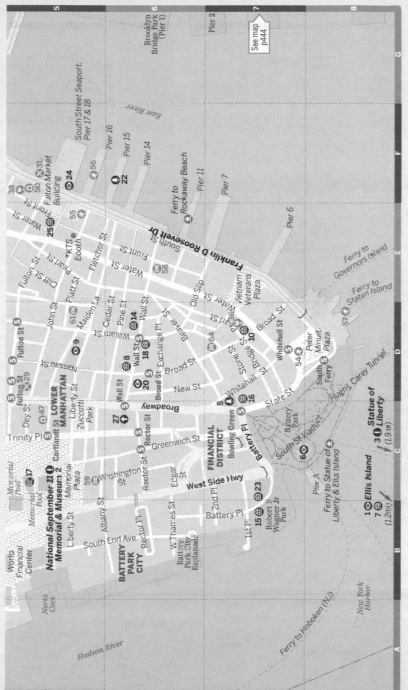

See map p444

SOHO, NOHO & NOLITA

THE FINANCIAL DISTRICT

Key on p412

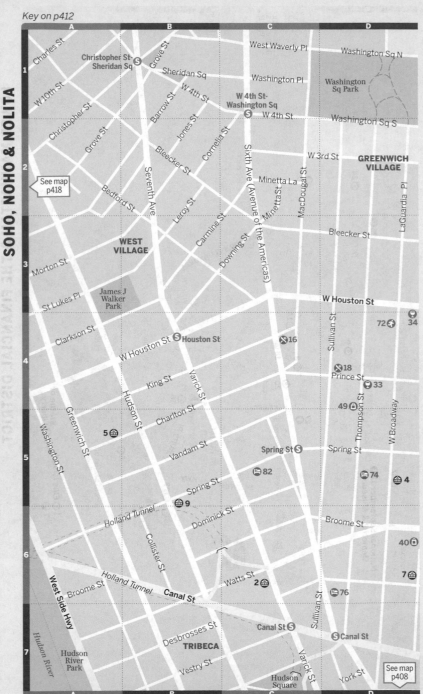

Charles St
W 10th St
Christopher St
Christopher St-Sheridan Sq
Grove St
Sheridan Sq
West Waverly Pl
Washington Sq N
Washington Pl
Washington Sq Park
W 4th St
W 4th St-Washington Sq
W 4th St
Washington Sq S
Barrow St
Jones St
Cornelia St
Sixth Ave (Avenue of the Americas)
Minetta La
Minetta St
MacDougal St
W 3rd St
GREENWICH VILLAGE
See map p418
Bedford St
Seventh Ave
Bleecker St
Leroy St
Carmine St
Downing St
Bleecker St
LaGuardia Pl
Morton St
WEST VILLAGE
St Lukes Pl
James J Walker Park
W Houston St
Sullivan St
72
34
Clarkson St
W Houston St
Houston St
16
Greenwich St
Washington St
King St
Hudson St
Varick St
Charlton St
18
Prince St
33
49
Thompson St
W Broadway
5
Vandam St
Spring St
82
Spring St
Spring St
74
4
Holland Tunnel
9
Dominick St
Broome St
40
Collister St
7
Holland Tunnel
Broome St
Canal St
Watts St
2
Sullivan St
76
West Side Hwy
Desbrosses St
TRIBECA
Canal St
Canal St
Hudson River Park
Hudson River
Vestry St
Hudson Square
Varick St
York St
See map p408

SOHO, NOHO & NOLITA *Map on p410*

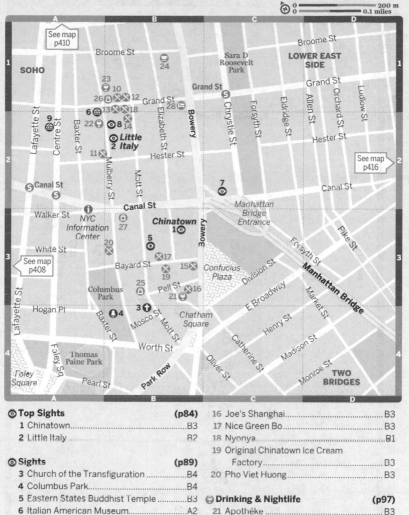

EAST VILLAGE

LOWER EAST SIDE

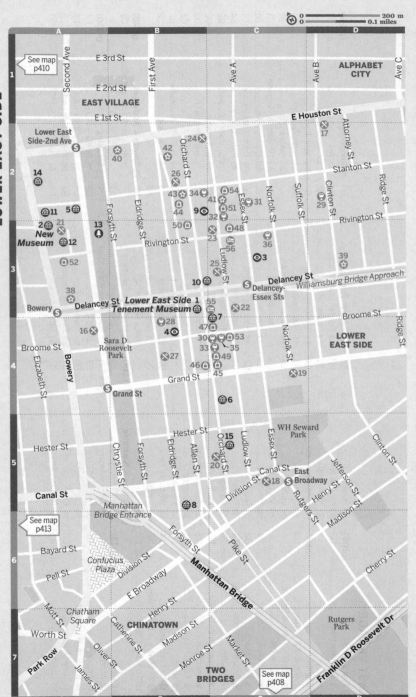

See map p410

See map p413

See map p408

0   200 m
0   0.1 miles

EAST VILLAGE

E 3rd St

E 2nd St

E 1st St

Second Ave

First Ave

Ave A

Ave B

Ave C

E Houston St

ALPHABET CITY

Attorney St

Stanton St

Ridge St

Clinton St

Rivington St

Suffolk St

Norfolk St

Essex St

Orchard St

Eldridge St

Forsyth St

Lower East Side-2nd Ave

New Museum

Rivington St

Ludlow St

Delancey St

Delancey-Essex Sts

Williamsburg Bridge Approach

Broome St

LOWER EAST SIDE

Ridge St

Delancey St

Lower East Side Tenement Museum

Bowery

Broome St

Elizabeth St

Sara D Roosevelt Park

Grand St

Norfolk St

Grand St

Hester St

Hester St

Allen St

Ludlow St

Essex St

WH Seward Park

Clinton St

Jefferson St

Canal St

Chrystie St

Forsyth St

Eldridge St

Orchard St

Canal St

Division St

East Broadway

Rutgers St

Henry St

Madison St

Manhattan Bridge Entrance

Manhattan Bridge

Bayard St

Confucius Plaza

Division St

Pike St

Cherry St

Pell St

E Broadway

Henry St

Rutgers Park

Mott St

Chatham Square

CHINATOWN

Madison St

Market St

Worth St

Catherine St

Monroe St

Franklin D Roosevelt Dr

Park Row

Oliver St

James St

TWO BRIDGES

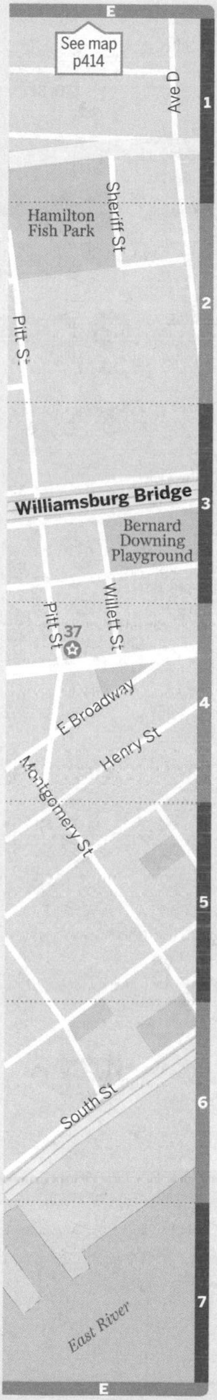
E
See map p414
Ave D
Hamilton Fish Park
Sheriff St
Pitt St
Williamsburg Bridge
Bernard Downing Playground
Willett St
Pitt St
37
E Broadway
Henry St
Montgomery St
South St
East River
E
1
2
3
4
5
6
7

Top Sights (p106)

1 Lower East Side Tenement Museum B3
2 New Museum A3

Sights (p112)

3 Essex Street Market C3
4 Kehila Kedosha Janina Synagogue & Museum B4
5 Lehmann Maupin A2
6 Lesley Heller C4
7 Mark Miller Gallery C4
8 Museum at Eldridge Street Synagogue B5
9 Orchard Street Bargain District B2
10 Rox B3
11 Salon 94 Bowery A2
12 Salon 94 Freemans A3
13 Sara D Roosevelt Park A3
14 Sperone Westwater A2
15 Untitled C5

Eating (p116)

16 Boil A4
17 Clinton Street Baking Company D2
18 Dimes C5
19 Donut Plant C4
20 Fat Radish C5
21 Freemans A3
22 Hotel Chantelle C3
23 'inoteca C3
24 Katz's Delicatessen B2
25 Kuma Inn C3
26 Meatball Shop B2
27 Vanessa's Dumpling House B4

Drinking & Nightlife (p123)

28 Attaboy B4
29 Barramundi D2
30 Barrio Chino C4
31 Beauty & Essex C2
32 Cake Shop C2
33 Casa Mezcal C4
34 Stanton Social B2
35 Ten Bells C4
36 Welcome to the Johnsons C3

Entertainment (p125)

37 Abrons Arts Center E4
38 Bowery Ballroom A3
39 Delancey D3
40 Landmark Sunshine Cinema B2
41 Pianos C2
42 Rockwood Music Hall B2
43 Slipper Room B2
Sweet .... (see 43)

Shopping (p127)

44 Bluestockings B2
45 By Robert James C4
46 Dressing Room B4
47 Earnest Sewn (Lower East Side) C4
48 Edith Machinist C3
49 Moo Shoes C4
50 Reed Space B3
51 Reformation C2
52 Spiritual America A3
53 Top Hat C4
54 Yumi Kim C2

Sleeping (p330)

55 Blue Moon Hotel C3
56 Hotel on Rivington C3

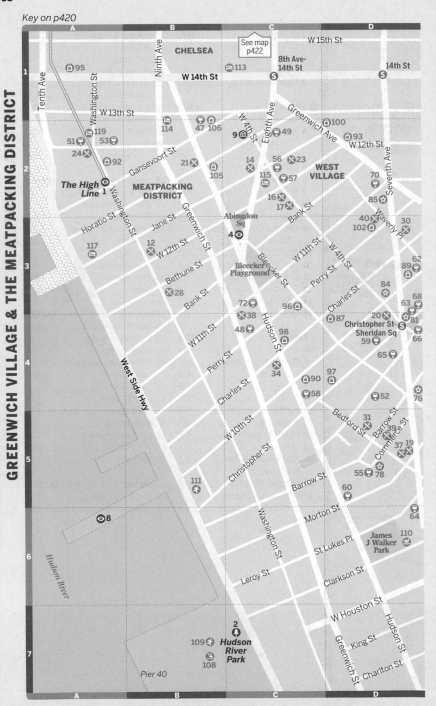

Key on p420

GREENWICH VILLAGE & THE MEATPACKING DISTRICT

See map p422

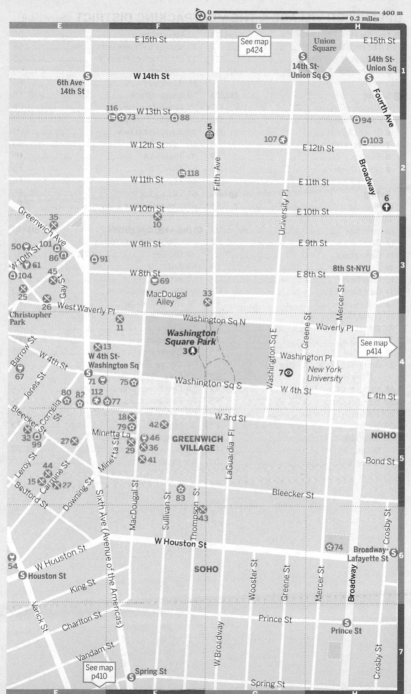

See map p424

See map p414

See map p410

GREENWICH VILLAGE & THE MEATPACKING DISTRICT

Union Square

E 15th St

14th St-Union Sq

14th St-Union Sq

6th Ave-14th St

W 14th St

Fourth Ave

Broadway

W 13th St

116 73 88 94

103

5

W 12th St

107 E 12th St

E 11th St

Fifth Ave

W 11th St

118

W 10th St

E 10th St

University PI

6

35

Greenwich Ave

10

W 9th St

E 9th St

50 101 86

91

W 10th St

61 45

104

Gay St

W 8th St

8th St-NYU

E 8th St

Mercer St

25

69

26

West Waverly PI

MacDougal Alley

33

Christopher Park

11

Washington Sq N

Greene St

Waverly PI

Washington Square Park

3

Washington Sq E

13

W 4th St-Washington Sq

Barrow St

W 4th St

67

Jones St

71

75

Washington PI

Washington Sq S

7

New York University

W 4th St

E 4th St

80 82

112

77

Bleecker St

Cornelia St

18

79

42

W 3rd St

NOHO

32

99

27

Minetta La

46

36

GREENWICH VILLAGE

LaGuardia PI

Bond St

Leroy St

44

15

Carmine St

22

Minetta St

29

41

Bedford St

Downing St

Sixth Ave (Avenue of the Americas)

MacDougal St

Sullivan St

83

Thompson St

43

Bleecker St

Wooster St

Greene St

Mercer St

Crosby St

W Houston St

54

W Houston St

Houston St

King St

SOHO

74

Broadway-Lafayette St

Charlton St

Vandam St

W Broadway

Prince St

Broadway

Prince St

Crosby St

Varick St

Spring St

Spring St

GREENWICH VILLAGE & THE MEATPACKING DISTRICT *Map on p418*

GREENWICH VILLAGE & THE MEATPACKING DISTRICT

CHELSEA

CHELSEA & THE MEATPACKING DISTRICT

400 m
0.2 miles

KOREA TOWN

W 29th St
W 27th St

W 28th St

Chelsea Park

See map p430

W 28th St

W 29th St

W 26th St

W 25th St

W 27th St

London Terrace

W 24th St

Eleventh Ave

Chelsea Waterside Park

Hudson River Park

Twelfth Ave (West Side Hwy)

Pier 66

26

Hudson River

Pier 62

Chelsea Piers

Pier 61

Pier 60

Pier 59

Eleventh Ave (West Side Hwy)

W 27th St

23

23rd St

39

54

32

Sixth Ave (Avenue of the Americas)

See map p424

41

11

23rd St

28th St

21

Seventh Ave

18th St

17th St Market

23rd St

31

4

30

20

35 28

27

42

40

49

43

45

Eighth Ave

23rd St

51

16

CHELSEA

W 23rd St

W 22nd St

W 21st St

50

29

33

W 20th St

W 19th St

W 18th St

W 17th St

55

52 25

22

Ninth Ave

W 16th St

13

18

12

14

7

15

Tenth Ave

38

8

44

19

The High Line

48

24

53

36

17

2 3

9

10

5

34

6

47

46

23

CHELSEA

UNION SQUARE

WEST VILLAGE

MEATPACKING DISTRICT

Chelsea Market

Hudson St

W 15th St

W 14th St

See map p418

⊙ Top Sights (p133)
1 Chelsea Market.....................D5

◎ Sights (p136)
2 Andrea Rosen Gallery C2
3 Barbara Gladstone Gallery....C2
4 Chelsea Hotel.......................F3
5 David Zwirner......................C3
6 Gagosian.............................B2
7 General Theological Seminary...D3
8 Matthew Marks Gallery.........C3
9 Pace Gallery........................C2
10 Paula Cooper Gallery...........C3
11 Rubin Museum of Art...........G4

✕ Eating (p143)
Amy's Bread.....................(see 1)
12 Billy's Bakery.......................D3
13 Blossom..............................D3
Chelsea Market.................(see 1)
14 Co......................................D2
15 Cookshop.............................C3
Eleni's.............................(see 1)
16 Foragers City Table..............E3
17 Heath.................................C1
l'Arte Del Gelato..............(see 1)
18 Le Grainne..........................D3
19 Tia Pol...............................C3
Tuck Shop.......................(see 1)

🍸 Drinking & Nightlife (p151)
20 Bar Veloce...........................F3
21 Barracuda............................F3
22 Bathtub Gin.........................D4
23 Chelsea Brewing Company.....B4
24 Eagle NYC............................C1
25 Electric Room.......................E4
26 Frying Pan............................A2
27 G Lounge.............................D3
Gallow Green....................(see 36)

28 Peter McManus Tavern F4

🎭 Entertainment (p154)
29 Atlantic Theater Company E3
30 Chelsea Bow Tie Cinema F3
31 Gotham Comedy Club............F3
32 Irish Repertory Theater.........G3
33 Joyce Theater......................E4
34 Kitchen...............................C4
35 New York Live Arts...............F4
36 Sleep No More.....................C1
37 Upright Citizens Brigade
   Theatre.............................E1

🛍 Shopping (p158)
38 192 Books............................C3
39 Antiques Garage Flea Market...G2
40 Behaviour............................A2
41 Housing Works Thrift Shop.....G4
42 INA (Chelsea).......................F4
43 Nasty Pig............................E4
Posman Books....................(see 1)
44 Printed Matter......................C3
45 Universal Gear......................E4

🚴 Sports & Activities (p159)
46 Chelsea Piers Complex...........B3
47 Little Athletes Exploration
   Center...............................B3
48 New York Gallery Tours.........C2

🛏 Sleeping (p331)
49 Chelsea Hostel.....................F3
50 Chelsea Lodge......................E3
51 Colonial House Inn................E3
52 Dream Downtown..................D4
53 Hôtel Americano...................C1
54 Inn on 23rd St......................G2
55 Maritime Hotel.....................E4

Lobster Place....................(see 1)

UNION SQUARE, FLATIRON DISTRICT & GRAMERCY PARK

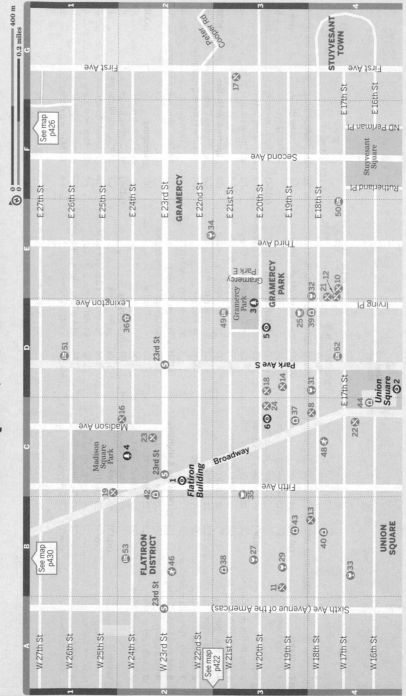

UNION SQUARE, FLATIRON DISTRICT & GRAMERCY PARK

MIDTOWN EAST & FIFTH AVENUE

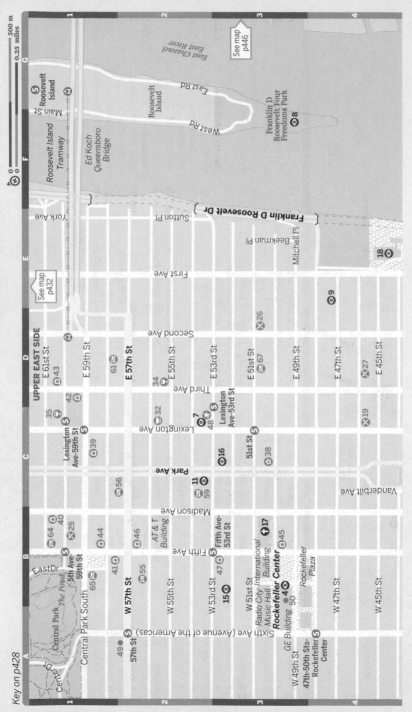

Key on p428

See map p446

See map p432

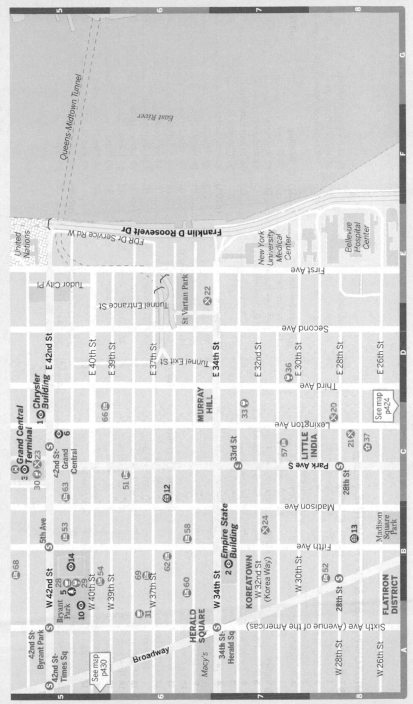

MIDTOWN EAST & FIFTH AVENUE Map on p426

Top Sights (p179)
1 Chrysler Building....................C5
2 Empire State Building.............B7
3 Grand Central Terminal...........C5
4 Rockefeller Center..................B3

Sights (p189)
5 Bryant Park............................B5
6 Chanin Building......................C5
7 Citigroup Center.....................C2
8 Franklin D Roosevelt Four
   Freedoms Park.....................F3
9 Japan Society.........................E4
10 Le Carrousel.........................A5
11 Lever House..........................C2
12 Morgan Library &
    Museum..............................C6
13 Museum of Sex.....................B8
14 New York Public Library.........B5
15 Paley Center for Media...........B3
16 Seagram Building..................C3
17 St Patrick's Cathedral............B3
   Top of the Rock................(see 4)
18 United Nations......................E4

Eating (p197)
19 99 Cent Pizza.......................C4
    Breslin...........................(see 52)
20 Curry in a Hurry...................C8
21 Dhaba.................................C8
22 El Parador Cafe....................E6
23 Grand Central Oyster
    Bar & Restaurant................C5
24 Hangawi..............................B7
    John Dory Oyster Bar.....(see 52)
25 Rouge Tomate......................B1
26 Smith..................................D3
27 Sparks................................D4

Drinking & Nightlife (p200)
28 Bryant Park Cafe...................B5
29 Bryant Park Grill...................B5
30 Campbell Apartment..............C5
31 Culture Espresso...................A6
32 Little Collins.........................C2
33 Middle Branch......................C7
34 PJ Clarke's...........................D2
    Stumptown Coffee
    Roasters.......................(see 52)

35 Subway Inn..........................C1
36 Terroir.................................D7
    Top of the Strand............(see 69)

Entertainment (p202)
37 Jazz Standard.......................C8
    New York Public Library....(see 14)
38 St Bartholomew's
    Church...............................C3

Shopping (p206)
39 Argosy.................................C1
40 Barneys...............................B1
41 Bergdorf Goodman................B1
42 Bloomingdale's.....................D1
43 Dylan's Candy Bar................D1
44 FAO Schwarz........................B1
    Grand Central Market......(see 3)
45 Saks Fifth Ave......................B3
46 Tiffany & Co.........................B2
47 Uniqlo.................................B3

Sports & Activities (p209)
48 24 Hour Fitness....................C2

49 Municipal Art Society.............A2
50 NBC Studio Tours..................B3
    Rink at Rockefeller Center....(see 4)

Sleeping (p334)
51 70 Park................................C6
52 Ace Hotel.............................B8
53 Andaz Fifth Avenue...............B5
54 Bryant Park Hotel..................B5
55 Chambers.............................B2
56 Four Seasons........................C2
57 Hotel 31...............................C7
58 Hotel 373.............................B6
59 Hotel Elysée.........................C2
60 Hotel Metro..........................B6
61 Ivy Terrace...........................D1
62 Langham Place......................B6
63 Library Hotel.........................C5
64 Pierre..................................B1
65 Plaza..................................B1
66 Pod 39................................C5
67 Pod 51................................D3
68 Royalton..............................B5
69 Strand.................................B6

MIDTOWN WEST & TIMES SQUARE

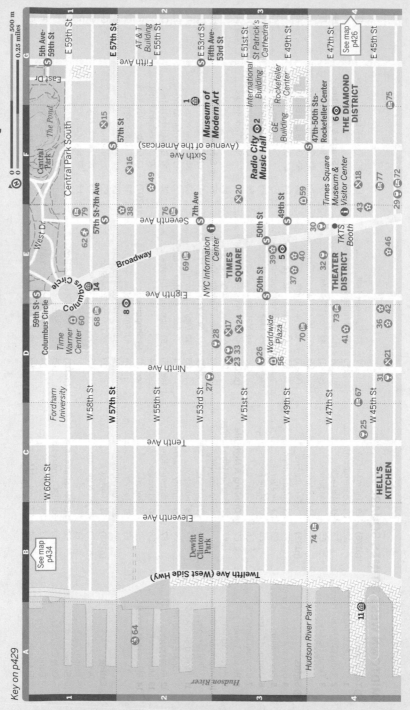

Key on p429

See map p434

500 m
0.25 miles

W 60th St
W 58th St
W 55th St
W 53rd St
W 51st St
W 49th St
W 47th St
W 45th St

Fordham University

Eleventh Ave

Tenth Ave

Ninth Ave

Eighth Ave

Twelfth Ave (West Side Hwy)

Hudson River

Hudson River Park

Dewitt Clinton Park

HELL'S KITCHEN

64

74

11

25
67
31
21
41
73
70
36
42
32
40
37
39
5
23 33
27
26
56
Worldwide Plaza
17
24
28
8
68
60
14
Columbus Circle
Time Warner Center
59th St-Columbus Circle
Central Park
West Dr
Columbus Circle
Broadway
NYC Information Center
TIMES SQUARE
50th St
50th St
49th St
59
20
30
TKTS Booth
THEATER DISTRICT
Times Square Museum & Visitor Center
43
18
77
29
72
46
THE DIAMOND DISTRICT
6
47-50th Sts-Rockefeller Center
75
GE Building
Rockefeller Center
International Building
GE
Radio City Music Hall
2
Museum of Modern Art
1
Sixth Ave (Avenue of the Americas)
Fifth Ave
Fifth Ave-53rd St
St Patrick's Cathedral
See map p426

E 45th St
E 47th St
E 49th St
E 51st St
E 53rd St
E 55th St
AT & T Building
E 57th St
E 59th St
5th Ave-59th St

W 57th St

Central Park South

57th St-7th Ave
57th St
Seventh Ave
7th Ave
Central Park
The Pond
East Dr

15
16
49
79
62
38
76
69

The Pond

Central Park South

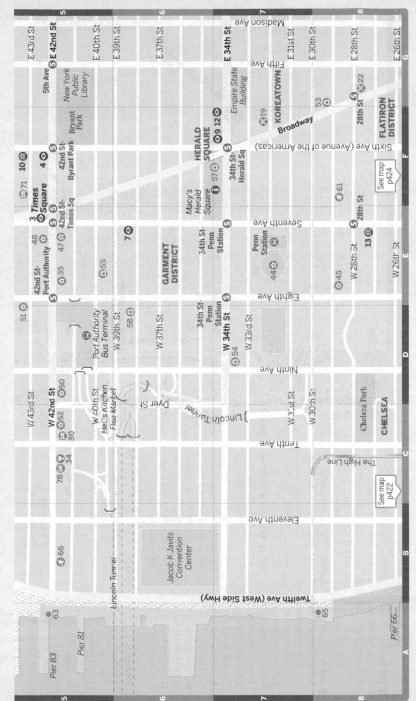

MIDTOWN WEST & TIMES SQUARE

See map p424

See map p422

Upper East Side

Top Sights (p212)
1 Guggenheim Museum ... A3
2 Metropolitan Museum of Art ... A5

Sights (p218)
3 Asia Society & Museum ... B7
4 Cooper-Hewitt National Design Museum ... A3
5 Frick Collection ... A7
6 Gracie Mansion ... D3
7 Jewish Museum ... A3
8 Museum of the City of New York ... A1
9 National Academy Museum ... A3
10 Neue Galerie ... A4
11 Temple Emanu-El ... A7
12 Whitney Museum of American Art ... A6

Eating (p222)
13 ABV ... B2
Cafe 3 ... (see 1)
14 Café Boulud ... A6
Café Sabarsky ... (see 10)
15 Candle 79 ... B5
16 Candle Cafe ... B6
17 Earl's Beer & Cheese ... B2
18 James Wood Foundry ... C6
19 JG Melon ... B6
20 Sandro's ... C5
21 Sant Ambroeus ... A5
22 Tanoshi ... D6
Untitled ... (see 12)
23 Via Quadronno ... A6
24 William Greenberg Desserts ... A4
Wright ... (see 1)

Drinking & Nightlife (p225)
25 Metropolitan Museum Roof Garden Café & Martini Bar ... A5
Bar Pleiades ... (see 14)
26 Bemelmans Bar ... A6
27 Drunken Munkey ... C3
28 JBird ... C6
29 Oslo Coffee Roasters ... D6
30 Penrose ... C4
31 Vinus and Marc ... C2

Entertainment (p226)
32 92nd St Y ... B3
Café Carlyle ... (see 26)
33 Comic Strip Live ... C5
Frick Collection ... (see 5)

Shopping (p226)
34 Blue Tree ... A3

0 400 m
0 0.2 miles
A
B
C
D
1
2
3
4
See map p436
East Meadow
Fifth Ave
Madison Ave
Park Ave
Lexington Ave
Third Ave
Second Ave
First Ave
York Ave
East End Ave
E 103rd St
103rd St
E 102nd St
E 101st St
E 100th St
E 98th St
96th St
E 96th St
E 94th St
E 92nd St
E 90th St
E 88th St
86th St
E 86th St
E 84th St
Carl Schurz Park
Franklin D Roosevelt Dr
East River
Jacqueline Kennedy Onassis Reservoir
Guggenheim Museum
East Dr
UPPER EAST SIDE

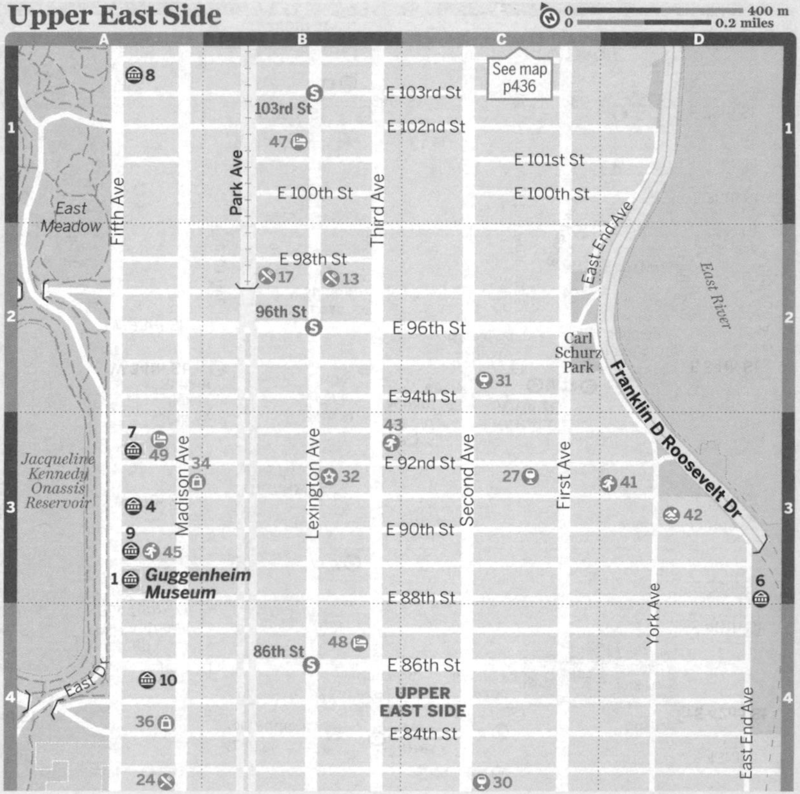

UPPER EAST SIDE

Metropolitan Museum of Art

See map p434

See map p446

See map p426

Conservatory Road

Central Park

The Pond

John Jay Park

Rockefeller University

East River

Franklin D Roosevelt Dr

Roosevelt Island Tramway

Ed Koch Queensboro Bridge

East End Ave

York Ave

First Ave

Second Ave

Third Ave

Lexington Ave

Park Ave

Madison Ave

Fifth Ave

E 82nd St
E 80th St
E 78th St
E 76th St
E 74th St
E 72nd St
E 70th St
E 68th St
E 65th St
E 63rd St
E 61st St

77th St
68th St-Hunter College
Lexington Ave-63rd St
Lexington Ave-59th St
5th Ave-59th St
59th St

Hunter College

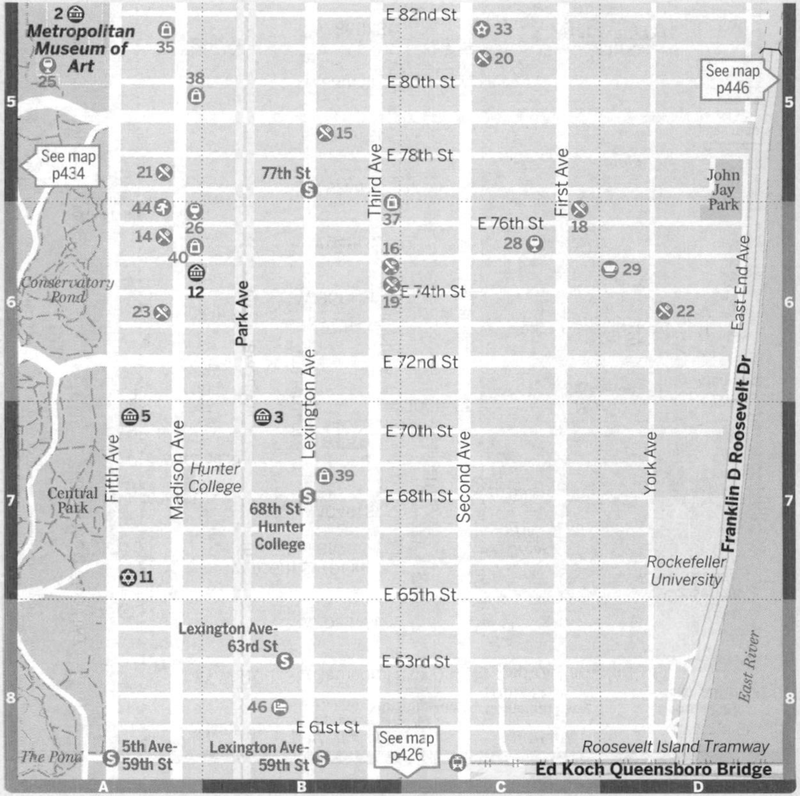

UPPER WEST SIDE

UPPER WEST SIDE

⊙ Entertainment (p242)

American Ballet
Theatre..................(see 49)
44 Beacon Theatre...................B6
45 Cleopatra's Needle..............B3
46 Delacorte Theater...............C5
47 Eliror Bunin Munroe
Film Center.......................B7
48 Merkin Concert Hall............B7
49 Metropolitan Opera
House..............................B7
50 New York City Ballet..........B7
51 New York
Philharmonic....................B7
52 Smoke..............................B2
53 Symphony Space..................B3
54 Walter Reade Theater..........B7

⊙ Sports & Activities (p245)

64 Belvedere Castle..................C5
65 Bike and Roll......................C3
66 Central Park Tennis
Center.............................C3
67 Champion Bicycles Inc. B2
68 Charles A Dana
Discovery Center..............D1
69 Downtown Boathouse
(Upper West Side)...........A6
Loeb Boathouse.............(see 31)
70 Toga Bike Shop...................B7
71 West S de YMCA................C7
72 Wollman Skating Rink........D8

⊙ Sleeping (p340)

73 Empire Hotel......................C7
74 Hostelling
International New
York.................................B2
Hotel Beacon...................(see 44)
75 Hotel Beleclaire..................E6
76 Hotel Newton.....................B3
77 International Student
Center.............................C4
78 Jazz on the Park
Hostel..............................C2
79 Lucerne............................BE
80 NYLO Hotel.......................B5

⊙ Shopping (p245)

55 Barneys Co-op.....................B6
56 Century 21..........................B7
57 Comptoir des
Cotonniers.......................E7
58 Greenflea...........................B6
59 Harry's Shoes......................B5
60 Time for Children...............B5
61 West Side Kids....................B5
62 Westsider Books..................B5
63 Westsider Records...............BE

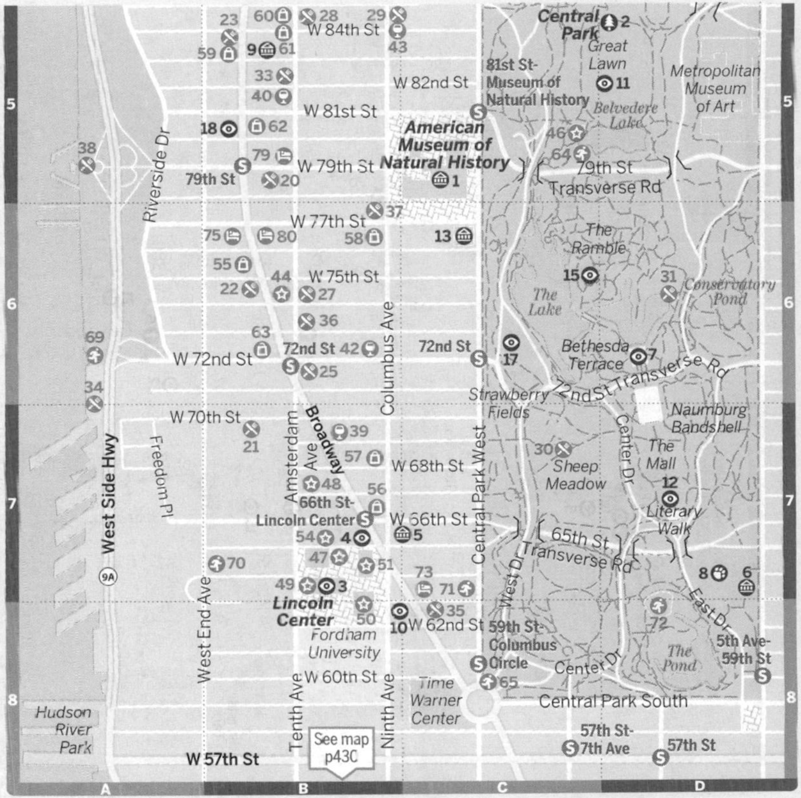

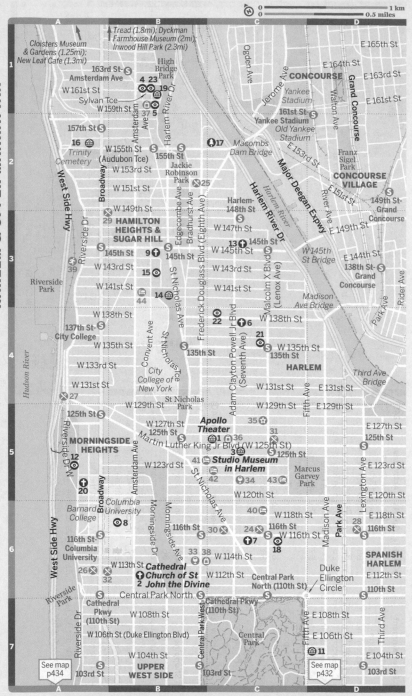

0 1 km
0 0.5 miles

Cloisters Museum
& Gardens (1.25mi);
New Leaf Cafe (1.3mi)

Tread (1.8mi); Dyckman
Farmhouse Museum (2mi);
Inwood Hill Park (2.3mi)

E 165th St

E 164th St

CONCOURSE

E 163rd St

163rd St
Amsterdam Ave

High
Bridge
Park

Ogden Ave

Jerome Ave

Yankee
Stadium

E 161st St

W 161st St

4 23

19

Yankee
Stadium

Walton Ave

Grand Concourse

161st St-
Yankee Stadium
Old Yankee
Stadium

Sylvan Tce

37 5

W 159th St

157th St

Amsterdam Ave

Harlem River Dr

E 153rd St

Franz
Sigel
Park

CONCOURSE
VILLAGE

16

Trinity
Cemetery

W 155th St
(Audubon Tce)

155th St

17

Macombs
Dam Bridge

Major Deegan Expwy

River Ave

E 151st St

149th St-
Grand
Concourse

W 153rd St

Jackie
Robinson
Park

25

Harlem River Dr

E 149th St

Broadway

W 151st St

Harlem River

Harlem-
148th St

W 149th St

138th St-
Grand
Concourse

29 HAMILTON
HEIGHTS &
SUGAR HILL

W 147th St

W 145th
St Bridge

E 144th St

Rider Ave

Park Ave

145th St

9

145th St

13 145th St

W 145th St

E 138th St

Riverside
Park

15

W 143rd St

W 143rd St

Malcolm X Blvd
(Lenox Ave)

39

W 141st St

Edgecombe Ave

Bradhurst Ave

Frederick Douglass Blvd (Eighth Ave)

W 141st St

Madison
Ave Bridge

44 14

Riverside Dr

137th St-
City College

W 138th St

22

St Nicholas Ave

6

W 138th St

Third Ave
Bridge

W 135th St

21

135th St

W 135th St

W 133rd St

Convent Ave

St Nicholas Tce

HARLEM

Fifth Ave

W 131st St

City
College of
New York

St Nicholas
Park

W 131st St

E 131st St

27

Hudson River

W 129th St

Adam Clayton Powell Jr Blvd
(Seventh Ave)

W 129th St

E 129th St

125th St

Apollo
Theater

35

E 127th St

W 127th St

31

125th St

125th St

Martin Luther King Jr Blvd (W 125th St)

1 36

MORNINGSIDE
HEIGHTS

3

12

Riverside Dr W

W 123rd St

41 Studio Museum
in Harlem

E 123rd St

42

Amsterdam Ave

34 43

Marcus
Garvey
Park

20

Broadway

Morningside Dr

W 120th St

40

Lexington Ave

Barnard
College

Columbia
University

8

116th St

30

W 118th St

E 118th St

28

24

116th St

E 116th St

116th St-
Columbia
University

Morningside Ave

St Nicholas Ave

7

18

Madison Ave

SPANISH
HARLEM

33 38

W 114th St

26

W 113th St

Cathedral
Church of St
John the Divine

W 112th St

Duke
Ellington
Circle

E 112th St

32

2

Central Park North (110th St)

110th St

Central Park North

Cathedral
Pkwy
(110th St)

W 108th St

Central Park West

Cathedral Pkwy
(110th St)

E 108th St

W 106th St (Duke Ellington Blvd)

Fifth Ave

E 106th St

Riverside
Park

Riverside Dr

West Side Hwy

West Side Hwy

Central
Park

11

E 104th St

W 104th St

Park Ave

Third Ave

See map
p434

103rd St

UPPER
WEST SIDE

103rd St

103rd St

See map
p432

103rd St

A B C D

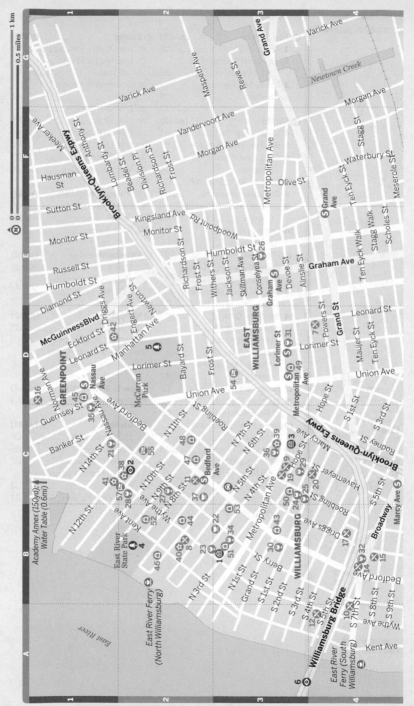

Sights (p271)
1 Brooklyn Art Library B3
2 Brooklyn Brewery C2
3 City Reliquary C3
4 East River State Park B2
5 McCarren Park D2
6 Williamsburg Bridge A3

Eating (p280)
7 Champs D4
8 Cubana Social B2
9 Fette Sau C3
10 Marlow & Sons A4
11 Meatball Shop C2
Ides ...... (see 57)
12 Miss Favela A4
13 Momo Sushi Shack G5
14 Motorino B4
15 Peter Luger Steakhouse B4
16 Peter Pan Bakery D1
17 Pies-n-Thighs B4
18 Roberta's G5
19 Rosebug Tea Room C3
20 Rye C4

Drinking & Nightlife (p290)
21 Berry Park C1
22 Blue Bottle Coffee B3
23 Brooklyn Oenology B2
24 Clem's C3
25 Desnuda C3
26 Harefield Road E3
27 Hotel Delmano C2
Ides ...... (see 57)
28 Kinfolk Studios C2
29 Larry Lawrence G5
30 Maison Premiere B3
31 Metropolitan D3
32 OTB B4
33 Pine Box Rock Shop G5
34 Radegast Hall & Biergarten B3
35 Spritzenhaus C1
36 Spuyten Duyvil C3
37 Toby's Estate C2

Entertainment (p293)
38 Brooklyn Bowl C2
39 Knitting Factory C3
40 Music Hall of Williamsburg B2
41 Output C1
42 Warsaw D1

Shopping (p295)
43 Adobe New York C2
44 Artists & Fleas C3
45 Beacon's Closet (Greenpoint) D3
46 Brooklyn Flea Market (Williamsburg) B2
47 Brooklyn Industries C2
48 Buffalo Exchange C2
49 Desert Island Comics D3
50 Fuego 718 ...... C3
51 Mast Brothers B3
52 Rough Trade B2
53 Spoonbill & Sugartown B3

Sports & Activities (p298)
Brooklyn Bowl ...... (see 38)

Sleeping (p343)
54 Hotel Le Jolie B3
55 King & Grove B2
56 New York Loft Hostel G5
57 Wythe Hotel D1

BOERUM HILL, CARROLL GARDENS, COBBLE HILL, FORT GREENE & RED HOOK

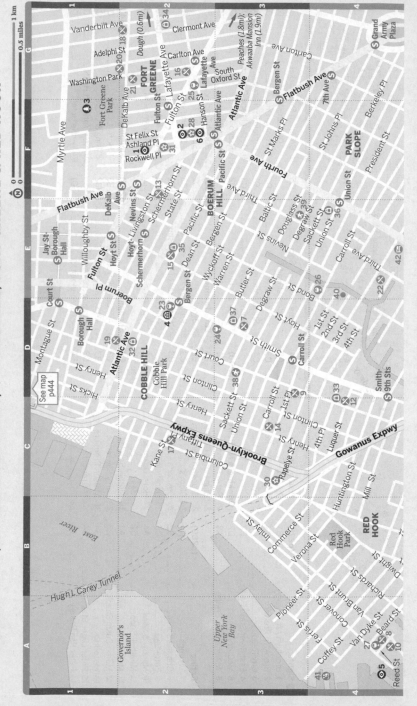

BOERUM HILL, CARROLL GARDENS, COBBLE HILL, FORT GREENE & RED HOOK

See map p442

PARK SLOPE & PROSPECT PARK

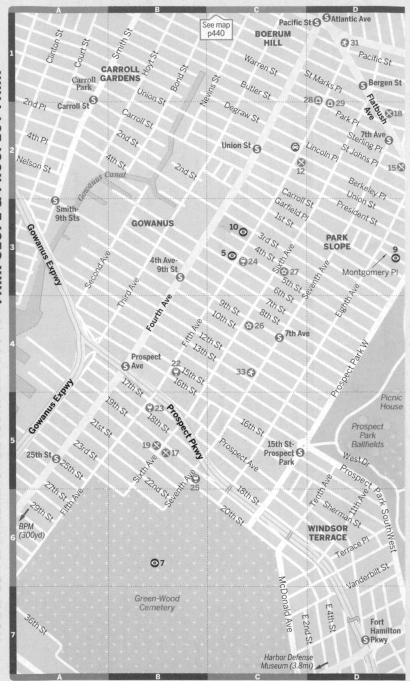

See map p440

BOERUM HILL

CARROLL GARDENS

Clinton St
Court St
Smith St
Hoyt St
Bond St
Nevins St

Carroll Park
Carroll St

Pacific St **S**
S Atlantic Ave

31
Pacific St

Warren St

St Marks Pl
S Bergen St

Butler St

28 **29**
Park Pl
18

Flatbush Ave

2nd Pl
Carroll St
Union St
2nd St

Degraw St

Union St **S**

Lincoln Pl

Sterling Pl
7th Ave **S**
St Johns Pl

4th Pl

Carroll St

12

Nelson St
4th St

Berkeley Pl
Union St
President St

15

Gowanus Canal

2nd St

Carroll St
Garfield Pl
1st St

Smith-9th Sts **S**

GOWANUS

10

3rd St

PARK SLOPE

9

Second Ave

5 **24**

4th St
5th St

27

Montgomery Pl

4th Ave-9th St **S**

Third Ave

6th St

7th St

Fourth Ave

Fifth Ave

9th St
10th St

26

8th St

7th Ave **S**

Eighth Ave

Gowanus Expwy

12th St
13th St

Prospect Ave **S**

22
15th St
16th St

33

Prospect Park W

Picnic House

17th St

Gowanus Expwy

19th St

23
18th St

Prospect Pkwy

Prospect Park Ballfields

21st St

19 **17**

16th St

15th St-Prospect Park **S**

West Dr

25th St **S** 25th St

23rd St

Sixth Ave
22nd St
Seventh Ave
25

Prospect Ave

18th St

20th St

Prospect Park Southwest

Tenth Ave
Sherman St
11th Ave

BPM (300yd)

27th St
29th St
Fifth Ave

WINDSOR TERRACE

Terrace Pl

Vanderbilt St

7

Green-Wood Cemetery

McDonald Ave

E 2nd St
E 4th St

Fort Hamilton Pkwy **S**

36th St

Harbor Defense Museum (3.8mi)

◎ **Top Sights** (p267)
1 Brooklyn Museum F3
2 Prospect Park............................... E4

◎ **Sights** (p278)
3 Brooklyn Botanic Garden F3
4 Brooklyn Public Library.................. E3
5 Brooklyn Superhero Supply Co C3
6 Grand Army Plaza......................... E3
7 Green-Wood Cemetery................... B6
8 Lefferts Historic House.................. F4
9 Montgomery Place D3
10 Old Stone House........................... C3
11 Prospect Park Zoo........................ E4

✷ **Eating** (p288)
12 Bierkraft.................................... C2
13 Cheryl's Global Soul E3
14 Chuko....................................... E1
15 Franny's.................................... D2
16 Kimchi Grill F2
17 Lot 2 .... B5
18 Marco's..................................... D2
   Saul .... (see 1)
19 Southside Coffee B5
20 Tom's Restaurant F3
21 Vanderbilt.................................. E2

○ **Drinking & Nightlife** (p293)
22 Der Kommissar B4
23 Freddy's.................................... B5
24 Ginger's.................................... C3
25 Greenwood Park B5

✿ **Entertainment** (p293)
26 Barbes...................................... C4
   Brooklyn Public Library................. (see 4)
27 Puppetworks C3

▣ **Shopping** (p297)
28 Beacon's Closet (Park Slope) D1
29 Flirt... D2
30 Grand Army Plaza Greenmarket E3

✤ **Sports & Activities** (p298)
31 Barclays Center D1
32 Lakeside.................................... F6
33 On the Move C4
34 Prospect Park Tennis Center........... E7

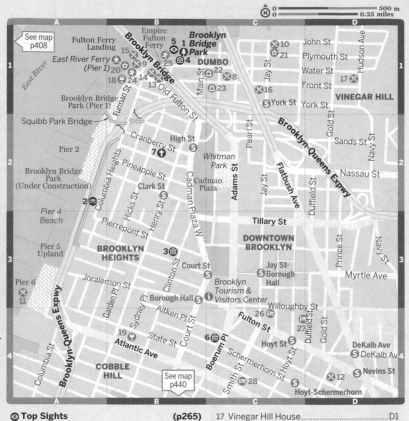

CONEY ISLAND & BRIGHTON BEACH

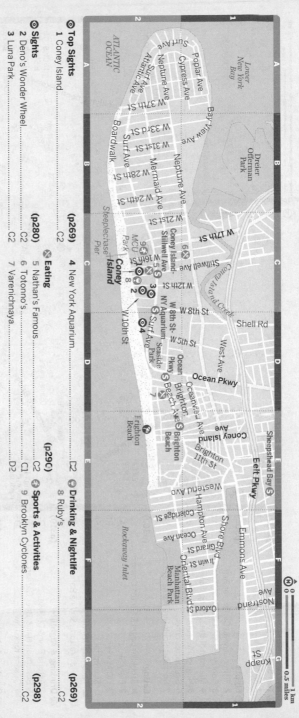

ASTORIA

◎ Top Sights	(p302)
1 MoMA PS1	B4

◎ Sights	(p306)
2 Fisher Landau Center for Art	B3
3 Gantry Plaza State Park	A4
4 Museum of the Moving Image	C3
5 Noguchi Museum	B2
6 SculptureCenter	B4
7 Socrates Sculpture Park	B2

⊗ Eating	(p307)
8 Brooklyn Bagel & Coffee Company	C2
9 El Ay Si	A4
10 LIC Market	B4
11 Sripraphai	E4
12 Taverna Kyclades	D1
13 Vesta Trattoria & Wine Bar	C2

◔ Drinking & Nightlife	(p310)
14 Astoria Bier & Cheese	C2
15 Bohemian Hall & Beer Garden	D1
16 Queens Kickshaw	D3

✪ Sports & Activities	(p311)
17 Cliffs	A4
18 New York Trapeze School	A4

⌂ Sleeping	(p344)
19 Country Inn & Suites	B3
20 Ravel	A3
21 Z Hotel	B3

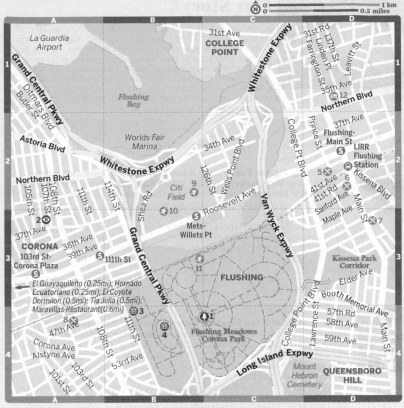

Our Story

A beat-up old car, a few dollars in the pocket and a sense of adventure. In 1972 that's all Tony and Maureen Wheeler needed for the trip of a lifetime – across Europe and Asia overland to Australia. It took several months, and at the end – broke but inspired – they sat at their kitchen table writing and stapling together their first travel guide, *Across Asia on the Cheap*. Within a week they'd sold 1500 copies. Lonely Planet was born.

Today, Lonely Planet has offices in Franklin, London, Melbourne, Oakland, Beijing and Delhi, with more than 600 staff and writers. We share Tony's belief that 'a great guidebook should do three things: inform, educate and amuse'.

Our Writers

Regis St Louis

Coordinating Author; East Village & Lower East Side; Greenwich Village, Chelsea & the Meatpacking District; Upper East Side; Upper West Side & Central Park; Brooklyn A Hoosier by birth, Regis grew up in a sleepy riverside town where he dreamed of big-city intrigue and small, expensive apartments. In 2001 he settled in New York, which had all that and more. He has written more than three dozen Lonely Planet guides, covering destinations from Spain to Papua New Guinea. His articles have appeared in many publications including the *Chicago Tribune* and the *San Francisco Chronicle*. When not out on the road, Regis lives in Boerum Hill in Brooklyn.

Regis also wrote the Plan Your Trip, Day Trips and Survival Guide sections of this guide and cowrote the Sleeping chapter.

Read more about Regis at:
lonelyplanet.com/members/regisstlouis

Cristian Bonetto

Lower Manhattan & the Financial District; SoHo & Chinatown; Union Square, Flatiron & Gramercy; Midtown; Harlem & Upper Manhattan; Queens Planet-roaming Cristian has played both visitor and local in New York City, a place he has been obsessed with since his Sesame Street diaper days. From mainstream Midtown to the far-flung corners of outer Queens, the one-time TV and theater scribe has explored countless corners of the city, his musings appearing in newspapers, magazines and online publications across the world. He also tweets at twitter.com/cristianbonetto.

Cristian also contributed to the Plan Your Trip and Sleeping sections, as well as writing the Understand New York City features.

Published by Lonely Planet Publications Pty Ltd
ABN 36 005 607 983
9th edition – August 2014
ISBN 978 1 74220 882 4
© Lonely Planet 2014   Photographs © as indicated 2014
10 9 8 7 6 5 4 3 2 1
Printed in China